A Companion to Film Theory

Blackwell Companions in Cultural Studies

Advisory editor: David Theo Goldberg, University of California, Irvine

This series aims to provide theoretically ambitious but accessible volumes devoted to the major fields and subfields within cultural studies, whether as single disciplines (film studies) inspired and reconfigured by interventionist cultural studies approaches, or from broad interdisciplinary and multidisciplinary perspectives (gender studies, race and ethnic studies, postcolonial studies). Each volume sets out to ground and orientate the student through a broad range of specially commissioned articles and also to provide the more experienced scholar and teacher with a convenient and comprehensive overview of the latest trends and critical directions. An overarching *Companion to Cultural Studies* will map the territory as a whole.

1. A Companion to Film Theory
   Edited by Toby Miller and Robert Stam

2. A Companion to Postcolonial Studies
   Edited by Henry Schwarz and Sangeeta Ray

3. A Companion to Cultural Studies
   Edited by Toby Miller

4. A Companion to Racial and Ethnic Studies
   Edited by David Theo Goldberg and John Solomos

5. A Companion to Art Theory
   Edited by Paul Smith and Carolyn Wilde

6. A Companion to Media Studies
   Edited by Angharad Valdivia

Forthcoming:
A Companion to North American Indian Studies
Edited by Ward Churchill

A Companion to Gender Studies
Edited by Philomena Essed, Audrey Kobayashi, and David Theo Goldberg

A Companion to Television Studies
Edited by Janet Wasko

A Companion to African American Studies
Edited by Lewis Gordon and Jane Anna Gordon

A Companion to Third Cinema
Edited by Teshome Gabriel

A Companion to Literature and Film
Edited by Robert Stam and Alessandra Raengo

A Companion to American Studies
Edited by John Carlos Rowe

A Companion to Museum Studies
Edited by Sharon Macdonald

A Companion to Lesbian, Gay, Bisexual, Transgender, and Queer Studies
Edited by George Haggerty and Molly McGarry

A Companion to Film Theory

Edited by

Toby Miller and Robert Stam

Blackwell Publishing

BLACKWELL PUBLISHING
350 Main Street, Malden, MA 02148-5020, USA
108 Cowley Road, Oxford OX4 1JF, UK
550 Swanston Street, Carlton, Victoria 3053, Australia

First published 1999
First published in paperback 2004 by Blackwell Publishing Ltd
Reprinted 2004

Library of Congress Cataloging-in-Publication Data

The Blackwell companion to film theory / edited by Toby Miller and Robert Stam.
p. cm.—(Blackwell companions in cultural studies; 1)
Includes bibliographical references and index.
ISBN 0-631-20644-2 (hardback); ISBN 0-631-20645-0 (paperback)
1. Motion pictures. 2. Motion pictures—Social aspects.
I. Miller, Toby. II. Stam, Robert, 1941– . III. Series.
PN1995.B495 1999
791.43'01—dc21   99–20206   CIP

A catalogue record for this title is available from the British Library.

Set in 11 on 13pt Ehrhardt
by Kolam Information Services Pvt Ltd, Pondicherry, India

The publisher's policy is to use permanent paper from mills that operate a sustainable forestry policy,
and which has been manufactured from pulp processed using acid-free and elementary chlorine-free
practices. Furthermore, the publisher ensures that the text paper and cover board used have met
acceptable environmental accreditation standards.

For further information on
Blackwell Publishing, visit our website:
http://www.blackwellpublishing.com

Contents

Contents

CHAPTER ONE

Introduction

Toby Miller

Metz? How do you spell that? – *James Bond*
M . . . . Get out, you irritating little man – *Dr Metz*
Diamonds Are Forever, Guy Hamilton, 1971

Signs may be analyzed, for few love them. But films are somehow delicate, like roses, and pulling the petals off a rose in order to study it is often viewed as an act of destruction.
Sol Worth, *Studying Visual Communication*

[T]he motion picture house . . . is . . . the first enemy of King Alcohol with real power where that king has deepest hold . . . . The people will have a shelter where they can readjust themselves . . . a substitute for many of the lines of pleasure in the groggery.
Vachel Lindsay, *The Art of the Moving Picture*

Going to the Cinema is part of a British book series from the 1950s that instructs readers on how to enjoy culture. It notes that film "has to cater for millions, and to do so, must make no demands on the public. . . . Films are easy to understand." The book undertakes to rectify this lack of demands by offering "increased powers of perception," thus developing spectators' pleasure and making them more discriminating. To aid in this task, a list of "Films everyone should see" is included (Buchanan and Reed 1957: 13, 155–7).

Such a project reiterates longstanding concerns of film theory, from the silent era's faith in "the moving picture man as a local social force . . . the mere formula of [whose] activities" keeps the public well tempered (Lindsay 1970: 243), through 1930s research into the impact of cinema on American youth via the Payne Studies (Blumer 1933; Blumer and Hauser 1933), to post-World War II concerns about Hollywood's intrication of education and entertainment and the need for counter-knowledge among the public (Powdermaker 1950: 12–15; Mayer 1946: 24).

We are sometimes told today that there has been "a general movement in approaches to film from a preoccupation with authorship (broadly defined), through a concentration upon the text and textuality, to an investigation of

1

audiences" (Hollows and Jancovich 1995: 8) or a consecutive pursuit of know-ledge about film form, then realism, followed by language, and, finally, cultural politics (Braudy and Cohen 1999: xv–xvi). Such accounts approximate the history of some humanities-based academic work, but forget the hardy perennials of cinema criticism, social-science technique, and cultural policy: textual analysis of films; identification of directors with movies; and studies of the audience through psychology and psychoanalysis (Worth 1981: 39). The twin tasks of elevation identified in *Going to the Cinema* – addressing spectators and examining texts – have always informed film theory (Manvell 1950). The relevant dilemmas were echoed and elaborated by reviewer Andrew Sarris's 1960s search for "dedicated moviegoers in the reading public" capable of engaging the "adven-turous speculations" of his pantheon of titles (1968: 17) and scholar Christian Metz's mid-1970s dictum – "[a] film is difficult to explain because it is easy to understand" (1974: 69).

To repeat, the tasks of elevation address audiences and textual ranking. Over time, they branch out and converge. Audience concerns include psychological, sociological, educational, consumer, criminological, and political promises and anxieties. Textual ranking involves authorship, genre, form, style, and represen-tational politics. They cross over in the area of mimesis, with audiences inter-preting films against their own worlds of race, gender, class, region, age, religion, language, politics, and nation.

The question of pleasure has been central, as analysts have sought to account for and resist narrative stereotypes and explain "why socialists and feminists liked things they thought they ought not to" (Dyer 1992: 4). This difficulty over pleasure accounts for film theory being highly critical of prevailing cultural politics but never reifying itself into the puritanism or orthodoxy alleged by critics of political correctness. The extraordinary diversity of latter-day film anthologies makes this point clear. A feminist film anthology certainly focusses on issues of representation and production that are shared by many women, but it also attends to differences of race, history, class, sexuality, and nation, alongside and as part of theoretical difference (Carson, Dittmar, and Welsch 1994), while a black film anthology will divide between spectatorial and aesthetic dimensions (Diawara 1993), and a queer anthology will identify links between social oppres-sion and film and video practice (Gever, Greyson, and Parmar 1993; Holmlund and Fuchs 1997).

Concerns about representation and audience are, then, relatively stable across time. What has changed is the implicit and explicit Eurocentrism and universal-ism of earlier theory, as social movements and Third and Fourth World dis-courses have pointed to silences and generated new methods (Shohat/Stam 1994; Carson and Friedman 1995). Even here, though, there is a long history of protest at, for example, Hollywood's portrayal of foreigners and minorities (Vasey 1997).

This continuity of concern with audiences and representational politics does not, however, mean that there is agreement over the constitution, history, practice, or value of film theory. Alan Parker, Chair of the world's leading film-culture site, the British Film Institute, and also a noted Hollywood director, has famously stated that: "Film needs theory like it needs a scratch on the negative" (quoted in Lapsley and Westlake 1988: vi), a reaction to the complaint that such writing "is unreadable to the uninitiated" and "often sounds like gobbledygook to filmmakers" (Barbash and Taylor 1997: 3). Students frequently argue that theorizing film removes its pleasure (to which their professors frequently reply that pleasure is only one aspect of study and that new forms of enjoyment may flow from new forms of knowledge).

Parker and other critics of film theory generally follow a tripartite line of reasoning: (a) filmmakers use imagination and practical knowledge; (b) filmgoers work with common sense; and (c) film theorists unravel the magic and escape of cinema. But each time a director selects a location or angle, or asks for a script to be rewritten, she or he is operating from various implied understandings of space, time, vision, and meaning. The same is true of viewers. The task of film theory is to make those processes available for debate, whether they are deliberate or unconscious, individual or collective, human or institutional. The chapters in this book assist this task by examining a wide variety of approaches to cinema, summarizing them in a scholarly and readable fashion, and offering some new directions. We have sought diversity of intellectual, geographical, and cultural background in our authors, in keeping with the plural approaches to film theory they address. Some contributors are well known to cinema studies while others are newer figures on the landscape, and their backgrounds criss-cross literature, philosophy, communications, education, sociology, and anthropology. They come from five continents, as part of our desire to push the field further toward deprovincialization.

In almost all cases, the material in these chapters has political implications. Of course, some film academics separate their work from politics, seeking instead a means of registering and developing aesthetic discrimination "in a relationship of tutelage, to the more established disciplines" (Bennett, Boyd-Bowman, Mercer, and Woollacott 1981: ix). They seek to isolate the "basic features of film which can constitute it as an art" (Bordwell and Thompson 1997: ix). But even that old-fashioned cultural elitism, whereby professors define what is art and then instruct others, can be of use. First, a seemingly abstracted formalism necessarily looks at the materiality of cinema, its sound and image, in ways that encourage a careful explanation of meaning. And second, the avowed project of "art" is doomed to failure in its attempt to cordon off the social. Film always exceeds attempts to institute such New-Critical readings, because of its history. As a governmental and business technology that spread with urbanization and colonialism, alongside multifarious attempts to comprehend the modernity that it brought into vision (Shohat/Stam 1994: 100–36), film is impossible to delimit in a fetishized manner for very long in all but the most intramural cloisters. The medium's promiscuity points every day and in every way toward the social. It is three things, all at once: a *recorder* of reality (the unstaged pro-filmic event); a *manufacturer* of reality (the staged and edited event); and *part of* reality (watching film as a social event on a

3

Saturday night, or a protest event over sexual, racial, or religious stereotyping). Film is a marker of culture:

> not even the final target of enquiry, but part of a wider argument about *representation* – the social process of making images, sounds, signs stand for something ... In effect, film theory becomes part of the wider field of disciplines and approaches called cultural studies. (Turner 1988: 38)

This suggests that the study of cinema is about how consciousness and systems of value are created and either bind society together or illuminate its fissures. Film attained its majority as one of the principal new forms of inter-war communication. Along with the popular press and radio, it was designated as ideal for propaganda and social uplift (choose your terms). The imbrication of audiences and aesthetics through questions of representation is an abiding effect of this history (Lopez 1985: 57, 59). Depending on your politics, that may lead to uncovering "the cultural codes of patriarchy" (Wexman 1985: 62) or the "*mode of representation of otherness*" (Bhabha 1983: 34). This history ensured Siegfried Kracauer's preference for "a *material* aesthetics, not a formal one" (1965: ix).

Perhaps the most significant innovation in recent film theory has been a radical historicization of context, such that the analysis of textual properties and spectatorial processes must now be supplemented by an account of occasionality that details the conditions under which a text is made, circulated, received, interpreted, and criticized. The life of any popular or praised film is a passage across space and time, a life remade again and again by institutions, discourses, and practices of distribution and reception – in short, all the shifts and shocks that characterize the existence of cultural commodities, their ongoing renewal as the temporary "property" of varied, productive workers and publics, and their stasis as the abiding "property" of businesspeople. Ana Lopez asks:

> Is *Gone with the Wind* the same kind of theoretical object on the TV screen today as it was in Radio City Music Hall in 1939? Should we study this phenomenon through a feminist, formalist, semiotic, or hermeneutic methodology? (1985: 56–7)

I would add the lens of black film theory to the list of textual methods, and ask social history, Africana, and American studies to assist with locating the film's intertexts, notably white racism of the 1860s, the 1930s, and today.

Despite the continuity of textual and audience axes within film theory, latter-day lines have been drawn dividing media, communication, cultural, and film studies for reasons of rent-seeking academic professionalism. The theorization of production and spectatorship relations between film and television, for instance, continues to be dogged by the separation of mass communication's interest in economics, technology, and policy from film theory's preoccupations with aesthetics and cultural address, although attempts are underway to transform both sides of the divide (Balio 1990; Hill and McLoone n.d. [1997]).

4

The push for a radical contextualization of interpretation is aided by a surprising turn – the early history of film as part of a vaudeville bill is being reprised. The moving image is again part of a multi-form, animated, diverse network of entertainment, via CD-ROMs, computer games, the Web, and multiplexes. The brief moment when cinema could be viewed as a fairly unitary phenomenon in terms of exhibition (say, 1930 to 1950) set up the prospect of its textual fetishization in academia, something that became technologically feasible with videocassette recorders – just when that technology's popularity compromised the very discourse of stable aestheticization! Now that viewing environments, audiences, technologies, and genres are so multiple, the cinema is restored to a mixed-medium mode. At this crucial juncture, the division between the analysis of text and context is breaking up. Contemporary approaches model themselves on the abiding discourses identified at the beginning of this introduction, rather than on text alone (Hill and Church Gibson 1998).

In keeping with the argument that there is as much repetition as difference in film theory, this *Companion* is organized conceptually rather than developmentally. We begin with five chapters on film form and style (James Naremore on authorship, Sarah Berry-Flint on genre, André Gaudreault and François Jost on narration, Lucy Fischer on editing, and Warren Buckland on semiotics). These chapters cover methods of cataloging and analyzing films as well as unpacking the sounds, images, and tendencies of the cinema and its critical apparatus. They are matched by three chapters addressing spectatorship (Gregory Currie on cognitivism, Richard Allen on psychoanalysis, and E. Deidre Pribram on subjectivity). These papers represent dominant and competing theories of the film audience.

The second half of the volume looks at topics that cross these boundaries, starting with two meta-critiques of film scholarship (Julia Erhart on queer theory and David James on class politics). We then take up marginalized approaches in film theory that are nevertheless central to understanding the cinema (Douglas Kellner on the culture industries and Janet Wasko on political economy) before examining three emergent developments (Henry Jenkins on digitalization, Tom O'Regan on cultural exchange, and Faye Ginsburg on First People's film and media ethnography). The *Companion* concludes with four applications of some of the precepts illustrated in earlier chapters, modeling meta-criticism (Ira Bhaskar and Ismail Xavier) and textual analysis (Charles Ramírez Berg and Toby Miller).

Although this book is designed to stand alone, it can also be used in concert with two other projects from Blackwell: Robert Stam's *Film Theory: An Introduction* and our coedited *Film and Theory: An Anthology*. *Film Theory: An Introduction* takes readers through the history of the subject, summarizing and debating the field from early film theory, such as formalism and montage; through structuralism, early Third World critiques, and auteurism; on to psychoanalysis, feminisms, and post-structuralisms; and later queer theory and cultural studies, amongst others. *Film and Theory: An Anthology* includes key writings since the 1960s. Various rubrics (such as authorship, film language, class and the culture industries, the historical spectator/audience, and the nature of the gaze, plus many more) are introduced by analytic essays, followed by selections of the most significant (and sometimes surprising) papers on the subject over the past 30 years.

For all its pluralism, this project is not proclaiming a happy moment of Whiggism, where all feasible methods of understanding films can be distilled. A scholarly paper combining *all* the methods outlined in this book, for example, would be not only unwieldy, but internally contradictory, striving to deny the incommensurability of various discourses (such as cognitivism and psychoanalysis, or auteurism and political economy). Attempts to marry neoformalist textual analysis, where politics is accidental, with neo-Marxist analysis of production, where politics is central, have not always ended happily (Clark 1995: x; Wasko 1994: 17–18).

If you walk away from reading this book with one message, however, it might be the necessity for a plural and political approach to film that follows Roger Chartier's *dicta* from the history of books: (a) a reconstruction of "the diversity of older readings from their sparse and multiple traces"; (b) a focus on "the text itself, the object that conveys it, and the act that grasps it"; and (c) an identification of "the strategies by which authors and publishers tried to impose an orthodoxy or a prescribed reading on the text." Such syncretism looks for meaning in the interstices, the interactions, and the relative autonomy of each part of a film: how technology, labor, image, sound, paratext, intertext, and social text change (Chartier 1989: 157, 161–3, 166).

In short, theory should produce "a verbal representation of the film complex" (Andrew 1984: 3). As such, it must acknowledge that "film is not only entertainment but . . . part of industrial and political culture" (Kolker 1999: xi). Our aim in compiling this *Companion* has been to encourage readers to utilize the full wealth of the human sciences in order to make a credible intervention into film culture. We trust it is useful and thank our contributors for their efforts in generating a summary of the past and the present and a challenge to the future.

References

Andrew, J. Dudley. 1984. *Concepts in Film Theory*. Oxford: Oxford University Press.

Balio, Tino, ed. 1990. *Hollywood in the Age of Television*. Boston: Unwin Hyman.

Barbash, Ilisa, and Lucien Taylor. 1997. *Cross-Cultural Filmmaking: A Handbook for Making Documentary and Ethnographic Films and Videos*. Berkeley: University of California Press.

Bennett, Tony, Susan Boyd-Bowman, Colin Mercer, and Janet Woollacott. 1981. "Preface." In *Popular Television and Film*. Ed. Tony Bennett, Susan Boyd-Bowman, Colin Mercer, and Janet Woollacott. London: British Film Institute/Open University Press. ix–xi.

Bhabha, Homi K. 1983. "The Other Question . . . The Stereotype and Colonial Discourse." *Screen* 24: 18–36.

Blumer, Herbert. 1933. *Movies and Conduct*. New York: Macmillan.

———, and Philip M. Hauser. 1933. *Movies, Delinquency and Crime*. New York: Macmillan.

Bordwell, David, and Kristin Thompson. 1997. *Film Art: An Introduction*, 5th edn. New York: McGraw-Hill.

Braudy, Leo, and Marshall Cohen. 1999. "Preface." In *Film Theory and Criticism: Introductory Readings*, 5th edn. Ed. Leo Braudy and Marshall Cohen. New York: Oxford University Press. xv–xviii.

Buchanan, Andrew, and Stanley Reed. 1957. *Going to the Cinema*. London: Phoenix House.

Carson, Diane, Linda Dittmar, and Janice R. Welsch, eds. 1994. *Multiple Voices in Feminist Film Criticism*. Minneapolis: University of Minnesota Press.

Carson, Diane, and Lester D. Friedman, eds. 1995. *Shared Differences: Multicultural Media and Practical Pedagogy*. Urbana: University of Illinois Press.

Chartier, Roger. 1989. "Texts, Printings, Readings." In *The New Cultural History*. Ed. Lynn Hunt. Berkeley: University of California Press. 154–75.

Clark, Danae. 1995. *Negotiating Hollywood: The Cultural Politics of Actors' Labor*. Minneapolis: University of Minnesota Press.

Diawara, Manthia, ed. 1993. *Black American Cinema*. New York: Routledge.

Dyer, Richard. 1992. *Only Entertainment*. London: Routledge.

Gever, Martha, John Greyson, and Pratibha Parmar, eds. 1993. *Queer Looks: Perspectives on Lesbian and Gay Film and Video*. New York: Routledge.

Hill, John, and Pamela Church Gibson, eds. 1998. *The Oxford Guide to Film Studies*. Oxford: Oxford University Press.

Hill, John, and Martin McLoone, eds. n.d. [1997]. *Big Picture Small Screen: The Relations Between Film and Television*. Luton: University of Luton Press/John Libbey Media.

Hollows, Joanne, and Mark Jancovich. 1995. "Popular Film and Cultural Distinctions." In *Approaches to Popular Film*. Ed. Joanne Hollows and Mark Jancovich. Manchester: Manchester University Press. 1–14.

Holmlund, Christine, and Cynthia Fuchs, eds. 1997. *Between the Sheets, In the Streets: Queer, Lesbian, and Gay Documentary*. Minneapolis: University of Minnesota Press.

Kolker, Robert. 1999. *Film, Form, and Culture*. Boston: McGraw-Hill.

Kracauer, Siegfried. 1965 [1960]. *Theory of Film: The Redemption of Physical Reality*. New York: Oxford University Press.

Lapsley, Robert, and Michael Westlake. 1988. *Film Theory: An Introduction*. Manchester: Manchester University Press.

Lindsay, Vachel. *The Art of the Moving Picture*. 1970 [1922]. New York: Liveright.

Lopez, Ana. 1985. "From Photoplays to Texts: Film Theory, Film Studies, and the Future". *Cinema Journal* 24: 56–61.

Manvell, Roger. 1950. *Film*. Harmondsworth: Penguin.

Mayer, J. P. 1946. *Sociology of Film: Studies and Documents*. London: Faber and Faber.

Metz, Christian. 1974. *Film Language: A Semiotics of the Cinema*. Trans. Michael Taylor. New York: Oxford University Press.

Powdermaker, Hortense. 1950. *Hollywood: The Dream Factory: An Anthropologist Looks at the Movie-Makers*. Boston: Little, Brown.

Sarris, Andrew. 1968. *The American Cinema: Directors and Directions 1929–1968*. New York: E. P. Dutton.

Shohat, Ella/Robert Stam. 1994. *Unthinking Eurocentrism: Multiculturalism and the Media*. New York: Routledge.

Turner, Graeme. 1988. *Film as Social Practice*. London: Routledge.

Vasey, Ruth. 1997. *The World According to Hollywood, 1918–1939*. Madison: University of Wisconsin Press.

Wasko, Janet. 1994. *Hollywood in the Information Age: Beyond the Silver Screen*. Cambridge: Polity Press.

Wexman, Virginia Wright. 1985. "Evaluating the Text: Canon Formation and Screen Scholarship." *Cinema Journal* 24: 62–5.

Worth, Sol. 1981 [1969]. *Studying Visual Communication*. Ed. Larry Gross. Philadelphia: University of Pennsylvania Press.

CHAPTER TWO

Authorship

James Naremore

Motion pictures and television are often described as collaborative media, but their modes of production are hierarchical, involving a mixture of industrialized, theatrical, and artisanal practices. Given the circumstances under which particular films are made, it is possible to think of any of the creative individuals who contribute to them as a kind of author. In books about classic Hollywood, the term has been applied with more or less justification to writers (Anita Loos, Raymond Chandler), photographers (John Alton, Gordon Willis), composers (Max Steiner, Bernard Herrmann), choreographers (Busby Berkeley, Michael Kidd), and stars (the Marx Brothers, Bette Davis). It has even described the old-style corporate executives (David Selznick, Darryl Zanuck), who functioned as impresarios and who wanted to keep their names before the public. For the most part, however, film authorship is associated with directors, who are said to play the most important role in the production process. Directorial names such as D. W. Griffith and F. W. Murnau have been fundamental to the establishment of movies as "respectable" art, and until recently histories of film styles and institutions were organized around them, just as literary history is organized around the names of poets or novelists. As a result, "Sergei Eisenstein," "Robert Flaherty," and "Alfred Hitchcock" have come to signify not only persons but also traditions, theories, and genres.

The study of authorship is not in itself a theory, only a topic or theme. It can involve a great variety of political positions and theoretical assumptions; and, like all types of criticism, it can be performed well or badly. And yet the discourse on the director-as-author has always been problematic – not only because of the industrial basis of the film medium, but also because the film director emerged as a creative type at the very moment when authorship in general was becoming an embattled concept. At no point was the irony of the situation more evident than during the 1950s and '60s, when certain directors in classic Hollywood and the international art cinema became known throughout the world as "auteurs," and when film criticism as a whole underwent a kind of revolution. This was the period of the French *politique des auteurs*, or "policy" of canonizing directors in the name of art, and it remains crucial to an understanding of contemporary film studies. I therefore want to postpone my discussion of theoretical debates surrounding authorship until I have commented on film culture in the middle decades of the century. In this way, I can historicize recent film theory, making a useful distinction between the study of authors (which, although it involves all the arts, has strong literary associations) and the more influential, movie-specific phenomenon called auteurism.

1 Auteurism

As its suffix implies, auteurism is less a scientific approach to the problem of the author than a kind of aesthetic ideology or movement. Like countless other movements, it was generated by what Raymond Williams terms a "cultural formation" – a loose confederation of intellectuals and critics (in this case made up almost entirely of white males) who had roughly similar objectives, and who developed a body of polemical writing to justify their opinions. Such formations are especially important to the modern era, and sociological research might help us to understand their significance. As Williams notes, they are typically centered in a metropolis, at points of "transition and intersection" within a complex social history; and the individuals who both compose and are composed by them always have a "range of diverse positions, interests and influences, some of which are resolved (if at times only temporarily)..., others of which remain as internal differences" (1981: 85–6). In every modern case, the formations are ephemeral, spinning off into individual careers or breakaway movements; but they some-times disseminate their ideas widely, leaving more or less permanent traces on the general culture.

Auteurism fits the profile of a modern cultural formation almost perfectly. It originated in Paris during the 1950s, at a moment when France was becoming increasingly Americanized, and in many respects it imitated what Peter Burger and other writers have called the "historical" avant-garde of the 1910s and '20s. Like the old avant-garde, it possessed an intellectual or "left bank" aura; it made iconoclastic or shocking value judgments; it was articulated in specialized maga-zines (the most famous of which was *Cahiers du cinéma*); it embraced certain elements of pop culture and used them as a weapon to attack bourgeois values; it published manifestos (such as François Truffaut's "A Certain Tendency of the French Cinema"); and it served as a kind of banner to help publicize the early work of its own adherents.

The last point is especially important, because many of the auteurists (includ-ing Truffaut, Jean-Luc Godard, Claude Chabrol, Eric Rohmer, and Jacques Rivette) were themselves directors who wanted to foreground their own creativ-ity. Their call for a "personal" cinema was inspired to some extent by Alexandre Astruc's 1948 essay, "The Birth of a New Avant-Garde: La Camera-Stylo," published in the socialist film journal *L'Ecran français*, which spoke metaphorically of the camera as a pen, the screen as a piece of paper, and the director as an author. Astruc, who was both a novelist and a director, strongly emphasized the inscribable properties of cinematic mise-en-scène, locating them "in every gesture of the characters, in every line of dialogue, in those camera movements that relate objects to objects and characters to objects." The auteurists strongly supported such ideas, and gave them a practical application by moving from critical writing into filmmaking. Meanwhile, their reviews and essays were filled with flamboyant descriptions of directors as existentialist authors. Godard remarked apropos of Ingmar Bergman that "The cinema is not a craft. It is an art. It does not mean teamwork. One is always alone on the set as before the blank page" (1972: 76). Truffaut, speaking of Robert Aldrich's *Kiss Me Deadly*, declared, "It is easy to picture its author as a man overflowing with vitality, as much at ease behind a camera as Henry Miller facing a blank page" (1978: 94).

As Godard himself wittily remarked about this attitude, "Nothing could be more classically romantic" (76). There was also a certain irony in the French fascination with the American cinema: the auteurists' rise to success as filmmakers was facilitated by the decline of the Hollywood studios, which had dominated the marketplace in the years between the two world wars. In the United States, the major production companies were no longer in control of exhibition, censorship regulations were becoming liberalized, and European art films were making significant inroads in urban theaters. The French New Wave was particularly well suited to the period, because it managed to fuse certain elements of Italian neorealism with a fond, insouciant, distinctively Gallic attitude toward old-fashioned Hollywood genres and directors. In certain American contexts, its name became useful as a kind of marketing strategy.

This does not mean, however, that either the New Wave or auteurism can be reduced to a device for self-promotion. The latter began as a purely critical undertaking, and in some of its most impressive cinematic instances it dissolved the distinctions between criticism and art. Equally significant, auteurism marked an important change in the history of taste. One of the best sources for an understanding of what the French movement achieved is Jim Hillier's intelligently edited *Cahiers du Cinéma in the 1950s*, which illustrates the diversity of opinion among the writers of the period, and places French debates over American cinema in the context of larger concerns about neorealism, modernism, and the French film industry. As Hillier indicates, auteurism was never a product of *Cahiers du cinéma* alone, and was not simply about American-based directors such as Samuel Fuller, Alfred Hitchcock, and Nicholas Ray. All the Parisian cineastes were interested in American auteurs, including the left critics at *Positif* and the right critics at *Présence du cinéma*; in general, however, French writing about Hollywood was tempered by an even stronger admiration for Roberto Rosselini, Michaelangelo Antonioni, Alain Resnais, and the authors of the "nouveau roman." Nor were the auteurists exclusively concerned with authorship. Particularly at *Cahiers*, their practice usually implied a contradictory set of theories about the phenomenology and semiotics of the cinema, and it produced excellent

11

essays on stars and genres. Above all, it generated a relentlessly evaluative kind of criticism, involving a policy of liking some directors and films more than others. Thus if you wrote for *Cahiers*, you tended to favor Jean Renoir, Howard Hawks, and Kenji Mizoguchi over Eisenstein, John Huston, and Akira Kurosawa; you disliked well-made literary adaptations of Great Books, especially when they suggested a slick, middle-brow attitude toward Art; you had a quasi-surrealistic passion for *l'amour fou* in pictures like *Gun Crazy*, *Letter from an Unknown Woman*, and *Vertigo*; you preferred low-budget films noirs such as *Kiss Me Deadly* over Big Productions with Important Themes such as *Bridge on the River Kwai*; and you praised wide-screen, color-coded melodramas like *Some Came Running* instead of Academy-Award-winning "little" movies like *Marty*.

Much of the philosophical underpinnings of 1950s criticism at *Cahiers* derived from André Bazin, the editor of the journal. It must be emphasized, however, that Bazin himself was never an auteurist in the sense I have described above. Although he produced seminal writings on a number of directors (Renoir, Robert Bresson, William Wyler, Orson Welles, and the Italian neorealists), he chastised his younger colleagues for their habit of falling into uncritical hero worship, and he was explicitly disapproving of the "Hichcocko-Hawksian" tendency in Truffaut's work. For his own part, Bazin wrote a great deal about well-made literary adaptations, and praised "the genius of the system" in classic Hollywood. His influence on the younger generation lay not so much in the authors he favored as in his broad historical knowledge of the cinema and the arts generally, his ability to take Hollywood genres and technical developments seriously, and his keen understanding of the way style gives rise to meaning. Above all, Bazin imbued the early New Wave with a spirit of existential humanism, which placed great emphasis on the cinema's ability to view the world from an objective standpoint. (The very word for the photographic lens in French is *objectif*.) He and the auteurists repeatedly favored "realistic," "democratic," or untendentious uses of the camera; as a result, *Cahiers* in the 1950s was preoccupied with the "ethics" of mise-en-scène, and with directors who used invisible editing, long takes, or sequence shots rather than montage. Sometimes this ideology was joined with a belief that the best American auteurs were existentialists *avant la lettre*. In his excellent 1960 review of Fuller's *Verboten!*, for example, Truffaut describes the director of the film as if he were an action painter, making instinctive or primal decisions about what should be put on the screen: "This is direct cinema, uncriticizable, irreproachable, 'given' cinema, rather than assimilated, digested, or reflected upon. Fuller doesn't take time to think; it is clear that he is in his glory when he is shooting" (1978: 108).

There was a tension, however, between Truffaut's existentialist ideas, which made him sympathetic to a Bazinian or "open" cinema of the kind practiced by Renoir and Rosselini, and his equally strong love of genre directors like Fuller and modernist auteurs like Welles. Whatever attitude he may have had toward phenomenal reality, it seems clear that what chiefly attracted Truffaut to the Americans was their sense of fairy tales or pure artifice. As Leo Braudy has pointed out, Truffaut and Godard were part of a movie-obsessed generation who were hyper-aware of the conventions of the medium, and who "showed their involvement with the special aesthetics of film most clearly when they considered genre films – the westerns, the detective films, the musicals – in which realistic materials were used unrealistically in a structure dictated less by story than by myth." Even when Truffaut discussed *Citizen Kane*, Braudy notes, "he implicitly contradicted Bazin's assumption of a realist teleology in film history by celebrating the virtues of self-conscious stylization" (1991: 47).

Where the auteurists chiefly differed from Bazin was in the delirious style of their cinephilia, and in their tendency to place directors of pop genres or assembly-line films alongside the work of more highly respected artists. One of their favorite devices for achieving these effects was the ten-best list, which could be used as a weapon against prevailing opinion. (Godard announced not only the ten best films of each year, but also such things as the "Ten Best American Sound Films" and the "Six Best French Films Since the Liberation.") The typical list in *Cahiers* contained several key works of the Nouvelle Vague, together with such unexpected choices as *Hatari!*, *Bigger Than Life*, or *A Time to Love and a Time to Die*. Both here and in their more discursive writings, the auteurists loved to elevate the low-brow over the middle-brow. Godard was perhaps better than anyone at the technique – as when he remarked that "an alert Frank Tashlin is worth two Billy Wilders" (1972: 35). His reviews repeatedly blurred the distinction between mass media and the avant-garde, and balanced sophistication with a swooning idealism about certain Hollywood films. In most cases, he employed a language of puns, epigrams, and breathtakingly unorthodox pronouncements that turned the dominant critical values on their heads. Thus in 1952, writing under the name "Hans Lucas," he answered the Bazinian question, "What is Cinema?," with a single phrase, basing his response on the work of old-fashioned auteurs like Griffith, Flaherty, Renoir, and Hitchcock: "the expression of lofty sentiments" (31).

Godard's Olympian pronouncement illustrates one of the fundamental paradoxes of auteurism. Although the movement was in every sense youthful, impetuous, and romantic (some would say adolescent), it was often dedicated to antique virtues, and to praising the work of directors who were entering their twilight years. We should recall that Josef von Sternberg's *Jet Pilot*, Fritz Lang's *The Thousand Eyes of Dr. Mabuse*, Renoir's *Le Dejeuner sur l'herbe*, John Ford's *Seven Women*, and Hawks's *Red Line 7000* were all made during roughly the same period as the early films of the Nouvelle Vague. These pictures occupied a world apart from both the current Hollywood hits and the new European art cinema, as if they were still clinging to dated formulas or dead modes of production. Few mainstream critics in the Anglo-Saxon world took them seriously, but the auteurists passionately embraced them, sometimes ranking them above the same directors' more celebrated films of the 1930s and '40s. One of the most sweetly charming features of auteurism lay in its love for old pros or cinematic father-figures who were still alive, making unpretentious genre movies or quiet, meditative films such as Ford's *The Sun Shines Bright*. Truffaut, who could be devastatingly sarcastic in some contexts, was quite touching when he spoke of such films, or when he used them to rebuke current fashions.

The paradoxes or tensions I have been describing – between old and new, between pop and modernism, between a humanist philosophy and a nascent idea of cinematic *écriture* – are also apparent in the early films of the Nouvelle Vague. Truffaut's directorial style, for example, rises out of two apparently incompatible approaches to cinema: Renoir's free-flowing tolerance, which breaks down generic conventions, and Hitchcock's "murderous gaze," which exploits generic conventions to the utmost. Godard's *Breathless* employs a similar dialectic, but the effect is much more conflicted or ambivalent. A highly personal movie (at least in the intellectual sense), *Breathless* gives its auteur an opportunity to identify with both Michel (Jean-Paul Belmondo), a French wise guy who is infatuated with everything American, and Patricia (Jean Seberg), a sensitive, rather intellectual young woman from America who fears that she might be getting too deeply involved with the underworld. The two facets of the director's imaginary identity are represented in the form of a perversely romantic and failed relationship, much like the ones in Hollywood film noir; and the relationship is echoed in a dense pattern of allusions to two different kinds of text: genre movies, mostly associated with Michel, and high-cultural literature, music, or painting, mostly associated with Patricia. The film alludes not only to Aldrich, Fuller, Budd Boetticher, Otto Preminger, and Raoul Walsh, but also to William Faulkner, Rainer-Marie Rilke, Louis Aragon, Guillaume Apollinaire, and William Shakespeare. Godard is the implicit source of these allusions and is therefore identified with both the man of action and the would-be artist, with both the rebel and the conformist – although it may be significant that he makes a cameo appearance (imitating Hitchcock) as a man on the street who points Michel out to the cops.

In retrospect, both French auteurism and the Nouvelle Vague could be understood as early symptoms of what Andreas Huyssen, in *After the Great Divide* (1986), describes as a "postmodern" sensibility. Huyssen chooses 1960 as the date when the postmodern style became dominant in Western culture, manifesting itself in the Pop Art movement, the criticism of Susan Sontag and Leslie Fiedler, and the architectural theory of Robert Venturi. Auteurism is contemporary with these events, and it shares one of their defining characteristics: a tendency to blur or dissolve the boundaries between high and mass art. Godard in particular often seems like a Pop Artist, especially when he writes about Hollywood directors like Fuller or Douglas Sirk, or when he inserts loving tributes to pulp thrillers or big-budget musicals into his films. Notice, moreover, that auteurism is contemporary with the end of the Fordist system in Hollywood and the sale of old movies to television. By 1960 the postmodern economy of electronic communication had fully arrived, and viewers everywhere were becoming accustomed to an aesthetic based on allusion, pastiche, or recycled photographic imagery.[1]

14

Although the Nouvelle Vague was fostered by postmodernity or "late capitalism," it also retained certain features of romanticism and critical modernism. However it might be described, the important point is that French success in the art theaters gave the auteurist writings of Godard, Truffaut, Rohmer, and Chabrol a special authority. By the early 1960s the movement had spread far beyond France. In England, it influenced the best critics of the period, including Robin Wood, Raymond Durgnat, Victor Perkins, Peter Wollen, David Thomson, and the group of writers associated with *Movie*. Over the next decade, it had a similar influence in America, shaping the work of critic–filmmakers Paul Schrader and Peter Bogdanovitch, and eventually affecting what came to be known as "New American Cinema." During the 1960s, its presence was quite strong in New York, where the avant-garde filmmaker Jonas Mekas briefly provided a space for auteurist criticism in the pages of *Film Culture*, where select revival cinemas featured retrospectives of Hollywood auteurs, and where *Film Comment* became an important auteurist journal.

The maverick critic Manny Farber, who anticipated many of these developments, had written his famous essay on "Underground Films" in 1957, praising Hollywood's male-action genre movies and attacking the middle-brow or "quality" tradition in America (meanwhile persuading us that Howard Hawks, one of the most successful producer–directors of the previous two decades, was somehow an underground artist). The most influential American exponent of auteurism, however, was Andrew Sarris, whose columns for *The Village Voice* and writings on directors in *The American Cinema* (1968) helped to establish the canonical works of classic Hollywood. Sarris's major achievement was to reinterpret the French movement for America. Like Truffaut, he launched a polemical attack against a tradition of quality, made up chiefly of literary adaptations and social-problem pictures; his principal targets, however, were not Claude Autant-Lara, Marcel Carné, and Jean Delannoy, but John Huston, William Wyler, and Elia Kazan. Along similar lines, he attacked prevailing intellectual opinions (especially the disdain for Hollywood glamour and the taste for movies with "proletarian" significance). But because Sarris was a university teacher rather than a would-be director, he gave auteurism a strong academic inflection, using its basic assumptions to write a full-scale history. One of the explicit aims of *The American Cinema* was to make film historiography less of an amateur calling. To this end, Sarris modeled himself to some degree on the New Critics in American literary studies: he placed great emphasis on personal style and was contemptuous of the positivists, the sociologists, and their nonprofessional allies, the hobbyists or "stamp collectors." His most powerful technique was the evaluative list, which he borrowed from the French and elaborated into a map of popular movies from Griffith to the present. In *The American Cinema* he listed approximately two hundred directors, placing them in hierarchical categories; he listed each director's films chronologically, italicizing the pictures he favored; and he listed the best films of each year from 1915 onward (after their directors' names), italicizing the masterpieces.

At the time *The American Cinema* was written, Sarris's evaluations were iconoclastic and politically incorrect. With the exception of Rouben Mamoulian, Lewis Milestone, and William Wellman, all the directors he placed in the "Less Than Meets the Eye" and "Strained Seriousness" categories were active, and most were highly regarded. Ford's greatest pictures were generally thought to be *The Informer* and *The Grapes of Wrath* (Sarris preferred *Steamboat 'Round the Bend* and *Wee Willie Winkie*), and melodramatists such as Sirk or low-budget action directors such as Fuller and Anthony Mann had nothing like their present reputations. Even so, the overwhelming majority of names in Sarris's "Pantheon" belonged to the old-time producer–directors who worked slightly apart from studio executives. There was nothing especially unusual about a book that praised these individuals. Sarris was most unorthodox not when he argued on behalf of Chaplin or Welles, but when he defended *Limelight* or *The Lady from Shanghai*. He was also challenging when he showed admiration for Hollywood soap operas, and when he placed an unfashionable director such as Cecil B. de Mille (the very symbol of Hollywood vulgarity and right-wing bombast) on the "Far Side of Paradise," next to the most honored figures.

In this respect and others, *The American Cinema* is a book of sharp but productive contradictions – a mixture of populism and elitism, of appeals to individual expression and vigorous praise for Hollywood. Even while it offers a montage of epigrammatic comments on directors, it shares Bazin's fondness for long takes and the continuity style. Notice, too, that while its critical opinions reflect the latest continental trends, its basic values are old. Sarris is skeptical of art-house modernism (which he describes more than once as "Antonionien-nui"), and he greatly admires the cinema of nostalgia or memory – especially the films of Griffith, Chaplin, Ford, and Welles, all of whom look back to the nineteenth century. By the same token, he responds passionately to the old-world aestheticism of Sternberg and Max Ophüls, and he insists that proper appreciation of their films should not be confused with the 1960s vogue for camp or kitsch.

Sarris, like all the other auteurists, is a latter-day aesthete (albeit a heterosexual one), finding autonomous personal expression in places where the studio bosses, the puritans of the American left, and the artistic trend-setters had not thought to look. He and his colleagues were surely among the last romantics. Their judgments of specific films and directors, however, have withstood a great many changes in intellectual fashion; furthermore, as I hope to indicate, their interest in creative agency still has relevance and ought to be taken seriously by anyone who thinks of the movies as an art.

2 The Death (and Survival) of the Author

Auteurism had a significant impact. It profoundly affected Hollywood's view of its own past, and in the process greatly enhanced the reputation of directors like

Hawks and Hitchcock, who were making their late films at the height of the movement.[2] Equally important, it influenced the spread of college film societies, inspired a new generation of academics to write about film, and contributed to the growth of film studies as an academic discipline.

In the Anglo–Saxon world especially, film study proliferated in literature departments rather than in drama or art-history departments, probably because the very term "auteur" tended to encourage an association with literature. Literary specialists found auteurism especially compatible because it offered a provisional canon and a program for research into a vast, largely unexplored area of twentieth-century narrative; it also required a scholarly effort to see everything, not for the purpose of cataloging or building an archive, but for the purpose of making informed value judgments. To British auteurists such as Robin Wood, this project had something in common with the severely evaluative, somewhat anti-modernist literary criticism practiced by F. R. Leavis and his followers at *Scrutiny* in the 1930s and '40s. Thus Wood began his famous book on Hitchcock with a chapter entitled "Why We Should Take Hitchcock Seriously," and went on to stress the "complex moral implications" of certain Hitchcock films (1989: 4). In a more qualified and complex fashion, the first edition of Peter Wollen's *Signs and Meaning in the Cinema* (1969) concluded with the suggestion that film study might join forces with the dominant, Arnoldian form of education:

> Hitchcock is at least as important an artist as, say, Scott Fitzgerald, much more important than many other modern American novelists who have found their way on to the university curriculum. I do not think time is wasted in writing about these novelists, all things being equal, and I do not think it would be wasted if hundreds of post-graduates were writing research theses on Jean Renoir, Max Ophuls or John Ford. (160–1)

Arnold and Leavis, however, were strange models for film critics to imitate. Leavis in particular had been a thoroughgoing opponent of mass culture, who offered literature as a civilizing defense against industrial modernity. To apply his methods to film was to unwittingly parody or appropriate the British culture-and-society debates of the previous century; it was also to realign or decenter the academic canon, and to encourage a certain curiosity about how canons are formed in the first place. In this regard and in many others, auteurism began to deconstruct at the very moment when it achieved its greatest success. Ultimately it fell victim to a variety of internal contradictions in its own practice, to growing acceptance by the culture industries, to the professionalism of academia, and to theoretical challenges from both the right and the left.

The first of the theoretical challenges, barely noticed at the time, was already inherent in the literary methodology that some of the American auteurists had adopted. Disregarding the question of what kind of work directors actually perform, we do not need to know their names (just as we do not need to know the names of stars) in order to comprehend the stories we see on the screen, or to construct a sophisticated poetics of the cinema. The very idea of modern poetics in the Anglo-Saxon world derives from an "objective" formalism of a type best exemplified by T. S. Eliot, who argued in "Tradition and the Individual Talent" (1919) that "Honest criticism and sensitive appreciation is directed not upon the poet but upon the poetry." In the literary sphere, Eliot and the New Critics mounted a devastating attack on a dusty, genteel, academic historicism, in which the names of great writers figured prominently. In the process, they warned us not to commit the "intentional fallacy," and always to trust the tale, not the teller.

Prior to the 1920s, the study of literature in the United States was essentially a branch of intellectual biography, guided by the Arnoldian attempt to shape the morality and taste of young gentlemen, and by the idea that art was something in the "real" world, existing prior to language. In sweeping aside major parts of this tradition, the New Criticism had democratic effects: it called attention to the way sign systems construct the world, and, in the words of Jonathan Culler, it enabled "the meanest student who lacked the scholarly information of his betters" to make "valid comments on the language and structure of the text" (1981: 3–4). Even though the New Criticism gradually died out, all subsequent developments in textual analysis – including structuralism, post-structuralism, and contemporary narratology – have been equally formalist or objective in their methodologies. Moreover, the overwhelming majority of introductory classes on media "language" taught in the universities are still based on New-Critical precepts. The most influential textbook in film studies, David Bordwell and Kristin Thompson's *Film Art*, argues that films should be evaluated along formal lines, according to internal criteria such as unity, coherence, complexity, originality, and intensity. Given this advice, we have not moved as far as we might think from the New-Critical ideal of the "well-wrought urn."

But here we encounter another paradox. Although the main current of instruction and analytic criticism tends to leave the question of the author to one side, the major achievements in modern poetics, as represented by such diverse figures as Erich Auerbach, Leo Spitzer, Roland Barthes, or Emile Benviniste, are derived from close analysis of the Western canon. For its part, *Film Art* is replete with the names of celebrated directors, and David Bordwell himself is the author of fine books on Carl Dreyer, Yasujiro Ozu, and Eisenstein. There would appear to be an unstated link between formalism, aestheticism, and the tendency to favor certain artists. In this context, we should recall that for all its apparent objectivity of method, the New Criticism advanced implicit ideological agendas, some of which were anti-democratic, and it created both a canon of modernist authors and a kind of priesthood of interpretation. It achieved such ends despite (or perhaps because of) the fact that it bracketed the important issue of historical authors and readers, leaving them outside the field of study, as unexamined entities who were extraneous to the understanding of self-sufficient works of art. Auteurism was different, not only because it validated Hollywood, but also because it openly fostered a cult of authorship and an impulse toward historical research. There were nevertheless a good many affinities between the New-Critical study of language and the auteurist emphasis on the "camera-stylo."

The auteurists faced much greater challenges from inside film culture, which was deeply affected by the radical politics of the Vietnam years, and by a new and more truly avant-garde movement centered in Paris. The late 1960s and '70s were a period when the "Langois affair" led to student riots and a general strike, when the Situationists made collage films, when Godard joined the "Dziga Vertov collective," and when the radicalized elements of the French film industry began to express dissatisfaction with any system that designated directors as "bosses of meaning."[3] At roughly the same time, "Third Cinema" developed in Latin America and in several nations that had once been colonized; this led to a militantly political type of filmmaking which, although it was indebted in certain ways to the Italian neorealists and the French New Wave, defined itself in opposition to both Hollywood entertainment and personalized European art.

Meanwhile, French anti-humanist "Theory" (a term that hardly existed in the Anglo-Saxon world) began to change the priorities for academic film criticism throughout the West. Outside France, the change first became widely apparent in the British journal *Screen*, which published Colin MacCabe's writings on Brecht, Stephen Heath's two-part analysis of *Touch of Evil*, Laura Mulvey's study of "Visual Pleasure," and many other seminal essays. *Screen* theory as a whole was indebted to the program outlined in "Cinema/Ideology/Criticism," a 1968 *Cahiers du cinéma* manifesto by Pierre Narboni and Jean-Louis Comolli, which marked a turn away from auteurism. Like Narboni and Comolli, *Screen* was suspicious of Hollywood entertainment. It tended to subsume individual practices under generalized formal categories, to which it attributed ideological effects; it closely examined the ways a hypostasized "subject" was positioned by narrative conventions and the technical apparatus; and it repeatedly argued on behalf of a modernist or avant-garde cinema that was both politically activist and critically self-reflexive.

Although nearly all theory in this period was Marxist (via Louis Althusser), it was just as disdainful of social realism as the auteurists had been. Nearly all of it was also in some sense Freudian (via Jaques Lacan), but it was not at all interested in the neuroses of individual artists; instead, it argued that the dominant tradition of cinematic language (described by Christian Metz as an "imaginary signifier") was structured by a systemically patriarchal unconscious. On every front, theory replaced the study of the author with the study of the sign systems through which ideology was represented. The author became a kind of epiphenomenon – an ideological or historical construction. Two French essays strongly influenced this tendency: in "What Is an Author?" Michel Foucault deconstructed the authorial "function," showing its relationship to early Christian exegesis, to the rationalist episteme of bourgeois society, and to legal or property rights; and in "From Work to Text," Roland Barthes contrasted the authorized work of art – which, he argued, was little more than a reified commodity – with the open-ended process of textuality, which seemed to belong to the reader, or to nobody in particular.

19

Where film study was concerned, the names of theorists now became more important than the names of directors. The new writing nevertheless favoured a wide range of filmmakers who could be interpreted in avant-garde terms – including Soviet radicals (Eisenstein, Dziga Vertov), pre-Hollywood pioneers (Edwin Porter and the photographers who worked before Griffith), certain Japanese directors (Ozu and Nagisa Oshima), and a group of contemporaries who practiced "counter cinema" (Godard, Jean-Marie Straub and Daniel Huillet, Peter Wollen and Laura Mulvey). Moreover, the auteurist canon did not completely disappear from the advanced film journals. When the editorial collective at *Cahiers du cinéma* undertook a close ideological analysis of Hollywood, the representative text they chose was John Ford's *Young Mr. Lincoln*; most of the French essays on cinema and psychoanalysis were centered on Hitchcock; and even in "Cinema/Ideology/Criticism," Narboni and Comolli said a good word about Jerry Lewis's *The Bellboy*. Several of the original British auteurists, including Wollen and Wood, who for some time had been associated with the New Left, made increasing use of post-structuralist theory; but again and again they chose to write about pictures by Hitchcock or Welles. In the pages of *Screen* and elsewhere, cutting-edge theoretical papers were often devoted to films by Hawks, Walsh, Sirk, and Ophüls. These papers did not try to establish particular individuals as artists; nevertheless, they had the indirect effect of keeping artistic reputations and auteurist tastes alive.

Over the next decade, the Vietnam era gave way to the Reagan–Thatcher years. Hollywood learned to profit from blockbusters; the media were increasingly consolidated and globalized; and social protest fragmented along generational, ethnic, and gender lines. The succeeding generation of academic writers on film became skeptical of authoritarian or top-down models of communication (in part because Barthes had already pointed to the importance of the reader), and the theoretical conjunction of Saussurian linguistics, Althusserian Marxism, and Lacanian psychoanalysis was gradually replaced by another paradigm, associated with such figures as Antonio Gramsci, Michel de Certeau, Pierre Bourdieu, and the British and Australian exponents of cultural studies. The critical emphasis shifted from the avant-garde to the popular, and from the "interpellating" effects of cinematic narrative to the techniques of "resistance" or "poaching" employed by audiences. As a result, we began to hear more about reception than production, and more about Jean-Luc Picard than about Jean-Luc Godard.

Today, after more than two decades of sophisticated film theory, academic writing tends to oscillate between large-scale arguments about the Hollywood "apparatus" and studies of genres or particular audiences. The critical study of authors is no longer a central activity. A great deal of contemporary historiography continues to treat the author in the manner of Foucault, as little more than a discursive "function," and this tendency is reinforced by a long tradition of cultural theory, ranging from radicals like Walter Benjamin to conservatives like Daniel Bell, who argue that technology and the mass media systematically undermine the bourgeois values of originality, autonomy, and aestheticism upon which the idea of authorship depends. Each new technical development since the beginning of the century helps to confirm the theory. Thus in the age of the computer, the media are able to generate "hypertexts" – apparently author-less words, sounds, and images manipulated by the reader/viewer according to structural conventions and a repertoire of older styles. A great many postmodern artists adopt a similar strategy; more like *bricoleurs* than creators, they make new texts out of borrowed or retro motifs, becoming ironic about their originality.

And yet, as anyone can see from the latest movies, individual style has not gone away, and the star director is more visible than ever. Timothy Corrigan has argued that such figures are especially important to the contemporary market-place because they serve as a "commercial strategy for organizing audience reception . . . bound to distribution and marketing aims that identify and address the potential cult status of an auteur" (1991: 103).[4] I would agree, although Corrigan tends to overstate the differences between the past and the present. Orson Welles was a vastly more important artist than Kenneth Branagh or Woody Allen, but he was deeply involved in vulgar showbusiness, and the marketing of his early pictures depended heavily on RKO's ballyhoo about his "genius." In their own day, Cecil B. DeMille and Frank Capra were publicized no less than Steven Spielberg and James Cameron. What makes the contempor-ary situation relatively new is the presence of a well-organized boutique cinema, geared to an up-market audience. In America, this cinema is promoted by high-profile film festivals such as Sundance (which is regularly featured in *The New York Times*), and by the large advertising budgets of distributors such as Mir-amax. Its films are aimed at people who read reviews, and who make discrimina-tions on the basis of directorial names like David Lynch, Sally Potter, and Atom Egoyan. Meanwhile, in Europe, the international art cinema is more alive than ever, and is still dependent upon auteurs. *Cahiers du cinéma* recently acknow-ledged this situation by speculating on the question, "What happened to the *politique des auteurs?*" The ultimate answer: nothing. As proof of an ongoing *"auteuromorphisme"* (defined as a persistent desire to make the film resemble the body of its creator), the journal offered interviews with five directors – Pedro Almodovar, Takeshi Kitano, Alain Resnais, Robert Guediguian, and Abbas Kiarostami – whose work had opened in Paris within the preceding month.[5]

The academic deemphasis on authors seems oddly out of key with this situa-tion, although in one sense it has been salutary, offering a counterweight to the overwhelming emphasis on stars, celebrities, and biographies in the mainstream market. Perhaps, however, we have reached a point where an author criticism could join with cultural studies and contemporary theory in productive ways, contributing a good deal to our understanding of media history and sociology. French auteurism as a historical movement may be dead (its greatest influence lasted roughly two decades), but so are the tedious debates about the death of the author. The residual "auteur theory" in its various manifestations still affects our view of film history, and it still has lessons to teach us – among them, the three I have listed below:

1.   The author is just as real (or as illusory and fetishized) as the money and the mechanical apparatus behind the cinema. The classic auteurs such as Hitchcock and Hawks imposed a style upon their films (as do contemporary directors), and any "materialistic" criticism needs to take this fact into account. It is of course true that authors are "written by" a series of historical, social, and cultural determinants; but the author does not become less real simply because she is socially constructed. Critics need to understand the phenomenon of the author dialectically, with an awareness of the complicated, dynamic relationship between institutions and artists, and with an appreciation of the aesthetic choices made by individual agents in particular circumstances.

2.   The study of authors is useful because it enables us to differentiate films more precisely. To be sure, we can make valid generalizations about Hollywood genres, studios, and the dominant ideology; but every western and every film noir is not the same. Within the institutional context of the classic studios, for example, the name "Hitchcock" points to a different nexus of ideological and psychological concerns from the name "Capra." The two individuals were themselves situated differently in history, and a study of their careers can produce a fine-grained understanding of both film style and the general culture. A similar point has been made by Robin Wood, who, in an echo of a famous statement by F. R. Leavis, argues that it is "only through the medium of the individual that ideological tensions come into particular focus" (1989: 292).

3.   Contrary to what Foucault suggests in his famous essay on the idea of the author, it is very important indeed for us to know who is speaking. Readers or viewers always decode messages by positing a source, even if only an imaginary or unconscious one, and the source has a political meaning. A good deal is at stake, for example, when we decide to view *Citizen Kane* as an accident of collaboration at RKO rather than as a product of Orson Welles's career. One way of looking at the film makes it seem like a Hollywood classic, whereas the other recognizes its critical or subversive edge. We can of course derive a political interpretation from purely internal evidence, avoiding the question of the source altogether. When we do, however, we fail to engage with what Andreas Huyssen calls "the *ideology of the subject* (as male, white, middle-class)," and we forsake the chance of "developing alternative and different notions of subjectivity" (1986: 213). In other words, there is no good reason why everyone needs to follow the example of Barthes and Foucault – who, as European male intellectuals, were deeply invested in the attempt to kill off the paternal creator. On the contrary, a good many previously marginalized groups need some identification with authors to help shape their identities. Thus in a recent book on Italian director Elvira Notari, Giuliana Bruno poses a rhetorical question: "Can or should we consider as dead an author, such as the female author, who is yet to be fully established in the public sphere and theorized?" (1993: 234).[6]

In the current situation, writing about authors ought to be encouraged, if only because it is a remarkably adaptable form of criticism that can make use of theory while at the same time focussing on particular cases. Such writing does not need to center on directors: for example, it has a natural affinity with books or essays about stars, performance, and celebrity. Nor does it need to ignore studios, genres, and "collaboration." As one instance of the synthetic quality it can achieve, I would point to Peter Wollen's excellent monograph on MGM's *Singin' in the Rain*, which views the film as a summation of Gene Kelly's career, while at the same time discussing the work of the other contributors, the history of dance in movies, and the politics of American entertainment in the 1950s. Wollen notes that "*Auteur* structures can be superimposed in the same film . . . but, in any one instance, there is an implicit hierarchy of *auteurs* and, in the end, a threshold below which individual input becomes increasingly difficult to single out" (1992: 29). Whatever limitations such an approach might have, in Wollen's hands it gives the film a dense historical specificity, and it greatly enhances our understanding of popular art.

In many cases the study of authors is an exclusionary, conservative activity, bound up with the perpetuation of traditions and the manufacture of commodities. But in certain contexts it can also serve as an attack on convention and a form of resistance. The best of the early auteurist criticism had these last qualities; it was romantic, but it flew in the face of received wisdom; it was ironic, but it never used irony as a defense against popular pleasure; it was subjective, but it implicitly demonstrated that the personal is the political. We can learn from what it accomplished without sacrificing theoretical insights or cultural critique. The canon of Hollywood, largely established by the original French auteurists, has yet to be explored, expanded, and challenged. We have plenty of biographies on major directors, but surprisingly few good books of criticism on their films. Meanwhile, the vast area of post-1970s cinema and made-for-TV movies is largely uncharted territory, containing undiscovered auteurs. Perhaps the old French strategy of announcing ten-best lists of directors and films (which survives today in lists of box-office receipts, kitsch, "guilty pleasures," and the appallingly bad "100 best films" chosen by the American Film Institute) ought to be revived, with the understanding that canons are not monuments graven in stone – only provisional tables of value or expressions of enthusiasm, meant to tell others about ourselves and to stimulate debate. We need to develop more of them, shaped by new constituencies who work outside the studio marketing departments. Above all, we need to restore to film criticism the sense of iconoclasm and aesthetic sensitivity it had in the days of the *politique des auteurs*.

Notes

1 I have discussed the connections between auteurism, the avant-garde, and postmodernism in Naremore 1990.
2 For an account of auteurism's influence and effect on the reputation of one of the most famous directors, see Kapsis 1992.

3 For a useful summary of these years, see Harvey 1978.
4 Other commentaries on postmodern authorship include Andrew 1993 and Lehmann 1997. For an interesting essay on the signature of an auteur, see Thomas 1998.
5 See Baecque 1997.
6 Additional commentary on authorship from a feminist perspective may be found in Silverman 1988.

References

Andrew, Dudley. 1993. "The Unauthorized Auteur Today." In *Film Theory Goes to the Movies*. Ed. Jim Collins, Hillary Radner, and Ava Preacher Collins. New York: Routledge. 77–85.

Baecque, Antoine de. 1997. "Qui reste-t-il la politique des auteurs?" *Cahiers du cinéma* 518 (November): 22–5.

Bordwell, David, and Kristin Thompson. 1996. *Film Art*, 5th edn. New York: McGraw Hill.

Braudy, Leo. 1991. "The Rise of the *Auteur*." In Leo Braudy, *Native Informant*. New York: Oxford University Press. 43–50.

Bruno, Giuliana. 1993. *Streetwalking on a Ruined Map*. Princeton: Princeton University Press.

Corrigan, Timothy. 1991. *Cinema Without Walls*. New Brunswick: Rutgers University Press.

Culler, Jonathan. 1981. *The Pursuit of Signs: Semiotics, Literature, and Deconstruction*. Ithaca: Cornell University Press.

Godard, Jean-Luc. 1972. *Godard on Godard*. Ed. Jean Narboni and Tom Milne. New York: The Viking Press.

Harvey, Sylvia. 1978. *May '68 and Film Culture*. London: British Film Institute.

Hillier, Jim. 1986. *Cahiers du Cinéma: The 1950s*. Cambridge: Harvard University Press.

Huyssen, Andreas. 1986. *After the Great Divide*. Bloomington: Indiana University Press.

Kapsis, Robert E. 1992. *Hitchcock: The Making of a Reputation*. Chicago: University of Chicago Press.

Lehmann, Courtney. 1997. "Kenneth Branagh at the Quilting Point." *Post Script* 17, 1 (fall): 6–27.

Naremore, James. 1990. "Authorship and the Cultural Politics of Film Criticism." *Film Quarterly* 44, 1 (fall): 14–23.

Silverman, Kaja. 1988. *The Acoustic Mirror: The Female Voice in Psychoanalysis and Cinema*. Bloomington: Indiana University Press.

Thomas, François. 1998. "La Signature effacée: Welles et la notion d'auteur." *Positif* 449/450 (August): 6–10.

Truffaut, François. 1978. *The Films of My Life*. New York: Simon and Schuster.

Williams, Raymond. 1981. *Culture*. London: Fontana.

Wollen, Peter. 1969. *Signs and Meaning in the Cinema*. Bloomington: Indiana University Press.

—— 1992. *Singin' in the Rain*. London: British Film Institute.

Wood, Robin. 1989. *Hitchcock's Films Revisited*. New York: Columbia University Press.

CHAPTER THREE

Genre

Sarah Berry-Flint

The books in a library must be arranged in one way or another.... Who can deny the
necessity and the utility of such arrangements? But what should we say if some one began
seriously to seek out the literary laws...of shelf A or shelf B, that is to say, of those
altogether arbitrary groupings whose sole object was their practical utility?

Benedetto Croce, *Aesthetic*

According to popular usage, film genres are ways of grouping movies by style and
story; a "genre film" is one that can be easily categorized with reference to a
culturally familiar rubric. Genres offer prospective consumers a way to choose
between films and help indicate the kind of audience for whom a particular movie
was made. This emphasis on genres as means of popular market segmentation is,
however, fairly recent. This chapter will offer a brief overview of how genres
have been defined within film studies, beginning with post-war mythology and
iconology studies and ending with contemporary debates about genres as broad
discursive practices.

Western genre theory is often traced back to Aristotle's *Poetics* and its influence on eighteenth-century European classicism, when genres were seen as ideal
types of artistic expression to be emulated and refined. Classical genres, however,
quickly turned into academically defined rules governing style and content in the
arts. With the nineteenth-century Romantic movement, many artists and writers
came to see classical genres as an over-regulation of both representation and
reception (Jameson 1981: 106; Buscombe 1995: 11). By the time of cinema's
arrival in the 1890s, genres had become even more discredited through association with mass-market publishing, which displaced the Victorian "gentle reader"
at the center of the publishing world (Wilson 1983: 41). As a result, genres were
associated with popular culture and a "brand name system against which any
authentic artistic expression must necessarily struggle" (Jameson 1981: 107).

Early film critics thus tended to see genre as something to be derided or
overlooked, since Romantic and nascent modernist aesthetics defined art in terms
of individual formative vision, not commercial or popular forms. Although

individual critics and avant-garde groups like the surrealists admired slapstick comedy or Feuillade's detective serials, it was not until after World War II that film writers began to question the priority of authorship over genre in critical evaluation. Under the influence of the *Cahiers du cinéma*, mainstream film critics began to take genre films more seriously, but their praise of individual genre films still implied that such works transcended generic mediocrity thanks to their directors' personal vision. Andrew Sarris, for example, used the term "genre film" to describe works without distinction – although he occasionally described genre films as having "unexpected deposits of feeling" (cited in Alloway 1969: 11).

In 1969, however, British writer Lawrence Alloway argued for a radically different approach to film criticism. In his catalog for a screening of popular American crime films at the Museum of Modern Art, Alloway wrote:

> The proper point of departure for a film critic who is going to write about the movies is membership in the large audience for whom they are intended . . . the majority of film reviewers write as a hostile minority interested primarily in works that are above obsolescence. The emphasis in this book is on a description of popular movies, viewed in sets and cycles rather than as single entities. It is an approach that accepts obsolescence and in which judgments derive from the sympathetic consumption of a great many films. In terms of continuing themes and motifs, the obsolescence of single films is compensated for by the prolongation of ideas in film after film. (1969: 19)

Alloway's argument that genre films should be seen as part of "sets and cycles" has resonance today in relation to television studies and the recognition of how intertextuality and repetition structure individual television programs (cf. Browne 1987). Alloway's work offered a significant challenge to criticism that evaluated popular films solely in terms derived from more elite, individualized forms of cultural production. Instead, Alloway supported an approach based on the recurring "themes and motifs" of popular films, grouping them into loosely defined categories to be described and interpreted by genre critics.

1   Problems of Definition

Current debates on the status of film genres arise, in part, because of the different reasons for invoking them: film scholars tend to define genres for purposes of interpretation and critical analysis, while producers, publicists, and audiences may use them as descriptive tools. Genres are part of film production and reception around the world, and although many Hollywood genres are internationally recognized, they always have culturally specific meanings. The variety of contexts and uses for generic labels is important because it indicates the provisional nature of such categories. In practical terms, genres are vehicles for the circulation of films in industrial, critical, and popular discourses. As the culture industries rapidly expand their global reach, questions of the cross-cultural circulation of genres become increasingly central to an understanding of how cinematic meaning is constructed and "translated."

One might argue for a more limited, textual definition of genres by pointing out that generic conventions are not merely part of the circulation and reception of films, but are often inscribed as central aspects of film form and intelligibility. The film *Singin' in the Rain* (1952), for example, is not merely considered a musical by broad consensus; it also comments on and formally typifies the conventions of the "Hollywood musical." But generic meaning can never be inscribed within a single film – the repetition of genre motifs can only be experienced intertextually. Genre studies set out to define and codify such intertextual fields, and thereby create their own objects rather than simply discovering them. Certain formal or narrative patterns are seen as paradigmatic and thus serve, as Derrida suggests, to demarcate sameness and difference (Derrida 1980: 204). If we assume, however, that each film culture tends to generate some broadly agreed-upon generic categories, the question remains as to what significance they have. Are genres part of the dominant ideological bias of entertainment industries, functioning primarily to reconcile viewers to the status quo? Are they manifestations of the popular imagination, selected and repeated because of the viewing habits of sovereign film consumers? Are they simply stylistic and narrative patterns that engage viewers in pleasurable kinds of cognitive hypotheses and variations?

These questions have often been addressed by seeing genres as part of an interdependent relationship between audience, industry, text (Ryall, cited in Gledhill 1985: 58), although most genre studies tend to focus on one of these three sites of genre use. For example, audience reception studies tend to define genres as "reading practices": socio-discursive frameworks and "horizons of expectation" brought by viewers to each new film they see. In this sense, genres are social rather than textual constraints, allowing viewers to modify their generic frameworks and participate in the construction of meaning rather than simply "absorbing" it from the screen. For industry analysts, the ways that genres are used in relation to marketing strategies (advertising, merchandising, the star system, etc.) are seen to have a definitive influence on such reading practices. Lastly, texual and formal analysis in film studies tends to focus on the ways that narrative and stylistic conventions are "encoded" with genre-specific meanings. These aesthetic devices are seen to cue viewers to anticipate certain experiences (music or editing patterns that create suspense, for example, or the use of filters and sepia tones to indicate a period film). The history of such aesthetic codes is significant even when they are seen, ultimately, as dependent on larger discourses for their meaning (once we know we are watching a period film, for example, what kind of reading practices might come into play?). Ultimately, this circulation of meaning between audience, industry, and film text is irresolvable, but it is also central to any discussion of the significance of film genres.

2   Early Genre Study: Classicism and Myth

Early film genres were derived by the transposition of visual, narrative, and discursive patterns from older media onto cinematic forms. Early Japanese films, for example, not only adapted traditional storytelling and theatrical "content" for the screen, but they were also incorporated into theatrical productions, with films projected as backdrops for Kabuki and *shimpa* plays (Nolletti and Desser 1992: ix). In the US and Europe, early film categories were primarily derived from other popular forms such as melodrama, religious and occult spectacle, journalistic and pictorial photography, the Wild West show, the travel or scientific lecture, and the dime novel. In spite of this history of polyglot genre formation, the task of genre analysis in film studies has often been seen as one of clarifying the key qualities and limits of each genre. Like Aristotle's *Poetics*, such approaches imply that genres have highly specific qualities which, like art forms more generally, demonstrate their essence when developed into a classical or ideal form. David Bordwell has detailed the degree to which early film scholars adopted such developmental models of art, which proposed:

> a progressive development from simpler to more complex forms, treated according to that biological analogy of birth/childhood/maturity so common among art historians since Vasari. (1997: 9)

But Bordwell also notes that early film criticism adopted many tenets of aesthetic modernism, such as "the need for perpetual breaks with academicism" and a "radical' interrogation" of the medium (1997: 9). Early film critics thus tended to valorize individual works and see most genre films as formulaic products of a low-brow industry. Individual genre films were occasionally canonized, but it was not until the post-war reappraisal of Hollywood cinema by critics like André Bazin that the relationship between genre filmmaking and the Romantic/modernist model of artistic production was seriously explored.

The advent of genre criticism was marked by a shift in focus away from film's aesthetically "transformative" and medium-specific attributes toward a more sociological interest in relations between style, popular narrative, and myth. André Bazin's praise of the western, for example, centered on its representation of an imaginary past, and he described its formal motifs as "signs or symbols of its profound reality, namely the myth" (Bazin 1971b: 142). But Bazin also maintained the developmental assumptions and genre essentialism of traditional art history, seeing *Stagecoach* (1939), for example, in highly Platonic terms:

> *Stagecoach* is the ideal example of the maturity of a style brought to classic perfection. John Ford struck the ideal balance between social myth, historical reconstruction, psychological truth, and the traditional theme of the Western *mise-en-scène* . . . [it] is like a wheel, so perfectly made that it remains in equilibrium on its axis in any position. (Bazin 1971a: 149)

Post-war westerns, he argued, often abandoned this sense of the "profound reality" of the myth by becoming more self-conscious and thematically diverse (149).

This model of film genres' birth, evolution to a classical form, and inevitable decline is derived from art historians' periodization of stylistic movements into "experimental," "classical," and "baroque" phases. Although Bazin wrote that he did not claim to "explain everything by the famous law of successive aesthetic periods," such a teleology is implicit in his statement that "by 1938 or 1939 the talking film . . . had reached a level of classical perfection" due to the "maturing" of its dramatic and technical vocabulary (cited in Alloway 1969: 11). Thomas Schatz has cited art historian Henri Focillon's notion that the life-cycle morphology is "inherent in [art] forms themselves," although Schatz also draws on Russian formalist theory, which proposes that "as a genre gains popularity it loses its defamiliarizing role and moves inevitably into decadence, giving way to new forms" (Schatz 1981: 37; Gunning 1990: 87).

In early genre criticism, this genre morphology was frequently combined with a genre/myth analogy, relating generic rise and fall in a mimetic relationship to changes in social consciousness. This audience-driven morphology assumes that film viewers either validate existing mythological forms or require that they undergo revision. John Cawelti has argued, for example, that following their phases of innovation and classicism, genres go through a period of revisionist "self-awareness on the part of both creators and audiences," resulting in the popularity of "parodic and satiric treatments," and the eventual formation of new genres (Cawelti 1979: 578). Although invoked by numerous film theorists, many have noted that this model of generic change relies on the degree to which commercial film genres "reflect" the collective sensibilities of a mass audience – a problematic thesis that will be explored in more detail below.

On the other hand, Steven Neale has argued that when seen in a larger historical context, the formalist approach to generic change can indicate the social dimensions of genre as a changing set of reading practices, rather than a fixed one. He notes that this requires equal attention to all three sites of generic meaning, however: audiences, industries, and texts. Citing Hans Robert Jauss, Neale argues that each new film seen by a particular viewer becomes part of the "founding and altering" of that viewer's horizon of generic expectations (Neale 1990: 57). Such an approach appeals to individual experience, since every film spectator has a personal viewing history and a set of cinematic associations and expectations; but how generic change is implemented remains unclear. Neale cites Jauss's suggestion that: "[s]uccessful genres . . . gradually lose their effective power through continual reproduction; they are forced to the periphery by new genres" (Neale 1990: 60). How a genre's "effective power" is determined, and how generic innovation is derived from reader responses remains unspecified, however; Neale concludes that the model "allows for a variety of factors" (61).

Earlier genre theorists often argued that, like myths, genres have an organic relation to social consciousness – an assumption that arises from traditional literary studies as well as art history. Post-Enlightenment models of literary history, following Kant and Hegel, described literary works as functioning to mirror a culture back to itself in a process of dialectical evolution toward cultural self-realization and -understanding (Corngold 1988: 139). The film/myth analogy applied this model of art as a form of cultural self-reflection to the more populist context of cinema. Significantly, this helped to dissolve film criticism's tendency to dismiss genre films as "formulaic" and thus unartistic: if the formulas themselves could be shown to be significant aspects of cultural self-awareness and evolution, they could be incorporated into "high-art" methods of articulating aesthetic value and meaning.

One disadvantage of this model, however, is that the search for the mythological essence of a particular genre is inevitably retrospective and elegiac. For if a genre is seen as a mythical form, how can the myth's essential meaning be defined unless it has already reached its "classical" phase of articulation? One can only interpret a set of films definitively by closing it off from new additions and thus locating its expressive acme in the past. It is not surprising, therefore, that the genre most easily characterized as mythological was the Hollywood western. By the mid-1950s, the western had enough canonical exemplars to be seen as having reached a "classical" peak in the 1930s and '40s, subsequently entering a period of "reinterpretation" and decline.

The American critic Robert Warshow was, along with Bazin, an early interpreter of film genre, and his book *Movie Chronicle: The Westerner* (1954) offered a comparative analysis of the heroes of Hollywood gangster films and westerns. Warshow points out that these "men with guns" represent a basic American fascination with violence, but he is more interested in the differences between the two types of hero and their relationship to violence. The gangster is, for example, a figure of "enterprise and success" whose frenetic career is nevertheless "a nightmare inversion of the values of ambition and opportunity." The western hero, on the other hand, is "the last gentleman," demonstrating such a restrained sense of purpose that he often "appears to be unemployed" (Warshow 1979: 471). His nobility is always somewhat anachronistic, as well as morally ambiguous, due to the fact that, "whatever his justifications, he is a killer of men." What makes the western compelling for Warshow is its "serious orientation to the problem of violence" and its ritualistic repetition of the "value" of violence under certain moral conditions. The fact that such heroic vigilantism is incompatible with the legal precepts of democracy simply adds to the western hero's mythical potency:

> What redeems him is that he no longer believes in this drama and nevertheless will continue to play his role perfectly: the pattern is all. (Warshow 1979: 480)

The consistency and purity of purpose that Warshow values in the western hero is also central to his definition of the "classical" western form. He writes, for example, that the western is "an art form for connoisseurs, where the spectator derives his pleasure from the appreciation of minor variations within the working out of a pre-established order" (1979: 480). Like Aristotle, Warshow is highly prescriptive in his definition of the genre's essence: he argues that westerns should avoid excesses of realism or stylization as well as the incorporation of any new motifs not present in the exemplary classical works. *The Virginian* (1929), for example, is "an archetypal Western movie" about the leader of a posse (Gary Cooper) who must oversee the lynching of his best friend for stealing cattle. But *The Ox-Bow Incident* (1943), which deals with the injustice and psychological implications of a lynching, is regarded as an "anti-Western" (Warshow 1979: 475). Purity of generic form is thus predicated on the anti-realist abstraction of its thematic content. Women, for example, represent "civilization" in the classic western, but in this capacity their role must remain marginal; Warshow complains that "in *The Gunfighter* the women and children are a little too much in evidence, threatening constantly to become a real focus of concern instead of simply part of the given framework" (Warshow 1979: 481; cf. Modleski 1997). Thus, while raising important issues about the representation of violent masculinity in American film, Warshow's work demonstrates the drawbacks of defining a genre's essential or "classical" qualities, which requires their abstraction from the socio-political and discursive contexts that organize their meaning.

The genre studies of Bazin, Warshow, and Alloway, together with the *Cahiers du cinéma* critics' valorization of mise-en-scène over script in regard to Hollywood film, allowed genres to be seen as expressive vocabularies rather than simply as constraints imposed by the film industry (cf. McArthur 1972). They were also compared positively by some scholars to classical traditions in the arts; in the mid-1970s, for example, Leo Braudy argued that by returning to pre-Romantic models of artistic production, genre films could be seen as "the equivalent of conscious reference to tradition in the other arts." The vision of the film auteur was seen as a process of "picking and choosing among possible conventions" in order to revivify classical forms. Braudy's ideal genre film is thus a "self-conscious mastery" of formal and narrative patterns that could raise genre films to the same level of expressivity as less generically coded films (Braudy 1979: 448). Jean-Loup Bourget has pointed out that genre auteurism reconciled "two apparently antagonistic approaches: the auteur theory, which claims that a film is the work of one creative individual, and the iconological approach, which assumes that a film is a sequence of images whose real meaning may well be unconscious on the part of its makers" (Bourget 1995: 51). As a result, Hollywood's conventionality could be seen, paradoxically, as the "reason for its creativity," forcing talented directors to transcend hackneyed plots through the "pure poetry" of visual elements (50).

3 Iconology and Genre Structuralism

In addition to the genre/myth analogy outlined by Bazin and Warshow, a primary influence on early genre studies was the work of art historian Erwin

Panofsky (cf. Alloway 1969; McArthur 1972). His 1939 book *Studies in Iconology* concerned itself with the denotative and symbolic content of art, rather than its formal qualities. For Panofsky, the recognition of conventional meanings attached to images ("that a male figure with a knife represents St. Bartholomew, that a female figure with a peach in her hand is a personification of Veracity") constitutes iconographic analysis in a "narrow" sense. The deeper sense of iconographic meaning, however,

> is apprehended by ascertaining those underlying principles which reveal the basic attitude of a nation, a period, a class, a religious or philosophical persuasion. (Panofsky 1939: 7)

Works of art are thus directly mimetic of their *Zeitgeist*, and culture itself is seen as an expressive totality. The visual motifs found in a particular period and art form thus allow the art historian to:

> deal with the work of art as a symptom of something else which expresses itself in a countless variety of other symptoms, and ... interpret its compositional and icono- graphical features as more particularized evidence of this "something else." (8)

Panofsky's iconology was useful to the study of film genre because it emphasized the visual motifs and symbolic language of art rather than individual authorship or mythic narrative. To some extent, it can be seen as a kind of visual content analysis, especially when iconology is applied to cinematic motifs without Panofs- ky's emphasis on interpretation. Alloway, for example, suggests that since "there is no body of literature" that defines the meaning of cinematic imagery, "it is necessary to derive the information from adequate samples of the films them- selves" (Alloway 1969: 41). Alloway also rejects the notion that film iconology amounts to a kind of myth analysis, since he emphasizes the constant change and ephemerality of visual patterns in popular art (54). His application of iconology to film genres is thus more descriptive than interpretive. But Panofsky's own method presupposed that symbolic vocabularies reflected the essential concerns of a particular culture and period, which could be conceived as an organic essence manifesting itself consistently in all forms of expression. His work thus typifies E. H. Gombrich's critique of art history as "Hegelianism without metaphysics" (cited in Bordwell 1997: 44).

In "The Idea of Genre in the American Cinema," Ed Buscombe takes a position similar to Alloway's use of iconology, suggesting that generic visual conventions can be productively analyzed without assuming that they are part of a comprehensive thematic structure. For Buscombe, describing the western in terms of its mise-en-scène (the landscapes, towns, clothes, guns, horses, etc.) is not comprehensive or definitive of what westerns are about, but it is saying "something both intelligible and useful," namely that "the visual conventions provide a framework within which the story can be told" (Buscombe 1995: 15). Iconography is thus a palette of familiar motifs that can be recombined creatively (or ironically) in ways that provide both familiarity and variety. Buscombe's emphasis on familiarity and variation is reminiscent of Warshow's notion of the western as a genre for "connoisseurs," but without the nostalgia for a "pure" western form that had died out. A more thematic definition may nevertheless be implicit, since Buscombe notes that:

> the essential theme of *Guns in the Afternoon* (1962; U.S. title, *Ride the High Country*) is one that, while it could be put into other forms, is ideally suited to the one chosen. The film describes the situation of men who have outlived their time. Used to a world where issues were decided simply, on a test of strength, they now find this way of life threatened by complications and developments they do not understand. Since they cannot, or will not, adapt, all that remains to them is a tragic and bitter heroism. (24)

But the question of why this story is "ideally suited" to the western's iconographic language is not really addressed in Buscombe's descriptive paradigm. Definitions of genre based on loosely grouped sets of repeated motifs are thus open to shifting, intertextual, and historical meanings, but they often rely on implicitly mythological or auteur-based interpretations (Kitses and McArthur both combine iconographic genre analyses with auteur studies). What is lacking in most iconological analyses is a more historical approach to visual and thematic intertextuality, which might address the social semiotics of specific genre motifs for particular audiences.

Panofsky emphasized the art historian's search for "symptomatic" meanings, which must be inferred based on the totality of cultural production from any one period. The uptake of iconographic analysis in film studies, however, was equally informed by structural linguistics and anthropology. Structuralism assumes that the meanings attributed to signs within any symbolic language arise comparatively – they do not express a pre-existing cultural essence. No object or word can have meaning in a vacuum – its meaning must be derived by contrast with a different kind of meaning. Symbolic systems are thus structured by core tensions or differential values, and it is the task of the analyst to perceive those "deep structures." The difference between this model and Panofsky's is that a structuralist one sees forms of communication not as the expressions of a pre-existing social essence, but as systems of meaning that structure the social itself by encouraging certain forms of conceptualization and not others.

The structuralist genre studies of Jim Kitses (*Horizons West*, 1969), Will Wright (*Sixguns and Society*, 1975), and Thomas Schatz (*Hollywood Genres*, 1981) thus viewed genres as structures of differential meaning and as part of larger frameworks of difference between generic paradigms. Kitses, for example, begins his analysis of the Hollywood western by looking at the opposition proposed by Henry Nash Smith in *Virgin Land* between representations of the US West as garden and desert. Kitses defines this dichotomy as a core opposition between the wilderness and civilization, with additional oppositions aligned as sub-themes: tradition vs. change, restriction vs. freedom, community vs. individuality, etc. (Kitses 1969: 11). In addition to this thematic structure, Kitses sees the genre as drawing its meanings from frontier history, the chivalric codes of medieval romance, and pre-cinematic representations of the West. The core binary oppositions that structure the western film are thus seen to offer a certain socio-historical, narrative, and visual "language" for filmmakers to work within. For Kitses this structure has social significance because it is rooted in mythological and historical tensions, but it produces meaning dialectically by incorporating new approaches rather than evolving to a "classical" form and then dissipating.

Thomas Schatz's *Hollywood Genres* is explicitly informed by Lévi-Strauss's structuralist reading of myth. Schatz thus defines genres around sets of thematic binary oppositions, arguing that their narrative patterns work to temporarily resolve particular cultural tensions. However, as Lévi-Strauss suggests, such stories only provide a temporary resolution of these tensions and therefore must be told repeatedly in various ways. Schatz divides the major Hollywood genres into those that work to reestablish social order (westerns, crime and detective films) and those that work to establish social integration (the musical, comedy, and melodrama). Central to each of these genres is the social community they define, which consists of a set of character types who enact the conflicts inherent within that community. Often opposing value systems are mediated by an individual, or a romantic coupling signifies their integration. The resolution of these conflicts, according to Schatz, constitutes "the genre film's function as cultural ritual." Will Wright, in *Sixguns and Society*, made a similarly comprehensive analysis of the western, drawing on the work of Russian formalists such as Vladimir Propp and his analysis of narrative and character types in folktales. In this way, Wright analyzes not only the core conflicts that structure the western, but also the "character functions" that structure its plot patterns and offer "a conceptual response to the requirements of human action in a social situation" (Wright 1975: 17).

Both Schatz and Wright thus utilize analytical models drawn from earlier forms of narrative (myth and folktale) and apply them to the commercial cinema. The relatively close relations between producers and users of pre-industrial folkways are thus transposed to the capitalist marketplace for entertainment, which raises a number of problems. Schatz refers, for example, to generic change as the result of a "conversation" between filmmakers and audiences, whereby "the genre film reaffirms what the audience believes both on individual and on communal levels" (Schatz 1981: 38). On this point, he cites Leo Braudy's description of film audiences as agents of generic development: "change in genre occurs when the audience says 'that's too infantile a form of what we believe. Show us something more complicated'" (Schatz 1981: 38). Like Schatz, Will Wright proposes that the popularity of Hollywood film, measured in box-office dollars, stands as evidence of viewer demand for just such films and genres (Wright 1975: 12). Wright thus limits his study to films that grossed at least $4,000,000 on initial release.

Schatz and Wright, in other words, base their interpretation of Hollywood genres' social significance on the presumed existence of a feedback loop between audiences and film industries. This popularity, however, is measured in terms of attendance, just as television ratings are used in the US to argue that viewers get exactly what they want. This argument assumes that the market for entertainment works democratically, with each potential viewer having the financial power to "vote" by making consumer choices. The American film industry, however, has long controlled markets through vertical integration and anti-competitive distribution systems. To read profitability as a blanket endorsement of mainstream genres assumes a model of consumer sovereignty and "free market" competition inappropriate to highly monopolized media industries. In addition, as Steven Neale notes, it collapses the "multiplicity of reasons for consumer 'choices'" and varieties of viewing pleasure into a fictive unanimity of taste (Neale 1990: 64; cf. Jowett 1985).

Rick Altman has usefully summarized the differences between iconographic and structural approaches to genre in his essay "A Semantic/Syntactic Approach to Film Genre." Altman points out that these debates center on the classification of genres according to either broadly inclusive, iconographic definitions (a western is a film with cowboys and horses) or more interpretive definitions (a western is about historical tensions between American individualism and society). Altman notes that inclusive definitions, like Buscombe's and McArthur's, are descriptively useful but do not explain the social significance of genres. Interpretive definitions, such as Schatz's "genres of order/genres of integration" model, explain their social significance by simply excluding films that do not repeat those patterns found significant by the analyst. Altman calls inclusive definitions "semantic," since they describe the "building blocks" of genres; explanatory definitions are called "syntactic," since they describe the "structures" into which these elements are narratively presented. Altman proposes that these two definitional strategies are complementary, and that the full significance of film genre can only be understood by utilizing both approaches. He points out that:

> not all genre films relate to their genre in the same way or to the same extent . . . . In addition, a dual approach permits a far more accurate description of the numerous inter-generic connections typically suppressed by single-minded approaches . . . numerous films . . . innovate by combining the syntax of one genre with the semantics of another. (1995)

Such an approach indicates, for example, that the category of film noir is semantically distinctive (noir lighting, framing, and character types) but shares its syntactical patterns with larger categories like the thriller and detective film. It also facilitates analysis of how a film like *The Right Stuff* (1983), which is about astronauts, also uses many of the visual and characterological patterns of the western; or how *Blade Runner* (1982) combines a science-fiction narrative with film noir mise-en-scène.

35

4   Genres and Ideology

In melodrama two themes are important: the triumph of moral virtue over villainy, and the consequent idealizing of the moral views assumed to be held by the audience. In the melodrama of the brutal thriller we come as close as it is normally possible for art to come to the pure self-righteousness of the lynching mob. We should have to say, then, that all forms of melodrama, the detective story in particular, were advance propaganda for the police state, in so far as that represents the regularizing of mob violence, if it were possible to take them seriously. But it seems not to be possible.

Northrop Frye, *Anatomy of Criticism*

At roughly the same time that Schatz and Wright proposed a ritual significance for Hollywood genres as expressions of collective imagination, the film journals *Cahiers du cinéma* and *Screen* were arguing, instead, that Hollywood film imposed dominant ideological meanings on audiences. In the 1980s, genre theory was thus marked by two very contradictory definitions of genre – as social ritual and ideological tool. Robert Kapsis has described the ritual model as a "reflection of society perspective," while the argument that genres are ideological is referred to by Kapsis as the "production of culture perspective" (1991: 68–9). He offers a critique of Wright, Schatz, and Cawelti's "reflection" approach based on his analysis of the "interorganizational relationships" that dominate the American film industry's decision-making processes, arguing that although historical audiences may exercise some influence over general market trends, "the very existence of genre films and cycles is a product of the film industry's attempt to overcome the problem of uncertainty, that is, of not knowing the future tastes of the mass audience" (70).

For the most part, however, ideological readings of film genre have been based on textual rather than industrial analysis. The 1970s and '80s genre debates in *Screen*, for example, tended to see genre as a sub-set of the journal's broader ideological critique of classical Hollywood narrative, since genres provided and regulated variety while still binding the viewer to the cinematic institution as a whole in a position of textually inscribed subjectivity. There were also those who argued for a more straightforward ideological interpretation of genre. For example, in an article called "Genre Film and the Status Quo," Judith Hess Wright argued that, as products of the capitalist culture industry, genre films "serve the interests of the ruling class by assisting in the maintenance of the status quo" (Hess Wright 1995: 41). This, as Steven Neale pointed out, amounts to "reductivism, economism, and cultural pessimism" (Neale 1990: 65). Such a position, like the "reflection of culture" perspective, uses an overly simplified model of spectatorship, seeing only the influence of industry over audience rather than the ritual theory's inverse schema. Text-based ideology critique often assumes a degree of textual determinism, whereby viewers are more passive than active in relation to cinematic meaning. However, in the 1980s, specific genres such as melodrama and film noir were also seen as textual structures that manifested ideological contradictions and thus invited viewers to negotiate or question the conventional resolutions and patterns of Hollywood narrative.

In the case of melodrama, critical interest in the dynamic between auteurs and the limits imposed by generic Hollywood scripts (in journals such as *Movie* and *Positif*) focussed attention on the ability of filmmakers like Douglas Sirk, Nicholas Ray, Max Ophüls and Vincente Minnelli to transform familiar melodramatic stories through mise-en-scène and the "formal play of distanciation and irony" (Gledhill 1985: 73). Eventually, as Barbara Klinger notes, "critics began to consider the relation of melodramatic form to ideology, without an exclusive emphasis on the director as enabler of critique" (1994: 20). Christine Gledhill states, for example, that, "through discovery of Sirk, a genre came into view" (cited in Klinger 1994: xii). For example, in 1978, when Laura Mulvey's "Notes on Sirk and Melodrama" was published in *Movie*, it took a somewhat critical view of Paul Willemen's earlier praise of Sirk for subverting the normatively conservative melodramatic form. Instead, Mulvey argued that the ideological tensions foregrounded in Sirk's films were "not produced by the exercise of a special authorial agency, but are a congenital feature of melodrama as a genre filled with ideological inconsistencies" (cited in Klinger 1994: 20).

The notion that genres can manifest "unconscious dynamics" which contradict the ideological values implied by their narratives suggests that they are both symptomatic and ideologically structured. Such an account rests on Althusser's notion of overdetermination, whereby texts are seen as sites of unconsciously conflicting structural forces. For example, one can argue that 1950s American melodrama "raised the contradictions inherent in bourgeois and patriarchal ideologies" (Klinger 1994: 22) or that American film noir exposed the misogyny of post-war angst over masculine self-determination. Such descriptions see the "subversive" genre as a particularly rich constellation of tensions within the dominant culture that structures mainstream filmmaking. Such readings, however, tend to rely on a definition of genres as loosely defined sets of expressive and narrative tropes. In his 1981 article "The 'Force-Field' of Melodrama," Stuart Cunningham argues that the inevitable problems of such textual definitions arise "only if melodrama is approached as an exclusively aesthetic category" (1981: 348). Instead, he proposes that melodrama be seen as a broader discursive category of "religious, moral, political, as well as aesthetic experience." Like Peter Brooks, Cunningham sees melodramatic discourse as a response to modernity and its shift from "the traditional Sacred and its representative institutions (Church and Monarch)" to a democratic society that must "propagate the new 'sacred' in purely ethical and personal terms" (Brooks 1976: 14–15; Cunningham 1981: 348). Melodrama thus becomes "the principal mode for uncovering, demonstrating, and making operative the essential moral universe in a post-sacred era." Cunningham argues that melodrama should be seen as a broadly discursive "mode, function, or effect," because its meaning is produced socially, historically, and "in a wide variety of media, narrative structures and aesthetic forms" (354).

37

If genres are seen as inter-media modes of discourse, then the problem of whether film industries or audiences are the source of generic meaning is displaced by the question of how film genres relate to other social, political, and aesthetic formations in particular historical contexts. This concept of genres as aspects of social discourse draws on a post-structuralist model of the ways texts take on meaning according to the epistemological and rhetorical modes to which they are linked. Discourses, in other words, are culturally specific frameworks of knowledge that determine what can be considered fiction, news, entertainment, obscenity, history, etc. From this perspective, it is not only a question of how genres work, but also what kind of "truth" they both presume and preclude. As Tony Bennett has argued, genres can thus be seen as socially rather than textually constituted:

> texts constitute sites around which the pre-eminently social affair of the struggle for the production of meaning is conducted, principally in the form of a series of bids and counter-bids to determine which system of inter-textual coordinates should be granted an effective social role in organising reading practices. (1990: 59–60)

In practice this approach is not incompatible with Altman's synthesis of semantic and syntactic genre analysis, but a discursive approach also requires attention to the historically particular cultural norms that govern both aesthetics and reception. Such an approach to genre does not disregard the importance of textual organization; it simply sees films as *sites* rather than *sources* of meaning. Their reception is thus primarily determined socio-culturally because of the ways that social discourses organize what sense viewers make of films' aesthetic and phenomenological effects.

5   From "Genre" to Generic Readings

If genres are most productively seen as aspects of historically specific discourses, what are the implications for genre studies? One, as Barbara Klinger summarizes, is that the object of study shifts,

> from the text to the intertext – the network of discourses, social institutions, and historical conditions surrounding a work.... Such contextual analysis hopes to reveal the intimate impact of discursive and social situations on cinematic meaning. (1997: 108)

Second, the transnational circulation of film genres becomes more clearly constituted as an arena for culturally specific, contextual research. As Mitsuhiro Yoshimoto argues with regard to melodrama,

> An examination of melodrama in the postwar Japanese cinema merely from a formal perspective does not lead to any significant conclusion; instead, we must

place melodrama in a particular sociopolitical background of postwar Japan. Although various studies of what the melodramatic form of the Hollywood cinema signified in the 1950s' America are extremely significant, they cannot be a direct model. (1993: 101)

The hegemony of the American film industry has ensured that Hollywood genres are globally familiar; but their meanings in relation to localized generic structures are complex. For example, in his analysis of Hong Kong action film, Julian Stringer argues that while American genres are gender-coded as "male action or 'doing' genres (the Western, war films) and female 'suffering' genres (melodrama, the woman's film)", the Hong Kong action films of John Woo "collapse these two paradigms of masculinity into one. They combine simultaneously doing and suffering heroes" (1997: 29–30). Stringer concludes that Woo's work needs to be seen in relation to events such as the 1989 Tiananmen Square massacre and the 1997 handover of Hong Kong in order to see how:

> Hong Kong action cinema is somewhat unique in its crisis-ridden logic precisely because it cannot provide the system within which any new masculinity can be reconsolidated. (40)

Although the uneven global flow of media has made non-Western cinemas particularly marked by such genre hybridity due to the negotiation of Hollywood influence, hybridity is itself a hallmark of genre. Derrida even suggests that the tendency of critics to identify "mixed" generic objects simply confirms the fantasy that an "essential purity" of unmixed genres is possible (cited in Brunette and Wills 1989: 46). As Peter Brunette and David Wills conclude, "[g]enre is thus always indispensable and impossible at the same time" (49). Historical research on "classical Hollywood" genres certainly supports a Bakhtinian or Kristevan model of texts as multi-vocal and citational; even in the studio era the use of genre categories was far from consistent, and usually involved mixed-genre descriptions. Similarly, film audiences have been found to utilize a wide variety of descriptive categories; for example, Richard Koszarski has described a 1923 poll of high school students that produced the following categories: "not true to life," "bad artistically," "immoral," and "brutality" (1990: 28–9). What is interesting is that these categories blur narrative, aesthetic, and ethical criteria, underscoring the regulatory aspect of genre classifications and their similarity to content ratings (the determination of who is allowed to see certain kinds of film). This raises the question of whether genre definition, as a social practice, can be separated from attempts to define the effects of film on audiences. Since the definition of concepts like "obscenity" ultimately rely on assumptions about what a text's effect will be on the typical viewer, how do assumptions about audiences underpin the definitions of categories like "romance" or "documentary"? Genre's relationship to fictive audiences is not limited to the targeting of particular markets as demographic and cultural types. As film theorists have pointed out, popular genre definitions are often made according to films' presumed effect:

horror, suspense, "thrillers," "weepies," or "tear-jerkers" (cf. Williams 1995; Sobchack 1995). This practice of categorizing films according to their effects on particular kinds of viewers underscores the extent to which genres organize reading practices as much as they organize texts, by indicating to viewers what kinds of experiences to expect.

The instability of generic labels thus arises not only from the Bakhtinian "heteroglossia" of generic allusion that limits any attempt at film classification, but from the fact that genres function as tools for predicting and regulating the reception of texts. A text that cannot be located within some sort of genre is, for practical purposes, unreadable. What is important from an analytical standpoint, however, is that generic readings are not produced from a "virtual continuum of meaning containing all possible genres, but from a particular historical matrix supporting a handful of actual genres" (Hunter 1988: 219). The object of genre analysis should thus be the social constitution of their uses: the way they organize texts, identify them with certain modes of rhetoric and of discourse, and thus suggest the kind of reception and significance they should have.

6   Conclusion: The Politics of Genre

> I take it...as one of the moments of "high seriousness" in the history of recent Marxist thought that when the aging Lukács felt the urgency of supporting Solzhenitsyn's denunciation of Stalinism but also of responding to the religious and antisocialist propaganda to which the latter lent his talent and the authority of his personal suffering, he did so by sitting down at his desk and producing a piece of genre criticism.
>
> Fredric Jameson, *The Political Unconscious*

It has been suggested that the confusion over film genre definition might be addressed by focussing on the more general categories of "narrative film, experimental/avant-garde film, and documentary" (Williams 1984: 121). This approach, modeled on traditional literary distinctions, would simply define westerns, melodramas, action films, etc., as narrative film sub-genres. As sensible as this may seem, it does not address the question of how genres function in relation to cinematic meaning: how, for example, do we differentiate between narrative fiction and documentary? In the United States, the 1980s and 1990s have seen a remarkable resurgence of popular interest in documentary film, indicated by the theatrical success of Errol Morris's *The Thin Blue Line* (1987), Michael Moore's *Roger and Me* (1989), Jennie Livingston's *Paris is Burning* (1991), and Michael Apted's *35 Up* (1991), among others. At the same time, the rise in the US of numerous television-based, hybrid formats has blurred the hypothetical line between documentary and fictional representation (verité-style programs like *Cops*, "infotainment" magazine formats such as *20/20*, *48 Hours*, and *Dateline*, fact-based reenactment shows like *Emergency 911* and *America's*

Most Wanted, and televised trials on Court TV) (cf. Corner 1995; Petley 1996; Bondebjerg 1996). Ironically, however, the 1990s has also seen the repeal of laws requiring television networks to air a minimum amount of public affairs programming. The notion that the television documentary functions, like the news, to provide viewers with information necessary for active citizenship has, in the US, been superseded by the documentary's ability to rate reasonably well as entertainment. Such a shift is not merely a textual one from, say, the civic exhortation of Edward Murrow's *Harvest of Shame* (1960) to the video-game images of US government-censored Gulf War coverage. It is an institutional and political one, based on a redefinition of the viewer as a consumer rather than a citizen.

Genres are socially organized sets of relations between texts that function to enable certain relations between texts and viewers. Because they organize the framework of expectations within which reading takes place, they help to enable the possibility of communication; the blurring of certain genres, therefore, can be seen as a political move to discourage certain forms of communication. For example, the 1934 US Federal Communications Act codified the notion that commercial broadcasters were responsible for producing programs in "the public interest"; the genres of television documentary, public affairs, and news were later defined as sites for the potential articulation of such public interests. But the potential viewer-use of these television genres has been increasingly limited since the deregulation policies of the Reagan-era Federal Communications Commission. American nonfiction television still shows the impact of Reagan's FCC Director Mark Fowler, who argued that "broadcasting is simply a business, and should be freed from myths . . . about service to the community" (cited in Kellner 1990: 92).

The loss of public financing for American documentary film due to attacks on the National Endowments for the Arts and Humanities has also had a direct effect on what kinds of discourse viewers can expect from nonfiction formats. The deregulation of television and the radical privatization of film funding thus constitute a more significant form of "genre revisionism" than any maverick auteur could provide. As Linda Williams has noted, contemporary documentary is marked by the postmodern recognition that the screen is less a "mirror with a memory" than a hall of mirrors. But, as she points out, epistemological reflexivity does not threaten the significance of documentary as a commitment to communicating "the 'truths' which matter in people's lives but which cannot be transparently represented" (Williams 1993: 13). With the loss of any generic (i.e. institutional and economic) protection for representations of "public interest," however, film and television viewers may become hard pressed to find any "truths" represented that run counter to the economic interests of corporate media owners and sponsors. Genre is thus about social as well as textual rules. Genres indicate what kind of communication will be facilitated in specific social formations, and it is in this regard that genre criticism can be a matter of "high seriousness."

References

Alloway, Lawrence. 1969. *Violent America: The Movies, 1946–1964*. Greenwich: New York Graphic Society and the Museum of Modern Art.

Altman, Rick. 1995. "A Semantic/Syntactic Approach to Film Genre." In *Film Genre Reader II*. Ed. Barry Keith Grant. Austin: University of Texas Press. 26–40.

Bazin, André. 1971a. "The Evolution of the Western." In *What is Cinema? Vol. 2*. Ed. and trans. Hugh Gray. Berkeley: University of California Press.

Bazin, André. 1971b. "The Western, or the American Film *Par Excellence*." In *What is Cinema? Vol. 2*. Ed. and trans. Hugh Gray. Berkeley: University of California Press.

Bennett, Tony. 1990. *Outside Literature*. London: Routledge.

Bondebjerg, Ib. 1996. "Public Discourse/Private Fascination: Hybridization in True-Life-Story Genres." *Media, Culture and Society* 18: 27–45.

Bordwell, David. 1997. *On the History of Film Style*. Cambridge: Harvard University Press.

Bourget, Jean-Loup. 1995. "Social Implications in the Hollywood Genres." In *Film Genre Reader II*. Ed. Barry Keith Grant. Austin: University of Texas Press. 50–8.

Braudy, Leo. 1979. "From *The World in a Frame*: Genre: The Conventions of Connection." In *Film Theory and Criticism: Introductory Readings*. 2nd edn. Ed. Gerald Mast and Marshall Cohen. New York: Oxford University Press. 443–68.

Brooks, Peter. 1976. *The Melodramatic Imagination: Balzac, Henry James, Melodrama, and the Mode of Excess*. New Haven: Yale University Press.

Browne, Nick. 1987. "The Political Economy of the Television (Super) Text." In *Television: The Critical View*. 4th edn. Ed. Horace Newcomb. Oxford: Oxford University Press. 585–99.

Brunette, Peter, and David Wills. 1989. *Screen/Play: Derrida and Film Theory*. Princeton: Princeton University Press.

Buscombe, Edward. 1995. "The Idea of Genre in the American Cinema." In *Film Genre Reader II*. Ed. Barry Keith Grant. Austin: University of Texas Press. 11–25.

Cawelti, John. 1979. "*Chinatown* and Generic Transformation in Recent American Films." In *Film Theory and Criticism: Introductory Readings*. 2nd edn. Ed. Gerald Mast and Marshall Cohen. New York: Oxford University Press. 559–79.

Corner, John. 1995. *Television Form and Public Address*. London: Edward Arnold. 20–31.

Corngold, Stanley. 1988. *Franz Kafka: The Necessity of Form*. Ithaca: Cornell University Press.

Croce, Benedetto. 1978 [1909, revised 1922]. *Aesthetic: As Science of Expression and General Linguistic*. Trans. Douglas Ainslie. Boston: Nonpareil Books.

Cunningham, Stuart. 1981. "The 'Force-Field' of Melodrama." *Quarterly Review of Film Studies* 6, 4 (Fall): 347–64.

Derrida, Jacques. 1980. "The Law of Genre." *Glyph* 7 (July): 202–29.

Frye, Northrop. 1957. *Anatomy of Criticism: Four Essays*. Princeton: Princeton University Press.

Gelman, Morrie. 1994. "Shop Around the Clock." *Emmy* 16, 3 (May–June): 30–3.

Gledhill, Christine. 1985. "Genre." In *The Cinema Book*. Ed. Pam Cook. New York: Pantheon Books.

Gunning, Tom. 1990. "Non-Continuity, Continuity, Discontinuity: A Theory of Genres in Early Films." In *Early Cinema: Space, Frame, Narrative*. Ed. Thomas Elsaesser. London: BFI Publishing.

Hess Wright, Judith. 1995. "Genre Films and the Status Quo." In *Film Genre Reader II*. Ed. Barry Keith Grant. Austin: University of Texas Press. 41–9.

Hunter, Ian. 1988. "Providence and Profit: Speculations in the Genre Market." *Southern Review* 22, 3: 211–23.

Jameson, Fredric. 1981. *The Political Unconscious: Narrative as a Socially Symbolic Act*. Ithaca: Cornell University Press.

Jowett, Garth S. 1985. "Giving Them What They Want: Movie Audience Research Before 1950." In *Current Research in Film: Audience, Economics, and Law, Vol. 1*. Ed. Bruce A. Austin. Norwood: Ablex Publishing Corporation.

Kapsis, Robert E. 1991. "Hollywood Genres and the Production of Culture Perspective." In *Current Research in Film: Audiences, Economics, and Law Vol. 5*. Ed. Bruce Austin. Norwood: Ablex Publishing Corporation. 68–85.

Kellner, Douglas. 1990. *Television and the Crisis of Democracy*. Boulder: Westview Press.

Kitses, Jim. 1969. *Horizons West: Anthony Mann, Budd Boetticher, Sam Peckinpah: Studies of Authorship within the Western*. Bloomington: Indiana University Press.

Klinger, Barbara. 1994. *Melodrama and Meaning: History, Culture, and the Films of Douglas Sirk*. Bloomington: Indiana University Press.

——. 1997. "Film History Terminable and Interminable: Recovering the Past in Reception Studies." *Screen* 38, 2 (Summer): 107–28.

Koszarski, Richard. 1990. *An Evening's Entertainment: The Age of the Silent Feature Picture, 1915–1928*. Vol. 3 of *History of the American Cinema*. General Ed. Charles Harpole. New York: Scribner's.

McArthur, Colin. 1972. *Underworld USA*. London: Secker and Warburg/BFI.

Modleski, Tania. 1997. "A Woman's Gotta Do . . . What a Man's Gotta Do? Cross-Dressing in the Western." *Signs: Journal of Women in Culture and Society* 22, 3: 519–44.

Neale, Steve. 1990. "Questions of Genre." *Screen* 31, 1 (Spring): 45–66.

Nolletti jr., Arthur, and David Desser. 1992. "Introduction." In *Reframing Japanese Cinema: Authorship, Genre, History*. Bloomington: Indiana. University Press. ix–xviii.

Panofsky, Erwin. 1939. *Studies in Iconology: Humanistic Themes in the Art of the Renaissance*. New York: Harper and Row.

Petley, Julian. 1996. "Fact Plus Fiction Equals Friction." *Media, Culture and Society* 18: 11–25.

Ryall, Tom. 1978. *Teachers Study Guide No. 2: The Gangster Film*. London: BFI Education.

Schatz, Thomas. 1981. *Hollywood Genres: Formulas, Filmmaking, and the Studio System*. New York: Random House.

Sobchack, Vivian. 1995. " 'Surge and Splendor': A Phenomenology of the Hollywood Historical Epic." In *Film Genre Reader II*. Ed. Barry Keith Grant. Austin: University of Texas Press. 280–307.

Stringer, Julian. 1997. " 'Your Tender Smiles Give Me Strength': Paradigms of Masculinity in John Woo's *A Better Tomorrow* and *The Killer*." *Screen* 38, 1 (Spring): 25–41.

Warshow, Robert. 1979 [1964]. "Movie Chronicle: *The Westerner*." Rpt. in *Film Theory and Criticism: Introductory Readings*, 2nd edn. Ed. Gerald Mast and Marshall Cohen. New York: Oxford University Press. 469–87.

Williams, Alan. 1984. "Is a Radical Genre Criticism Possible?" *Quarterly Review of Film Studies* 9, 2 (Spring): 121–5.

Williams, Linda. 1993. "Mirrors Without Memories: Truth, History, and the New Documentary." *Film Quarterly* 46, 3 (Spring): 9–21.

Williams, Linda. 1995. "Film Bodies: Gender, Genre, and Excess." In *Film Genre Reader II*. Ed. Barry Keith Grant. Austin: University of Texas Press. 140–58.

Wilson, Christopher. 1983. "The Rhetoric of Consumption: Mass-Market Magazines and the Demise of the Gentle Reader, 1880–1920." In *The Culture of Consumption: Critical Essays in American History, 1880–1980*. Ed. Richard Wightman Fox and T. J. Jackson Lears. New York: Pantheon Books. 39–64.

Wright, Will. 1975. *Sixguns and Society: A Structural Study of the Western*. Berkeley: University of California Press.

Yoshimoto, Mitsuhiro. 1993. "Melodrama, Postmodernism, and Japanese Cinema." In *Melodrama and Asian Cinema*. Ed. Wimal Dissanayake. Cambridge: Cambridge University Press. 101–26.

CHAPTER FOUR

Enunciation and Narration[1]

André Gaudreault and François Jost

There are no stories without a storytelling instance. Virtually all narratologists agree on this point. Films differ, however, from novels in that a film can *show* an action rather than *tell* it. In that regime of showing (monstration), notably in theatrical staging or in the "documentary" recordings of the Lumière Brothers, the discursive instance is less apparent than in a written tale. Events seem to tell their own stories. Yet this is misleading, because without any mediation there would have been no recording and we would not have seen the events at all. This perception of events recounting themselves, which some spectators might have (for example in watching a surveillance video) or certain critics might argue for (such as André Bazin, when he invokes the "impartiality of the camera" or "the fragment of 'raw reality' in Italian neorealism" [Bazin 1981: 280–1]), does not stand up to analysis.

We are confronted with a key question: should narratology start from spectatorial perception, however flawed, or look for a system of narrative instances capable of explaining the textuality of film? This question was posed at a time when the possibility of a film as a narrative was no longer accepted as a postulate and after the decline of the euphoria of those who believed there was a necessary correspondence between messages sent and messages understood in a communication system where every message encoded by a sender was supposed to be received intact, or almost intact, by a receiver.

Since then, narratologists have responded diversely to this methodological question. To simplify what is at stake, consider this image: a ventriloquist and his dummy, for example the impertinent Hugo of *Dead of the Night* (Alberto Cavalcanti, 1945). Here, the dummy has a monologue, confiding his love for this or that well-known singer. If the situation seems comic, that is because the spectator believes (or pretends to believe) that the dummy is responsible for what it "says". But if it turns to the man holding it on his knee to begin a dialogue, the spectator momentarily adheres to the fiction that these two figures are autonomous subjects, sometimes in disagreement with one another. That belief will be strong or weak, depending on whether the viewer is a child or an adult, a "good" or "bad" audience. This can only work if spectators bracket their knowledge that dummies do not actually talk. When, by error, the dummy's voice changes itself into the ventriloquist's, it becomes clear that we are being deceived. Now, if we are asked to explain what the ventriloquist has been doing, we could simply state that a man is speaking the words that seem to come from the toy while keeping his own lips still.

Back to film. As a double narrative, in such cases where the soundtrack allows us to hear the words of a narrator, film calls on two narrative instances. But while one tells one story in an overt manner, as in a living voice, the grand image-maker does now show himself. For example, "a fictional, invisible person turns the leaves of an album, drawing our attention to a specific item" (Laffay 1964: 81–2). How should we conceptualize the narrative relationship between this instance and those characters who, from within the films themselves, tell us oral or written stories? There are two approaches:

1 The first answer focusses on the spectator's grasp of what is seen and heard. This solution envisions the ways that the presence of a grand image-maker can be made more or less felt as responsible for the filmic enunciation, an organizer of various narratives (as if one looked at the earlier example from the perspective of the dummy, then moved to the ventriloquist as manipulator).
2 The second answer focusses on the properties of the film. This concentrates on film narrative per se, leaving to one side spectatorial reading.

We shall examine these two methods in turn.

1   First Approach to Narratology: Moving from Film to Narrative Instances

1.1   From enunciation to narration

Enunciation has several meanings. In the broadest sense, it signifies "the relations between what is said and the different sources that produce statements:

– the protagonists of discourse [sender and receiver]
– the situation of communication."

In a more restricted sense, enunciation refers to everything from the narrow sense of "linguistic traces of the speaker's presence within his utterance" (Kerbrat-Orecchioni 1980: 30–1) to the broader phenomena that Benveniste groups under "subjectivity in language." The latter conception is undoubtedly the most common one among narratologists, notably in Benveniste's celebrated opposition between "histoire" and "discours," or "story" and "discourse." If, in the story, "events seem to recount themselves," then in discourse we see a mode of enunciation that "presumes the presence of both a speaker and a listener" (Benveniste 1966: 241).

In order to study narrative instances in novels, Genette takes off from Benveniste's distinction and stresses its ambiguity: the opposition between story and discourse is less an absolute boundary than the product of perceiving, in a varying way, the presence of the speaker in what he says. This is more obvious in the case of a statement such as "For a long time, I had always gone to bed early" (from Marcel Proust's *Remembrance of Things Past*) than in an historical story such as "Napoleon died at Saint-Helena," but the latter still comes from somewhere, since it uses the past tense, "a time before the narration that is the story" (Genette 1972: 225), and therefore implies a storytelling instance. No story exists without discourse. Nevertheless, one can see discourse as a sort of "cyst," because language has marks, signs, that bear the trace of the teller, the holder of the discourse: these marks are *deictics*.

When a novel begins with "I am alone here, now, sheltered" (from *The Labyrinth*, Alain Robbe-Grillet, 1959), the reader immediately asks: who is this "I?", when is "now" in the story? and what defines "here" and being "sheltered"? These questions cannot be answered until we can identify the storyteller with a name or description, along with the place or moment of speaking. In a situation of oral discourse, it is as if "the correlatives of the situation allow one not to describe the places, situations, and objects in great detail, because it is common knowledge" (Slama-Cazacu 1961: 213). Without this knowledge, which is not offered by the written text, the signification of "I am alone here, now, sheltered" varying in meaning with its speaker. Think of what happens to that remark when spoken in a bunker, a phone box, or said softly by James Bond near a swimming pool to the "Bond girls," while under surveillance from above by a spyglass.

An utterance that only uses deictics (the adverbs "here" and "now," the pronoun "I," and the present tense) can only be deciphered when we know the speaker's identity, unlike a statement such as: "On 12th April 1979, Corporal Wilson was alone in his nuclear shelter," which can be understood without knowing who is saying it.

Starting from these phenomena of subjectivity in language, linguistics moved from "the analysis of utterances to the analysis of the relationship between these utterances and their productive instances" (Genette 1972: 225), their enunciation, which Genette tried to study at "the productive moment of narrative discourse, narration." Naturally, theorists of cinematographic enunciation have looked for such deictic markers in film. Within that paradigm, we can discern six cases where the subjectivity of the image is clear (Jost 1983):

1   an exaggerated foreground, suggesting the proximity of the lens, produced by either discrepancy of scale (obtained, for example, by deep focus: see, at the end of *Citizen Kane* [Welles, 1942], the moment when Susan, seated on the ground, tries to finish a puzzle, her face as high as Kane's figure, which

appears at the door, in the background), or by an opposition between fuzziness and clarity (as when one sees, across almost indistinct bushes, a landscape);

2   a point of view below eye level: Orson Welles's work provides many examples;

3   representation of a body-part in the foreground, which makes it look as though the camera is anchored in a point of view: the countryside seen from the flick of hair (*Notorious*, Hitchcock, 1946), the road that is seen as double when drunk (*North by Northwest*, Hitchcock, 1959), and, more widely, all those images that seem to conflict with "normal" vision – double vision, deliberately fuzzy focus, and so on, that replicate the perception of drunkenness or myopia;

4   a character's shadow;

5   seeing the viewfinder, framing devices, or a keyhole in the image;

6   a shaking camera, its motion jerky or so mechanical that we notice the point of view is that of an apparatus.

To all these criteria, we must add the look at the camera.

Without embarking on a comprehensive account of point of view, which we have addressed elsewhere (Jost 1989; Gaudreault and Jost 1990), the most important thing for our purposes here is this: in language, deictics construct a "speaker-observer" (Kerbrat-Orrechioni 1980: 49), the person who offers the discourse and his position in space. "I am alone *here*; on *my* right is the chest of drawers, on *my* left the window" reveals not only a discourse situation, but a discourse situation from a perspective. In the case of film the marks of subjectivity suggest someone watching the scene, a person located in the diegesis, while, on other occasions, they trace the presence of something beyond the diegesis, a "grand image-maker." Consider category (6), comparing its use in two celebrated pictures: *Dark Passage* (Delmer Daves, 1947) and *Citizen Kane*.

The former begins with a turning landscape shot, seen through a circular matte, then a barrel fallen from a truck, rolling down a slope. Then a hand, in the foreground, is visible pushing back the foliage. The camera moves from one end of the landscape to the other to follow motorbikes on the road.

In Welles's film, the newsreel "News on the March" shows us images of Kane at the end of his life between the fretwork of a barrier in the foreground, which conceals much of the view; the camera shakes.

While in the first extract the spectator understands quite quickly, thanks to the image of the barrel and the voice-over, that he is seeing through the eyes of a character, in the second the marks of subjectivity don't belong to anyone from within the story. They are there only to give the impression that the shots of Kane have been stolen, as it were, from reality, as if by some paparazzi. They imitate the difficulties of filming for journalistic purposes. Unlike deictics in language, these marks can construct a look internal to the diegesis, a character as much as the grand image-make, who by definition is situated outside the diegetic world. To a certain extent, therefore, there is in the cinema only enunciative use of signs and not enunciative signs per se. But there is something else: experience shows that when we screen the "News on the March" sequence to film studies students, some of them bracket the trembling camera, from the moment when the camera pans to follow the movement of the wheelchair. As J.-P. Simon notes, the "distortions (wide angle, high angle, low angle) don't have the same effect in all types of film because of the discursive context, since the marks of enunciation often get buried in the utterance itself" (Simon 1979: 113).

Perception of enunciation therefore varies according to both the audiovisual context and the sensibility of the spectator. Throughout its history, the cinema has created procedures for concealing these marks, to the point where it has been said that "the special trait of the classical text was to hide the discursive instance that produced it, as if it were nothing more than the simple transcription of an anterior and homogeneous continuity" (Marie 1976: 24), so that, strictly speaking, "the events seem to recount themselves." The eyeline matches, the matches on movement and action, are part of these procedures, so that if a Wellesian angle appears so forcefully, it's because it doesn't have to do with a character lying on the ground, and therefore seems to come from a grand image-maker who is "speaking cinema."

Here we have an example of cinematic enunciation: the moment where spectators, escaping the fiction-effect, find themselves confronted by cinematic language as such – from "This is cinema," acknowledged by various cinematic devices, to "I am at the cinema" (Sorlin 1984: 306). This realization does not arise only from the traits we have already mentioned. It can also arise from the observation of light (it is rarely night in the films: for example, we still see a person after they have turned off all the lights), makeup (blood as red paint in Godard), montage (jump cuts), punctuation (iris, superimposition). The perception of cinematic enunciation varies according to the spectator, as differentiated by knowledge, age, social class, and historical period.

Thus, in early cinema, the famous look at the camera, which was commonly in use, was not often noticed by spectators, as films often replicated the conditions of the vaudeville attraction, which were based on the relationship between an on-stage artist and his audience. It was only when film began to develop continuous stories, which required the creation of an autonomous diegetic world, that the look at the camera was systematically banished (cf. Woods 1911, cited in Gunning 1984: 130). In the same way, narrative cross-cutting might have been seen as shocking when it was introduced at the beginning of the century, whereas today it is a normal montage figure, no longer noticed, as long as the rules of cutting are respected.

Pastiche offers very revealing exercises of cinematic enunciation. We have already cited Welles's "News on the March," but *Zelig* (Woody Allen, 1983), which generalizes this procedure, would merit a detailed analysis. All of the paramaters of filming sounds and images, framing, and music that we associate with classical Hollywood and TV reportage are imitated, reworked, and, in this way, designated as enunciative marks. The pastiche here culminates in the end scene, during which an actor replays a part of the life of the character previously played by Allen himself. The cutting, the gestures, the mise- en-scène, mimic the Hollywood B-film.

Without expressly using the term "enunciation," in the same spirit Iouri Lotman defines cinematic language as a system of gaps in relation to a system of expectations dictated by experience. Supposing, on the one hand, "a spectator who knows nothing of cinematic language, and on the other, a spectator formed by the history of film" (Lotman 1977: 59), he demonstrates that for the former there is cinematic language only where an element is marked as different from what he expected, whereas for the latter meaning is created in the opposition between marked and unmarked.

1.2   The explicit narrator and the grand image-maker

If a certain modernist cinema accentuates the marks of filmic enunciation (Resnais, Robbe-Grillet, Godard, Duras, etc.), classical cinema always tried, as we have suggested, to suppress these marks to stress what was happening to the characters or what was told by explicit narrators. In the same way, documentaries are generally made in such a way that we pay more attention to what an interviewee says than the manner in which the interviewee is filmed.

Nevertheless, in both cases, the presence of the grand image-maker stays more or less perceptible. Let's take the case of the flashback in which a character becomes a storyteller, such as Walter Neff in *Double Indemnity* (Billy Wilder, 1944) who confesses his crime to a colleague on a dictaphone. After recording a few sentences of his story, images come to show us his life and his story: he drives to a villa where he will meet the woman who will turn his life upside down. How does this movement, from the said to the shown, operate?

To understand the story, the spectator must suppose that the narrator, Walter Neff, takes responsibility for this audiovisual story, which covers the images of the recording of his confession. The spectator must assume that this "audio-visualization", this trans-semioticization, is faithful to the verbal narrative that Neff is supposedly still dictating. It's in the name of this postulate of sincerity that the spectator is ready to tolerate a number of bizarre occurrences, or forget them: the narrator himself is, within the diegetic world of the story that he's telling, shown from outside; each of the characters has his own voice and not that of the narrator; and every detail is shown, even though the memory of the narrator would logically be limited. These strange phenomena, which create a veritable "paralepsis" (Genette's [1972: 212] term), are conventions we accept in order to believe in the diegesis, to identify with characters and their points of view.

But sometimes there are narrative delinkages which go beyond the conventions of a given period. In other words, there are gaps that create a canyon between the verbal narrative and its trans-semioticization. For example:

1   Gaps between what the character is supposed to have seen and what we see. In this sense, the audiovisualizations of the narratives of Thatcher and Bernstein in *Kane* are very different. The fact that the first shows us Thatcher from outside doesn't surprise us, since most flashbacks function in this way and to the degree that we only see scenes that he witnessed. On the other hand, Bernstein's narrative begins with a shot of Kane and Leland arriving at the *Inquirer* building. The fact that we hear their conversation is somewhat strange because the narrator, Bernstein, only enters the shot a few seconds later on a pile of furniture, behind his two friends – so he wasn't a witness to these events, unlike Thatcher in the previous example, which nevertheless he is supposed to be relating to the journalist Thompson who came to interview him. Even less explicable, in the story of Susan singing opera, are the multiplicity of the shots which describe the opera house, the prompter, Kane in the balcony seat, Leland ripping up his program – in this case, we see multiple actions which the narrator, Susan, could not possibly have witnessed.

2   Gaps between what the character tells us and what we see. In *Diary of a Country Priest* (Robert Bresson, 1951), for example, which seems to show only what the priest notes day by day in his notebooks, we see behind him the countess's daughter, who witnesses the conversation between her mother and the priest. In the diegesis, the priest has no idea about this indiscretion until the priest from Torcy tells him, much later, "You were seen while you were speaking with the countess," and it is hard to comprehend how such a shot could be a visualization of his diary. Furthermore, in the Bernanos novel, there is no equivalent to this image – at least, not at this point, in the priest's narrative. We learn about the daughter's indiscretion only much later, thanks to the Torcy priest's revelation: "I imagine that she was in the garden, beneath the window, where the sill is high above the ground." Here, the authority of the author/ narrator of the diary is questioned. What is said can be contradicted by what is shown. The audiovisualization implies and constructs for the spectator, more obviously than other films with voice-over, a superior narrator whose existence is even more perceptible since the intimate-diary genre usually entails only a single narrative instance – that of the diarist.

These gaps can also be found in documentaries and news reports. The first – between what the interviewee is supposed to see and what we see – is when images are superimposed that are not invoked in his speech, whether with an ironic intention or to evaluate him. The second, revealing a disparity of enunciative instances, occurs when, in the case of an on-camera interview, there is a jump in the image, revealing that something has been edited out (as mocked by Welles in "News on the March").

In all these cases, if the spectator is not sensitive to the enunciation, if he has mentally erased the specifically cinematic procedures, he is suddenly reminded that alongside this verbal narrator (explicit, intradiegetic, and visualized) whom he took at his word, there is also a grand filmic image-maker (implicit, extradiegetic, and invisible) manipulating this audiovisual network. This un-mistakable realization is reaffirmed in a new way. In the case of fiction, we would call this organizing function the implicit narrator. But in the case of a document-ary or news report, we would call it a documentarist or journalist.

To move from the perception of cinematic language to the idea of enunciation, or from the visualization of an explicit story to an implied one – these are two ways to deduce the cinematic discourse. That does not mean that it ever disappears. It only means that its presence is always more or less perceptible. And this way of thinking about the narrative instances of film is very close to certain linguistic theories about language.

What happens, in fact, when Pierre says "Jean told me: 'I shall come'"? There are two speakers: Jean and Pierre. Nevertheless, says the linguist Ducrot (1984: 196), "it is also possible that parts of the utterance generally imputed to a primary speaker, nevertheless can be imputed to a secondary speaker [...] just as, in the novel, a principal narrator can insert into his own narrative another narrative told to him by a secondary narrator." One tends to think that the primary speaker, Pierre, doesn't betray the words of the secondary narrator, Jean. Nevertheless, it is enough that Pierre appears to be lying to make one doubt the postulate of sincerity that is the condition of one's listening. Then one strongly dissociates the primary speaker and the secondary one.

This embedding of speakers brings with it a double attribution of the utter-ance, according to the linguist. This does not mean that two people speak physically in the utterance: the speaker is not the speaking subject. In the novel, diacritical marks permit us to distinguish the primary narrator from the secondary one: they speak the same language, "natural language." In the cinema, the primary speaker, the implicit narrator, speaks cinema using images and sounds; the explicit narrator only uses words. That explains why, as the film's spectator, I tend to attribute the narrative to the one who claims to be telling it, just as I attribute the phrase "I shall come" to Jean, even though Pierre is telling me about it. It is only in the gap that the second level becomes necessary for my comprehension, just as in language it is at the moment when something tells me that Pierre is not relating Jean's words correctly, or that he lies, that I have to dissociate the two speakers and attach differential credence to them.

Silent cinema already worked with different visualizations of verbal narratives (for example, the contradictory versions of the two lawyers in *Les Deux timides* [René Clair, 1928]).

2   Second Approach to Narratology: Moving from Narrative Instances to Film

2.1   From narration to sub-narration

Cinema has an almost natural predilection for narrative delegation, for embedded discourses. The reason for this is quite simple: the cinema shows characters in action who imitate human beings in their diverse daily activities, and one of these activities, in which all of us are involved some time or another, is to speak. And in speaking, many human beings are led, by circumstance, to use the narrative function of language, to tell, and to tell themselves. And for the cinema this phenomenon is accentuated even more by the fact that it deploys five modes of expression – that is to say, images, sounds, words, written materials, and music – and that film, as we said, is always a double narrative.

In a sense, we can therefore claim that in the cinema, a narrative that is the product of a visualized narrator (e.g. Leland, Bernstein, Susan, and Raymond in *Citizen Kane*) is merely a sub-narrative (in the same sense that Genette [1972: 239] speaks of a meta-narrative and Mieke Bal [1977: 24] of a hypo-narrative). In effect, at a primary level cinema always already tells, if only in showing the visualized narrator, himself in the process of telling, or to be more precise, in the process of undertelling.

Here we see what is tendentious in the expression "undertelling" (*sous-raconter*). The expression is a function of this second narratological approach, which tries to respect the order of things versus how they appear to the spectator. It makes the only real narrator of the film the grand image-maker, or the meganarrator (Gaudreault 1988), the equivalent of the implicit narrator mentioned earlier. From this perspective, all the other narrators present in the film are only delegated narrators, second narrators, whose activity is a sub-narration, an activity which could be distinguished from first-degree narration. *Citizen Kane*, once again, is a prime example for clarifying this model.

2.2 Secondary narrators

The problem of sub-narration varies depending on whether we are referring to written or filmic narrative. In the first case, the sub-narration of the secondary narrator is conveyed through the same semiotic medium that is used by the primary narrator: verbal language (even if, in certain cases, the movement to writing down the oral involves difficulties of transcription, such as how to convey intonations, accents, nervous tics, etc.).

Consider the case of *The Thousand and One Nights*. The primary narrator of this written story, the first one to speak, tells the story of a king who, in order to take vengeance on women, successively marries several women who must be killed immediately after the wedding night. When Scheherazade's turn comes, in order to delay the deadly fate that awaits her, she undertakes to tell a story each night, each more captivating than the last. As a result, the king indefinitely postpones her execution. Each of these stories is told by this sub-narrator, Scheherazade, who is herself part of the primary diegesis on the level told by the primary narrator (she is in this sense what Genette would call an "intradiegetic narrator").

Summing up, in such a case, a verbal narrator tells verbally what another verbal narrator has (under)told verbally. There is a homogeneity of materials. It is notable that in such cases of narrative delegation the primary narrator is almost invisible; when Scheherazade speaks, the reader completely forgets the very existence of the primary narrator. It is almost as if the primary narrator were literally drowned in the flow of words of the secondary narrator.

This situation, which belongs to written narrative, is less frequent in the case of cinematic narrative. This is due to the homogeneous nature of written narrative, which engages only one mode of expression, language, compared to the essentially polyphonic character of filmic narrative. Given the homogeneous matter of linguistic expression, narrators within written narratives, like that of *The Thousand and One Nights*, delegate the narration to a sub-narrator, giving up their own role. This explains the ease with which many sub-narrators and many second narrators, such as Scheherazade, manage to recover the "voices" of and conceal the presence of the primary narrator.

This is clearly a paradoxical situation, which is not unknown in the cinema, even if to a lesser degree. In this sense, the cinema seems to have an exemplary value for narratology as a whole because, unlike verbal stories, in the cinema it is relatively difficult to make invisible the presence of the primary instance, which is the grand image-maker, the meganarrator, by interposing a secondary one. This allows various combinations between narrative levels, much more complex than in literature, and enables the double narrative to be completely manifest. Thus the film narratologist is very sensitive to the hierarchization of these different instances.

2.3   Oral narrative, audiovisual

In effect, in film the double narrative is hierarchized, as we have seen, and it is speech, above all, that effects these narrative articulations. Let's take the case of Leland in *Citizen Kane*. Thompson visits him in the hospital, where Leland begins to tell him about Kane's life with his first wife:

> She was like all the young girls I knew in dancing school. Charming. Utterly charming. Emily was a little more charming than the others. Well, after the first couple of months, they never saw much of each other except at breakfast. It was a marriage like any other.

If Leland gives an oral narration, or more precisely a sub-narration, it is nevertheless true that the meganarrator continues, throughout this verbal storytelling, to show Leland in his wheelchair, to have us hear him and also follow his "own" narration. In this case, the narrative is an audiovisual narrative, which tells us, by showing it, the story of Thompson, the journalist, paying a visit to Leland and making him (under)narrate his own story. Therefore, the narrative is truly double to the extent that the narrative voice of the filmic meganarrator, responsible for the audiovisual narrative, is simultaneous to that of the verbal (sub-) narrator, responsible for the oral (sub-)narrative.

The situation becomes more complex on the narratological plane when the image of the secondary narrator vanishes, as when Leland in his wheelchair gives way to the visualization of the diegetic world he is telling us about. The plot of the audiovisual story thus gives way to the sub-narrative, which is just as audiovisual as the first. And as in the case of the primary narrator of the written narrative, the filmic meganarrator erases himself in favor of a secondary narrator who, just as polyphonous as he, occupies the five tracks of transmission of the filmic narration. Here, too, we find identity between the semiotic materials of storytelling (the primary narrative which is the film *Citizen Kane*) and the semiotic materials of that which is told (the secondary narrative which tells of the deterioration in relations between Kane and his wife), and thus we confront a phenomenon of the primary narrator becoming invisible, a situation comparable, at least apparently, to the case of *The Thousand and One Nights*.

However, the difference between these two situations is that in the latter, the story is told through the device of a semiotic mechanism – the verbal language – which the responsible, the secondary narrator (for example, Scheherazade, who is a speaking subject) uses. Quite a different situation applies in the case of the transvisualized sub-narratives in film, such as the one which accompanies, or more precisely substitutes for, Leland's verbal narration (he is in effect not a filming subject). Once the verbal narrative of the secondary narrator (Leland) has undergone its transmutation, its transcoding, into an audiovisual language of which Leland himself is not a user, it becomes difficult to answer the question, who speaks and who is telling the story? It is either the grand image-maker speaking or the secondary narrator. Since the latter is not a user of the audiovisual language (he is not supposed to communicate with his narratee [here the journalist Thompson] and with words), who is then telling this audiovisual sub-narrative? This question must be asked because often such transvisualized sub-narratives give us information not available to the secondary narrator (for example, see the particularly clear example cited above: the sub-narrative of Kane's arrival at the *Inquirer* as told by Bernstein). In such cases we must recognize that the meganarrator is the one responsible for that . . . . But how do we distinguish the respective fields of intervention of the filmic meganarrator and the verbal sub-narrators?

The history of the cinema is very instructive concerning the relationship between certain sub-narrators and the transvisualization that stems from their verbal narrative. In a film like *The Sultan of Love* (Le Somptier and Burguet, 1918), when the heroine tells the story of meeting the sultan, she looks off into the distance; we have the impression that she is seeing the images which she is describing verbally to her servant (i.e. her narratee). In the first decade of sound film, this codification of the look sometimes signaled the beginning of the sub-narrative. Thus, in *The Story of a Poor Young Man* (Abel Gance, 1935), when the conductor begins his story, we see him superimposed on the events he is telling. We don't hear him anymore, but he continues to speak, his gaze lost in the void. It is only very slowly that the verbal narration becomes dissociated from the marked position of the narrator in relationship to the visualization of his story.

2.4   Instances in collusion

Let's return to the breakfast sequence mentioned earlier. How can we think that its contents, which visualize Leland's discourse, are a perfectly faithful representation of what he says? Isn't it extremely unlikely that Leland's verbal discourse would have been so cinematic and allusive in showing the degradation of their conjugal relationship? Let's remember that we see a series of shots separated by swishpans in which Kane and his wife have breakfast, at first gazing into each other's eyes, then talking in a more and more tense manner, until each is reading a different newspaper at the end of a very long table. Admittedly, Leland begins his story by alluding directly to the breakfasts ("Well, after the first couple of months, they never saw much of each other except at breakfast. It was a marriage like any other"), but it is hard to imagine that the contents of this sequence are in any way a literal transcription of Leland's words. These breakfast scenes only have an exemplary and symbolic value: there were obviously other breakfasts, and Leland never witnessed them.

The case is a bit different when we think about Thatcher's memories. This sub-narrative has a hybrid status if only because it is through the device of a written narrative, rather than an oral one (as with Leland, Susan, Bernstein, and Raymond), that the retrospective narrative information about Kane's life is delivered to the journalist–investigator and thus to the spectator. Unlike Leland's narrative, which is told to Thompson here and now, Thatcher's narrative has been written before, at a time prior to the moment where Thompson becomes aware of it.

Nevertheless this apparently changes nothing in terms of the audiovisual narrative designed to illustrate the words of the filmic sub-narrator, Thatcher. At bottom, it doesn't matter whether these words come in oral or written form. In order to establish the illocutionary origin of an audiovisual sub-narrative of this type, in order to parcel out the responsibility of the diverse narrative instances implied in such cases, it is more important to examine carefully the gaps between the diverse forms of knowledge, what the characters might have seen, etc. In a case like Thatcher's memoirs, we must agree that the point of view inscribed in the audiovisual sub-narrative matches that of the secondary narrator, even though he is seen from outside. In this case there is collusion between the filmic meganarrator and the verbal sub-narrator: nothing is shown that isn't known to Thatcher and *perhaps* written by him (for we must remember that the spectator doesn't know exactly what Thatcher wrote since we only see a few lines of the text of the memoirs).

But as we saw with the breakfast sequence, the collusion between the filmic meganarrator and the verbal sub-narrator is not always so extensive. That explains the progressive increase in the gaps between the knowledge of the sub-narrator and that of the meganarrator in *Citizen Kane*, from Kane's arrival at the *Inquirer* office, as told by Bernstein, to the evening at the opera, as told by Susan.

The multiplicity of modes of expression provokes, or permits, a variety of "narrative situations" that go far beyond those available in written literature. It follows therefore that cinematic narratives are particularly good at superimposing discourses over one another, and working from a variety of planes of enunciation and points of view, which might even enter into collision. Cinematic polyphony, its signifying density, means that, contrary to the situation in any written narratives, "covering over" the voice of the basic narrator, i.e. the meganarrator, with the voice of the secondary narrator, the sub-narrator, is far from being the rule.

Nevertheless, we do encounter in the cinema a situation analogous to that of Scheherazade's speaking in *The Thousand and One Nights*, which allows a complete covering over of the primary narrator's voice by the secondary narrator's. This rendering invisible supposes that the secondary narrator utilizes, in telling the sub-story, the same means as those of the former, the primary narrator. If in a narrative written in one language, this presumes that the sub-narrator also begins to speak in that language and occupies the transmission channel of the narration; in the cinema the analogous situation presumes that the sub-narrator begins literally to "speak cinema." We see this process in the sequence "News on the March" within *Citizen Kane*. This film-within-a-film demonstrates very clearly, as a sub-narrative, the diverse channels of narrative transmission (i.e. the five filmic modes of expression) and its hidden agent, in its way and for a short period, the fundamental filmic meganarrator, responsible for the cinematic narrative that is *Citizen Kane*.

2.5   Who recounts the film?

In the model we have just developed, we see that the fundamental instance of filmic narration is not unitary, since the cinema, as a mixture of modes of expression, is not unitary. From this perspective we have proposed a model where the primary narrator, responsible for communicating the filmic narrative, could be said to manipulate the diverse modes of filmic expression, to orchestrate them, make them function, and regulate their play in order to provide the spectator with diverse narrative information. One could even imagine regrouping the modes of expression in terms of their particular sub-instances: thus André Gardies (1987) divides into three sub-groups the diverse narrative responsibilities of the real conductor, who is the "filmic enunciator" who would modulate the voice of three sub-enunciators, each one responsible, respectively, for the iconic, the verbal, and the musical.

To the extent that the filmic process implies a certain kind of articulation between diverse operations of signification (mise-en-scène, framing, and sequencing), it is also possible to mold a "story system" which takes account of what has been called "the process of filmic discursivization" (Gaudreault 1988: 119). This hypothesis is based on the diverse operations necessary to the material making of a film and on the diverse manipulations by the agency responsible for the production of a film. It identifies two superimposed layers of narrativity. The first of these layers, resulting from the combined work of mise-en-scène and framing, is limited to what has been called *monstration*. It arises from a first form of cinematic articulation, that between frames, which forms the very basis of cinematic process and permits the presentation, in continuity on the screen, of successive photographic frames.

Once articulated with each other, these first-level units, called frames, create the illusion of continuous movement, giving birth to second-level units – the shot. The second layer of narrativity, at a level superior to that of monstration, according to this hypothesis, is equivalent to narration, if only as a function of its greater possibilities for a temporal modulation. It arises from the activity of sequencing called montage, a procedure that filmmakers have used to tell their stories. This second layer of narrativity is thus based on a second cinematic articulation: that between shots.

These two layers of narrativity presuppose at least two different instances, the monstrator and the narrator, responsible respectively for each. Thus, in order to make a pluri-punctual filmic narrative, we would need a monstrator, or show-er, who would be this responsible instance, during the shooting of the film and the putting into the can of this multitude of micro-narratives called shots. Then the filmic narrator would intervene and would inscribe, through montage, a reading, after having looked at the primary narrative substance – the shots. At a higher level, the voice of these two instances would be modulated and regulated by the primary instance, which is the filmic meganarrator responsible for the meganarrative – the film itself. Hence the following figure (from Gaudreault 1988: 116):

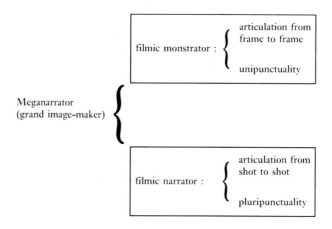

3   Filmic Narratology in Perspective

The ideas we have just outlined here conform, to a certain extent, to the narratological tradition, in the sense that the models follow the same axis of research opened up recently by Gérard Genette, whose principles were elaborated in his book *Figures III* – despite the relative distance between what is being said here and Genette's hypotheses.

Other researchers have explored the problem of filmic narration from different angles, notably Roger Odin (1988), who developed a semio–pragmatic approach. Within this approach, spectators and their diverse affects must be taken into account from the beginning, to the extent that the production and the reception of films are "socially programmed practices" (Odin 1988: 121). For Odin, the consumer of a filmic narrative fiction, known as the "reader–actant," is called upon to make, in a relatively imperative fashion, a "network of fictionalizing determinations" identifiable as seven operations: figurativization (recognition of analogical signs); diegetization (construction of a world); narrativization (production of a narrative); monstration (construction of the world shown as "real"); belief (a corollary of the preceding); the synchronization of phases (homogenization of narration via the collusion of diverse instances), and fictivization (recognition of the fictionalizing status of the enunciator). The story thus communicated to the spectator always presupposes, for Odin (127), the intervention of a narrator: "a story is always told, in the cinema as elsewhere."

There has also been, from a more semiological angle and more involved with the problematic of enunciation, the work of Metz (1988 and 1991) and of Francesco Casetti (1990). In his 1991 book, Metz made a series of proposals which, if they are primarily concerned with questions of enunciation, equally address the problematic of narration. This is hardly surprising in relation to cinema, given the extent to which enunciation and narration are intimately connected. Metz mobilizes a conceptual apparatus which aims to get to the bottom of the illusions that surround the issue of enunciation, this "capacity of many utterances to fold in on themselves, to appear here and there as if in bas relief, to create a thin layer which is engraved with cues revealing another level, which has to do with the production and not the product" (Metz 1988: 22). The phrase "to do with the production and not the product" explains why Metz can claim that "enunciation is the semiological act through which some parts of the text speak to us of this text as of an act." For Metz, filmic enunciation is, above all, "metadiscursive," in the sense that what it indicates in the first place is the film itself as an object – so much so that "the enunciator" becomes for Metz the film itself, and not some instance situated below or above (or, at any rate, outside) the film. Hence his option of having his analysis remain at the level of the text, eliminating from the metafilmic discourse any anthropomorphic instance, such as "narrator," "enunciator," "addressee," and other such concepts, basing himself rather on those "sites of enunciation," which are, at the beginning of the text, at its source, the "focus" of the utterance, and at the other end, its target: "the enunciator is the film, the film as focus, acting as such, oriented as such, the film as an activity" (1988: 26).

Basing his argument on the idea that, by its nonverbal nature, the filmic utterance, unlike the linguistic utterance, is not attributed to a specific person, Metz makes the following claim:

Those who believe that "enunciation in the cinema" means something, should not take this argument lightly, for it is very strong. It obliges us to change our conception: to conceive an enunciative apparatus which is not essentially deictic, and therefore anthropomorphic, not personal, as one says of pronouns, and which does not imitate in any close way a specific linguistic apparatus, because the linguistic inspiration is more successful at a distance. (1988: 21)

For his part, Francesco Casetti founds his enterprise on Greimas's principles about narrativity. For that school, the founding principle of narrative discourse is "shifting out," that operation by which the enunciative instance projects beyond itself categories of time, place, and subject: the action of telling, like any other discursive form, "appears as a creative schism, on the one hand of the subject, the space, and the time of the representation, and on the other of the actantial, spatial, and temporal representation of the utterance" (Greimas and Courtés 1979: 79). It is on this basis that Casetti (1990) identifies the filmic enunciator with the "I," the *enunciataire*, that is the addressee of the utterance as "you," and finally, the utterance itself as "he." The three instances of I, you, and he, for Casetti, are always present in the text, but their relative value and function can vary. Hence Casetti's four "discursive figurations" of point of view, potentially inscribed in the narrative filmic discourse are as follows:

1   The configuration said to be objective: those shots, the most common of all, which present profilmic reality as if it were a question of seizing the essence of the action without underlining who runs through the shots or shows them, that is to say without showing either the enunciator (or narrator) or the *enunciataire* (or spectator). This is the "nobody's shot": a neutral shot, which represents the point of view of "no one" and where "he" (the utterance) is more important than the "I" (the enunciator) or the "you" (the addressee).

2   The configuration of the addressee: in this case, the character acts as if he were the one offering and showing the film and directly interpellates those to whom the film is addressed: the spectator–addressee. An example would be the look at the camera. In this configuration, the "I," the enunciator, is concealed in the "he" that constitutes the whole of the utterance to interpellate the "you," the addressee–spectator.

3   The subjective configuration, for example the figure, usually produced through montage, which is the famous "subjective shot" and which has the looking activity of the character coincide with that of the spectator. Melding with the "he"-character, the "you" (addressee–spectator) shares what is seen with the "I"-enunciator.

4   The objectively unreal configuration: this arises, for example, every time the camera overtly manifests its omnipotence, when the camera opens up a perversion, since things no longer have their "normal" appearance. Thus Wellesian low-angle shots indicate, in a powerful way, through their out-

rageous character, the presence of an "I"-enunciator who affirms himself as such and reaffirms to the "you"-spectator his power over the "he" utterance.

Cassetti's theorization is relevant because what is at stake here is quite crucial, if only because of the importance that film theorists, and especially those concerned with cinematic narrative, have always accorded to different "enunciative postures." Those postures which bring closer the enunciator and the addressee, for example with the look at the camera and the subjective shot, are of central interest to those who are concerned with cinematic narration, like Marc Vernet with his chapters revealingly titled "the look at the camera" and "the look of the camera," which also draws on the fundamental figures of narrative cinema that engage the diverse instances of narration (Vernet 1988).

4   Narration without Narrator

As we have seen, the story given to the spectator always presupposes for Odin, as for most film narratologists, the intervention of a narrator. On this question, the narratological theory of cinema, even when it was not yet formally constituted, has always enjoyed a broad consensus. The "tradition" has always recognized the beautiful unanimity, the necessity (the theoretical necessity, obviously) of a basic narrative instance, responsible for the filmic narrative utterances. And it matters little what name has been given to these instances (shower of images, grand image-maker, narrator, filmic narrator, enunciator, etc.). Since the cinema, unlike literature, is an audiovisual rather than a strictly verbal medium, such unanimity might seem astonishing, and one might expect it to be broken. And indeed it was: a rare discordant voice has appeared, that of David Bordwell, who rejects the necessity for film theory of recognizing the existence of an illocutionary source to narrative utterances, the narrator.

Basing himself on the rejection of the application to filmic stories of Jakobson's famous communication schema, Bordwell claims the following: "On the principle that we ought not to proliferate theoretical entities without need, there is no point in positing communication as the fundamental process of all narration, only to grant that most films 'efface' or 'conceal' this process" (1985: 62). We thus see that, for Bordwell, this condemnation is complete. And actually his condemnation applies to any form of narration, not only the cinema. Bordwell points out, with some acuity, certain problems in enunciation theory as applied to the cinema, but the solutions he proposes often appear more difficult to work with than the problems they have been created to solve. Let's look at the problems more closely.

In fact, Bordwell doesn't completely liquidate the theory of the narrator. For him, there exist at least two types of text: those which presuppose the existence of a narrator and those in relation to which it is useless to posit a narrator. His first suggestion is only to recognize the narrator when there are evident traces of the presence of such an organizing instance. On the one hand, there are classical films in which, apparently, no one "speaks cinema": in this case there is no need to posit a narrator. Such a position would entail an anthropomorphic fiction. On the other hand, basing his argument on a very different corpus, which includes the work of the Soviets and also those of Godard, Resnais, and Bresson, these are narrative texts which present multiple indices suggesting the existence of a narrational figure.

Such a position is problematic to the extent that it doesn't manage its own relation with anthropomorphism, of which, as we saw earlier, we are supposed to be suspicious. However, Bordwell is nevertheless conscious of the dangers, since he has shown earlier a concern with deanthropomorphizing narrative instances. It is exactly from this perspective that he substitutes for the word "narrator" the word "narration," in order to identify the agent responsible for the cinematic narrative. But through a boomerang, the operation is accompanied by a return of anthropomorphism, since this instance of "narration" is granted clearly human attributes: "Furthermore, the pensive ending [to Antonioni's *La Notte*] acknowledges the narration as not simply powerful but humble: the narration knows that life is more complex than art can ever be" (Bordwell 1985: 209–10).

This seems to us to constitute a paradoxical and indefensible position. What use is it to emphasize further the abstraction of narration, by naming it "narration" rather than "narrator," in a first movement, and thus distance it even more from the authorial instance, the manifest empirical author, the concrete author, if it is only, with a swing back of the pendulum, to grant this abstract instance with some concrete characteristics, which could only apply to a concrete author? For who knows, after all, that life is more complex than art, if not Antonioni himself?

Whether it is a question of cinema or any other form of narrative, it is impossible, in our view, without running useless risks, to do away with the notion of the "narrator."

Note

1   English version of chapter 2 from their book *Le Récit cinématographique* (1990). Translated by Robert Stam and Toby Miller.

References

Bal, Mieke. 1977. *Narratologie*. Paris: Klincksieck.
Bazin, André. 1981. *Qu'est-ce que le cinéma?* Paris: Le Cerf.
Benveniste, Emile. 1966. *Problèmes de linguistique générale*, vol. I. Paris: Gallimard.
Bordwell, David. 1985. *Narration in the Fiction Film*. Madison: University of Wisconsin Press.

Casetti, Francesco. 1990. *D'un regard l'autre: le film et son spectateur*. Lyon: Presses Universitaires de Lyon.

Ducrot, Oswald. 1984. *Le Dire et le dit*. Paris: Editions de Minuit.

Gardies, André. 1987. *L'Espace dans la narration filmique: l'exemple du cinéma d'Afrique noire francophone*, unpublished Ph.D. thesis. Paris: Université de Paris VIII.

Gaudreault, André. 1988. *Du Littéraire au filmique: système du récit*. Paris/Québec: Méridiens Klincksieck/Presses de l'Université Laval. Reissued at Armand Colin (Paris) 1999.

——and François Jost. 1990. *Le Récit cinématographique*. Paris: Nathan.

Genette, Gérard. 1972. *Figures III*. Paris: Seuil.

Greimas, Algirdas-Julien, and Joseph Courtés. 1979. *Sémiotique: dictionnaire raisonné de la théorie du langage*. Paris: Hachette.

Gunning, Tom. 1984. "Présence du narrateur: l'héritage des films Biograph de Griffith". In *David Wark Griffith*. Ed. Jean Mottet. Paris: Publications de la Sorbonne/L'Harmattan, 1984.

Jost, François. 1983. "Narration(s): en deçà et au-delà". *Communications* 38, "Enonciation et cinéma."

——. 1989. *L'Œil-caméra: entre film et roman*, 2nd edn. Lyon: Presses Universitaires de Lyon.

Kerbrat-Orecchioni, Catherine. 1980. *L'Enonciation: de la subjectivité dans le langage*. Paris: Armand Colin.

Laffay, Albert. 1964. *Logique du cinéma*. Paris: Masson.

Lotman, Iouri. 1977. *Esthétique et sémiotique du cinéma*. Paris: Editions Sociales.

Marie, Michel. 1976. "Analyse textuelle." In *Lectures du film*. Paris: Albatros.

Metz, Christian. 1988. "L'Enonciation impersonnelle, ou le site du film." *Vertigo* 1.

——. 1991. *L'Enonciation impersonnelle, ou le site du film*. Paris: Méridiens Klincksieck.

Odin, Roger. 1988. "Du spectateur fictionnalisant au nouveau spectateur: approche sémio-pragmatique." *Iris* 8. 121–39.

Rousset, Jean. 1983. "Le journal intime, texte sans destinataire?" *Poétique* 56 (November).

Simon, Jean-Paul. 1979. *Le Filmique et le comique*. Paris: Albatros.

Slama-Cazacu, Tatiana. 1961. *Langage et contexte*. Paris: Mouton.

Sorlin, Pierre. 1984. "L'Enonciation de l'histoire." In *David Wark Griffith*. Ed. Jean Mottet. Paris: Publications de la Sorbonne / L'Harmattan.

Vernet, Marc. 1988. *Figures de l'absence*. Paris: Cahiers du cinéma.

CHAPTER FIVE

Film Editing

Lucy Fischer

Editing is one of the most significant instruments of effect possessed by the film technician.
V. I. Pudovkin, *Film Technique and Film Acting*

Of all the technical properties of film, the most general and indispensable is editing.
Siegfried Kracauer, *Theory of Film*

As the quotes above indicate, editing has long been viewed by film critics and practitioners alike as a major component of cinematic form. As such, it has received considerable attention in the annals of film theory. Yet, it is not a simple term to define.

While some scholars speak of editing entirely in relation to film production (Ephraim Katz deems it: "The process of selecting, assembling, and arranging motion picture shots and corresponding sound tracks in coherent sequence and flowing continuity" [1994: 405]), others extend it to the film text itself. Reflecting this, David Bordwell and Kristin Thompson conceive editing in a double sense as: "1. In filmmaking, the task of selecting and joining camera takes [and] 2. In the finished film, the set of techniques that govern the relations among shots" (1990: 409).

While Katz specifically includes sound within his description of editing, Bordwell and Thompson sidestep the issue, mentioning only the assembly of "camera takes." None of the critics highlights the liminal case of "editing *within* the camera" – shooting film footage (either planned or unplanned) in the order in which it will ultimately appear, thus nullifying the need for recombining images (and sounds) at a later point. Finally, biases can surface in definitions of editing. Katz speaks of the editor creating "coherent sequence and flowing continuity," thus assuming conventional narrative form and denying the possibility of abstraction. Clearly, the best definition will reveal the *full* complexity of editing: its status as production craft and discursive mode; its efficacy for structuring dramatic and experimental works; its potential application to sound and image.

In discussing the theorization of film editing, it is also necessary to invoke an historical perspective. On a certain level, in the early years of cinema (during its so-called "Primitive" stage, from around 1895 to 1900), there really was no film editing. Producers (like the Brothers Lumière in France, or Thomas Alva Edison in the United States) supervised the making of one-shot films: a subject was selected for shooting; it was suitably framed for the lens; then the camera ran until the film "magazine" was depleted. There were no changes in camera set-up (to be conjoined later in a multi-shot format). Among such notable one-shot works (made between 1894 and 1896) are Edison's *Sandow the Strongman*, *Morning Bath*, *Black Diamond Express*, *Serpentine Dances*, and *The Kiss*, as well as the Lumière Brothers' *Feeding the Baby*, *The Arrival of a Train*, *Workers Leaving the Lumière Factory*, and *Leaving Jerusalem by Railway*.

There was one major exception to this rule in the early years, though it was not labeled as film editing per se. I refer to the in-camera device known as the "substitution trick" – generally used for "special" effects. For example, in a film by Georges Méliès (a former stage magician), a woman might suddenly disappear (as one does in *The Vanishing Lady* [1896]). Méliès achieved this by shooting the first part of the footage with the woman before the camera, then stopping the apparatus while she was removed from the scene. Filming was then resumed and her body (in projection) seemed, mysteriously, to have evaporated. Similar techniques (of in-camera/stop-motion photography) were used in more serious works. In *The Execution of Mary Queen of Scots* (1895) – an historical event which took place in the sixteenth century – an actress poses while an axe is lowered to her neck, then (with the camera shut off) her body is "exchanged" for that of a dummy (whose head eventually "rolls").

By 1903, with works like Edwin Porter's *The Great Train Robbery* (made for the Edison Company), one finds the rudiments of sophisticated film editing – at least within a dramatic context. The story unfolds in multiple shots: those of bandits riding toward the train; those of the robbery within the bank car; those of men scurrying atop the train; those of the posse riding to the rescue. Beyond the narrative genre, editing became important in other modes. The primitive one-shot documentary (like Edison's *President McKinley at Home* [1897]) was replaced by such multi-shot films as Cricks and Martin's *A Visit to Peek Frean and Company's Biscuit Works* (1906) – a British actualité that, in sequential images, shows every aspect of the bakery's production process ("Rolling out Dough," "Packing Biscuits").

As the craft of film editing evolved through the 1910s and '20s, critics and theorists struggled to explain its techniques and to formulate its significance: How does film editing work? Does it constitute a language? Does it mimic the workings of the human mind? What formal principles guide its use? As an aesthetic tool, how does it compare to those of the more established arts (e.g. literature and theater)? Which filmmakers have been masters of the technique?

As is clear from these questions, theorists invoked editing in a variety of different contexts. For some, it shored up notions of the "specificity" of the film medium. For others, it fueled arguments championing experimentation or realism. For some, it demonstrated film's relation to cognition or the psyche. For others, it helped characterize the style of film auteurs.

Hence, if the physical act of editing entails a juxtaposition of film images, providing an overview of its theorization requires a "montage of theories" (to borrow the title of Richard Dyer MacCann's pioneering anthology of film criticism).

1   Editing and Realism

> Even while being shot, a film must be thought of already as an editable sequence of separate pieces of celluloid. The filmic form is never identical with the real appearance, but only similar to it.
>
> V. I. Pudovkin, Film Technique and Film Acting

One of the major ways in which an art form can be valorized and justified is in terms of its difference from everyday reality – a feature that, ostensibly, bestows upon it an elevated status. In the early years of cinema, such an argument was made by Rudolph Arnheim, a German critic. Significantly, for Arnheim, one of the major synthetic aspects of the cinema was its recourse to editing. His theorization of the issue appears in his influential book *Film* (1933),[1] as part of his discussion of cinema's absence of the normal "Space–Time Continuum":

> In real life every experience or chain of experiences is enacted for every observer in an uninterrupted spatial and temporal sequence .... There are no jerks in time or space in real life. Time and space are continuous. Not so in film. The period of time being photographed may be interrupted at any point. One scene may be immediately followed by another that takes place at a totally different time. And the continuity of space may be broken in the same manner. (1971: 20–1)

While Arnheim does not specifically use the term "editing," it is clear from his remarks that this is the practice to which he refers – speaking of "jerks" in time and space, of the camera being "interrupted," of "broken" continuity, of one scene (by which he means shot) being followed by another.

Arnheim also attempts to explain why film's aesthetic distance from reality does not, ultimately, disturb the spectator or cause her "a physical discomfort akin to seasickness" (27). He concludes that it fails to do so because we apprehend the cinema as only a "partial illusion":

> Up to a certain degree it gives the impression of real life .... On the other hand, it partakes strongly of the nature of a picture. (26)

While Arnheim sees the discourse of editing as entirely unconstrained (as compared to the rules of the world's space–time axis), he understands that montage can be used to create a sense of reality on-screen:

To be sure, in practice this freedom [of editing] is usually restricted in that the subject of the film is an account of some action, and a certain logical unity of time and space must be observed into which the various scenes are fitted. (21)

On the other hand, for Arnheim, montage often reflects the abstraction of the editing process itself: "Sometimes... shots are associated by montage whose connection is not realistic but conceptual or poetic" (89).

While Arnheim champions a cinema which is distinguished from the quotidian universe through editing, other critics have taken the reverse position. Among them is the German writer Siegfried Kracauer, who, in *Theory of Film: The Redemption of Physical Reality* (1960), argues (as the title indicates) for cinema's ability to capture the material world. Of the two major tendencies he sees in film history (Lumière and realism vs. Méliès and formalism), he prefers the former and praises Lumière for "avoid[ing] any personal interference with the given data" (31). Méliès, on the other hand, with his edited illusions, "did not take advantage of the camera's ability to record and reveal the physical world" (33). Summing up his position, Kracauer sees the film director as uneasily pulled between two opposing tendencies of the medium – the impulse to edit or not:

> Any film maker evolving a narrative is faced with the task of simultaneously living up to two obligations which seem to be difficult to reconcile. On the one hand, he will have to advance the action by assigning to each shot a meaning relevant to the plot.... [T]his reduction of meanings falls to editing.... On the other hand, the film maker will wish to exhibit and penetrate physical reality for its own sake. And this calls for shots not yet stripped of their multiple meanings, shots still able to release their psychological correspondences. (69)

Clearly, the "stripping" process is one Kracauer ascribes to editing. Ultimately, for Kracauer, editing is only useful to the extent that it supports the "basic property" of the film medium – its pull toward realism:

> The interest lies not with editing in itself, regardless of the purposes it serves, but with editing as a means of implementing – or defying... such potentialities of the medium as are in accordance with its substantive characteristics. (11)

Like Kracauer, French critic André Bazin, in a famous essay, "The Evolution of the Language of Cinema" (1950), celebrates those filmmakers who "put their faith" in reality instead of the plastic image. Clearly, Bazin does not imagine a cinema devoid of editing. Rather, he favors the kind of "invisible" cutting identified with D. W. Griffith (and the classic American cinema) over the aesthetics of "montage" (associated with the assertive editing of the revolutionary Soviet cinema [1967: 24–5]). While the former is fairly subtle, providing a "window" onto the world, the latter creates "meaning not proper to the images themselves but derived exclusively from their juxtaposition" (25). Ultimately, Bazin lends a moral tone to his distinction between a cinema of editing and that of photographic representation. He uses the term "cheat" to describe the "tricks of montage" (27) and concludes that filmmakers who eschew showy editing have a "*respect* for the continuity of dramatic space and, of course, of its duration" (34).

Writing in later years, French theorist Christian Metz sees the cinema as tracing a similar binary trajectory. In the first camp are filmmakers who downplay editing. Here, Metz quotes Roberto Rossellini: " 'Things are. Why manipulate them?' " (1974: 41). In the second camp are the "montage or bust" filmmakers. As Metz remarks of the Soviet director Sergei Eisenstein, "all he can see anywhere are prefragmented pieces, which ingenious manipulation will then join together.... Eisenstein refused to admit any kind of descriptive realism into the cinema" (33). To some degree, Metz sees his own work (on the semiotics of cinema) as striking a median position between the two poles.

2   Editing and Creativity

> Film editors speak eloquently using their splicers. They make order out of chaos...
> Vincent LoBrutto, *Selected Takes*

For theorists like Arnheim, cinema's distance from crude reality was not simply an ontological point. Rather its recognition demonstrated cinema's status as a high cultural form (hence the title of Arnheim's major work, *Film as Art*). For Arnheim (and those who shared his perspective), editing was a privileged aspect of cinematic craft, since it gave clear evidence of the artist's hand. As Arnheim notes, montage is "the royal road to film art" (1971: 87). He continues:

> The single image, after all, arises from a recording process, which is controlled by man but which, regarded superficially, does no more than reproduce nature. But when it comes to montage man takes a hand in the process – time is broken up, things that are disconnected in time and space are joined together. This looks much more like a tangibly creative and formative process. (87–8)

In a similar vein, theorist–filmmaker Maya Deren saw editing as one of the primary tools of the cinema artist:

> In film, the image can and should be only the beginning, the basic material of the creative action. All invention and creation consist primarily of a new relationship between known parts.... The editing of a film creates the sequential relationship which gives particular or new meaning to the images. (1992: 66–7)

For Deren, tour-de-force editing involved both a rejection of conventional narrative and a negation of the space–time continuum so beloved of Kracauer and Bazin. She remarks:

68

[Film] must relinquish the narrative disciplines it has borrowed from literature and its timid imitation of the causal logic of narrative plots, a form which flowered as a celebration of the earthbound, step-by-step concept of time, space and relationship which was part of the primitive materialism of the nineteenth century. Instead, it must develop the vocabulary of filmic images and evolve the syntax of filmic techniques which relate those. It must determine the disciplines inherent in the medium, discover its own structural modes, explore the new realms and dimensions accessible to it and so enrich our culture artistically. (70)

It was, in fact, such editing that Deren used in her own films – seminal works of the New American Cinema. In *A Study in Choreography for Camera* (1945), sequential shots depict a male dancer beginning a leap in one space and landing in another. In *Meshes of the Afternoon* (a dream-like fantasy starring the director), Deren arises (with dagger in hand) to approach a second sleeping figure of herself. She then takes a series of steps which are edited into a synthetic continuity – by the sea, on soil, on grass, on pavement, and on carpet. Clearly, through editing, Deren achieves her goal of forging a "creative film form" (69).

3   Editing and the Other Arts

[O]ur cinema is not altogether without parents and without pedigree, without a past, without the traditions and rich cultural heritage of past epochs.
Sergei Eisenstein, "From 'Dickens, Griffith and the Film Today'"

One of the principal ways in which film theorists have traditionally framed their discussion of the cinema has been to compare it to other established arts. On one level, this impulse bespeaks an aesthetic curiosity: How does a new medium extend or revamp our understanding of earlier artistic forms? On another plane, however, such diatribes are meant to "legitimize" the cinema – by heralding its ancestry and origins in more respectable forms. For some critics, editing played a prominent role in their line of "hereditary" argument.

Since cinema borrowed significantly from nineteenth-century theater (and was known as the "photo*play*"), it was natural for writers to compare the two media. As regards editing, it was cinema's capacity for presenting shifting perspectives that was seen to distinguish it from the stage. As Arnheim notes:

Whereas the theater stage differs from real life only in that the fourth wall is missing, the setting of the action changes, and the people talk in theatrical language, the film deviates much more profoundly. The position of the spectator is continually changing since we must consider him located at the station point of the camera. (1971: 28)

Pudovkin, however, stresses other issues. While, for him, the theater director works with "reality," the film artist's "active raw material is no other than those *pieces of celluloid*"; hence, film craft is more plastic and material than theatrical art (1970: 84). Pudovkin also recognizes that, due to editing, screen acting requires a different skill from that of the stage:

The editing of separate camera angles in the cinema is the more vivid and expressive equivalent of the technique that obliges a stage actor who has inwardly absorbed his acting image to "theatricalise" its outer form.

The film actor must clearly understand that the moving of the camera from place to place is not simply a means of realising purely directorial methods. The understanding and feel of the possibilities of the shooting of shots from various angles must be organically included in the process of the actor's own work on the external shaping of his role. (285)

Finally, Sergei Eisenstein sees in the style of Japanese classical theater a prototype for cinematic montage. He writes of one such performance:

[I]n the Kabuki play *Narukami* the actor Sadanji must change from drunkenness to madness. This transition is solved by a mechanical cut . . . . This method is organic to film. (1992a: 136)

If comparisons between cinema and theater have been legion in the history of film theory, so have analogies to literature. One of the earliest and most well-known treatises on the topic was Eisenstein's "Dickens, Griffith and the Film Today." Significantly, the essay identifies film editing as the central feature that connects the two arts. As Eisenstein notes: "Griffith arrived at montage through the method of parallel action, and he was led to the idea of parallel action by – Dickens!" (1974: 303). Having stated this, Eisenstein proceeds to analyze the "montage structure" of Dickens's writing, along with its strong visual quality (304). Seeing the limitations of overstating the parallels between literature and film, Eisenstein warns:

Analogies and resemblances cannot be pursued too far – they lose conviction and charm. They begin to take on the air of machination or card-tricks. (303)

4   Editing and the Psyche

The photoplay obeys the laws of the mind rather than those of the outer world.
Hugo Munsterberg, *The Film*

For many theorists, the major interest of film editing (and the textual discourse it creates) has been its capacity to "mimic" the workings of the human mind. Prominent among these critics is Hugo Munsterberg, who, in the very early years of the cinema, wrote *The Film: A Psychological Study (The Silent Photoplay in 1916)*. While Munsterberg does not specifically use the term "editing," his focus on cinema's propensity for "rapid changes of scenes" is clearly a way of referencing the device (1970: 47).

Munsterberg deals with editing primarily in his section on "Memory and Imagination" – often comparing the cinema with theater in order to emphasize film's unique psychological mode. In speaking of memory, for example, he notes:

> The theater cannot do more than suggest to our memory this looking backward.... The photoplay can. We see the jungle, we see the hero at the height of his danger; and suddenly there flashes upon the screen a picture of the past. For not more than two seconds does the idyllic New England scene slip into the exciting African events. When one deep breath is over we are stirred again by the event of the present. That home scene of the past flitted by just as a hasty thought of bygone days darts through the mind. (40)

Thus, for Munsterberg, the cinema provides "an objectivation of our memory function.... It is as if the outer world itself became molded in accordance with our ... passing memory ideas" (41). In addition to rendering a sense of reverie, the cinema, for Munsterberg, has particular powers for visualizing the human imagination:

> Just as we can follow the reminiscences of the hero, we may share the fancies of his imagination.... We see the boy who is to enter the navy and who sleeps on shipboard the first night; the walls disappear and his imagination flutters from port to port. (43)

While the previous examples pertain to editing's capacity for representing the consciousness of screen *characters*, Munsterberg is equally interested in how cutting affects the mind of the *spectator*. Here, he finds that movies allow the viewer a certain mental "omnipresence" and distraction:

> The photoplay alone gives us our chance for ... omnipresence. We see the banker, who had told his young wife that he has a directors' meeting, at a late hour in a cabaret feasting with a stenographer from his office. She had promised her poor old parents to be home early. We see the gorgeous roof garden and the tango dances, but our dramatic interest is divided among the frivolous pair, the jealous young woman in the suburban cottage, and the anxious old people in the attic. Our mind wavers among the three scenes. The photoplay shows one after another. Yet it can hardly be said that we think of them as successive. It is as if we were really at all three places at once. (45)

So, for Munsterberg, film works by "overcoming the forms of the outer world, namely, space, time, and causality, and by adjusting the events to the forms of the inner world, namely, attention, memory, imagination, and emotion" (74).

Though Munsterberg wrote in 1916, the issues he examines remain vital in contemporary film theory. Recently, Maureen Turim has extended Munsterberg's concern with film and memory by tracing the history of the "flashback" – a crucial editing structure in film. As she notes: "We can easily suggest that the flashback developed as a means of mimetic representation of memory, dreams, or confession" (1989: 6). While many conventional films have had significant flashback sequences – ones that are, generally, well marked (*Humoresque* [1946], *Casablanca* [1943], *Body and Soul* [1947], *The Snake Pit* [1948]) – there are some innovative works that are structured around the indeterminate borders between past and present, fantasy and reality. Among the most intriguing is Alain Resnais's *Hiroshima, Mon Amour* (1959) – a work of the French New Wave, which constitutes a high point of modernist cinema. In that film, a contemporary tryst between a French woman and a Japanese man (which occurs during her visit to Tokyo) is ambiguously interlaced with references to a prior love affair between the woman (as a young girl in wartime France) and a German soldier. Continually, the narrative shifts abruptly from her present-day activities to such unexplained scenes as that of her, as a young girl, hidden in her parents' basement – her head shaven by an angry mob. Gradually, the tragedy of her romance is revealed through temporally scrambled flashbacks that portray her liaison with a forbidden lover. While, by the 1990s, such enigmatic flashbacks have become quite common, in the late 1950s they were groundbreaking.

5   Editing and Cognition

[T]he filmmaker carefully structures the motion picture to interact directly with the mind of the viewer.

John D. Anderson, "A Cognitive Approach to Continuity"

While Munsterberg was interested in film's relation to the psychological states of memory and fantasy, other critics have been concerned with cinema's association with cognition. Again, a theorization of editing has been central to their investigation.

In the early years of the cinema, V. I. Pudovkin both analyzed narrative film editing and offered prospective directors a "guide" for constructing cinema dramas. Paramount, in his theory, was the use of editing to guide the viewer's consciousness:

We have established . . . the basic significance of the constructive editing of scenes. It builds the scenes from separate pieces, of which each concentrates the attention of the spectator only on that element important to the action. The sequence of these pieces must not be uncontrolled, but must correspond to the natural transference of attention of an imaginary observer (who, in the end, is represented by the spectator. (1970: 70–1)

In recent years, other writers have confronted the issue of cognition and film form. Noël Carroll has focussed on how cinematic discourse interacts in a "natural" way with the workings of the spectator's mind, offering the viewer cinematic tropes that hold his or her attention. For example, he sees the shifting assortment of shots presented through editing as a form of movement that keeps "the screen palpitating with visual activity" (1996: 18). This strategy works to insure the viewer's interest, because, as humans, "we are naturally disposed to shift our attention to other sectors of the environment, unless some change, such as a movement, keeps us focused on the object of our present attention" (19). Editing is such a "change," and the straight cut its most abrupt and effective transition (22). According to Carroll, other editing techniques enjoy a "natural" fit with human perception. For example, the common "point-of-view" trope is an "elaboration of our ordinary cognitive and perceptual experience" (39), which impels us to follow the trajectory of another person's sight line. As Carroll notes, this functions as:

> a way in which one animal derives information about another animal. The glance of a creature exhibits its interests and often its practical intents. In this respect, following the gaze of another creature possesses survival value. (39)

Carroll also sees the structure of point-of-view editing as dictated by the dynamics of human emotion: "The function of the point/object shot [the shot which depicts what a character apprehends] is to supply the audience with the cause or object of the character's emotional state" (43). Hence, it is "natural" that if we see a character appearing shocked in one shot, we would want to see, in the next, a representation of the reason for that reaction. Similarly, for John Anderson, editing's "fit" with the dynamics of human perception explains the popularity of mainstream cinema:

> the wide accessibility of Hollywood film rests in no small part upon the discovery and subsequent incorporation into convention of a number of rules for filmic construction which allow the film to interact directly with the human perceptual system. (1993: 65)

While the guidance of attention is a part of all film construction and apprehension, certain works (both experimental and mainstream) have foregrounded this issue as part of their discourse. Jacques Tati's comedy *Playtime* (1968) embeds myriad sight gags within a single long-shot/long-take image, highlighting each through methods of composition, color, and movement. Nonetheless, each shot is so complex and confusing that it constitutes a cognitive challenge or "game" for the spectator (Fischer 1980: 83–8). American independent filmmaker Robert Nelson models his work *Bleu Shut* (1970) on the television quiz show, and the viewer is instructed, by an off-screen voice, to keep track of time by watching a small on-screen clock. Similarly, George Landow's *Institutional Quality* (1969) – which parodies an instructional movie about film projection – asks viewers to

73

respond, as though to a standardized exam – including marking answers in a nonexistent test booklet. The ironic joke in both these texts is the impossibility or unsuitability of the cognitive acts required of the audience.

6   Editing as Communication and Language

Editing is the language of the film director. Just as in living speech, so, one may say, in editing: there is a word – the piece of exposed film, the image; a phrase – the combination of these pieces.

V. I. Pudovkin, *Film Technique and Film Acting*

If Carroll is interested in issues of editing and cognition, he is also concerned with cinema as a means of human communication. As he writes:

editing involves more than chemistry and mechanics. It is a means of communication within the social institution of world cinema. It provides a means of articulation whose practice enables filmmakers to convey stories, metaphors and even theories to spectators. (1978/9: 79)

Once more, in his view, cinema's communicative powers interface with propensities of the human mind – especially its ability to reason. As Carroll notes, when a spectator is presented with a series of sequential film shots:

the task engages the viewer's inductive capacities. The viewer must infer the relation between the new material and antecedent information. Editing does not supply the whole story; the very concept of editing implies that it is only a partial representation. The viewer must fill in the gaps. (80)

Clearly, the more conventional the film, the less intellectual work is required of the audience.

While other critics have embraced the notion of cinema as communication, they have tended to regard the tropes of montage as less "natural" than Carroll, likening them to linguistic structures or codes. Early on in film theory, Sergei Eisenstein targeted the Japanese "ideogram" as a model for montage. What appealed to him was the pictorial/hieroglyphic nature of the Japanese language. As he notes, "their writing is primarily representational" (1992a: 127).

More recently, parallels between cinematic and linguistic systems have been proposed by French theorist Christian Metz. He has been careful, however, to avoid implying that film editing creates a formal linguistic *system* (1974: 48). Rather, he catalogs a series of features of the cinema (based on its reliance on the photographic image) that are opposed to verbal modes: its instant intelligibility, its suppression of abstraction, its heterogeneity, its universality, its lack of "double articulation," its excess of connotation, its one-way communicative dynamic. Despite these differences, Metz is "persuaded . . . that the 'filmolinguistic' venture is entirely justified" (60), but prefers to speak of a "semiotics" of cinema (89). Here, the proper area of study is the dramatic film. As Metz states: "*it was precisely to the extent that the cinema confronted the problems of narration* that, in the course of successive groupings, it came to produce a body of specific signifying procedures" (95). Thus, he studies the *syntagmatic* units of film (created by editing) and attempts to answer the following questions:

> How does the cinema indicate successivity, precession, temporal breaks, causality, adversative relationships, consequence, spatial proximity, or distance, etc.? These are central questions to the semiotics of the cinema. (105)

For Metz (and others who conceive of cinema as "language"), its discursive structures (fashioned, in part, through editing) must be learned. Opposing this view, Carroll denies that films "are decoded by audiences who have learned the conventions of cinema" (1996: 11). Rather, he finds that such comprehension depends more upon "recognition" (14).

7 Editing and Ideology

> [Ideology] must hide its operations, "naturalizing" its functioning and its messages in some way.
>
> Daniel Dayan, "The Tutor-Code of Classical Cinema"

As we have seen, certain theories of editing have ideological implications. André Bazin's preference for filmmakers who "put their faith" in the realistic image has a quasi-religious tone to it. His love of the long-take format (which, allegedly, leaves the spectator more "freedom" of interpretation) also harbors a pro–democratic resonance – especially since Bazin contrasts it with the school of editing championed by Soviet artists.

7.1 Editing and dialectics

For Sergei Eisenstein, "art is always conflict" (1992b: 138), and in the cinema this is realized through montage. Arguing against the notion of editing as shot-to-shot "linkage" (a theory associated with Lev Kuleshov), Eisenstein poses and answers the following question:

> By what, then, is montage characterized and, consequently, its cell – the shot?
>
> By collision. By the conflict of two pieces in opposition to each other. By conflict. By collision. (1992a: 133)

Clearly, this dynamic notion of creation relates to Eisenstein's embrace of revolutionary Soviet politics. As he remarks:

According to Marx and Engels the dialectic system is only the conscious reproduction of the dialectic course (substance) of the external events of the world. (138)

Hence, while, on a dramatic level, a film like *Strike* (1925) depicts a socio-economic conflict between workers and industrialists, its editing reflects a sense of aesthetic struggle through the "principle of optical counterpoint." Potentially, this may involve shot-to-shot contrasts of scale, volume, mass, depth, direction, illumination, color, and/or duration (134–5).

7.2   Editing and the construction of gender

In the contemporary era, with the rise of feminist criticism, a major concern of film theory has been the consideration of cinema's elaboration of gender. Central to this debate is the notion of point-of-view editing and the articulation of the so-called "gaze." According to such arguments, the "look" (both on-screen and in the audience) is selectively identified with the male. Typically, the editing trope that renders the masculine gaze of an on-screen character involves two shots: that of a man looking, and that of the woman he apprehends. According to Laura Mulvey:

> Traditionally, the woman displayed has functioned on two levels: as erotic object for the characters within the screen story, and as erotic object for the spectator within the auditorium, with a shifting tension between the looks on either side of the screen.... As the spectator identifies with the main male protagonist, he projects his look on to that of his like, his screen surrogate, so that the power of the male protagonist as he controls events coincides with the active power of the erotic look. (1992: 751).

Mulvey sees such editing tropes as evoking psychoanalytic notions of scopophilia – giving the male spectator "the satisfaction, pleasure and privilege of [an] 'invisible guest' and highlight[ing] how film has depended on voyeuristic active/passive mechanisms" (757).

7.3   Editing and "bourgeois style"

Beyond the sexual politics of the point-of-view trope, critics have seen it as more broadly tainted by bourgeois ideology. Daniel Dayan examines the shot-reverse structure, by which he means a sequence in which "shot one" frames a person or object and "shot two" portrays the individual who apparently has sighted the contents of shot one. For Dayan, this type of sequence works in the following manner:

> The spectator's pleasure, dependent upon his identification with the visual field [of shot one], is interrupted when he perceives the frame. From this perception he

infers the presence of the absent-one and that other field from which the absent-one is looking. Shot two reveals a character who is presented as the owner of the glance corresponding to shot one. That is, the character in shot two occupies the place of the absent-one emanating from shot one's other stage into a presence. (1992: 188)

According to Dayan, the ideological problem with such editing is that it "tricks" the spectator (189): rather than acknowledging that shot one is simply framed by the camera, it presents a figure in shot two who stands in for the mythical "absent-one" and appropriates the camera's visual field. Thus, "[u]nable to see the workings of the code, the spectator is at its mercy. His imaginary is sealed into the film; the spectator thus absorbs an ideological effect without being aware of it" (188). So Dayan sees classical cinema as "present[ing] itself as a product without a producer, a discourse without an origin" (191). Rather than revealing who really "speaks" (director, actor, camera, screenwriter, etc.), bourgeois cinema makes things seem to "speak for themselves". Hence, such a form is "establishe[d] as the ventriloquist of ideology" (191).

Since its publication, Dayan's interpretation of classical film editing has been hotly contested. William Rothman, for example, feels that Dayan's analysis of the shot/reverse-shot structure is wrong-headed, and concludes that "[n]o ghostly sovereign is invoked by the point-of-view sequence" (1992: 196).

8   Editing and Authorship

Now, by the *auteur* theory, if a director has not technical competence, no elementary flair for the cinema, he is automatically cast out from the pantheon of directors.
Andrew Sarris, "Notes on the Auteur Theory in 1962"

We have already seen how certain theorists, in their discussion of film history and aesthetics, identify styles of editing with various directors. Bazin, for example, in proclaiming his preference for the long-shot/long-take/deep-focus mode, singled out particular filmmakers as exemplary of that tradition: F. W. Murnau, Jean Renoir, Orson Welles, William Wyler, Roberto Rossellini. Similarly, in writing of the major tendencies of film editing, Christian Metz linked Eisenstein to the "montage or bust" camp. These diverse formulations illustrate how film critics see cinematic authorship as tied to styles of editing (as well as to a director's other aesthetic and thematic leanings).

Of course, the major theorists to advance conceptions of cinema authorship were the French "auteurist" critics identified, in the post-World War II era, with the journal *Cahiers du cinéma*. One of those writers was Jean-Luc Godard, who later was championed as a modernist film author himself. Writing on Godard, David Bordwell sees the filmmaker's status as "auteur" linked, historically, to his association with nontraditional (anti-continuity) editing. In particular, it is

Godard's fame for the "jump cut" (starting with *Breathless* [1960]) that "proves" his cinematic genius. As Bordwell notes:

> If we take a simple but uncommon stylistic device, we can see how it became identified and analyzed only after changes within the cinematic institution were able to link it to conceptions of the author – author as the source of the film, as unique creative temperament and as the "narrator" in film. (1984: 4)

Significantly, the "jump cut" had existed in some form as far back as the days of Méliès (5).

Also concerned with questions of editing and authorship is theorist Gilles Deleuze, who, in *Cinema 1: The Movement-Image*, devotes a chapter to "Montage" (1986: 29–56). Deleuze sees four types of editing as characterizing the broad sweep of film history. While each is identified with a particular national style, it is also linked to a specific director. The American school of montage (tied to Griffith) is "organic" and "empiricist"; the Soviet school (affiliated with Eisenstein) is "materialist" and "dialectical"; the French school (associated with Abel Gance) is "quantitative–psychic"; and the German school (identified with Paul Wegener, Fritz Lang, and F. W. Murnau) is "intensive–spiritual" (55).

9   Technological Development and Editing

> It is an easy self-deception to assume that better editing is related to the latest tools for the job.... We do well to remember this as we sit in front of our very expensive electronic wizardry.
>
> Roger Crittenden, *Film and Video Editing*

Given that film theory has generally favored the image, most writings have concentrated on visual editing at the expense of sound. At a particular moment in cinema history, however, the question of acoustic montage was paramount. This period was, of course, the "Coming of Sound," which lasted from the mid-1920s to the mid-1930s (depending upon which national industry was involved).

There was great fear that sound would ruin the poetic art of cinema developed in the silent era – reducing all film to banal talking heads or ringing phones. In response to that depressing scenario, various theorists proposed more radical conceptions of the sound/image relation. Primary in such formulations (especially among Soviet artists) was the notion of liberating the screen from literal sound/image-matching (lips moving as a person speaks) in favor of "audiovisual counterpoint" (Eisenstein 1992b: 144). As Pudovkin notes: "it is not generally recognised that the principal elements in sound film are the asynchronous and not the synchronous" (1970: 185). In "A Statement [on Sound]", signed by Eisenstein, Pudovkin, and G. V. Alexandrov, it is noted that:

To use sound in [an illusionistic] way will destroy the culture of montage, for every ADHESION of sound to a visual montage piece increases its inertia as a montage piece and increases the independence of its meaning – and this will undoubtedly be to the detriment of montage, operating in the first place not on the montage pieces but on the JUXTAPOSITION. (1992: 318)

The writers conclude: "[s]ound, treated as a new montage element (as a factor divorced from the visual image), will inevitably introduce new means of enormous power to the" cinema (318).

One of the most stunning instantiations of this theory occurs in the work of Soviet filmmaker Dziga Vertov (not a signatory to the document). In *Enthusiasm* (1931) he applies the notion of acoustic montage to the documentary film – a genre which had not received great attention in the early years of sound, due to theorists' focus on drama and talking heads. What is most striking about *Enthusiasm* is the incredible tension that exists between the sound and visuals – as though the acoustic track were physically pushing itself away from the screen. This happens because of the film's hyperbolic asynchronization. For example, a shot of some interior is matched to an exterior sound; a shot of drunks is matched to the voices of a church choir. Vertov also edits the sound itself in highly complex ways – drawing upon techniques of superimposition, collage, reversal, and distortion. Throughout the film, a woman (who seems to be a stand-in for filmmaker and audience) is shown wearing headphones – as though to remind us of the technical/synthetic nature of sound recording and montage.

Despite such tour-de-force films as *Enthusiasm*, and the early outcries of Soviet theorists, most sound films were made in a standard fashion – with voices and lips matched. Subsequently, many theorists struggled to comprehend this relation – one created through synchronous audiovisual editing. Mary Ann Doane stresses classical cinema's impulse to create a sense of the real human body, with the voice contributing to the feel of its corporeal presence:

The attributes of this fantasmatic body are first and foremost unity (through the emphasis on a coherence of the senses) and presence-to-itself. The addition of sound to the cinema introduces the possibility of re-presenting a fuller (and organically unified) body. (1980: 34)

For Doane, there are moments in mainstream cinema when the illusionist sound/ image relation is threatened. One of them occurs when the shot is edited with a "voice-off" (e.g. depicting a close-up of a door with a character heard talking behind the door – outside of the visual range). As she notes:

the use of the voice-off always entails a risk – that of exposing the material heterogeneity of the cinema. Synchronous sound masks the problem and this at least partially explains its dominance.... There is always something uncanny about a voice which emanates from a source outside the frame. (40)

Less radical is the case of "voice-over" used as interior monologue. Here, "the voice and body are represented simultaneously, but the voice, far from being an extension of that body, manifests its inner lining.... The voice here is the privileged mark of interiority, turning the body 'inside-out'" (41).

Rick Altman, on the other hand, wants to reverse the established priority of image over sound, using the metaphor of ventriloquism to establish sound as the controlling force:

> [T]he sound track is a ventriloquist who, by moving his dummy (the image) in time with the words he secretly speaks, creates the illusion that the words are produced by the dummy/image whereas in fact the dummy/image is actually created in order to disguise the source of the sound. Far from being subservient to the image, the sound track uses the illusion of subservience to serve its own ends. (1980: 67)

Because "[s]ound editing is first and foremost word editing," Altman argues that the basic tenet of the cinema is "*I speak, therefore I am seen*" (68).

To some degree, Altman also shares the kind of ideological concerns about classical cinema raised by Dayan – seeing synchronous sound/image editing as, essentially, manipulative:

> The fundamental scandal of sound film – and thus the proper starting point for a theory of sound film – is that sound and image are different phenomena, recorded by different methods, printed many frames apart on the film, and reproduced by an illusionistic technology. (79)

Some noteworthy films have especially foregrounded this "scandal." One thinks of Fritz Lang's *The Testament of Dr. Mabuse* (1933), an early sound film in which an unseen criminal leader is revealed to be a phonograph behind a curtain. One thinks, as well, of Hollis Frampton's experimental work *Critical Mass* (1971), in which an argument between a young man and woman is made to seem comic and bizarre through a purposeful failure in voice/lip synchronization. Finally, one recalls a Hollywood film like *Singin' in the Rain* (1952) – set in the early sound period – which mocks silent screen actors whose vocals must be dubbed because their voices are sub-par.

Like Altman, Kaja Silverman finds sound editing inflected by ideological implications – especially those relating to gender. In her view, female screen characters are far more likely to be edited with synchronous sound than are male:

> To allow [a female character] to be heard without being seen would be ... dangerous, since it would disrupt the specular regime upon which dominant cinema relies .... Finally, to disembody the female voice in this way would be to challenge every conception by means of which we have previously known woman within Hollywood film, since it is precisely *as body* that she is constructed there. (1988: 164)

Feminist cinema, on the other hand, "generally pulls away from any fixed locus within the image track, away from the constraints of synchronization" (141).

This tendency can be seen in such experimental women's films as Laura Mulvey and Peter Wollen's *Riddles of the Sphinx* (1977), which counterpoises dramatized domestic scenes with free-associative interior monologues. Similarly, in Su Friedrich's *The Ties that Bind* (1984), a film portrait of the artist's mother, the viewer never sees Friedrich or her parent speak in synchronous sound. Finally, Chantal Akerman's *News from Home* (1976) is comprised of footage of city streets linked to the voice of Akerman reading letters.

While in the 1920s and 1930s the coming of sound created one kind of crisis in editing, today the advent of new, high-tech methods precipitates another. In 1992, *Needful Things* became one of the first features to be entirely cut on a digital computer editor; and since then, according to David Ansen and Ray Sawhill, "a quiet revolution has occurred in the world of . . . filmmaking" (1996: 64). Because of this new technology, the tasks of film editing and special-effects designing have merged, with editors able to seamlessly combine parts of separate shots within the same image. As technician Rob Kobrin notes: " 'I'm now editing within the frame' " (Ansen and Sawhill 1996: 64). The implication of such gadgetry is truly radical as "all live action films [now] have the potential to become animation" (64).

Moving beyond cinematography itself, in Spielberg's *Jurassic Park* (1993) and *The Lost World* (1997), while certain dinosaur figures derive from elaborately crafted three-dimensional models (some of them life-size), others are entirely computer-generated – "absent," in the photographic sense, from profilmic space, though eventually inserted (by editing) within the frame. Hence, in the era of virtual reality, we find ourselves in a virtual cinema – one that questions the "integrity" of the shot. As writer James Gleick notes: "We have long had distorting lenses and airbrushes. Still we trust photographs, or we did. We admit them into evidence." Clearly, this confidence erodes as a "new visual virtuosity becomes the . . . norm" (1997: 22).

Whereas, for the theorists considered in this essay, film editing meant plastic relationships *between* shots, for the theorists of the future, editing equally implies synthetic relations *within* shots. Given the consequent transformation of cinema's traditional association with realism, a new philosophy or ontology of the medium may be in order.

Note

1 Arnheim's *Film* has been long out of print. Most of it was republished in sections of *Film as Art* (1957, 1971).

References

Altman, Rick. 1980. "Moving Lips: Cinema as Ventriloquism." *Yale French Studies* 60: 67–79.

Anderson, John D. 1993. "A Cognitive Approach to Continuity." *Post Script: Essays in Film and the Humanities* 13, 1 (fall): 61–6.

Ansen, David, and Ray Sawhill. 1996. "The New Jump Cut." *Newsweek* (September 2): 64–5.

Arnheim, Rudolph. 1971. *Film as Art*. Berkeley, Los Angeles, and London: University of California Press.

Bazin, André. 1967. "The Evolution of the Language of Cinema." In *What is Cinema?* Trans. Hugh Gray. Berkeley and Los Angeles: University of California Press. 23–40.

Bordwell, David. 1984. "Jump Cuts and Blind Spots." *Wide Angle* 6, 1: 4–11.

——, and Kristin Thompson. 1990. *Film Art: An Introduction*, 3rd edn. New York: McGraw Hill.

Carroll, Noël. 1978/9. "Toward a Theory of Film Editing." *Millennium Film Journal* (winter/spring): 79–99.

——. 1996. "Film, Attention, and Communication." In Noël Carroll, *The Great Ideas of Today*. Chicago: Encyclopedia Britannica. 4–49.

Crittenden, Roger. 1995. *Film and Video Editing*, 2nd edn. London: Chapman and Hall.

Dayan, Daniel. 1992 [1974]. "The Tutor-Code of Classical Cinema." In Mast, Cohen, and Braudy 1992: 179–91.

Deleuze, Gilles. 1986. *Cinema 1: The Movement-Image*. Trans. Hugh Tomlinson and Barbara Habberjam. Minneapolis: University of Minnesota Press.

Deren, Maya. 1992 [1960]. "Cinematography: The Creative Use of Reality." In Mast, Cohen and Braudy 1992: 59–70.

Doane, Mary Ann. 1980. "The Voice in the Cinema: The Articulation of Body and Space." *Yale French Studies* 60: 33–50.

Eisenstein, Sergei. 1974. "From 'Dickens, Griffith and the Film Today.'" In Mast and Cohen 1974: 302–13.

—— 1992a. "The Cinematographic Principle and the Ideogram." In Mast, Cohen, and Braudy 1992: 127–38.

—— 1992b. "A Dialectic Approach to Film Form." In Mast, Cohen, and Braudy 1992: 138–54.

——, V. I. Pudovkin, and G. V. Alexandrov. 1992. "A Statement [on Sound]." In Mast, Cohen, and Braudy 1992: 317–19.

Fischer, Lucy. 1980. "*Playtime*: The Comic Film as Game." *West Virginia Philological Papers* 26 (summer): 83–8.

Gleick, James. 1997. "Fast Forward: Reality Check." *New York Times Magazine* (May 18): 20, 22.

Katz, Ephraim. 1994. *The Film Encyclopedia*. New York: HarperCollins.

Kracauer, Siegfried. 1960. *Theory of Film: The Redemption of Physical Reality*. London, Oxford, and New York: Oxford University Press.

LoBrutto, Vincent. 1991. *Selected Takes: Film Editors on Editing*. New York, Westport, and London: Praeger.

MacCann, Richard Dyer, ed. 1966. *Film: A Montage of Theories*. New York: Dutton.

Mast, Gerald, and Marshall Cohen, eds. 1974. *Film Theory and Criticism: Introductory Readings*, 1st edn. New York and Oxford: Oxford University Press.

Mast, Gerald, Marshall Cohen, and Leo Braudy, eds. 1992. *Film Theory and Criticism: Introductory Readings*, 4th edn. New York and Oxford: Oxford University Press.

Metz, Christian. 1974. *Language and Cinema*. Trans. Donna Jean Umiker-Sebeok. The Hague: Mouton.

Mulvey, Laura. 1992. "Visual Pleasure and Narrative Cinema." In Mast, Cohen, and Braudy 1992: 746–57.

Munsterberg, Hugo. 1970. *The Film: A Psychological Study (The Silent Photoplay in 1916)*. New York: Dover.

Pudovkin, V. I. 1970. *Film Technique and Film Acting*. Trans. Ivor Montagu. New York: Grove Press.

Rothman, William. 1992 [1975]. "Against 'The System of the Suture.'" In Mast, Cohen, and Braudy 1992: 192–8.

Sarris, Andrew. 1974. "Notes on the Auteur Theory in 1962." In Mast and Cohen 1974: 500–15.

Silverman, Kaja. 1988. *The Acoustic Mirror: The Female Voice in Psychoanalysis and Cinema*. Bloomington and Indianapolis: Indiana University Press.

Turim, Maureen. 1989. *Flashbacks in Film: Memory and History*. New York and London: Routledge.

CHAPTER SIX

Film Semiotics

Warren Buckland

Twentieth-century thought is marked by a shift from idealist philosophy to the Language Analysis tradition (see Apel 1976). The structural linguist Ferdinand de Saussure and the American semiotician C. S. Peirce initiated a radical critique of Descartes's and Kant's philosophy of the subject, in which language and signs replaced mental entities as the locus of knowledge. Language Analysis therefore rejects idealism, transforming its "first-person perspective" (focus on private mental events, as in Descartes's method of introspection) to the public, "third-person perspective" of language and signs. The problem with introspection, writes Thomas Daddesio, is that "it was perceived as being unable to provide the objective, repeatable observations that science requires" (1995: 49). Prior to the Language Analysis tradition philosophers believed that mental processes founded knowledge (including self-knowledge). But Daddesio adds:

> once this privilege came to be viewed as illusory, introspection was replaced by methods relying on a third-person perspective. From this new perspective, the access individuals have to their own thoughts could no longer be taken as the foundation for knowledge and, consequently, private events were replaced, in discussions of language, meaning, and reason, by events that were open to public scrutiny such as the behavior of others, the words they utter, and the uses to which they put words. (50)

The Language Analysts' assumption of indirect access to one's thoughts via language and other intersubjective sign systems replaced the idealists' assumption of immediate access to the thoughts in one's own mind.

In the late 1950s cognitive processes made a decisive return *within* the Language Analysis tradition, beginning with Noam Chomsky's transformational generative grammar (together with his decisive critique of B. F. Skinner's behaviorism). In the form of Chomsky's linguistics, the Language Analysis tradition created a synthesis of both idealism and the intersubjective nature of language, thus (in principle at least) avoiding the idealism and first-person perspective and the (quasi-)behaviorism of the Language Analysts' third-person perspective.

This history of twentieth-century thought is reflected in film theory, particularly in the shift from "classical film theory" (of Arnheim, Bazin, etc.) to "classical film semiotics" (the early research of Christian Metz, based on structural linguistics) and finally to "cognitive film semiotics", influenced by Chomsky and cognitive science generally (the research of Dominique Chateau, Michel Colin, Francesco Casetti, and Roger Odin). In this chapter I aim to outline the foundations of semiotics, summarize its institutional context, analyze the basic tenets of classical film semiotics, and answer a number of its critics (particularly Gregory Currie), before ending with an overview of cognitive film semiotics.

1 Linguistic and Semiotic Models

The ultimate objective of structural linguistics is to offer a theoretical description, or model, of the nonobservable underlying linguistic reality. For Rudolf Botha a model is not a mere summary of directly recorded data, but a description offering "an image, representation or replica of something which cannot be observed in any direct manner" (1981: 129). The function of a model is to mediate between a theory and its object of study. The relation between theory and its object is therefore indirect. For this reason, theory does not *discover* its specific object of study, but must *construct* it, for this object is defined as being inaccessible to empirical perception. Saussure realized this in relation to the specific object of linguistic study when he stated that "The object is not given in advance of the viewpoint: far from it. Rather, one might say that it is the viewpoint adopted which creates the object" (1983: 8). For Samuel Weber: "This assertion marks out the epistemological space of Saussure's theoretical effort, and to neglect its far-reaching implications has inevitably meant to misconstrue the status of his arguments." (1976: 916).

Structural linguistics and semiotics, including film semiotics, therefore construct hypotheses and models, founded on the hierarchy between underlying (latent, nonobservable) reality and surface (manifest, observable) reality. Structural linguistics is founded on the hierarchy between *langue/parole*, and its ultimate objective is to construct a model of *la langue*. For Chomsky, the hierarchy consists of competence and performance, and the ultimate aim of his linguistics is to model competence. The specific underlying reality of film to be modeled is called cinematic language, which is opposed to individual films.

I shall now outline some of the concepts Saussure developed to model *la langue* – particularly arbitrariness, language as speech circuit, commutation, recursivity, syntagmatic and paradigmatic relations, as well as André Martinet's concept of double articulation. These concepts are important because Metz used them to construct his semiotic theory of film.

Saussure delimited the specific object of linguistic study – *la langue* – by the metaphor of speech as a circuit, as Roy Harris explains: "The *Cours* is the first treatise on language to insist that speech communication is to be viewed as a 'circuit,' and to attach any theoretical significance to the fact that individuals linked by this circuit act in turn as initiators of spoken messages and as recipients of such messages" (1987: 24–5). The metaphor "speech circuit" enabled Saussure to conceive a language as an intersubjective (or social) system of communication.

To study a language as a system of communication, Saussure developed a deductive method to analyze the "invisible" boundaries within the continuous speech chain, boundaries that confer meaning upon the signs in this chain. This method involved segmentation and classification, carried out by means of commutation which enables linguists to identify the boundaries of a phoneme – the units that distinguish one phoneme from another. In principle, a commutation involves the correlation between a change on the surface level and a change on the underlying level. A change on the surface may either be a variation of the same phoneme (or other linguistic unit) or a new phoneme. By means of commutation, linguists are able to identify the changes on the surface level that correlate with the changes on the underlying level.

Saussure described *la parole* as an infinitude of manifestations generated by *la langue*, which is necessarily finite. Generating an infinity of utterances with finite means is possible by recognizing that all utterances are composed from the same small number of signs used recursively in different combinations. All the infinite manifestations could thereby be described in terms of the finite system that evoked them. This system is not a mere conglomerate of signs, but consists of interdependent, formal relationships. Furthermore – and here Saussure located the "ultimate law of language" – signs were defined only in terms of their relation to, or *difference* from, other signs – both the paradigmatic relations they enter into in *la langue*, and the syntagmatic relations they enter into in *la parole*.

André Martinet (1964) characterized *la langue* as a doubly articulated system, consisting of the first (the higher) level, analyzable into meaningful units (morphemes, or monemes), and a second, lower level, consisting of non-meaningful units (phonemes), which have no semantic content in themselves but combine with one another on the higher level to form morphemes. Roman Jakobson and Morris Halle (1971) then broke down the phoneme into a bundle of distinct features, which were defined in terms of binary oppositions.

In identifying *la langue* Saussure justified his idea that the relation between each signifier and signified is arbitrary. This implies that *la langue* does not "inherit" properties from what it represents, but is an autonomous system of differential values that structures each language user's experience of reality.

One fundamental difference between the various underlying realities studied by linguists and semioticians is that natural language's underlying system, *la langue*, is of a much higher level of organization than the underlying systems of other semiotic languages. Care needs to be taken to qualify the term "language" to indicate whether we mean natural language (a narrow use of the word "language") or semiotic language (a much broader use of the word). To argue that a semiotic language is the same as natural language is to commit a category mistake, one that confuses the logical type of the semiotic language under discussion.

2 Institutional Context

I shall briefly review Niilo Kauppi's analysis of the institutional context in which linguistics and semiotics emerged in France in the 1950s (Kauppi 1994). He shows that there were two simultaneous forces shaping French universities at that time: (1) the rapid expansion of higher education, which allowed for the setting up of new university departments that distinguished themselves from other departments by teaching novel subjects, such as semiotics; and (2) the decline of some traditional areas of research, such as Romance philology, history of the French language, and lexicology. Kauppi notes that in the 1950s both Roland Barthes and A. J. Greimas initially worked in lexicology but were unable to obtain funding. Both, therefore, had to expand their research interests in order to encompass more novel and dynamic subjects such as anthropology, which was well funded partly due to the influence of Lévi-Strauss. To accommodate the rapid increase in university departments, new journals and book series were published. Like the departments they addressed, these new publishing ventures had to distinguish themselves from traditional university research, either by applying novel theories to traditional French culture (Derrida on Rousseau, Barthes on Racine and Michelet) or by combining novel theories with novel subject matter (Barthes's *Mythologies*).

Kauppi also points out that the institutions that introduced semiotics into the university were marginal to the French university system. It was in the Sixth Section of the Ecole Pratique des Hautes Etudes that semiotics originated in France. This school is unique in that it does not give awards to its students. It therefore attracts students by distinguishing itself from other, more established institutions (such as the University of Paris), placing itself at the vanguard of intellectual development and functioning primarily as a research institution. It attracts the most innovative researchers to its staff and, uniquely, acts as an intermediary between academics and artists, particularly avant-garde artists. As Kauppi points out, "in the 1950s the faculty of the Sixth Section included names like Lévi-Strauss, Fernand Braudel, Lucien Febvre, and in the 1960s in semiotics, Barthes, Greimas, Christian Metz as Barthes's assistant, Barthes's student Gérard Genette, Oswald Ducrot, and Louis Marin" (1994: 190). It is precisely from this innovative context that semiotics emerged in France in the late 1950s.

The Ecole Pratique also publishes its own journal, *Communications*. It is in this journal that Metz presented much of his most important research, including his essay "Cinéma: langue ou langage?" (*Communications* 4, 1964), the first version of his *grande syntagmatique* ("La Grande Syntagmatique du film narratif,"

Communications 8, 1966), and his essay "Le Signifiant imaginaire" (*Communications* 23, 1975).

3   Classical Film Semiotics

What type of inquiry is film semiotics? What role does linguistic theory play in its study of film? Is there any justification for using semiotics to study an iconic medium such as film? And how does film semiotics analyze, describe, construct, and evaluate problems? I shall approach these fundamental questions in this section.

Film semiotics does not conceive "film" to be a pre-given, unproblematic entity. Instead, it defines film's specificity – its uniqueness in terms of its underlying reality, rather than its immediately perceptible qualities. The role of theory is to make visible this invisible reality by constructing a model of it. Like other semiotic studies, film semiotics adopted the two-tier semiotic hierarchy (between manifest/latent levels of reality) and formulated hypotheses describing that underlying reality. One way to justify the linguistic analysis of film is to determine if it carries out its own agenda – modeling film's underlying reality.

But first, I need to clarify a few misunderstandings. The very idea of "film language" for film semioticians is not a simple analogy (as it was in the pre-linguistic film–language comparisons of Raymond Spottiswoode, the filmology movement, etc.) but suggests that film is a coded medium like natural language and possesses a specific, autonomous, underlying system – again, as does natural language. The semioticians' claim that film is a language was therefore made, not through any direct resemblance between film and natural language, but on methodological grounds: film's specific, underlying reality could be reconstructed by the methods of structural linguistics. At least from this methodological viewpoint, film semioticians were justified in using structural linguistics to study film because this discipline is the most sophisticated for analyzing a discourse's underlying reality.

Theory therefore consists of "hypothetical systems of concepts which represent an underlying . . . reality" (Botha 1981: 20). A theory is a system of interrelated hypotheses, or tentative assumptions, about the unobservable nature of reality (a reality assumed to be a regular, economical, cohesive structure underlying a chaotic, heterogeneous, observable phenomenon). Formulating hypotheses is dependent upon heuristic strategies: "A heuristic strategy represents any means which may be systematically used to create more favourable circumstances for the construction of hypotheses" (Botha 1981: 109). Botha lists three common heuristic strategies: (1) problem decomposition, in which large problems are broken down into smaller, more elementary problems; (2) analogies, in which the analyst looks for previously solved problems in similar areas of research; and (3) abstraction/idealization, in which a problem is simplified to make it manageable. In classical film semiotics, Metz borrowed strategies (1) and (3) from Saussure and therefore employed Saussure's analysis of natural language to research the semiotics of film (strategy (2)).

As well as offering the most sophisticated method for analyzing underlying codes, Saussure's work also enabled linguistics to become an autonomous discipline. For Saussure linguistics can only become autonomous when it identifies and studies a specific object (or dimension of language – *la langue* for Saussure), an object not studied by other disciplines. Like Saussure, Metz argued that film studies could only become an autonomous discipline by adopting a methodology that studied the irreducible specificity of film (cinematic language).

By transporting structural linguistics into film studies, Metz established a new object of study, new problematics to be confronted, and a new methodology with which to approach film, therefore making it possible to identify and establish film studies as an autonomous discipline. The new object of study was of a new level of filmic reality – the unobservable, latent level that makes filmic meaning possible and defines its specificity. The first immediate objective of film semiotics was to identify and describe this specific object of study, which Metz did by employing the three heuristic strategies mentioned above (problem decomposition, analogies, abstraction/idealization).

I shall now examine the activities involved in formulating theoretical problems and then illustrate this activity at work in three canonical texts by Metz: "Cinema: Language or Language System?" (in Metz 1974a: 31–91), "Problems of Denotation in the Fiction Film" (in Metz 1974a: 108–46), and *Language and Cinema* (1974b).

Botha (1981: 54) lists four activities involved in formulating theoretical problems: (a) analyzing the problematic state of affairs; (b) describing the problematic state of affairs; (c) constructing problems; and (d) evaluating problems with regard to well-formedness and significance. This list is based on the distinction between a "problematic state of affairs" and "problems." Whereas the former refers to an aspect of reality not understood by a theorist, a problem formulates what the theorist needs to look for in order to resolve the problematic state of affairs.

In carrying out (a), analysis, the theorist must know exactly what is problematic, isolate each component of the problematic state of affairs, determine how they are interrelated, and identify the background assumptions informing her inquiry, such as the nature conferred upon the object of analysis. The background assumptions of semiotics include: the object of analysis consisting of a hierarchy of two levels – manifest and latent; and the latent being the more significant level to analyze.

In carrying out (b), description, the problematic state of affairs must be accurately recorded and formally described. For Botha (66), this involves three processes: (i) collecting data; (ii) systematizing data; (iii) symbolizing the results. In collecting data, the theorist must determine whether the data or the theory generates the problematic state of affairs. Systematizing data involves the activities of classifying, correlating, and ordering. These activities enable the theorist to identify common properties among data, put similar data into classes, and determine the relations between the classes. Finally, symbolizing simply involves representing data in a concise and accurate manner.

In carrying out (c), the construction of problems, the theorist employs several different concepts (since a problem is made up of concepts). Botha (85) identifies four types of concept involved in the construction of problems: *phenomenological* concepts, which concern factual data and are intuitively known; *grammatical* concepts (here, *filmic* concepts), which concern general background assumptions concerning the nature of individual languages (or the nature of film); *general linguistic* concepts (here, *semiotic* concepts), which concern background assumptions about the nature of linguistic/semiotic inquiry; and *metascientific* concepts, which concern the aims and nature of linguistic/semiotic inquiry.

Finally, in carrying out (d), evaluating problems, Botha recognizes that only problems satisfying the criteria of well-formedness and significance are relevant problems worth pursuing. A well-formed problem is solvable – that is, it is based on correct assumptions and is clearly formulated. A significant problem is one that expands our existing knowledge of film. A problem may, therefore, be well formed but not significant.

3.1 *"Cinema: Language or Language System?"*

(a) Analyzing the problematic state of affairs. The problem analyzed in Metz's first essay in film semiotics is conveniently stated in the essay's title: is there a filmic equivalent to *la langue* (translated in Metz's essay as language system)? An answer to this question would then offer a definition of filmic specificity, the primary objective of film semiotics. In other words, filmic specificity should be defined in terms of an underlying reality (modeled on natural language's underlying reality – *la langue*), not in terms of the immediately perceptible level of film, as classical (pre-semiotic) film theorists had attempted to do. Metz's background assumption in this essay is that film must possess an equivalent to *la langue* to be defined as a language (*langage*).

(b) Describing the problematic state of affairs. Not surprisingly, with a background assumption listed in (a), Metz describes the state of affairs negatively (he concludes by stating that cinema is a *langage sans langue*). Much of his description involves documenting how the underlying reality of film does *not* resemble *la langue*.

The negative results are not unexpected, for the semiotic language of film obviously does not possess the same system specific to natural language. For example, Metz states: "the image discourse is an open system, and it is not easily codified, with its nondiscrete basic units (the images), its intelligibility (which is too natural), its lack of distance [i.e. lack of arbitrariness] between the [signified] and the signifier" (1974a: 59). Metz emphasizes that the image does not derive its meaning in opposition to other images, but from a direct correspondence to profilmic events. In other words, film has no paradigm on the level of the image; consequently, it has no *langue*, and no double articulation.

The reasons are twofold: (1) Metz believed, under the influence of the classical film theorist André Bazin, that the image is analogical, not coded, for it is constituted by a continuous, nondiscrete resemblance to the thing it represents; and (2) "The image is always actualized" (67). That is, filmic images do not belong to a collective, non-manifest, closed system existing prior to usage; rather, each image is at the outset a complete, manifest, and individual unit of discourse. In Metz's famous example: "A close-up of a revolver does not mean 'revolver' (a purely virtual [non-manifest] lexical unit [morpheme]), but at the very least, and without speaking of the connotations, it signifies 'Here is a revolver!'" (67). This led Metz to state that "the cinematographic image is primarily speech [*parole*]" (69), which is the same as saying that "The filmic shot is of the *magnitude of the sentence*" (86).

But this terminology has often confused how the linguistic status of the image is understood. Metz merely characterized the relation between image and sentence in exterior terms, in which there is no structural similarity between them, because the sentence is also analyzable into units that signify paradigmatically: "The difference [between sentence and image] is that the sentences of verbal language eventually break down into words, whereas in the cinema, they do not: A film may be segmented into large units ('shots'), but these shots are not *reducible* (in Jakobson's sense) into small, basic, and specific units" (88). The "irreducibility" of filmic images suggests that they are potentially infinite in number and that each one is unique. This explains why they cannot be formed into a closed paradigm.

Metz also concluded that the cinema does not form a speech circuit: "The cinema is not a language system, because it contradicts three important characteristics of the linguistic fact: a language is a *system* of *signs* used for *intercommunication*. Three elements to the definition. Now, like all the arts, and because it is itself an art, the cinema is one-way communication" (75). Language as a "speech circuit," so crucial for Saussure, does not, therefore, apply to film.

Two reasons explain Metz's failure to establish a semiotics of the cinema on the level of the image. (1) The first is a genuine inability to articulate a new perspective on film by means of two fundamental criteria that make linguistics scientific (at least for Saussure) – the arbitrary relation between signifier and signified, and the metaphor of language as a speech circuit – for these two criteria do not hold on the level of the filmic image. To achieve his objective – to define filmic specificity in semiotic terms – Metz sought the above two criteria on the level of image sequences. (In fact, it was evident that film does not form a speech circuit on any level, so Metz attempted to establish a principle of arbitrariness in the filmic chain.) (2) The second reason has to do with Metz's unnecessary adoption of Barthes's reversal of Saussure's hierarchy between linguistics and semiotics (resulting in a translinguistics). This reversal simply forced Metz into a strait-jacket; it meant he did not directly apply structural linguistics to film (i.e.

91

the methodological concepts syntagm/paradigm, signifier/signified, etc.) but took the *results* of the analysis of the system of articulation specific to natural language and attempted to find the *same system (la langue)* in film. Hence, at this stage he did not search for filmic paradigms, for example, but for paradigms organized along double articulation. And because the filmic image does not conform to the same system of articulation as that revealed by the structural linguistic analysis of natural language, Metz concluded that the structural linguistic research into the specificity of film language on the level of the image is an inappropriate starting point for a film semiotics. This is because, for him, semiotics must operate within the narrow confines of structural linguistics, which is geared exclusively to the study of systems such as *la langue*, rather than to analogical systems (such as *la parole*), to a system of arbitrary signs systematically organized into paradigms. He believed all semiotic systems to be regulated by *la langue* composed of nonsignifying – that is, purely differential – units (such as phonemes), which constitute *la langue* as a doubly articulated system. The lack of all these features on the level of the image forced Metz to conclude that film is, in some sense, a *"langage sans langue."* And in later essays he attempted to clarify this statement by arguing that the specific system of filmic language begins on the level of the syntagm.

Stephen Heath writes that, for Metz in "Cinema: Language or Language System?," "cinema lacks any equivalent to the double articulation of linguistic *langue*, its very economy, the combination of systematically defined units of a lower level (phonemes) to form units of a higher level (monemes); instead of articulation, duplication, instead of economy, an infinity of analogical resemblance" (1981: 142). Because Metz could not codify the filmic image in terms of *la langue*, he concluded that it is completely uncoded, a mechanical duplication or analogical resemblance. In Saussurean terms, Metz thought of images as *parole* – as uncoded actualized discourse. Furthermore, he concluded that cinema is a *langage sans langue* because it is one-way communication (or expression, rather than communication), unlike natural language, which is two-way communication; it lacks signs (since filmic images are motivated); and it does not form a system (precisely because filmic images are motivated they do not require a system of paradigms and syntagms to generate meaning). There is no system of virtual, or non-manifest, images that a film then manifests; instead, each image is an invention. In one sentence, cinema suffers from a paradigmatic poverty. This wasn't the most promising start for initiating a semiotics of the cinema!

(c) Constructing problems. In transposing linguistic concepts to film, Metz confused filmic concepts with linguistic concepts (the background assumptions concerning the nature of film with the background assumptions concerning the nature of natural language). In other words, he believed that the reality underlying all languages should conform to the reality underlying natural language (here we encounter one problem with translinguistics). More positively, "Cinema: Language or Language System?" employs general and metascientific

concepts: it uses the hierarchy between underlying/manifest levels and identifies the aim of film semiotics as the activity of identifying pertinent underlying units (although here modeled on *la langue*).

(d) Evaluating problems.   It is doubtful whether "Cinema: Language or Language System?" formulated a well-formed and significant problem, since it is not a significant problem whether film is a *langue* or *langage*, for the simple reason that *la langue* is unique to natural language – it is natural language's underlying reality. Metz did not perceive that film has its own underlying reality that does not resemble the structure of *la langue* (Metz therefore directly compared film to natural language, an erroneous activity which inspired pre-semiotic film theorists). In effect, Metz was attempting to define filmic specificity in terms of the specificity of natural language as formulated by structural linguistics, since he believed that double articulation is the only form of articulation. He even contradicted the basic semiotic premise that the aim of film semiotics is to define filmic specificity in terms of an underlying reality, since he argued that film is always actualized. But if film has no *langue*, what is actualized? Surely, to say that film is actualized implies a prior set of terms that are actualized. However, Metz did manage to identify a prior set of terms in his subsequent work.

3.2   "Problems of Denotation in the Fiction Film"

(a) Analyzing the problematic state of affairs.   The assumption that film is a *langage sans langue* led Metz, in "Problems of Denotation," to explore the syntagmatic dimension of film, which in turn generated another background assumption – that filmic specificity (or cinematic language) is to be identified with narrativity (a single, superstructural code): "*it is precisely to the extent that the cinema confronted the problems of narration that* . . . it came to produce a body of specific signifying procedures" (1974a: 95).

(b) Describing the problematic state of affairs.   Above all else, "Problems of Denotation" is concerned almost exclusively with classifying, correlating, and ordering data. The main purpose of the essay is to identify a prior set of sequence (or syntagmatic) types operative in classical cinema, a paradigm of syntagmas from which a filmmaker can choose to represent profilmic events in a particular sequence. Each syntagma is identifiable by the particular way it structures the spatio-temporal relations between the profilmic events it depicts. Syntagmas are commutable because the same events depicted by means of a different syntagma will have a different meaning.

These spatio-temporal relationships between the images constitute cinematic language for Metz because they articulate the profilmic events in terms of a *specific* cinematic space and time. In other words, this cinematic space and time confers upon these events a meaning that *goes beyond* their analogical relation to the image. These image orderings therefore conform to the principle of arbitrariness, since there is no strict motivation governing the choice of one syntagma over another in representing a particular profilmic event.

Metz detected eight different spatio-temporal relationships in total, which constitute eight different forms of image ordering syntagmas. Metz called the resulting "paradigm of syntagmas" the *grande syntagmatique* of the image track. These image syntagmas form a paradigm to the extent that they offer eight different commutable ways of constructing an image sequence. As Metz himself has said: "These montage figures [film syntagmas] derive their meaning to a large extent in relation to one another. One, then, has to deal, so to speak, with a paradigm of syntagmas. It is only by a sort of *commutation* that one can identify and enumerate them" (1976: 587).

The *grande syntagmatique* identifies syntagmatic units only when a change in shot produces a change in meaning – that is, when a spatio-temporal transition (the cut, etc.) on the level of the filmic signifier correlates with a change in meaning on the level of the signified (the spatio-temporal relationship between the profilmic events). Each filmic syntagma is constituted by the same spatio-temporal relationship between its images. As long as the same relation holds across cuts, there is no commutation. A commutation, or change in meaning, therefore occurs when a spatio-temporal transition on the level of the filmic signifier is correlated with a *new* spatio-temporal relation between profilmic events, for a new relation signals the end of one syntagma and the beginning of another. (See Metz 1974a: 124–33, for an outline of the eight syntagmatic types.)

(c) Constructing problems. Metascientific and general problems: in "Problems of Denotation" Metz employs the hierarchy between underlying/manifest levels (in which the system of syntagmas constitute the underlying level) and identifies the aim of film semiotics as the activity of identifying pertinent underlying units (codes) and their rules of combination. Filmic concepts: Metz makes the well-known assumption that film language is to be equated with narrative. This is one of the major limitations of the *grande syntagmatique*, with the result that Metz equates narrative with filmic specificity (cinematic language), because narrative in the cinema conforms to the principle of arbitrariness. In other words, narrative is presented as being intrinsic, rather than contingent, to film form.

(d) Evaluating problems. "Problems of Denotation" formulates a well-formed and significant problem, since it successfully identifies an autonomous level of articulation in the cinema (syntagmas) and constructs a paradigm of eight syntagmas (thus overcoming cinema's paradigmatic poverty). As Heath points out: "The focus on syntagmatic relations 'saves' semiology (in so far as it is held in the *language* or *langage* debate) in the face of the paradigmatic poverty of cinema" (1981: 144). Yet two problems remain: Metz's identification of filmic specificity with narrativity (confusion of types), and the uncoded, transparent nature conferred on the image (a problem carried over from "Cinema: Language

or Language System?" and merely displaced in the *grande syntagmatique*). Metz approached both problems in *Language and Cinema*.

3.3   Language and Cinema

(a) Analyzing the problematic state of affairs: "We could summarize the task of the semiotics of the filmic fact as follows: to analyze film texts in order to discover either textual systems, cinematic codes, or sub-codes" (Metz 1974b: 150).[1] In *Language and Cinema* Metz continues to pursue the question "What is the specificity of film?" but now answers by distinguishing between film and cinema and then defining specificity in terms of a combination of cinematic codes and sub-codes:

> We shall call *filmic*... all the traits which appear in films (i.e., in the messages of the cinema), whether they are or are not peculiar to this means of expression, and no matter what idea one has of this specificity or of its absence. We shall call *cinematic* certain filmic facts which are supposed to play a part... in one or the other of the codes specific to the cinema. The cinematic is but a part of the filmic. Certain phenomena are filmic and cinematic, others filmic but not cinematic. (47)

Metz now regards the study of singular filmic systems to be an equally important dimension of film semiotics. In other words, he no longer limits film semiotics to the study of filmic specificity, but also includes study of the way specific and nonspecific codes combine in single films.

The study of film (the filmic) involves the analysis of singular textual systems, while the study of cinema (the cinematic) involves the analysis of codes: "In this sense, film and cinema are opposed as a real object to an ideal one, as an *utterance* to a *language system*" (24).[2] In *Language and Cinema* Metz no longer uses the term *la langue* to discuss cinematic language, but replaces it with the more general term *code*, which has no linguistic connotations; there is therefore no obligation to search for double articulation, etc.

"Cinematic language" refers to a generality not exhausted by any film, whereas "singular textual system" refers to the specific organization of one film. A singular textual system therefore lacks the generality of a code, and is not concerned with cinematic specificity but with the way specific and nonspecific codes combine in a particular film.

Two background assumptions of *Language and Cinema* not evident in Metz's previous film semiotics are that: "(1) the specificity which interests semiotics is the specificity of codes, not the 'crude' specificity of physical signifiers; (2) the specificity of specific codes nevertheless refers to certain features of the material of expression" (Metz 1974b: 219) Earlier, Metz stated:

> there is a great difference between a specificity defined directly according to material criteria and one that is defined in terms of codes, even if the specification of codes cannot be accomplished without a consideration of certain traits of the

material of the signifier (and not of this material itself, taken as a whole and without further analysis). (43)

No single code is unique to the cinema, although this doesn't prevent Metz from defining codes as specific: "A code may . . . be specific for *several* languages . . . . This notion of an *obviously multiple specificity* is paradoxical only in appearance. Sameness is not the only form of specificity, and a circumscribed multiplicity also forms a specific group; a specific field is not necessarily a very small one" (224). Instead, he defines cinematic language in terms of a combination of (more or less) specific codes. A consequence of this is that Metz identifies a hierarchy of specificity amongst these codes, a hierarchy defined in terms of material of expression. This adds a degree of complexity to the second and third aspects of the activities involved in constructing theoretical problems.

(b) Describing the problematic state of affairs. Metz systematizes his data (cinematic and filmic codes, and their relation to film's matter of expression) in the form of concentric circles, which enables him to establish classes of codes and define their relation to one another. Each circle represents a code and also a group of languages associated with it. In chapter 10.4 of *Language and Cinema*, Metz defines the specificity of film's image track in terms of a specific combination of the following codes: iconicity, mechanical duplication, multiplicity, and movement. Metz's lengthy description can be represented visually (see figure 1), a practice Metz would have done well to follow.

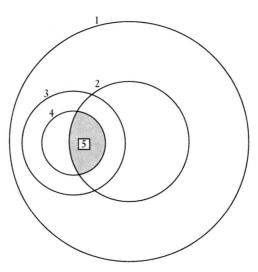

1. Iconicity
2. Mechanical duplication
3. Multiplicity
4. Movement
5. Mechanically produced multiple moving images

Figure 1

This description of film semiotics' problematic state of affairs is motivated by the fact that the relation between these codes is one of inclusion (as well as intersection). Iconicity is a code specific to all visual languages; its degree of specificity therefore remains rather low. More specific is the fact that filmic images are produced by mechanical duplication (circle 2) and are multiple (circle 3). The combination of these three codes attains a high degree of specificity but does not define film's unique specificity. Moreover, multiplicity is not included within circle 2 but intersects with it (as well as with circle 1), because some languages (such as cartoons) are made up of a multiplicity of non-mechanically produced images. A fourth characteristic of filmic specificity is that its multiple mechanical images move. Because movement depends upon a multiplicity of images, it is included within circle 3 (multiplicity) and also intersects mechanical duplication and iconicity (circles 2 and 1 respectively). Film belongs to a fifth group of languages included within circle 4 – namely, mechanically produced multiple moving images (the shaded area in figure 1). This fifth group is the logical product of 4 and 2.

In terms of the image track, filmic specificity has been defined by a combination of codes and their material of expression. Because all these codes can be manifest in film's material of expression, they attain a degree of specificity. However, both film and television images belong to the shaded area of figure 1. It seems, then, that cinema has no unique codification. Metz (1974b: 235–40) resorts to a technological criterion to distinguish them: a televisual image is electronically rather than photographically produced, although both modes of production function to manifest the same code – that of movement. Furthermore, there is, of course, a purely perceptual difference, in that filmic images are projected on a large screen, whereas televisual images are electronically transmitted on a small screen. Nonetheless, what appears on the big and small screens is still the same set of codes.

(c) Constructing problems. Metascientific and general: *Language and Cinema* rigorously employs the hierarchy between underlying/manifest levels (cinema and film respectively), and continues to identify the aim of film semiotics as the activity of identifying pertinent underlying units (codes) and their rules of combination. Filmic: the nature of film is significantly expanded in *Language and Cinema*, overcoming the two problems identified in "Problems of Denotation": iconicity is defined as coded, and film consists of a combination of codes (rather than one code – narrativity); furthermore, some of those codes are defined in terms of the matter of expression in which they are manifest. This directly leads to the employment of phenomenological concepts: a definition of specific codes with reference to film's sensory dimension.

The latter two types of concept are significant additions to film semiotics in that they show Metz tackling the issue of iconicity within a semiotic framework. In "Cinema: Language or Language System?" and "Problems of Denotation in the Fiction Film," Metz worked with the realist conception of the image-as-analogue (as a mechanical duplication of reality). Heath called this "the blind spot of Metz's formulations" for it is "the point at which the articulation of significance collapses in the face of analogy" (1981: 141). Metz overcame this blind spot under the influence of Umberto Eco. Eco was one of the first semioticians to successfully study the image in terms of codes, which enabled him to define its apparent analogical (nonsemiotic) nature as a system of iconic codes organized into a triple hierarchy (Eco 1976a).[3]

Once semiotic analysis had overcome the problem of analogy, the rich semiotic field of the cinema was opened up to analysis because film theorists were able to analyze the multiple systems of codes that constitute the complex act of filmic signification. Within this framework the social and ideological determination of all semiotic systems were finally recognized. Heath commented that: "It is this recognition of codes at work in the image, of the possibility of analogy being itself the result of codes, which marks a decisive process of rethinking in Metz's writings" (1981: 143).

Language and Cinema represents this process of rethinking. In earlier work, Metz preferred to reject the status of film as a complete semiotic system rather than challenge the realist status of the photographic image. But using the concept of code in *Language and Cinema* developed "a response to cinema as a complexity of codes of differing kind and degree of systematicity" (Heath 1981: 144).

(d) Evaluating problems. It is arguable whether all the answers Metz formulates to the problems he poses in *Language and Cinema* (see (a) above) are well formed, since some of the logic is dubious (Metz's argument that some codes are not specific to one language, and that there is a hierarchy of specificity amongst codes). In *Language and Cinema* Metz reaches the limits of the question of filmic specificity and the limitations of a structuralist answer to this question. (These are, of course, interrelated, since the study of filmic specificity – of an autonomous realm of film – is approached by film semioticians with the methodology of structural linguistics.) These two limitations are evident in Metz's use of classical set theory to represent filmic specificity, which gives the impression that it can be defined simply in terms of an addition, or culmination, of codes. That is, the single component codes are seen to culminate into a complex set of component codes. But such a representation of information can be misleading, as George Lakoff has shown (1987: ch. 9). He gives many examples showing how the intersection of two components does not necessarily form a complex set of components. For one of his examples, "pet fish," he writes: "A guppy might be a good example of a pet fish, but a bad example of a pet, and a bad example of a fish" (141). "Pet fish" is not therefore a simple combination of "pet" and "fish."

This criticism also applies to Metz's representation of filmic specificity in *Language and Cinema*. Iconicity, mechanical duplication, movement, and multiple images do not simply overlap and intersect with one another (i.e. culminate) but interact in more dynamic ways to form filmic specificity. Metz did in fact begin to explore this issue at the end of *Language and Cinema*, with the concept of filmic writing, in which the codes are thought to displace one another rather than simply culminate. But the whole book is built upon a classical theory of classification, and the theory of filmic writing sits uneasily within that context.

In conclusion, we can say that in *Language and Cinema* Metz attempted to develop a complex definition of filmic specificity (based on a combination of codes) using the methodology employed to develop a simple definition of filmic specificity (defined in terms of a single, master code). But such a methodology is not equipped to develop a complex definition (since it cannot adequately represent the way the multiple codes combine without resorting to the simple principle of culmination).

4   Critiques of Classical Film Semiotics

My criticism in the previous section of Metz's early research is based on identifying and clarifying its internal logic and inconsistencies. However, it is now fashionable to reject film semiotics outright. Here I shall briefly review Gregory Currie's recent critique.

Currie considers two hypotheses from film semiotics: the strong hypothesis that film is like a natural language, and the weak hypothesis that film is a semiotic system. Most of chapter 4 of his book *Image and Mind* (1995) is devoted to refuting the strong hypothesis. Currie has made an unfortunate choice because he is simply repeating the arguments Metz presented back in 1964, in "Cinéma: langue ou langage?" As we saw above, in this essay Metz compared film images with natural language (*un langage avec langue*) and found that no similarities exist, which led him to conclude that film is a *langage sans langue* (that film is not a natural language).

Metz abandoned the direct comparison between film and natural language (*langue*) and argued, in his subsequent work on image sequences, that film is a language in the sense of a semiotic system (the second hypothesis that Currie does not attempt to reject, even though it characterizes the dominant position in film semiotics). Currie has not considered the history of film semiotics, nor has he adequately characterized its basic hypotheses. When Currie writes "I shall argue that, in crucial respects, film is very unlike natural language" (119), he is simply repeating Metz's statement that film is a *langage sans langue*. There is no disagreement between Metz and Currie, simply Currie's misunderstanding, caused by his failure to grasp the status of Metz's arguments and the history of film semiotics.

Even though Metz tried without success to compare film to natural language, he never argued that film is like a natural language. He did not commit the category mistake of arguing that film has the same status as English, French, Japanese, and so on. Yet Currie attributes this view to film semiotics. To repeat: film semiotics argues that film is a language (a semiotic system) but does not argue that film is like a natural language, such as English, French, or Japanese.

By attributing the proposition "film is like a natural language" to film semiotics, Currie has simply constructed his own straw man to attack. This is due to his narrow definition of the term "language," in which it always means "natural language." Film is not a language for Currie because it is not like a natural language. But for Metz, even though film is not like a natural language, it is still a language (a semiotic system).

The clearest moment when Currie collapses the distinction between language and natural language is in the last section of chapter 4 of *Image and Mind*, when he briefly considers whether the comparison between film and natural language can be made in the study of image sequences:

> Perhaps the claim that there is a language of cinematic images is not the claim that these images themselves have a language-like structure, but rather that these images enter into language-like combinations with each other. In films, there are combinations of images; sometimes these combinations form identifiable and recurrent patterns, and these combinations can have a meaning which partly depends on the manner of their combination. Isn't there something here like the articulated structure of a sentence? No. As many film theorists have recognized, the representational content of a cinema image cannot be equated with that of a name, predicate, or other sub-sentential part of speech. (134)

I agree with Currie that we can only give the answer "no" to the question: "Isn't there something here [in the recurrent patterns of image combinations] like the articulated structure of a sentence?" But this is because it is the wrong question, since film semioticians do not fall into the trap of making comparisons between the specific structure of natural language sentences and image combinations. (Or if they do, their results are negative.) If Currie asked "Isn't there something here [in the recurrent patterns of image combinations] like semiotic articulation?" (that is, articulation not reducible to natural language's specific system of codes, *la langue*), the answer would be "yes." Metz's *grande syntagmatique* is a model of the eight recurrent types of image combinations (syntagmas) that dominate classical cinema. The problem here is Currie's purely argumentative engagement with film semiotics, an engagement that only offers decontextualized criticism. Murray Smith's claim that "Currie's argument [in chapter 4 of *Image and Mind*] is in stark contrast to the lingering and vague belief in the language-like structure of film among semiotic thinkers, and constitutes perhaps the most comprehensive demolition of this article of faith to date" (1998: 326) is entirely misplaced.

5   Cognitive Film Semiotics

David Bordwell has noted the absence of references to the work of Chomsky in film theory: "it is surprising that theorists who assign language a key role in determining subjectivity have almost completely ignored the two most important contemporary developments in linguistic theory: Chomsky's Transformational

Generative Grammar and his Principles-and-Parameters theory" (1996: 22). He adds that: "no film theorist has mounted an argument for *why* the comparatively informal theories of Saussure, Emile Benveniste, or Bakhtin are superior to the Chomskyan paradigm. For over two decades film theorists have made pronouncements about language without engaging with the major theoretical rival to their position" (22). The truth is that over the last two decades a number of film theorists have been engaging with Chomskyan linguistics and, furthermore, have deemed it to be superior to structural linguistics. Here I shall briefly chart the relation between classical film semiotics and cognitive film semiotics.

During the 1970s Metz's classical film semiotics was modified and transformed. Its fundamental problems lay in its total reliance upon structural linguistics. One major transformation came from post-structural film theory, which did not draw upon autonomous linguistic theories, but based itself primarily upon the Marxism of Louis Althusser and the psychoanalysis of Jacques Lacan.

The second transformation was carried out by cognitive film semiotics. For most Anglo-American film scholars, film semiotics takes only one form – namely, Metz's early film semiotics, represented by the three pieces of research analyzed above. But as Metz himself acknowledged in the opening chapter of *Language and Cinema*, "By its very nature, the semiotic enterprise must expand or disappear" (1974b: 19). Although *Language and Cinema* marks the logical conclusion to classical film semiotics, it does not mark the end of film semiotics per se. In his subsequent work – particularly his essay "The Imaginary Signifier" (1982: 1–87) – Metz adopted a psychoanalytical framework, which aided the formation of post-structural film theory. However, many of his students and colleagues continued to work within a semiotic framework, which they combined with cognitive science. Research in film semiotics has continued unabated in the 1970's, '80s, and '90s, especially in Europe. Far from disappearing, film semiotics has expanded into a new framework, one that overcomes the problems of classical film semiotics by embracing three new theories: (1) transformational generative grammar and cognitive science generally (in the work of Dominique Chateau [e.g. 1986, 1995] and Michel Colin [1995]); (2) a renewed interest in enunciation theory (particularly in the work of Francesco Casetti [1986, 1995] and Metz of *L'Enonciation impersonnelle, ou le site du film* [1991]); and (3) pragmatics (in the work of Roger Odin [1988, 1995a, 1995b]).

In his essay "The Grande Syntagmatique Revisited" (1995) Michel Colin redefined Metz's eight syntagmatic types in terms of selectional (or semantic) features. Selectional features represent the inherent grammatical and semantic components of lexical items (or "words"). For example, the lexical item "cat" can be represented in terms of the following selectional features: +Common, +Count, +Animate, −Human. Every lexical item can be characterized in terms of these and other selectional features. The most remarkable outcome of Colin's rereading of Metz's work is that, as with all generative models, the actual, manifest syntagmatic types are posited as merely the result (the epiphenomenon) of the generative process. Within the generative framework, we can identify and analyze not only actual syntagmas, but also possible (i.e. potential) syntagmas and impossible syntagmas. Once all the finite selectional features have been identified, the potentially infinite number of syntagmatic types can be conceived and generated. These selectional features constitute the finite underlying level of filmic discourse (or its system of codes) from which a potentially infinite number of film sequences can be generated. For Colin, then, the primary aim of the *grande syntagmatique* is not to identify actual syntagmatic types, but to identify the more fundamental selectional features that combine to form these syntagmatic types. (See Buckland 1995a for a detailed analysis of Colin's research.)

In linguistics, cognitive pragmatics designates a discipline that describes a type of linguistic competence that governs the relation between utterances and the appropriate contexts in which they are uttered. Cognitive pragmatics is therefore a study of the immediate discursive nature of language. Roger Odin (1995a, 1995b) develops a cognitive–pragmatic theory of film semiotics. He distinguishes between institutions, modes, and operations in order to characterize the film spectator's pragmatic competence in comprehending films. From this he identifies the different filmic institutions, modes, and operations, with particular focus on fiction films, documentaries, home movies, and what Odin calls the "dynamic" mode of filmmaking (1988).

Enunciation designates the activity that results in speech, in the production of utterances (*énoncés*). Emile Benveniste identified two form of utterance: discourse (*discours*) and story (*histoire*). *Discours* employs deictic categories – words such as personal, possessive, and demonstrative pronouns that grammaticalize within the utterance particular aspects of its spatio-temporal context (e.g. the speaker and hearer), whereas *histoire* is a form of utterance that excludes deixis. Francesco Casetti (1986, 1995) takes to its logical conclusions the analysis of the deictic dimension of film – of film as *discours*. Using the deictic categories "I," "you," and "he," he develops a seminal typology of four shot types, which aim to describe the way film orients itself in relation to the spectator. However, in his final published book Metz (1991) disputes this deictic theory of film, and instead argues that film can only be studied as *histoire*.

The psychologist Karl Bühler used the term "deixis" to refer to systems of orientation that position an individual's body and consciousness in relation to her environment. In the sense of systems of orientation, deixis refers to a general cognitive process. Deictic systems of orientation include bodily gestures (e.g. pointing), language expressions, and imagination. Casetti conducted his research within the framework of one of these general systems of orientation – personal pronouns in linguistic expressions. Metz criticizes Casetti's use of personal pronouns to describe how the spectator is oriented in relation to film. (He is therefore criticizing Casetti's over-reliance on linguistic concepts.) Metz then replaces orientation by means of personal pronouns with orientation by means of anaphora – a narrow system of orientation in which one textual element points to another textual element. Moreover, Metz identifies anaphora as a reflexive moment in a film, which results in his identifying filmic enunciation with reflexivity.

The work of the cognitive film semioticians represents the current state of film semiotics, which is united by the same project – to combine film semiotics and cognitive science with the aim of modeling filmic competence. Far from disappearing, film semiotics has continued to expand, even though its results haven't been in the spotlight of Anglo-American film theory.

Notes

1   The distinction between cinematic codes and sub-codes is irrelevant to my discussion here. But briefly, cinematic codes are codes specific to film, whereas cinematic sub-codes, while also specific to film, are specific only to some films. Moreover, whereas codes syntagmatically combine with one another (lighting, montage, etc.), sub-codes (of the same code) are in a paradigmatic relation of substitution. Hence, the code of punctuation is a cinematic code, whereas the fade and the dissolve are sub-codes of this code. As such, they cannot appear at the same time in the same film (this being due to their paradigmatic nature) and may not appear in a film at all (this being due to their nature as sub-codes).
2   Raymond Bellour's film semiotics focusses primarily on this issue of singular textual systems. See Buckland 1993 for an overview of Bellour's film semiotics.
3   For additional semiotic studies of iconicity, see Eco 1976b: 191–217, Kjorup 1978, and Prince 1993.

References

Apel, Karl Otto. 1976. "The Transcendental Conception of Language-Communication and the Idea of First Philosophy." In *History of Linguistic Thought and Contemporary Linguistics*. Ed. Herman Parret. Berlin and New York: Walter de Gruyter.

Bordwell, David. 1996. "Contemporary Film Studies and the Vicissitudes of Grand Theory." In *Post-Theory: Reconstructing Film Studies*. Ed. David Bordwell and Noël Carroll. Madison: University of Wisconsin Press.

Botha, Rudolf. 1981. *The Conduct of Linguistic Inquiry: A Systematic Introduction to the Methodology of Generative Grammar*. The Hague: Mouton.

Buckland, Warren. 1993. "From System to Structure: The Film Semiology of Raymond Bellour." *Essays in Poetics* 18, 2: 42–68.

——. 1995a. "Michel Colin and the Psychological Reality of Film Semiology." *Semiotica*, 107, 1/2: 51–79.

——, ed. 1995b. *The Film Spectator: From Sign to Mind*. Amsterdam: Amsterdam University Press.

Casetti, Francesco. 1986. *Dentro lo sguardo: il filme e il sou spettatore*. Milano: Bompiani.

——. 1995. "Face to Face." In Buckland 1995b: 118–39.

Chateau, Dominique. 1986. *Le Cinéma comme langage*. Bruxelles: AISS – Publications de la Sorbonne.

——. 1995. "Towards a Generative Model of Filmic Discourse." In Buckland 1995b: 35–44.

Colin, Michel. 1995. "The Grande Syntagmatique Revisited." In Buckland 1995b: 45–86.

Currie, Gregory. 1995. *Image and Mind: Film, Philosophy, and Cognitive Science*. Cambridge: Cambridge University Press.

Daddesio, Thomas. 1995. *On Minds and Symbols: The Relevance of Cognitive Science for Semiotics*. Berlin: Mouton de Gruyter.

Eco, Umberto. 1976a. "Articulations of the Cinematic Code." In *Movies and Methods*. Ed. Bill Nichols. Berkeley: University of Calfornia Press. 590–607.

——. 1976b. *A Theory of Semiotics*. Bloomington: Indiana University Press.

Harris, Roy. 1987. *Reading Saussure*. London: Duckworth.

Heath, Stephen. 1981. "The Work of Christian Metz." In *Screen Reader 2*. London: SEFT. 138–61.

Jakobson, Roman, and Morris Halle. 1971. *Fundamentals of Language*, 2nd edn. The Hague: Mouton.

Kauppi, Niilo. 1994. *The Making of an Avant-Garde: Tel Quel*. Berlin and New York: Mouton de Gruyter.

Kjorup, Soren. 1978. "Iconic Codes and Pictorial Speech Acts." In *Danish Semiotics*. Ed. Jorgen Dines Johansen and Morten Nojgaard. Orbis Litterarum, supplement 4. Munksgaard/Copenhagen. 101–22.

Lakoff, George. 1987. *Women, Fire, and Dangerous Things: What Categories Reveal About the Mind*. Chicago: University of Chicago Press.

Martinet, André. 1964. *Elements of General Linguistics*. Trans. Elizabeth Palmer. London: Faber and Faber.

Metz, Christian. 1974a. *Film Language: A Semiotics of the Cinema*. Trans. Michael Taylor. New York: Oxford University Press.

——. 1974b. *Language and Cinema*. Trans. Donna Jean Umiker-Sebeok. The Hague: Mouton.

——. 1976. "On the Notion of Cinematographic Language." In *Movies and Methods*. Ed. Bill Nichols. Berkeley: University of California Press. 582–9.

——. 1982. "The Imaginary Signifier." In *Psychoanalysis and Cinema: The Imaginary Signifier*. Trans. Ben Brewster et al. London: Macmillan. 1–87.

——. 1991. *L'Enonciation impersonnelle, ou le site du film*. Paris: Méridiens Klincksieck.

Odin, Roger. 1988. "Du spectateur fictionnalisant au nouveau spectateur: approche sémio-pragmatique." *Iris* 8: 121–39.

——. 1995a. "A Semio-Pragmatic approach to the Documentary Film." In Buckland 1995b: 227–35.

——. 1995b. "For a Semio-Pragmatics of Film." In Buckland 1995b: 213–26.

Prince, Stephen. 1993. "The Discourse of Pictures: Iconicity and Film Studies." *Film Quarterly* 47, 1: 16–28.

Saussure, Ferdinand de. 1983. *Course in General Linguistics*. Trans. Roy Harris. London: Duckworth.

Smith, Murray. 1998. Review of Currie 1995. *British Journal of Aesthetics* 38, 3: 325–7.

Weber, Samuel. 1976. "Saussure and the Apparation of Language: The Critical Perspective." *Modern Language Notes*, 91: 913–38.

CHAPTER SEVEN

Cognitivism

Gregory Currie

This survey is the work of a philosopher with an intense interest in the relations between film and the mind, and sympathy for, if not a universal admiration of, the work of cognitivist film theorists so far. It emphasizes the broader, more programmatic and philosophical aspects of cognitivism and seeks always to place doctrines in the context of a view of method – surely the most distinctive feature of cognitivism. My apologies go to those cognitivists and their allies whose work on film history and on particular genres, directors, and films I have passed over.

1 The Growth of Cognitivism

Elements of broadly cognitivist thinking can be found in work on film through-out this century (e.g. Munsterberg 1970). But cognitivism as a distinctive and self-conscious research program took shape in the 1980s.[1] It has been gaining impetus since then and has recently been brought to bear on topics well beyond what is sometimes thought to be its natural domain: classical Hollywood narrative and the European/Japanese "art cinema." We now have cognitivist studies, at least of a preliminary kind, of the avant-garde (Carroll 1981/2; Peterson 1996), the documentary (Carroll 1996c; Currie 1999), film music (J. Smith 1999), the woman's film (Leibowitz 1996), horror (Carroll 1990; Freeland 1996), mass art generally (Carroll 1998), and industry studies focussing on corporate and global marketing aspects (Vasey 1997). A series of recent and forthcoming books and essay collections showcase the multiple strengths of the cognitive program, while offering important criticisms of other, more institutionally established views (Carroll 1988; Bordwell, 1989b; Bordwell and Carroll 1996; Allen and Smith 1997; Plantinga and Smith 1999). Yet cognitivism remains at some distance from the center of the film/screen studies enterprise, often dismissed or ignored, sometimes castigated for a supposed adherence to positivism and hence for a betrayal of the new, radical insights of those approaches to film that have emerged in the wake of structuralism.

2   The Content of Cognitivism

What, then, is the claim of cognitivism? Several things stand in the way of a sharp characterization, despite the cognitivist's commitment to clarity of exposition and argument. First, there are few, if any, specific doctrines with which all or most people who regard themselves as cognitivists would agree – one sign that cognitivism is a program rather than a specific theory. Second, there is a strand in cognitivist thought that is chary of system-building, opting instead for an eclectic mix of theories and models determined by the purpose in hand (see the "Introduction" to Bordwell and Carroll 1996).

But we shall get nowhere without at least a rough characterization, and the following corresponds to at least a central theme of cognitivist thought. It comes in two parts. It is important to see that both parts are assertions about where it is necessary to start one's inquiries, rather than putatively exceptionless generalizations; they are, in other words, heuristic rules. The first part says that our response to film is primarily to be seen as a rationally motivated and informed attempt to make sense of the work at each of the levels it presents: sensory stimulus in light and sound, narrative, and object charged with higher-order meanings and expression. Second, the cognitive and perceptual resources we deploy in this project of making sense of film are, to a significant degree, those that we deploy in the project of making sense of the real world. Thus there is a strong realist tendency in cognitivism – a tendency to emphasize ways in which our experience of cinematic images and cinematic narrative resemble our experiences of seeing and comprehending events and processes in reality. Thus characterized, cognitivism is capable of being embodied in various more specific and more tightly knit bodies of propositions, some of them mutually contradictory.

The leading idea suggests a method as well as a doctrine: in seeking to understand our responses to film, apply the best available theories of perception, information-processing, hypothesis-building, and interpretation. Thus cognitivism in film theory leans toward cognitive science, and toward the kind of philosophy that is its natural ally – a philosophy that is science-oriented, committed to the power of rigorous argument, and focussed on particular problems rather than on building a grand historical synthesis.

3   Cognitivism as Criticism

In doctrine, method, and style, cognitivism stands in sharp contrast to the program that has been its main rival: this program combines ideas from Marxist theories of ideology, psychoanalytic theories of dream, fantasy, and voyeurism, and semiotic theories of signification. It has been for some time sufficiently dominant within the world of film-theory writing and teaching, as well as within the institutions of job placement, tenure, and promotion, to be called "the orthodox view." Its approach is political and often polemical, especially in its treatment of what it conceives of as standard tropes of narrative representation. Thus it has been argued by the feminist theorists who represent one important line of thought within the orthodox view that much or even all filmmaking emanating from or influenced by Hollywood privileges an essentially male perspective, both in the literal sense of a point of view and in the more extended sense of an outlook on the world – the world of the fiction, and also the social world the viewer inhabits.

While acknowledging the tremendous economic and ideological power of movies and their capacity to reinforce, if not to impose, systems of value through the artifice of representation, cognitivists have generally rejected the methods and doctrines of the orthodox program. Thus the psychologist of film perception Virginia Brooks described the semiotic work of Christian Metz as "devoid of any experimental content or even any suggestions as to how decisions might be reached as to the rightness or wrongness of its assertions" (1984: 118).[2] Cognitivists expect that claims about how people respond to and are affected by movies would be treated as matters to be investigated by observation and experiment, and to be formulated within the context of psychological theories judged the best available by those best able to make those judgments. But orthodox theorists show little interest in experimental work in this area and appeal to psychological theories (such as Lacan's version of psychoanalysis) that are rarely given serious consideration by academic psychologists.[3] In recent years there has been an explosive growth in our understanding of the psychological processes underlying the child's development of both language and comprehension of self and other.[4] While no body of data–cum–theory is inviolable, cognitivists hold that this material – often deriving from large-scale and statistically sophisticated studies – should at least be taken into account by those film theorists who claim, for example, that a sense of self is intimately linked to the development of language, or who explain the drive to filmic horror in terms of infantile male helplessness.[5]

4 Cognitivism, Deep Psychology, and Folk Psychology

While cognitivists have occasionally spoken as if their hostility to psychoanalytic approaches to cinema is definitive of their position, this is not really so. For a start, cognitivism and psychoanalysis are not strictly at odds. Someone convinced of the basic soundness of a cognitive approach to human psychology might hold, for example, that some version of psychoanalysis has an important role to play in explaining irrationality (Gardner 1993). Presumably we are as capable of responding irrationally to cinema as to anything else, so there is little reason a priori to exclude psychoanalysis as a potential tool for understanding our response to cinema. The most a cognitivist need hold is that psychoanalysis is

107

not the central or, *a fortiori*, the exclusive means by which we understand the psychology of film.

Also, cognitivists do not regard it as signifying progress if, as happens from time to time, theorists abandon psychoanalytic models for some *other* large-scale psychodynamic theory with similar features: neglect of systematic empirical testing, heavy reliance on metaphor, analogy and other rhetorical devices, a technical but not clearly defined terminology, etc.[6] The cognitivist's fundamental objection is to a certain kind of theorizing, of which psychoanalysis-applied-to-cinema is just one example. But what then would they put in its place? As we shall see, cognitivists have made use of theories and results in the more academically mainstream areas of psychology, particularly studies of perception and cognition. But a point that seems to underlie a good deal of cognitivist work is this: it is a mistake to think that we can speak and write productively about the experience of film only by appealing to a "deep" psychological theory, that is, one which postulates states, processes, and mechanisms not acknowledged by our quotidian psychological knowledge – the "folk psychology" we unreflectively use every day in order to predict and explain the behavior of others and perhaps of ourselves. Much of the revolt against traditional humanistic studies of the arts has been based on a rejection of that tradition's casual assumption of a community of values, concerns, and interests – indeed of a whole conception of human flourishing – which many contemporary scholars reject as unsystematic, subjective, and deriving from the unacknowledged hegemony of a certain class, race, and sex. The "common-sense" view of human beings having been unmasked as the insidious creature of interest, an alternative had to be found: thus the appeal of psychoanalysis and similar constructions.

All this, the cognitivist might say, is a bad mistake. Folk psychology is, in fact, a subtle and successful instrument for helping us make sense of the community of minds in which we find ourselves immersed.[7] We employ it so often, with such facility and success, that it can be surprising to learn that one is using "knowledge of other minds." While a cognitive film theorist's official position is that we should use the best available psychological theory, her strong and well-founded impression may be that folk psychology fits that description very well.

Now a commitment to the explanatory power of folk psychology is not the same as a casual acceptance of everything you, I, or anyone else happens unreflectively to say or think about the mind, still less an acceptance of one group's articulation of the folk theory. Folk psychology must be regimented, refined, and indeed corrected by more academic constructions, so long as the supplements show signs of explanatory fecundity. The point is that it is not necessary to jettison the concepts, terminology, and principles of our folk-theoretic wisdom in favor of a radical, more scientific-sounding, but probably less reliable "depth psychology" in order to say illuminating things about the appeal of images, the lure of narrative, the fascinations of horror, the emotional power of melodrama, and a range of other matters that engage the film theorist.

5   Cognitivism and Perceptual Psychology

As well as rejecting the orthodox theorist's commitment to depth psychology, cognitivists have questioned the semiotic assumption that film can be understood as, or in any interesting way akin to, a language, arguing that there is a fundamental difference between the ways in which words and sentences on the one hand, and images on the other are processed (Carroll, 1988; Currie 1995a: ch. 4). While studies in the perceptual psychology of film-viewing do not seem to have been explicitly directed at this issue, some work here (see Hochberg and Brooks 1978, 1996) has tended to confirm this view by showing that the visual processing and interpretation of cinematic images is done in much the same way as the visual processing of objects in the real world. For example, the cues that indicate to us such things as shape, object identity, depth, relative size, the occlusion of one object by another when we look at objects in the real world are also the cues we use to determine those features of what is represented in a cinematic image.[8] This is hard to reconcile with the view that there is some interesting affinity between cinematic images and signs in a conventional language; one thing we can be fairly sure of with respect to our linguistic competence in this post-Piagetian age is that it is not a function of our perceptual skills or experience. Nor is it plausible to maintain that the connections between cinematic images are substantially a matter of rules, as are the connections between the elements within a natural language like English or Mandarin. Contemporary linguistic theory is by and large committed to the view that such languages need to be described in terms of rules which determine the meaning of a combination of signs as a function of the meanings of the components. While a few kinds of shot-combination in cinema have acquired the status of recurrent and familiar patterns (e.g. point-of-view editing),[9] these in no sense constitute or even approach the status of meaning-determining rules: no combination of shots, however unorthodox, is strictly meaningless, there are no "basic" or word-like elements of meaning from which filmic meanings can be built, and one does not need exposure to a large or even a modest body of shot-combinations before one can follow a conventional cinematic narrative. All this contrasts sharply with the linguistic case. Of course most films employ language in the ordinary sense, as when the characters speak or the intertitles announce, but the "language of film" thesis was supposed to be something more exciting than the platitude that you have to be competent with English to understand the utterances of English characters: it was the claim that there is a specifically cinematic language or "sign system," and this is a claim unsupported by the psychology of language and of perception.

But if understanding cinematic images is not assimilable to understanding language, how is it done? The central puzzle of cinematic perception is basically the same as that of pictorial perception in general: how is it that a flat, colored surface presents to us the appearance of three-dimensional objects and their relations? The fact that film images are moving pictures merely adds further relations, for it seems that cinematic pictures present to us the appearance of change as well as shape, color, relative position, and other static properties of objects we are familiar with from painting and drawing. Now a particularly thoroughgoing cognitivism might insist that the answer to this problem must invoke mental activity that is, exactly, cognitive: that is, involving processes defined over contentful states (beliefs, for example) and which can be seen as rationally sensitive to those contents (Pylyshyn 1981: 159). That way we arrive at the picture of the viewer struggling to make rational sense of a "deviant" input and doing so by structuring it in accordance with beliefs and presuppositions. But if pictorial perception is a matter of interpretation, we might well expect considerable interpersonal and especially intercultural variation in how and whether pictures are understood.

Such views have had distinguished supporters (Goodman 1976) but have come under heavy fire from three directions: anthropological studies, which has dealt unkindly with the notion that non-Western people have to "learn" to comprehend photographs and other perspectival representations (Messaris 1994); philosophical arguments in favor of the natural interpretability of pictures (Schier 1986); theories of perception, which have emphasized the extent to which the workings of vision are insulated from the subject's general beliefs (Marr 1982). On current evidence the more reasonable view would seem to be that the human visual system is built to respond quickly and decisively to stimuli and therefore operates by means of mechanisms that do not depend on calling up general knowledge. Such a system is naturally prone to error: the visual stimuli which a horse will cause can be approximated by a mule, a stuffed horse, a picture of a horse – and a cinematic image of one (Currie 1995a: ch. 3).

It is therefore natural to think that cinematic and other pictures work by means of illusion, and indeed it has been suggested that illusions such as the "Ames room" provide a model for cinematic perception.[10] But in a crucial respect we seem to be dealing with very different phenomena. In the case of the Ames room (or the simpler Muller–Lyer illusion, whereby lines of equal length can be made to look unequal by the addition of differently directed arrowheads), the content of one's perceptual experience contradicts reality and indeed what one believes about reality. The people in the room are of roughly equal size, and I know this to be the case, yet my visual experience when looking through the peephole is stubbornly of one person much larger than the other. And try as I may, I cannot reconcile my knowledge that the lines in the Muller–Lyer illusion are of the same length with their appearance of distinctness (Fodor 1983). It is this tension between appearance and reality which entitles us to say that we have here cases of perceptual illusion. By contrast, the content of even an engrossed experience of watching cinematic images does not in the same way contradict belief: one is not constantly struggling to avoid believing that acts of violence and passion are being perpetrated right in front of one, however intensely one responds to them at the level of the fictional.

110

If we are going to speak of illusions in this context, it will be useful to distinguish two kinds of illusion here: personal and sub-personal. The Ames-room illusion is a personal one: *I* am subject to the illusion, and the illusory experience, being one I have, conflicts with my beliefs. In the case of film-viewing, it seems better to say that it is a part of my visual object-recognition system that is subject to an illusion, registering as output "there is a horse directly ahead" when I see an image of a horse; but *my* perceptual experience, only partially determined by that output, is one of there being a cinematic image of a horse, and that experience does not have an illusory content.[11]

6 Cognitivism and Meaning

Studies of film-viewing from the point of view of perceptual psychology have so far had a limited impact on our understanding of how films, considered as works of cinematic narrative rather than merely cinematic presentations of objects and scenes, are responded to. Indeed, one advocate of cognitive film theory has said that the role of psychological studies of film-viewing is limited to the discovery of "causal generalization," leaving to film theory proper the discovery of "systems of signification," thereby suggesting that psychology cannot help us to uncover cinematic meaning (Carroll 1981/2).[12] One argument for this would appeal to the well-known philosopher's distinction between the world of science and the world of appearances (Sellars 1956): meanings are part of the world as it appears to us; a causal–scientific story about how cinematic images are processed can tell us no more about what they mean for us than a causal story about light waves and spectral reflectance properties can tell us about how red things look to us.

We should agree that we cannot decide specific questions about the meanings of particular narratives by carrying out experiments, for the meaning that the work makes available to us has to be available through the ordinary process of attentive watching. But there is much that is located within the viewer which is relevant to understanding the signification of the work, and here experiments might give us more than mere causal generalizations. We might, for example, follow this line of thought: a major issue to be sorted out before we can understand the meaning of a cinematic narrative is the nature of the viewer's imagined relation to that narrative. It is frequently assumed, for example, that the viewer imagines himself to be located within the space of the action, moving as the camera moves. But is this standardly the case? I have argued that such imaginings would be a cause of distraction from the narrative and would sometimes collide with the project of imagining the events of the story. How, for instance, would I reconcile my own imagined presence within the room of dismally crated objects at the end of *Citizen Kane* and my own imagined looking at the objects within that room, including the "rosebud" sledge, with imagining – what the narrative surely requires me to imagine – that no one sees this key to the mystery (Currie 1995a: ch. 5)?

111

Here we surely have a substantive general issue about narrative meaning that can be resolved only by empirical psychology, possibly, at least in principle, in the following way. We identify, using the most refined techniques of brain-imaging, those brain areas implicated in imagined movement, and we see whether those areas are activated by viewing film scenes that, on independent grounds, we regard as those most apt to induce imaginings as of movement. Subject of course to the normal doubts that attend the interpretation of psychological experiments, the outcome would be strong evidence either for or against the hypothesis of imagined movement. And our decision to accept or to reject that hypothesis will have profound implications for the kinds of meaning we are prepared to attribute to films. For we shall think one way about the meaning of a film if we suppose the viewer to be an imagined participant in its action, and another way if we don't.

7 Cognitivism and Constructivism

To say this is, of course, to say that filmic meaning must be in some way dependent on the ways in which an audience is apt to respond to it and cannot be considered as something intrinsic to the work. This raises the question: to what extent is cinematic meaning a construction of the viewer rather than something the viewer finds in the work? David Bordwell, a founder of cognitivism, has said that audiences construct meaning (1989b). His arguments are very much in the spirit of a Gombrichian thesis of the "beholder's share" and stand in opposition to the orthodox view, which, with obvious Marxist antecedents, tends to see the viewer as a passive receiver of signification in need of the semiotician's skillful analysis of the film's (probably sinister) message. For Bordwell, everyone, from the unreflective casual movie-watcher to the self-conscious, professional interpreter whose work we read in academic journals, is a constructor of meaning. Thus the contrast between the passive viewer and the penetrating critic/theorist, able to see the truth about meaning, dissipates.

On reflection, Bordwell's constructivism seems poorly motivated. There need be no more (or less) mental activity involved in constructing meaning than in decoding or interpreting it. From the point of view of stressing mental activity, there is nothing to choose between saying that the viewer creates meaning and saying that she finds it, for of course found meaning is not simply stumbled across. In the philosophy of mathematics there is a question about whether numbers are human constructs or pre-existent entities that we discover. But this debate has no implications for whether we should think of mathematicians as active or passive; on both views the mathematician's art is one of activity, and to think of the numbers as created by thought is not to attribute greater efforts to the thinker.

So the inference "cognition implies activity implies construction" will not do. Nor will it do to observe that the meaning of a narrative depends, in some sense, on the responses to it of the audience – a point I emphasized earlier. The audience-dependent nature of meaning in narrative is consistent with thinking of that meaning as residing in the narrative, and not in us, just as the observer-dependent nature of color – the way the color of a thing can be specified only in relation to a community of observers who normally see it as having a certain color – is consistent with thinking that colors reside in the objects themselves, and that perceiving color is the way we have of finding out what colors things have.

What would convince us that color is constructed rather than discovered? A relevant factor is consensus, across persons and times. Most of us, most of the time, agree with each other and with our earlier selves about the colors of things, and where we disagree we can usually find independently verifiable causes that constitute disturbance. If we could not, the colors might seem to be subjective constructions, projected onto the world (as moral values seem to be, at least according to some philosophers).

If we give strong weight to consensus or the lack of it, the question of whether the meaning of a filmic narrative is constructed or found can have no *general* answer. The right thing to say seems to be that some aspects of the work's meaning command a broad consensus and some do not. So the conclusion would be that while, for example, the thought that Ethan Edwards (in Ford's *The Searchers*) is a civil-war veteran is itself part of the work and therefore discovered by the audience, who generally agree about this feature of the narrative, some particular – and disputed – view about his motives for pursuing his search might fairly be called a construct.

But why should consensus decide the issue as between discovery and construction? There is after all no consensus in some areas of science, but we ought not to conclude that in such areas discovery is off the agenda. In science, it makes sense to think of "the world out there" holding an answer to our questions, even when there is nothing we can do to determine what the answer is.[13] With fiction, on the other hand, such a picture makes no sense (that would be too extreme a realism, even for a cognitivist). There is no real Ethan Edwards whose mental states determine the truth about his motives. If, with all the relevant evidence in, we can still rationally disagree about Ethan's motives, those motives are indeterminate. That's why lack of consensus, as long as it represents irresolvable disagreement, is grounds for thinking that we are in the business of constructing filmic meanings rather than finding them (Currie 1993).

To the degree that one is a constructivist about narrative meaning, one is also an anti-realist about it, in the sense that one rejects the idea of a narrative meaning "really there" to be discovered. But there are different senses of realism, and one can be a constructivist *and* a realist (as Bordwell is) on the important issue of the existence and significance of connections between the narrative and the real world. I began by noting that cognitivists have a prejudice in favor of a realism that says we make sense of films in substantially the same ways as we make sense of the real world. We have seen this exemplified in the arguments about the perceptual realism of cinematic images. This is not to say that viewers mistake the film's narrative for a "slice of life" or that there are no substantial differences between the experience of film and of reality. But cognitivists hold that when we understand, interpret, and respond to filmic narratives we are bringing to them a good deal of the knowledge and skills we deploy to understand, interpret, and respond to people and events in the real world. Thus Bordwell argues that we simply could not make sense of fictional narratives if we did not bring to them something like a default assumption that the characters have motives and feelings of basically the same kinds as real people do, that physical and social processes operate in much the same way in the world of the fiction as they do in reality (1989b).[14] Like the guiding principles of cognitivism, this is a default assumption and not an iron rule, so there are many occasions where fictions deviate from the "background conditions" of reality; the point is that the default assumptions are abandoned only when there is positive evidence that they should be.

So the cognitivist's realism demands of her that she develop theories of our emotional and other responses to fictions and their characters based on the best psychological theories of our responses to real people. Let us now see how the cognitivist might do this.

8   Cognitivism and Emotion

As the discussion of theories of perception indicated, the cognitivist is always in danger of being too much a cognitivist, believing that every aspect of our response to film is an act of interpretation. Thus Schacter and Singer's "attribution theory of emotions" has appealed to some cognitivists because it says that emotions are the product of our attempt to make sense of our bodily reactions to stimuli (Schacter and Singer 1962, cited in Brooks 1984). But the data produced by Schacter and Singer simply do not support the idea that all or even most emotions result from an act of self-interpretation; many emotions are more than simply feelings or their bodily correlates and involve thoughts of various kinds. Shame, for example, is not separable from the thought that one has done wrong.[15] And since such a thought is typically a purely reflexive response to a situation, an emotion can be cognitive in this sense without being something the subject constructs. At least in the case of shame and like emotions, the bodily feeling results from the thought, not the other way around. Also, there seems to be a significant and highly noncognitive connection between certain emotions and the perception of facial expression. Faces that express an emotion can, to a certain extent, transmit that emotion to the viewer – an important facet of the earliest interactions between infants and caregivers. Thus cinematic images share with other pictorial media an important capacity to transmit emotions via cognitively quite primitive mechanisms.[16] And film's capacity to do this is heightened by its use of moving images: the visual experience of a changing facial expression seems to be more affecting than that of a static one.

While cognitive theorists have acknowledged these probably "hard-wired" aspects of the emotional transaction between film and viewer, they have devoted greater attention to a more sophisticated kind of emotion transmission which may be important for understanding film. *Empathy* is a notion first systematically developed by the English moral philosophers of the eighteenth century and revived by philosophers of history and the social sciences early this century.[17] The basic idea is that we are capable of putting ourselves imaginatively in the position of another, coming thereby to feel and also to think as the other does, and that this act of imaginative projection can be the basis of our prediction or explanation of the other's behavior. Orthodox theorists of cinema often speak of a process of "identification," which they believe to be central to the experience of film, and cognitivists have complained that this notion, taken literally, is too blunt an instrument to explain cinematic experience: wholesale identification with a character is surely a rare thing. If, on the other hand, "identification" is a theorist's term of art, its justification and domain of application are unclear and anyway derive from theories the cognitivist is unlikely to accept. However, at least part of what people have intended to convey by means of identification may be reconstructible within a theory of empathy, since empathy is, of its nature, a kind of partial identification (Smith 1995). And recent developments in cognitive science suggest that empathy is itself a notion capable of being made more precise and therefore subject to the kind of empirical investigation cognitivists look for. "Simulation theory" offers a hypothesis about the mental mechanism underlying empathy and suggests that there may be identifiable pathologies that derive from a malfunction of the mechanism (Gordon 1986; Currie 1996).

Empathy / simulation has the potential to play two distinct roles in explaining our engagement with the fiction film. First of all, if we think of the film as an elaborate prop in a game of make-believe (Walton 1990) and the viewer as a game-player who engages imaginatively with that prop, the viewer would seem naturally to be describable as one who projects himself imaginatively into the situation of one who is learning facts about the acts and events the fiction describes (Currie 1995a: ch. 6). Second, our responses to the characters and events of the film (and here I include emotional responses but also judgments, unemotional desires, etc.) may be, to some extent, explicable as the result of our coming to think, to desire, and to feel as the characters do themselves (Neill 1996). But cognitivists are by no means united in their enthusiasm for empathy/ simulation, and cognitive theories of horror, suspense, and other genres have been elaborated without substantial appeal to the notion (Carroll 1990, 1996e).

Empathy/simulation theory is also well placed to validate the cognitivist's insistence on one kind of realism in cinema: that to some extent we respond to the cinema as we do to reality. For simulation postulates a mechanism of empathetic response in order to explain, exactly, our capacity to cope with real people, their thoughts, feelings, and behavior; that mechanism can then be pressed into service to explain our response to the fictions we see on screen. But simulation theory challenges, at least in part, an assumption made by the most influential cognitivist thinker, David Bordwell: that our response to film is mediated by "schemata," or bodies of often unarticulated knowledge and belief that we can bring to bear on particular real-world situations. Thus it is crucial to the simulation theory that my understanding, via empathetic contact, of your decisions, feelings, and other psychological responses is not a matter of my inferring those responses from a tacit and perhaps rudimentary theory of human psychology. Rather, it is a matter of my modeling those responses within my own mind, a process which can take place independently of whether I know anything about how the process works. Simulation/empathy does not suggest that all knowledge or belief is irrelevant to the cinematic experience, but it does suggest that we might get by with less appeal to specifically psychological knowledge than we would otherwise think.

9   Fictional and Nonfictional Cinema

Orthodox theorists are sometimes skeptical of the distinction between the fiction and the nonfiction film, partly on the grounds that all films embody a subjective point of view. Cognitivists have protested that the fiction/nonfiction divide is neither the same as nor a function of the subjective/objective distinction and that the highly subjective vision of a Leni Riefenstahl or a Michael Moore can give rise to something describable as documentary and distinguishable from fictions like *The Great Dictator* or *Blue Collar*. How?

Before answering that question, the cognitivist might want to set some ground rules for the debate. She might reject a characterization of the debate as one concerning whether there is, after all, such a thing as the documentary, claiming instead that it is sensible simply to presuppose this. The cognitivist's enterprise would then be to show where the difference between documentary and non-documentary lies, and failure to achieve that goal would not count as reason for thinking that there is, after all, no such thing as documentary. After all, philosophers cannot agree on what precisely is the difference between right and wrong, error and opinion, and a host of other traditional contrasts. But few (at least among those inclined to cognitivism) would want to conclude from this that there are no such contrasts, and the cognitivist may well take it to be part of the mistake of "grand theory" to suppose that the onus is on those who want to defend a common-sense distinction like that between documentary and non-documentary. She may also remind us that the difference between documentary and nondocumentary can be vague or a matter of degree, without ceasing to be a real difference; not every man is bald, despite the fact that there is no minimum number of hairs which constitutes hirsuteness.

So far I have moved without qualification between the nonfiction/fiction divide and the documentary/nondocumentary divide. And indeed some theorists do take the project of analyzing documentary to be tantamount to the construction of a theory of the nonfiction film. Thus Noël Carroll has focussed on what he calls the film of "presumptive assertion," within which category would fall dramatic reconstructions as well as documentaries in the narrower sense. Carroll's analysis suggests that films of presumptive assertion form a natural and coherent category within which one could distinguish between documentaries proper and other nonfiction films in an artificial way (Carroll 1996c). On the other hand one might argue for a quite distinctive characterization of the documentary, as does Currie, who appeals to the idea of a *cinematic trace*. A photographic film is a trace of its subject, and that is true whether we are speaking of the sober documentary or the wildest fantasy: shots from *Drifters* are traces of the fishing boats that reflected light into the camera when the film was exposed, and shots from *Bringing up Baby* are traces of Cary Grant and Katherine Hepburn. Simplifying somewhat, we can then say that *Drifters* is a documentary because the maker's primary intention was to get an audience to form beliefs about the things and events of which the shots they see are traces. But with *Bringing up Baby* it is different: the intention primary to the project of the fiction film is to get the audience to have imaginings (rather than beliefs) concerning events other than those of which the shots they see are traces, in this case events involving a hapless paleontologist, a young woman with Connecticut connections, and a lost bone (Currie 1999).

10   The Limits of Cognitivism

Cognitivism is too recent a theory to be judged with much confidence; its most striking success is probably the negative one of having inspired important criticism of the orthodox view. But cognitivism as a program in film theory cannot be given credit simply for the weakness of its rivals. There has been little illuminating connection made so far between the analysis of film style, narrative, and genre and the researches of cognitive and perceptual psychologists. Cognitive work on film and emotion is just beginning; analyses of the documentary and nonfiction films are barely announced.

Cognitivists will need to sort out some fairly basic issues for themselves, primarily what their commitment to the label "cognitive" entails for their view of psychological processes and mechanisms. Which of these are to be understood as interpretive (as is fairly obviously the case with acts of narrative reconstruction) and which automatic and brute-causal (as may be the case with much visual processing and possibly also with some acts of empathetic contact)? And what exactly is it to be a *cognitivist* if you recognize a significant contribution to filmic experience from processes of the latter kind? At a more parochial level, cognitivists ought to decide where they stand on the specific doctrines that have shaped cognitivism more or less through an accident of history. Without detracting from the achievement of David Bordwell in having done so much to set the cognitivist program in motion, it needs to be remembered that many of his specific views are not constitutive of that program. His anti-intentionalism, his constructivism about interpretation, and his enthusiasm for notions of "schemata" and "semantic field" are all, I believe, logically detachable from the basic cognitivist program and may indeed be questioned from within that program.

As I have characterized it, cognitivism is a realist position, insofar as it emphasizes the similarities between our responses to film and to events and processes in the real world. But of course no cognitivist supposes that film and reality are interchangeable; film is not just "more reality," and if it were it would be hard to see what its interest for us could be. Again influenced by Gombrich, cognitivists are likely to assert that the aesthetic and other kinds of interest that film has for us are determined by the boundaries between its realism and unrealism, and especially by attempts to shift, or to highlight, or to comment on those boundaries. As with much else, there is no one theory of the mechanisms involved here to which a cognitivist must assent. But we do need better-developed theories of the unrealism of film than we currently possess.

But the most significant challenge ahead for cognitivists must surely be in the area of normative issues. What will they say about issues of value generally? Much recent film theory has tended to combine an official relativism about the value, particularly the aesthetic value, of films with a clear preference in practice for films that can be seen in some way to undermine conventional social assumptions, particularly if they combine this with anti-classical stylistic and generic moves. Cognitivists are more likely to want a positive theory of value and a practice of distinguishing judgments about the aesthetic or more generally artistic value of filmic works from their moral values (though this would not preclude the natural thought that moral value can, in complex ways, contribute to or detract from aesthetic value). Cognitivists are also more likely to be hospitable to the idea of a canon than are their orthodox colleagues, though they may want to tailor that notion to the specific needs of an industrialized mass art. It is currently unclear how such a theory of value will relate to the doctrines of cognitive and perceptual processing espoused by cognitivists.

Some cognitivists will see the success or failure of their program ultimately in terms of the illumination it brings to particular films. For cognitivists regard themselves as the servants rather than the masters of the works they study, complaining of a tendency, which they claim to detect in orthodox theorists, to use particular works to validate their own world-view, even at the cost of distorting and even falsifying those works. Cognitivists have neither the resources nor the inclination to closely constrain criticism by theory; certainly they will not wish to relive the Bazinian nightmare of equivocation, inferring from the doctrine of filmic realism to the exhortation "make more realistic films." Perhaps their victory will be a resurgence of imaginative criticism not tightly confined by a commitment to a view about what film in general does or should mean.

Notes

1   Probably the single most important work of this period was Bordwell, *Making Meaning* (1989b). But this cannot be regarded as a "founding document"; as I shall

suggest below, there is too much in it logically separable from the cognitivist's project.

2 The comment was directed explicitly against Metz's *Film and Language* (1974), but would apply as well to later writing.

3 For criticisms of psychoanalytic theories of spectatorship along these lines, see Prince 1996, as well as the comprehensive attack on the orthodox program in Carroll 1988.

4 For accessible introductions to this material see e.g. Wellman 1990, Baron-Cohen et al. 1993, and Gopnik and Meltzoff 1997.

5 See e.g. Carroll 1996a.

6 Most cognitivists would regard the work of Derrida and of Deleuze as falling into this category.

7 The assumption here of a community of minds is the relatively weak assumption that, as a matter of fact, we are good at knowing what other people think, want, and decide in a broad range of day-to-day settings. (Conversational success supports this assumption; mundane talk exchange would be impossible if we were not able to presuppose a shared background of knowledge, interest, and intended direction.) It is not the assumption that the minds of others are "wholly transparent" to us, which they clearly are not.

8 Hochberg and Brooks also note that we perceive cinematic motion and real-world motion in the same way (which is somewhat surprising, given that they are such different phenomena): "A continuous motion in the world is, of course, captured by successive displaced images on film (or their video equivalent). For most events these displacements are small, and within the range of the low-level sensory receptors of the visual system; these respond identically to the small displacements on the screen and to the differences provided from one moment to the next by smooth physical motion in the world" (1996: 368–9).

9 For a cognitivist account of point-of-view editing which treats the device not as a "code" but as a rational response to certain natural human perceptual tendencies, see Carroll 1996b. See also Bordwell 1996.

10 See e.g. Anderson and Anderson 1996. At this point cognitivist thinking converges with the "illusionistic" strand in orthodox theory.

11 This issue is briefly touched on in the debate between Dom Lopes and Gregory Currie, in Currie 1998.

12 But he more recently suggests that this is "too conservative" (1996d: 159).

13 At least, cognitivist film theorists will be liable to see science in this way, even if students of cultural phenomena with different theoretical commitments may think of science as "all a matter of social construction."

14 This principle of narrative has a parallel in a principle of perception, Helmholtz's Likelihood Principle: "We perceive that which would in our normal life most likely have produced the effective sensory stimulation we have received" (see Hochberg and Brooks 1996: 373).

15 Ed Tan, in some ways an advocate of cognitivism, seems to be committed to the view that we can decide whether a state is genuinely one of fear by measuring responses like breathing rate, and disregard the accompanying thought contents (see Tan 1996, and the discussion at pp. 230–2 of Carroll 1990).

16 See e.g. Plantinga 1999 for a discussion of the ways that film exploits this mechanism and for references to the psychological literature. The expression and recogni-

tion of emotion is also, to a considerable extent, invariant across cultures (see e.g. Ekman 1982; Izard 1977; see also Hatfield et al. 1994).

17 "Empathy" or "Einfuhlung" is most directly associated with the psychological–aesthetic theories of the late nineteenth-century writer Theodor Lipps, whose work is now largely forgotten but has clear connections to the moral theories of Adam Smith and David Hume, and to the theory of historical explanation of R. G. Collingwood.

References

Allen, Richard, and Murray Smith, eds. 1997. *Film Theory and Philosophy*. Oxford: Clarendon Press.

Anderson, Joseph, and Barbara Anderson. 1996. "The Case for an Ecological Meta-theory." In Bordwell and Carroll 1996.

Baron-Cohen, Simon, Helen Tager-Flusberg, and Donald Cohen, eds. 1993. *Understanding Other Minds*. Oxford: Oxford University Press.

Bordwell, David. 1985. *Narration in the Fiction Film*. Madison: University of Wisconsin Press.

——. 1989a. "A Case for Cognitivism." *Iris* 9: 11–41.

——. 1989b. *Making Meaning: Inference and Rhetoric in the Interpretation of Cinema*. Cambridge: Harvard University Press.

——. 1996. "Convention, Construction, and Cinematic Vision." In Bordwell and Carroll 1996.

——, and Noël Carroll, eds. 1996. *Post-Theory*. Madison: University of Wisconsin Press.

Brooks, Virginia. 1984. "Film, Perception and Cognitive Psychology." *Millennium Film Journal* 14: 105–26.

Carroll, Noël. 1981/2. "Causation, the Ampliation of Movement and Avant-Garde Film." *Millennium Film Journal* 10/11: 61–82. Reprinted in Carroll 1996d.

——. 1985. "The Power of Movies." *Daedalus*: 79–103.

——. 1988. *Mystifying Movies: Fads and Fallacies in Contemporary Film Theory*. New York: Columbia University Press.

——. 1990. *The Philosophy of Horror: Or Paradoxes of the Heart*. New York and London: Routledge.

——. 1996a. "Cracks in the Acoustic Mirror." In Carroll 1996d.

——. 1996b. "Film, Attention, and Communication." In *The Great Ideas of Today*. Chicago. Encyclopedia Britannica.

——. 1996c. "Nonfiction Film and Postmodern Skepticism." In Bordwell and Carroll 1996.

——. 1996d. *Theorizing the Moving Image*. Cambridge: Cambridge University Press.

——. 1996e. "The Paradox of Suspense." In *Suspense*. Ed. P. Vorderer, H. Wuff, and M. Friedrichsen. Mahwah: Lawrence Erlbaum.

——. 1998. *A Theory of Mass Art*. New York: Oxford University Press.

——. 1999. "Film, Emotion and Genre." In Plantinga and Smith 1999.

Currie, Gregory. 1993. "Objectivity and Interpretation." *Mind* 102: 413–28.

———. 1995a. *Image and Mind: Film, Philosophy and Cognitive Science*. New York: Cambridge University Press.

———. 1995b. "Imagination and Simulation: Aesthetics Meets Cognitive Science." In *Mental Simulation*. Ed. Martin Davies and Tony Stone. Oxford: Blackwell.

———. 1996. "Theory-Theory, Simulation Theory and the Evidence from Autism." In *Theories of Theories of Mind*. Ed. Peter Carruthers and Peter K. Smith. New York: Cambridge University Press.

———. 1998. "Reply to My Critics." *Philosophical Studies* 89: 355–66.

———. 1999. "Traces of the Real: Documentary and the Content of Photographs." *Journal of Aesthetics and Art Criticism* 57.

Ekman, Paul, ed. 1982. *Emotion and the Human Face*. Cambridge: Cambridge University Press.

Fodor, Jerry. 1983. *The Modularity of Mind*. Cambridge: MIT Press / Bradford Books.

Freeland, Cynthia. 1996. "Feminist Frameworks for Horror Films." In Bordwell and Carroll 1996.

Gardner, Sebastian. 1993. *Irrationality and the Philosophy of Psychoanalysis*. Cambridge and New York: Cambridge University Press.

Gaut, Berys. 1995. "Making Sense of Films: Neoformalism and its Limits." *Forum for Modern Language Studies* 31, 1: 8–23.

Goodman, Nelson. 1976. *Languages of Arts*, 2nd edn. Indianapolis: Hackett.

Gopnik, Alison, and Andrew Meltzoff. 1997. *Words, Thoughts and Theories*. Cambridge: MIT Press / Bradford Books.

Gordon, Robert. 1986. "Folk Psychology as Simulation." *Mind and Language* 1: 158–71.

Hatfield, Elaine, John Cacioppo, and Richard Rapson. 1994. *Emotional Contagion*. Cambridge: Cambridge University Press.

Hochberg, Julian, and Virginia Brooks. 1978. "The Perception of Motion Pictures." In *Handbook of Perception: Vol. 10, Perceptual Ecology*. Ed. Edward C. Carterette and Morton P. Friedman. New York: Academic Press.

———. 1996. "Movies in the Mind's Eye." In Bordwell and Carroll 1996.

Izard, C. E. 1977. *Human Emotions*. New York: Plenum Press.

Leibowitz, Florence. 1996. "Apt Feelings, or Why 'Women's Films' Aren't Trivial." In Bordwell and Carroll 1996.

Lopes, Domenic. 1997. "Imagination, Illusion and Experience in Film." *Philosophical Studies* 89: 343–53.

Marr, David. 1982. *Vision*. New York: W. H. Freeman.

Messaris, P. 1994. *Visual Literacy*. Boulder: Westview Press.

Metz, Christian. 1974. *Film and Language*. Trans. Michael Taylor. New York: Oxford University Press.

Munsterberg, Hugo. 1970 [1916]. *The Film: A Psychological Study* (an unaltered and unabridged republication of *The Photoplay: A Psychological Study*). New York: Dover Publications.

Neill, Alex. 1996. "Empathy and (Film) Fiction." In Bordwell and Carroll 1996.

Peterson, James. 1996. "Is a Cognitive Approach to the Avant-Garde Cinema Perverse?" In Bordwell and Carroll 1996.

Plantinga, Carl. 1996. "Motion Pictures and the Rhetoric of Nonfiction Film: Two Approaches." In Bordwell and Carroll 1996.

———. 1999. "Scene of Empathy and the Human Face on Film." In Plantinga and Smith 1999.

——, and Greg Smith, eds. 1999. *Passionate Views*. Baltimore: Johns Hopkins University Press.

Prince, Stephen. 1996. "Psychoanalytic Film Theory and the Problem of the Missing Spectator." In Bordwell and Carroll 1996.

Pylyshyn, Zenon. 1981. "The Imagery Debate: Analog Media vs Tacit Knowledge." In *Imagery*. Ed. N. Block. Cambridge: MIT Press.

Schacter, S., and J. Singer. 1962. "Cognitive, Social and Psychological Determinants of Emotional State." *Psychological Review* 69: 379–99.

Schier, Flint. 1986. *Deeper into Pictures*. Cambridge: Cambridge University Press.

Sellars, Wilfred. 1956. "Empiricism and the Philosophy of Mind." In *Minnesota Studies in the Philosophy of Science*, vol. 1. Ed. M. Scriven, P. Feyerabend, and G. Maxwell. Minneapolis: University of Minnesota Press.

Smith, Jeff. 1999. "Movie Music as Moving Music: Emotion, Cognition and the Film Score." In Plantinga and Smith 1999.

Smith, Murray. 1995. *Engaging Characters: Fiction, Emotion, and the Cinema*. Oxford: Clarendon Press.

Tan, Ed S. 1996. *Emotion and the Structure of Narrative Film*. Trans. Barbara Fasting. Mahwah: Lawrence Erlbaum.

Vasey, Ruth. 1997. *The World According to Hollywood, 1918–1939*. Exeter: University of Exeter Press.

Walton, Kendall. 1990. *Mimesis as Make Believe*. Cambridge: Harvard University Press.

Wellman, Henry. 1990. *The Child's Theory of Mind*. Cambridge: MIT Press.

CHAPTER EIGHT

Psychoanalytic Film Theory

Richard Allen

In this chapter I shall outline some of the main contours of psychoanalytic film theory in the Anglo-American context since the late 1960s. I shall begin with a number of methodological remarks. First, since a vast amount of words have been expended on the subject, my account will necessarily be selective. Second, since the field is so wide and varied, I have, where possible, focussed on the elucidation of key concepts, positions, and arguments that cut across the writings of different authors. Third, psychoanalytic film theory is a notoriously opaque discourse and often assumes a large amount of prior knowledge on the part of the vexed and taxed reader. In order to remain intelligible, I have employed the strategy of trying to reconstruct the arguments of psychoanalytic theorists in my own words. Fourth, the history of psychoanalytic film theory is one that often displays an arbitrary selection and deployment of psychoanalytic ideas and manifests a blurred or distorted self-understanding by film theorists of the status of the concepts they are using. This chapter seeks to diagnose some of the conceptual confusions and misunderstandings that are manifested in psychoanalytic film theory, as well as to plot a history of ideas. The result, I hope, is an account of psychoanalytic film theory that will provide impetus for reflection and reconsideration, rather than simply regurgitate a seemingly obscure and arguably moribund set of doctrines.

In the first section I shall sketch the reasons why psychoanalysis has occupied such a prominent place in thinking about cinema and lay out a series of distinctions that will serve as a framework for subsequent discussion. In section 2, I shall sketch in more detail the ways in which Freudian and Lacanian theories have been used to explain the affinities of cinema with the irrational and the nature of the spectator's identification with the cinematic image and with visual fictions. In section 3 I shall explore how, by using psychoanalysis to diagnose the hypnotic power of mass culture, cultural theorists in the Marxist tradition sought to explain the seemingly irrational allegiance of the masses to a system that perpetuated their own subordination, and how Freud's dream analysis became a model for decoding and thereby exposing the ideological character of specific films.

Psychoanalysis seemed to offer feminist theorists a way of understanding how film and kindred forms of representation have served to perpetuate gender imbalance and oppression. In section 4 I shall present some of the ways in which psychoanalysis has been used by feminist film theorists to argue this. In conclusion, I shall reflect more generally on the relationship between psychoanalytic theory and interpretation.

1   Psychoanalysis and Cinema: Some Preliminary Distinctions

Film theorists, critics, and commentators have been drawn to psychoanalytic ideas to explain cinema, because cinema seems to display a fundamental kinship with the irrational that psychoanalysis seeks to explain. This kinship between cinema and irrationality is suggested by two distinct aspects of the cinema: the distinctive visual properties of the medium, and the character and quality of mass cultural narratives. The relationship between the visual properties of film and irrationality has been pursued in two related but distinct ways. The first stresses the affinity of film to irrational thought and dream. The second explores the significance for human understanding of cinema's augmentation of perception; it emphasizes what and how the cinema allows us to see, and how this effects our self-understanding. The second kinship between cinema and the irrational has its roots in the goal of mass culture to mobilize the whole population in the consumption of pleasure. To this end, it has been argued, the cinema mobilizes the most primitive (and therefore least differentiated and most universal) desires of the spectator by telling stories of everyday romance that take on mythic proportions and by casting the human being, in the figure of the star, as a transcendent, god-like creature.

From his initial encounter with female hysterics in Charcot's clinic, Freud was interested in trying to understand and explain the phenomenon of irrational behavior. Freud hypothesized the existence of unconscious mental states of archaic infantile origin that motivated this behavior. They consist in powerful inchoate wishes that emerge in a person's life before they have the capacity to be conscious of them or to own them. These wishes center on the child's sexualized desire for its parent or parents (the Oedipus complex) and its prohibition which, Freud argued, the male child experienced in fantasy as the threat of castration at the hands of a punitive, all-powerful, internalized father figure (the super-ego). Successful negotiation of the Oedipus complex, issuing in self-individuation, is predicated on the repression of these wishes – they are barred from rational articulation – for they contain ideas that are intolerable for the newly formed ego to consciously entertain. Since little girls do not experience the threat of castration like little boys (they are already castrated) their individuation is less complete, and the mechanism of repression is less rigorously installed in their psychic life.

Repression explains how unconscious mental states exist, but how are these mental states sustained? Freud argued that unconscious mental states gain their effectivity in the life of the mind through the imagination in its capacity to evoke, to varying degrees, the force and significance of an event we have actually lived through, even though the event is merely represented to us in the imagination. The imagination thus provides a stage upon which the mind can represent to itself, in the form of fantasies, desires that are otherwise unrealizable. Dreams are the stage of the imagination that are perhaps most readily apprehensible. The narrative forms that fantasy adopts disguises the desire that animates it and, by disguising it, at once prevents it from being consciously entertained and simultaneously ensures that it continues to be directly, though unconsciously, experienced in the life of the mind. Under certain conditions fantasy may break through the fabric of reality and manifest itself in what might otherwise seem inexplicable human activity. Material that is ready to hand, especially the agent's own body, is mobilized as the stage upon which fantasy is acted out or projected, such as in hysteria.

The way psychoanalytic theory is applied to the cinema depends upon which aspect of the medium is being illuminated. Apparatus theories use psychoanalysis to illuminate the peculiar way that cinema seems to augment or transform vision. Some emphasize the analogy between film and dream and use psychoanalytic theory to explain how film works upon the mind of the spectator as an image that is akin to the screen upon which we may imagine our dreams are projected (Eberwein 1984). Others emphasize the real rather than the imaginary quality of looking at motion pictures and suggest the way in which the intensification or omnipotence of vision in the cinema yields perverse pleasures. Psychoanalytic film criticism takes its cue from the way in which the visual fictions of mass culture function as wish-fulfilling narratives or collective fantasies and employs Freud's method of dream analysis in order to interpret their meaning. This follows the practice of Freud's disciples, who analyzed art not simply as a method of investigating the psychology of the artist behind the work but to demonstrate the ways in which characteristic forms taken by fiction and kinds of fiction demonstrate a kinship with fantasy and dream (see Jones 1951; Bonaparte 1949).

There is a second fundamental distinction to be drawn within the practice of psychoanalytic film theory that cuts across the distinction between apparatus theory and psychoanalytic interpretation. This distinction turns upon how the kinships between cinema and the irrational are to be evaluated. One tradition of psychoanalytic film theory construes the power of cinema to circumvent reason and sobriety as a wonderful thing; the second construes the power of cinema as profoundly dangerous and manipulative, as something that must be diagnosed and defended against by the cool light of reason. The first tradition originates in the writings of the French surrealists and their commentators (see Hammond 1978) that is resumed in the remarkable and neglected writings of Parker Tyler (1944, 1947). The second tradition originates in the arguments of Western Marxists such as Theodor Adorno in the 1940s and 1950s, who drew on Freud's analysis of group psychology to describe the way in which the irrational powers of cinema were orchestrated by capital to create a docile and compliant population.

125

The Marxist critique of culture was reinvigorated through the intoxicating mix of Althusserian Marxism, Lacanian psychoanalytic theory, and semiotics in the 1970s, which was itself sustained and transformed through the 1970s and 1980s through the work of feminist psychoanalytic theorists who argued that the perverse pleasures of the cinema operated at the expense of women. This Marxist–feminist tradition, until recently, formed the dominant strand of psychoanalytic film theory.

While this distinction between the celebration and condemnation of irrationality and perversity is a fundamental cleavage in psychoanalytic film theory, it is nonetheless less straightforward than it first appears. Laura Mulvey's famous psychoanalytic diagnosis of the subjection of women in cinema, "Visual Pleasure and Narrative Cinema," is predicated upon a call for the abandonment of the pleasures of cinema, which forcefully suggests that those pleasures held their lure (Mulvey 1989b; see also Mulvey 1989a). Furthermore, although the writings of Christian Metz on psychoanalysis were appropriated by the Marxist and feminist tradition of psychoanalytic film theory, their relationship to that tradition is an ambivalent one. For in his psychoanalytic essays Metz writes as a cognitive semiotician whose anatomization of the perverse pleasures of cinema could be considered evaluatively neutral. There is also an important intellectual tradition that combines Marxism and surrealism, represented in film theory through Walter Benjamin's one-of-a-kind but enormously influential essay "Art in the Age of Mechanical Reproduction" (1969), which seeks to combine a Marxist diagnosis of mass culture with a surrealist celebration of its liberatory potential afforded by cinema's augmentation of vision (see Hansen 1999). Furthermore, it was the psychoanalytic theory of Jacques Lacan rather than Freud that was most influential upon psychoanalytic film theorists of the 1970s and 1980s, yet Lacanian psychoanalysis was profoundly informed by surrealism, in which psychoanalysis was used to subvert rather than restore rationality. The writings of Lacanian Slavoj Žižek arguably redeem the surreal dimension of Lacan's thought within a Marxist diagnosis and analysis of the narratives of popular culture.

The centrality of Lacanian psychoanalysis to psychoanalytic film theory requires observation of a third distinction, one that separates Freudian psychoanalysis from Lacan, and that is the difference between science and metaphysics. Although I would argue that Freud's discovery is better understood as one that involves conceptual innovation rather than empirical discovery (see Cioffi 1969; Allen 1997b), it has traditionally been construed as an empirical discovery of hitherto unrecognized causal processes that govern mental life. Freudian psychoanalysis is considered to be a science of the mind that uncovers and explains these causal processes. The cogency of Freudian psychoanalysis and its application to film theory can be judged on the grounds of whether or not the phenomena explained through psychoanalysis bear the requisite hallmarks of irrationality, and where cinema is ascribed causal effects, the cogency of this ascription may be judged by reference to the behavior of actual spectators. However, Lacan recasts

Freud's psychological theory of unconscious agency as a philosophical theory that describes the essential or constitutive paradox of self-representation. Lacanian theory is given an aura of empirical legitimacy by borrowing the language of psychological (and linguistic) theory, but because it is a metaphysical theory it is actually immune from empirical confirmation or refutation and cannot be used to justify or support causal hypotheses.

Lacan's theory has its roots in the philosophy of Hegel, but its metaphysical foundations are perhaps best displayed by comparing Lacanian themes to the ideas of Sartre, who was hostile to and repudiated psychoanalytic theory. For Sartre, human self-consciousness is defined by a perpetual struggle between being-for-itself (*pour-soi*), expressing absolute freedom, nonfixity, mobility, transformation, and change, and being-in-itself (*en-soi*), expressing fixity, thinghood, and stasis. In bad faith, the for-itself defines itself as an entity, but while Sartre condemns this as inauthentic, he offers no way out of the dilemma or paradox of self-representation. When I represent myself to another being-for-itself by expressing my desire for them, I necessarily misrepresent myself, for I am fixed in the look of the other as a being-in-itself. The perpetual process of self-alienation that defines the condition of consciousness and the relationship of self to the other is stabilized for Sartre only by the gaze of a third person who stands for the social order as whole, bestows an apparent equivalence between self and other, and gives the illusion of commonality and community (see Sartre 1958).

It's not hard to see how Sartrian themes are rehearsed by Lacan (see Samuels 1993). The dialectic of being-in-itself and being-for-itself is recast by Lacan (via Heidegger) in the drama of the subject before the mirror of the other. Self-consciousness is articulated in the moment that the subject *qua* no-thing-ness (Heidegger's subject) recognizes itself in a mirror or in the gaze of the other. But what it recognizes is "an armor of alienating identity" that gives it a form, shape, fixity, and thinghood which it is not, albeit, at this stage, one that is provisional and unstable. The role of Sartre's being-for-others is transformed by Lacan, who identifies the "third term" as the structure of meaning relationships engendered by language and culture (the Other), in which the subject discovers a (wholly) fictitious identity at the cost of cementing his self-alienation. For Lacan, therefore, the castration of the subject refers not simply to the repressed fantasy of penile loss at the hands of the internalized castrating father figure, which, for Freud, lay at the core of unconscious mental life. Instead, the fantasy described by Freud is a figuration of a quite general, metaphysical "lack in being" that is made permanent in the self-understanding achieved by the subject, who begins to inhabit language and culture through identifying with the place of the father.

The appeal of Lacan's theory to Marxist and feminist film theorists was undoubtedly as much due to the imaginative way Lacan theorized the role of representation in "constructing" subjectivity as to his melancholy metaphysics of lack. While the two aspects of the theory are conjoined – it is because the subject is metaphysically nothing that the subject is also the necessary fiction that is fabricated in representation – nevertheless film theorists used Lacan's theory of subject construction to make quasi-empirical claims about the effects of cinema upon the film spectator. (I use the term "quasi-empirical" because film theorists employ a distinction between the ideal spectator of theory and actual, empirical viewers, but unless the two entities are correlated in some way the theory loses its point.) In this way, psychoanalytic film theorists routinely conflated the distinction between science and metaphysics: they promiscuously melded Freudian and Lacanian psychoanalytic concepts that have distinct, indeed incompatible, intellectual pedigrees, and they made sweeping empirical claims on wholly metaphysical grounds. In my view, this conceptual confusion vitiates much of the work discussed in these pages.

2   Psychoanalytic Theories of Cinema

As I have already outlined, there are two broad kinds of applied psychoanalysis according to which aspect of the cinema is being illuminated. The first kind focusses upon the visual properties of cinema, the second upon the qualities of cinema fiction. This section will be concerned mainly with the first kind of psychoanalytic film theory.

The surrealists and their commentators were the first to celebrate these affinities between the visual in film and irrational thought and the capacity of cinema to augment human powers of perception, and these ideas received persuasive articulation in surrealist practice in the work of filmmakers such as Epstein, Dulac, and Buñuel. As early as 1926 Jean Goudal, in an essay that was praised by Breton, argued that the experience of cinema, in conformity with the goals of surrealist art, was lodged at the boundary of the conscious and unconscious: "The cinema," he writes, "constitutes a conscious hallucination" (Hammond 1978: 51). As in the theater, the cinema spectator sits in a darkened auditorium, but, unlike the theater, what we see is not actually present to us; rather, it is presented to us in the form of a "simulacrum of a uniquely visual kind." For Goudal, cinema has a kinship to the dream world on account of its lack of three-dimensionality, sound, and color. The concreteness of the film, together with its temporality, makes cinema an ideal medium for escaping the tyranny of reason and staging the associative processes of condensation and displacement that, for Freud, characterized unconscious thought. In a later essay, Jacques Brunius compares dissolves and fade-outs/ins to transitions in dreams and writes that "the disposition of screen images in time is absolutely analogous with the arrangement thought or the dream can devise. Neither chronological order nor relative values of duration are real" (Hammond 1978: 61).

Other surrealist writers reflected more upon the impact of cinema on our powers of perception. Parker Tyler writes: "In moving with a more pyrotechnic virtuosity than the human eye, . . . [the camera] has displaced the body of the

128

spectator and rendered it, as a carriage of perception, fluid; the eye itself has become a body capable of greater spatial elasticity than the human body, insofar as it seems a sort of detachable organ of the human body" (Tyler 1944: 23). It is not simply that the camera brings human beings closer in the manner of a scientific instrument, but by replacing or displacing the body as the locus of perception, the camera seems to challenge the apparent division between inner and outer, between mind and world, and hence the coordinates of rational understanding itself, transmuting perception into trance or dream: "The camera seems to possess the wildness, the compulsiveness, and the interior meaning of the most instinctive life, such as that symptomatic in dreams, romantic poetry and surrealist art" (35). Perhaps a similar idea is echoed in Benjamin's utopian conception "unconscious optics," where the camera–eye released from the constraints of the body can reverse the alienating effects of technology and reveal to us "the secret life of things" (see Hansen 1999). It was the hidden, or secret, aspects of things as they are revealed by the camera's automatic registration of the profilmic event that inspired the surrealists' critical practice of "irrational enlargement" of scenes from otherwise dull American movies.

Subsequent theoretical elaboration of the analogy between the visual properties of cinema and unconscious mental states in the writings of Baudry, Metz, and Allen continue to be divided between theories that focus on the relationship between film and fantasy or dream and theories that focus upon the augmentation of perception and its implications for human self-understanding. However, these writings contrast with surrealist writings on film by taking on the aspect of a psychological theory: that is, cinema is conceived as an apparatus that has certain causal effects on the spectator which psychoanalysis can illuminate. Metz and Baudry restate Goudal's argument that the cinema provides the spectator with a simulacrum of reality that is endowed with illusion of presence. It is for this reason that Metz dubs cinema "the Imaginary Signifier." Furthermore, Baudry and Metz contend that by externalizing the form taken by fantasy, the cinema actually serves to mobilize and sustain wish-fulfillment. The cinema, Baudry writes, "*causes* the subject to regress to an early state of development with its own forms of satisfaction which may play a determining role in his desire for cinema and the pleasure he finds in it" (1986b: 313, my emphasis). In my book *Projecting Illusion* I try to refine the theories of Metz and Baudry to account for the fact that the experience of cinema they describe, which I term "projective illusion," is at once a normal rather than a pathological activity and also a contingent rather than necessary feature of film spectatorship (1995).

However, it was psychoanalytic theories of cinematic vision rather than the film–dream analogy that came to define the terms of modern psychoanalytic film theory. The two kinds of apparatus theory are connected by the idea that the cinema stimulates or causes archaic regression, but while the first emphasizes the "inner" aspect of this process, the retreat of the subject into a boundary undifferentiated state, the latter emphasizes the impact of archaic desire on how and what we see. Since archaic desire characteristically manifests itself in adult life through perversions, psychoanalytic film theorists proposed that the cinema is distinctive in mobilizing a whole range of perverse pleasures.

Metz argues that the cinema, conceived as an imaginary signifier, is like a fetish, and the film spectator is a fetishist (1982). For Freud, the fetish object functions as a prop for a fantasy that denies sexual difference – *the* fundamental difference for the child to deny in order to affirm its own sense of imaginary wholeness and lack of psychic differentiation from the (m)other. In his imagination, the fetishist fills in the apparent gap caused by the perceived absence of the female phallus with the fetish. He disavows what he knows (rationally) to be the case in favor of a primitive belief in sexual undifferentiation that the fetish serves to sustain. According to Metz, the cinematic image functions as a fetish because it allows us to *perceive* what is imaginary as being real and hence to disavow our knowledge that what we see is only an image. Metz thereby takes the fetish object and the disavowal it sustains out of the domain of fantasy and into the realm of visual illusion. Although influential, Metz's assimilation of fetishism to illusion is incoherent, as Jacqueline Rose first pointed out, for whereas knowledge of an illusion functions rationally to contradict a false belief, knowledge of a fetish does not (Rose 1980).

Metz also argues that the cinema, *qua* imaginary signifier, promotes scopophilia in the form of voyeurism that always, he suggests, includes sadism. Scopophilia describes a sexual pleasure derived from looking. Voyeurism can be distinguished from scopophilia on the grounds that the pleasure of the voyeur is derived from looking at a person who is unaware of the voyeur's presence (although this distinction is not always made). Metz argues that the cinema installs the spectator in a situation in which his gaze is inoculated from reciprocal awareness. Spectatorial voyeurism is further promoted by the keyhole effect of the screen which suggests we are looking through an aperture/apparatus upon the actors (a feature it shares with the television screen). The salience of the keyhole effect to the idea of voyeurism seems to contradict Metz's overall argument that bases voyeurism upon the idea of the imaginary signifier, since the keyhole effect depends upon recognition of the aperture/apparatus that we are looking through rather than a disavowal of it. However, the fact that the keyhole argument survives a critique of the general idea of the imaginary signifier may be in its favor. Cinema may not be constitutively voyeuristic, but it does seems to be particularly conducive to satisfying voyeuristic desires, as any trip to the local video store attests.

Thus far I have focussed on the Freudian aspect of apparatus theory. I shall now turn to the influence of Lacan and the screen–mirror analogy, whose formulation by Baudry was explicitly inspired by Althusser (as we shall see) but takes on an independence from Marxism in the writings of Metz. Metz claimed that the cinema screen was akin to Lacan's idea of mirror-misrecognition, with the significant difference that one does not see an image of oneself in the cinema. Just as the subject in front of the mirror (of the other) is bestowed with an illusory sense of identity, cinematic representation engenders in the spectator an illusory sense of herself as someone who "identifies" with the position of the camera and therefore authors and owns the visual field of the film. However, the visual field the viewer purports to own and the position from which she purports to own it are actually the product of the system of representation.

While some theorists emphasized the way in which the image constituted the subject as the author of their own visual field, others emphasized the effect of the cut on spectatorial omnipotence – namely, castration – and theorized how narrative cinema works to contain or "suture" (like stitches over a wound) the potentially catastrophic nature of this cut. For suture theorists the cut in cinema represents or enacts the castration that defines the subject's relationship to discourse according to Lacanian theory. Narrative cinema consists of alternating moments of identification with the plenitude of the image (imaginary wholeness) followed by a severance of that imaginary wholeness through the cut, which raises the possibility that the spectator may recognize the status of the image and discover the relation to lack that defines her position as spectator, and, by grandiose extrapolation, as a "subject." Film "constructs" the subject of self-misrepresentation, but it also has the power to expose the nature of that construction. Classical cinema avoids this through deploying strategies of reverse-field cutting, in which the visual field of an image that is lost to the spectator by the cut is restored to her vicariously through identification with the look of a character whom we see in the next image and who, it transpires, claims ownership of the visual field of the first.

This theory has been thoroughly discredited for many different reasons and from many different intellectual perspectives:

1 Analytic film theory focusses on flawed arguments. Apparatus theory involves argument by analogy, but the analogy is mistakenly conceived as identity (Carroll 1988; Allen 1995). Apparatus theory also misunderstands the nature of character identification (Carroll 1988; Smith 1995).
2 Cognitive film theorists point out that psychoanalytic theory overlooks the pre-conscious and conscious aspects of the spectator's cognitive and emotional engagement with narrative film (Bordwell 1985).
3 Narratologists demonstrate that character identification does not depend upon point of view in the manner required by the theory (Rothman 1976; Browne 1985; Smith 1995).
4 Film aestheticians point out that the theory depends on a naive, reductive analysis of film style that precludes the fine-grained distinctions the theory itself requires (Bordwell 1985).
5 Feminists argue that the idea of the spectator as a transcendent, omnipotent figure is a patriarchal one (Penley 1989).
6 Most importantly in this context, Lacanians point out that film theorists misconstrue the nature of Lacanian psychoanalysis and offer a different conception of psychoanalytic film theory (Copjec 1982, 1995).

As the failings of apparatus theory became evident, some psychoanalytic film theorists began turning away from medium-specific arguments based on the visual properties of film toward an exploration of the kinship between the fiction film and fantasy. Perhaps it is self-evident that popular narratives are narratives of wish-fulfillment offering imaginary and wholly fantastic solutions to the complex and messy problems of how to live, how to love, and how to deal with death. Tyler writes: "A thousand small wishes are symbolically satisfied by the humblest and worst Hollywood movie, and the excellence or triteness of a movie has little to do with satisfying the average customer" (1944: 238). However, film theorists have sought a more general explanation of the kinship between fiction and fantasy at the level of the way fantasy operates upon the subject rather than what it contains. Elizabeth Cowie argues that fictions are congruent in their form with the mechanisms that govern fantasy on the grounds that our engagement with visual fictions is predicated upon (a) disavowal and (b) wish-fulfillment.

Cowie's first argument recapitulates Metz's own citation of Octave Manoni, now shorn of Metz's visual bias. When I consume a fiction, "I know very well that this is a story but all the same it is real"; thus my engagement with fiction is akin to the way I inhabit fantasy. The second argument stresses the way in which narrative form engages the wish to know, where desire is mobilized in relation to a lack and the point lies in the process rather than the result: Cowie writes:

> Reading or viewing is a relation of desire, which is, at the very least, the wish to know. The corollary of this wish is that the spectator is a subject of lack – we lack the knowledge of what will happen in the narrative, and the narration will feed us or tease us until it draws us to its already determined conclusion. (1997: 45)

Of course both arguments depend on a move characteristic of much psychoanalytic theory which tends to assimilate imagination to fantasy. Make-believe in a fictional world surely does not intrinsically involve imagination informed by sexualized desire, but merely imagination. Our engagement with narrative process, suspense, involves, to be sure, the "desire to know," but is the desire to know always or necessarily a sexual desire? These questions are moot only if our point of departure is the Lacanian one that the subject as lack is always and everywhere the subject that is engaged. And, as I have suggested, it is not even necessary to adhere to a theory of fiction as fantasy in order to endorse the relevance of thinking about films as fantasies; it perhaps only requires some pre-theoretical reflection.

Lacanian theorists have shown that apparatus and suture theory involve a fundamental misapplication of a Lacanian understanding of the relationship between vision and desire. I would argue that this confusion derives from the fundamental misappropriation of Lacanian psychoanalysis by film theorists as a psychological rather than a metaphysical theory. Furthermore, it was a confusion that was fostered by the intent of apparatus theorists to develop a causal theory of how cinema affects spectators. It is scarcely surprising, then, that what appears to Lacanians as bad psychoanalysis looks to cognitive theorists like bad science. In

Lacanian theory, looking that is informed by desire is defined by the gaze. The gaze is not something that guarantees the subject's self-assurance; on the contrary, it renders the subject paranoid, someone who is ensnared by a look that is imagined to come from the other but cannot actually be seen. The gaze is that which lies outside the field of what is perceived (whether representation or physical object), sustaining the fantasy of subjectivity, not by purporting to guarantee the subject a mastery of that visual field, but by ceaselessly engaging the subject's desire. Such a desire is necessarily mobilized by the world of appearances, whether or not those appearances take the form of visual representations, and whether or not those visual representations are fictional. However, visual representations, such as film, do afford the possibility of overtly symbolizing the gaze in the form of a stain or a grimace in the visual field that, so to speak, looks back at the observer and challenges their complacency, revealing the kernel of disorder and chaos beneath the calm surface of appearances in the fictional world. This grimace of the real is a ubiquitous motif in the films of Hitchcock, which Žižek terms the "Hitchcockian Blot" (1991, 1992a, 1992b). I shall return to this question at the end of the next section.

3 Marxism, Psychoanalysis, and the Critique of Mass Culture

In this section I will discuss four main schools of thought that attempt to synthesize Marxism and psychoanalysis in the study of cinema: the Frankfurt School critique of mass culture (focussing on the work of Adorno), Althusserian–Lacanian film theory, what might be dubbed the *Cahiers du cinéma* school of ideological criticism, and the "new Lacanianism" of Žižek and his followers that I have already introduced. The first three schools of thought synthesize Marxism and psychoanalysis within the framework of a political modernism that stands implacably opposed to mass culture and its products, save in the case of those mass cultural texts which show evidence of their own undoing. Psychoanalysis becomes a tool for diagnosing the lure of cinema and laying bare the contradictions of dominant ideology. Žižek rejects the opposition between ideological illusion / mass culture / pathology and enlightenment / the avant-garde / authenticity that defined political modernism. In Žižek's hands psychoanalysis reveals the necessity of ideological illusion to which there is no outside. Valuable works of fiction, high and low alike, are those that mirror this truth.

Following Wilhelm Reich, who used Freud to analyze the mass psychology of fascism (1946), Theodor Adorno explained the allegiance of the German population to Hitler through Freud's analysis of group psychology (Adorno 1991; Freud 1955). Freud argued that identification with a group is dependent on the relationship the group bears to the leader. In this pattern of identification, the individual (partly) relinquishes his identification with a punitive super-ego and reidentifies instead with a collective ego-ideal he shares with other members of the group. In the classical Freudian model, identification with the super-ego affords individuation and differentiation of the male child from the mother and prepares the way for heterosexual object choice. This "straightforward" development is denied the female child since the female has little inducement to give up her relationship with her father. As a result, the female may form a regressive, melancholic identification, in her fantasy, with the father, an identification that takes the place of heterosexual object choice. This identification eroticizes the father in fantasy (it renders him perverse), diminishes individuation, and impedes the development of conscience. Of course, a parallel condition may afflict the male child who regressively identifies with his mother (one Freudian explanation for the etiology of homosexuality). Freud implies that mass psychology is modeled precisely upon the collective investiture of a regressive "feminine" super-ego (see Lebeau 1995), and he compares the capacity of this figure, thus installed, to manipulate his or her subjects with the authority of the hypnotist.

Adorno contends that mass culture functions as ideology in a manner akin to fascist propaganda as a substitute form of socialization to the traditional patriarchal family. Traditional patriarchal culture under liberal capitalism produced an individuated citizenship with the capacity to imagine social change and form a genuine collectivity (albeit one that privileged masculinity). Consumer capitalism produces a de-individuated citizen whose imagination is colonized by a culture industry which functions as a collective feminine super-ego that reduces all its citizens to a collectivity of isolated monadic identical subjects. Through a combination of administration and hypnosis, the culture industry tutors its subjects into believing it is addressing needs that are really manufactured by it: "The culture industry not so much adapts to the reactions of its customers as it counterfeits them. It drills them in their attitudes by behaving as if it were itself a customer" (Adorno 1974: 200–1). The success of the culture industry is achieved through the application of the capitalist methods of industrial organization to the production of art. The technology of filmic representation is ideally suited to the calculation and control of the audience's most primitive pre-ego impulses through the "transparency" of the cinematic image and the way in which the spectator's imaginative engagement with film is controlled by the temporality and rhythm of the work (see Adorno and Horkheimer 1972).

Adorno's psychoanalysis of cinema did not enter into the mainstream of psychoanalytic film theory, but aspects of his work are echoed in the profoundly influential theories of French Marxist Louis Althusser. For Althusser, ideology describes the process through which society cultivates compliant social subjects by appealing to their need to be recognized, to acquire a social identity. Social institutions call upon individuals to take up socially recognized positions and thereby become "subjects." Individuals enter these positions believing they are freely chosen, though in fact they are determined in advance by the system that "interpellates" or hails the subject. Althusser compared this "error" of the subject to the "error" of the subject before Lacan's mirror who misrecognizes herself as an entity within it (collapsing the formation of the social subject with Lacan's psychic subject). This comparison allowed film theorists such as Jean-

Louis Baudry (1986a) to map Althusser's interpellated subject onto an analysis of cinematic representation, through an analogy between the film screen and Lacan's mirror as illusion-generating apparatuses. The film spectator, Baudry argues, is captivated by an "impression" or illusion of reality in the cinema. The viewer actually perceives an image but imagines that what she perceives is real, an unmediated perception of the world. However, both the world that the spectator appears to perceive and the point of view upon that world are created by the apparatus. In this way the cinematic apparatus serves to perpetuate the specta-tor's disavowal of the fact that her perception of reality is determined only through representation. "What emerges here," Baudry writes, "is the specific function fulfilled by the cinema as support and instrument of ideology. It con-stitutes the 'subject' by the illusory delimitation of a central location – whether this be that of a god or of an other substitute" (1986a: 295). The task of the film theorist is to expose the construction of the subject as an illusion and thereby to reveal the truth of ideology from a cognitive standpoint that is outside it.

As we shall see, Althusserian-influenced apparatus theory seemed to afford a detailed analysis of cinematic representation and narration, but it did so at the expense of the analysis of content that characterizes Adorno's version of that theory. However, Althusser also offered a model for psychoanalytic textual criticism, for he pitched his interpretation of the work of Marx as a "symptomatic reading" designed to reveal a meaning that was concealed beneath the surface of his writing and yet determined its contours in the way that, in Freud's dream analysis, the manifest content of a dream conceals its latent content and yet is explained by it. Drawing upon Althusserian literary theorist Pierre Macherey, the *Cahiers* critics undertook a similar ideological diagnosis of Hollywood films that sought "to make them say what they have to say within what they leave unsaid, to reveal their constituent lacks; these are neither faults in the work, nor a deception on the part of the author; they are structuring absences, . . . the unsaid included in the said and necessary to its constitution" (*Cahiers du cinéma* editors 1976: 496). In their famous analysis of John Ford's *Young Mr. Lincoln*, the *Cahiers* editors purported to reveal how the myth of Lincoln as upholder of the law is established in Ford's film only by representing Lincoln as a castrated figure whose authority paradoxically derives from the mother. In the *Cahiers* reading of the film, popular narrative is seen to enact a kind of fantasy or utopia of social coherence and conflict resolution, whose underlying oedipal logic based on castration and repressed desire can be unmasked through a detailed attention to the film's formal structure and style that exposes the cracks and fissures in the myth of social authority articulated by it.

Althusserianism therefore bestowed a dual legacy on psychoanalytic film theory: apparatus theory and symptomatic criticism. Although a few texts, most notably Stephen Heath's (1975) analysis of *Touch of Evil*, sought to synthe-size the analysis of subject construction with textual analysis, such a synthesis was difficult to achieve. Subject-construction theory is a quasi-scientific theory which explains how spectator response is causally produced by the cinematic apparatus,

135

although it is a theory that rests on metaphysical premises. However, symptomatic criticism is an activity of interpretation that requires the imaginative resources of the critic to discover meanings that a film does not appear to mandate. The dual legacy of Althusserianism has been overcome in recent years through Slavoj Žižek's breathtaking synthesis of Lacanian psychoanalysis and ideology critique. Žižek retains the underlying concern of apparatus theorists with the way that cultural representations serve as supports for subjectivity, but he rejects the idea that this can be explained in terms of the causal effects of an apparatus upon subjects. Instead, the texts of popular culture serve to allegorize the drama of lack-in-being that defines the condition of the subject, and, if we are attentive critics, these can tutor us in grasping more deeply the ways in which the subject's lack-in-being sustains and is sustained by the social order.

Central to Žižek's voluminous writings is the concept of fantasy and its relationship to the real, or that which always exceeds (self-)representation. "Ideology," he writes, "is a fantasy construction which serves as a support of our 'reality' itself: an 'illusion' which structures our effective, real social relations and thereby masks some insupportable, real-impossible kernel" (1994: 50). Žižek's analysis of popular culture implicitly rejoins Freud's analysis of the ego-ideal in the fantasy of group identification in the context of Adorno's extension of this idea to the popular culture, but it is shorn of the normative underpinnings of both thinkers – of an attachment to the masculine super-ego, to the distinction between the normal and pathological (however attenuated in Adorno's case), and to the hierarchy between art and mass culture – and recast in Lacanian terms. For Žižek, the relationship between the consumer and the texts of popular culture is a form of super-ego identification that is not degraded or pathological, but normative. It is not a question of standing outside ideology that exposes its pathology or its fictive character in the manner of apparatus theorists, for there is nowhere outside ideology to stand. Instead it is a question of exposing the necessity of ideological fictions. Žižek writes:

> It would be wrong to conclude from "non existence of the big Other," i.e. from the fact that the big Other is just a retroactive illusion masking the contingency of the real, that we can simply suspend this "illusion" and "see things as they really are." The crucial point is that this "illusion" structures our social reality itself: its disintegration leads to a "loss of reality" – or, as Freud puts it in *The Future of Illusion*, after conceiving religion as an illusion: "Must not the assumptions that determine our political regulations be called illusions as well?" (1991: 71)

Whereas apparatus theorists privileged modernist films that self-reflexively exposed the illusory character of representation, Žižek privileges those works of popular culture that self-consciously expose the fictive nature of the social order, which is nonetheless required to support and to make possible subjectivity. So even while Žižek rejects the distinction between false transparency and enlightened self-reflexivity so dear to political modernism, he retains the distinction between pathology and enlightenment in attenuated form. There are those who understand how the necessary fiction of subjectivity is sustained by the social order to ward off the abyss of the real and those who do not. Equally some texts serve as privileged guides: Hitchcock is Žižek's exemplary instance (1991, 1992a, 1992b). It is as if Hitchcock occupies the place for postmodern theory that Godard occupied for political modernists. In his relentless exposure of the "real-impossible" kernel that the social order serves to mask, Žižek has crafted a fin-de-siècle negative theology whose breathless aphorisms seem to emerge from the jaws of authorial extinction. Žižek is Nietzsche reincarnated for the millennium, with all the strengths and weaknesses that implies.

4   Psychoanalysis, Feminism, and Film Theory

The starting point for modern feminist psychoanalytic film theory is Laura Mulvey's essay "Visual Pleasure and Narrative Cinema" (mentioned above). Mulvey's purpose was to diagnose and analyze the structure of gender hierarchy and inequality in narrative cinema, and she proposed that psychoanalytic theory provides the requisite tools to do it. Mulvey shared with Metz the assumption that the "conditions of screening and narrative conventions give the spectator an illusion of looking in on a private world" (Mulvey 1989b: 17) and hence that cinema was voyeuristic (though she does not assume as forthrightly the idea that the spectator identifies with the camera). However, she also asserts what is perhaps implicit but not stated by Metz, that this voyeuristic gaze is active, sadistic, and male. Why? One answer might be that the voyeuristic gaze is defined by Freud as being active, sadistic, and male. A second answer is that the voyeuristic male gaze is mobilized through a structure of identification in which the male spectator, through identification with the gaze of the male star, looks upon the spectacle of the female body. However, as psychoanalysis shows, the female body evokes castration threatening the authority of the voyeuristic gaze. This threat is neutralized, Mulvey claims, by two characteristic strategies: the first is to fetishize the image of woman (as in von Sternberg films), the second is to punish the woman (as in certain Hitchcock films).

In 1969 Raymond Bellour commenced a series of essays on American cinema, primarily on the work of Hitchcock, which also identified a gender hierarchy and inequality in narrative cinema (see Bellour 1980). However, as Janet Bergstrom (1979) pointed out in a detailed presentation of Bellour's analysis of Hitchcock, while Bellour identifies a relentless male oedipal logic, in classical Hollywood cinema in general and in the films of Hitchcock in particular, that works to constrain female desire to become the mirror of male desire, his analysis, unlike Mulvey's, is not predicated simply upon the hierarchy seen/being seen, nor does it simply deny female characters control of the gaze. For example, in his detailed analysis of the Bodega Bay sequence from Hitchcock's film *The Birds*, Bellour demonstrates the way in which a gender hierarchy is created across a series of formal contrasts, seen/being seen, close-up/long shot, stasis/movement (1969).

137

Furthermore, it is a hierarchy in which, initially at least, Melanie Daniels (Tippi Hedren), the heroine of the film, is in control of the narrative and the gaze, brazenly seeking out Mitch Brenner (Rod Taylor) as a potential mate. For Bellour, the male oedipal narrative allows space for the autonomous articulation of female desire in order for that desire to be contained. If Bellour's analysis had become the paradigmatic example of how Hollywood narrative is gender-bound, the history of feminist film theory may have been different, for his analysis is predicated upon the structure of visual fictions, not upon the structure of the apparatus. While Bellour's male oedipal narrative appears both ubiquitous and closed, his reading can, in principle, be challenged on the grounds that not all fictions have this structure and that even his interpretation of Hitchcock is only a partial one. However, Mulvey's argument turned primarily not on the kind of story narrated through the formal strategies of classical editing, but upon the putative active, sadistic, masculine, voyeuristic quality of the gaze in cinema, and feminist theory became mired in the question of how to conceptualize the place of the female spectator in a system of looks that seemed to exclude her. Retrospectively, it is clear that this was quite simply the wrong question to ask, for it was framed by a series of erroneous assumptions.

There is a fundamental ambiguity in Mulvey's theorization of the look: either it is contingent upon the narrative context of a male character gazing at to-be-looked-at women, or it is intrinsic to the apparatus as such. Making the male gaze intrinsic renders it inescapable and hence questionable as a theory. However, if it is merely contingent upon context then it cannot implicate the spectator in the manner required by the theory, for a character's gaze, represented in the fiction as voyeuristic, is not necessarily experienced by the spectator as a voyeuristic gaze. In this sense, Mulvey's analysis of Hitchcock's self-conscious presentation and critique of male voyeurism in *Rear Window* contradicts her general theory.

Kaja Silverman (1988) offers an ingenious way to rescue Mulvey's argument. The (voyeuristic) look in cinema is not intrinsically male, and it evokes lack (through the cut) for all spectators. Mulvey demonstrates the way that, in classical cinema, the burden of lack belonging to all becomes a property of the female character (and hence the female spectator) in the repetitive scenarios in which man is bearer of the look and woman its object. However, Silverman's solution has to confront all the criticisms of apparatus theory, which, as we have seen, there are good reasons to reject (for criticisms, see Carroll 1996).

Pace Silverman, who recasts Mulvey's argument as one about specific narrative scenarios, albeit ones that are ubiquitous, and makes that argument relative to a gender-neutral apparatus theory, the response of Mary Ann Doane to this ambiguity in Mulvey's argument moves in the opposite direction. For Doane, Mulvey's position was interpreted in the light of French Lacanian feminist arguments that denied woman access to representation entirely on the grounds that the subject constituted in discourse was male: "The man alone has access to the privileged specular process of the mirror's identification" (Doane 1987: 16). Once the opposition "woman as image / man as bearer of the look" was understood as a structural feature of representation itself, the problem confronting feminist theorists became how to conceptualize the role of the female spectator. The options reduced themselves to four (nonexclusive) possibilities. The female spectator could (1) assume a transvestite identification with the male gaze at the expense of her like (see Mulvey 1989b), or (2) identify masochistically with the lack by which she is defined (Doane 1987). Alternatively, the female spectator could become a theorist who either (3) imagines a position for women outside any representational system that defines her as lack, or (4) exposes the way representation ceaselessly structures the subordination of woman (see Hammett 1997). However, a number of feminist theorists, including Doane, also pursued a line of reasoning that would eventually undermine all the above (Doane 1987; Penley 1989). For, they argued, not only was representation structured in a manner that produced gender asymmetry, but this gender asymmetry was produced by the theorist who characterized cinematic representation in patriarchal terms. That these two contradictory propositions could be held simultaneously attests to the power that the theory of the male gaze held over a whole generation of film theorists. Ultimately, though, one horn of the dilemma, "apparatus theory," gave way in favor of theories of fiction as fantasy that reconceptualized the relationship of gender to psychoanalysis.

The dilemma of conceptualizing female spectatorship within the framework of the Mulvey–Metz paradigm is illustrated by a debate that took place in the pages of *Cinema Journal* over the reponse of the female spectator to the film *Stella Dallas* (1937). At the conclusion of the film, the audience watches Stella, who gazes through a window at her daughter's wedding to an upper-class man, excluded from the scene, yet triumphant in the knowledge that she has secured her daughter's social ascent. Linda Williams concedes that the conclusion of the film subordinates the chastened Stella to the position of passive spectator of her "properly fetishized" daughter but argues that the film appeals to female readers who have a different reading competence from men "that derives from the different way women take on their identities under patriarchy and is a direct result of the social fact of mothering" (1984a: 8). She refers here to feminist object-relations psychology that has emphasized the role of the mother–child bond in the development of the girl's identity in contrast to the sharp separation from the mother that defines phallic masculinity (Chodorow 1978). In this way the female subject identifies with the position of the mother as well as the position of the father and may criticize the latter from the standpoint of the former.

In her reply to Williams, Ann Kaplan responds correctly, if literal-mindedly, that women's different socialization has no bearing on how identification in the cinema is structured by the patriarchal gaze of film (1985). It is left to Christine Gledhill to point out that "a mainstream feature film is not constituted simply by a series of looks; it is above all fiction, deploying a range of strategies . . . which assist in the viewer's construction of a mental/emotional fictional arena" (1986: 46). The Metz–Mulvey model cannot be undermined by an appeal to female spectatorship; the model itself is misconstrued. If object-relations psychology has a bearing upon understanding identification in cinema, it is not because it can contribute to understanding the psychology of spectatorship but in the way it can illuminate the portrayal of mother–daughter relationships in the cinema and hence women's experience in Western culture (see Byars 1991).

Many revisionist critics contested the universality of the scenario of oedipal narrative that enshrined phallic mastery and female to-be-looked-at-ness without challanging the underlying assumptions of the model. Steve Neale (1983) and others showed the way in which certain genres of classical cinema made a spectacle of the male body, though within action stories that allowed the hetero-sexual male spectator to identify with male narrative agency rather than the spectacle of masculinity. Tania Modleski (1988), Patrice Petro (1986), and others identified the importance of the female oedipal scenario in popular films in which the female protagonist does not relinquish her bonds with her mother. Linda Williams (1984b) and Barbara Creed (1993) identified scenarios of female empowerment in the horror film in which the threat of castration was not contained but acted out in the narrative through the figure of the monstrous feminine. Carol Clover (1992) argued that slasher films elicit a "masochistic" identification with the suffering female victim on the part of male and female spectator alike, preparing the way for the empowerment of the girl as hero in the final scenes. Kaja Silverman (1992) analyzed how, under the pressure of history (the trauma of World War II), the dominant strategy of narrative cinema in which male lack is displaced onto the figure of woman breaks down, and male maso-chism is explicitly staged.

Gaylyn Studlar (1985, 1988) proposed a fundamental revision of the Metz–Mulvey paradigm to support her interpretation of the films of von Sternberg. Studlar argued that Baudry's comments about the psychic regression of the spectator in the cinema, and the analogy between cinema spectatorship and dreaming pursued by both Baudry and Metz, point in an altogether alternative direction to the idea of spectatorial voyeurism and sadism, and phallic fetishism, enshrined in the Metz–Mulvey model. Studlar suggests that the cinema spectator is characteristically not a sadistic voyeur but a masochist who swoons before the image which overwhelms him or her in its size and proximity. Since the origins of masochism lay in the child's fantasies of an all-powerful mother rather than in the child's relationship with the father (an argument drawn from Deleuze), the perverse pleasures of cinema are undifferentiated according to gender and there-fore available (after all) for feminists and their antagonists alike. Carol Clover (1992) contested (along with other psychoanalytic theorists) the putatively pre-oedipal character of masochism in Studlar's theory and returned to Metz's forgotten formulation of the projective and introjective gaze, as well as Lacan's conception of vision bifurcated between the gaze and the look, to argue that spectatorial voyeurism cuts both ways: it can be both active and passive, mascu-line and sadistic by turns. However, these revisionist theories, while they offer a fundamental challenge to the Metz–Mulvey paradigm, remain locked in the implausible assumption that perversion, whether masochistic or sadistic, male or female, is intrinsic to the experience of cinema and they therefore fail to escape the shadow cast by apparatus theory (see Gaut 1994).

As I have already argued, theories of visual fiction as fantasy offered an alternative way to understand identification in psychoanalytic terms that seemed to avoid the pitfalls of apparatus theory. They also provide a way to divest the more localized discoveries of feminist critics from the standard oedipal scenario toward a more general theory of audience response. A number of feminist film theorists draw on Freud's analysis of typical fantasies in "A Child is Being Beaten" to show that a person does not necessarily identify with a person of like gender, that active and passive, "sadistic" and "masochistic" forms of identification are not gender-bound in the manner presupposed by Mulvey, and that popular narratives are not simply patriarchal and oedipal in the manner described by Barthes and Bellour (Donald 1989; Rodowick 1992; Cowie 1997). Thus Cowie contends that Max Ophüls' film *The Reckless Moment* (1949) offers diverse "positions" of identification – "father, mother, child, lover, wife, husband" – that involve a wish "both to have and to be the father, and to both have and to be the mother" (1997: 162, 163). To be sure, some feminist theorists sought to map Freud's analysis of the female role in psychoanalytic theories of fantasy onto visual fictions in order to emplot identificatory positions for the female spectator that were excluded by the Mulveyan model. However, this kind of analysis risks forcing textual interpretation and understanding into yet another procrustean theoretical mold (cinema as fantasy apparatus), and it runs contrary to idea that the investigation of fantasy reveals the fluid, contingent, even performative character of all identities (see chapter 10 on queer theory). Yet fantasy theories of (visual) fiction contain their own pitfalls for feminist theory. Not only should the general equation between fantasy and fiction be contested (as opposed to identifying fantasies in particular fictions or groups of fiction) on the grounds that it conflates fantasy with imagination, but it is not immediately clear what the theory of fiction as fantasy per se contributes to a feminist politics committed to discovering the ways in which patterns of gender inequality are perpetuated or subverted in popular narratives. For if all popular narratives offer the identificatory positions that subvert normative gender roles, then the theory seems to lack explanatory power for feminism. To be sure, with sufficient ingenuity, all films become available for a feminist *reading* thus conceived, but what then does this really tell us about the meaning of the film itself and, in particular, its political significance?

5 Conclusion: Psychoanalysis and the Ethics of Interpretation

The history of the application of psychoanalysis to cinema has been driven by two main politically motivated goals: theories of how cinema in general effects spectators, and symptomatic readings of individual texts. I have tried to show the limitations of psychoanalytically informed theories of film and fiction, but I would now like to address, by way of conclusion, the status of psychoanalytic interpretation and its relationship to what I will call the ethics of interpretation.

Symptomatic readings purport to show the meaning behind the text that is concealed by its manifest content, but it is not clear that this is what psychoanalytic readings of Hollywood cinema achieve. A striking feature of Hollywood filmmaking (and American popular culture in general) is the way that psychoanalytic narratives become a shorthand for emplotting contradictions and conflict in the lives and loves of the rational goal-oriented character of Hollywood cinema, while avoiding the motivational ambiguities characteristic of art cinema: the unconscious motive provides a clear-cut alternative to the conscious one. Thus, arguably, far from providing an objective code to unlock the real (hidden) meaning of the text, psychoanalytic criticism quite frequently describes what is going on at the surface of it: a case in point would be the innumerable psychoanalytic interpretations of the works of Hitchcock. However, if this is the case, the psychoanalytic critic posing as theorist erroneously claims for himself the insight that rightly belongs to the text itself. Psychoanalytic film theorists often proceed as if they were in the position of an analyst who explains the symptoms of the patient. Yet, as Stanley Cavell has suggested, the interpersonal ethics of the analytic situation suggest the reverse: the good analyst is one who listens to her patient in order to discover something about themselves, to become a wiser analyst (Cavell 1996). This suggests that a film theorist who is informed by the ethics rather than simply the theory of psychoanalysis will listen to what a film or text might say to them, rather than impose their theory upon it. Laura Mulvey has learned this lesson well; her analysis of *Citizen Kane* uncovers the way the film itself is formally structured to reveal to the attentive viewer a pattern of unconscious motivation that gives the lie to Kane's populism and serves to critique American political culture in general. That is, the film itself is understood to be a work of symptomatic criticism (Mulvey 1992; see also Bates and Bates 1987 for a similar argument about the film).

If psychoanalysis is not a privileged code for unlocking the meaning of texts, then it surely should be one among many conceptual frameworks to be deployed by the critic who is seeking to understand a film or body of films; too often psychoanalysis is the sole or dominant tool in the arsenal of the critic who deploys it in the belief that he possesses the philosophers' stone. Furthermore, if it is the film itself that bestows authority on an interpretation (a claim that obviously requires more defense than I can give it here), then one should not assume, prima facie, that either Freudian psychology or one singular version of psychoanalytic theory is the key to understanding a text: Hitchcock's *The Birds* may be informed by more than just the oedipal trajectory Bellour discovers within it (Allen 1997a); David Lynch's work may be most fruitfully understood by self-psychology and theories of narcissistic personality that are contemporaneous with it (Layton 1994); Nicolas Roeg's films might be understood in terms of the Jungian psychology that is their acknowledged source of inspiration (Izod 1992). This kind of culturally embedded, interpretative use of psychoanalysis is not likely to persuade Lacanians (who possess the philosophers' stone), but it may persuade the rest of us.

Note

Thanks to Malcolm Turvey, Alexandra Seibel, and the editors for their suggestions.

References

Adorno, Theodor. 1974. *Minima Moralia: Reflections from a Damaged Life*. Trans. E. F. N. Jephcott. London: Verso.

———. 1991. "Freudian Theory and the Pattern of Fascist Propaganda." In *The Culture Industry*. Ed. Jay Bernstein. London: Routledge.

———, and Max Horkheimer. 1972. *Dialectic of Enlightenment*. Trans. John Cumming. New York: Herder and Herder.

Allen, Richard. 1995. *Projecting Illusion: Film Spectatorship and the Impression of Reality*. New York: Cambridge University Press.

———. 1997a. "Avian Metaphor in *The Birds*." *Hitchcock Annual* (1997/8): 40–67.

———. 1997b. "Psychoanalysis after Wittgenstein." *Psychoanalysis and Contemporary Thought* 20, 3: 299–322.

Bates, Robin, with Scott Bates. 1987. "Fiery Speech in a World of Shadows: Rosebud's Impact on Early Audiences." *Cinema Journal* 26, 2 (winter): 3–26.

Baudry, Jean-Louis. 1986a [1970]. "Ideological Effects of the Basic Cinematographic Apparatus." In *Narrative, Apparatus, Ideology*. Ed. Philip Rosen. New York: Columbia University Press.

———. 1986b [1975]. "The Apparatus: Metaphysical Approaches to Ideology." In *Narrative, Apparatus, Ideology*. Ed. Philip Rosen. New York: Columbia University Press.

Bellour, Raymond. 1969. "*Les Oiseaux*: Analyse d'une sequence." *Cahiers du cinéma* 216 (October): 24–38.

———. 1980. *L'Analyse de film*. Paris: Albatros.

Benjamin, Walter. 1969. "Art in the Age of Mechanical Reproduction." In *Illuminations*. New York: Schocken Books.

Bergstrom, Janet. 1979. "Enunciation and Sexual Difference." In *Feminism and Film Theory*. Ed. Constance Penley. New York: Routledge.

Bonaparte, Marie. 1949. *The Life and Works of Edgar Allan Poe: A Psychoanalytic Interpretation*. Trans. John Rodker. London: Imago.

Bordwell, David. 1985. *Narration in the Fiction Film*. Madison: University of Wisconsin Press.

Browne, Nick. 1985 [1975]. "The Spectator-in-the-Text: The Rhetoric of *Stagecoach*." In *Movies and Methods Vol. II*. Ed. Bill Nichols. Berkeley: University of California Press.

Byars, Jackie. 1991. *All that Hollywood Allows: Re-Reading Gender in 1950s Melodrama*. Chapel Hill: University of North Carolina Press.

Cahiers du cinéma editors. 1976 [1972]. "John Ford's *Young Mr. Lincoln*." In *Movies and Methods*. Ed. Bill Nichols. Berkeley: University of California Press.

Carroll, Noël. 1988. *Mystifying Movies: Fads and Fallacies in Contemporary Film Theory*. New York: Columbia University Press.

——. 1996. "Cracks in the Acoustic Mirror." In *Theorizing the Moving Image*. New York: Cambridge University Press.

Cavell, Stanley. 1996. *Contesting Tears: The Hollywood Melodrama of the Unknown Woman*. Chicago: University of Chicago Press.

Chodorow, Nancy. 1978. *The Reproduction of Mothering: Psychoanalysis and the Sociology of Gender*. Berkeley: University of California Press.

Cioffi, Frank. 1969. "Wittgenstein's Freud." In *Studies in the Philosophy of Wittgenstein*. Ed. Peter Wind. New York: Routledge.

Clover, Carol. 1992. *Men, Women and Chainsaws: Gender in the Modern Horror Film*. Princeton: Princeton University Press.

Copjec, Joan. 1982. "The Anxiety of the Influencing Machine." *October* 23: 43–59.

——. 1995. *Read My Desire: Lacan Against the Historicists*. Cambridge: MIT Press.

Cowie, Elizabeth. 1997. *Representing the Woman: Cinema and Psychoanalysis*. Minneapolis: University of Minnesota Press.

Creed, Barbara. 1993. *The Monstrous-Feminine: Film, Feminism and Psychoanalysis*. New York: Routledge.

Doane, Mary Ann. 1987. *The Desire to Desire: The Woman's Film of the 1940s*. Bloomington: Indiana University Press.

Donald, James, ed. 1989. *Fantasy and the Cinema*. London: BFI.

Eberwein, Robert. 1984. *Film and the Dream Screen*. Princeton: Princeton University Press.

Freud, Sigmund. 1955 [1922]. "Group Psychology and the Analysis of the Ego." *Standard Edition* 18: 65–143.

Gaut, Berys. 1994. "On Cinema and Perversion." *Film and Philosophy* 1: 3–17.

Gledhill, Christine. 1986. "On *Stella Dallas* and Feminist Film Theory." *Cinema Journal* 25, 4 (summer).

Hammett, Jennifer. 1997. "The Ideological Impediment: Epistemology, Feminism, and Film Theory." In *Film Theory and Philosophy*. Ed. Richard Allen and Murray Smith. Oxford: Clarendon Press.

Hammond, Paul. 1978. *The Shadow and Its Shadow: Surrealist Writings on Cinema*. London: BFI.

Hansen, Miriam Bratu. 1999. "Benjamin and Cinema: Not a One-Way Street." *Critical Inquiry* 25, 2 (winter): 306–43.

Heath, Stephen. 1975. "Film and System: Terms of Analysis Parts 1 and 2." *Screen* 16, 1 (summer): 7–77; *Screen* 16, 2 (summer): 91–113.

Izod, John. 1992. *The Films of Nicolas Roeg: Myth and Mind*. London: St. Martin's Press.

Jones, Ernest. 1951. *On the Nightmare*. New York: Liveright.

Kaplan, Ann. 1985. "Reply to Linda Williams." *Cinema Journal* 24, 2: 40–3.

Layton, Lynne. 1994. "*Blue Velvet*: A Parable of Male Development." *Screen* 35, 4 (winter): 374–93.

Lebeau, Vicky. 1995. *Lost Angels: Psychoanalysis and Cinema*. London: Routledge.

Metz, Christian. 1982. *Psychoanalysis and Cinema: The Imaginary Signifier*. Bloomington: Indiana University Press.

Modleski, Tania. 1988. *The Women Who Knew Too Much: Hitchcock and Feminist Theory*. New York: Routledge.

Mulvey, Laura. 1989a. "Individual Response to Questionnaire on The Spectatrix." *Camera Obscura* 20–1 (May–September): 248–52.

——. 1989b. *Visual and Other Pleasures*. Bloomington: Indiana University Press.

——. 1992. *Citizen Kane*. London: BFI.

Neale, Steve. 1983. "Masculinity as Spectacle." *Screen* 24, 6: 2–16.

Penley, Constance. 1989. *The Future of an Illusion: Film, Feminism, and Psychoanalysis*. Minneapolis: University of Minnesota Press.

Petro, Patrice. 1986. "Rematerializing the Vanishing 'Lady': Feminism, Hitchcock, and Interpretation." In *A Hitchcock Reader*. Ed. Marshall Deutelbaum and Leland Poague. Ames: Iowa State University Press. 122–33.

Reich, Wilhelm. 1946. *The Mass Psychology of Fascism*. New York: Orgone Institute Press.

Rodowick, D. N. 1992. *The Difficulty of Difference: Psychoanalysis, Sexual Difference and Film Theory*. New York: Routledge.

Rose, Jacqueline. 1980. "The Cinematic Apparatus: Problems in Current Theory." In *The Cinematic Apparatus*. Ed. Teresa de Lauretis and Stephen Heath. New York: St. Martin's Press.

Rothman, William. 1976 [1975]. "Against 'The System of the Suture.'" In *Movies and Methods*. Ed. Bill Nichols. Berkeley: University of California Press.

Samuels, Robert. 1993. *Between Philosophy and Psychoanalysis: Lacan's Reconstruction of Freud*. New York: Routledge.

Sartre, Jean-Paul. 1958. *Being and Nothingness*. Trans. Hazel E. Barnes. London: Methuen.

Silverman, Kaja. 1988. *The Acoustic Mirror: The Female Voice in Psychoanalysis and Cinema*. Bloomington: Indiana University Press.

——. 1992. *Male Subjectivity at the Margins*. New York: Routledge.

Smith, Murray. 1995. *Engaging Characters: Fiction, Emotion, and the Cinema*. Oxford: Clarendon Press.

Studlar, Gaylyn. 1985. "Masochism and the Perverse Pleasures of the Cinema." In *Movies and Methods Vol. II*. Ed. Bill Nichols. Berkeley: University of California Press.

——. 1988. *In the Realm of Pleasure: Von Sternberg, Dietrich, and the Masochistic Aesthetic*. Urbana and Chicago: University of Illinois Press.

Tyler, Parker. 1944. *The Hollywood Hallucination*. New York: Simon and Schuster.

——. 1947. *Magic and Myth of the Movies*. New York: Henry Holt.

Williams, Linda. 1984a. "Something Else Besides a Mother: *Stella Dallas* and the Maternal Melodrama." *Cinema Journal* 24, 1: 2–27.

——. 1984b. "When the Woman Looks." In *Re-Vision: Essays in Feminist Film Criticism*. Ed. Mary Ann Doane, Patricia Mellencamp, and Linda Williams. Frederick: University Publications of America.

Žižek, Slavoj. 1991. *Looking Awry: An Introduction to Jacques Lacan Through Popular Culture*. Cambridge: MIT Press.

——, 1992a. *Enjoy Your Symptom!: Jacques Lacan in and out of Hollywood*. New York: Routledge.

——, ed. 1992b. *Everything You Always Wanted to Know about Lacan But Were Afraid to Ask Hitchcock*. New York: Verso.

——. 1994. *The Sublime Object of Ideology*. London: Verso.

145

CHAPTER NINE

Spectatorship and Subjectivity

E. Deidre Pribram

The study of spectatorship is an attempt to understand why we choose to sit in the movie theater seat or on the living-room sofa captivated by a screen. What is it that makes the experience so pleasurable, desirable, meaningful – given that viewing subjects position themselves as filmic or televisual spectators voluntarily, in very large numbers, and with frequent repetition? What are the relationships between individual and filmic process: how are we linked to screen, narrative, character? Who exactly is the subject seated before the screen, involved in an activity which has been described as everything from passive absorption to active production of the text?

Concepts of the spectator are inseparable from theories of the human subject. That is, notions of spectatorship, while not identical to, change in conjunction with, evolving or altering conceptualizations of subjectivity. The three "subjects" discussed here – psychoanalytic, discursive, and social – are all poststructuralist in that they are constructed through socio-cultural and ideological forces. This is in contrast to the humanist subject of the age of Enlightenment through modernism, a unified, coherent being who is able to know "truth." In the latter schema, the universe operates according to rules of logic and reason which "man" can ascertain. Rationality and science, emanating from the humanist subject, replace the earlier ordering of divine providence.

Post-structuralism, in contrast, posits a decentered, noncoherent, externally constructed rather than internally originating subject. The study of (post-structuralist) spectatorship is the search for what constitutes the person seated in front of the movie or television screen, and an exploration of which configurations, out of limitless possibilities, constitute viewing subjects so that they see themselves, the text, and the world(s) it represents within specific systems of meaning.

1 The Psychoanalytic Subject

The psychoanalytic concepts used in film studies are based on the work of French theorist Jacques Lacan, who, in turn, built upon Sigmund Freud's pioneering work on the unconscious, sexuality, and subject formation. Freud hypothesized that children are introduced into sexuality in the first few, formative years of life. Believing that the myth of Oedipus Rex mirrors the desires and events of infant sexuality, Freud based his description on the Greek myth in which Oedipus, unwittingly, kills his father and marries his mother. In the Oedipus complex, the male infant develops a desire for his mother and comes to perceive his father, who is the rival for his mother's affection, as the obstacle to the fulfillment of his desire. The outcome is that the boy identifies strongly with the father in order that he can take the father's place vis-à-vis the mother. In other words, he *becomes* the father so that he can desire the mother, and so, "woman." For female infants, the process is similar but the inverse: the object of desire is the father and identification occurs in relation to the mother.

But in either case, the oedipal stage and its resolution enable the child to take up its assigned place in terms of gender identification, or "sexual difference." It is at this moment that the infant emerges into a world ordered by sexed selfhood, that is masculinity and femininity.

Indebted to Freud, Lacan was also extremely influenced by linguistics and structuralism, which attributed culture and consciousness to the acquisition of language. Without language, we cannot develop a sense of ourselves as individuated, cognitive beings. Integrating Freudian analysis with contemporary work on structural linguistics, Lacan's description of human formative development tracks how the infant becomes acculturated, how he or she is brought into being as a member of society. The penis of Freudian sexuality (which the girl infant is aware she lacks, the boy infant fearing a similar "castration") becomes the phallus – the bearer of male identity, that is, of patriarchal power. In this scenario the child emerges not only into sexual difference but into a larger patriarchal order. To resolve the Oedipus complex in language is to take one's place as a member within phallocentric culture.

In Lacan's analysis, the first stage of this process for the infant is the Imaginary – "Imaginary" not only in the sense of illusory, but as a pre-linguistic order dominated by images. This is the world of the mother, a world of unity, connectedness, fullness, and satisfaction, in which the infant and mother are one. The infant has no sense of itself as a separate being but only as part of the mother. The second stage is the Mirror Phase, in which the infant recognizes its own reflected image, suggesting that it is a separate being. Finally, there is the Symbolic. This is the world of the father, the world of language, of meaning production, of law in the sense of cultural order, concepts of justice and morality, and so on. It is into the Symbolic that the infant steps at the end of its early, formative years, at the resolution of the Oedipus complex and at the moment of language acquisition. These three stages – the Imaginary, the Mirror Phase, and the Symbolic – together constitute the subject; in Lacan's system, the process of moving through these phases establishes the infant as subjective being.

As the stage of oneness with the mother, the Imaginary is considered illusory because such unity does not materially exist and because the phase, of necessity, must pass. However, the infant, as she or he grows, is "haunted by the memory of this original illusory experience of plenitude when baby and world were one" (Gledhill 1984: 30). This is the desire for the mother outlined in the Oedipus complex; it is a desire for connectedness and the longing to return to a state of fullness which stays with the child as he or she grows up and long after having entered the Symbolic.

The entry into the world of language occurs when the child realizes the concept of difference. The illusion of unity with the mother, and therefore with the world, is broken, and the infant becomes aware of itself as a separate being. The world becomes differentiated into the self or subject versus objects and others. The moment of entry into the Symbolic, into culture, is a function of realizing the difference between self and Other. The establishment of one's subjectivity cannot occur without comparison to an objectified Other.

While the Imaginary is a world of unity, the Symbolic is a world of separation and loss. But the child must accept entry into the Symbolic as the process of becoming an adult and taking up one's position as a social being. Simultaneously, however, the longing for the Imaginary is never lost, establishing the unconscious as the location for these unfulfilled desires. Further, the unity of the Imaginary can never be retrieved in its original state of wholeness or plenitude, but only as phantasy, in which other objects or representations act as temporary replacements or equivalences. This produces a never-ceasing sense of lack, provoking the subject into a constant search for the replenishment of unity and fullness, the achievement of which must always be deferred.

Film scholars such as Christian Metz have taken Lacan's work and theorized that the cinematic experience is one of the locations in which the drives and desires of the Imaginary surface and are played out. In *The Imaginary Signifier*, Metz examines cinema's role as "a technique of the imaginary":

> [T]he subterranean persistence of the exclusive relation to the mother, desire as a pure effect of lack and endless pursuit, the initial core of the unconscious. . . . All this is undoubtedly reactivated by the play of that *other mirror*, the cinema screen, in this respect a veritable psychical substitute. (1982: 3–4)

In this analysis, the viewing experience triggers unconscious desires and phantasies in such a way that the screen–spectator relationship replicates – or substitutes for – the very operations of the unconscious. Moreover, it is film's activation of desires associated with the Imaginary which explains cinematic pleasure, the gratifying sensation of which prompts spectators to return to the film-viewing experience repeatedly.

Metz then attempts to account for the mechanisms by which the material base of the medium, the images and sounds of the text, reenact or retrieve the unconscious. From "The Fiction Film and its Spectator" in *The Imaginary Signifier*:

[H]ow does the spectator effect the mental leap which alone can lead him [*sic*] from the perceptual *donnée*, consisting of moving visual and auditory impressions, to the constitution of a fictional universe, from an objectively real but denied signifier to an imaginary but psychologically real signified? (116)

Incorporating such work as Jean-Louis Baudry's "Ideological Effects of the Basic Cinematographic Apparatus," Metz describes the "filmic state," the institutional, technological, and psychological conditions in which, or from which, the spectator views the film. It is this filmic state which causes the viewer to be lulled into a "waking sleep," a semi-regressive or phantasy state which accesses the unconscious.

However, the interaction of spectator and screen/film text doesn't simply pleasure a fixed, pre-existing subject, but actually produces or constitutes the viewer as subject in the process. "[F]ilm-viewing and subject-formation [are] reciprocal processes: something about our unconscious identity as subjects is reinforced in film viewing, and film viewing is effective because of our unconscious participation.... [T]he cinema 'reinscribes' those very deep and globally structuring processes which form the human psyche" (Flitterman-Lewis 1992: 124). In semiotic and post-structuralist conceptions of subjectivity, the subject is continually constructed through signifying or meaning-producing practices such as cinema.

In other words, psychoanalytic film theory is concerned with establishing the complex, myriad mechanisms by which the relationship of spectator to screen links the human psyche, particularly the unconscious, to the film text. Through the circulation of psychoanalytic attributes such as desire, phantasy, and identification, the spectator–screen process, among other cultural processes, constructs the psychoanalytic subject, also variously referred to as the desiring subject, the sexual subject, and the screen subject.

Another important cinematic arena that utilized Lacanian concepts of psychoanalysis was feminist film theory, investigating and adapting those concepts to fit, more appropriately, a political agenda. Combining Freudian/Lacanian psychoanalysis with studies in ideology, in the work of Louis Althusser and others, feminist film theory managed to invert psychoanalytic theories so that the theories fundamentally critiqued the phallogocentric structures they previously seemed to be simply describing or otherwise naturalizing.

The appeal of psychoanalytic theories for feminist film studies could be found in their description of gender as a culturally acquired series of attributes, rather than the effect of biological determinism (anatomy as destiny, women's "natural" place, etc.). The concept of cultural acquisition implies the potential for change, crucial to a political movement, while deterministic notions foreclose the pursuit of altered gender relations. The idea that gender acculturation occurs in the first few years of life, prior to the advent of memory, also seemed to account for the persistence of male domination over women across diverse cultures and historical eras, without proscribing the possibility of altered relations. Further, the contention that sexual difference is such a primary source of self-identity, of subjectivity, opened up many possibilities for further feminist analyses.

The initiatory work of Laura Mulvey, Pam Cook, and Claire Johnston outlined how, within a patriarchal order, the male is constructed as subject while women are relegated to object, to the Other, against which male subjectivity is produced. In a short article first published in 1973, "Fears, Fantasies and the Male Unconscious or 'You Don't Know What Is Happening, Do You, Mr. Jones?',", Laura Mulvey writes about sculptor Allen Jones and his "Women as Furniture" series, "in which life-size effigies of women, slave-like and sexually provocative, double as hat-stands, tables and chairs" (1989a: 6). Mulvey's point is that the sculptures, as with dominant forms of representation in general, do not reflect "real" women, that is, social beings existing in a material world. Nor do culturally pervasive representations of women reflect the female unconscious or women's phantasies. Rather, images of women mirror the male unconscious which produces those representations, and which does so on the basis of deep psychic structures of fear and desire. In "Visual Pleasure and Narrative Cinema" (1989b), Mulvey goes on to describe the specific, complex processes, including scopophilia, voyeurism, and fetishism, by which the male unconscious is enacted or performed upon the image/body of woman in cinema. Such "enactments" on women as an objectified Other, in film and other forms of representation, are central to the process of male subject formation, the primary controlling, organizing, and signifying presence in patriarchal culture. But women are necessary in this process of male subject formation, if only as Other, as sexual difference. In psychoanalytic terms, he is aware of his phallus because of her lack. In order to know who he is, he needs to have before him who he is not. In Claire Johnston's words, feminist film theory and practice "revealed how the economy of the classic realist text works towards the unquestioned Imaginary of the patriarchal order" (1992: 297).

In such feminist analyses, the look of the camera, the look of the characters within the text, and the position of narrative enunciation are all male. The film speaks from, for, and is addressed to the male unconscious, regardless of the gender of specific viewers. The cinematic apparatus and the film text position or construct an ideal male spectator as the terms in which the screen–spectator relationship occurs.

The contribution of feminist film theory based in psychoanalysis is its attempt to explain – with the hopes of dismantling – the exclusion of women from the dominant discourses and institutions of socio-cultural life as the function of male needs and drives for power. It was able to describe many of the mechanisms of phallic oppression (including psychoanalytic theory itself) and certainly opened up a wealth of new ways to read films.

However, psychoanalytically informed feminist film theory, and psychoanalytically based theories of cinema in general, pose significant, perhaps insurmountable, limitations as well. In the first instance, the theories are universalizing or totalizing, and so exclusionary, that is, they ignore historical and cultural differences. The subject, the individual psyche, appears to be the same, once gender differences are established, over time and social categories, despite class, race and ethnicity, nationality, sexual preference, and so on. The theory generalizes singular subject identities regardless of obvious differences between people, cultures, and eras.

In the second instance, it is difficult to accept the spectator as normatively male in the face of large numbers of social subjects – women who repeatedly attend the cinematic (and televisual) experience and do so with evident pleasure. Rather, one assumes that some manner of divergent signifying process(es) must occur for female spectators as well.

For feminist film theory, the theoretical conceptualizations, not solely the surrounding phallic economy, are monolithic and restrictive. Women are excluded from any legitimate position from which to view or to speak. As scholars such as Teresa de Lauretis have argued, the theory leaves us caught in the orbit of the male and not-male, while what is necessary (and desirable) aren't considerations of what it means to be "not-male," but rather what it means to be "women." The theories themselves, not just patriarchal culture, limit the ability to explore women's own fears and desires, and to give voice to women's psychic lives.

Feminist scholars originally were drawn to psychoanalytic theories because of their capacity to explain gender identity in cultural rather than biological terms. However, psychoanalytic theory led to similarly reductive or absolutist notions in which the problem of how to alter the psychoanalytic construction of sexual difference, so apparently early and fundamentally formative of identity, seemed nearly as insurmountable as arguments based on biological determinism.

The response of early feminist film theorists to such an apparently exclusionary and detrimental positioning of female spectators by dominant cinematic forms was to call for a denial of films which embodied traditional visual and narrative pleasures, as the title of Mulvey's article suggests (initiatory feminist analyses and critiques were very much aimed at classic realist film and not at the concept of cinema in toto). Films of traditional narrative pleasure were to be replaced, instead, by avant-garde work which made evident the workings of those traditional pleasures or created alternative modes of gratification for viewers. While a number of the films that resulted were striking, original, and successful, much of the work was textually difficult, tending to create specialized audiences, and so, ignoring or excluding wider bands of spectators, including, potentially and contradictorily, large numbers of women.

At the same time, the refusal to participate in forms of dominant culture seemed to position the feminist avant-garde as exacerbating or actively participating in the exclusion of women from the centers of cinematic production and reception. As it was unrealistic to assume that mainstream cinema was going to cease to be either mainstream or dominant, it made more sense to attempt to appropriate such forms in ways that benefited women. This entailed exploring other, more productive ways in which popular narrative cinema might provide its audiences with pleasures. The development of less restrictive theories and

151

practices was necessary in order that women could be represented in and addressed by cinema, as social subjects and as spectators, in alternative, independent, and dominant arenas – in other words, wherever and whenever film occurs.

2   The Discursive Subject

Feminist awareness of the need for reconceptualizing psychoanalytic theories coincided with – and helped enable – important shifts in the concepts of cinema, culture, and subjectivity. Evolving notions of subject formation, and therefore spectatorship, moved to respond to the two large problematics incurred by psychoanalysis. First, in post-structuralist theories beyond Lacan, the universalizing "sameness" of subjectivity is superseded by the discursive subject, a much more complex, multi-layered understanding of how the self is constituted. Second, the posited absence of social beings from the mechanisms and interactions of spectatorship is redressed in the audience studies and reception theories of cultural studies, via close examination of the viewing practices of specific social subjects (discussed in the following section).

In discursive theory, individual identity is not a function of singular, solely psychic or unaltering processes, but rather, subjectivity is constructed by the cultural forces of multiple, overlapping, and sometimes competing discourses. Sexual difference or gender, then, is one (or a plurality of) shaping discourse(s) among many others in the formation of identity. It is in Michel Foucault's work that notions of the discursive subject are most clearly delineated.

In Foucault's terms, discourses are systems of thought or domains of knowledge which form around certain thematics or ideologies, for instance, "justice." A discursive practice, in this instance the juridical system, would involve institutions (courts, etc.) and technologies (laws, means of enforcing them). Together, the discourses, institutions, and technologies interact as the discursive formation of the law. The discursive formation of heterosexuality would involve institutions and technologies such as marriage, and discourses such as romance, love, and so on.

In discursive theory, the (humanistic) subject does not predate, conceive of, or invent the discourse; discourse is not a "phenomenon of expression" by a "transcendental subject" (Foucault 1972: 54–5). Rather, and very importantly, the subject is constituted by the discourse. So, the law-abiding citizen and the criminal are constructs of the discursive practice of the law, husbands and wives are the subjective effects of heterosexuality, and so on. In this account, the individual is the intersection or collection of discourses which constitute or articulate him or her. In other words, the self is the effect of cultural processes.

Originally influenced by structural linguistics, in Foucault's later work discourse came to be inseparable from power. Speaking of the "traditional theme" in philosophy that "truth does not belong to the order of power, but shares an original affinity with freedom," Foucault argues that this conceptualization needs to be overturned because "truth is not by nature free" but "thoroughly imbued with relations of power" (1978: 60). Power is dispersed everywhere throughout culture, which is not to say that it is dispersed evenly or equitably, but that instances of the exertion of and struggle for power occur continually, at every level and in every configuration of culture.

Instead of the benevolent, forward-progressing, and freeing version of reason projected since the Enlightenment, Foucault argues a "reason," that is, regimes of knowledge, that are coercive, controlling, and driven by the mechanisms and forces of power – although it should also be said that Foucault does not understand power as simply oppressive, but sees it as a much more "productive" force, in its capacity for producing cultural relations.

Theorizing the discursive formation of sexuality, Foucault describes how experience – sexuality in this instance – is organized as a regime of knowledge/ power in a threefold process. Sexuality is treated as "the correlation of a domain of knowledge, a type of normativity and a mode of relation to the self." The domain of knowledge is created by the constitution of sexuality as "a field of study (with its own concepts, theories, diverse disciplines)." Normativity is imposed by "a collection of rules (which differentiate the permissible from the forbidden, natural from monstrous, normal from pathological, what is decent from what is not, etc.)." And a mode of relation to the self occurs "between the individual and himself [sic] (which enables him to recognize himself as a sexual subject amid others)" (1984b: 333–4).

While the thematic of a discourse may remain constant, the meanings produced over historical eras change. To continue with the instance of sexuality, its occurrences in the seventeenth century marked a departure from previous experiences of it. "[T]hings were said in a different way; it was different people who said them, from different points of view, and in order to obtain different results" (Foucault 1978: 27).

The function of systems of discourse and relations of power is precisely to constitute subjectivity, to organize "techniques for 'governing' individuals – that is, for 'guiding their conduct' – in domains as different as the school, the army, and the workshop" (1984b: 337–8). In the modern era, regimes of knowledge/ power are less physically or externally coercive (punishment) than they are internalized or self-regulated (control), through the process of normatization.

The process of normatizing entails a discipline describing its own field of operation and creating its own object of study. So, for instance, psychiatry as a domain of knowledge was created by emerging discourses on madness. "[M]ental illness was constituted by all that was said in all the statements that named it, divided it up, described it, explained it, traced its developments, indicated its various correlations, judged it, and possibly gave it speech by articulating, in its name, discourses that were to be taken as its own" (Foucault 1972: 32). However, in the process of constituting the object of study, the object in the sense of subject/object is also formulated. The conceptualization of the insane is necessary to the process of normatizing acceptable behavior, the criminal is necessary to the description of the boundaries and parameters of law and order, and so on. By deploying the concept of 'insane,' the identity of the sane subject is described, or proscribed. Thus, discourses of what constitutes healthiness must always incorporate the ill, sanity include the mad, law-abiding the criminal, 'normal' sexuality the deviant, and so forth.

In a hypothesis structurally similar to the function of sexual difference in psychoanalytic theory, social relations are constructed upon conceptions of otherness or alterity. "The history of madness would be the history of the Other – of that which, for a given culture, is at once interior and foreign, therefore to be excluded (so as to exorcise the interior danger)" (Foucault 1973: xxiv). By attempting to make the danger of madness entirely "foreign" or exterior to the subject and instead locate it as embedded in the object or other – of the insane in this instance – the potential for its interiority or effect on the self is denied, and thereby its threat or the anxiety of its threat diminished.

It is critical in post-structuralist discursive theory to understand subjectivity as the invention or articulation of discourse. In the process of naming someone as mad, as object of study, or as Other, what is assembled are interpretations or judgments, not facts; what is constructed are *meanings*, not "truths."

Although extremely influential, Foucaultian discursive theory has not been applied to cinema studies in any kind of systematic manner, as was attempted by Metz and Mulvey with Lacanian psychoanalytic theory. To date, most efforts have been deployed in the study of cultural discourses invoked by a particular text or set of texts which cite, group, or contest varying notions of the law, say, or sexuality. Those discursive practices specifically considered by Foucault have proven most accessible to film and television scholars – in the instance of sexuality, in gay and lesbian studies, in studies of the uses of the body, and so on.

While there are reasons that make it particularly difficult to systematically apply post-structuralist discursive theory to cinema studies (the polymorphous origins of discourse, its multiply produced effects, and the delineation of a fluid rather than a fixed subject), the theory's potential productivity for representational studies is enormous. Foucault's own preoccupation with the human or social sciences precluded specific analyses of forms of representation, but his work has certainly contributed to and enriched the way film and television studies are pursued, including, pivotally, their conceptions of the subject and spectatorship.

The result has been a broader, more complex notion of representation as a reflection of and a site for cultural struggles over meaning formation, that is, as a place where meaning production occurs and also where its structures of operation can be viewed. This is so because of the ability of representational forms to "stand in for" social processes via aesthetic and narrative codes (e.g. characters for social subjects), as well as their capacity to invoke or put into circulation wide-ranging occurrences of discursive formations or domains of knowledge (what films are "about"). At the core of these operations of meaning formation is the notion of the subject, and its cinematic version, the spectator, as the convergence, accumulation, and reconfiguration of complementary/competing discourses. It is this spectator who has displaced the fixed, meaning-producing spectator of humanism/modernism, and the fixed, meaning-effect spectator of psychoanalysis.

Two examples of studies of representational forms consonant with discursive understandings of subjectivity, and so taken up and utilized by film theorists, are Stuart Hall's notions of encoding/decoding and Mikhail Bakhtin's concept of heteroglossia. Both theories focus on a diversity of subject positions and a multiplicity of textual meanings.

Stuart Hall understands encoding – the production of media texts – and decoding – the reception of media texts – as discursive practices. "Before this message can have an 'effect' (however defined), satisfy a 'need' or be put to a 'use,' it must first be appropriated as a meaningful discourse and be meaningfully decoded" (1993: 93). The spectator has the potential to interpret, construct, or meaningfully produce the text from one of several positions in relation to it. First, he or she can make a dominant or preferred reading. Hall calls such readings "preferred" because while they are dominant in having "the institutional/political/ideological order imprinted in them and have themselves become institutionalized," they are not singular, fixed, or closed, "not univocal or uncontested" (98).

The viewer can also forge a negotiated reading which is "a mixture of adaptive and oppositional elements: it acknowledges the legitimacy of the hegemonic definitions to make the grand significations (abstract), while, at a more restricted, situational (situated) level, it makes its own ground rules – it operates with exceptions to the rules" (102). Third, the spectator can secure an oppositional reading in which the message is decoded in a "globally contrary way. He/she detotalizes the message in the preferred code in order to retotalize the message with some alternative framework of reference" (103).

In this formulation, the spectator's own varying relationship to the discourses invoked by the text, and the ways they are invoked, allow for a slippage between potential readings or viewing positions in relation to the material of the text. However, while the spectator is no longer "sutured" to the text in a particular way, preferred, negotiated, and oppositional readings continue to imply judgments of "better or worse" interpretations of the text for that particular viewer (depending on the viewer's or the interpreting critic's politics). A hierarchy is structured in which one kind of reading is chosen or prioritized over another – preferred, negotiated, oppositional – displacing or occurring in place of the others. This problematizes a more complex Foucaultian notion of multiple, varied, and simultaneous discourses operating on the subject, some of which may be complementary to each other, while others are competing.

Mikhail Bakhtin's concept of heteroglossia, as outlined in *The Dialogic Imagination*, helps redress the limitations of a "pick or choose" or hierarchizing concept of readership, while retaining the complexity of Foucault's perspectives on discourse and subjectivity. Heteroglossia ia "a notion of competing languages and discourses applying equally to 'text' and 'context.' The role of the artistic text, within a Bakhtinian perspective, is not to represent real life 'exist-ents' but to stage the conflicts, the coincidences and competitions of languages and discourses, inherent in heteroglossia" (Stam 1992: 197). As well as the simultaneity of complementary/competing discourses, Bakhtin's heteroglossia accounts for the simultaneous circulation and interaction of representational discourses (the text) and other socio-cultural discourses beyond representation (the context).

The most persistent criticism of Foucault's concept of discursive subjectivity is that it eliminates the possibility of "agency," that is, motivated, intentional action and reaction on the part of the subject. If the discursive subject is entirely the construct of culturally determining forces via discursive institutions and systems of knowledge, then the potential for internally driven response is pre-empted. How are individual or self-willed thoughts and actions possible? How can spectators actively select or reject readings if they, themselves, are the product or effect of cultural and textual processes? Much post-structuralist theory, certainly Foucault's, has been accused of negating the agency of the subject and therefore eliminating necessary conditions for the possibility of political activity and social change.

Such accusations have been countered by theorists such as Chantal Mouffe and Judith Butler. Mouffe finds that a frequent misunderstanding of the anti-essentialist position "consists in believing that the critique of an essential identity must necessarily lead to the rejection of any concept of identity whatsoever" (1992: 381). Mouffe contends:

> It is only when we discard the view of the subject as an agent both rational and transparent to itself, and discard as well the supposed unity and homogeneity of the ensemble of its positions, that we are in the position to theorize the multiplicity of relations of subordination.... We have rather to approach it [the social agent] as a plurality, dependent on the various subject positions through which it is constituted within various discursive formations.... To deny the existence of an a priori, necessary link between subject positions does not mean that there are not constant efforts to establish between them historical, contingent, and variable links. (371–2)

She calls for the identification and investigation of the multiple and changing links between subject positions, within and between subjects, which together produce "identity." These are not an impediment to understanding the subject, but rather the only means to ascertain the equally multiple and changing forms of power and subordination.

In a similar argument, Judith Butler objects to the notion that questioning the construction of subjectivity is equated to "doing away with" the subject (1992: 15). "[T]o claim that the subject is constituted is not to claim that it is deter-mined" (12). If the subject is constructed, then agency, too, is a construction, not an a priori given.

[I]f we agree that politics and power exist already at the level at which the subject and its agency are articulated and made possible, then agency can be *presumed* only at the cost of refusing to inquire into its construction. . . . We need instead to ask, what possibilities of mobilization are produced on the basis of existing configurations of discourse and power? Where are the possibilities of reworking that very matrix of power by which we are constituted, of reconstituting the legacy of that constitution, and of working against each other those processes of regulation that can destabilize existing power regimes? (13)

While both Mouffe and Butler argue that the subject and her or his agency do not disappear but, instead, are constituted relationally, not absolutely, are never fixed but always evolving, many questions remain. Indeed, the areas insufficiently theorized by Foucault (What precisely causes discourses to alter historically? How do various, multiple discourses construct specific subjects and in what proportions or relations of impact? What are the mechanisms by which change and agency operate?) remain insufficiently understood in terms of their application to film studies as well as other disciplines. While the work of Hall, Bakhtin, Mouffe, Butler, and many other scholars marks fruitful beginnings, much is yet to be done on questions of representation and the discursive subject of film/media/art, and further, on the ways representation conflicts and collaborates with other cultural discourses.

How do viewers operationalize specific readings? That is, how do spectators select a specific reading(s) or shift among readings? Do different information effects, such as those provided by close readings, political engagement, etc., alter earlier, or what might have otherwise been different, subject positions and therefore alter interpretations of a text? What mechanisms are required in order to deploy particular readings or deactivate others?

How does the individual operationalize certain identities at specific moments: for instance, what enables a specific female spectator to read a text from the position of her gendered subjectivity and simultaneously understand its "intended" preferred meanings? What are the mechanisms which might account for that specific female spectator constructing an oppositional reading from her gendered subject position but a dominant reading from her perspective as a racialized identity? Among competing or simply differing discourses invoked by a text, what allows specific readings to take on greater significance – significance in both its senses of meaning and importance? Why do some readings "matter" to a given spectator more than others? What permits a viewer to change his or her "mind" about previously held interpretations?

Do systems of representation such as film and television form their own discursive formation, or are they the confluence of multiple discourses, such as, in film, the narrative discourse(s) of the script, the cinematographic discourse(s) of the image, and so on? Do genres represent their own discrete discourses within a system of representation such as cinema or cut across modes of representations (film, TV, novels, poems), encompassing many diverse socio-cultural practices and artifacts? Do the romance genres – the "women's weepies" of the 1940s or today's "date movies" – form part of a discursive formation on romance which includes Harlequin romances, Hallmark cards, and Valentine's Day (rendering discipline-based analyses insufficient, thus helping to explain the prominence of cultural studies)? To what degree and in what ways are the many films (and TV shows) that follow the conventions of courtroom dramas, or resolve their dramatic dilemmas in courtrooms, part of a representational system of narrative conventions or an armature of dominant social discourses surrounding justice and the juridical system? While the likely answer is "both" to questions concerning the particular (representational) and general (socio-cultural) discursive formations invoked by any text, how do we conceptualize and articulate this? How we do so is of significance because, as a site where representational and social discourses intersect (and perhaps the media's impact can be partially explained by their ability to invoke both sorts of discourse relationally), it marks a promising point for agency and political intervention.

As a series of discursive formations, what kinds of knowledge/power are deployed by the representational to construct what kinds of subjectivity? In such post-structuralist theoretical configurations, spectatorship/readership are "technologies of the self," historical and cultural modes of subject formation. While Foucault's work does not focus on the relations of representation in detail, in an interview he offers a provocative suggestion concerning the need for creativity to displace Sartrean (and humanist) notions of authenticity. "I think that the only acceptable practical consequence of what Sartre has said is to link his theoretical insight to the practice of creativity – and not of authenticity. From the idea that the self is not given to us, I think that there is only one practical consequence: we have to create ourselves as a work of art" (1984a: 351). While Foucault's statement can be interpreted as invoking a romantic and modernist conception of art, it can also be understood as extending an alternative cultural metaphor or paradigm in which the truth-generating agency of authenticity and rational subjectivity are displaced by the meaning-generating agency of the creative subject.

3   The Social Subject

Although the discursive subject has not, to date, been formulated specifically in terms of spectatorship, it has had significant impact on cultural studies and the latter's concern with the social subject and identity formation.

Cultural studies marks a theoretical return to the "everyday experiences" or lived specificities of the material, historical subject. This realignment occurs in the face of the seeming "death of the subject" – because an entirely cultural construct – predicted by (or, some would argue, predicated on) post-structuralism.

Cultural studies' interest in the social subject is not, however, a replication of the humanist subject who creates "himself" and controls the surrounding world.

Acknowledging that individual subjects are multiply and complexly constructed, cultural studies is an attempt to integrate the discursive subject of post-structuralism as, on the one hand, the effect of representational and other signifying practices, and, on the other hand, an agent of socio-cultural constructs and institutions. While a Foucaultian might argue that the distinction between the signifying and the social is illusory in that all is signifying practice, cultural studies maintains the distinction in order to preserve a recognition of people's material existences, which can be made better or worse through political activity. "The problem for cultural studies has been to incorporate the significance of sliding signifiers and disappearing signifieds without asserting that meaning no longer exists, without giving up a politics, without lapsing into a radical moral relativism, without abandoning the interventionist commitment which has motivated the research of cultural theorists" (Slack and Whitt 1992: 583).

The concern to maintain a position for political intervention is consonant with the Marxist origins of cultural studies, as well as the considerable impact feminism, race and ethnicity studies, gay and lesbian studies, and other identity formations have had upon it, in addition to class. However, the formulation of an identity politics, or a politics of difference, seemingly necessitates the existence of a social subject with some range of conscious agency in order to enact or affect a political agenda.

More specifically, cultural studies works to apply varying notions of the post-structuralist subject to forms of representation in popular culture. It does so while seeking to avoid the totalizing overdetermination of psychoanalytic theory and Althusserian-based concepts of ideology, in which the subject is determined by dominant ideology as it is embedded in the text, that is, the text instructs the viewer how to understand it and so positions the spectator in subjectivity. Cultural studies is also a reaction against earlier paradigms of audience research that tended to focus on quantitative data such as audience demographics (what has been skeptically referred to as the "bums in the seats" approach), and that presumed a passive viewership, which surrendered itself to the overpowering effects of the media.

Instead, cultural studies argues that the spectator is the result of various discourses put in play by the text, but also the subject of social, economic, and political practices beyond the text, which are brought to bear at the moment of screen/viewer interaction. While the potentially innumerable configurations of such a balance have yet to be sufficiently mapped out, David Morley explains the intentions shaping this notion of the audience member / social subject:

> The Althusserian drift of much early cultural studies work ... would reduce [the individual subject] to the status of a mere personification of a given structure, "spoken" by the discourses which cross the space of his subjectivity. However, it is not simply Althusser who is at issue here; much of the psychoanalytic work on the theory of ideology generates an equally passive notion of subjectivity, in which the subject is precisely "spoken" by the discourses which constitute that person. I

want to try to formulate a position from which we can see the person actively producing meanings from the restricted range of cultural resources which his or her structural position has allowed them access to. (quoted in Turner 1992: 193–4)

In contrast to approaches in which spectators are "spoken" by the text, cultural studies theorists began to ask: What is actually occurring for viewers? How are social subjects using texts specifically, and to what ends? These concerns led to the ethnographic methodology associated with cultural studies, and to investigations of specific subordinate communities or sub-cultures, as exemplified in the work of David Morley, Janice Radway, Ien Ang, Dick Hebdidge, Angela McRobbie, and others.

Their work posited a much more active viewer than had been theorized previously in either textual/ideological studies or earlier audience research, a viewer capable of resisting dominant encodings and forging oppositional readings, readers who actively and continuously participate in the formation of their own identities. Analyzing the results of her study of elderly viewers of the British soap *Crossroads*, Dorothy Hobson comments:

> Communication is by no means a one-way process and the contribution which the audience makes to *Crossroads* is as important as the messages which the program-makers put into the program. In this sense, what the *Crossroads* audience has revealed is that there can be as many interpretations of the program as the individual viewers bring to it. There is no overall intrinsic message or meaning in the work, but it comes alive and communicates when the viewers add their own interpretations of a program. (quoted in Turner 1992: 133)

The emergent spectator of cultural studies, then, contributes two significant variations to the notion of spectatorship. First, the text is produced only at the moment of interaction with the audience member, bringing the spectator/reader/viewer to the forefront of the mediated event (which in cultural studies, to date, has been far more extensively television analysis, not film). It becomes impossible to speak of the meanings of a text separately from its viewing subject, the two becoming indissoluble. Second, the viewing subject is composed of the interaction between the effects of discourses invoked by the text/representation *and* the effects of social and material discourses beyond. Spectatorship is formulated as the convergence of textual subjects and social subjects. "[T]he focus of critical attention in cultural studies switched from ideology and its effects toward audiences or readerships, since it is at this point that meanings generated in and by media discourses actually go live socially, where textual and social power intersect, and where the distinction between them is meaningless" (Hartley 1996: 225).

Further, the spectator is no longer positioned in subjectivity by the text, but, under the concept of hegemony, can offer resistance to the ideologies of the text. Indeed, cultural studies understands popular culture as the terrain where cultural power, relationships, and systems of meaning are negotiated and established – and, consequently, can be resisted and/or reestablished otherwise.

John Fiske describes one of the projects for cultural studies theorists as the discovery of:

> how actual audience groups actively use television as part of their own cultures – that is, use it to make meanings that are useful to them in making sense of their own social experiences and therefore of themselves.... Exploring the strategies by which subordinate subcultures make their own meanings in resistance to the dominant is currently one of the most productive strands of cultural studies. (1992: 300, 304)

While this avenue of inquiry has indeed been productive, resulting in the identification and analysis of numerous specific communities of social and viewing subjects in terms of their uses of representational forms, it has also been critiqued for displaying a Utopian or ideal notion of resistance. That is, any sub-cultural manifestation of distinct identity can be received as a potential form of resistance beyond the parameters of dominant ideologies. No means have yet been established to determine which sub-cultural configurations of identity might prove beneficial or detrimental to that community vis-à-vis the resistance to or imposition of dominant discursive practices and institutions. What remains for cultural studies is to forge a position that avoids what David Morley has referred to as "the improper romanticism of consumer freedoms" while continuing to avert an earlier "paranoid fear of global control" (quoted in Ang 1996: 260).

Another problematic facing the ongoing endeavor of cultural studies is to develop what Janice Radway describes as "a rich and complex understanding of the different, multiple, everchanging configurations of subjectivity dialectically produced through the negotiation between historically produced individuals and material, social and discursive contexts" (1996: 238). Using her own work with women readers of romance novels as an example, Radway continues: "To construct her, then, as a 'romance reader' may be to isolate only one small portion of her life and to mistake that part for the whole.... The womanhood or femininity constructed through romance reading may well be at odds with the femininity constructed in the process of doing aerobics, watching *Roseanne*, or playing softball" (244–5). Audience (or any subject) analysis, then, is an attempt to contain what is the constant stream of subjectivity in order to study it, isolating one or a few of its aspects, applicable only for a given moment and specific location.

This complex stream of interwoven and changing subjectivities is what Ien Ang refers to as "radical contextualism," which she welcomes as an opportunity to better understand the "chaotic" empirical landscape of audience experiences (1996: 257). Ang argues that the way to approach such a chaotic landscape of subjectivity is to work "within the framework of a particular cultural politics," which then allows the researcher to "meaningfully decide which contexts we wish to foreground as particularly relevant, and which other ones could, for the moment, within this particular political conjuncture, be left unexplored" (258). While Ang's approach addresses the difficulty of imagining "where to begin and where to end the analysis" (253), it raises the question of an a priori politics, and therefore of an a priori social subject. Radway's suggestion is that cultural studies embrace the daunting task and "take the fluid process of articulation as its topic, that is, the process whereby the historical human subject is constructed through the linkage, clash and confluence of many different discourses, practices, and activities" (1996: 245).

In addition to mapping the complex processes of subjectivity, cultural studies has yet to delineate the mechanisms between text and society. As John Hartley points out:

> If the media exert power and influence over their audiences – that is, socially – how is it done textually? And if media texts exert power, what is the place of meaning in the analysis of power? ... In spite of Foucaultian, postmodernist, feminist and other interventions, or perhaps because of them, it seems as hard as ever to explain the link between textual and social power. (1996: 221, 224)

Additionally, cultural studies' emphasis on sub-cultural groups raises questions about the relationship of the individual to identifying communities, and the relationship of both, respectively, to dominant discourses. In what ways and to what degree is the individual merely a representative of the group(s) or the configuration of a "unique" individual in its accumulation of a multiple but specific series of subject positions?

Angela McRobbie suggests that: "What really is at stake is the nature and form of the relationships which bind these differences together and from which they accrue their meaning. It is in relation to each other that identity is formed. If meaning is relational, so too is identity" (1992: 726). If identity is the relational process of the confluence of differences within the individual, between the individual and specific communities of identity formation, and between identifying communities, how might this multitude of simultaneous registers of subject positions enact or allow slippage, selection, agency, and intervention?

Spectatorship has been theorized, variously and to date, as the construction of the viewing subject through psychic processes, discursive formations, and social and historical relations. It seems most productive to consider the spectator as the effect of such processes, formations, and relations as they operate concurrently, rather than thinking of each dynamic as singular or exclusive of the others. Less clear, then, are the complex and simultaneous interconnections between these dynamics, which may render the spectator as anything along a barometer of viewership from passive imbiber of pre-packaged ideology to active and successful resistent of these same oppressive psychic, discursive, and socio-historical forces. Each theorization – psychoanalytic, discursive, social – has contributed to the concept of spectatorship, while not managing to address all the problematics summoned up by the other, differing approaches.

While the social subject of cultural studies regains a political position in that the act of viewing and the meanings created are sites of struggle and contestation, the theory doesn't yet sufficiently explain the operations by which the viewing subject attains a position of (some) power as the participant in the process of his or her own subject formation, able to resist, in however limited a manner, the dominance of social and cultural discourses. Similarly, although discursive theory offers a more complex way of understanding subjectivity than psychoanalytic theory, rendering the subject fluid rather than fixed, it has the same difficulties as cultural studies in elaborating the mechanisms by which such subjectivities might occur.

Limited and erroneous in its universalizing, unverifiable claims for the unconscious and its lack of participatory (hence political) position in the process of "becoming" a subject, psychoanalytic theory did, however, attempt to account for reasons why the viewer is "captured" by the text. Addressing the questions of what mechanisms operate to "fix" the viewer into an oppressive position in seeming opposition to her or his self-interests, and why, once the spectator realizes these are the operative mechanisms, she or he can't break free of that captivation, psychoanalytic theory's responses were the concepts of pleasure and desire, operating alongside social and ideological coercion.

Cultural studies developed, in part, out of resistance to the notion of the spectator/subject as "psychic dupe," determined entirely by the robotic effects of his or her own unconscious processes – similar to the criticized concept of the public as cultural dupes, simplemindedly affected by the dominant ideologies embedded in the popular. Yet, neither the social subject nor the discursive subject adequately explains the determinants, the "why" of specific subject or spectatorial articulations, remaining open projects for both cultural studies and post-structuralism.

References

Ang, Ien. 1996. "Ethnography and Radical Contextualism in Audience Studies." In *The Audience and Its Landscape*. Ed. James Hay, Lawrence Grossberg, and Ellen Wartella. Boulder: Westview Press. 247–62.

Baudry, Jean-Louis. 1992 [1970]. "Ideological Effects of the Basic Cinematographic Apparatus." In *Film Theory and Criticism*. Ed. Gerald Mast, Marshall Cohen, and Leo Braudy. Oxford: Oxford University Press. 302–12.

Butler, Judith. 1992. "Contingent Foundations: Feminism and the Question of 'Postmodernism.'" In *Feminists Theorize the Political*. Ed. Judith Butler and Joan W. Scott. New York: Routledge. 3–21.

de Lauretis, Teresa. 1988. "Aesthetic and Feminist Theory: Rethinking Women's Cinema." In *Female Spectators: Looking at Film and Television*. Ed. E. Deidre Pribram. London: Verso. 174–95.

Fiske, John. 1992. "Cultural Studies and Television." In *Channels of Discourse, Reassembled: Television and Contemporary Criticism*, rev. edn. Ed. Robert C. Allen. Chapel Hill: University of North Carolina Press. 284–326.

Flitterman-Lewis, Sandy. 1992. "Part IV: Psychoanalysis." In Robert Stam, Robert Burgoyne, and Sandy Flitterman-Lewis. *New Vocabularies in Film Semiotics: Structuralism, Post-Structuralism and Beyond*. New York: Routledge. 123–83.

Foucault, Michel. 1972 [1971]. *The Archaeology of Knowledge and the Discourse on Language*. Trans. A. M. Sheridan Smith. New York: Pantheon.

——. 1973 [1966]. *The Order of Things: An Archaeology of the Human Sciences*. New York: Vintage Books.

—— 1978 [1976]. *The History of Sexuality, Volume I: An Introduction*. Trans. Robert Hurley. New York: Penguin Books.

—— 1984a. "On the Genealogy of Ethics: An Overview of Work in Progress." In *The Foucault Reader*. Ed. Paul Rabinow. New York: Pantheon Books. 340–72.

—— 1984b. "Preface to *The History of Sexuality, Volume II.*" In *The Foucault Reader*. Ed. Paul Rabinow. New York: Pantheon Books. 333–9.

Gledhill, Christine. 1984. "Recent Developments in Feminist Film Theory." In *Re-Vision: Essays in Feminist Film Criticism*. Ed. Mary Ann Doane, Patricia Mellencamp, and Linda Williams. Los Angeles: AFI. 18–48.

Hall, Stuart. 1993. "Encoding, Decoding." In *The Cultural Studies Reader*. Ed. Simon During. London: Routledge. 90–103.

Hartley, John. 1996. "Power Viewing: A Glance at Pervasion in the Postmodern Perplex." In *The Audience and Its Landscape*. Ed. James Hay, Lawrence Grossberg, and Ellen Wartella. Boulder: Westview Press. 221–33.

Johnston, Claire. 1992 [1980]. "The Subject of Feminist Film Theory/Practice." In *The Sexual Subject: A Screen Reader in Sexuality*. London: Routledge. 295–300.

McRobbie, Angela. 1992. "Post-Marxism and Cultural Studies: A Post-Script." In *Cultural Studies*. Ed. Lawrence Grossberg, Cary Nelson, and Paula A. Treichler. New York: Routledge. 719–30.

Metz, Christian. 1982 [1977]. *Psychoanalysis and Cinema: The Imaginary Signifier*. Trans. Ben Brewster, Alfred Guzzetti, Ceila Britton, and Annwyl Williams. Bloomington: Indiana University Press.

Mouffe, Chantal. 1992. "Feminism, Citizenship and Radical Democratic Politics." In *Feminists Theorize the Political*. Ed. Judith Butler and Joan W. Scott. New York: Routledge. 369–84.

Mulvey, Laura. 1989a [1973]. "Fears, Fantasies and the Male Unconscious or 'You Don't Know What Is Happening, Do You, Mr. Jones?'" In *Visual and Other Pleasures*. Bloomington: Indiana University Press. 6–8.

—— 1989b [1975]. "Visual Pleasure and Narrative Cinema." In *Visual and Other Pleasures*. Bloomington: Indiana University Press. 14–26.

Radway, Janice. 1996. "The Hegemony of 'Specificity' and the Impasse in Audience Research: Cultural Studies and the Problem of Ethnography." In *The Audience and Its Landscape*. Ed. James Hay, Lawrence Grossberg, and Ellen Wartella. Boulder: Westview Press. 235–45.

Slack, Jennifer Daryl, and Laurie Anne Whitt. 1992. "Ethics and Cultural Studies." In *Cultural Studies*. Ed. Lawrence Grossberg, Cary Nelson, and Paula A. Treichler. New York: Routledge. 571–92.

Stam, Robert. 1992. "Part V: From Realism to Intertextuality." In Robert Stam, Robert Burgoyne, and Sandy Flitterman-Lewis. *New Vocabularies in Film Semiotics: Structuralism, Post-Structuralism and Beyond*. New York: Routledge. 184–221.

Turner, Graeme. 1992. *British Cultural Studies: An Introduction*, 2nd edn. London: Routledge.

164

CHAPTER TEN

Laura Mulvey Meets Catherine Tramell Meets the She-Man: Counter-History, Reclamation, and Incongruity in Lesbian, Gay, and Queer Film and Media Criticism

Julia Erhart

What are the specific contributions lesbian, gay, and queer theorists have made to the fields of film and media studies? That the answer to this question is the subject of a chapter in this film theory companion is a testament to the positive growth of an area that, until recently, was characterized largely by censorship and absence. In the early 1990s the factor that united lesbian, gay, and queer media researchers was the dearth of representation – on-screen, in production, in print, and in the classroom. Initially an effect of more than 25 years of institutional censorship that forbade even the vaguest references to "sex perversion" (let alone depictions of it), pre-1960s, US-produced representations of homosexuality fared much the same as homosexuality itself before the gay liberation movements – as a closeted and little seen thing. In contrast, the queer pulse of film and media studies today is strong and vibrant. It is audible on conference panels, editorial boards, and the pages of academic journals: *Screen*, *Wide Angle*, and *Media International Australia* have all featured one or more special issues on the topic, and *Camera Obscura*, *Cineaste*, *Jump Cut*, and *Continuum* regularly showcase lesbian, gay, and queer research. Lesbian, gay, and queer work is recognized by academic publishers, which, during the years 1993–97, produced no fewer than nine English-language film or popular culture anthologies with the word "lesbian," "gay," or "queer" in the title.[1] And, mentioning only scholarly books and journals is to overlook more popular publishing venues where significant queer film work has also appeared.[2]

The question I hope to answer is how this increased presence has impacted on the theories and methods in film and media studies per se. It is my aim in this chapter to show how lesbians, gays, and queers have challenged, altered, intervened in, as well as benefited from film and media studies discussions. By no means are scholars in agreement on how to pose such challenges, making for a compelling diversity in queer media studies in terms of method, aim, and object. Divisions exist as to where to do work, in the New York City Public Library, in the Gay Museums of Berlin or Amsterdam, in the UCLA Film Archives, or in the local cineplex. Splits occur over the matter of method, with some wishing to identify a gay cinematic language in the tradition of *écriture féminine*; some wanting to focus exclusively on self-declared and typically avant-garde or independent "lesbian" or "gay" films by lesbian, gay, or queer authors; others wishing to work concertedly on popular culture, reading hegemonic texts against the grain, looking for the queer within the straight. Lesbian, gay, and queer work further divides over who or what is the proper subject of research – queers? straights? texts? culture? whose texts? whose culture?

This chapter is a thematic account of the recent major strands of lesbian, gay, and queer film and media studies work. Touchstones like Parker Tyler's *Screening the Sexes* (published in 1972), the first edited scholarly volume entitled *Gays and Film* (Dyer 1977), Vito Russo's *The Celluloid Closet* (1981), and the *Jump Cut* Special Section on "Lesbians and Film" (Becker et al. 1981) tell us that there is indeed a history to contemporary lesbian, gay, and queer film and media research. While I will not be discussing those works in any detail, I will attempt to provide, whenever possible, a genealogy of methodological antecedents to contemporary trends in hopes of explaining the shape of research at present. This chapter does not portray a seamless development of the field but emphasizes rather the divergent approaches lesbian, gay, and queer scholars are currently choosing. It is divided into three sections, which comprise key threads in contemporary lesbian, gay, and queer research. These are: historiography; text-oriented, psychoanalytic approaches; and queer theory. Now, admittedly, this division suggests a discreteness that is organizationally beneficial but in reality artificial. For example, several of the historiographies I consider in section 1 employ psychoanalytic modes of analysis, which is the subject of section 2; some of the theorists I examine in the third "queer theory" section have been influenced by feminist film theory, which is also discussed in section 2. And some of the authors mentioned in sections 1 and 2 identify as "queer theorists," a term that I reserve for work I discuss in the section 3. My intention in creating the three groupings is to suggest neither an absolute difference between work of different sections nor a fundamental sameness between research within sections, but to convey that lesbian, gay, and queer scholars form at least virtual communities, which in turn produce and sustain different clusters of research.

1   Queer Stories, Counter-Histories: Reviewing the Past

How have lesbian and gay representations changed from one era to the next, and what can these changes tell us about historical homosexualities? What do films from periods prior to our own say about homosexual life during those times? How would a queer perspective add to or interrupt histories of media censorship, film genres, or national media? What specific concerns must we bring to bear to theorize historical images of lesbianism or gayness? These are the questions that both inspire and unravel from lesbian, gay, and queer historiographic film and media work, whose most elementary function, in the US at least, is to inform present-day viewers of the presence of gays in cinema before the demise of the Censorship Code.[3] Lesbian, gay, and queer film and media historiography also counters the misapprehension, common in gay studies, that the material of gay history is not visual, adding an important component to a field that has demonstrated a passion for gay history but not, as Tom Waugh notes, in its visual dimensions (1996: 5). Finally, lesbian, gay, and queer film and media historiography makes a significant methodological contribution: given the multi-leveled operations of censorship that functioned for decades to circumscribe homosexual representation, queer film and media historians know how to circumvent seeming dead-ends and to give shape to subjects from frequently scant or unconvincing information.

A recurring challenge to lesbian, gay, and queer film and media historiography is that of presentism, or what I would call the anachronistic fallacy. It is well known that homosexual identities and the terms that designate them are protean, subject to change from one period to the next. The referent of "homosexual" in the 1990s is entirely different from its inter-war one; yet should this preclude our analogizing between the social positionings of a female-to-male cross-dresser in 1914 and a contemporary dyke, as R. Bruce Brasell has done? The most convincing lesbian, gay, and queer historiographic film and media work has been sensitive to both sides of the matter, refraining from imposing current-day language on archival images while permitting productive comparisons between representations from different decades. The most effective historiographies, one of which continues to be Ruby Rich's 1981 study of the lesbian classic *Maedchen in Uniform* (Leontine Sagan, 1931), scan films not for images of queerness (an entirely recent invention) but for how they represent historical attitudes to gender and sexuality, including spinsterhood, independent women, bachelorhood, and so forth. Aware of the fact that homosexual identities are not the same as contemporary lesbian and gay ones, historiographies like Rich's put their readers in the place of the historical viewer, contextualizing images in terms of such a viewer's potential perceptions.

The scarcity of popular pre-1960s representations is a problem facing nearly all lesbian, gay, and queer film and media historiographers. What images do exist are recognized as being predominantly straight-authored and as having little to do with historical gayness due to the operations of the notoriously strenuous Code. This is expressly the problem Chon Noriega grapples with in his 1990 survey of changing attitudes toward homosexuality during the Code years. Knowing that depictions within films, from *These Three* (1936) through *Advise and Consent* (1962), yield little reliable information about gayness, Noriega shifts the focus to the paratextual material of the films' reviews in search of what had not been permitted to be represented on-screen. For Noriega, the question is not "whether certain films have – in retrospect – gay and lesbian characters, subtexts, stars, or directors as an anodyne to censorship, but how homosexuality was 'put into discourse,' and the role censorship played during the Code era" (1990: 21). Showing how to look beyond or around distorted screen representations, the essay provides a counter-discursive response to the deformations caused by the Code.

Noriega's essay continues to be one of the most successful examples of the use of paratextual elements to delineate historically specific practices of film consumption. Taking account of marketing and publicity strategies, Rhona Berenstein's *Attack of the Leading Ladies* (1996) also makes use of paratextual data and is a good example of a topic that remains important in contemporary lesbian, gay, and queer historiographic research, which is genre analysis. *Attack of the Leading Ladies* is one of two relatively recent academic press publications on the horror genre, which has long attracted lesbian, gay, and queer film and media interest (Zimmerman 1981; Weiss 1993). Published within a year of each other, Berenstein's book and Harry Benshoff's *Monsters in the Closet* (1997) could not be more different in method and focus; for these reasons they are useful illustrations of some of the choices facing lesbian, gay, and queer researchers in this area. Not focussed on "queerness" per se, Berenstein's book takes as its subject matter a specific series of films (Hollywood horror movies made between 1931 and 1936) to consider how they demonstrate the precarious nature of normative white reproductive sexuality under threat from homosexual men, lesbians, people of color, and women. Benshoff's book, in contrast, surveys images of monstrousness in English-language horror films from the classical Hollywood era to the present, primarily insofar as they serve as a vehicle for homosexuality. Whereas Berenstein's book is a synchronic study of a discrete set of films in terms of the cultural anxieties they represent, Benshoff's presents a transhistoric view of the concurrent development of two cultural tropes, "monster" and "queer."

The discrepancy in Berenstein's and Benshoff's research in method and object of labor is typical of most lesbian, gay, and queer genre work. Many researchers strive to delineate the queer significance of media previously considered primarily interesting to straight viewers, as Benshoff does, frequently by drawing attention to the prevalence of stock lesbian or gay characters within a genre and/or the artificiality of heterosexual coupling; others name homosexuality as but one of several contexts helpful to understanding a genre, as Juan A. Suárez's (1996) book on the American avant-garde does. Some research celebrates the sheer fact of bringing previously unseen work to print, as Tom Waugh's elegant historical study of pornography succeeds in doing. Almost all lesbian, gay, and queer genre analyses seek to recognize a gay presence within texts, forms, and genres that previously had gone unrecognized.[4]

Highlighting the gay-relevance of subjects previously considered to be straight is also the aim of work that is organized around a single director or artist. Some of this, like Mark Gatiss's 1995 book on James Whale, is more or less straightforwardly biographical in scope; in contrast, a 1996 anthology on Warhol (Doyle et al.) seeks a broader discussion of the audiences and contexts that produce the artist. Still other research, like the dossier on Hitchcock included in the *Out in*

Culture anthology (Creekmur and Doty 1995), attempts to explore how a single director's films can challenge normative ideas about sexuality in spite of the fact that the director did not identify as gay. Most of these studies foreground, or at least problematize, the individual's (homo)sexuality as an important authorial component which deserves to be reclaimed by contemporary queers. This is true even of the work on Hitchcock, whose membership in this category may strike some as precarious, but which editor Doty defends on the basis that " 'being' queer (homosexual, gay, bisexual, or lesbian) [may be] a case not only of naming yourself but of being named by your pleasures, desires, and even your anxieties" (183). Writing with a comparable intention, the editors of the Warhol anthology state that their aim is to counter the "degaying" that occurs in high-art assessments of Warhol's work. Demanding recognition of Warhol's sexuality, they go on to say: "to ignore Warhol's queerness is to miss what is most valuable, interesting, sexy, and political about his work" (Doyle et al. 1996: 2).

As the Warhol editors do, most biographical writing touches upon experiences of marginalization and self-censorship; it thus has the potential to expose the social circumstances of a particular period, as Judith Mayne's (1994) book on Arzner does. Not a traditional biography, Mayne's book is an examination that names the director's sexuality as the key but not the sole salient epistemological frame through which to consider her films. Less interested in plotting every aspect of the director's life than in delineating a broad context for her work, Mayne both works within and against conventional auteur studies. Interestingly, one of the by-products of Mayne's biographical work has been a resuscitation of the organizational trope of the author. Due in part to Mayne's and, notably, Richard Dyer's interest, the topic has enjoyed something of a revival. Both Mayne and Dyer have named the author's death premature arguing that a director's sexuality, along with his or her gender, race, and class background, are indeed salient factors (Mayne 1991; Dyer 1991). For lesbians and gay men, the sexed, raced, classed, and gendered body of the director is not an outmoded modernist critical concept, but an idea that should never have been abandoned to begin with. Proof of this are the number of author-oriented studies that have appeared in the past few years of potential interest to lesbian, gay, and queer students, which include the aforementioned Warhol anthology and dossier on Hitchcock as well as a book on Laurel and Hardy (Sanders 1995).[5]

In sum, interest in lesbian, gay, and queer film and media historiography is strong, as is positive concern for the historical presence of lesbians, gays, and queers on-screen during prior decades (which is related but not precisely equivalent to the former). This latter interest is particularly visible in the domain of nonacademic publishing, where an outpouring of multi-national guides and reference works, whose focus is contemporary as well as historical images of gayness, indicates a burgeoning, extra-academic epistemophilia for this aspect of the gay past. To date, I count at least eight English-language anthologies that catalogue in one way or another past representations of gayness in film, on television, and on the radio, in the US, the UK, and Australia.[6] The popularizing of this strand of queer film history is in many ways very exciting, suggesting a concern for queer-film matters outside the realm of the university.

Before concluding this section on "queer-storiography," there is a cautionary note to add. In her bibliographic essay on queer theory and cinema, Fabienne Worth (1993) notes the tendency for lesbian and gay cinema research to split up according to sex, with gay men conducting historiographic archival work and lesbians carrying out text-based, psychological analyses of, more often than not, contemporary films. While there is certainly sufficient gay male interest in non-historiographic textual analysis, and though the above discussion testifies to the presence of some lesbian historiographic work, overall I agree with Worth that there is a paucity of lesbian historiography, which isn't the case for feminist film historiography more generally. Antonia Lant's 1991 research on women in wartime Britain and Shelley Stamp Lindsey's 1996 analysis of US women viewers in the 1910s are but two testaments to the vigor and vitality of feminist historiography, as is Lea Jacobs's 1991 study of the negotiations between directors and censors over the "sensitive" subjects of adultery and prostitution. However, what I find curious is that none of these admirable historical projects has been a "lesbian" project per se.[7] My point here is not why lesbians have been "excluded" from the above-mentioned analyses; rather, it is why they have not conducted more of their own. The early and mid-1980s witnessed the publication of two ethnographies (Whitaker 1981; Ellsworth 1986), but since the last was published, nothing more has emerged in this area. While one could well imagine a range of compelling lesbian historiography, including more ethnographic work as well as archival projects that would scrutinize censorship files for conversations about "sex perversion," such studies have not been quick to materialize.

2   Laura Mulvey Meets Catherine Tramell: Paradigm Shifts

In contrast to the relative paucity of lesbian historiography, there has been an abundance of lesbian as well as gay research in the area of contemporary spectatorship. In overall method and aim, lesbian and gay spectatorship work takes as its point of departure heterosexual feminist film theory of the 1970s and early 1980s. Initially, this theory aimed to qualify from a feminist point of view many of the concepts delineated by the "apparatus theorists," as Jean-Louis Baudry, Stephen Heath, and Christian Metz were called. Research by, among others, Pam Cook, Claire Johnston, and in particular an early essay by Laura Mulvey established several basic premises: first, that there exists a relationship between power, objectification, and looking that neatly divides up along sexual lines, with men being the agent of the look and women the object viewed; second, that the mechanisms of cinema foster such relationships; third, that psychoanalysis helps delineate and indeed undo such mechanisms; and fourth, that the mode of analysis needed to bring about change must engage at the level of the signifier, i.e. the text.

170

Whereas Mulvey had limited herself to the concerns of male viewers, others, such as Mary Ann Doane and Tania Modleski, worked to outline the vicissitudes of viewing for the female spectator. Given shape by the language of psycho-analysis, this spectator was not a product of empirical or ethnographic research but an idealized subject divorced from cultural or historical context, whose class, racial, national, and sexual orientation generally went unnamed – at least in the ten years immediately following "Visual Pleasure." Simply, this first phase of post-Mulvey theory could not envision exceptions to structures of looking which positioned men as agents and women as objects, let alone a gay or lesbian spectator. Though not articulated from an explicitly gay or lesbian point of view, two essays carved out a space for such spectators, Dyer's 1982 essay on the male pin-up (see Dyer 1992), and de Lauretis's 1984 chapter, in *Alice Doesn't*, entitled "Desire and Narrative." Without challenging Mulvey's findings, both Dyer and de Lauretis extended their analyses to areas not covered by Mulvey. Dyer examined the consequences of objectifying men (rather than women), detailing the configuration of the look in the case of the male "pin-up." De Lauretis, in turn, added to Mulvey's observation of the sexedness of narrative, the idea that narrative was *hetero*sexed, detailing how narrative nearly always involves the movement of a male hero through female-gendered space. Though homosexuality was not a matter of concern at this point to either critic, both essays made room for speculations about the difference lesbianism or gayness might make to Mulvey's paradigm, signaling that spectating need not conform to a sexist or heterosexist paradigm.

Following these initial formulations, lesbian and gay theorists began to qualify how feminist film theory's notions of looking, desire, and identification would manifest themselves in lesbian or gay contexts. While earlier feminist elabora-tions of such processes were useful to lesbians and gays, many took feminist film theory to task for failing to question the sexuality of the viewer and for theorizing a system of viewership that, without exception, associated men with vision, desire, and agency, and women with passivity and desiredness. The list of grievances was long and sustained; critics noted that what had been termed a *sexual* division of labor was in fact a *heterosexual* division of labor and sub-sequently castigated feminist film theory for not recognizing that desire and identification need not be patterned after the model of heterosexuality (Becker et al., 1981; Stacey 1987; Straayer 1996; de Lauretis 1991; Mayne 1991; Roof 1991; White 1991).

In spite of these negative appraisals, gays' and lesbians' debt to feminist film theory is certain. Nowhere is it more clear than in work that invokes feminist psychoanalytic theory directly. Lizzie Thynne's (1995) essay on the Canadian *Anne Trister* (Lea Pool, 1986) and Patricia White's (1995) reading of the British film *Nocturne* (Joy Chamberlain, 1991) both rehearse heterosexual feminist read-ings of the mother–daughter relation for their understanding of lesbian specta-torship, as other work does (Holmlund 1989). However, an important forerunner to those articles, Teresa de Lauretis's 1991 essay "Film and the Visible," on *She*

Must Be Seeing Things, circumvents feminist versions of psychoanalysis altogether to return to an earlier pre-feminist model. Significantly invested in Laplanche and Pontalis's notion of primal fantasy as a setting of desire, de Lauretis is concerned with Sheila McLaughlin's 1987 film because of how it articulates such a scene – and especially because it does so with female characters. Delineating how the film is addressed to a lesbian subject, in terms that Laplanche and Pontalis outline, the essay shows how concepts such as "primal fantasy" are relevant for lesbians, as well as the significance, for psychoanalysis, of a lesbian film such as McLaughlin's.

De Lauretis's essay is one of several which functioned to update the psychoanalytic vocabulary from a lesbian, gay, or queer perspective. Work also emerged claiming the importance for lesbians, gays, and queers of classical scenarios or mechanisms such as fetishism (Knapp 1993), the primal scene (Miller 1991), castration (ibid.), paranoia (White 1991; Barton 1995), and identification (Stacey 1987; Vermeule 1991; de Lauretis 1991), as well as the psychoanalytic dimension of cultural processes like homophobia and lesbophobia. Mulvey's description of the nonequivalence of cinematic identification and desire – the resolute difference between the character that the viewer identifies with and the one she or he desires – has been a matter of particularly heated debate. While de Lauretis has insisted on the theoretical validity of Mulvey's distinction, Jackie Stacey has argued that representations that show the two mechanisms to be co-present, in films like *All About Eve*, provide models lesbians would do well to embrace. Stacey's point has been taken up to some extent by Blakey Vermeule (1991), which has in turn generated further commentary from de Lauretis (1994).

At the very least, the critical activity that I am detailing indicates the dramatic amplification of the psychoanalytic vocabulary with the materialization of lesbian and gay work. Simply, lesbian and gay research brought new life to the field at the very moment when some heterosexual feminists were beginning to express frustrations about the limitations of feminist film theory, as I have said elsewhere (Erhart 1997).[8]

Further shifts followed the amplification of the psychoanalytic vocabulary. Whereas the focus of Mulvey's address had been the central male protagonist, lesbian and gay theorists scanned the entire frame, looking well beyond the activities of the leading heterosexual couple to consider relationships between a range of minor characters. Renée Hoogland's (1997) essay on *Basic Instinct* is one of several that demonstrate this. Hoogland's thesis is that the lesbian is a paradoxical figure made invisible by culture yet simultaneously endowed with privileged powers of sight. To substantiate this, she examines the film's treatment of the infamous, ice-pick-wielding Catherine Tramell and her lesbian lover, Roxy, in light of cultural narratives of lesbianism, specifically looking at the scene in which Catherine and the male hero are in bed as Roxy watches from a distance. From this scene, Hoogland deduces that the banishment of Roxy to the margins of the frame recycles an earlier narrative of sexual subject constitution – that of the little boy looking on during the primal scene, with the result of reducing the lesbian to what she calls an "aspiring male" (35). Hoogland's analysis is important because it considers the positions and points of view of *all* the characters, apart from those of the male lead, to determine how the film recycles dominant myths of sexual subject constitution. Like other work I have discussed, the essay significantly corrects, updates, and expands feminist film theory, the psycho-analytic models it employs, and the textual material it considers, augmenting both the theoretical paradigms and our knowledge of lesbian subjectivity.

While lesbian and gay spectatorship work has undoubtedly gone beyond feminist film theory, it has preserved an essential component, which is the belief in the primacy of sexual difference in the constitution of human subjects. For each of the theorists I have discussed, gender has remained just as key as it did for Mulvey, even as new factors were added. In contrast, a considerable number of lesbian, gay, and queer film and media researchers have bypassed the debates with feminist film theory and have articulated modes of sexuality beyond and apart from debates about sexual difference. Three key things must be said about such research. First, it sees sexual difference as, to quote Chris Straayer, a "forced system [which] produces false conclusions" (1996: 7); second, it is critical of feminist film theory's understanding of the visual text as the sole determinant of the viewing experience; and third, it identifies with the word "queer" in terms of its practice and subject of research.

3 Everyone Has Their "Queer Moments":[9] Reception and the Bisexed Body

Appropriated in the late 1980s by the North American activist group Queer Nation and the special "Queer Theory" issue of *differences* more or less simultaneously, the term "queer" was fast adopted by activists and academics throughout the anglophone First World as both more "in your face" *and* more inclusive than earlier terms had been. To begin with, "queer" was intended as a productively disruptive alternative to what was seen as the assimilationist and conservative aims of post-liberation movement majority gay culture. If liberal gay rights advocates located homosexuality within the separate-but-equal discourse of difference, "queer" was impatiently oppositional in its stance, celebrating and drawing attention to rather than minimizing its difference from the hegemonic (hetero)sexual norm. Second, "queer" emerged as a more inclusive alternative to terms such as "lesbian" and particularly "gay," which tended to refer to specific sub-sets of the gay communities while excluding others. Third, "queer" was seen as a more economical alternative to cumbersome taxonomical listings like "lesbian, gay, bisexual, transgender..." which themselves had evolved when the universality of "gay" was called into question. In its very lack of specificity, "queer" promoted itself as a term "beyond labels," as a term that included lesbians, queers of color, bisexuals, cross-dressers, transgendered people, and sexual others of all stripes, in addition to gay white men. Whereas lesbian or gay

173

politics could be attacked on account of their unrepresentativeness, "queer" claimed to represent everyone. By avoiding prioritizing any single identity group, "queer" aimed to include all groups, mitigating the divisions that separated communities. "Queer" thus contained a strong Utopian element, to which this passage attests:

> queer . . . includes people who might also self-identify as gay and/or lesbian, bisexual, transsexual, transvestite, drag queen, leather daddy, lipstick lesbian, pansy, fairy, dyke, butch, femme, feminist, asexual, and so on – any people not explicitly defining themselves in "traditional" heterosexual terms. (Benshoff 1997: 5)

Utopian, indeed. Almost immediately after the term appeared, objections were raised as to whether "queer" really could represent such strands of diversity or whether it was merely a spruced up and more contemporary version of the earlier, recognizedly problematic word, "gay." If "gay" had come to seem too male- and white-specific, what made the word "queer" any different?[10]

At the same time as criticisms began to be voiced, in specifically academic realms "queer" was welcomed as an alternative to the constraints of identity-politics-driven appellations of the 1970s and '80s. What was deemed particularly useful about the term was the way it defied easy definition in terms of both the subject(s) to which it referred and the practices that it comprised. Throwing into question traditional or accepted understandings of sexuality but also, more broadly, gender, maleness, femaleness, love, sex, and desire, "queer" provoked a reevaluation of the object of the critical enterprise itself. This was particularly true in the area of film and media studies, where the notion stimulated discussions about aesthetics, marginality, and the relationship between art and audience, in addition to conversations about the difference between "queer" and the terms "gay" and "lesbian" (Smyth 1994). Critics identifying with the word went so far as to ask: What is the object of criticism? What determines the relationship between viewers and texts? Are our disciplinary models adequate to describe it? What makes a film or a television show queer to begin with?

In the area of film and media studies, a good deal of effort initially went into determining what the term "queer" referred to, as critics attempted to decide what exactly a queer image or narrative looked like. Typically "queer" was defined oppositionally, that is, as representation that possessed qualities of being non-, contra-, or anti-straight (Doty 1993; Benshoff 1997; Evans and Gamman 1995; Burston and Richardson 1995; Robertson 1996). "Queer" was representation that "makes heterosexuality strange" (Nataf 1995: 59). "Queer" continued to signify images that were deemed homosexual, but stood also for non-homosexual imagery that fell outside of hegemonic representation, such as representations of s/m sexuality, intergenerational sex, or interspecies sex. Whereas the earlier categories "lesbian" and "gay" were suited to analyzing discrete lesbian and gay images from (respectively) lesbian and gay films like *Desert Hearts* and *Boys in the Band*, a queer approach helped analyze images that appealed to both lesbians and gay men (not to mention bisexuals and transgendered people). For example, images meriting a queer reading included Katherine Hepburn dressed as a young man in *Sylvia Scarlett* as well as the relationship between Russell, Monroe, and the male athletes in *Gentlemen Prefer Blondes* (Doty 1993).

In addition to trying to figure queer content, queer researchers initially attempted to clarify where exactly *queerness* (as the status of being queer was designated) could be found. Three relatively uncontroversial areas emerged: first, queerness could appear in scripts by lesbian, gay, or queer authors; second, it could be conveyed to a scene via a lesbian, gay, or queer director; or third, it could be seen in performances of actors who were lesbian, gay, or queer (Benshoff 1997: 13–16). Alexander Doty additionally proposed that queerness could arise from the viewing situation as a response of a certain audience to specific imagery. A product of contextual relationships, queerness could result from the reception position adopted by self-identified lesbian, gay, or queer audiences to queer as well as non-queer texts, or by straight-identified viewers to lesbian, gay, or queer images. In this formulation, queerness was not an essential attribute inhering within either the text or the viewer, but arose from their co-configuration.

The consequence of Doty's definition of queerness was a radical reevaluation of the previously impermeable border between "gay" and "straight." If queerness could emerge from particular practices and moments regardless of the identities or experiences of viewers, it could just as easily be apprehended – maybe even performed – by "heterosexuals" as by "homosexuals." Queerness could materialize regardless of the self-termed identity of a viewer or the socially recognized gayness of the object viewed. Queerness was no longer experienced solely by self-declared queers watching "out" texts, but was produced within and circulated by so-called "straight" culture too.

What should be noted about the intervention I have just described is its fundamental anti-essentialism; this is visible in Doty's reluctance to name, as immutable, homosexual and heterosexual identities. The mutability of identity is key to contemporary queer film and media theory, a good part of which has rejected, as I have said, established categories of gayness, preferring to think of sexuality as a performance. Influenced by the writing of Eve Sedgwick and Judith Butler (themselves influenced by Joan Riviere, Monique Wittig, and J. L. Austin, among others) as well as by work going on in science studies, queer media theorists have noted the insufficiency of binarily opposed and mutually exclusive terms such as "man" and "woman." Chris Straayer, for example, has posited the arbitrariness of biology's two-sex system, suggesting that the notion of an "embraced incongruity" of maleness and femaleness may be more appropriate (1996: 88).

According to Straayer, both popular-culture forms such as music video and modernist genres like video art already suggest the existence of such an incongruity. Figures that manifest traits of both sexes not only destabilize the opposition between masculinity and femininity but are culturally empowered by this fact, rather than castrated, as psychoanalysis would have it. In her writing on the "bisexed" figure that she calls the She-man, Straayer shows how signifiers of femaleness such as certain kinds of clothing (in music video) magnify the power of a biologically male performer; she compares this to the way in which women's donning of male clothing sometimes results in masculine privilege (82). In both cases, the co-presence of seemingly mutually exclusive body parts and accoutrements (male bodies decked out in women's clothing, female bodies adorned with mustaches or dildos) undermines normative understandings of two-sexedness *and* renders powerful the respective performers. Intersexuals, hermaphrodites, dildo-wearing women, and others not fitting easily into either "male" or "female" categories are the beneficiaries in this new (but, Straayer says, already existing) system that privileges instability and contradictoriness over seamlessness.

What should be said about Straayer's work on the She-man is how far it has traveled from the concerns outlined in my second section, on lesbian and gay revisions to psychoanalytic feminist film theory.[11] For Straayer, queerness has more to do with performance and the figuration of the body than with the matter of object choice, that is, with what I would call sexual presentation rather than sexual *orientation*. Second, the *queerness* (to continue with that term) of the material Straayer discusses lies less in a spectator's against-the-grain response than within the texts themselves. For these reasons, it is not surprising that the matter of the spectator is not especially high on Straayer's list of concerns. Does it make a difference whether the She-man is viewed by a lesbian, a straight woman, a queer man, or a straight man? That this question is in many ways beside the point is a welcome exception to a body of theory that is more at ease discussing Hollywood than self-produced lesbian, gay, and queer work.

4 Conclusion

The presence of lesbian, gay, and queer work in film and media studies has been steadily on the rise, at the same time as it is consistently under revision. To discuss this work solely in the context of film and media studies, however, is to skew the reality of its origins and influences. In addition to film and media studies, gay, gender, and women's studies have all aided the field's development, providing inspiration and reading material to researchers who were perhaps not finding them in film and media departments. Lesbian, gay, and queer film and media researchers, in turn, have injected new life into the areas of gay, lesbian, and women's studies, contributing significantly at international queer and women's studies conferences, to anthologies, to journals, and in interdisciplinary teaching situations.

How queers fare in the world of production is a closely related matter. Though statistics on both behind-the-camera and on-screen participation in mainstream cinemas are lacking, the 1990s saw a flowering in lesbian and gay film and video festivals world-wide, 69 active ones being listed by Jackson and Tapp (1997).

While the majority of these happen in the US, indicating the bias that characterizes production as well as research, festivals currently take place in locations as widespread as Riga, Budapest, Hong Kong, Reykjavik, Leningrad, Jerusalem, Cork, Cape Town, and Turku. How much of the work seen at such festivals makes it back to the classroom, on to public television, or through other means to audiences unable to reach the metropolis is not entirely clear; but the increase in queer film (which has been produced in practically all of Latin America in addition to Cuba, Egypt, Thailand, Singapore, India, and Kazakhstan, as well as in Europe and North America) leaves me hopeful. However, the midnight-hour ban on the first Seoul Queer Film and Video Festival that occurred in September 1997, and on Wong Kar-Wai's gay-themed film *Happy Together* which occurred at the same time, reminds us that the internationalization of queer film and video is still partial.

Nonetheless, the range and breadth of lesbian, gay, and queer work has been impressive, as I have tried to show. Lesbians, gays, and queers have brought a visual dimension to gay history, have archived images and figures from the past, have delineated the lesbian and gay relevance of methods such as psychoanalysis, and have redefined the borders between previously discrete subjects like "gay" and "straight," image and audience, and male and female. How lesbians, gays, and queers keep on negotiating the thorny terrain of popular culture – especially film, which is irresistible and everywhere, stunningly affirmative and furiously homophobic, engaging a legion of desires, anxieties, and fantasies, sometimes all at once – is a matter which none of us can afford to ignore.

Notes

1 Burston and Richardson 1995; Creekmur and Doty 1995; Doan 1994; Doyle, Flatley, and Muñoz 1996; Gever, Greyson, and Parmar 1993; Gibbs 1994; Hamer and Budge 1995; Holmlund and Fuchs 1997; Wilton 1995.
2 Boffin and Fraser 1981; Burston 1995; Hadleigh 1993, 1994; Weiss 1993.
3 It is probably safe to say that the processes of regulation and liberalization that representations of homosexuality underwent in some European cinemas paralleled such processes in the United States. For example, *Victim* (Basil Dearden, 1961), Britain's first film to represent homosexuality in a favorable way, was released only one year prior to *Advise and Consent* in the US, suggesting similarities between the liberalization timetables of the British Board of Censors and the Censorship Code. For an older, comparative account of censorship regulations in Britain, the US, India, Canada, Australia, Denmark, France, and the USSR, from a legal point of view, see Hunnings 1967. A more recent collection of writings on censorship is edited by Petrie 1997; for a history of censorship in Britain, see Robertson 1989.
4 For good examples of work that defines new queer genres, see Holmlund 1991, 1994, and Straayer's chapter on the "Temporary Transvestite Film" in Straayer 1996. An example of a contemporary queer reclaiming of an already established genre is Holmlund and Fuchs' anthology on documentary (1997).

177

5 Additional recent examples of author-oriented studies would be individual chapters from Smith 1992 and Suárez 1996. The books treat homosexuality in a national context and in the context of the 1960s underground (respectively), but feature individual chapters on directors Pedro Almodóvar and Eloy de la Iglesia (in Smith), and Kenneth Anger, Andy Warhol, and Jack Smith (in Suárez).

6 Bourne 1996; Facets 1993; Howes 1993; Jackson and Tapp 1997; Murray 1996; Olson 1996; Parish 1993; Roen 1994; Steward 1994.

7 More perplexing, when lesbian scholars have authored "historical" studies, such work has not prioritized lesbian issues. This is the case for Jackie Stacey's 1994 study.

8 Lesbians and gays were of course not alone in their critiques of feminist film theory, whose blind spots to differences in race, ethnicity, age, and nationality were beginning to be voiced around the same time. These blind spots were centrally addressed in the introductory article to a special issue of *Camera Obscura* entitled "The Spectatrix," on female spectatorship (Doane and Bergstrom 1989). In that introduction, the editors reviewed criticisms by Ellen Seiter, Chris Straayer, Jacqueline Bobo, and numerous others, who identified a "single-mindedness" in feminist theory that made it extremely problematic (9). Agreeing with such critics about the need for divergent interests and methodologies, the editorial is characterized by a receptiveness to other methods and perspectives that had not often been seen before this moment.

9 This quote is from Burston and Richardson 1995 (6), paraphrasing Evans and Gamman.

10 For a recent critique of the term's masculinism, see Smyth 1994; Graham 1995. For a critique of its whiteness, see Dhairyam 1994.

11 While Straayer uses the terms "lesbian," "gay," and "queer" with equal ease, there are moments when she grants special privilege to the latter, as when she opposes "queer" lesbianism to "assimilationist" lesbianism (1996: 276). It is for this reason that I consider her a "queer theorist."

References

Barton, Sabrina. 1995. " 'Crisscross': Paranoia and Projection in *Strangers on a Train*." In Creekmur and Doty 1995. 216–38.

Becker, Edith, Michelle Citron, Julia Lesage, and B. Ruby Rich, eds. 1981. Special Section: "Lesbians and Film." *Jump Cut*: 17–21, 24–5.

Benshoff, Harry M. 1997. *Monsters in the Closet: Homosexuality and the Horror Film*. Manchester: Manchester University Press.

Berenstein, Rhona J. 1996. *Attack of the Leading Ladies: Gender, Sexuality, and Spectatorship in Classic Horror Cinema*. New York: Columbia University Press.

Boffin, Tessa, and Jean Fraser, eds. 1981. *Stolen Glances: Lesbians Take Photographs*. London: Pandora.

Bourne, Stephen. 1996. *Brief Encounters: Lesbians and Gays in British Cinema, 1930–1971*. London: Cassell.

Brasell, R. Bruce. 1997. "A Seed for Change: The Engenderment of *A Florida Enchantment*." *Cinema Journal* 36, 4 (summer): 3–21.

Burston, Paul. 1995. *What Are You Looking At? Queer Sex, Style and Cinema*. London: Cassell.

——, and Colin Richardson, eds. 1995. *A Queer Romance: Lesbians, Gay Men and Popular Culture*. London: Routledge.

Creekmur, Corey K., and Alexander Doty, eds. 1995. *Out in Culture: Gay, Lesbian, and Queer Essays on Popular Culture*. Durham, NC: Duke University Press.

de Lauretis, Teresa. 1984. *Alice Doesn't*. Bloomington: Indiana University Press.

——. 1991. "Film and the Visible." In *How Do I Look? Queer Film and Video*. Ed. Bad Object-Choices. Seattle: Bay Press. 223–76.

——. 1994. *The Practice of Love: Lesbian Sexuality and Perverse Desire*. Bloomington: Indiana University Press.

Dhairyam, Sagri. 1994. "Racing the Lesbian, Dodging White Critics." In Doan 1994. 25–46.

Doan, Laura, ed. 1994. *The Lesbian Postmodern*. New York: Columbia University Press.

Doane, Mary Ann, and Janet Bergstrom, eds. 1989. "The Spectatrix." *Camera Obscura* 20–1.

Doty, Alexander. 1993. *Making Things Perfectly Queer*. Minneapolis: University of Minnesota Press.

Doyle, Jennifer, Jonathan Flatley, and José Muñoz, eds. 1996. *Pop Out: Queer Warhol*. Durham, NC: Duke University Press.

Dyer, Richard, ed. 1977. *Gays and Film*. London: BFI.

——. 1991. "Believing in Fairies: The Author and the Homosexual." In Fuss 1991. 198–201.

——. 1992 [1982]. "Don't Look Now: The Instabilities of the Male Pin-Up." In Richard Dyer, *Only Entertainment*. London: Routledge.

Ellsworth, Elizabeth. 1986. "Illicit Pleasures: Feminist Spectators of *Personal Best*." *Wide Angle* 8, 2: 45–58.

Erhart, Julia. 1997. "She Must Be Theorizing Things: Fifteen Years of Lesbian Criticism, 1981–1996." In *Straight Studies Modified: Lesbian Interventions in the Academy*. Ed. Gabriele Griffin and Sonya Andermahr. London: Cassell. 86–101.

Evans, Caroline, and Lorraine Gamman. 1995. "The Gaze Revisited, or Reviewing Queer Viewing." In Burston and Richardson 1995. 13–56.

Facets Multimedia, Inc. (principal writer: Patrick Z. McGavin). 1993. *Facets Gay and Lesbian Video Guide*. Chicago: Facets.

Fuss, Diana, ed. 1991. *Inside/Out: Lesbian Theories, Gay Theories*. New York: Routledge.

Gatiss, Mark. 1995. *James Whale: A Biography or The Would-be Gentleman*. London: Cassell.

Gever, Martha, John Greyson, and Pratibha Parmar, eds. 1993. *Queer Looks: Perspectives on Lesbian and Gay Film and Video*. New York: Routledge.

Gibbs, Liz, ed. 1994. *Daring to Dissent: Lesbian Culture from Margin to Mainstream*. London: Cassell.

Graham, Paula. 1995. "Girl's Camp? The Politics of Parody." In Wilton 1995. 163–81.

Hadleigh, Boze. 1993. *The Lavender Screen: The Gay and Lesbian Films, Their Stars, Makers, Characters and Critics*. New York: Citadel.

——. 1994. *Hollywood Lesbians*. New York: Barricade.

Hamer, Diane, and Belinda Budge, eds. 1995. *The Good, the Bad, and the Gorgeous: Popular Culture's Romance with Lesbianism*. London: Pandora.

179

Holmlund, Christine. 1989. "I Love Luce: the Lesbian, Mimesis, and Masquerade in Irigaray, Freud, and Mainstream Film." *New Formations* 9: 105–24.

——. 1991. "When Is a Lesbian Not a Lesbian? The Lesbian Continuum and the Mainstream Femme Film." *Camera Obscura* 25–6: 145–80.

——. 1994. "Cruisin' for a Bruisin': Hollywood's Deadly (Lesbian) Dolls." *Cinema Journal* 34, 1: 31–51.

——, and Cynthia Fuchs, eds. 1997. *Between the Sheets, In the Streets: Queer, Lesbian, and Gay Documentary*. Minneapolis: University of Minnesota Press.

Hoogland, Renée C. 1997. *Lesbian Configurations*. London: Polity.

Howes, Keith. 1993. *Broadcasting It: An Encyclopedia of Homosexuality on Film, Radio and TV in the UK 1923–1993*. London: Cassell.

Hunnings, Neville March. 1967. *Film Censors and the Law*. London: Allen and Unwin.

Jackson, Claire, and Peter Tapp. 1997. *The Bent Lens: A World Guide to Gay and Lesbian Film*. Melbourne: Australian Catalogue Company.

Jacobs, Lea. 1991. *The Wages of Sin: Censorship and the Fallen Woman Film, 1928–1942*. Madison: University of Wisconsin Press.

Knapp, Lucretia. 1993. "The Queer Voice in *Marnie*." *Cinema Journal* 32, 4 (summer): 6–23.

Lant, Antonia. 1991. *Blackout: Reinventing Women for Wartime British Cinema*. Princeton: Princeton University Press.

Lindsey, Shelley Stamp. 1996. "Is Any Girl Safe? Female Spectators at the White Slave Films." *Screen* 37, 1: 1–15.

Mayne, Judith. 1991. "A Parallax View of Lesbian Authorship." In Fuss 1991. 173–84.

——. 1993. *Cinema and Spectatorship*. London: Routledge.

——. 1994. *Directed by Dorothy Arzner*. Bloomington: Indiana University Press.

Miller, D. A. 1991. "Anal *Rope*." In Fuss 1991. 119–41.

Murray, Raymond. 1996. *Images in the Dark: An Encyclopedia of Gay and Lesbian Film and Video*. New York: Plume.

Nataf, Z. Isiling. 1995. "Black Lesbian Spectatorship and Pleasure in Popular Cinema." In Burston and Richardson 1995. 57–80.

Noriega, Chon. 1990. " 'Something's Missing Here!': Homosexuality and Film Reviews during the Production Code Era, 1934–1962." *Cinema Journal* 30, 1: 20–41.

Olson, Jenni, ed. 1996. *The Ultimate Guide to Lesbian and Gay Film and Video*. London: Serpent's Tail.

Parish, James Robert. 1993. *Gays and Lesbians in Mainstream Cinema: Plots, Critiques, Casts and Credits for 272 Theatrical and Made-for-Television Hollywood Releases*. Jefferson, NC: McFarland.

Petrie, Ruth, ed. 1997. *Film and Censorship: The Index Reader*. London: Cassell.

Rich, B. Ruby. 1981. "From Repressive Tolerance to Erotic Liberation: *Maedchen in Uniform*." In Becker et al. 1981. 44–50.

Robertson, James C. 1989. *The Hidden Cinema: British Film Censorship in Action, 1913–1975*. London: Routledge.

Robertson, Pamela. 1996. *Guilty Pleasures: Feminist Camp from Mae West to Madonna*. Durham, NC: Duke University Press.

Roen, Paul. 1994. *High Camp: A Gay Guide to Camp and Cult Films*, vol. 1. San Francisco: Leyland.

Roof, Judith. 1991. *A Lure of Knowledge: Lesbian Sexuality and Theory*. New York: Columbia University Press.

Russo, Vito. 1981. *The Celluloid Closet.* New York: Harper.

Sanders, Jonathan. 1995. *Another Fine Dress: Role-Play in the Films of Laurel and Hardy.* London: Cassell.

Smith, Paul Julian. 1992. *Laws of Desire: Questions of Homosexuality in Spanish Writing and Film: 1960–1990.* New York: Oxford University Press.

Smyth, Cherry. 1994. "Beyond Queer Cinema: It's in Her Kiss." In Gibbs 1994. 194–213.

Stacey, Jackie. 1987. "Desperately Seeking Difference." *Screen* 28, 1: 48–61.

——. 1994. *Star Gazing: Hollywood Cinema and Female Spectatorship.* London: Routledge.

Steward, Steve. 1994. *Gay Hollywood: Film and Video Guide: 75 Years of Gay and Lesbian Images in the Movies.* Laguna Hills: Companion.

Straayer, Chris. 1996. *Deviant Eyes, Deviant Bodies: Sexual Re-orientations in Film and Video.* New York: Columbia University Press.

Suárez, Juan A. 1996. *Bike Boys, Drag Queens, and Superstars: Avant-Garde, Mass Culture, and Gay Identities in the 1960s Underground Cinema.* Bloomington: Indiana University Press.

Thynne, Lizzie. 1995. "The Space Between: Daughters and Lovers in *Anne Trister*." In Wilton 1995. 131–42.

Tyler, Parker. 1972. *Screening the Sexes: Homosexuality in the Movies.* New York: Holt.

Vermeule, Blakey. 1991. "Is There a Sedgwick School for Girls?" *Qui Parle?* 5, 1 (autumn/winter): 53–72.

Waugh, Thomas. 1996. *Hard to Imagine: Gay Male Eroticism in Photography and Film from Their Beginnings to Stonewall.* New York: Columbia University Press.

Weiss, Andrea. 1993. *Vampires and Violets: Lesbians in Film.* London: Penguin.

Whitaker, Judy. 1981. "Hollywood Transformed." In Becker et al. 1981. 33–5.

White, Patricia. 1991. "Female Spectator, Lesbian Specter: *The Haunting*." In Fuss 1991. 142–72.

——. 1995. "Governing Lesbian Desire: *Nocturne*'s Oedipal Fantasy." In *Feminisms in the Cinema.* Ed. Laura Pietropaolo and Ada Testaferri. Bloomington: Indiana University Press. 86–105.

Wilton, Tamsin, ed. 1995. *Immortal, Invisible: Lesbians and the Moving Image.* London: Routledge.

Worth, Fabienne. 1993. "Of Gayzes and Bodies: A Bibliographical Essay on Queer Theory, Psychoanalysis and Archeology." *Quarterly Review of Film and Video* 15, 1: 1–13.

Zimmerman, Bonnie. 1981. "Lesbian Vampires." In Becker et al. 1981. 23–4.

CHAPTER ELEVEN

Is There Class in this Text?: The Repression of Class in Film and Cultural Studies[1]

David James

1   Academic Identity Politics

During the last quarter-century, questions about social class have been pushed to the margins of the academic study of cinema and related cultural phenomena. Feminism and other forms of sexuality studies, and projects mobilized by and on behalf of people of color, have transformed the humanities; but in the remarkable extension of the limits of discourse that has resulted, the topic of class has become all but unspeakable, and so the possibility that socialism might shape a common struggle for women, blacks, and in fact oppressed groups of all kinds now has less of a command on either the popular or the intellectual imagination than at any time in the twentieth century. The devasting global assault on the working class itself, which these academic trends both reflect and assist, merits some initial reference.[2]

The toppling of the Berlin Wall on November 9, 1989, and the rapid collapse of Soviet-sponsored governments in Eastern Europe were everywhere touted as marking, not simply the West's victory in the Cold War, but the final, world-historical victory of capitalism *tout court*. Coming little more than a year after the events in Tienanmen Square had ended any remaining illusions about the Chinese Communist Party (which had in any case already abandoned socialism in its embrace of a market economy and a social order premised on class division and the future widening of it), these events signaled the complete integration of Second- and Third-World economies into the global market that had been accelerating over the previous two decades. Now only racial superstition and religious fanaticism interrupted a triumphant new world order dominated, if no longer controlled, by US capital.

The previous decade had brought parallel traumas to the working people of the anglophone West. Begun in the late 1960s in the United States, the radical reconstruction of the right matured in the 1980s' "Revolt of the Haves": the termination of the New Deal, the pseudo-populism of Reaganomics, and other attacks on the working class of a ferocity unprecedented in the twentieth century. In President Reagan's first administration, welfare cutbacks and regressive tax policies (for example, the top rate on unearned income was reduced from 70 to 50 percent) cost low-income families $23 billion, while high-income families gained more than $35 billion.[3] Families with annual incomes over $200,000 profited by $60,000, while those receiving below $10,000 lost an average of $1,100. Combined with the 1970s' transformations within the domestic economy and in its position in the global economy, Reaganomics widened income disparities and produced a substantially new social stratification. Figured as the "Brazilianization" of the economy or as the reshaping of the American income pyramid into an hourglass, the reproduction of global core–periphery relations within the First-World working class split the workforce into a small, more skilled sector and a very much larger, less skilled sector. Stably employed and sustained by corporate-subsidized welfare, the former gravitated toward and identified its interests with the capitalists and top business managers, while the latter declined into irregular employment or even permanent unemployment and, dependent on defunded state welfare, disintegrated in an overall immiseration of barbaric proportions.

The crucial site of this sustained offensive against working people was the attacks on those welfare programs most identified with the underclass (cuts in food stamps, child nutrition, aid to families with dependent children, and low-income housing, but not, for example, tax deductions on home mortgages) and especially on trade unions. Newly elected President Reagan's destruction of the Professional Air Traffic Controllers' Organization (ironically, the only union to have supported his candidacy) escalated the offensive that had been developing since the 1970s: the relocation of manufacturing to union-free Sunbelt regions, the closing of unionized shops and their reopening as open shops, and the use of wage differentials between unionized and nonunionized labor to divide the working class. Eviscerated by its failure to embrace the black, women's, and Third World solidarity movements after the 1960s and shackled by its cooperative ties to management, organized labor lost two million members during the 1980s, and at the end of the decade union membership was half what it had been at its high point after World War II. Fleeing a sinking ship, the Democrats (like the British Labour Party) abandoned their traditional constituencies – and working people abandoned the ballot box.

Nationally and in fact internationally coordinated, this objective reduction of the life opportunities of *all* working-class people cut across the New Social movements that had replaced class in post-1960s identity politics. While these movements had scored impressive gains for those members of them capable of entering the newly opened avenues for success in bourgeois society, far greater numbers of working-class women and blacks walked with the rest of the working class down the road to poverty and hopelessness. The same era that saw gender and ethnic identity politics make their momentous ideological advances also saw

183

the "feminization of poverty" (continued increases in female-headed households beyond the 1980 figure, when women comprised 66 percent of all adults officially classified as poor); the flight of the new black middle class and the further decline of living standards in urban African-American communities (by 1984, while a quarter of all children lived in poverty, twice that proportion of black children did); and the increase of sweatshop exploitation of both illegal and legal immigrants. Far from demonstrating the obsolescence of class divisions, bourgeois identity politics in fact concealed and so facilitated increased class polarizations. Taken together, these developments mark the fading of the vision of a rational, nonalienated, nonexploitative, and fully participatory democracy that had been the great imaginative achievement of Marxism, itself one of the great intellectual achievements of modernity.

Although the repression of consideration of class in cultural studies reflects these global developments, it was most immediately determined by the functions of the academy itself, where the emergence of discourses around sexual and ethnic identity simultaneously ensured the silencing of class theory. The social movements of the 1960s and then the mutually incommensurate micropolitics that split the left thrived in the university largely to the extent that they negotiated the personalization of the political into academic practices. Thus, in the case of feminism, the struggle for women's rights generally, the struggle to increase the presence of women in higher education, and the struggle to empower women as cultural producers all played their part in the struggle to develop feminist hermeneutics and historiography in the university, and were all understood as interdependent components of a broadly unified cultural initiative. Both the trace and the medium of the interdependence of these projects was a new, postmodernist discourse, a mixed autobiographical and critical mode based, to use Lyotard's (1984) terms, on narrative rather than science, whose immense rhetorical and analytic force was supplied by the heritage of shared subjectivity discovered in consciousness-raising.

Subsequent identity groups aspired to their own similarly united fronts, in which advances in academic theory, disseminated through para-academic institutions, would both nourish and be nourished by advances in the relevant constituencies in society at large. But though, in the academy and on its slopes, these interdependencies made possible great gains in the theoretical consideration of ethnic and sexual identity, the practice of constructing academic programs around the political interests of academics themselves in fact inhibited the emergence of parallel discourses around class. First, the crucial social agency that might have created an equivalent identity group was not present; the working class is not generally admitted into higher education, certainly not to elite research universities where theoretical work is done, in sufficient numbers to create the critical mass of working-class-identified subjects that could develop such a theoretical offensive in class terms.[4] Second, where affirmative action programs did fortuitously occasion the enrollment of working-class women or working-class people of color to these institutions, they were admitted (and interpellated), not *as* working class, but under the designation of their sexual or ethnic identities, identities that were subsequently invoked and affirmed by a panoply of methodologies, courses, journals, and other apparatuses, while their class background was ignored and any residual class consciousness and class loyalties they might have had were systematically inhibited.

And so, third, while all other identities have been eminently assimilable to the bourgeois academy, allowing female, black, and queer people to live privileged lives as female, black, and queer academics, such a richly rewarded career as the voice and image of a social identity is not even theoretically possible for a working-class person. Of course, the corporatization of higher education increasingly depends on the exploitation of graduate students and peripatetic adjuncts; but for those who attain it, a tenured life of college teaching and research is hardly alienated labor. Whatever its anxieties, it provides more of the rewards and satisfactions of bourgeois life than the exigencies and perils of the proletarian's.[5] In this respect, the best that a person from the working class can hope for is precisely that, to be *from* the working class, and in this displacement to be deprived of the possibility of speaking either as or for the working class, or even as or for her- or himself.[6] The back of a working-class identity must be broken across the abyss of a class migration to a station where feelings of pride and success will always be gnawed by those of estrangement and betrayal.[7]

Such institutional repression of working-class consciousness is not accidental. As Samuel Bowles and Herbert Gintis (1976) have shown, reforms in the US educational system have historically entailed the extension of privileges. But the schooling of the previously excluded has always been determined by the requirements of their roles in the structural transformations of capital: in the early nineteenth century, when public day schools replaced the family to complement the developing factory system; in the Progressive Era, when the expansion of high schools saw the common curriculum sacrificed to the ideology of vocationalism, with special tracking for working-class children that broke the control of trade unions in skill training; and since World War II, where acceptance of demands for expanded access to higher education by minorities and women has simultaneously satisfied corporate and state needs for technical, clerical, and other service skills – the creation of a reserve army of underemployed white-collar labor.[8] There is no reason not to suppose that contemporary curricular reforms and admissions programs are part of a similar historical process. However humanly necessary and objectively good they currently seem to be, and however they empower those few, selected members of minority groups that they incorporate, they are similarly instrumental in displacing class consciousness and otherwise legitimating and reproducing the class structure of a diversified postmodern economy. And indeed, despite pockets of resistance, multi-culturalism has itself long been a major corporate priority.

The point here is not to propose an academic identity politics based on class. The university already – sometimes loudly, sometimes silently – sustains a bourgeois identity politics, and a working-class identity politics within it will be structurally infeasible as long as the university maintains its present functions, that is to say, as long as the present social order and its systemic dependence on exploitation lasts. And in any case, whatever impossible identity working-class intellectuals sustain is fundamentally different from all others; rather than seeking to create a society in which its own interests are paramount, it looks forward to its own supersession, either in the terms of Marx's own proposal that "a *real* possibility of emancipation" demands the formation of "a class which is the dissolution of all classes," or in the now century-old commitment made by the Social Democrats who met at Erfurt in 1891 to struggle "against not only the exploitation and oppression of wage workers, but also every form of exploitation and oppression, be it directed against a class, a party, a sex, or a race."[9] Where they are not simply unimaginable, such conceptions are now so ubiquitously denigrated that any approach to the role of culture in class society is obliged to begin from the recognition of two absences: first, the absence of a generally accepted theory of class and of its articulation with other forms of structural social division, and hence second, the absence of any single systematic or comprehensive theory of the way class could inform the study of cinema. As a preliminary to remedying these absences, a synopsis of some of the overall issues involved in the concept of class and a review of the processes by which class came to be excluded from film studies may have its uses.[10]

2   Classical Marxism

Marx himself never systematically developed a theory of class, and in fact he died leaving the manuscript of volume 3 of *Capital* unfinished a few lines after he had asked the crucial question, "What constitutes a social class?" (Tucker 1978: 441). Nevertheless, in his work and in the traditions of Marxism, class is one of the key theoretical formulations. Fundamentally, it designates a position in the economic structure of society. As each historical era finds its own way of organizing material production, around the raw materials, tools, factories, and so on from which goods are produced (*the means of production*), it generates specific social divisions. These social divisions are classes; the relation between them is the hidden foundation of the social formation, and their conflictual interaction has driven history through a series of stages, or *modes of production*. If the latest of these, capitalism, were ever to exist in a pure form, it would allow two social positions in relation to the means of production: that of the few capitalists, who own them, and that of the many workers, who own nothing but their ability to work, which they are obliged to sell in order to live and from which the capitalists extract and appropriate more value than the labor power itself costs to reproduce. Capitalist society consists, in essence, then, of two classes, bourgeois and proletarian. Marx expected nineteenth-century capitalism to continue to develop the conflict between these until the proletariat would communally seize control of the means of production for themselves, eventually to create a society without a division between exploiter and exploited, "the *abolition of all classes* and . . . *a classless society*" (220). Beyond this premise of the historically specific, adversarial relation between capitalists and workers, almost everything in Marx about class is debatable. A number of issues, however, are both primary and recurrent: the apparent existence of classes or class factions other than those of capitalist and worker; the relation between the objective and subjective components of a class position; and the modes of activity in spheres outside the economic that follow from a given position in production.

The period in which Marx wrote was not one of pure capitalism, but rather one in which capitalism was in the process of replacing the previous mode of production, feudalism, with its class division between landowners and peasants, while signs of a future socialism were already perceptible. Class positions remaining from a previous era, as well as those harbingers of the next, thus complicated the social polarization. In the early 1880s, when he was writing the last page of *Capital*, Marx observed that whereas "middle and intermediate strata even here obliterate lines of demarcation," nevertheless "three great social classes" existed: "wage-labourers, capitalists and landlords" (441–2). But because the last of these, vestigial of feudalism, were progressively assimilating to capital, the situation as a whole fundamentally ratified the polarization thesis announced more than 30 years before in *The Communist Manifesto*: "Society as a whole is more and more splitting up into two great hostile camps, into two great classes directly facing each other: Bourgeoisie and Proletariat" (474).

Marx's prediction of the inevitability of class polarization was challenged as early as the 1890s, when, largely as a result of gains made by the labor movement, class conflict appeared to be diminishing in Western Europe, and economic crises and the immiseration of the proletariat seemed, if anything, to be becoming less likely. *Revisionism*, initially theorized by Eduard Bernstein, proposed that class fractions between capitalist and proletariat would not disappear but would continue to expand. The expansion of these middle classes indicated a reconciliation of the class conflicts of early capital and the progressive amelioration of workers' conditions through electoral politics of the kind that produced the traditions of social democracy. In the longer perspective, the proliferation of such fractions and other social reforms, together with the failure of the working class to emerge as the agent of revolutionary change in the Western democracies, has continued to challenge Marx's teleology, while simultaneously authorizing social movements premised on reconciliation between classes, or on structural division along lines other than class.

Marxism itself has provided several responses to these challenges. While in the West recent deindustrialization and the expansion of service and high technology sectors have allowed a small number of blue-collar workers to rise economically, a much greater number of previously skilled and unionized workers have slid down into unskilled service jobs and even unemployment, creating a new social polarization with a new and highly fragmented working class that traditional forms of working-class organization find difficult to access. And in any case, Marx's expectation of increasing class polarization was predicated on capitalism's assimilation of the entire global economy, and while he may not have theorized this fully, others did, most notably Lenin, in *Imperialism, the Highest Stage of Capitalism*, where he diagnosed the shift from the industrial to the financial form of capital as the vehicle of its expansion. Today, as the relocation of heavy manufacturing industries from the West to East Asia reconfigures the global division of labor and as the capitalist world market has come to control even the vestigial instances of pre-capitalist production, the "new world economy" and similar umbrellas for the unregulated internationalization of capital may temporarily obscure class polarization in the First World, but only as the exploitation of First-World proletariat is refracted in core–periphery relations and the spatial extension of capitalism generally. Thus, employing a simple, objective definition of class (the bourgeois are those who receive surplus value and are in a position to reinvest it, while all others are proletarian), Immanuel Wallerstein has argued that world-wide the process of increasing dependence on wage labor has continued, so that polarization remains "a historically correct hypothesis, not a false one . . . provided we use as the unit of calculation . . . the capitalist world-economy" (Balibar and Wallerstein 1991: 128).

The other, entirely different response to the apparent plurality of classes is to make a distinction between an objective position in relation to production (like Wallerstein's above, for example) and one that includes other factors, such as the notion that in the actual historical organization of classes, economic relations interact with political and ideological processes, especially the consciousness of specific historical subjects.[11] Marx himself proposed the basis for this latter response in a distinction between class *an sich* and class *für sich*, first adumbrated in 1847 in *The Poverty of Philosophy*: industrialization, he argued, has in fact "transformed the mass of the people of the country into workers. The combination of capital has created for this mass a common situation, common interests. This mass is thus already a class as against capital, but not yet for itself" (Tucker 1978: 218). But neither the specific point at which a social aggregate constituted around production actually forms a class nor the role played by ideological self-consciousness in the process was fully explained. Thus, in a parallel discussion of small peasants in mid-century France in *The Eighteenth Brumaire of Louis Bonaparte*, Marx implied the need for quite extensive activity outside the realm of the purely economic for a class formation properly to congeal. The peasants were, he argued, "a vast mass . . . which live in similar conditions"; but they were nevertheless so isolated from each other in the process of their work that they remained politically inchoate, "much as potatoes in a sack form a sackful of potatoes":

> In so far as millions of families live under economic conditions of existence that divide their mode of life, their interests and their culture from those of other classes, and put them in hostile contrast to the latter, they form a class. In so far as there is merely a local interconnection among these small peasants, and the identity of their interests begets no unity, no national union and no political organization,

they do not form a class. They are consequently incapable of enforcing their class interest in their own name. (608)

In his commentaries on the revolutions in nineteenth-century France, particularly *The Eighteenth Brumaire* (1852) and *The Civil War in France* (written in 1871), Marx explored the process by which class as an economic category is re-created in the more complex forms of class as a political category and function. The process includes the overlapping of modes of production to produce multiple class fractions (the aristocracy of finance, the industrial bourgeoisie, the middle class, the petite bourgeoisie, the army, the lumpenproletariat, the intellectual lights, the clergy, the rural population, as well as the proletariat proper of France in 1848, for example), the shifting alliances among these as they form "ruling blocs," the consolidation of such blocs in the formation of the state, and the subsequent degree of the state's autonomy and/or its implementation of specific class interests, either overtly or through some form of masquerade.

The question of class consciousness that runs through all these considerations is framed by the issues of ideology and ideological determination generally. Again, key formulations are not a little ambiguous. In *The German Ideology* (written 1845–6), Marx proposed a schema according to which the class that controls material production is also able to control mental production, with the result that the "ideas of the ruling class are in every epoch the ruling ideas.... The ruling ideas are nothing more than the ideal expression of the dominant material relationships" (172). Elsewhere, most clearly in the summary statement of the general principles of historical materialism in *A Contribution to the Critique of Political Economy* (1859), he strongly implied that different classes possess different ideologies: if "it is not the consciousness of men that determines their being, but, on the contrary, their social being that determines their consciousness" (4), then because different classes have different social beings, their different consciousnesses must follow.

Because intentional social reorganization would seem to require some degree of conscious opposition to the received status quo, the Marxist tradition has produced a number of positions about the consciousness of the agents of such historical change, especially about working-class self-consciousness. One tradition emphasizes its importance. Rosa Luxembourg, for example, believed that the working class could generate its own class consciousness through its own mass political action; and Georg Lukács argued, in *History and Class-Consciousness*, that although the working class is the only class capable of true self-knowledge, practically speaking the conditions of working-class people's lives inhibit its emergence, necessitating its construction from outside by the party, a position fully developed by Lenin. On the other hand, the need for or possibility of such a self-consciousness posited in this "Hegelian" tradition has been denied by "structural" Marxists, notably Louis Althusser and Nicos Poulantzas. Referencing the anti-humanism of late Marx, instanced in his claim in *Capital* that he was dealing with individuals "only in so far as they are the personifications of economic categories, embodiments [or bearers, *Träger*] of economic categories, embodiments of particular class-relations and class-interests" (297), Althusser theorized classes as objective social structures, whose nature and development are independent of any immanent subjectivity, even in the members of the working class themselves.

Multiplied by the details of subsequent political history as well as by transformations in the nature of capital, these indeterminacies in Marx have generated the body of Marxist class theory. This is beyond even the meagerest summary here, but three issues do merit mention: the main non-Marxist theories of class; debates about class in contemporary sociology; and "post-Marxist" attacks on the primacy of the working class in left politics.

3   Other Theories of Class

Besides Marx, the main contributor to classical sociological theories of class was Max Weber (1864–1920), who conceived of class somewhat more loosely as a specification of "life chances," defined by a position not in productive relations but in market relations, determined by ownership of property and possession of skills and education. He subsumed the resulting plurality of market situations into four "social classes": the working class; the petite bourgeoisie; technicians, specialists and lower-level management; and those who were privileged through property and education. In addition to rejecting Marx's notion of necessary structural conflict among these groups, he also rejected any distinction between conscious and unconscious positioning and hence the possibility of economistic historical development. *The Protestant Ethic and the Spirit of Capitalism*, his analysis of the origins of modern society, thus emphasized the role of ideology, specifically Calvinism, as producing rather than reflecting economic transformation. The importance of economic class for Weber is further qualified in its relation to an alternative formulation, that of the "status group," according to which individuals derive social identity from common cultural patterns, including consumption and other lifestyle priorities.

Much post-war sociology effected various forms of Marx–Weber synthesis in functionalist theories of the relation between (objective) class formation and (subjective) class action. The most prominent neo-Weberian, John Goldthorpe, for example, devised a class scheme closely resembling those used by market researchers and census bureaus, which combined market and work situations to differentiate seven levels aggregated into three categories: service, working, and intermediate classes. On the basis of this analysis, he then explored the degree to which these positions have produced actual demographic identities capable of social action and also tracked social mobility across class positions (Crompton 1993: 57–60, 63–9).[12]

Erik Olin Wright, on the other hand, retained the Marxist principle of class positions generated in production; his work has attempted to demonstrate that the plurality of new middle classes may actually be reduced back to primary economic relations, so as to sustain the polarization thesis. To the bourgeoisie, proletariat, and petite bourgeoisie – the three basic positions developed in orthodox Marxism in respect of ownership or nonownership of the means of production – he added three *contradictory* class locations: managers and supervisors; small employers; and semi-autonomous wage earners. Occupants of these locations are contradictorily determined: managers, for instance, do not own the means of production yet they do control both means of production and labor power, whereas semi-autonomous wage earners do not own or control the material means of production, but nor do they sell their labor power (Wright 1985: 19–57). In subsequent work, as he shifted his emphasis from forms of domination to processes of exploitation, Wright (1989) was forced to double the number of classes in the occupational scheme, as well as to develop increasingly sophisticated theoretical and statistical procedures to map synchronic positions and mobility among them. Although he has not been able to produce a model that can satisfactorily account for multiple intermediary classes, neither has he abandoned either the general project or its Marxist foundations.

Given the economic emphasis of these Weberian and neo-Marxist traditions, it is not surprising that their reverberation in cultural studies has been slight; but other Marxist–Weberian sociologies oriented toward consumption, particularly symbolic consumption, have been heard, most notably the work of Pierre Bourdieu.[13] His *Distinction: A Social Critique of the Judgement of Taste* (1984), a self-designated "ethnography of France," synthesized a Marxist understanding of class as an objective structural position in relation to production with an extensive system of stratification based on subjective values – a broadly Weberian attention to symbolic practices, including lifestyles and consumption preferences. Occupation categories supply the major social strata (working, middle, and upper classes) and the internal divisions within them, but positions in these – and the operations of power generally – are seen as sustained through other social and cultural factors, which Bourdieu defines as educational and cultural "capital." An individual's or social group's possession of social and cultural capital produces a characteristic system of dispositions, which Bourdieu calls the *habitus* – "the internalized form of class condition and of the conditioning it entails" (101). Together, the economic, social, and cultural conditions constitute class: "Social class is not defined solely by a position in the relation of production, but by the class habitus which is 'normally' (i.e. with a high statistical probability) associated with that position" (372).

Generally, Bourdieu argues, the hierarchies of occupation and taste are homologous; higher social class reproduces itself with better education, which produces more cultural capital, leading to superior social standing and power, including a greater capacity to process works of "legitimate" culture. But there are significant variations within the three major class divisions that reflect not only the different overall volume of a given capital, but also its different "composition," that is, the relative proportion of the economic, social, and cultural

191

forms. These variations engender the different tastes and consumption habits of the various groups within each stratum. Within the dominant class, for example, the economic capital of industrial employers dominates their cultural capital, whereas the opposite is the case for intellectuals (115); for recreation, then, the former prefer golf "with its aristocratic etiquette, its English vocabulary and its great exclusive spaces, together with extrinsic profits, such as the accumulation of social capital," while the latter get high ascetically, in mountaineering for example, which "offers for minimum economic costs the maximum distinction, distance, and spiritual elevation" (219).

Distinction was based on surveys taken in France, some as long ago as 1963. In anglophone countries 30 years later, neither the occupational class patterns, which are its basis, nor the codes of cultural differentiation are nearly as clear; a working-class taste for *La Traviata* against an haute bourgeois taste for *Well-Tempered Clavier* will not register in a leveled cultural milieu where both works are denigrated as "high" culture. Bourdieu's understanding of cultural preferences is, moreover, strongly deterministic, and although it allows for extremely fine gradings of class location and is extraordinarily responsive to cultural factors that internally stratify occupational categories, it makes no place for individual or sub-cultural resistance to them or movement through them. Nevertheless, his demonstration of how class situation not only permeates and controls all forms of subjectivity, but in fact comprises it – in Bourdieu's words, how a class "condition" in fact "impos[es] conditionings" (101) – remains a powerful challenge to the end-of-class ideologies that now dominate the academic study of culture. Of these, Ernesto Laclau and Chantal Mouffe's use of post-structural theory to authorize the replacement of class by other forms of identity in radical politics became widely fashionable.

In their *Hegemony and Socialist Strategy* (1985), Laclau and Mouffe developed a "post-Marxism" in which the proletariat's inability to hegemonize over the "New Social movements" has caused the disintegration of the historical role proposed for it in Marxism:

> What is now in crisis is a whole conception of socialism which rests upon the ontological centrality of the working class, upon the role of Revolution, with a capital "r," as the founding moment in the transition from one type of society to another, and upon the illusory prospect of a perfectly unitary and homogenous collective will that will render pointless the moment of politics. The plural and multifarious character of contemporary social struggles has finally dissolved the last foundation for that political imaginary. (2)

Their revisionism is distinguished by a highly sophisticated repertoire of discourse theory drawn especially from Saussure, Wittgenstein, Foucault, and Derrida – a theoretical apparatus that they use to read the classic Marxist texts from Bernstein to Althusser deconstructively. Their reading, they claim, discloses the persistence of a fundamental economic determinism that has caused all Marxists to give an ontological priority to the working class, even in social analyses that propose forms of class alliance; although a plurality of social actors are recognized, the search for a "true working-class subject" forces their reduction back into class politics. Against such an essentialism and against an undifferentiated pluralism, they argue the need for new forms of "*social logics* which ... acquire their meaning in precise conjunctural and relational contexts where they will always be limited by other – frequently contradictory – logics; but none of them has absolute validity, in the sense of defining a space or structural moment which could not in its turn be subverted" (142–3).

Laclau and Mouffe have encountered some resistance from the left.[14] Their historical rereading of the Marxist tradition has been criticized as reductionist, a straw-man caricature that conceals the actual complexity of the relations between the economic and political developed in it, and the argument that economic production does generate social relations and hence classes prior to their discursive articulation has been reasserted. The political programs their conclusions project have likewise been dismissed as merely a new pluralism or as so abstract and vague as to be virtually useless. But since some version of the crisis in Marxist theory they describe is all but axiomatic in the entire New Left tradition (articulated in its essentials 30 years earlier by C. Wright Mills) as well as in many post-war Marxisms (Eurocommunism, for example), by and large the academy has received their work with relief and gratitude. Their argument that class need no longer be considered *the* hegemonic formation of political alterity in a model of "radical democracy" that still necessarily included a socialist dimension, "the abolition of capitalist relations of production" (192), has slipped into justification for the abandonment of class as even one among other categories of resistance – a specifically anti-working-class politics that their subsequent writings have endorsed. Here we cannot explore that process in the realm of political thought, but a virtually identical itinerary may be traced in the displacement of class from two of the bodies of cultural theory engendered by the New Left: 1970s film theory and 1980s cultural studies.

4   The Displacement of Class from Film Theory and Cultural Studies

Especially after the Comintern adopted Popular Front Policies, in the late 1930s many forms of populist film culture in which class politics were paramount flourished across Western Europe and the United States; but in the renewal of radical politics after the 1950s the importance of class was radically diminished, especially in the US.[15] The reasons for this are complex, though beyond whatever plausibility remained to arguments for "American exceptionalism," clearly the revelations about Stalin, followed by the Cold War and McCarthyism, had virtually destroyed any popular currency Marxism might still have had. With the notable exceptions of the Black Panthers and certain sectors of the Vietnam War resistance, the main social movements of the 1960s such as Civil Rights and Women's Liberation – the immediate sources of contemporary ethnic and sexual identity politics – developed more in opposition to Marxism than in articulation with it. But in France, following the success of the union of students and workers in the May events and the challenge to Gaullism, the vocabulary of cultural criticism was not only self-consciously Marxist, but its Marxism was to some degree class-oriented. So, initially, were both radical film and radical film theory in the period immediately after 1968. The subsequent evaporation of class from this Marxism and then the general failure of French Marxism reverberated through the anglophone adoption of French film theory, particularly around the heritage of Louis Althusser.

Of Althusser's various interventions – the proposal of the autonomy of the economic, political, and ideological practices; the theory of the epistemological break between the conceptual frameworks of the early and the late Marx; the replacement of a Hegelian, humanist conception of the subject by one determined by the lived social structures – the most fateful for film studies was his theory of ideology. Given his strictures on Marx's early Hegelian writings, it is ironic that Althusser should have taken up the general model of ideology proposed in *The German Ideology*, that is, as pandemic and consistent in the social formation as a whole rather than class-specific. As early as 1967, he recognized the limitations that resulted; he was "not equipped for an adequate treatment of certain questions," and so he "did not examine... the 'fusion' of Marxist theory and the *workers' movement* ... did not examine the *concrete forms of existence* of this 'fusion' (organization of the class struggle – trade unions, parties – the means and methods of direction of the class struggle by these organizations)" (1977: 15). But he never redressed the deficiency, and with the sole exception of the autonomy allowed to certain intellectual activity designated as science (or "theoretical practice"), all the other social, material, and ideological apparatuses that call the subject into being were understood as promoting each other uniformly, and were lived so completely across all social classes as to amount to a general conditioning that structured even the unconscious. Developed through Lacanian psychoanalysis, this theory of ideology was appropriated by film studies with a similar essentialism; the ideological effects of cinema were seen as socially uniform because they were intrinsic to its apparatus, to the historical conditions of its invention, and to all cases of its use apart from deliberate avant-gardist ruptures of its fundamental and enabling mechanism, primary identification.

Since the British importation of French theory took place in the mid-1970s at exactly the time when its psychoanalytic component was being most forcefully developed, the early 1970s' concern with the rediscovery of early Soviet cinema (also imitated from French journals) was hardly in place before a psychoanalytic theory of the subject was dropped like a cuckoo's egg into the nest of historical materialism. Thus, to take one example, in the 1974 special issue of *Screen* devoted to a reconsideration of Brecht as exemplary for a contemporary revolutionary cinema, his use of techniques of formal rupture and negation as a means to critical distanciation were re-presented via a Freudian rather than a Marxian theory of fetishism (Heath 1974). The combination of semiology and psycho-analysis that comprised *Screen*'s "Marxism," especially as it moved to disentan-gle a purely Lacanian concern with subject formation from its previous Althusserian concern with ideology, was challenged in both Britain and the United States – in the first case, from a position which sought to sustain concern with working-class cultural values (e.g. Buscombe et al. 1975: 129–30), and in the second, where *Jump Cut* was beginning to nurture a populist radical film criti-cism that did include elements of class consciousness, from a working-class feminist position (e.g. Lesage 1974). But with the fading of the suspicion of Freud common in US feminism in the early 1970s, Lacanian psychoanalysis came to dominate US film theory almost entirely. As it did so, the only social difference that film theory could thenceforth register was the specificity that psychoanalysis itself could theorize, that is sexual difference. After this point, given that even the historically specific family structure was not admissible as a mediating agency in the structuration of the unconscious and of language around the phallus or its lack, the main currents of cinema studies had no theoretical means of addressing issues of class. That they have also had no desire to do so has been confirmed in the generally parallel itinerary followed by the other New Left tradition of cultural criticism, cultural studies.

The founders of British cultural studies – Richard Hoggart, Raymond Wil-liams, and E. P. Thompson – were committed to working-class politics, and the first two were themselves of working-class origin. Their early critical and histor-iographical writing was informed by their political commitments as well as by their address to specific constituencies, especially as they found them through their participation in adult education programs for working-class people. In this, their project paralleled later feminist practices, even though (in the case of Williams and Hoggart) its autobiographical component was displaced into novels and autobiography, rather than being combined with criticism to form the mixed objective/subjective mode that made early feminist writing so powerful. Initially, their project entailed not the repression of class content from Marxism so much as the gradual discovery that European Marxism could in some cases supply a vocabulary for the analysis of working-class culture. With the conspicuous exception of Thompson's (1978) attack on Althusserianism and "theory" in general and his own correlative subjectivist (and empiricist) theory of class as something that "happens when some men, as a result of common experiences (inherited or shared), feel and articulate the identity of their interests as between themselves, and as against other men" (1963: 9), British cultural studies profited from the translation into English of the texts of Western Marxism: Lukács, the Frankfurt School, and, especially, Gramsci. By the early 1970s, "a decisive second ... break into a complex Marxism" (Hall 1980a: 25) allowed researchers at the Birmingham Centre for Contemporary Cultural Studies to jettison Anglo-Amer-ican structural–functionalist sociology, and so to produce the mid-1970s projects of reading working-class life for its "lived meanings," and the initial studies of deviant sub-cultures, schooling, and workplace relations, as well as sophisticated metatheoretical considerations (e.g. Clarke et al. 1979). These were thoroughly informed by Althusser, but structural Marxism's inability to pose the concept of class from within a general theory of ideology and its lack of a theoretical means of conceptualizing ideological resistance made it less and less useful, especially as text-based, semiological studies were increasingly linked to sociological studies of actual audiences. The consequent "turn to Gramsci" – a turn away from the concept of monolithic, virtually irresistible ideological determination toward that of a dialectical relation among the interests of several classes under the hegemony of one of them – was incompatible with the *Screen* problematic.

Birmingham's implicit challenge to Althusserianism and "*Screen* theory" was taken up by Rosalind Coward. Admitting (more than charitably) that "in *Screen* itself, there has been little work which deals explicitly with the problems of class analysis," she nevertheless argued that its Lacanian theories of subject formation invalidated the Birmingham Centre's papers, in which "the ideological and political are finally reduced to being an expression of a class interest or position" (1977: 75–6). Denying reductionism, Birmingham retorted that *Screen*'s view of the autonomy of discursive practices and the refusal of any "determinacy in, articulation with or pertinent specific effects for other levels of the social formation" (Chambers at al. 1977: 116) discredited any theory of ideology it might otherwise propose, certainly any Marxist one. Presumably spurred by this interchange, the Media Group at Birmingham spent the next year (1977–8) studying *Screen* theory and reevaluating its own premises, but without finding anything to make them amend their position. Stuart Hall's summary response (1980b) again attacked *Screen*'s exclusive concern with the psychoanalytic construction of the subject as an essentialism that excluded any other determination that the social formation, in its historically specific forms, might exert and made any concept of ideological struggle impossible. In advancing Birmingham's alternative, David Morley (1992) did invoke Michel Pêcheux's concept of an interdiscourse, by which the differential effects of specific discursive practices are seen as inflecting the uniformity of primary subject positioning; but, practically, his work was still based on Hall's "decoding" model, published some seven years earlier. Indeed his empirical studies of the reception of British television news programs (made with Charlotte Brunsdon) presupposed precisely the self-identical, humanist subject which *Screen* had worked so hard to dispose of.

The progress of this and of Morley's independent work was not, however, immune to the prevailing currents. The early study of the audience for the television program *Nationwide* was overtly concerned with class and had demonstrated very clear, if direct, correlations between class position and patterns of decoding.[16] But Morley's discontent with the imprecision of the model of the class structure used, which might well have prompted him to develop a more sophisticated model, instead caused him to abandon class for an exclusive concern with gender. His subsequent studies of the contexts of television reception still focussed on working-class families, but since they were *all* working class, class was a constant; it thus became invisible in all the analyses, which in any case made no attempt to explore the class specificity of the gender relations discovered or to compare them with gender relations in more privileged families. Though Morley eventually recognized that "gender analysis was prioritized more exclusively than had originally been intended, and the effectivity of this particular factor was isolated from that of others – such as class and age" (1992: 160), he did not return to class.

Otherwise, in attempting to combine a historically and socially specific semiotics with a nonreductionist sociology, and in walking a thin line between recognition of the ways people actively and creatively make over industrial culture to their own uses and acknowledgment of the constraints that surround such interventions, Morley's work was representative of the best of 1980s media studies. In general, however, what became the main current of cultural studies in the United States abandoned not only Birmingham's concern with the working class, but also the Marxist and feminist critical components of the early projects. What Morley himself designated as "the 'don't worry, be happy' school of (principally American) cultural studies" (11) became essentially accommodationist, preoccupied with affirmative models of the consumption of industrial culture as itself a form of empowerment, the site of resistance. Where the ethereal heat of *Screen* theory had boiled off Althusser's Marxism, so, amid the political defeats and defeatism of the Reagan/Thatcher and then the Clinton eras, the lowlier ambitions of cultural studies drained the Marxism out of Gramsci.[17]

Notes

1   This essay includes material previously published in James 1996a and 1996b.
2   There are, of course, exceptions: some work in labor history; less in literary criticism, with Barbara Foley's (1993) study of proletarian fiction being especially noteworthy; and some essays in cinema studies, such as Auster and Quart 1978; Biskind and Ehrenreich 1980; Hansen 1983; Jameson 1990; Kleinhans 1974; Mayne 1982; Nichols 1972; Ross 1991; Ryan and Kellner 1988; Sklar 1975; Stead 1989; Traube 1992; and several essays in Sklar and Musser 1990. Hansen and Philipson (1990) have assembled essential articles on socialist–feminism.
3   Figures here and below are variously from American Social History Project 1992; Chafe 1995; Davis 1986; and Ferguson and Rogers 1986.
4   See Bowles and Gintis 1976, especially pp. 209–13, for a survey of statistics on the stratification of higher education by family income. Bourdieu notes that only 6.7 percent of French professors come from working-class families (1988: 44).
5   Erik Olin Wright (1979) surveyed various models of the class position of intellectuals – that they are workers, that they belong to several different classes, that they are part of the petite bourgeoisie, and that they are part of a professional–managerial class – concluding that they occupy contradictory locations.
6   Bourdieu points out that the intellectual who attempts to put himself or herself in the place of the worker can actually experience neither the conditionings that position imposes nor, especially, the necessity that informs those conditionings; but he also

197

points out that migration out of the working class makes "true" representations of working-class experience similarly unavailable for people who "originate from these classes" (1984: 372–4, 587 nn. 1, 2). His whole section on the determination of working-class culture by the experience of domination is very important.

7　*Strangers in Paradise: Academics from the Working Class* (Ryan and Sackrey 1984) is a collection of autobiographical essays typically illustrating the fact that "to grow up working class, then to take on the full trappings of the life of the college professor, *internalizes the conflicts in the hierarchy of the class system within the individual, upwardly mobile person*" (5). This principle of the "hidden injuries of class" is adopted from the book of that title (Sennett and Cobb 1973), an account of the experience of working-class people in Boston.

8　Bowles and Gintis's (1976) "reproduction theory" of capitalist education, with its general principle that any "adequate explanation" of "the evidently critical relationship between education and the capitalist economy . . . must begin with the fact that schools produce workers" (10), recognizes that the "authoritarian classroom does produce productive workers, but it also produces misfits and rebels" (12), but it does not develop the alternative function. Bowles and Gintis's work is usefully supplemented by an important text from a quite different tradition, Paul Willis's *Learning to Labor: How Working Class Kids Get Working Class Jobs* (1981), an ethnography of the forms of cultural resistance mobilized by working-class youth, which nevertheless assures their reproduction as working class. In its contrast with Bowles and Gintis's functionalism – which can find hope only in "a socialist movement [and] the creation of working-class consciousness" to replace "the divisive and fragmented consciousness of US working people" (285) – Willis's recognition of the "deep disjunctions and desperate tensions within social and cultural reproduction" that allows for "challenging and subversive and . . . threatening" sub-cultural contestation (175) was a major contribution to the Gramscian phase of British cultural studies.

9　The first quote here is from *Contribution to the Critique of Hegel's Philosophy of Right* in Tucker 1978 (64); all subsequent references to Marx's writings are to this edition. The entire statement of principles adopted at Erfurt is reprinted in Laidler 1968 (233–6).

10　Johnson (1979) provides a useful overview of Marxist theories of class, especially as they affect issues of culture. Other useful introductions may be found in Bottomore 1983 (74–8) and Crompton 1993 (23–9).

11　Przeworski (1977) provides an especially useful survey of the history of this position in Marxist thought.

12　Crompton (1993) has made an excellent – and user-friendly – overview of the history and present state of debates about class in sociology. In addition to the theoretical class schemes deriving from the traditions of Marx and Weber, she considers other categories of class indexes, such as "commonsense" hierarchies based on occupation and subjective scales of social status.

13　Brubaker (1985) usefully surveys Bourdieu's work, though he underestimates the importance of social position in relation to production in Bourdieu's model of class identity.

14　Of these, Wood (1986) is especially useful in placing Laclau and Mouffe's disarticulation of the political from the economic in the "retreat from class" of 1970s anglophone post-Althusserianism generally, especially in the work of Barry Hindess and Paul Hirst.

15   A notable exception here is the school of radical historians fostered by William Appleman Williams at the University of Wisconsin, who in 1959 founded the seminal journal *Studies on the Left*. For an overview of this left historiography, see Wiener 1991. The relevance of this school's corporate liberalism thesis – that corporate capital's appropriation of popular protest movements within the ideology of liberalism prevents their challenging capitalism itself on specifically socialist grounds – continues to increase.

16   The conclusion was "that patterns of decoding should not be seen as being simply determined by class position, but by the way in which social position articulates with the individual's position in different discursive formations" (Morley 1992: 116). So whereas there were great differences in the decodings made by people of different classes, there were also differences within classes. Within working-class reception of *Nationwide*, for example, he found a "profound difference in decodings between those groups which are nonunion, or are simply 'members' of unions, and those groups with an active involvement in the discourses of trade unionism – although the two categories of groups have the same working-class background... union officials tend to produce forms of negotiated decoding; the shop stewards produce a fully oppositional form of decoding... and simply inactive union members ... tend to reproduce dominant decodings" (116). But Morley's conclusions here, which strikingly resemble Bourdieu's general model described above, were read in the United States as if they demonstrated that there were *no* correlations between decoding and class. See Morley 1992 (12–13) for his complaints about these mis-readings and his attempts to clarify.

17   For overviews of the erasure of the critical component in 1980s Gramscianism, see Budd et al. 1990 and Harris 1992. Morley 1992 (1–41) reviews some of the same issues.

References

Althusser, Louis. 1977. *For Marx*. London: New Left Books.

American Social History Project. 1992. *Who Built America? Working People and the Nation's Economy, Politics, Culture and Society. Vol. 2: From the Guilded Age to the Present*. New York: Pantheon.

Auster, Albert, and Leonard Quart. 1978. "The Working Class Goes to Hollywood." *Cineaste* 9, 1: 4–7.

Balibar, Etienne, and Immanuel Wallerstein. 1991. *Race, Nation, Class: Ambiguous Identities*. London: Verso.

Biskind, Peter, and Barbara Ehrenreich. 1980. "Machismo and Hollywood's Working Class." *Socialist Review* 50/51: 109–30.

Bottomore, Tom, ed. 1983. *A Dictionary of Marxist Thought*. Cambridge: Harvard University Press.

Bourdieu, Pierre. 1984. *Distinction: A Social Critique of the Judgment of Taste*. Cambridge: Harvard University Press.

——. 1988. *Homo Academicus*. Stanford: Stanford University Press.

Bowles, Samuel, and Herbert Gintis. 1976. *Schooling in Capitalist America: Educational Reform and the Contradictions of Economic Life*. New York: Basic Books.

Brubaker, Rogers. 1985. "Rethinking Classical Theory: The Sociological Vision of Pierre Bourdieu." *Theory and Society* 14: 745–75.

Budd, Mike, Robert M. Entman, and Clay Steinman. 1990. "The Affirmative Character of US Cultural Studies." *Critical Studies in Mass Communication* 7: 164–84.

Buscombe, Edward, et al. 1975. "Statement: Psychoanalysis and Film." *Screen* 16, 4 (winter): 119–30.

Chafe, William H. 1995. *The Unfinished Journey: America since World War II*. New York: Oxford University Press.

Chambers, Iain, et al. 1977. "Marxism and Culture." *Screen* 18, 4 (winter): 109–19.

Clarke, John, Chas Critcher, and Richard Johnson, eds. 1979. *Working-Class Culture: Studies in History and Theory*. London: Hutchinson.

Coward, Rosalind. 1977. "Class, 'Culture' and the Social Formation." *Screen* 18, 1 (spring): 75–105.

Crompton, Rosemary. 1993. *Class and Stratification: An Introduction to Current Debates*. London: Polity Press.

Davis, Mike. 1986. *Prisoners of the American Dream*. New York: Verso.

Ferguson, Thomas, and Joel Rogers. 1986. *Right Turn: The Decline of the Democrats and the Future of American Politics*. New York: Hill and Wang.

Foley, Barbara. 1993. *Radical Representations: Politics and Form in US Proletarian Fiction, 1929–1941*. Durham, NC: Duke University Press.

Hall, Stuart. 1980a. "Cultural Studies and the Centre: Some Problematics and Problems." In *Culture, Media, Language*. Ed. Stuart Hall et al. London: Hutchinson.

——. 1980b. "Recent Developments in Theories of Language and Ideology: A Critical Note." In *Culture, Media, Language*. Ed. Stuart Hall et al. London: Hutchinson.

Hansen, Karen V., and Ilene J. Philipson, eds. 1990. *Women, Class, and the Feminist Imagination: A Socialist–Feminist Reader*. Philadelphia: Temple University Press.

Hansen, Miriam. 1983. "Early Silent Cinema: Whose Public Sphere?" *New German Critique* 29.

Harris, David. 1992. *From Class Struggle to the Politics of Pleasure: The Effects of Gramscianism on Cultural Studies*. London: Routledge.

Heath, Stephen. 1974. "Lessons from Brecht." *Screen* 15, 3 (summer): 103–28.

James, David E. 1996a. "Introduction: Is There Class in this Text?" In *The Hidden Foundation: Cinema and the Question of Class*. Ed. David E. James and Rick Berg. Minneapolis: University of Minnesota Press.

——. 1996b. *Power Misses: Essays Across (Un) Popular Culture*. London: Verso.

Jameson, Fredric. 1990. "Class and Allegory in Contemporary Mass Culture: *Dog Day Afternoon* as a Political Film." In *Signatures of the Visible*. New York: Routledge.

Johnson, Richard. 1979. "Three Problematics: Elements of a Theory of Working-Class Culture." In *Working-Class Culture: Studies in History and Theory*. Ed. John Clarke et al. London: Hutchinson.

Kleinhans, Chuck. 1974. "Contemporary Working Class Film Heroes." *Jump Cut* 2: 11–17.

Laclau, Ernesto, and Chantal Mouffe. 1985. *Hegemony and Socialist Strategy: Towards a Radical Democratic Politics*. London: Verso.

Laidler, Harry W. 1968. *History of Socialism: A Comparative Survey of Socialism, Communism, Trade Unionism, Cooperation, Utopianism, and Other Systems of Reform and Reconstruction.* New York: Crowell.

Lesage, Julia. 1974. "The Human Subject – You, He, or Me?" *Jump Cut* 4 (summer): 77–83.

Lyotard, Jean-François. 1984. *The Postmodern Condition: A Report on Knowledge.* Minneapolis: University of Minnesota Press.

Mayne, Judith. 1982. "Immigrants and Spectators." *Wide Angle* 5, 2.

Morley, David. 1992. [1980] *Television, Audiences and Cultural Studies.* London: Routledge.

Nichols, Bill. 1972. "Horatio Alger Goes to Hollywood." *Take One* 3, 11 (May–June): 11–14.

Przeworski, Adam. 1977. "Proletariat into a Class: The Process of Class Formation from Karl Kautsky's *The Class Struggle* to Recent Controversies." *Politics and Society* 7, 4: 343–402.

Ross, Steven J. 1991. "Struggles for the Screen: Workers, Radicals, and the Political Uses of Silent Film." *American Historical Review* 96: 333–67.

Ryan, Jake, and Charles Sackrey. 1984. *Strangers in Paradise: Academics from the Working Class.* Boston: South End Press.

Ryan, Michael, and Douglas Kellner. 1988. *Camera Politica: The Politics and Ideology of Contemporary Hollywood Film.* Bloomington: Indiana University Press.

Sennett, Richard, and Jonathan Cobb. 1973. *The Hidden Injuries of Class.* New York: Knopf.

Sklar, Robert. 1975. *Movie-Made America: A Cultural History of American Movies.* New York: Random House.

——, and Charles Musser, eds. 1990. *Resisting Images: Essays on Cinema and History.* Philadelphia: Temple University Press.

Stead, Peter. 1989. *Film and the Working Class: The Feature Film in British and American Society.* London: Routledge.

Thompson. E. P. 1963. *The Making of the English Working-Class.* New York: Knopf.

——. 1978. *The Poverty of Theory.* London: Merlin.

Traube, Elizabeth. 1992. *Dreaming Identities: Class, Gender, and Generation in 1980s Hollywood Movies.* Boulder: Westview Press.

Tucker, Robert C., ed. 1978. *The Marx–Engels Reader,* 2nd edn. New York: Norton.

Wiener, Jon. 1991. *Professors, Politics and Pop.* London: Verso.

Willis, Paul. 1981 [1977]. *Learning to Labor: How Working Class Kids Get Working Class Jobs.* New York: Columbia University Press.

Wood, Ellen Meiksins. 1986. *The Retreat from Class: A New "True" Socialism.* London: Verso.

Wright, Erik Olin. 1979. "Intellectuals and the Class Structure of Capitalist Society." In *Between Labor and Capital.* Ed. Pat Walker. Boston: South End Press.

——. 1980. "Varieties of Marxist Conceptions of Class Structure." *Politics and Society* 9, 3: 323–70.

——. 1985. *Classes.* London: Verso.

——. 1989. "Rethinking, Once Again, the Concept of Class Structure." In *The Debate on Classes.* Ed. Erik Olin Wright. London: Verso.

201

CHAPTER TWELVE

Culture Industries

Douglas Kellner

In capitalist societies, film production has been by and large a form of commercial entertainment controlled by media corporations. Thus, the Frankfurt School coined the term "culture industries" to call attention to the industrialization and commercialization of culture under capitalist relations of production. This situation was most marked in the United States, which has had little state support of the film industry. Consequently, the concept of culture industries in film studies finds its paradigm in analysis of Hollywood as a distinctive mode of cinematic production, originating in the United States in a specific time and place, but spreading throughout the world as film became a global business and major form of commercialized culture.

Accordingly, I first discuss the development of the concept of the culture industries in the Frankfurt School and then delineate some conceptions of Hollywood film as ways of understanding how the culture industries shape the commercial mode of film production, resulting in a specific sort of cinema with distinctive effects.

1   The Frankfurt School, the Culture Industries, and Regimes of Capital

To a large extent, the Frankfurt School inaugurated critical studies of mass communication and culture and produced the first critical theory of the cultural industries (see Kellner 1982, 1989, 1995, 1997). During the 1930s, the Frankfurt School developed a critical and transdisciplinary approach to cultural and communications studies, combining critique of political economy of the media, analysis of texts, and audience reception studies of the social and ideological effects of mass culture and communications.[1] They coined the term "culture industries" to signify the process of the industrialization of mass-produced culture and the commercial imperatives that drove the system. The critical theorists analyzed all mass-mediated cultural artifacts within the context of industrial production, in which the commodities of the culture industries exhibited the same features as other products of mass production: commodification, standardization, and massification. The culture industries had the specific function, however, of providing ideological legitimation of the existing capitalist societies and of integrating individuals into the framework of its social formation.

Adorno's analyses of popular music (1978 [1932], 1941, 1982, 1989), Lowenthal's studies of popular literature and magazines (1961), Herzog's studies of radio soap operas (1941), and the perspectives and critiques of mass culture developed in Horkheimer and Adorno's famous study of the culture industries (1972; and Adorno 1991), which contain many, albeit unsystematic, references to Hollywood film, provide significant examples of the value of the Frankfurt School approach. Moreover, in their theories of the culture industries and critiques of mass culture, they were the first to systematically analyze and criticize mass-mediated culture and communications within critical social theory. They were the first social theorists to see the importance of what they called the culture industries in the reproduction of contemporary societies, in which so-called mass culture and communications stand in the center of leisure activity, are important agents of socialization and mediators of political reality, and should thus be seen as major institutions of contemporary societies with a variety of economic, political, cultural, and social effects.[2]

Furthermore, they investigated the cultural industries in a political context as a form of the integration of the working class into capitalist societies. The Frankfurt School were one of the first neo-Marxian groups to examine the effects of mass culture and the rise of the consumer society on the working classes, which were to be the instrument of revolution in the classical Marxian scenario. They also analyzed the ways that the culture industries and consumer society were stabilizing contemporary capitalism and accordingly sought new strategies for political change, agencies of social transformation, and models for political emancipation that could serve as norms of social critique and goals for political struggle. This project required rethinking the Marxian project and produced many important contributions – as well as some problematical positions.

The Frankfurt School focussed intently on technology and culture, indicating how technology was becoming both a major force of production and a formative factor of social organization and control. In a 1941 article, "Some Social Implications of Modern Technology," Herbert Marcuse argued that technology in the contemporary era constitutes an entire "mode of organizing and perpetuating (or changing) social relationships, a manifestation of prevalent thought and behavior patterns, an instrument for control and domination" (414). In the realm of culture, technology produced mass culture that habituated individuals to conform to the dominant patterns of thought and behavior, and thus provided powerful instruments of social control and domination.

Victims of European fascism, the Frankfurt School experienced first hand the ways that the Nazis used the instruments of mass culture to produce submission to fascist culture and society. While in exile in the United States, the members of the Frankfurt School came to believe that American "popular culture" was also highly ideological and worked to promote the interests of capitalism. Controlled by giant corporations, the culture industries were organized according to the strictures of mass production, churning out products that generated a highly commercial system of culture, which in turn sold the values, lifestyles, and institutions of American capitalism.

In retrospect, one can see the Frankfurt School work as articulation of a theory of the stage of state and monopoly capitalism that became dominant during the 1930s.[3] This was an era of large organizations, theorized in 1910 by Hilferding as "organized capitalism" (1981), in which the state and giant corporations managed the economy and in which individuals submitted to state and corporate control. This period is often described as "Fordism" to designate the system of mass production and the homogenizing regime of capital that wanted to produce uniform desires, tastes, and behavior. It was thus an era of mass production and consumption characterized by uniformity and homogeneity of needs, thought, and behavior, producing a "mass society" and what the Frankfurt School described as "the end of the individual." No longer was individual thought and action the motor of social and cultural progress; instead giant organizations and institutions overpowered individuals. The era corresponds to the staid, ascetic, conformist, and conservative world of corporate capitalism that was dominant in the 1950s with its organization of men and women, its mass consumption, and its mass culture.

During this period, mass culture and communication were instrumental in generating the modes of thought and behavior appropriate to a highly organized and conformist social order. Thus, the Frankfurt School theory of the culture industries articulates a major historical shift to an era in which mass consumption and culture were indispensable in producing a consumer society based on homogeneous needs and desires for mass-produced goods and a mass society based on social organization and homogeneity. It is culturally the era of highly controlled network radio and television, insipid top-forty pop music, glossy Hollywood films, national magazines, and other mass-produced cultural artifacts.

Of course, media culture was never as massified and homogeneous as in the Frankfurt School model, and one could argue that the model was flawed even during its time of origin and influence. One could also argue that other models were preferable (such as those of Walter Benjamin, Siegfried Kracauer, Ernst Bloch and others of the Weimar generation, and, later, British cultural studies). Yet the original Frankfurt School model of the culture industries did articulate the important social roles of media culture during a specific regime of capital and provided a model, still of use, of a highly commercial and technologically advanced culture that serves the needs of dominant corporate interests and plays a major role in ideological reproduction and in enculturating individuals into the dominant system of needs, thought, and behavior.

The form of culture industry in the mode of film production that became hegemonic in the United States and eventually became the dominant form of world cinema is usually designated "Hollywood film," referring to a highly industrialized and rationalized mode of commercial cinematic production driven by the logic of commodification and capital realization. Accordingly, in the next section I interrogate the form of Hollywood film as culture industry.

2 Hollywood, Film, and the Culture Industries

Film emerged as one of the first mass-produced cultural forms of the twentieth century. Based on new technologies of mechanical reproduction that made possible simulations of the real and the production of fantasy worlds, film provided a new mode of culture that changed patterns of leisure activity and played an important role in social life. From the beginning, film in the United States was a mode of commercial activity controlled by entertainment industries that attempted to attract audiences to its products. Film production was accordingly organized on an industrial model with a mass-produced output aimed at capturing a secure audience share and thus realizing a substantial profit. As a commercial enterprise, American film developed as an entertainment industry, rather than as an educational instrument or art form.

Early films were the inventions of technicians and entrepreneurs like the Lumière Brothers and Méliès in France and the Edison Corporation in the United States. The first films ranged from the documentaries and quasi-documentary realist fictions produced by the Lumières and Edison to the fantasy fictions of Méliès. The genres that would characterize Hollywood film began to appear during the first decades of the century with westerns like *The Great Train Robbery* (1903), the melodramatic social dramas of D. W. Griffith, costume and historical dramas like *Ben Hur* (the first of several versions appeared in 1899), horror films, and comedies by Mack Sennett, Charlie Chaplin, Buster Keaton, and others.

Hollywood soon emerged as the capital of the film industry in the United States. Benefiting from Californian weather, which provided good light and a lot of sunshine, and a varied environment that opened onto the sea, desert, mountains, small towns, and a bustling urbanscape, a film colony soon emerged which became the locus of the American and eventually world film industry. The demand for film was great, and the early film studios began repeating and reproducing the formulas and types of film that were most popular. Consequently, Hollywood films were divided into the most popular types of genres, like the western, melodrama, crime drama, costume film, horror film, and, with the coming of sound, the musical (Schatz 1981).

Film soon became the most popular and influential form of media culture in the United States (Sklar 1975; Jowett 1976). Indeed, for the first half of the twentieth century – from 1896 to the 1950s – movies were a central focus of leisure activity and deeply influenced how people talked, looked, and acted, becoming a major force of enculturation. The number of theaters grew from

205

about 10,000 storefront nickelodeons with daily attendance of four to five million in 1910 to around 28,000 movie theaters by 1928 (May 1983). In the 1920s the average audience was between 25 and 30 million customers a week, while by the 1930s from 85 to 110 million people paid to go to the movies each week (Dieterle 1941). Consequently, films were a central form of entertainment and an extremely popular leisure activity.

Moreover, films became a major force of socialization, providing role models and instruction in dress and fashion, in courtship and love, and in marriage and career. Early films were produced largely for working-class, immigrant, and urban audiences, and some critics of the movies thought that they had negative or subversive effects (Jowett 1976). For example, the comedies of Charlie Chaplin made fun of authority figures, romantic dramas were attacked by the Legion of Decency for promoting promiscuity, and crime dramas were frequently attacked for fostering juvenile delinquency and crime. On the other hand, films were believed to help "Americanize" immigrants, to teach their audiences how to be good Americans, and to provide escape from the cares of everyday life (Ewen and Ewen 1982).

Whereas some films from the silent and early sound era presented poverty and social struggle from progressive perspectives sympathetic to the poor and oppressed, many films focussed on the rich and celebrated wealth and power, serving as advertisements for the consumer society and the ruling elites. Cecil B. de Mille's comedies and dramas of modern marriage, for example, can be seen as marriage and fashion models, and the romantic films of the 1920s can be read as "manuals of desire, wishes, dreams" for those wanting to assimilate themselves to mainstream America (Ewen and Ewen 1982: 102). Consequently, films played an important socializing role by mobilizing desires into certain models. In particular, they helped socialize immigrant and working-class cultures into the emerging forms of the consumer society, teaching them how to behave properly and consume with style and abandon.

From the beginning, popular movie stars played an important role in Hollywood cinema and became fantasy figures for idealized romance and desire (Dyer 1979). Female stars like Clara Bow, Gloria Swanson, and Colleen Moore represented the glamour and vivacity associated with the 1920s, while Mary Pickford and Lillian Gish projected idealized fantasies of pure American women. Romantic male idols were represented by Rudolf Valentino, Douglas Fairbanks, John Gilbert, and Clark Gable. Becoming a Hollywood star became the fantasy of countless young men and women who flocked to the film capital in search of fame and fortune, and some of these aspirants indeed succeeded in becoming the stars of the Hollywood firmament.

Although films for the most part reflected mainstream American values, they represented modern and urban social values in particular, and so conservatives began attacking their alleged "immorality" and "subversiveness". Due to pressure from civic groups and the threat of government regulation, a set of censorship boards was established with the cooperation of the film industry, which produced a Production Code that was adopted by the industry by the mid-1930s. Explicit limits were set on the allowable length of kisses and no open-mouth kisses could be shown. No nudity or explicit sexuality was allowed, such things as prostitution and drugs could not be portrayed, criminals had to be punished, and religion and the church could not be criticized (the Code is reproduced and discussed in Jowett 1976). The Production Code held sway until the 1960s (although it was challenged in the 1950s) and set firm ideological and social parameters to Hollywood films.

But the crucial determinants of the ideological functions of Hollywood film had to do with control of film production by major studios and the emergence and subsequent dominance of the studio systems from around 1917 into the 1960s (Bordwell et al. 1985; Schatz 1988). Hollywood film production became dominated early on by big studios, which monopolized the patents necessary for film production and projection and which primarily produced films for profit. Since films must attract large audiences, they needed to resonate to audiences' dreams, fears, and social concerns, and thus inevitably reflected social mores, conflicts, and ideologies. Consequently, some of the first critical analyses of Hollywood film argued that films reflected American society, providing mirror images of its dreams, fears, and mode of life.

3 Hollywood Film and US Society

Since the culture industries sought masses audiences, Hollywood cinematic production attempted to resonate to audience tastes, desires, and fantasies, and so there was a close connection between Hollywood film and contemporary social life in the United States. Sociological and psychological studies of Hollywood film proliferated in the post-World War II era and developed a wide range of critiques of myth, ideology, and meaning in the American cinema. Parker Tyler's *The Hollywood Hallucination* (1944) and *Myth and Magic of the Movies* (1947) applied Freudian and myth-symbol criticism to show how Walt Disney cartoons, romantic melodramas, and other popular films provided insights into social psychology and context, while producing myths suitable for contemporary audiences. In *Movies: A Psychological Study* (1950), Martha Wolfenstein and Nathan Leites applied psychoanalytical methods to film, decoding fears, dreams, and aspirations beneath the surface of 1940s Hollywood movies, arguing that: "The common day dreams of a culture are in part the sources, in part the products of its popular myths, stories, plays and films" (13). In her sociological study of *Hollywood: The Dream Factory* (1950), Hortense Powdermaker studied an industry that manufactured dreams and fantasies, while Robert Warshow (1970) related classical Hollywood genres like the western and the gangster film to the social history and ideological problematics of US society.

Building on these traditions, Barbara Deming demonstrated in *Running Away from Myself* (1969) how 1940s Hollywood films provided insights into the social

207

psychology and reality of the period. Deming argued that: "It is not as mirrors reflect us but, rather, as our dreams do that movies most truly reveal the times" (1). She claimed that 1940s Hollywood films provided a collective dream portrait of its era and proposed deciphering "the dream that all of us have been buying at the box office, to cut through to the real nature of the identification we have experienced there" (5–6). Her work anticipates more sophisticated and university-based film criticism of the post-1960s era by showing how films both reproduce dominant ideologies and contain proto-deconstructive elements that cut across the grain of the ideology that the films promote. She also undertook a sort of gender reading of Hollywood film that would eventually become a key part of Hollywood film criticism.

Another tradition of film scholarship and criticism in the United States attempted to situate films historically and to describe the interactions between film and society in more overtly political terms. This tradition includes Lewis Jacobs' pioneering history of Hollywood film (1939), John Howard Lawson's theoretical and critical works (1953, 1964), Ian Jarvie's sociological inquiries into the relation between film and society (1970, 1978), D. M. White and Richard Averson's studies of the relation between film, history, and social comment in film (1972), and the social histories written by Robert Sklar (1975), Garth Jowett (1976), Will Wright (1977), Peter Biskind (1983), and Thomas Schatz (1988). While this tradition produced useful insights into the relationships between Hollywood film and US society in specific historical eras, it tended to neglect the construction of film form, the ways that specific films or genres work to construct meaning, and the ways that audiences themselves interact with film.

More theoretical approaches to the production of the works of the Hollywood culture industry began emerging in the 1960s, including the ideological analyses of *Cahiers du cinéma* and the extremely influential work associated with *Screen* which translated many key *Cahiers* and other works of French film theory, including Roland Barthes, Christian Metz, and others who generated much more sophisticated formal approaches to film (see Metz 1974; Heath 1981). The *Cahiers* group moved from seeing film as the product of creative auteurs, or authors (their *politique des auteurs* of the 1950s, taken up by Sarris [1968] and others) to focus on the ideological and political content of film and how it transcoded dominant ideologies. At the same time, French film theory and *Screen* focussed on the specific cinematic mechanisms that helped produce meaning.

During the same period of intense ferment in the field of film studies during the 1960s and 1970s, members of the Birmingham Centre for Contemporary Cultural Studies were discovering that gender, race, and sub-culture were also important elements in analyzing the relationships between culture, ideology, and society. Pushed by feminism to recognize the centrality of gender, it was argued that the construction of dominant ideologies of masculinity and femininity was a central aspect of Hollywood film (Kuhn 1982; Kaplan 1983). Studies of the ways that Hollywood films constructed race, ethnicity, and sexuality also became a key aspect of film studies, and various post-structuralist-influenced theories studied the role of film and media culture in the social construction of ideologies and identities.

Studies also began appearing in the 1970s of the business of film, dissecting the political economy of the Hollywood studio system (see Balio 1976, 1985; Wasko 1994). Combining these historical, socio-economic, and theoretical perspectives, Bordwell, Staiger, and Thompson (1985) provided a comprehensive and systematic approach to analyzing the "classic Hollywood film system" with specific studies of the production process, Hollywood style, and cinematic technology. They argued that Hollywood cinema is a highly distinctive economic and artistic phenomenon which blends a unique system of production, film style, and cinematic technology to produce a clearly recognizable product. Offering the concept of "a mode of film practice," they situated Hollywood film in its historically specific context and analyzed the system of production, style, and typical products.

There are now a multiplicity of approaches competing to theorize the relations between Hollywood film and US society. The theory wars of the 1980s and '90s have proliferated a tremendous amount of new theories that have in turn been applied to film. Consequently, structuralism and post-structuralism, psychoanalysis, deconstruction, feminism, postmodernism, and a wealth of other theoretical frameworks have generated an often bewildering diversity of approaches to theorizing film, which join and complicate previous film theory methods such as the genre theory, auteur theory, and historical–sociological approaches. My own take on the cacophony of contemporary approaches to film is that it is not a question of either/or which forces the theorist to adopt one option, but rather a variety of approaches can be deployed to engage the relations of film to society (see Kellner 1995 for elaboration of my multiperspectival model).

Consequently, the following section will discuss the genre approach to analyzing the intersection of film and society in the Hollywood culture industry, while in the concluding section, I note developments in contemporary Hollywood film that legitimate the use of auteur criticism and socio-ideological approaches to film. These approaches can be combined, I would argue, with the newer theoretical approaches to provide fuller and richer thematizations of the relation of Hollywood film to US society.

4 Hollywood Genres: The Coin of the Culture Industries

Although much of the best European art film can be interpreted as a result of the creative vision and talent of individual directors, Hollywood film from the beginning was deeply influenced by the dominant genres in its studio system. Hollywood culture industry film production was thoroughly industrialized and

209

rationalized, its films delineated into specific types with their familiar codes, conventions, iconography, and themes. Genres like the western or crime drama were a preferred type of film for the Hollywood studio system since they were popular, conventional, and easy to reproduce. The studios were set up like factories with big barns, rows of barracks, stock sets, and so forth, in a production process that thrives on formulas and conventions. Thus, following the economic imperatives of the capitalist system to produce products as quickly and cheaply as possible to maximize production and profits, the Hollywood cinema became a genre cinema.

The major Hollywood studios controlled not only film production, but also distribution, ensuring a guaranteed exhibition site for Hollywood product. This system first emerged in the 1910s, took its distinctive shape in the 1920s, reached maturity in the 1940s, and began to disintegrate in the 1950s due to anti-trust legislation, which caused the studios to divest themselves of their distribution and exhibition channels, and to competition from other entertainment media such as television (Schatz 1988).

The various Hollywood studios had their own distinctive style and favorite genres. Warner Brothers was known for a gritty 1930s-era realism, featuring tough gangster films, hard-edged domestic melodrama, crusading biopics, and energetic musicals; Universal was renowned for its atmospheric horror films, MGM for its colorful musicals and spectaculars, and David Selznick was associated with big-budget quality pictures, both when he worked for other studios and after he formed Selznick International Pictures in 1935 (Schatz 1988). Since the main Hollywood studios repeatedly reproduced the types of film that they thought were the most popular, Hollywood cinema became primarily a *genre cinema*, in which popular formulas are repeated in cycles of genres that in turn deal with central societal conflicts, problems, and concerns of its audiences. The western, for example, deals with conflicts between civilization and threats to civilization from disruptive forces, whereas the gangster film deals with threats to law, order, and social stability within an already established urban society. Melodramas, social comedies, and musicals deal with conflicts and problems within domestic arenas like the family and romance, whereas war films and adventure genres generally deal with conflicts in the public sphere outside of the private realm.

Genres become established when visual, stylistic, and thematic concerns become formalized into an immediately recognizable system of conventions. Genre films were thus the appropriate form of production for a culture industry geared toward commercial success. For the most popular genres become familiar artifacts that create certain expectations which, if fulfilled, bring audiences back again and again for their particular satisfactions. Thus, genre films combine narrative formula, audience expectation, and the industrial practice of a culture industry aiming at commercial success.

For instance, the cultural form of the western developed into a generic construct featuring conflicts between cowboy heroes and villains in the familiar setting of the US West. The plot contains standard conventions of gunfights, chase scenes, and the eventual defeat of forces of disorder; the visual imagery alternates small town or homestead scenes, with chase or action scenes in the desert and the mountain regions of the West. In this setting, the western pits sets of "bad" guys against the "good" townspeople, homesteaders, and cowboy hero in an epic struggle between "good" and "evil." This form in turn generated ideologies of racism and imperialism whereby the "enemies" of civilization (Indians, Mexicans, villains) were portrayed negatively, thus legitimating the "settlement" of the West by (white male-dominated) forces of "civilization." In addition, women were stereotyped as either whores or submissive representatives of the domestic order, thus reproducing patriarchical ideologies.

In order to resonate to audience fears, fantasies, and experiences, the Hollywood genres had to deal with the central conflicts and problems in US society and offer soothing resolutions, assuring its audiences that all problems could be solved within existing institutions. Western films, for example, assured their audiences that "civilization" could be maintained in the face of threats from criminals, outsiders, and villains of various sorts, and celebrated individualism, white male authority figures, and violence as a legitimate way of resolving conflicts. The western's mythologized vision of American history glossed over the fact that the "villains" were often the land's original inhabitants who had had their property stolen by the white settlers, presented as being forces of civilization.

Gangster films appealed to people's fear of crime and fascination with criminals; the classical Hollywood gangster films inculcated the message that "crime does not pay" and showed the police and legal system able to contain crime and to deal with criminals. But gangster films also explored cultural conflicts and contradictions central to American capitalism. Gangsters are, in fact, prototypical capitalists who will do anything to make a buck and thus are allegorical stand-ins for capitalist energy and will. Gangster films explore the tensions within American life between making money and morality, between self-interest and legality, and between private and public interests. The gangsters are fantasy characters who act out secret audience desires to get ahead no matter what, although it is still not clear if their repeated punishment (mandated by the Production Code) actually helped prevent crime or whether the films promoted crime by making the gangsters – often played by popular figures like James Cagney or Humphrey Bogart – extremely dynamic, attractive, and vital figures.

Melodramas, social comedies, and musicals in turn legitimated male-dominated romance, marriage, family, and moral rectitude as the proper road to happiness and well-being. Musicals followed formulas of boy meets girl, boy loses girl, and boy gets girl to celebrate the desirability of male-dominated romance. Melodramas dramatized what would happen to wayward women or willful men who failed to conform to dominant gender roles. They celebrated hardworking mothers who sacrificed their own happiness for their children, thus projecting the proper role for women (for example, *Imitation of Life*, *Stella Dallas*, *Mildred Pierce*, and others), and intimated that life's greatest happiness derived from marriage and family. And social comedies, too, celebrated marriage and family as the proper goals for men and women (Cavell 1982). Indeed, David Bordwell claims that in his random selection of 100 typical Hollywood movies, 95 made romance at least one important plot line while in 85 heterosexual romantic love was *the* major focus (Bordwell et al. 1985: 16).

Hollywood genre films thus tended to promote the American dream and dominant American myths and ideologies. They taught that money and success were important values; that heterosexual romance, marriage, and family were the proper social forms; that the state, police, and legal system were legitimate sources of power and authority; that violence was justified to destroy any threats to the system; and that American values and institutions were basically sound, benevolent, and beneficial to society as a whole. In this way, Hollywood film, supported by other forms of media culture, helped establish a certain *hegemony*, or cultural dominance of existing institutions and values to the exclusion of others. As Raymond Williams argued:

> I would say that in any society, in any particular period, there is a central system of practices, meanings and values, which we can properly call dominant and effective ... what I have in mind is the central, effective and dominant system of meanings and values, which are not merely abstract but which are organized and lived. That is why hegemony is not to be understood at the level of mere opinion or mere manipulation. It is a whole body of practices and expectations; our assignments of energy, our ordinary understanding of the nature of man and of his world. It is a set of meanings and values which as they are experienced as practices appear as reciprocally confirming. (1983: 8–9)

Hollywood film is thus implicitly "political" in the way it tends to support dominant American values and institutions. The more explicitly political functions of Hollywood cinema generally emerge in times of social crisis. During both World Wars, war films and other genres advocated patriotism and presented the "enemy" in stereotypical terms. During the Cold War anti-communist period, Hollywood produced a genre cycle of anti-communist films that depicted the threat to democracy and the "American way of life" by the "communist conspiracy." Whereas during World War II Russians were presented positively as US allies against fascism, from the late 1940s on through *Rambo* communists are generally presented as the incarnation of evil.

Yet the Hollywood system was flexible enough to allow individual cinematic statements and social critique within the genre system. Hollywood films prized difference and variation within accepted boundaries and allowed a limited range open for artistic expression and social commentary. Filmmakers like John Ford, Frank Capra, Sam Fuller, and Alfred Hitchcock used the genre system to articulate their own specific artistic concerns and visions, finding in the genre and studio system a congenial framework to produce their work. Other artistically inclined directors like Erich von Stroheim and Orson Welles constantly clashed with their production bosses and found their work edited against their will, eventually leaving the system and giving up filmmaking altogether, as von Stroheim did, or seeking alternative funding with mixed success, as in the case of Welles.

Indeed, it is not certain that the genre films always resolved the social contradictions portrayed and served as ideological advertisements for existing social institutions, discourses, and practices. As noted, the crime dramas often made the criminals' transgressions of societal norms more appealing and attractive than their punishment, and likewise women's transgressions of bourgeois norms in the melodrama often put in question established patriarchal institutions. The western could also be used to portray the victims of the frontier conquest sympathetically and to attack the crimes and barbarism of the "civilizing" forces. Genre films could thus be used to contest ideological norms as well as reproduce them, and thus to provide ideology critique as well as legitimation.

During the 1950s, the studio system that had produced genre cycles as the mode of production of Hollywood film broke up, and the genre system was challenged, opening the ways to new types of film. As we shall see in the next section, although the Hollywood system initially opened up, a new regime of production came to support the equivalent of genre cinema, and the desire for megaprofits continued to drive the system.

5 Hollywood Today, and into the Future

The break-up of the studio system in the 1950s forced film directors to find new sources of film-financing. The result was a very fertile period of production in the 1960s with film becoming more varied, diverse, and socially critical. The rise of new directors like Stanley Kubrick, Arthur Penn, and Robert Altman, who had distinctive artistic visions and style, seemed to give credence to the notion of a "New Hollywood" and provided a boost to auteur criticism that focussed on the cinematic style and form of key directors and films, while critics like Andrew Sarris insisted that the classical Hollywood directors also exhibited distinctive aesthetic styles which he canonized in his artistic pantheons (1968).

In retrospect, all one-sided approaches to theorizing Hollywood film are problematical. Although some "authors" had created distinctive and impressive bodies of work, they were often created within the constraints of a specific genre and studio system. So to fully understand Hollywood film, one needs insight into the production system, its codes and formulas, and the complex interaction of film and society, with film articulating social discourses, embedded in social struggles, and saturated with social meanings (Kellner and Ryan 1988). Thus, analyzing the connection between Hollywood film and US society requires a multi-dimensional film criticism that situates its object within the context of the social milieu within which it is produced and received.

213

It was widely perceived in the 1960s that youth constituted a major audience for Hollywood film, and so more youth-oriented films and directors emerged, creating new cycles of films which cinematically inscribed the discourses of the New Left student movements, as well as the feminist, black power, sexual liberationist, and counter-cultural movements, producing a new type of socially critical Hollywood film. These films transcoded (i.e. translated) representations, discourses, and myths of 1960s culture into specifically cinematic terms, as when *Easy Rider* transcodes the images, practices, and discourses of the 1960s counter-culture into a cinematic text. Popular films intervened in the political struggles of the day, as when 1960s films advanced the agenda of the New Left and the counter-culture. Films of the "New Hollywood," however, such as *Bonnie and Clyde*, *Medium Cool*, *Easy Rider*, and so on, were contested by a resurgence of right-wing films during the same era (e.g. *Dirty Harry*, *The French Connection*, and any number of John Wayne films), leading many to conclude that Hollywood film, like US society, should be seen as a contested terrain and that films could be interpreted as a struggle of representation over how to construct a social world and everyday life.

Throughout the 1970s, intense battles between liberals and conservatives were evident in Hollywood film, with more radical voices – of the sort that occasionally were heard in the late 1960s and early 1970s – becoming increasingly marginalized. The tremendous success of more generic films, like *Love Story*, *Airport* and other disaster films, *The Godfather* films, and *The Exorcist* and other horror films, led the Hollywood culture industry to search for the blockbuster film, leading to a return to genre cinema. But it was probably the huge success of *Jaws* (1975) that set the pattern for the blockbuster syndrome. Released in the summer of 1975, the film was introduced to an unprecedented ballyhoo of advertising and opened in a then-record "wide release" of 464 theaters. An all-time high of 25 million tickets were sold in the film's first 38 days of release, and it had soon earned a record $102 million in rentals. Henceforth, "high concept" films that could be clearly described and marketed became a major focus of the Hollywood film industry (Wyatt 1994), which sought "blockbuster" hits that would turn over a high profit.

In the 1970s, new technologies and cultural forces emerged that changed the nature of film culture and production. In August 1975, Home Box Office (HBO), a new nationwide movie channel, began disseminating an array of films by satellite transmission and cable systems to individual homes. Other movie channels followed, and a mushrooming of cable and satellite channels made available a cornucopia of films for home consumption. In addition, the Sony Betamax home video recorder appeared in 1975, followed by the more successful VHS format, and a proliferation of video-rental stores and businesses made it possible to see the history of film within one's own home. Henceforth, film culture became part of everyday life, and the most popular films could be seen via theater, television, or home video systems.

During this period as well, the culture wars that had raged since the 1960s were reproduced in Hollywood films. As the 1970s progressed, conservative films were becoming more popular (e.g. *Rocky*, *Star Wars*, *Close Encounters of the Third Kind*, *Superman*), indicating that conservative sentiments were growing in the public and that Hollywood was nurturing these political currents. Indeed, even liberal films ultimately helped advance the conservative cause. A cycle of liberal political conspiracy films (e.g. *The Parallax View*, *All the President's Men*, *The Domino Principle*, *Winter Kills*) vilified the state and thus played into the conservative/Reaganite argument that government was the source of much existing evil. Films that took a perspective sympathetic to the working class and critical of business (*Blue Collar*, *F.I.S.T.*, and many others) blamed corrupt unions for the working class's problems, while liberal films dealing with race (*Claudine*, *A Piece of the Action*, and the like) attacked welfare institutions and celebrated individual initiative and self-help – precisely the Reaganite position. And even the most socially critical films (such as the Jane Fonda films, *Network*, and other Sidney Lumet films) posited individual solutions to social problems, thus also reinforcing the conservative appeal to individualism and attack on statism. Consequently, reading Hollywood films of the decade politically allowed one to anticipate the coming of Reagan and the New Right to power by demonstrating that conservative yearnings were ever more popular within the culture and that film and popular culture were helping to form an ideological matrix more hospitable to Reagan and conservatives than to embattled liberals (Kellner and Ryan 1988).

On the other hand, even seemingly conservative film genres such as the horror film, or seemingly anti-gay films like *Cruising*, contain critical moments, problematizing hegemonic ideologies and putting in question dominant ideologies like the family (Wood 1986). Robin Wood argues that the "incoherent text" is a dominant cinematic mode of the 1970s, full of ideological contradictions and conflicts that reproduce existing social confusion and turmoil. Thus, film, like society, was very much a contested terrain, with the future of society and culture up for grabs.

With the election of Reagan in 1980, the conservative wave of films continued throughout the decade, though they were contested, as was Reaganism itself, by liberal and radical films like *Missing*, *Reds*, *Salvador*, *Platoon* and other Oliver Stone films, as well as a wealth of films by independent filmmakers like John Sayles. The blockbuster syndrome, however, continued to be the dominant trend, and with the teaming up of Steven Spielberg and George Lucas for the *Indiana Jones* series and the continued success of Lucas's *Star Wars* films and Spielberg's blockbusters, Hollywood went big-time for high-tech spectaculars in which the special effects often overwhelmed story and character.

Gender struggles were particularly intense, with a return to the "hard-body" masculine hero of an earlier era, replacing the more feminized male heroes of the late 1960s and early 1970s (Jeffords 1994). As part of the backlash against feminism, there was also a cycle of films that villainized independent women, showing single career women without families being driven into pathological behavior (*Fatal Attraction, Basic Instinct, The Hand that Rocks the Cradle*, etc.). On the other hand, there was also a cycle of gay and lesbian films that expanded the representations of sexuality, and many films written, directed, or produced by women or men wishing more complex, varied, and progressive representations of gender and gender relations.

Moreover, although there was a return to big-budget films, there was also a wave of successes by independent filmmakers like John Sayles, Susan Seidelman, Spike Lee, and Robert Rodriguez, who turned over respectable profits on low-budget films, and so Hollywood itself began financing some off-beat films and allowed a new generation of filmmakers to enter the mainstream. Many of these were women, people of color, or more socially critical types; hence more diverse representations of gender, race, and class were produced and circulated. At this time, a multi-cultural-focussed cultural studies developed as a major approach to film and cultural criticism, and a proliferation of new critical strategies emerged. There was an especially intense focus on audience research, on how audiences produced meanings, on how films mobilized pleasure and influenced audiences, and how audiences decoded and used the materials of media culture. Consequently, a wide range of positions appeared on the relationship between film, media culture, and its audiences (see the discussion in Staiger 1991).

During the 1990s, globalization has made Hollywood film an ever more familiar and popular artifact throughout the world. Whereas Hollywood films have dominated the world market for decades, it is even more the case today with American global corporations playing an important role in distributing its products throughout the world. Hollywood films are the most capital-intensive and thus have the most spectacular special effects; they are effectively marketed throughout the world and are popular everywhere. In Canada, for instance, about 95 per cent of films in movie theaters are American; US television dominates Canadian television; seven American firms control distribution of sound recordings in Canada; and 80 per cent of the magazines on newsstands are non-Canadian (*The Washington Post National Weekly Edition*, September 11–17, 1995: 18). In Europe, Hollywood films comprise 75–80 per cent of the box office, and the explosion of new TV channels has produced a boom in US television exports, bringing in revenues of more than one billion dollars a year (*Time*, February 27, 1995: 36, 40). In Latin America, Asia, and other parts of the world, the situation is similar, with American media culture, commodities, fast food, and malls creating a new global culture.

To some extent globalization = Americanization, and Hollywood film is an effective culture industry which serves to sell the "American way of life" (on globalization and cultural identity, see Cvetovich and Kellner 1996). Thus, there are debates throughout the world about limiting Hollywood film and other artifacts of US culture to a specific quota and providing government

216

support for national film cultures. The market ideology which has been dominant since the Thatcher/Reagan era, however, has militated against government regulation and quotas; hence Hollywood films continue to dominate the world market.

Consequently, the products of the Hollywood culture industry and their relationships to US society, and indeed the entire world, are quite complex and require a multi-perspectival approach that dissects the political economy of the film industry and the production of film, provides critical and analytical readings of cinematic texts, and studies how audiences appropriate and use film and other cultural artifacts (see Kellner 1995 for elaboration of this model). Of course, in specific case studies, one might want to focus intensely on a single topic or dimension, but to grasp the full range of meanings and effects of Hollywood film one needs more complex and multi-dimensional approaches.

Finally, we are currently undergoing one of the most dramatic technological revolutions of recorded history with new entertainment and information technologies emerging, accompanied by unprecedented mergers of the entertainment and information industries (see Wasko 1994). These new syntheses are producing novel forms of visual and multi-media culture, in which it is anticipated that film will appear in seductive new virtual and interactive forms, accessible through computer, satellite, and other new technologies. There is feverish speculation that the Internet and its assorted technologies will create a new entertainment and information environment, and currently the major corporations and players are envisaging what sort of product and delivery system will be most viable and profitable for films and other entertainment of the future. Thus, one imagines that the culture industries producing and distributing film and other forms of media culture will continue to be highly significant as we approach a new century and perhaps a new era that will supply novel forms of film and new types of culture industry.

Notes

1 On the Frankfurt School theory of the cultural industries, see Horkheimer and Adorno 1972; Adorno 1991; the anthology edited by Rosenberg and White 1957; the readers edited by Arato and Gebhardt 1982 and Bronner and Kellner 1989; the discussions of the history of the Frankfurt School in Jay 1973 and Wiggershaus 1994; and the discussion of the Frankfurt School combination of social theory and cultural criticism in Kellner 1989, 1997.

2 I've analyzed some of these effects from a reconstructed critical-theory perspective in studies of Hollywood film with Michael Ryan (1988), two books on American television (Kellner 1990, 1992), and a series of media cultural studies (Kellner 1995; Best and Kellner, forthcoming).

3 See Kellner 1989 and the texts in Bronner and Kellner 1989.

References

Adorno, T. W. (with G. Simpson). 1941. "On Popular Music." *Studies in Philosophy and Social Science* 9, 1: 17–48.

——. 1978 [1932]. "On the Social Situation of Music." *Telos* 35 (spring): 129–65.

——. 1982. "On the Fetish Character of Music and the Regression of Hearing." In Arato and Gebhardt 1982. 270–99.

——. 1989. "On Jazz." In Bronner and Kellner 1989. 199–209.

——. 1991. *The Culture Industry*. London: Routledge.

Arato, Andrew, and Eike Gebhardt, eds. 1982. *The Essential Frankfurt School Reader*. New York: Continuum.

Balio, Tino, ed. 1976 (2nd edn 1985). *The American Film Industry*. Madison: University of Wisconsin Press.

Benjamin, Walter. 1969. *Illuminations*. New York: Shocken.

Best, Steven, and Douglas Kellner. 1991. *Postmodern Theory: Critical Interrogations*. London and New York: Macmillan and Guilford Press.

——. 1997. *The Postmodern Turn*. New York: Guilford Press.

——. Forthcoming. *The Postmodern Adventure*. New York: Guilford Press.

Biskind, Peter. 1983. *Seeing Is Believing: How Hollywood Movies Taught Us to Stop Worrying and Love the 50s*. New York: Pantheon.

Bloch, Ernst. 1986. *The Principle of Hope*. Cambridge: MIT Press.

Bordwell, David, Janet Staiger, and Kristin Thompson. 1985. *The Classical Hollywood Cinema*. New York: Columbia University Press.

Bronner, Stephen, and Douglas Kellner, eds. 1989. *Critical Theory and Society: A Reader*. New York: Routledge.

Cavell, Stanley. 1982. *Pursuits of Happiness*. Cambridge: Harvard University Press.

Cvetovich, Ann, and Douglas Kellner, eds. 1996. *Articulating the Global and the Local: Globalization and Cultural Studies*. Boulder: Westview Press.

Deming, Barbara. 1969. *Running Away from Myself*. New York: Grossman.

Dieterle, William. 1941. "Hollywood and the European Crisis." *Studies in Philosophy and Social Science* 9, 1: 96–103.

Dyer, Richard. 1979. *Stars*. London: British Film Institute.

Ewen, Stuart, and Elizabeth Ewen. 1982. *Channels of Desire*. New York: McGraw-Hill.

Heath, Stephen. 1981. *Questions of Cinema*. Bloomington: Indiana University Press.

Herzog, Herta. 1941. "On Borrowed Experience: An Analysis of Listening to Daytime Sketches." *Studies in Philosophy and Social Science* 9, 1: 65–95.

Hilferding, Rudolf. 1981 [1910]. *Finance Capital*. London: Routledge and Kegan Paul.

Horkheimer, Max, and T. W. Adorno. 1972. *Dialectic of Enlightenment*. New York: Seabury.

Jacobs, Lewis. 1939. *The Rise of the American Film*. New York: Harcourt, Brace.

Jarvie, I. C. 1970. *Toward a Sociology of the Cinema*. London: Routledge and Kegan Paul.

——. 1978. *Movies as Social Criticism*. Metuchen: Scarecrow.

Jay, Martin. 1973. *The Dialectical Imagination*. Boston: Little, Brown.

Jeffords, Susan. 1994. *Hard Bodies*. New Brunswick: Rutgers University Press.

Jowett, Garth. 1976. *Film: The Democratic Art*. New York: William Morrow.

Kaplan, E. Ann. 1983. *Women and Film*. New York: Methuen.

Kellner, Douglas. 1982. "Kulturindustrie und Massenkommunikation: Die Kritische Theorie und ihre Folgen." In *Sozialforschung als Kritik*. Ed. Wolfgang Bonss and Axel Honneth. Frankfurt: Suhrkamp. 482–514.

———. 1989. *Critical Theory, Marxism, and Modernity*. Cambridge and Baltimore: Polity and Johns Hopkins University Press.

———. 1990. *Television and the Crisis of Democracy*. Boulder: Westview Press.

———. 1992. *The Persian Gulf TV War*. Boulder: Westview Press.

———. 1995. *Media Culture: Cultural Studies, Identity, and Politics Between the Modern and the Postmodern*. London and New York: Routledge.

———. 1997. "Critical Theory and British Cultural Studies: The Missed Articulation." In *Cultural Methodologies*. Ed. Jim McGuigan. London: Sage. 12–41.

———, and Michael Ryan. 1988. *Camera Politica: The Politics and Ideology of Contemporary Hollywood Film*. Bloomington: Indiana University Press.

Kracauer, Siegfried. 1947. *From Caligari to Hitler*. Princeton: Princeton University Press.

Kuhn, Annette. 1982. *Women's Pictures*. London: Routledge and Kegan Paul.

Lawson, John Howard. 1953. *Film in the Battle of Ideas*. New York: Mainstream.

———. 1964. *Film: The Creative Process*. New York: Hill and Wang.

Lazarsfeld, Paul. 1941. "Administrative and Critical Comunications Research." *Studies in Philosophy and Social Science* 9, 1: 2–16.

Lowenthal, Leo. 1961. *Literature, Popular Culture and Society*. Englewood Cliffs: Prentice-Hall.

Marcuse, Herbert. 1941. "Some Social Implications of Modern Technology." *Studies in Philosophy and Social Science* 9, 1: 414–39.

May, Larry. 1983. *Screening out the Past*. Chicago: University of Chicago Press.

Metz, Christian. 1974. *Language and Cinema*. The Hague: Mouton.

Powdermaker, Hortense. 1950. *Hollywood: The Dream Factory*. Boston: Little, Brown.

Rosenberg, Bernard, and David Manning White, eds. 1957. *Mass Culture*. Glencoe: The Free Press.

Sarris, Andrew. 1968. *The American Cinema: Directors and Directions, 1929–1968*. New York: Dutton.

Schatz, Thomas. 1981. *Hollywood Genres*. Philadelphia: Temple University Press.

———. 1988. *The Genius of the System*. New York: Pantheon.

Sklar, Robert. 1975. *Movie-Made America: A Social History of American Film*. New York: Random House.

Staiger, Janet. 1991. *Interpreting Films: Studies in the Historical Reception of American Cinema*. Princeton: Princeton University Press.

Tyler, Parker. 1944. *The Hollywood Hallucination*. New York: Simon and Schuster.

———. 1947. *Myth and Magic of the Movies*. New York: Simon and Schuster.

Warshow, Robert. 1970. *The Immediate Experience*. New York: Atheneum.

Wasko, Janet. 1994. *Hollywood in the Information Age*. Austin: University of Texas Press.

White, David M., and Richard Averson. 1972. *The Celluloid Weapon: Social Comment in the American Film*. Boston: Beacon Press.

Wiggershaus, Rolf. 1994. *The Frankfurt School*. Cambridge: Polity Press.

Williams, Raymond. 1983. "Base and Superstructure in Marxist Cultural Theory." *New Left Review* 82: 6–33.

Wolfenstein, Martha, and Nathan Leites. 1950. *Movies: A Psychological Study*. Glencoe: The Free Press.

Wood, Robin. 1986. *Hollywood from Vietnam to Reagan*. New York: Columbia University Press.

Wright, Will. 1977. *Six-Guns and Society: A Structural Study of the Western*. Berkeley: University of California Press.

Wyatt, Justin. 1994. *High Concept: Movies and Marketing in Hollywood*. Austin: University of Texas Press.

CHAPTER THIRTEEN

The Political Economy of Film

Janet Wasko

In the late 1970s, Thomas Guback wrote an essay entitled "Are We Looking at the Right Things in Film?" (1978), in which he argued that the study of cinema focussed overwhelmingly on criticism and theory, with a dash of atheoretical history. Guback's main point was that film studies typically neglected the analysis of cinema as an economic institution and as a medium of communication.

In his paper, Guback described an "institutional approach" to film, which looked very much like a political economic approach to the study of communication. While this approach has been distinctly identified in communication scholarship, it seems to be much less common within film studies. And while there may be more attention to the economics of film by cinema scholars these days, it might be argued that some of Guback's concerns are still quite valid.

This chapter is based on the assumption that film is a form of mediated communication, and is thus appropriate for many of the approaches used in studying other forms of media. The chapter begins with a brief discussion of the political economy of communication and then focusses more specifically on the political economy of film, pointing to the significance of the approach, as well as identifying questions raised and methods used in this type of analysis.

1 Defining the Tradition: Classical Political Economy

Many of the descriptions of political economy of communication or media begin with a discussion of the general study of political economy, drawing on eighteenth-century Scottish enlightenment thinking and its critique in the nineteenth century. For Adam Smith, David Ricardo, and others, the study of economic issues was called *political economy* and was grounded in social theory. Smith defined political economy as the study of "wealth" (material goods) or the allocation of resources, and was concerned with "how mankind arranges to allocate scarce resources with a view toward satisfying certain needs and not others" (1776). Further, political economy focussed on the production,

221

distribution, exchange, and consumption of wealth and the consequences for the welfare of individuals and society. More specifically, these economists studied one arrangement for the allocation of resources – *capitalism*, as a system of social production.

Classical political economy evolved as capitalism evolved, adding Marx and Engels' historical materialism and class analysis in the nineteenth century, and emphasizing a radical critique of the evolving capitalist system through a moral stance in opposition to the unjust and inequitable characteristics of that system.

During the second half of the nineteenth century, however, there was a fundamental shift in the study of economic issues. As the focus changed from macro- to microanalysis, emphasis was placed on individual rather than societal concerns, and the methods used came from the social sciences rather than from moral philosophy. These changes were represented in the basic shift in the name of the discipline – from *political economy* to *economics*.

The person responsible for the name change, William Jevons, suggested that economics was the study of "the mechanics of utility and self interest . . . to satisfy our wants to the utmost with the least effort . . . to maximize pleasure is the problem of economics" (1970). As a more recent economist has explained, the "neo-classical economists made a sharper distinction than their predecessors had done between the explanation of What Is in an economic system and the consideration of What Ought To Be" (R. D. Collison Black, quoted in Jevons 1970).

Although neoclassical economics prevails today, political economy has survived in different forms. In communication studies, radical, critical, or Marxian political economy has been applied to the study of communication and has been recognized as a distinct tradition. In *The Political Economy of Communication* (1996), Vincent Mosco has defined this version of political economy as "the study of the social relations, particularly power relations, that mutually constitute the production, distribution and consumption of resources" (25). He explains that political economy is about survival and control, or how societies are organized to produce what is necessary to survive and how order is maintained to meet societal goals. Mosco further delineates four central characteristics of critical political economy, which are helpful in understanding this approach:

1 *Social change and history.* Political economy continues the tradition of classic theorists, uncovering the dynamics of capitalism – its cyclical nature, the growth of monopoly capital, the state apparatus, etc.

2 *Social totality.* Political economy is a holistic approach or, in concrete terms, studies the relationship among commodities, institutions, social relations, and hegemony, exploring the determination among these elements, although some elements are stressed more than others.

3 *Moral philosophy.* Critical political economy also follows the classical theorists' emphasis on moral philosophy, including not only analysis of the economic system, but discussion of the policy problems and moral issues

which arise from it. For some contemporary scholars, this is the distinguishing characteristic of political economy.

4 *Praxis.* Finally, political economists attempt to transcend the distinction between research and policy, orienting their work toward actual social change and practice, or, as Marx pointed out, "Philosophers have sought to understand the system, the point is to change it."

Mosco's model draws strongly on the work of British political economists Peter Golding and Graham Murdock, who distinguished critical political economy from mainstream economics: it is holistic, historical, centrally concerned with the balance between capitalist enterprise and public intervention, and "goes beyond technical issues of efficiency to engage with basic moral questions of justice, equity and the public good" (Golding and Murdock 1991).

These explanations set the stage or provide the grounding for applying political economy to the study of communication.

2 Political Economy Applied to Communication

The academic study of communication has not always embraced economic analysis, much less a political-economic approach. During the 1940s and 1950s, communication scholars focussed primarily on individual effects and psychologically oriented research, with little concern for the economic context in which media is produced, distributed, and consumed.

In the 1950s and early 1960s, former Federal Communication Commission economist and University of Illinois professor Dallas Smythe urged scholars to consider communication as an important component of the economy and to understand it as an economic entity. In 1960, he presented one of the first applications of political economy to communication, defining the approach as the study of political policies and economic processes, their interrelations and their mutual influence on social institutions (1960). He argued that the central purpose of applying political economy to communication was to evaluate the effects of communication agencies in terms of the policies by which they are organized and operated, or to study the structure and policies of communication institutions in their social settings. Smythe further delineated research questions emanating from policies of production, allocation or distribution, and capital, organization and control, concluding that the studies that might evolve from these areas were practically endless.

In the 1970s, Murdock and Golding defined political economy of communication as fundamentally interested in studying communication and media as commodities produced by capitalist industries (1974). The article represented "a ground-breaking exercise ... a conceptual map for a political economic analysis of the media where none existed in British literature" (Mosco 1996: 102). A later work placed political economy within the broader framework of critical and

223

Marxist theory, with links to the Frankfurt School, as well as to other critical theorists (Murdock and Golding 1979). Nicholas Garnham further outlined the approach, noting that the political economy of communication involves analyzing "the modes of cultural production and consumption developed within capitalist societies" (1979: 125).

Political economy draws upon several disciplines – specifically history, economics, sociology, and political science. And while some may question whether or not a specific methodology is involved, the study of political economy draws on a wide range of techniques and methods, including not only Marxist economics, but methods used in history and sociology, especially power-structure research and institutional analysis.

Because historical analysis is mandatory, the approach is able to provide important insight into social change and movement. Political economy becomes crucial in order to document communication in total social context. Interrelationships between media and communication industries and sites of power in society are necessary for the complete analysis of communications and help to dispel some common myths about our economic and political system, especially the notions of pluralism, free enterprise, competition, etc. Through study of ownership and control, political economists analyze relations of power and confirm a class system and structural inequalities. In that the position includes economic *and* political analysis, it is therefore necessary grounding for ideological readings and cultural analysis. And through identification of contradictions, political-economic analysis provides strategies for intervention, resistance, and change.

While the approach does not claim to explain everything, political economists have examined a wide range of communication and media practices, including the traditional mass media and, more recently, computers and information technologies and users. As it is nearly impossible to briefly trace the rich history and wide range of communication theory and scholarship that draws on a political economic tradition, only a few examples will be mentioned here. (See Mosco 1996 for a detailed overview.)

Political economy has been especially relevant in analyzing international communication. For instance, Herbert Schiller's extensive work (beginning with Schiller 1969) has been important in critiquing the US communication system, its government and military ties, and its international extension. In Latin American and Europe, Armand Mattelart's various studies of international communication have made important contributions to the discussion of cultural imperialism (see Mattelart and Siegalaub 1979). Another good example is Gerald Sussman's work, especially on Southeast Asia, which has emphasized Third-World issues (for instance, Sussman 1984).

The analysis of media concentration and the implications for media content and democratic ideals have been the focus of many studies, including Edward Herman and Noam Chomsky's *Manufacturing Consent* (1988) and Ben Bagdikian's *The Media Monopoly* (1997).

New technologies have been examined in a number of political economic studies, such as Mosco's *The Pay-Per Society* (1989), Dan Schiller's *Telematics and Government* (1986), and a more recent collection edited by McChesney et al., *Capitalism and the Information Age* (1998).

Despite the broad definitions discussed previously, the study of the political economy of communication is still often considered narrow and deterministic, accused of focussing primarily on the economic or on the production side of the communication process, and neglecting texts, audiences, and consumption. Another common misconception is that political economists are concerned only with ownership and control questions.

Over the years, political economists have defended their theoretical positions and research from extreme and inaccurate accusations, but also have attempted to respond to reasonable criticism of the approach (compare Murdock and Golding 1974 and 1996). Some of this discussion has taken place in the flurries of theoretical debates between political economy and cultural studies (for instance, Garnham 1995; Grossberg 1995).

In addition, a few political economists have directed attention to the process of "rethinking" political economy (Meehan et al. 1994). Mosco's volume on the political economy of communication (1996) is subtitled "Rethinking and Renewal", with an attempt to redefine political economy in the broad terms of commodification, spatialization, and structuration, as well as examining political economy's relation to cultural studies and policy studies. Others have specifically combined political economy with other approaches, such as textual analysis, audience studies, or ethnographies (Pendakur 1993).

Thus, the tradition is actually much more complex than some critics claim. It is important to remember that the study of political economy encompasses political as well as economic analysis. Indeed, the political cannot be separated from the economic. Understanding interrelationships between communication industries, the state, other economic sectors, and key power bases is crucial for a complete analysis of the communication process, and thus involves research issues that are not always related directly to texts, audiences, or consumption. Though studies of ownership patterns and the dynamics of control are essential, political economic analysis is much more extensive than merely identifying and then condemning those who control media and communication resources.

3 Political Economy and Media Economics

It may be helpful to discuss another approach to studying economic issues in communication, that is, *media economics*. As mentioned previously, more specific attention to economics has been evident in the field of communication and media studies since the late 1980s, with scholars identifying media economics as a distinct focus of research activity. Examples include texts by Robert Picard (1989), Alan Albarron (1996), and Allison Alexander et al. (1993), as well as

The Journal of Media Economics, which was introduced in 1988. The goal of the journal is "to broaden understanding and discussion of the impact of economic and financial activities on media operations and managerial decisions." Generally, these media economics texts and the journal echo the concerns of mainstream (neoclassical) economics. As the journal's first editor explains:

> Media economics is concerned with how media operators meet the informational and entertainment wants and needs of audiences, advertisers and society with available resources. It deals with the factors influencing production of media goods and services and the allocation of those products for consumption. (Picard 1989: 7)

For the most part, the emphasis of media economics is on microeconomic issues rather than macroanalysis, and primarily on producers and consumers in media markets. Typically, the concern is how media industries and companies can succeed, prosper, or move forward. While competition may be assessed, little emphasis is placed on questions of ownership or the implications of concentrated ownership and control. These approaches avoid the kind of moral grounding adopted by political economists, as most studies emphasize description (or "what is") rather than critique (or "what ought to be"). A common approach is the industrial organization model, as described by Douglas Gomery:

> The industrial organization model of structure, conduct, and performance provides a powerful and useful analytical framework for economic analysis. Using it, the analyst seeks to define the size and scope of the structure of an industry and then go on to examine its economic behavior. Both of these steps require analyzing the status and operations of the industry, not as the analyst wishes it were. Evaluation of its performance is the final step, a careful weighing of "what is" versus "what ought to be." (1989: 58)

In addition, communication scholars have contributed organizational studies, which call attention to economic characteristics of media and communication industries, as well as emphasizing policy and regulatory developments (see Turow 1984; Tunstall and Palmer 1991).

4   The Study of the Economics of Film

It is clear that much more economic analysis has been done in film studies since Guback's critique in the 1970s. Generally, economic approaches to film can still be characterized as Allen and Gomery did in their discussion of economic film history in 1985. Allen and Gomery describe, and obviously favor, an *institutional* or *industrial organizational model*, following Gomery's description of media economics above. Examples of an industrial analysis include Gomery's early work on the introduction of sound, followed by studies of exhibition, etc. More recently, Justin Wyatt's analysis of "high concept" as a dominant force in contemporary Hollywood draws directly on industrial organization economics (Wyatt 1994: 65–6). Much of the work in edited collections on the film industry more or less explicitly follow an industrial model (see Balio 1976; Kindem 1982).

Allen and Gomery also describe a *Marxist critique* in economic film history, singling out Thomas Guback's work as an example. While Guback draws on Marxist theory, one might argue that his work could better be described as political economy of film, as described below. Allen and Gomery note that a Marxist economic critique typically has been linked to the analysis of a particular film or set of films, which has not necessarily been the goal of Guback's research. More appropriate is Janet Staiger's work (Bordwell et al. 1985), in which she outlines a "Hollywood mode of production" obviously drawing on Marxist concepts, but primarily interested in film style. Interestingly, Staiger's work is described on the University of Texas website as "the economic history and the dynamics of the industry and its technology."

5   Political Economy of Film

I would argue that political economy represents a distinctly different approach to the study of film, yet has not received as much recognition within cinema studies. The political economy of film must incorporate those characteristics that define political economy generally, as discussed previously: i.e. social change and history, social totality, moral grounding, and praxis.

Fundamentally, the political economy of film must understand motion pictures as commodities produced and distributed within a capitalist industrial structure. As Pendakur notes, film as a commodity must be seen as a "tangible product and intangible service" (1990: 39–40). Similar to industrial analysts, the approach is most definitely interested in questions pertaining to market structure and performance, but a political economist analyzing these issues more often would challenge the myths of competition, independence, globalization, etc., and view the film industry as part of the larger communication and media industry, and society as a whole. For instance, the US film industry is not only important because its films are popular worldwide. Indeed, that is only the tip of the iceberg. Rather than celebrate Hollywood's success, political economists are interested in how US films came to dominate international film markets, what mechanisms are in place to sustain such market dominance, how the state becomes involved, how the export of film is related to marketing of other media products, what the implications are for indigenous film industries in other countries, and what political/cultural implications may stem from the situation.

Most importantly, the political and ideological implications of these economic arrangements are relevant, as film must also be placed within an entire social, economic, and political context and critiqued in terms of the contribution to maintaining and reproducing structures of power.

Indeed, the focus on one medium or industry, such as film, may be seen as antithetical to political economy's attempt to go beyond merely describing the economic organization of the media industries. The political-economic study of film must incorporate not only a description of the state of the industry, but, as Mosco explains, "a theoretical understanding of these developments, situating them within a wider capitalist totality encompassing class and other social relations [offering a] sustained critique from a moral evaluative position" (1996: 115).

Some of the key distinctions between political economy and other models are the recognition and critique of the uneven distribution of power and wealth represented by the industry, the attention paid to labor issues and alternatives to commercial film, and the attempts to challenge the industry rather than accepting the status quo.

5.1   Examples of studies representing political economy of film

While perhaps not as recognized as other approaches, the political economy of film is represented in a wide range of research. Some classic economic studies fit much of the above description, but were not explicitly identified as political economy. For instance, Klingender and Legg's *Money Behind the Screen* (1937) examined finance capital in the film industry in 1937, tracing studio owners and their capitalist backers, while Mae Huettig's study of the film industry in the 1930s documented the power inherent in the various sectors of the industry (Huettig 1944).

More recently, Guback's work, especially those studies focussing on international film markets, represents an ideal example of political economy of film. *The International Film Industry* (1969) presented primary documentation about how the US domination of European film industries intensified after 1945, with the direct assistance of the US government. Guback followed this classic study with several articles documenting the international extension of US film companies in the 1970s and '80s, especially emphasizing the role of the state in these activities (in Balio 1976). In another article, Guback defended a nation's right to resist Hollywood's domination and develop its own film industry based on economic and cultural factors (1989). Guback's in-depth outline of the US film industry in *Who Owns the Media?* (Compaine 1982) represents a strong critique of Hollywood structure and practices, as opposed to the other industrially oriented articles in the volume.

Pendakur's study of the Canadian film industry employs a radical political economy of film, but also incorporates industrial organization theory to examine the market structure of Canadian film. "Marxian political economy's concern with power in class societies and its emphasis on a dialectical view of history help explain how the battle to create an indigenous film industry has been fought in Canada, in whose interests, and with what outcome" (1990: 39).

Pendakur (1998) and Wasko (1998) have also examined labor issues in film, adding to the growing literature documenting the history of labor organizations and workers in the US film industry. Wasko's other contributions include *Movies and Money* (1982), which presented the historical development of relationships between Hollywood and financial institutions, and *Hollywood in the Information Age* (1994), which examined continuity and change in the US film industry relating to the introduction of new technologies during the 1980s and early 1990s. In addition, Wasko, Phillips, and Purdie (1993) examined the ongoing commercialization of film, by focussing on growth of product placement, tie-ins, and merchandising activities in film marketing.

Meanwhile, many other scholars have taken a political-economic approach in looking at various aspects of film. Nicholas Garnham incorporated an analysis of the "Economics of the US Motion Picture Industry" to exemplify the production of culture in his collection *Capitalism and Communication* (1990). Aksoy and Robins's "Hollywood for the 21st Century" (1992) is also a good example of a study that focusses on issues of concentration and globalization and draws fundamentally on political economy. Another example is Prindle's *Risky Business: The Political Economy of Hollywood* (1993).

Despite these various studies, it still might be argued that political economy is much less common in film studies than in communication research. If so, then why? It is possible that Guback's explanations in the 1978 essay mentioned at the beginning of this chapter are still relevant. He argued that one of the reasons that there is so much textual film analysis is the relatively easy access to film texts. In other words, scholars depend on the material that is available for study, whether it be film texts or industry-supplied information. Even though more popular media attention now centers on the film or entertainment industry through stories and programs (such as *Entertainment Tonight*), including stories that explore film production and box office numbers, it is mostly coverage generated by the industry itself and hardly critical.

Indeed, it is sometimes still a challenge to find reliable and relevant data about the film industry on which to base a critical analysis. For instance, where can one find accurate production figures beyond the rumour mill, as reported in *Variety* or other trade publications? The recent attention to the box office receipts from *Titanic* again draws attention to the mystical accounting methods used by Hollywood to determine profit and loss for specific films. Other areas also remain mired in mystery: for instance, where is it possible to find accurate or meaningful figures on stock ownership of film companies or the corporations that own them?

The type of information that *is* available tends to lend itself especially well to congratulatory coverage of the industry's triumphs. But it also might be argued that much scholarly writing on the industry is not critical anyway, resisting any criticism of the status quo and basically supportive of the way things are. Even when information is available, the commercial and profit-motivated goals of the industry are assumed, and rarely questioned.

On the other hand, one might also wonder why film is less often included in much of the work in political economy of communication? While film appears in general overviews of communication or media industries, it seems to receive less

229

careful analysis than other forms of media or communication (Jowett and Linton 1980). One obvious reason may be the academic fragmentation that still sometimes separates film studies from media and communication studies in university organizational charts, professional organizations, and scholarly journals. Of course, one explanation is that film studies typically has been based in the humanities, while communication and media studies tend to draw more on the social sciences. Beyond this fragmentation, though, there also may be different perceptions of film's importance for communication scholars. Film still often represents "only entertainment," thus not as worthy of scholarly attention as news and information programming, or computer and information technologies.

These oversights need to be addressed if we are to understand film in its social context. These days, film *must* be considered as part of the larger communications and media industry. More than ever before, distribution outlets such as cable and satellite services link news, information, and entertainment programs; and sometime in the future it seems likely that there will be further links via new digital and multi-media forms. It is no longer novel to observe that news is looking more like entertainment, with new forms evolving, such as infotainment, docudramas, etc.

But importantly, these activities are, more than ever, under the same corporate ownership. Films are produced by the same companies that are involved with other media and communications activities, and it is no secret that fewer and fewer giant corporations control these activities. These multi-national corporations have diversified into all areas of the media, sometimes attempting to maximize profitability by building synergy between their corporate divisions. For some of these companies, film plays a key role in these synergistic efforts, as corporations such as the Walt Disney Company build product lines which begin with a film but continue through television, cable, publishing, theme parks, merchandising, etc. These days, companies like Disney not only distribute products to these outlets, but own the outlets.

In addition, it may be useful for communication scholars to look more closely at the international expansion of the US film industry to better understand the historical evolution of current globalization trends. While the expansion of global markets may be relatively new for some media, the US film industry developed global marketing techniques as early as the 1920s and continues its dominant position in international media markets today.

5.2 What is to be done?

In addition to the cross-media analysis that is called for above, there are other links that political economists need to make, responding to the critiques of the approach discussed earlier. It is apparent to many political economists that cultural studies, whether centered on film or other areas, offers important insights that are crucial to understanding the reception of media products and their ideological significance. As critical cultural analysts come to an awareness of the significance of political-economic grounding, productive links might be made to integrate research, policy efforts, and other practical activities.

Political economists have been accused of ignoring the audience or the consumption side of the production equation, an issue dealt with by Wasko and Hagen (1999) in a volume that includes both reception analysts and political economists discussing issues relating to audiences and consumption.

Other linkages need to be forged with researchers who share similar political commitments. For instance, political economy has neglected many of the issues posed by feminist theorists. A forthcoming collection by Eileen Meehan and Ellen Riordan specifically addresses this blind spot and promises to make an important contribution to forging these links.

Another area that needs more attention is the application of political-economic analysis to practice, or actually challenging the industries that we are critiquing. Many scholars contribute a great deal through teaching and "enlightening" students, who may ultimately go on to work for media companies. However, developing strategies to affect the policies and activities of the communication and entertainment industries is still a real challenge for critical researchers.

One indication that some of the issues raised in this chapter have been recognized within film studies is the theme for the 1999 Society for Cinema Studies conference: Media Industries: Past, Present and Future. It indicates how media beyond film have been integrated into previously exclusive cinema studies, but also concretely acknowledges the importance of economic and industry issues. The conference description reads:

> Topics for panels and papers might include media industry issues concerning production, distribution and exhibition, regulatory parameters, the relationship between technological change and industrial structure, international industry comparisons, institutional/industrial issues concerning independent, and alternative media and *studies in political economy of the mass media*. (from SCS website, my emphasis)

As the industry and its wealth become ever more concentrated, it will be increasingly difficult to avoid the issues and analysis that a political economy of film offers; thus one might expect the approach to become even stronger in the future.

References

Aksoy, A., and K. Robins. 1992. "Hollywood for the 21st Century: Global Competition for Critical Mass in Image Markets." *Cambridge Journal of Economics* 16, 1: 1–22.

Albarron, A. B. 1996. *Media Economics: Understanding Markets, Industries, and Concepts.* Ames: Iowa State University Press.

Alexander, A., J. Owers, and R. Carveth, eds. 1993. *Media Economics: Theory and Practice.* Hillsdale: Lawrence Erlbaum.

Allen, R., and D. Gomery. 1985. *Film History: Theory and Practice*. New York: Alfred A. Knopf.

Bagdikian, B. 1997. *The Media Monopoly*. Boston: Beacon Press.

Balio, T., ed. 1976. *The American Film Industry*. Madison: University of Wisconsin Press.

Bordwell, D., J. Staiger, and K. Thompson. 1985. *The Classical Hollywood Cinema: Film Style and Mode of Production to 1960*. New York: Columbia University Press.

Compaine, B., ed. 1982. *Who Owns the Media? Concentration of Ownership in the Mass Communications Industry*. White Plains: Knowledge Industry Publications.

Garnham, N. 1979. "Contribution to a Political Economy of Mass Communication." *Media, Culture and Society* 1: 123–46.

——. 1990. *Capitalism and Communication: Global Culture and the Economics of Information*. London: Sage.

——. 1995. "Political Economy and Cultural Studies: Reconciliation or Divorce?" *Critical Studies in Mass Communication* 12, 1: 62–71.

Golding, P., and Graham Murdock. 1991. "Culture, Communication, and Political Economy." In *Mass Media and Society*. Ed. J. Curran and M. Gurevitch. London: Edward Arnold.

Gomery, D. 1989. "Media Economics: Terms of Analysis." *Critical Studies in Mass Communication* 6, 1: 43–60.

Grossberg, L. 1995. "Cultural Studies vs. Political Economy: Is Anybody Else Bored with This Debate?" *Critical Studies in Mass Communication* 12, 1: 72–81.

Guback, T. 1969. *The International Film Industry: Western Europe and America Since 1945*. Bloomington: Indiana University Press.

——. 1978. "Are We Looking at the Right Things in Film?" Paper presented at Society for Cinema Studies Conference, Philadelphia.

——. 1989. "Should a Nation Have Its Own Film Industry?" *Directions* 3, 1: 489–92.

Herman, E., and N. Chomsky. 1988. *Manufacturing Consent: A Political Economy of the Mass Media*. New York: Pantheon.

Huettig, M. D. 1944. *Economic Control of the Motion Picture Industry*. Philadelphia: University of Pennsylvania Press.

Jevons, W. S. 1970. *The Theory of Political Economy*. Harmondsworth: Penguin.

Jowett, G., and J. M. Linton. 1980. *Movies as Mass Communication*. Beverly Hills: Sage.

Kindem, G., ed. 1982. *The American Movie Industry: The Business of Motion Pictures*. Carbondale: Southern Illinois Press.

Klingender, F. D., and S. Legg. 1937. *Money Behind the Screen*. London: Lawrence and Wishart.

McChesney, R., E. M. Wood, and John Bellamy Foster, eds. 1998. *Capitalism and the Information Age*. New York: Monthly Review Press.

Mattelart, A., and S. Siegalaub, eds. 1979. *Communication and Class Struggle, Vol 1: Capitalism, Imperialism*. New York: International General.

Meehan, E., V. Mosco, and J. Wasko. 1994. "Rethinking Political Economy: Change and Continuity." In *Defining Media Studies: Reflections on the Future of the Field*. New York: Oxford University Press.

Mosco, V. 1989. *The Pay-Per Society: Computers and Communication in the Information Age*. Toronto: Garamond.

——. 1996. *The Political Economy of Communication: Rethinking and Renewal*. London: Sage Publications.

Murdock, G., and P. Golding. 1974. "For a Political Economy of Mass Communications." In *Socialist Register*. Ed. R. Miliband and S. Saville. London: Merlin Press. 205–34.

——. 1979. "Capitalism, Communication and Class Relations." In *Mass Communication and Society*. Ed. J. Curran and M. Gurevitch. Beverly Hills: Sage Publications.

——. 1996. "Culture, Communications, and Political Economy." In *Mass Media and Society*, 2nd edn. Ed. J. Curran and M. Gurevitch. London: Arnold.

Pendakur, M. 1990. *Canadian Dreams and American Control: The Political Economy of the Canadian Film Industry*. Detroit: Wayne State University Press.

——. 1993. "Political Economy and Ethnography: Transformations in an Indian Village." In *Illuminating the Blindspots: Essays Honoring Dallas W. Smythe*. Ed. J. Wasko, V. Mosco, and M. Pendakur. Norwood: Ablex Publishing.

——. 1998. "Hollywood North: Film and TV Production in Canada." In *Global Productions: Labor in the Making of the "Information Society"*. Cresskill: Hampton Press.

Picard, R. 1989. *Media Economics: Concepts and Issues*. Newbury Park: Sage Publications.

Prindle, D. F. 1993. *Risky Business: The Political Economy of Hollywood*. Boulder: Westview Press.

Schiller, D. 1986. *Telematics and Government*. Norwood: Ablex Publishing.

Schiller, Herbert I. 1969. *Mass Communication and American Empire*. Boston: Beacon Press.

Smith, A. 1776. *An Inquiry into the Nature and Causes of Wealth of Nations*.

Smythe, D. 1960. "The Political Economy of Communication." *Journalism Quarterly* (August): 156–71.

Sussman, G. 1984. "Global Telecommunications in the Third World: Theoretical Considerations." *Media, Culture and Society* 6: 289–300.

Tunstall, J., and Michael Palmer. 1991. *Media Moguls*. London: Routledge.

Turow, J. 1984. *Media Industries: The Production of News and Entertainment*. New York: Longman.

Wasko, J. 1982. *Movies and Money: Financing the American Film Industry*. Norwood: Ablex Publishing.

——. 1994. *Hollywood in the Information Age: Beyond the Silver Screen*. Cambridge: Polity Press.

——. 1998. "Challenges to Hollywood's Labor Force in the 1990s." In *Global Productions: Labor in the Making of the "Information Society"*. Cresskill: Hampton Press.

Wasko, J., and I. Hagen, eds. 1999. *Consuming Audiences: Production and Reception in Media Research*. Cresskill: Hampton Press.

——, M. Phillips, and C. Purdie. 1993. "Hollywood Meets Madison Ave.: The Commercialization of US Films." *Media, Culture and Society* 15, 2: 271–93.

Wyatt, J. 1994. *High Concept: Movies and Marketing in Hollywood*. Austin: University of Texas Press.

CHAPTER FOURTEEN

The Work of Theory in the Age of Digital Transformation

Henry Jenkins

Don't you wish that somebody, in 1895, 1897 or at least in 1903, had realized the fundamental significance of the cinema's emergence and produced a comprehensive record of a new medium's emergence? Interviews with the audiences; a systematic account of the narrative strategies, scenography and camera positions as they developed year by year; an analysis of the connections between the emerging language of cinema and different forms of popular entertainment which co-existed with it, would have been invaluable. . . . In contrast to a hundred years ago, when cinema was coming into being, we are fully aware of the significance of this new media revolution. And yet I am afraid that future theorists and historians of computer media will be left with not much more than the equivalents of newspaper reviews and random bits of evidence similar to cinema's first decade. . . . They will find that analytical texts from our era are fully aware of the significance of the computer's takeover of culture yet, by and large, they mostly contain speculations about the future rather than a record and a theory of the present.

Lev Manovich, "Cinema as a Cultural Interface"

In his essay "Cinema as a Cultural Interface," Lev Manovich laments the failure of contemporary media scholars to record "the moment when the icons and the buttons of multimedia interfaces were like wet paint on a just completed painting, before they became a universal convention and slipped into invisibility." Historians of early cinema can return to the prints of early films preserved in archival collections around the world to trace the process of stylistic experimentation and discovery. Many significant early films no longer exist – but enough exist to make the reconsideration of early films a central focus of cinema studies today. A historian of the Web, even one writing today, would face much greater difficulties. The early websites, made less than a decade ago, no longer exist, swamped by rapid growth, quickly scuttled and replaced, leaving no archival records. Writing the history of digital media will be much more like writing the history of a transitory medium, like early radio or vaudeville, than like documenting the evolution of a textual medium, like the printing press or the cinema. Rapid technological transformation may prevent future generations from accessing and reading many surviving texts and artifacts (computer games, software, hypertext narratives). We can still project old films, but they won't have the operating systems to play old video games, which are more like the wax phonograph cylinders than like books or films. Media scholars are therefore obligated to record our observations, to document technological and aesthetic change, and to preserve evidence of new media's impact.

Manovich also correctly captures – and to some degree manifests – the temporal flux characteristic of contemporary digital theory, looking to the past (for antecedents) and to the future (for the fulfillment of utopian promises) but rarely at the present (for crude prototypes for what is to come). Yet Manovich's discussion, which distinguishes between "newspaper reports, diaries of cinema's inventors, programs of film showings and other bits and pieces" on the one hand and academic theory on the other, preserves distinctions that are breaking down as the function and status of theory responds to the digital revolution. From a contemporary perspective, one wonders why *Moving Picture World*'s Epes Winthrope Sargent, who articulated the core principles of the emerging classical Hollywood cinema, isn't as much an early film theorist as Sergei Eisenstein, who used theory to explain his own filmmaking practices. Many digital theorists have more in common with Sargent or Eisenstein than with Foucault or Derrida.

If academic writers cast their eyes on the future, journalists (Rheingold 1993; Katz 1997a; Dibble 1994; Brand 1988; Herz 1996) and media activists (Horn 1998; Dyson 1998; Cherny and Weise 1996) have provided accounts of the early days of the Internet, the evolution of the video game, women's hostile reception on-line, and MUD (Multiple User Domain) debates about democracy and virtual communities. Thomas McLaughlin (1996) has offered the term "vernacular theory" to refer to theorizing outside the academy, offering compelling case studies of the different modes of theory formation among school teachers, advertising executives, fans, media activists, or New Age visionaries, and vernacular theory abounds in the digital realm. We are often told that the Internet is a "world without gatekeepers," which opens public debates beyond the confines of elite universities. Amy Bruckman (1996) describes this new participatory culture: "Cyberspace is not Disneyland. It's not a polished, perfect place built by professional designers for the public to obediently wait on line to passively experience it. It's more like a finger-painting party. Everyone is making things, there's paint everywhere, and most work only a parent would love." Do-it-yourself theory-making is sloppy business which doesn't accept academic theory's rules or standards.

What counts as theory and what theory does are questions that rarely get asked in summary essays like this one. Theory will be understood here as any attempt to make meaningful generalizations for interpreting or evaluating local experiences and practices. When we make claims about what e-mail is, what it does, how it changes how we relate to people, its potentials for reshaping traditional practices and institutions, or how it differs from letter-writing or phone calls, we are theorizing digital media. Academic and vernacular theory carry different degrees

235

of prestige, speak different languages, ask different questions, and address different audiences, though the line between them is rapidly breaking down. For example, when someone like Nicholas Negroponte, the head of MIT's Media Lab, writes a regular column in *Wired*, does he write as an academic or a vernacular theorist? Is his status fundamentally different from the provocative political journalist John Heilman, who has also published in *Wired* but has no university affiliation? Even some early works of digital theory, such as Vannever Bush's influential "As We May Think," first published in *Atlantic Monthly* in 1945, appeared not in scholarly journals but in mass-market magazines. Allucquere Rosanne Stone (1995) has used the term "code switching" to refer to her shifts in tone, language, and address as she goes from chat groups to academic conferences, from corporate trade shows to avant-garde arts exhibitions. Marshall McLuhan's "global village" surfaces as the name of a corporate knowledge-management program, alongside quotations from *Understanding Media* (McLuhan and Lapham 1994). Theory has become central to how businesses operate, how politicians plan their campaigns, and how consumers make choices.

What counts as digital media may also be up for grabs. Digital theory may address anything from the role of CGI (Computer Graphics Interface) special effects in Hollywood blockbusters to new systems of communication (the Internet), new genres of entertainment (the computer game), new styles of music (techno), or new systems of representation (digital photography or virtual reality). All of these different things reflect a shift from the computer as a tool, primarily understood in terms of information storage and numerical calculation, to the computer as a medium of communication, education, and entertainment. Each attracts their own cadre of theorists asking different questions: e-mail poses questions about virtual community; digital photography about the authenticity and reliability of visual documentation; virtual reality about embodiment and its epistemological functions; hypertext about readership and authorial authority; computer games about spatial narrative; MUDs about identity formation; webcams about voyeurism and exhibitionism; and so forth. The multiplicity of digital media makes writing a totalizing account impossible. The same might be true of a theory of print culture or of the cinema. However, theorists working on those earlier media privilege one form or function over others. Literature becomes the study of novels, short stories, and philosophical essays, not, at least until recently, of manners books, instructional manuals, travel narratives, or reference works. Cinema studies focusses primarily on commercial feature-film production and not home movies, instructional films, corporate promotional videos, or exercise tapes. Cyberspace is not one place or one thing. Digital theory struggles with its multiplicity, hybridity, and fluidity.

In a period of prolonged change, digital theory is more than an academic exercise. Digital media impacts all aspects of Western society, from education to politics, from business to the arts. Journalists, science-fiction writers, ideologues, entrepreneurs, activists, classroom teachers, rock stars, Supreme Court judges, and government regulators are both consumers and producers of digital theory.

For many, theorizing restores predictability and stability to a world rocked by radical change, while for others, theory fuels change, directing the energies unleashed by the digital revolution toward altering the nature of political life or personal identity. Our fantasies and fears about change shape our theories (including supposedly disinterested academic theories) as much as our theories help master those fears and fulfill those fantasies. Theories often reflect our points of entry into digital culture, the difference between a generation that initially encountered digital media as technologies of the workplace (word-processing) and those for whom digital media are technologies of recreation (computer games) or personal communication (chat rooms). For one group, digital media will be likely understood as technologies counterposed to the fleshy and spiritual aspects of human life. For the other, digital media are understood in terms of the social relations they facilitate and thus as integral to how we live within families, make love, express intimate thoughts, and have fun in the late twentieth century.

Because digital media are changing rapidly, the state of digital theory is also evolving at a dramatic pace. One book editor who had sought to analyze and evaluate the CD-ROM disk as a new medium discovered that CD-ROM was surpassed by DVD in the time it took him to get his contract, solicit and edit contributions, and get the book published and into the stores (Smith 1999). An important study on the impact of race on access to the Internet (Hoffman and Novak 1998) was deemed out of date upon publication, well before we could process and respond to its challenges for cyberdemocracy. For those reasons, this chapter can, at best, represent a day in the life of digital theory, not an exhaustive map of an established field.

1   Bridging the Two Cultures: The Artist and the Engineer

This book is intended as an attempt to think about the object-world of technology as though it belonged to the world of culture, or as though these two worlds were united. For the truth is, they have been united all along. Was the original cave painter an artist or an engineer? She was both, of course, like most artists and engineers since. But we have a habit – long cultivated – of imagining them as separate, the two great tributaries rolling steadily to the sea of modernity, and dividing everyone in their path into two camps: those that dwell on the shores of technology and those that dwell on the shores of culture.

Steven Johnson, *Interface Culture*

In the early 1990s, a group of graduate students and junior faculty members met regularly in the basement of the MIT Media Lab to read and discuss cultural theory. Reflecting their interests in the intersection between narrative/reader-response theory and artificial intelligence, they called themselves the Narrative/Intelligence Reading Group. Some of what the group read was predictable – the hypertext theories of Ted Nelson (1981), Roger Schank (1995) on storytelling machines, Donna Haraway's "Cyborg Manifesto" (1985). Other selections were more idiosyncratic – Aristotle's *Rhetoric*, Clifford Geertz's "Thick Descriptions" (1977), André Bazin's "Myth of Total Cinema" (1971a), or *The Memory Palace of Matteo Ricci* (Spence 1994). Occasionally, a visitor to the Media Lab, such as Samuel R. Delaney, joined the ongoing dialogue, yet the group never received official recognition or funds from the Media Lab and the students received no academic credit. As group members graduated, they continued to follow the Narrative/Intelligence electronic mailing and, in some cases, conducted their own sessions with local research groups. As a founding member, I was often struck by how fluidly discussions moved from abstract principles to designing filtering systems, holograms, virtual reality programs, or interactive cinema projects. They looked upon theory not simply as a vocabulary for studying things but as a tool for making things. Their Media Lab projects were always grounded in theories, sometimes simple-minded, sometimes sophisticated. Project directors make assumptions not only about programming language or delivery systems but also about the nature of the society or the kinds of user their innovations would foster. For example, intelligent agents, digital entities that seek recommendations from like-minded users on the Web, depend upon the assumption that taste is systematic. If we share one set of preferences with someone else, we likely make other common judgments. These assumptions come very close to Pierre Bourdieu's theory of "habitus", the field of cultural choices (1984). And when some group members working on agents first looked at Bourdieu's cryptic maps and charts, they immediately saw them as interfaces to be operationalized, tested, and refined.

These conversations were not fundamentally different from those at universities and corporations around the world. The early International Conferences on Cyberspace have been often described in language approaching "alien encounters," as humanists and technologists saw each other as beings from other worlds, speaking unfamiliar languages, and asking out-in-orbit questions. Consider the titles of two representative essays from Michael Benedict's *Cyberspace: First Steps* (1994): "The Erotic Ontology of Cyberspace" (Heim 1994) and "Collaborative Engines for Multiparticipant Cyberspaces" (Tollander 1994). More recent gatherings, such as Harvard's Internet and Society conferences, find academic theorists, entrepreneurs, and computer scientists addressing a divergent yet shared body of concerns. Through such conversations, we are starting to find ways beyond the division, which C. P. Snow (1992) described, between the "two cultures," the utilitarian realm of science and engineering and the expressive realm of the humanities and the arts.

This new fusion of the humanities and engineering reflects the shifting nature of the technologies themselves, what Bruce Sterling (1988) describes as the change from the "steam-snorting wonders" and massive dam projects of the early twentieth century to "technologies that stick to the skin" and become intimate parts of everyday life. As Michael Menser and Stanley Aronowitz argue:

238

The technological is not so easily distinguished from the "human," since it is within (medical technologies, processed foods), beside (telephones) and outside (satellites). Sometimes we inhabit it (the climate-controlled office space), or it inhabits us (a pacemaker). Sometimes it seems to be an appendage or prosthetic (a pair of eyeglasses); at other times, human beings appear to serve as the appendages (as in an assembly line). (1996: 9)

Sherry Turkle documents the diverse ways that people are interacting with and conceptualizing computers, mapping sub-cultural responses (hackers, gamers), naive encounters (children), and gendered computing styles through sociological observation and psychological analysis. Her movement from *The Second Self* (1984) to *Life on Screen* (1997) maps the shift from personal computers to a world-wide network. The computer, she argues, is a "second self," an extension of our perceptions of our own identity, a vehicle for rethinking our relations with the world, and a metaphor for thinking about human intelligence.

Cultural critics often act as if their importance lay in dethroning the scientific community's entrenched power. Yet the best digital theory emerges when the lines between the scientist/engineer and humanist/artist are less clearly demarcated, when engineers integrate cultural theory into their design principles, when humanists learn how to program, and when digital artists theorize their own creative processes. Much important work on interactive fiction, for example, has come from people like Stuart Moulthrop (1990), Michael Joyce (1996), and Shelley Jackson (1997), who are also key hypertext authors. Eastgate Systems (http://www.eastgate.com) not only markets such pioneering works but also shapes their reception context, distributing theoretical and critical works, hosting conferences and seminars, publishing bibliographies. Marsha Kinder (1998) has translated her ideas about the needs to "deconstruct" race, sex, and gender into a computer game, *Runaways*. Digital composer Tod Makover has created and performed a musical work, *Brain Opera* (http://brainop.media.mit.edu), based on Marvin Minsky's *Society of Mind* (1988). Brenda Laurel (1990, 1993, forth-coming) works in Silicon Valley, not only theorizing the gendering of computer technology but creating new games for girls which put her ideas into practice. Digital theory often comes from humanists at technical institutes; its theorists list themselves as CEOs of start-up companies.

Such projects necessarily challenge the "critical distance" which has dominated much recent academic theory, though this ideal of "distance" has already undergone serious questions across many different disciplines.[1] Nothing would be served, either within the academy or in the business sector, by theorists' refusal to engage in designing digital technologies and critiquing practical developments. Often such conversations reveal strange and unexpected common interests, as in the discussions surrounding the development of "girls' games," where feminist academics interested in ensuring girls' early access to the technology and female entrepreneurs interested in broadening the software market found they might work together (Cassell and Jenkins 1998). The state of the technology at that time reflected the unexamined goals of male game designers, who developed products that reflected their own tastes and interests, and, as a result, game systems required faster reaction time for fighting games but not the memory and processing necessary to establish more complex character relationships. Both groups wanted to rethink what a computer game might look like and what kinds of pleasure it might incorporate, and they drew on similar intellectual perspectives to address those shared questions. The female game executives were themselves versed in feminist theory, often had liberal arts backgrounds, and did quantitative and qualitative research mapping girls' preferences and playing styles. Academic feminists, who sought more precise understandings of the gendering of game genres, sometimes found themselves consulting with the games companies.

One of my contributions to the discussions of the Narrative/Intelligence Group was the introduction of David Bordwell's work on the institutional and cultural contexts of early Soviet film theory, which closely parallels the activities of our contemporary humanities computing centers (1994). Early Soviet film-makers, such as Sergei Eisenstein and Dziga Vertov, had professional training in engineering, architecture, and graphic design. They were recruited into filmmaking in the wake of the Bolshevik revolution, seeking a fusion of arts and engineering at a time when technologization was seen as key in transforming Russia from a feudal state into a worker's utopia. They framed their theories in a language derived from those more technical backgrounds, with Vertov celebrating the "man with the movie camera" as part artist and part engineer, with Kuleshov speaking of his early works as "experiments," with Eisenstein writing about montage-editing in terms from Pavlovian reflexology. Their essays were written to justify their work to the Bolshevik Party leaders (a form of grant-proposal-writing) or to explain to each other the lessons they had learned from specific projects (a form of lab-reporting). Any theoretical understanding was immediately converted into practical applications. Many digital theorists work in this same *techne* tradition, merging theory and practice.

This fusion between theory and practice shapes not only the content of media theory but also the forms theory takes and the contexts within which it circulates. Digital theorists, such as William Mitchell (1996) and Seymour Papert (Papert and Negroponte 1996), have translated their books into interactive websites which allow readers to follow links relevant to their discussions and which support additional annotation, linkage, and electronic discussion from their readers. Digital ethnographer Ricki Goldman-Segall's website (1997) enables users to directly access video footage from her fieldwork and to form their own conclusions and interpretations. The most important developments in digital theory are often first introduced on-line and only belatedly appear in print. Stuart Moulthrop's Technocultures mailing list, for example, has facilitated an ongoing international conversation about core issues in the theory of hypertext and interactive cinema, substantially influencing its participants' theoretical writings. Phil Agre's *The Network Observer* (http://weber.ucsd.edu/~pagre/

tno.html), a monthly electronic newsletter, is a vehicle for computer professionals to debate the social and political implications of their work. Bruce Sterling's Dead Media Project (http://griffin.multimedia.edu/~deadmedia) focusses on media inventions that failed or died out so that we gain a more skeptical attitude toward computer entrepreneurs' sweeping claims. A special issue of *Postmodern Culture* (http://calliope.jhu.edu/journals/postmodern_culture/toc/pmcv008.html#v008.2), edited by Robert Kolker, focussed on the potential application of digital media for traditional film studies and allowed contributors to develop a range of different models for writing cyberessays on subjects as diverse as *Prospero's Books*, Dziga Vertov, *Casablanca*, *Singin' in the Rain*, and *The Killing*. Some essays link in clips; others digitally map narrative space or even produce fly-by quicktime diagrams. Often, digital media enables theorists to enlarge their potential audience, as in the case of Berkeley's Bad Subjects (http://english-www.hss.cmu.edu/bs), whose monthly webzine of cultural criticism and political theory attracts 20,000 connections a week. The Birmingham tradition of cultural studies originated in a context of open universities, which shaped not only its focus on the practices of everyday life, but also the tone and style of its early writing. Similarly, Bad Subjects' attempts to broaden the dialogue of cultural studies to a larger public is generating a more accessible, pragmatic, and forward-looking version of cultural theory. In general, the need to create theory one can use, the merger of humanities and engineering approaches, is producing a different style of scholarship from the more abstract theories that have dominated media studies in recent decades.

2 Inventing the Future: Digital Theory and the Utopian Imagination

If we don't invent the future, AT&T will.
David Rodowick, "Audiovisual Culture and Interdisciplinary Knowledge"

In "The Theory of the Virtual Class," Arthur Kroker and Michael A. Weinstein (1994) speak of "the growth of cyber-authoritarianism," which excludes from the debates about digital media all voices that are not "stridently pro-technotopia," bestowing an air of "inevitability" on the digital revolution. At the heart of this vision of a "wired shut" culture is their conception of the "virtual class," which theorizes, develops, and regulates cyberspace according to its own "radically diminished vision of human experience." Displaying the radical pessimism that has characterized critical theory since Adorno, "virtual life" gives Kroker and Weinstein a new way to speak about "false consciousness." Their depiction of the "virtual class" borders on conspiracy theory, seeing the "digerati" as totally calculating, totally coherent, totally in control.

A fundamental technophobia runs through not only traditional humanism but the theories and critical practices of the old Left. Technology is understood as inhuman or anti-human, as destroying more organic pre-technological cultures.

241

Technology is viewed as the instrumentation of surveillance, power, and social control, rather than as a toolkit for social and political transformation. These writers fit digital media into a longstanding Left "alienation" from "the machine," critiquing the Internet's original support from the military as displacing the old "military industrial complex" with the new "military–entertainment complex" (Herz 1997). Herbert Schiller writes:

> What the evidence here demonstrates is the strong, if not determining, influence of the social purpose that initially fostered the development of new technologies. The social uses to which this technology is put, more times than not, follow their originating purposes. When military or commercial advantage are the motivating forces, it is to be expected that the laboratories will produce findings conducive to these objectives. (1994: 45)

Despite some of its limitations, critical pessimism serves important functions. It questions the more fanciful and zealous claims made for digital media (such as John Perry Barlow's proclamation that the nations of the world have no sovereignty over the citizens of cyberspace [1996]).[2] They ask whether our hopes for democracy, social justice, political transformation, and free expression are getting coopted into the sales pitch for new software and hardware. In practice, Robert Adrian (1995) argues: "Increased bandwidth allows telephone space to be appropriated for commercial propaganda; occupied by infotainment commodities; turned into a shopping mall." We need to be vitally concerned with who controls our technological and economic base, recognizing that there is a significant overlap between those countries which have the greatest access to the Internet and those countries which consume the bulk of the world's resources. As in earlier industrial or technological revolutions, computers may displace workers from their jobs or bring employees under tighter supervision and control by their bosses. While we are busy celebrating a participatory medium without gatekeepers, most other sectors of the entertainment and information industries have increasingly fallen into the hands of a smaller and smaller number of media conglomerates. Critical pessimism stresses the dangers of information overload; too much information can be as disempowering as too little.

As Lev Manovich (1996b) has noted, there is something distinctly American about the dominant currents of digital theory:

> For the West, interactivity is a perfect vehicle for the ideas of democracy and equality. For the East, it is another form of manipulation, in which the artist uses advanced technology to impose his/her totalitarian will on the people.... A western artist sees the Internet as a perfect tool to break down all hierarchies and bring the art to the people.... In contrast, as a post-communist subject, I cannot but see the Internet as a communal apartment of the Stalin era: no privacy, everybody spies on everybody else, always present line for common areas such as the toilet or the kitchen.

The dominant language in cyberspace remains English, the dominant ideology a characteristically American mixture of rugged individualism and civic libertarianism. Not surprisingly, many foreign governments have built firewalls blocking their citizens from Internet access, much as they jam the Radio Free Europe signals coming over their borders. As some social critics note, the digital revolution may simply be another phase in the process of American cultural imperialism, though others suggest it is a more complex version, since it does allow some channels for messages to be shipped back to the United States and impact its development (Stratton 1997).

However, the old paradigms of critical pessimism ultimately lead to political paralysis and fatalism, another way of seeing technological expansion as inevitable and irreversible. Critical pessimism offers us few models of viable change, focussing only on the strength of entrenched power and the failure of all strategies of resistance. At its most reductive, critical pessimism scapegoats the media for all the faults of the current social order, rather than recognizing that digital media might offer new technical potentials for responding to the fragmentation of contemporary social life or the domestic isolation of children, housewives, and the elderly. Digital theory matters politically because of its ability to envision alternatives, to imagine a better future. Cyberspace provides a place to experiment with alternative structures of government, new forms of social relations, which may, at least on the most grassroots of levels, allow us to temporarily escape, if not fully transform, unacceptable social conditions in our everyday lives.

Feminist critics, such as Brenda Laurel (forthcoming) and Allucquere Rosanne Stone (1995), have embraced the Amerindian myth of Coyote, the shapeshifter, to characterize digital media as enabling a breakdown of fixed sexual and social identities and a transformation of stable alignments of power. Donna Haraway (1985) has promoted the "cyborg," which exists at the interface between human and machine, not as a figure of dehumanization but as one that "denatures" gender and sexuality (Gray et al. 1996). Summarizing this line of feminist argument, Anne Balsamo writes: "Cyborg identity is predicated on transgressed boundaries. They fascinate us because they are not like us and yet are just like us" (1996: 33). The metaphor of the cyborg as a hybrid identity helps us to recognize that our gender identities are, at least, partially culturally manufactured, and, as such, gender may be reinvented, retooled, or reprogrammed. Some argue, for example, that going on-line enables a radical reconceptualization of the relationship between our selves and our bodies, potentially liberating us from a long legacy of biological determinism. Others would insist, however, that cyborg identities still require a physical transformation, a reconceptualization of what it means to live within our bodies and that cyborg feminism pulls us back to the material world.

This prospect of "shapeshifting" or "cyborg" identities is being realized by gay and lesbian teens who go on-line to find a community where homophobia does not dominate, where the risks of "coming out" can be lowered, and where

243

they can experiment with more fluid conceptions of their sexuality. The digital realm allows them room to find out who they are and what they want outside of the constant pressures at home or at school. For those teens, cyberspace is not a "virtual life" but rather a temporary alternative to their rather dystopian real-world experiences at a time when gay and lesbian teens are three times more likely than their straight counterparts to commit suicide. However, many filtering technologies block access to websites and discussion groups on the basis of the use of such words as "gay" and "lesbian," regardless of whether the sites include sexually explicit content. Such filters threaten to render that realm of alternative social interactions invisible and thus inaccessible to many who need it most (http://www.glaad.org/glaad/access_denied/exec-sum.html).

Even the most utopian digital theory often contains some degree of skepticism about the future and criticisms of the present – even if it remains only implicit. Michael Heim has framed the term "virtual realism" to describe the position taken by many digital theorists: "Virtual realism walks a tight rope. The delicate balancing act sways between the idealism of unstoppable Progress and the Luddite resistance to virtual life.... Virtual realism is an existential process of criticism, practice, and conscious communication" (1998: 43–4). As computer scientist Langdon Winner (1995) explains:

> Right now it's anyone's guess what sorts of personalities, styles of discourse, and social norms will ultimately flourish in these new settings.... We can predict, though, that American society will continue to exclude ordinary citizens from key choices about the design and development of new technologies, including information systems. Industrial leaders present as fait accompli what otherwise might have been choices open for diverse public imaginings, investigations and debates.... People doing research on computing and the future could have a positive influence in these matters. If we're asking people to change their lives to adapt to new information systems, it seems responsible to solicit broad participation in deliberation, planning, decision making, prototyping, testing, evaluation and the like.

Winner's essay poses two different conceptions of the utopian imagination – one in which the process of change is presented as inevitable and another in which alternative visions for the future are proposed and debated. The utopian imagination performs important political work. The entertainment industries, as Fredric Jameson (1979) notes, can only attract popular interest by acknowledging real-world fears and aspirations. In Jameson's model, those tensions are redirected toward consumer capitalism's preferred solutions, utopian fantasies that can be satisfied through consumption. Alienation equals bad breath; mouthwash is the solution. Richard Dyer's account of utopianism in queer politics (1992), on the other hand, suggests that the utopian imagination can provide the basis for social critique. No meaningful change can occur until we can imagine a world different from our own: the queer teens' on-line experience of "what utopia feels like" may lead them to fight for it in their real lives. In that sense, the utopian

244

imagination is not a refusal to face problems but rather a rhetorical strategy which allows us to move from a preoccupation with problems toward a new conceptualization of solutions.

Digital theory is closely related to a much older strain of technological utopian discourse in American culture, one which originated as middle-class reformers and political radicals proposed alternatives to the problems surrounding the industrial revolution (Segel 1984; Ross 1991). Writers like Edward Bellamy felt that improvements in technologies of communication and transportation might overcome conditions of alienation, improvements in mass production might overcome problems of scarcity, and a greater mastery over nature might cleanse soot-filled environments. However, they also called for profound shifts in the social structures and economic base of industrial society, linking technological change with political change. This technological utopianism arose at the moment when Frederic Jackson Turner was declaring the closing of the American frontier. Social alternatives to undesirable social conditions needed to be mapped onto the future rather than projected onto unsettled real estate. Technological utopianism was also the founding myth of the American science-fiction tradition, which took shape under the guidance of pulp-magazine editor Hugo Gernsbeck. Gernsbeck saw "scientifiction" as a means of democratizing access to knowledge about science and as an extension of his own vision of a more democratic and participatory culture brought about through amateur radio. By mid-century, however, the discourse of technological utopianism had been coopted into a discourse about consumerism, one fully embraced by the nation's business leaders and promoted through advertising. The "world of tomorrow" envisioned by the 1939 New York World's Fair had more to do with creating a sense of inevitability that foreclosed popular debates about where we are going than with the earlier technological utopian movements' attempts to challenge current conditions. Both modes of the utopian imagination shape digital theory – both the bland boosterism, which sees the development of digital media as leading irreversibly toward a better way of life (*Wired*'s linkage of democratic ideals and high-price consumer items), and the more cautious utopianism, which uses the future to question troubling aspects of contemporary life (coupling the promotion of virtual communities with close scrutiny of issues of privacy, ownership, surveillance, and access).

Philip Hayward (1993) notes that digital media have been situated in relation to the counter-culture, introduced to the popular imagination in terms borrowed from science fiction (such as "cyberspace," which was coined by William Gibson), the drug culture (such as Timothy Leary's promotion of VR's mind-altering potential), and rock music (such as Grateful Dead stalwart John Perry Barlow's promotion of digital media). There is a surprisingly comfortable fit between cyberpunk's representations of the hacker sub-culture battling multinational media conglomerates and contemporary cultural studies' accounts of "poaching" and "resistance."[3] Cyberpunk representations differ profoundly from the prevailing images of computer scientists as nerds with pocket protectors

245

or the "virginal" astronauts in earlier science fiction (Sobchack 1990). Cyberculture was understood as a "revolutionary force" destroying the old media, such as television, which George Gilder (1994) describes as the "technology of tyrants." This same rhetoric of decentralization appealed to the libertarian impulses of both the Left and the Right, leaving unresolved whose side was going to win the "digital revolution."

As with earlier counter-cultures, there is a danger that culture jammers (Dery 1993), hackers (Sterling 1994), and netizens (Katz 1997a) will confuse the romance of existing on the fringes with the hard work of promoting social and political change. Gibson has noted, for example, that the more critical or dystopian elements of *Neuromancer* (1994) have been ignored amid the giddy excitement that compels computer scientists to try to build the cyberspace he imagined. Gibson wrote his fiction less as a celebration of the transformative power of digital media than as a warning about the dangers of divorcing human intelligence from the body, of isolating the self from real-life experience, and of transforming human culture into data that can be controlled by global corporations. It is as if someone read *Frankenstein* and decided that it would be a good idea to assemble and mass-market human beings from parts of dead bodies. This failure to preserve both the critical and the utopian dimensions of Gibson's "cyberspace" does not bode well for the digital counter-culture's chances of achieving radical change.

Almost as "revolutionary" on their own terms, hypertext theorists, such as Stuart Moulthrop (1991), Richard A. Lanham (1993), Robert Coover (1992, 1993), George P. Landow (1991, 1994), and Espen J. Aarseth (1997), build upon post-structuralist literary theory to imagine digital media as reconfiguring the relations between readers, writers, and texts. Moulthrop (1989) writes:

> Hypertext is not a definable artifact like a bound volume, it is a dynamic, expansible collection of writings whose contents will change from moment to moment. It is nothing at all like a book, only a bit like a library, and much more like the university itself in that it is shaped both by inherited resources and current contributions. Though part of the system will probably need to be permanent, it is probably better not to depend too heavily on a framework of canonical text or definitive discourse . . . . Every hypertext project should support writing as well as reading. The function of the hypertext is not simply to disseminate information but to create better conditions in which people can exchange, develop, and evaluate ideas.

Moulthrop's conception of hypertext seeks to dismantle all that was rigid, hierarchical, and unidirectional in print culture. Suggesting that defenders of the book act as if "defending the wrapper would protect what was in the box," Richard Lanham (1993) characterizes hypertext as the literary fulfillment of the computer's promise of "radical democratization." Hypertext will result in an education system where "you simply cannot be a critic without being in turn a creator."

246

At the heart of hypertext theory remains a constructivist epistemology, the belief that the best forms of learning require active participation and free exploration, a hands-on process of testing and manipulating one's surroundings. Hypertext theorists imagine new forms of literature or theoretical argument which enable the reader's more active participation and which open themselves to a much broader range of interpretations. As Aarseth explains:

> A reader, however strongly engaged in the unfolding of a narrative, is powerless. Like a spectator at a soccer game, he may speculate, conjecture, extrapolate, even shout abuse, but he is not a player .... The cybertext puts its would-be reader at risk: the risk of rejection. The effort and energy demanded by the cybertext of its reader raise the stakes of interpretation to those of intervention. (1997: 4)

Early hypertext advocates, such as Ted Nelson (1981), imagined a world in which all human knowledge was available in digital form, open to access, annotation, and manipulation by all. His ideal is realized in a much more modest (and corporately sponsored) fashion in the World Wide Web. Other writers, such as Moulthrop (1995), acknowledge the dangers of getting lost in hypertext and the need to "steer between the extremes of informational anarchy and despotism."

Paul Duguid has challenged the rhetoric of "liberation" which surrounds hypertext: "The desire for a technology to liberate information from technology is not far from the search for a weapon to end all weapons or the war to end all wars.... As with so much optimistic futurology, it woos us to jump by highlighting the frying pan and hiding the fire" (1996: 76). Technology always emerges within a social and cultural context that constrains or facilitates its designer's goals. Hypertext theory envisions new forms of learning, knowledge, and expression; it does not always address the institutional and social changes needed to prepare us to participate in such a culture. At present, teachers who have always taught from county-approved textbooks and prescribed syllabi (such as in the US), are understandably intimidated by the promise that the Internet is a world without gatekeepers, uncertain how to evaluate the information they receive, and frightened of losing what little control they maintain over their classrooms. Others question whether part of the pleasure of reading a novel or watching a film might lie in surrendering control and allowing expert storytellers to manipulate our emotions.

Formalist writers are also eager to use digital media as a vehicle for transforming culture. Janet Murray's *Hamlet on the Holodeck* (1997) sees contemporary manifestations of digital media as the crude predecessors of a much more robust art form. Imagining the future storyteller as "half hacker, half bard," Murray "see[s] glimmers of a medium that is capacious and broadly expressive, a medium capable of capturing both the hairbreadth movements of individual human consciousness and the colossal crosscurrents of human society" (9). Murray's "cyberbard" represents at once a dramatic break with print culture and the continuation of literary creation into a strange and unfamiliar future. *Feed* magazine editor Steven Johnson's *Interface Culture* (1997) similarly imagines computer interfaces developing ways of charting information and social structure in a highly mediated society, much as nineteenth-century authors turned to the novel to map what Charles Dickens called the "links of association" between different social classes. Murray and Johnson embrace change as a dynamic quality, which will generate new forms of human expression; both see digital media as offering new models for understanding psychological and social relations, for making coherence and order out of the information flow.

Digital theory is not predictive, any more than science fiction is. Theorists and science-fiction writers don't foretell the future; they comment on the present. Few digital theorists claim to know for sure what directions digital media will take or what impact they are likely to have upon our social, political, and economic life. Digital theory is, in Allucquere Rosanne Stone's terms, "thoroughly experimental and subject to recall for factory modification at any time" (1995). In the end, Murray or Moulthrop may have less to tell us about the potentials of digital media than about the perceived limitations of existing media or the constraints of contemporary education. Rather, the future-orientation of digital theory represents an attempt to participate in the process of inventing the future. Calling on humanists to be inventors rather than custodians of their culture, James J. O'Donnell writes: "The genuine spirit of our culture is not expressed in applying small pieces of cellotape to hold together the structure we have received, but in pitching in joyously to its ongoing reconstruction" (1998: 91). The most important thing digital theory can do is to refuse to accept the rhetoric of the sales prospectus and to continue to push the digital media to grow in new directions. Academic theorists have historically responded to static, if not moribund, media. Printed texts existed for centuries before there was an academic discipline focussed on the study of literature. Film studies arose only at the moment when the Hollywood cinema's influence as a central cultural institution was giving way to television. Television studies gained academic respectability at the moment when the dominance of network broadcasting was challenged by new delivery technologies such as cable or videotape. As Marshall McLuhan has noted, "media are often put out before they are thought out" (McLuhan and Lapham 1994), and the lag time can be enormous. Digital theory is responding to the process of change, describing and analyzing a medium (or cluster of media) still being born.

Digital theorists identify and focus attention on sites of experimentation and innovation that hold promise for future developments, even when those sites counter the prevailing commercial logic of the marketplace. The danger, of course, is that they will reconstruct old cultural hierarchies, elevating avant-garde digital works (*afternoon, Patchwork Girl, Victory Garden*) at the expense of recognizing the cultural impact and artistic innovation of commercial products (*Myst, Chop Suey*). Already, these new works are being treated in separate anthologies, some of which deal with "digital cinema" as a new high art form, while others deal with games and CD-ROMs as popular culture. The best work on digital aesthetics, such as Murray's *Hamlet on the Holodeck*, bridges that gap, imagining new forms of storytelling as both culturally meaningful and formally challenging, broadly accessible and innovative.

3 Mapping Change: Digital Theory and Historical Analysis

> The computer as hypertext, as symbol manipulator, is a writing technology in the tradition of the papyrus roll, the codex, and the printed book. The computer as virtual reality, as graphics engine, as perceptual manipulator, belongs to and extends the tradition of television, film, photography and even representational painting.
>
> David Jay Bolter, "Degrees of Freedom"

Describing digital theory in terms of its focus on a developing technology and its future capacities may be misleading, since it is also vitally concerned with framing a historical account of media in transition,[4] explaining changes and continuities between digital and earlier forms of media. Most of the participants at a 1994 conference on "The Future of the Book" (Nunberg 1996) found that they could not address the topic without also discussing how the culture of the book came into being. Our changing media environment has foregrounded the codex book's status as material practice sparking recent moves from the study of literature (which is often abstracted as "text") to renewed interest in the history of the book, theatrical performance, orality, and the printing press. Literary studies has become a branch of media studies. Recognizing that the book is a medium does not necessarily imply that its material form fully determines its function or status. The medium is not always the message. Carla Hesse writes:

> The historical record makes unquestionably clear that the most distinctive features of what we have come to refer to as "print culture" – that is, the stabilization of written culture into a canon of authored texts, the notion of the author as creator, the books as property and the reader as an elective public – were not inevitable historical consequences of the invention of printing during the Renaissance, but, rather, the cumulative result of particular social and political choices made by given societies at given moments. (1996: 21)

Similarly, the democratic and participatory ideals associated with "*interactive technologies*" are not the product of the technologies but of our social and cultural *interactions* with them. Recognizing this distinction reminds us of the need to struggle to define technology's future directions through social and political actions, not simply through our design principles.

Contemporary discussions of technological conversion – that is, the integration of existing communications technologies into a single megasystem – need to be framed in relation to what I call cultural convergence. Cultural convergence refers to the process by which people in their everyday life use media in relation to each other, form evaluations about which media best serve specific purposes, assemble information across multiple channels of communication, and embrace artworks that depend upon appropriation and remixing of cultural materials or upon the archiving and recirculating of previous media texts. Some of these changes reflect our initial encounters with digital media, but these shifts are being felt across the full range of contemporary popular culture, and some of them prepare for, rather than respond to, the increased penetration of the Internet, the World Wide Web, and the PC into our everyday lives. The popularity of the VCR had to do with its time-shift capability which, at a time when Americans were working longer hours and were moving toward a 24-hour work cycle, enabled people to keep in touch with the popular television programs which had become a central part of contemporary cultural literacy. The wide-spread embrace of e-mail reflects the mobility of a culture where one American in three moves in any given year; the Internet allows us to maintain contact with those we've left behind or to build new friendships and join new communities, despite the unmooring of our ties to geographically local communities. Similarly, properties of one medium may train us in the perceptual and cognitive skills we will need to embrace future media. As Lev Manovich (1996a) writes:

> Gradually cinema taught us to accept the manipulation of time and space, the arbitrary coding of the visible, the mechanization of vision, and the reduction of reality to a moving image as a given. As a result, today the conceptual shock of the digital revolution is not experienced as a real shock – because we were ready for it for a long time.

Such arguments require a move away from digital theory toward what might be described as comparative media studies, an approach that reads the emerging digital technologies against the backdrop of a much broader range of media, both historical and contemporary. Because digital media potentially incorporate all previous media, it no longer makes sense to think in medium-specific terms. The renewed interest in Marshall McLuhan (McLuhan and Lapham 1994) has more to do with his willingness to talk about what a range of different media have in common and how each of them defines a particular series of relations to time and space than with his sometimes wacky insights into specific media. Harold Innis (1991), James Carey (1988), and Ithiel De Sola Pool (1984), among others, offer alternative models for thinking across media. All of a society's media interact with and influence each other, requiring research to be conducted in a systemic or ecological way rather than a fragmentary fashion. David Rodowick (1994) has suggested the term "audiovisual" rather than "digital" to refer to the complex interplay of representational technologies which constitute our contemporary sensory environs. Marsha Kinder (1991) discusses the "entertainment super-system," the complex intertextual relations between the manifestations of popular narratives, such as *Batman, The Teenage Mutant Ninja Turtles, Star Trek*, or *The X Files*, as they move across film, television, comic books, and digital media. Such migrations are a logical consequence of the horizontal integration of modern media conglomerates (Meehan 1991).

250

Some adaptations from filmic to digital media prove more engaging than others. Digital manifestations of *Star Trek* (Murray and Jenkins 1999), for example, stress only those aspects of the series that fit comfortably into pre-existing game genres: the result is an emphasis on combat, exploration, and technology rather than on character relations, cultural diversity, or negotiation. Digital *Star Trek* narrows the range of fannish activities and interests facilitated by the original television series. Despite digital media's "encyclopedic" promise, the contemporary CD-ROM disk contains far less information than a videotape library of series episodes. Moreover, talk about digital interactivity often ignores the interaction and participation ethnographers and reader-response critics have long discussed in relation to traditional literary, television, or cinematic narratives. Digital media structure into the text certain opportunities for interactions, providing the resources for engaging with richer, more vivid representations of the story world, but also foreclose other interactions that might arise from a less impoverished narrative universe. By contrast, Greg Smith (1999) argues that CD-ROM adaptations of Monty Python's comedy preserve its improvisational and fragmented style, its anarchic comedy of interruptions and destabilizations, its search for unpredictable juxtapositions of material, and its parodic self-consciousness about its own medium. More than simply a recycling of previously produced materials, Monty Python is rethought for CD-ROM and, in the process, helps us to rethink digital technology. One set of instructions in the game, for example, states: "to waste more time, please click here again." The game's comic focus on delay, technical breakdown, and repetition pokes fun at the complex attitudes toward temporality surrounding CD-ROM games: playing games may be a good way to *spend* time, and yet players are impatient with any delays which *waste* their time.

Our initial encounters with any new medium focus attention on its breaks with predecessor media and, as a consequence, help to defamiliarize properties that were once taken for granted. In the case of literature, the computer reopened questions about the bound and linear qualities of books, resulting in hypertext theory. For cinema, the introduction of digital media poses questions about the screen and our relationship to cinematic space. According to Manovich (1994), the cinema reworks "the classical screen" (Renaissance perspective's attempts to represent three-dimensional space on a flat surface), creating "the dynamic screen" where the displayed image changes over time. In watching a film, we focus our full attention on the representation on screen and disregard the physical space outside it. This concentration is possible because the image fills the whole screen. The screen "functions to filter, to screen out, to take over, rendering non-existent whatever is outside its frame." The introduction of the computer screen, however, reveals the "stability" of the dynamic screen, creating, in the case of the Windows desktop, a world where multiple screens compete for our attention or, in the case of virtual reality, a world where "the screen disappears altogether" facilitating more immediate interaction.[5]

David Jay Bolter and Richard Grusin describe this process in somewhat different terms in *Remediations* (1998), suggesting that the history of media might be charted through competing impulses toward immediacy, which depends on the ability *to look through the screen* as if it were a window, and hypermediacy, which forces us *to look at the screen* as a graphical surface. Examples of immediacy include "a painting by Canaletto, a photograph by Edward Weston, a 'live' television broadcast from the Olympics, and the computer system for virtual reality," while earlier examples of hypermediacy include "medieval illuminated manuscripts, Renaissance decorated altarpieces, Dutch painting, Baroque cabinets, and modernist collage and photomontage." Digital media reflects both the push toward immediacy – to create transparent interfaces – and the push toward hypermediacy – to bring multiple forms of media together on the same page. Yet both impulses reflect a process of remediation – that is, the attempt to define the new media in relation to the old. Hypermediacy makes explicit the process of quotation or appropriation from earlier media, yet immediacy often depends upon an unconscious comparison to earlier media. Computers that promise photorealism aren't promising us reality; they are promising computer graphics that look like photographs.

The new medium may usurp some of the cultural functions or status once held by the earlier media. André Bazin (1971b) argued, for example, that the introduction of photography as a mechanism for more perfectly reproducing the material world "freed" painters to explore abstraction. Television's usurpation of radio's storytelling role forced radio to expand the centrality of music to its broadcast content. The introduction of digital media, for example, has had an enormous impact upon the contemporary cinema, not simply in obvious ways, such as the use of computer animation in *Toy Story* or of CGI special effects in *Jurassic Park*. The morph introduces a fundamental new structure to the rhetoric of cinema, one which, as Vivian Sobchack (1997) notes, depends upon the suggestion of similarity across previously perceived differences rather than on montage's graphic collisions. Michael Jackson's *Black or White* music video uses the morph to erase racial differences and construct an image of humanity united through the pleasure of music and dancing; *Terminator 2* uses the morph to transform humans into inanimate objects and back again; political advertisements used the morph to suggest that democratic candidates could not easily separate themselves from the faults of Bill Clinton.

More profoundly, these devices subtly yet dramatically undermine the ontological status of the photographic image, which André Bazin argued was the fundamental basis of cinema. Contemporary film theory insists that cinematic images are not indexical, but rather complex cultural signs constructed for the screen. These critiques of the realist tradition always ran against our culture's core faith in the authenticity of the image. As Manovich (1996c) writes:

> During cinema's history, a whole repertoire of techniques (lighting, art direction, the use of different film stocks and lens, etc.) was developed to modify the basic

record obtained by a film apparatus. And yet behind even the most stylized cinematic images we can discern the bluntness, the sterility, the banality of early nineteenth century photographs. No matter how complex its stylistic innovations, the cinema has found its base in these deposits of reality.

Yet, as writers like William Mitchell (1994) note, digital photographers can construct vivid, compelling, absolutely convincing photographs of architectural spaces or historic encounters (Abraham Lincoln and Marilyn Monroe) which never existed. Hollywood could make Fred Astaire dance on the ceiling (through elaborate manipulations of his physical environment), but digital artists could make the dead star dance with a Dustbuster for a contemporary television commercial. In such a world, seeing is no longer believing. The computer ignores photography's indexical relation to reality, translating images into pixels which can be transformed, reworked, and redesigned like text in a word-processing program. The line blurs between animation (which involves creating images where none existed previously) and editing (which involves recutting or rearranging fragments of events which occurred before the camera).

Theories of spectatorship that assume a relationship between optical point of view and narrative identification must be revised in light of the intense identification and participation experienced by players of Sega or Nintendo video games, which almost always depend upon third-person camera. Even more sophisticated accounts of character identification, such as Murray Smith's *Engaging Characters* (1995), may be unable to fully describe the difference it makes when we become an active participant controlling the fictional character as a cursor which we navigate through narrative space or when we choose which camera position will be employed. When I feel the acceleration of speed, spinning real fast and clearing the screen as the Tasmanian Devil, my pleasure has less to do with my moral alignment with those characters than with my ability to control them. Even given my ample facial hair and my sometimes anarchic sense of humor, I am not, in the end, terribly much like Taz. Yet, I often speak of the game-playing experience as if "I" died, "I" flew off a cliff, "I" beat my opponent, suggesting a fairly direct identification with the often simplistically rendered figure on the screen.

Film theory often stresses temporality at the expense of spatiality, while most recent accounts of digital media stress its status as a new form of "spatial story" (DeCerteau 1988), one that provides complex and compelling visual environments rather than complexly structured plots or rounded characters. Margaret Morse (1994) notes, for example, that what compels the development of virtual reality technologies is a consumer desire for "another world" outside everyday life's limitations and frustrations. Mary Fuller and I (1995) compare the structures of contemporary video games and earlier forms of travel narratives. We argue that video games create "spaces for exploration, colonization, and exploitation, returning to a mythic time when there were worlds without limits and resources beyond imagining." In the process, they rewrite the history of the founding of America to absolve us for our postcolonial guilt, restaging them in worlds which had no prior human inhabitants. These games partially compensate for increased restrictions upon children's access to the physical spaces of their environment, offering a "virtual playscape" through which they can experience the illusion of "complete freedom of movement" (Jenkins 1998). Other games, such as *Simcity*, give us a god-like vantage point for redesigning the world (Friedman 1995).[6]

Many have drawn meaningful parallels between the current transformation of digital media and cinema's own emergence from scientific experimentation and arcade attraction to become a central cultural institution, but this hardly exhausts the range of meaningful analogies. "Multi-media" works, which may combine audio, still photographs, moving images, digital animation, and text, pose questions about the interplay between different media forms, inviting comparison to collage, *Life Magazine* photoessays, comic strips, comic books, or the sound-and-slideshow extravaganzas of the 1960s pop underground. Brenda Laurel (1993) and Thyrza Goodeve Nichols (1997) have called for a reconsideration of the relevance of theatre history to an understanding of digital media, Laurel focussing on the relationship of interactivity to theatrical improvisation, Goodeve exploring the relationship between on-line personas and vaudeville performance styles that required performers to exaggerate their own ethnic identities. The immersive quality of virtual reality has invited comparison with the amusement-park rides of turn-of-the-century Coney Island and with the nineteenth-century tradition of cycloramas and panoramas. The grassroots many-to-many dimensions of digital communication closely parallel earlier attempts to create more broad-based participatory media, such as the amateur radio movement of the 1910s and 1920s, which envisioned a world where there would be as many transmitters as receivers. Examining the CD-ROM game *Phantasmagoria*, Angela Ndalianis (1999) relates it to a much longer tradition of employing emergent communications technologies as the basis for magic or horror performances. Understanding the circulation of e-mail involves a reconsideration of earlier attempts to construct communications networks, such as the postal service, the telegraph, and the telephone, leading to new research into earlier styles of "sociability," such as the telephone "party line." Another tradition, represented by the work of Lisa Cartwright (1995; Cartwright et al. 1998), has sought to link contemporary digital media with a much larger history of medical and scientific imaging technologies, such as the X-ray or the sonogram. Early television, as Pam Wilson (1996) reminds us, showcased its ability to form links between remote geographic locations to show us, for example, both the east and west coasts on screen at once, much as journalists often describe "web-surfing" as a form of "virtual tourism." Scott Bukatman (1994) argues that we should trace the historic links between the typewriter and the computer keyboard to learn how mechanical writing systems have altered the way we work and think. Some of these comparisons are more forced than others, yet most reveal something significant about digital media and their historical predecessors.

What, then, is the work of theory in the age of digital transformation? Digital theory offers us explanations, interpretations, and predictions that enable us to manage the process of technological change and its impact upon our social, cultural, economic, political, and personal lives. Digital theory provides a point of intersection between the languages and practices of science and engineering on the one hand and the arts and humanities on the other. Digital theory embraces the utopian imagination, not as a way of predicting the future but as a way of envisioning meaningful change and keeping alive the fluidity that digital media have introduced into many aspects of our social and personal lives. Digital theory identifies historical antecedents for contemporary media developments and, at the same time, defamiliarizes older media and opens them to reexamination. What is striking about the present moment is not simply that academic theorists have responded quickly to a changing media environment – itself a phenomenon virtually without precedent – but that theory production has been embraced by the larger society. Theorists are interviewed as media celebrities in the pages of mass-market magazines like *Wired*. Vernacular theory surfaces and is debated on almost every on-line discussion list and newsgroup as everyday citizens hope to better understand the nature of the transformations occurring around them. Theoretical arguments are forming the basis for the early court decisions that determine what model of regulation, intellectual property rights, or anti-trust litigation is most appropriate for cyberspace. The impact of digital communications on all aspects of modern life has made the process of mediation remarkably visible and has created a new demand to answer questions that once would have seemed the arcane interest of media scholars.

Notes

1   For further discussion of this shift in theory's relations to subjective experience, see Jenkins et al. Forthcoming.
2   As one wag asked, if the citizens of cyberspace have escaped their bodies, how come so many of them suffer from carpal tunnel syndrome?
3   For more background on the relationship between cyberpunk and cultural studies, see Henry Jenkins, "Cyberpunk," *Media in Transition* website, http://media-in-transition.mit.edu. For other work on the cyberpunk movement, see Balsamo 1996, Bukatman 1993, Hayles 1997, McCaffrey 1996, Ross 1991, and Springer 1996.
4   The theme of "Media in Transition" has been the focus of a two-year-long series of conferences and events at MIT, organized by David Thorburn and Henry Jenkins, which will result in a series of books for MIT Press. For more information, see http://media-in-transition.mit.edu.
5   For another take on the evolution of the screen, see Sobchack 1994.
6   For other examples of work which focusses on the spatiality of digital media, see Tashiro 1998 and Strain forthcoming.

References

Aarseth, Espen J. 1997. *Cybertext: Perspectives on Ergodic Literature*. Baltimore: Johns Hopkins Press.

Adrian, Robert. 1995. "Infobahn Blues." CTHEORY, article 21. http://www.CTHEORY.com.

Balsamo, Anne. 1996. *Technologies of the Gendered Body: Reading Cyborg Women*. Durham, NC: Duke University Press.

Barlow, John Perry. 1996. "A Declaration of Independence for Cyberspace." http://www.peg.apc.org/~obelisk/dec.html.

Barrett, Edward, ed. 1989. *The Society of Text: Hypertext, Hypermedia, and the Social Construction of Information*. Cambridge: MIT Press.

——, and Marie Redmond. 1997. *Contextual Media: Multimedia and Interpretation*. Cambridge: MIT Press.

Bazin, André. 1971a. "Myth of Total Cinema." In *What Is Cinema?* Chicago: University of Chicago Press.

——. 1971b. "The Ontology of the Photographic Image." In *What Is Cinema?* Chicago: University of Chicago Press.

Benedict, Michael, ed. 1994. *Cyberspace: First Steps*. Cambridge: MIT Press.

Bolter, David Jay. Forthcoming. "Degrees of Freedom." http://www.lcc.gatech.edu/~bolter/degrees.html.

——, and Richard Grusin. 1998. *Remediations*. Cambridge: MIT Press.

Bordwell, David. 1994. *The Cinema of Eisenstein*. Cambridge: Harvard University Press.

Bourdieu, Pierre. 1984. *Distinction: A Social Critique of the Judgement of Taste*. Cambridge: Harvard University Press.

Brand, Stewart. 1988. *The Media Lab: Inventing the Future at MIT*. New York: Penguin.

Bruckman, Amy. 1996. "Cyberspace is Not Disneyland: The Role of the Artist in a Networked World." http://www.ahip.getty.edu/cyberpub/bruckman.html.

Bukatman, Scott. 1993. *Terminal Identity: The Virtual Subject in Postmodern Science Fiction*. Durham, NC: Duke University Press.

——. 1994. "William Gibson's Typewriter." In *Flame Wars: The Discourse of Cyberculture*. Ed. Mark Dery. Durham, NC: Duke University Press.

Bush, Vannever. 1945. "As We May Think." *Atlantic Monthly* (July). http://www.isg.sfu.ca/~duchier/misc/vbush.

Carey, James. 1988. *Communication as Culture: Essays on Media and Society*. Boston: Unwin Hyman.

Cartwright, Lisa. 1995. *Screening the Body: Tracing Medicine's Visual Culture*. Minneapolis: University of Minnesota Press.

——, Paula Treichler, and Constance Penley, eds. 1998. *The Visible Woman: Imaging Technologies, Gender, and Science*. New York: New York University Press.

Cassell, Justine, and Henry Jenkins, eds. 1998. *From Barbie to Mortal Kombat: Gender and Computer Games*. Cambridge: MIT Press.

Cherny, Lynn, and Elizabeth Reba Weise, eds. 1996. *Wired Women: Gender and New Realities in Cyberspace*. Seattle: Seal.

Coover, Robert. 1992. "The End of Books." *New York Times Book Review* (June 21): 1.

——. 1993. "Hyperfiction: Novels for Computer." *New York Times Book Review* (August 29): 1.

DeCerteau, Michel. 1988. *The Practice of Everyday Life*. Berkeley: University of California Press.

Dery, Mark. 1993. *Culture Jamming: Hacking, Slashing and Sniping in the Empire of Signs*. Open Magazine Pamphlet Series.

Dibble, Julian. 1994. "A Rape in Cyberspace." In *Flame Wars: The Discourse of Cyberculture*. Ed. Mark Dery. Durham, NC: Duke University Press. 237–62.

Duguid, Paul. 1996. "Material Matters: The Past and Futurology of the Book." In *The Future of the Book*. Ed. Geoffrey Nunberg. Berkeley: University of California Press.

Dyer, Richard. 1992. *Only Entertainment*. London: Routledge.

Dyson, Esther. 1998. *Release 2.0: A Design for Living in the Digital Age*. New York: Broadway.

Friedman, Ted. 1995. "Making Sense of Software." In *Cybersociety: Computer-Mediated Communication and Community*. Ed. Steven G. Jones. Thousand Oaks: Sage Publications.

Fuller, Mary, and Henry Jenkins. 1995. "Nintendo and New World Travel Writing: A Dialogue." In *Cybersociety: Computer-Mediated Communication and Community*. Ed. Steven G. Jones. Thousand Oaks: Sage Publications.

Geertz, Clifford. 1977. *The Interpretation of Cultures*. New York: Basic Books.

Gibson, William. 1994. *Neuromancer*. New York: Bantam.

Gilder, George. 1994. *Life after Television: The Coming Transformation of Media and American Life*. New York: W. W. Norton.

Goldman-Segall, Ricki. 1997. *Points of Viewing Children's Thinking: A Digital Ethographer's Journey*. New York: Lawrence Erlbaum. http://www.pointsofviewing.com.

Goodeve Nichols, Thyrza. 1997. "Houdini's Premonition: Virtuality and Vaudeville on the Internet." *Leonardo* 30, 5 (October).

Gray, Chris Hables, Heidi J. Figuroa-Sarriera, and Steven Mentor, eds. 1996. *The Cyborg Handbook*. New York: Routledge.

Haraway, Donna. 1985. "A Manifesto for Cyborgs: Science, Technology and Socialist Feminism in the 1980s." *Socialist Review* 80, 2: 65–108.

Hayles, N. Katherine. 1997. "Virtual Bodies and Flickering Signifiers." In *Electronic Culture: Technology and Visual Representation*. Ed. Timothy Druckrey. New York: Aperture.

Hayward, Philip. 1993. "Situating Cyberspace: The Popularization of Virtual Reality." In *Future Visions: New Technologies of the Screen*. Ed. Philip Hayward and Tana Wollen. London: British Film Institute.

Heim, Michael. 1994. "The Erotic Ontology of Cyberspace." In *Cyberspace: The First Steps*. Ed. Michael Benedict. Cambridge: MIT Press.

——. 1998. *Virtual Realism*. New York: Oxford University Press.

Herz, J. C. 1996. *Surfing on the Internet: A Nethead's Adventures On-Line*. New York: Little, Brown.

——. 1997. *Joystick Nation*. New York: Little, Brown.

Hesse, Carla. 1996. "Books in Time." In *The Future of the Book*. Ed. Geoffrey Nunberg. Berkeley: University of California Press.

Hoffman, Donna, and Thomas Novak. 1998. "Bridging the Digital Divide: The Impact of Race on Computer Access and Internet Use". http://www2000.ogsm.vanderbilt.edu/papers/race/science.html.

257

Horn, Stacy. 1998. *Cyberville: Clicks, Culture, and the Creation of an Online Town.* New York: Warner.

Innis, Harold. 1991. *The Bias of Communication.* Toronto: University of Toronto Press.

Jackson, Shelley. 1997. "Stitch Bitch: The Patchwork Girl." http://media-in-transition.mit.edu/articles.

Jameson, Fredric. 1979. "Reification and Utopia in Mass Culture." *Social Text* 1 (Winter).

Jenkins, Henry. 1998. "'Complete Freedom of Movement': Computer Games as Gendered Playspaces." In *From Barbie to Mortal Kombat: Gender and Computer Games.* Ed. Justine Cassell and Henry Jenkins. Cambridge: MIT Press.

——, Tara McPherson, and Jane Shattuc. Forthcoming. "Culture that Sticks to the Skin: Towards a New Cultural Studies." In *Hop on Pop: The Politics and Pleasure of Popular Culture.* Ed. Henry Jenkins, Tara McPherson, and Jane Shattuc. Durham, NC: Duke University Press.

Johnson, Steven. 1997. *Interface Culture: How New Technology Transforms the Way We Create and Communicate.* New York: HarperCollins.

Joyce, Michael. 1996. *Of Two Minds: Hypertext Pedagogy and Poetics.* Ann Arbor: University of Michigan Press.

Katz, Jon. 1997a. *Media Rants: Postpolitics in the Digital Nation.* San Francisco: HardWired.

——. 1997b. *Virtuous Reality.* New York: Random House.

Kinder, Marsha. 1991. *Playing with Power in Movies, Television, and Video Games: From Muppet Babies to Teenage Mutant Ninja Turtles.* Berkeley: University of California Press.

——. 1998. Interview. In *From Barbie to Mortal Kombat: Gender and Computer Games.* Ed. Justine Cassell and Henry Jenkins. Cambridge: MIT Press.

Kroker, Arthur, and Michael A. Weinstein. 1994. "The Theory of the Virtual Class." In *Data Trash: The Theory of the Virtual Class.* New York: St. Martin's Press.

Landow, George P. 1991. *Hypertext: The Convergence of Contemporary Critical Theory and Technology.* Baltimore: Johns Hopkins Press.

——, ed. 1994. *Hyper/Text/Theory.* Baltimore: Johns Hopkins Press.

Lanham, Richard A. 1993. *The Electronic Word: Democracy, Technology and the Arts.* Chicago: University of Chicago Press.

Laurel, Brenda. 1990. *The Art of Human–Computer Interface Design.* New York: Addison Wesley.

——. 1993. *Computers as Theatre.* New York: Addison Wesley.

——. Forthcoming. *Shrunken Heads: Notes on Computers, Art and Nature.*

McCaffrey, Donald, ed. 1996. *Storming the Reality Studio: A Casebook on Cyberpunk and Postmodern Science Fiction.* Durham, NC: Duke University Press.

McLaughlin, Thomas. 1996. *Street Smarts and Critical Theory: Listening to the Vernacular.* Madison: University of Wisconsin Press.

McLuhan, Marshall, and Lewis H. Lapham. 1994. *Understanding Media: The Extensions of Man.* Cambridge: MIT Press.

Manovich, Lev. 1994. "Archeology of the Computer Screen." http://jupiter.ucsd.edu/~manovich/text/digital_nature.html.

——. 1996a. "Cinema and Digital Media." http://jupiter.ucsd.edu/~manovich/text/digital-cinema-zkm.html.

——. 1996b. "On Totalitarian Interactivity (Notes from the Enemy of the People)." http://jupiter.ucsd.edu/~manovich/text/totalitarian.html.

——. 1996c. "What Is Digital Cinema?" http://jupiter.ucsd.edu/~manovich/text/digital-cinema.html.

——. 1998. "Cinema as a Cultural Interface." Lev Manovich Home Page. http://jupiter.ucsd.edu/~manovich/text/cinema-cultural.html.

Meehan, Eileen. 1991. "Holy Commodity Fetish, Batman!" In *The Many Lives of the Batman*. Ed. Roberta Pearson and William Urrichio. New York: Routledge.

Menser, Michael, and Stanley Aronowitz. 1996. "On Cultural Studies, Science and Technology." In *Technoscience and Cyberculture*. Ed. Stanley Aronowitz, Barbara Martinsons, and Michael Menser. New York: Routledge.

Minsky, Marvin. 1988. *The Society of Mind*. New York: Simon and Schuster.

Mitchell, William. 1994. *The Reconfigured Eye: Visual Truth in the Post-Photographic Era*. Cambridge: MIT Press.

——. 1996. *City of Bits: Space, Place and the Infobahn*. Cambridge: MIT Press. http://mitpress.mit.edu/e-books/City_of_Bits/contents.html.

Morse, Margaret. 1994. "Enthralling Spaces: The Aesthetics of Virtual Environments." http://www.uiah.fi/bookshop/isea_proc/spacescapes/j/02.html.

——. 1998. *Virtualities: Television, Media Art, and Cyberculture*. Bloomington: Indiana University Press.

Moulthrop, Stuart. 1989. "In the Zones: Hypertext and the Politics of Interpretation." *Writing on the Edge* 1, 1: 18–27. http://www.ubalt.edu/www/ygcla/sam/essays/zones.html.

——. 1990. "Reading from the Map: Metaphor and Metonymy in the Fiction of Forking Paths." In *Hypermedia and Literary Studies*. Ed. G. P. Landow and P. Delany. Cambridge: MIT Press. 119–32.

——, ed. 1991. *Special Issue of Hypertext* "Writing on the Edge 2."

——. 1993. "You Say You Want a Revolution? Hypertext and the Laws of Media." In *Essays in Postmodern Culture*. Ed. A. Amiran and J. Unsworth. New York: Oxford University Press.

——. 1994. "Rhizome and Resistance: Hypertext and the Dreams of a New Culture." In *Hypertext and Literary Theory*. Ed. G. P. Landow. Baltimore: Johns Hopkins University Press.

——. 1995. "Traveling in the Breakdown Lane: A Principle of Resistance for Hypertext". http://www.ubalt.edu/www/ygcla/sam/essays/pre_breakdown.html.

Murray, Janet. 1997. *Hamlet on the Holodeck: The Future of Narrative in Cyberspace*. New York: Free Press.

——, and Henry Jenkins. 1999. "Before the Holodeck: Translating *Star Trek* into Digital Media." In *On a Silver Platter*. Ed. Greg Smith. New York: New York University Press.

Ndalianis, Angela. 1999. "'Evil Will Walk Once More': *Phantasmagoria* – the Stalker Film as Interactive Movie?" In *On a Silver Platter*. Ed. Greg Smith. New York: New York University Press.

Nelson, Ted. 1981. *Literary Machines*, 5th edn. Swarthmore, PA: self-published.

Nunberg, Geoffrey, ed. 1996. *The Future of the Book*. Berkeley: University of California Press.

O'Donnell, James J. 1998. *Avatars of the Word: From Papyrus to Cyberspace*. Cambridge: Harvard University Press.

Papert, Seymour, and Nicholas Negroponte. 1996. *The Connected Family: Bridging the Digital Generation Gap*. New York: Longstreet. http://www.ConnectedFamily.com.

259

Pool, Ithiel De Sola. 1984. *Technologies of Freedom*. Cambridge: Harvard University Press.

Rheingold, Howard. 1993. *The Virtual Community: Homesteading on the Electronic Frontier*. New York: Addison Wesley.

Rodowick, D. N. 1994. "Audiovisual Culture and Interdisciplinary Knowledge." http://www.rochester.edu/College/FS/Publications/AVCulture/AudiovisualCultureText.html.

Ross, Andrew. 1991. *Strange Weather: Culture, Science, and Technology in the Age of Limits*. London: Verso.

Schank, Roger C. 1995. *Tell Me a Story: Narrative and Intelligence*. Chicago: Northwestern University Press.

Schiller, Herbert. 1994. "Media, Technology, and the Market: The Interacting Dynamic." In *Culture on the Brink: Ideologies of Technology*. Ed. Gretchen Bender and Timothy Druckrey. Seattle: Bay Press.

Segel, Howard P. 1984. "The Technological Utopians." In *Imagining Tomorrow*. Ed. Joseph E. Com. Cambridge: MIT Press.

Smith, Greg M. Forthcoming. " 'To Waste More Time, Please Click Here Again!': Monty Python and the Quest for Film/CD-Rom Adaptation." In *On a Silver Platter*. Ed. Greg Smith. New York: New York University Press.

——, ed. 1999. *On a Silver Platter: Cd-Roms and the Promises of a New Technology*. New York: New York University Press.

Smith, Murray. 1995. *Engaging Characters: Fiction, Emotion, and the Cinema*. Oxford: Clarendon Press.

Snow, C. P. 1992. *The Two Cultures*. Cambridge: Cambridge University Press.

Sobchack, Vivian. 1990. "The Virginity of the Astronauts: Sex and the Science Fiction Film." In *Alien Zone: Cultural Theory and Contemporary Science Fiction Cinema*. Ed. Annette Kuhn. London: Verso.

——. 1994. "The Scene of the Screen: Envisioning Cinematic and Electronic 'Presence.' " In *Materialities of Communication*. Ed. Hans Ulrich Gumbrecht and K. Ludwig Pfeiffer. Stanford: Stanford University Press.

——. 1997. "Meta-Morphing". http://www.heise.de/tp/deutsch/special/film/6122/1.html.

Spence, Jonathon. 1994. *The Memory Palace of Matteo Ricci*. New York: Penguin.

Springer, Claudia. 1996. *Electronic Eros: Bodies and Desire in the Postindustrial Age*. Austin: University of Texas Press.

Sproull, Lee, and Sara Kiesler. 1992. *Connections: New Ways of Working in the Networked Organization*. Cambridge: MIT Press.

Sterling, Bruce, ed. 1988. *Mirrorshades: A Cyberpunk Anthology*. New York: Ace.

——. 1994. *The Hacker Crackdown: Notes from the Computer Underground*. New York: Bantam. http://www.dina.kvl.dk/~abraham/crackdown/crackdown_1.html1#SEC1

Stone, Allucquere Rosanne. 1995. *The War of Desire and Technology at the Close of the Mechanical Age*. Cambridge: MIT Press.

Strain, Ellen. Forthcoming. "Narrativizing Cyber-Travel: CD-ROM Travel Games and the Art of Historical Recovery." In *Hop on Pop: The Politics and Pleasures of Popular Culture*. Ed. Henry Jenkins, Tara McPherson, and Jane Shattuc. Durham, NC: Duke University Press.

Stratton, Jon. 1997. "Cyberspace and the Globalization of Culture." In *Internet Culture*. Ed. David Porter. London: Routledge.

260

Tashiro, Charles. 1998. *Pretty Pictures: Production Design and the History of Film*. Austin: University of Texas Press.

Tollander, Carl. 1994. "Collaborative Engines for Multiparticipant Cyberspaces." In *Cyberspace: The First Steps*. Ed. Michael Benedict. Cambridge: MIT Press.

Turkle, Sherry. 1984. *The Second Self: Computers and the Human Spirit*. New York: Simon and Schuster.

———. 1997. *Life on Screen: Identity in the Age of the Internet*. New York: Touchstone.

Wilson, Pamela. 1996. "Virtual Reality, Fifties-Style: NBC's Wide Wide World." Society for Cinema Studies, Dallas (March).

Winner, Langdon. 1995. "Who Will We Be in Cyberspace?" *The Network Observer* 2, 9 (September) http://dlis.gseis.ucla.edu/people/pagre/tno/september-1995 .html#who.

CHAPTER FIFTEEN

Cultural Exchange

Tom O'Regan

A film...circulates in a sphere which can be described as transnational with none of the specificity so desired by nationalists. It does so because its mode of communication doesn't rely exclusively on the local or the national for success.

Ron Burnett, "The National Question in Quebec"

It almost goes without saying that what distinguishes the cinema from a good proportion of broadcasting and book publishing is that it is from inception international (McQuail 1994: 16–20). In most cinema markets and those parts of the television schedule dedicated to movies, including pay-TV movie channels, international productions dominate. Films circulate across national, language, and community boundaries reaching deep into social space. Audiences, critics, and filmmakers appropriate, negotiate, and transform this international cinema in various ways. It is in cinema's nature to cross cultural borders within and between nations, to circulate across heterogeneous linguistic and social formations. This is an internationalism in production and in reception, in the making of films and in their consumption. And if we agree that an internationalism is intrinsic to the cinema then what must underwrite this are systems of cultural exchange. We can say then that cultural exchange is fundamental to cinema at every level.

Cultural exchange is intrinsic to the cinema's production, circulation, and uptake. A normal – even unexceptionable – feature of the film milieu, cultural exchange can be found in filmmaking and film criticism, film reception, and film marketing. Processes of cultural exchange are intrinsic to the circulation of filmmaking across national and cultural borders – among and within states. They facilitate the lending and redisposition of cultural materials from one filmmaking and cultural tradition to another. A powerful force for innovation in filmmaking and the development of international understanding and misunderstanding alike, cultural exchange is a critical component of wider processes of cultural identity formation and cultural development. Cultural exchange matters to processes of cultural definition, loss, reconstruction, and renewal. It is constitutive of the cinema and of culture and identity more generally. As such, it is both unexceptionable and controversial. In this chapter I establish and evaluate the ways filmmaking and film studies alike have conceptualized and ordered the compelling evidence for cultural exchange.

By cultural exchange we mean the circulation – the giving, receiving, and redisposition – of cultural materials among differentiated socio-cultural formations. The component parts of the cultural exchange process – from the distribution mechanisms to the materials circulated and the formations that send and receive – are immensely varied in incidence, form, and purpose.

The central disputes within film studies about cultural exchange turn on how we identify its nature and how we evaluate its standing and direction. At issue here is not whether such exchange either does or should take place, as everyone agrees that it is a structural given at some level and is indeed committed to at least some forms of international, intercultural, or intercommunal cultural exchange. How we describe and judge cultural exchange is tied up with our very notions of culture, identity, and exchange itself. Our theoretical and normative positions on these concepts determine not only the range of cultural-exchange practices and processes in the cinema that are selected for investigation and discussion, but also the kind of position on cultural exchange that we adopt.

A vocabulary has built up within film studies to attempt to capture the various modalities of this handling of exchange. We speak of film, filmmakers, and audiences alike indigenizing, adapting, appropriating, poaching, resisting, coopting, and remaking films, filmmaking styles, practices, and technologies drawn from other filmmaking traditions – national and otherwise. We speak of filmmakers entering into a dialogue with the dominant international cinema and other cinema traditions. We speak of the cross-cultural reception of film and television. We speak of too little and too much cultural exchange, of unequal and reciprocal exchanges.

To discuss these matters we need to grasp the sheer dimensions of cultural exchange in terms of the materials that are exchanged, the peculiar standing of cultural exchange in the cinema in its broader contexts, the cultural communities involved in that exchange, and the economics of cultural exchange.

1   The Materials of Cultural Exchange

The cultural materials involved in this exchange can be diverse. They can be films like *Titanic* (James Cameron, 1997), circulating almost wherever films are screened commercially in theaters around the world. They can be concepts for films, as when the French film *Trois hommes et un couffin* (Coline Serreau, 1985) was remade in Hollywood as *Three Men and a Baby* (Leonard Nimoy, 1987). Filmmakers routinely draw on stories from other cultural traditions: how many times have Shakespeare's plays been remade or used as concepts for stories in various cultural traditions from the Russian to the Japanese to the American?

They can be the adjustments made to films with the explicit purpose of facilitating international circulation: this impinges on the selection of content (is it too parochial?), of actors and directors (are they known in other territories?), and even of accents and dialogue (will they be comprehensible?). The original *Mad Max* (George Miller, 1979) was dubbed from Australian into American English to facilitate its circulation; and the children's film *Babe* (Chris Noonan, 1995) strove for accents that would be acceptable to North American school children. Such factoring in of international circulation and therefore a film's potential for cultural exchange is a consistent consideration for investors, producers, directors, and scriptwriters.

The cultural materials can be filmmaking practices. Italian neorealist aesthetics and production practices of the late 1940s – particularly the enthusiasm for location shooting and the use of nonprofessional actors – evident in films such as *Roma: Citta aperta* (Roberto Rossellini, 1945, *Rome: Open City*) and *Ladri di biciclette* (Vittorio de Sica, 1951, *Bicycle Thieves*) were diffused among a variety of other national cinemas over the late 1940s and 1950s. These aesthetics created critical expectations as to what the cinema (generally) should look like.

The materials can be the reception of films and filming, which in turn inform those who produced the films in the first place. Provocatively, Thomas Elsaesser claims that the New German Cinema of Rainer Fassbinder, Wim Wenders, Werner Herzog, Volker Schlöndorff et al. was "discovered and even invented abroad, and had to be reimported to be recognised as such" within Germany (1989: 300). Such refashioning is part of the general circulation of any national cinema as it "travels" outside its domestic context and enters new contexts. Elsaesser writes of how:

> European films intended for one kind of (national) audience or made within a particular kind of aesthetic framework or ideology, for instance, undergo a sea change as they cross the Atlantic and on coming back find themselves bearing the stamp of yet another cultural currency. (1994a: 25)

Audiences routinely take up and reshape films made in other places, from other times, and yoke them to their purposes. They can create "imaginary Americas," turning film's purposes in alternate directions, creating aberrant interpretations and the like. Non-American audiences, John Caughie writes, routinely "play at being American" in their consumption of Hollywood movies. There is, he claims, a curious game of identification and nonidentification being played by audiences, such that the non-American "plays at being American" with all the "tactics of empowerment" and "games of subordination" that this implies (1990: 45). As Alison Butler observes:

> the refunctionalization of texts is not just a manifestation of occasional resistances, but the very condition of possibility of such border crossings. Productive – and indeed unproductive – misreading is perhaps the paradigmatic operation which

governs the reception of films outside – and sometimes inside – their original national contexts. (1992: 419)

Identifying much the same processes, Henry Jenkins writes of fans raiding "mass culture, claiming its materials for their own use, reworking them as the basis for their own cultural creations and social interactions" (1992: 18). Fans like Caughie's non-American are situated "outside" but reconstruct this status so as to inscribe themselves within that creative process.

The cultural materials can also include our ways of conceiving cinema itself. These consist of ideas about what cinema is, what it can be, how it can be important, in what ways its study should be approached. André Bazin (1967, 1971) and his colleagues at *Cahiers du cinéma* in the 1950s and 1960s developed ideas about the cinema of great international significance. Their ideas arguably underwent something of a sea-change also, as they were refashioned into the auteurist criticism of Andrew Sarris in North America and in that circulation helped found contemporary Anglo-American film studies.

People can be cultural materials too, as skills honed and developed in one cultural milieu are redisposed in another. Film directors often contribute to a number of national cinemas. Luis Buñuel made Spanish, Mexican, US, and French films. For his part Joseph Losey, "compelled to leave America at the time of Senator McCarthy...had to digest the mores of a new environment and struggle to obtain work" in the UK (Thomson 1980: 358). There he made classics of British cinema such as *The Servant* (1963) and *The Go-Between* (1971). The peripatetic Hungarian, Emeric Pressburger, worked in the film industry in Germany, then France, before settling in England, becoming one half of British cinema's most creative partnership, "Powell & Pressburger" (see MacDonald 1994). And it was he more than his collaborator who was responsible for the extraordinary wartime propaganda film *The 49th Parallel* (1941), aimed at shoring up wavering American public opinion for involvement in World War II. Pressburger's contributions did not end with his British involvements. In the 1960s he wrote the script from England for an Australian film, *They're a Weird Mob* (Powell, 1966).

Such freewheeling internationalism for actors, cinematographers, and directors is now an ordinary, even customary, way of inhabiting a film milieu. This experience of crossing borders is often driven by the needs of the receiving culture. Australian director Fred Schepisi is on record as saying that the Americans "want you [meaning non-Americans like him] to be original within formula frameworks" (Koval 1992: 43). They want "your originality but not for original films, they want it applied to their kind of films" (42) – in his case the results include *Russia House* (1990), *Roxanne* (1987), and *Six Degrees of Separation* (1993).

The cultural materials exchanged include particular technologies of exhibition, production, and marketing. Film festivals, for example, provide a machinery for films of various local cinemas to, in Bill Nichols's words, "circulate globally, within a specific system of institutional assumptions, priorities and constraints" (1994: 68). Screened at film festivals, these films are "never only or purely local"; instead they "circulate, in large part, with a cachet of locally inscribed difference and globally ascribed commonality." Film festivals as a distribution mechanism allow for the recognition of "the uniqueness of different cultures and specific filmmakers," while at the same time affirming "the underlying qualities of an 'international cinema.'"

Another example of cultural materials in circulation is provided by the adoption of different cinema exhibition venues. Take the example of the multiplex – the phenomenon of multi-screen theatrical exhibition spaces. It begins in Canada in the late 1950s, is extended to the US over the 1960s, and from there becomes dispersed around the world. Or take the siting of exhibition venues in giant shopping malls in the US and their slow spread throughout the global system since the late 1970s and into the twenty-first century. Here developments in real estate, site management, and city-planning are part of the diffusion of cinema developments internationally.

Exchangeable cultural materials are also of a more generalized character – such as the ideas, practices, and conceptions of everything from modernity to the role and functions of the state – and flow across cultural borders impacting upon film form, content, and the very organization of the cinema. John Orr, for example, identifies a "neo-modern moment" which "has its origin in the national cinemas of Western Europe and the United States where it engages with Western capitalist modernity" and has been extended to other cinematic traditions (1993: 6). John Tomlinson argues that a feature of the contemporary period is one where the "the simultaneous advantages and demerits of 'modernity' are being extended to powerful and impoverished nations alike" (1992: 175; see also Downing 1996: 223). In this context the cinema is, as Hamid Naficy has pointed out, one of those institutions of modernization, as "Third World" filmmakers, "wooed to cinema by Western films," trained in many cases in Europe, the US, and to a lesser extent the USSR, upon return made "films that critiqued the West and attempted to create a national identity in contradistinction to it" (1996: 4).

Another instance of such general exchanges is in policy models, where the ideas, the phrases, the arguments are borrowed and redisposed. Not long after the publication of the South African Film White Paper in 1996 (see Tomaselli and Shepperson 1996), Zimbabwe released its own film "white paper" which bore a remarkable resemblance to the South African document. The South Africans involved in the original white paper were surprised by these similarities. Although the Zimbabweans seem to have had no other agenda than to use an available African-based policy, one consequence of this kind of ad hoc borrowing is that it aligns, mirrors, and therefore helps integrate various regional film industries. Such policy-learning is important internationally. And it happens everywhere. Canadian film policy-making of the late 1960s and early 1970s directly impacted on Australian film policy development in the same period, with Canadian officials advising their Australian counterparts. The prevalence of

266

the overseas "fact-finding mission" is a more general instance of this on most government horizons. It is replicated by the obligatory visit of previously domestic filmmakers to international festivals, not only to learn the festival system but to assimilate the prevailing international standards of everything from imaging standards to deal-making.

Such cultural materials provide the glue holding together the more-or-less integrated international film system of production, circulation, distribution, and exchange.

2   The Communities for Cultural Exchange

Alongside the various cultural materials that can be exchanged and the mixed standing of this exchange we also need to recognize the various partners involved – the community terrain on which cultural exchange takes place. The cultural formations involved are as varied as are the cultural materials of the exchange and generate distinctive cultural-exchange dynamics.

They can be smaller and larger, richer and poorer nations. They can be groupings of nations, as in Europe, Africa, Latin America, as in the North and the South, as in the developed and the underdeveloped world, as in the Occident and the Orient. They can be communities of language-speakers of varying size and collective wealth – francophones, Zulu-speakers, Japanese-speakers, and anglophones. They can be religious communities embracing groups of nations, as in the so-called Islamic and Catholic countries. Such faith communities, like their language-community counterparts, can exist within and across a number of nations. The nation states involved in cultural exchange can be of various types. There are the "new world," neo-European nations of the Americas and Australasia defined by settler invasions and the dispossession of indigenous populations; there are the "old world" nations of Europe with their predominantly indigenous populations; and there are the postcolonial nations of Africa and South-East Asia.

The cultural formations involved in exchange also include smaller and larger sub-groupings within nation states. They might be the various "national communities," such as the Quebeckers and the Inuit "first nation" in Canada. They include the various minorities defined by ethnicity, region, sub-culture, sexual orientation, and gender. And they include the various cultural communities within national borders and those – such as various diasporic communities – who persist across national borders.

The cultural communities can be at greater or lesser cultural distance from each other. Some can be partly derived from each other and share a common language, such as the US, Canada, Australia, New Zealand, and South Africa, which are all former British colonies. Unsurprisingly, Hollywood has some of its best markets in English-speaking territories, leading to the perennial complaint of Britons, Australians, and English Canadians that they are cursed with sharing the English language with the dominant international cinema and wearing the consequences of this cultural proximity. Some national communities, like the Scandinavian and Benelux countries, are particularly open to cultural exchange. As small countries these nations look to a variety of import sources for television and cinema as a means of maintaining a sense of a distinctive identity, whereas bigger countries like Britain, France, and Germany look principally to their own local productions to secure these same objectives (Sepstrup 1990: *passim*). Smaller countries tend to regard imports in a different way from big countries, seeing in them advantages as much as disadvantages and often putting effort into diversifying the sources of film and program imports. Other national communities are remarkably closed, with international productions making up a negligible amount of the US box office and television schedules (but this negligible amount is enough to make the US Britain's best television and cinema export market).

The communities involved in cultural exchange can operate at a large cultural distance from each other – think of the gap between, say, a small Pacific Island nation such as Vanuatu and the People's Republic of China. And this large gap may be replicated within a nation, as when we compare traditional Aboriginal communities in central Australia with their "mainstream" European and increasingly Asian equivalents. Underwriting the complexity of cultural exchange are systems of mutual attraction and repulsion. We might assume that culturally contiguous communities would be more likely to be involved as partners in cultural exchange than communities at some distance from each other. But this does not always hold. In situations of conflict or histories of invasion, such communities may prefer, as a matter of policy, more culturally distant materials. Croatians prefer German and Hollywood filmmaking to that of their Serbian neighbours; Pakistan prefers Western programming over that of its neighbour India. Sometimes, among diasporic refugee communities, the films and television-programming of a proximate community are preferred to the local cultural materials of a homeland still under a despised political dispensation.

Sometimes this cultural exchange can be equal: French and German cultural trade is roughly balanced and both have larger populations. Mostly, however, cultural exchange is unequal. Some countries – like the US, Japan (in television at least), and India – are cultural producers, others cultural importers. Studies of the flow of cinema and television have quantified this cultural exchange, indicating the largely one-way cultural flows from the richer to the poorer, from the developed to the underdeveloped, from the North to the South, from the English language to other languages, from the larger language groups to the smaller ones, from the US to the rest of the world (Varis 1988). Such studies have also indicated the substantial role in cultural exports of highly populated countries in Europe (France, Germany, and Italy), Latin America (Mexico and Brazil), the Middle East (Egypt), and Asia (India, Japan, and Hong Kong/China) and the minor but significant role played by more sparsely populated countries such as Australia and Canada (see Sinclair et al. 1996).

This unequal character of cultural exchange is longstanding. In 1946 Gordon Mirams concluded his study of New Zealand filmgoing with the observation that "if there is any such thing as 'a New Zealand culture,' it is to a large extent the creation of Hollywood" (cited in Lealand 1988: 83). *The Moving Picture World* (Jan 7) of 1922 observed: "The American control of foreign market with respect to motion pictures is approximately the following: South America, 95%; Australian 90%; continental Europe, 85%; Britain, 85%; Far East, 8%" (quoted in de Usabel 1982: xv). Even in the world's second largest economy, Japan, international productions make up half the cinema box office (though negligible amounts on television).

Such unequal cultural-exchange dynamics have their origins in the structural dynamics of the cinema – its system of scale production with mass distribution and exhibition – requiring expensive technology, specialized screening venues, continuously improving standards of image-making and large-scale administrative coordination (Tunstall 1977). The international film industry is, unsurprisingly, dominated by a handful of major transnational corporations. Such multinationals conduct a largely unequal relationship with weaker domestic producers, exhibitors, and policy-makers. This industry is geographically concentrated in a handful of wealthy film centers, and its international scale shapes the production possibilities and contexts of peripheral film industries, nations, peoples, and centers (Guback 1969; Thompson 1985). The international industry is both dominant and predatory. It is predatory in that it is naturally expansive. It seeks new markets, new personnel for its productions (many national cinemas – British, Australian, Canadian, Dutch, and New Zealand – have their most talented directors for only so long), new commercial opportunities (in theme parks, product tie-ins, new media). And it seeks to extract the maximum benefit from its productions by, for example, forcing cinema-, video-, and television-buyers to take a package of products, whether sight unseen to get continuous access to valued products or in order to purchase that handful of productions that are most desired. As Janet Wasko notes, "it seems undeniable that the media business has increasingly become even more concentrated and unified" with "corporate mergers and diversification activities" intensifying this trend (1994: 18).

Yet this same Hollywood cinema, along with the other dominant international cinemas, plays an important role in cinema capacity-building globally, providing the incentive to invest in building or renovating exhibition infrastructures. For these reasons, much national cinema policy-making, while wanting to do much more to redress the imbalance, ends up leaving substantially intact the exhibition, distribution, and production nexus which aids the dominant international cinemas. Typically there is some fiddling at the edges through various national cinema supplements – based sometimes on minor imposts on the distribution and exhibition sectors, but mostly on various government-funded production support mechanisms. The commercial order of the cinema is one where unequal exchanges, dominance, hierarchies, the size and length of the multi-national and national exhibition and distribution networks rule. It is onto this basic structure that various governments and local industries graft their local filmmaking activities.

The partners to cultural exchange in the cinema come to that exchange on an undeniably and permanently unequal basis with disparities of language, wealth, size, resources, infrastructures, and culture. Few film relations are based on free and open exchange. There are many one-way cultural flows and little reciprocity. There are two broad ways in which community agents and film critics have understood the economic domination of cinema exchange by the larger players and in particular Hollywood. In the first, they see it as evidence of fundamental and structural inequality in the international system amounting to discriminatory economic dynamics (Schiller 1969; Mattelart et al. 1984). In the second, it is a pragmatic and improvised economic response to a set of given cultural conditions (Wildman and Siwek 1988). In one, Hollywood's dominance represents the distortion of markets, and in the other, a response to market conditions.

What the concentration on audiovisual flows and distribution dynamics tends to neglect is the use made by communities of the cultural materials that are exchanged. Clearly the producers and viewers in this international cultural exchange system only weakly share cultural resources. Both are required to negotiate cultural cleavages to create meanings. Eric Michaels suggests that this circumstance has had important textual consequences: it has encouraged Hollywood producers to adopt a "highly complex rhetorical stance which makes it quite difficult to say what the intended meaning of many programs might be" (1990: 19). In other words, the "conversation" between producers and audiences is designed to minimize obstacles to local and international participation alike on the part of potential audiences. But this strategy of incorporation is achieved through a communicative inefficiency (which is exploited most efficiently): as propositional contents are bent further, opportunities for partial misunderstanding are increased and even encouraged. And this is not a problem. For Hollywood, it does not particularly matter that wildly divergent or astonishingly convergent interpretations are routinely accomplished by audiences through Hollywood's global circulation so long as tickets are sold and videos rented. But equally, as Michaels elsewhere contends:

> It would seem difficult to see in the introduction of imported video and television programs the destruction of Aboriginal culture. Such a claim can only be made in ignorance of the strong traditions and preferences in graphics, the selectivity of media and contents, and the strength of interpretation of the Warlpiri. (1994: 95)

Heterogeneous cultural communities of region, race, and ethnicity make for various kinds of internal cultural exchange dynamics which can be profoundly unequal, dysfunctional, and to the disadvantage of the weaker party to the exchange. Taking the USA as an example, the cultural communities involved in this exchange include the "mountain" communities that are the subject of

J. W. Williamson's study *Hillbillyland* (1995), which has as its subtitle *What the Movies Did to the Mountains and what the Mountains Did to the Movies*. In this exchange, the mountains, with their associations of inbreeding, mental degeneration, and quaintness, become ciphers for a metropolitan imagination exercising its cultural power.

Similar unequal dynamics sustain many representational politics. Film scholarship speaks to the systematic and questionable representational dynamic involving African-American, Amerindian, and other minority populations in the content and practices of mainstream cinema, in its institutions, and among its mainstream white audiences (see Bogle 1973; Bataille and Silet 1980). Cultural exchange is routinely condemned here for the distorted lens it provides, leading to calls for the taking over of the representation of minorities to the mainstream by the minorities themselves so as to fashion a more inclusive image. Such internal cultural diversity is itself a leitmotif in much cultural studies and contemporary screen scholarship. It shifts attention to contingent processes of integration, differentiation, and assimilation of the cultural materials of the host and minority culture by minorities themselves, displacing the mainstream from its assumed center stage. So we find Hamid Naficy's Iranian immigrant viewers of film and television in California adapting aspects of their Persian heritage and taking on elements of American culture to construct composite, hybrid identities in symbolic cultural practices which simultaneously disavow and recognize their difference (1993: 86). Homi Bhabha's immigrant and marginal diasporic communities further make a claim for the centrality of their experience to the constitution of the nation itself: "the Western metropole must confront its postcolonial history, told by its influx of postwar migrants and refugees, as an indigenous or native narrative internal to its national identity" (1994: 6). For their part, gay and lesbian communities interacting with a filmmaking largely premised on heterosexual orientations produce not only their own resistances but proactive readings and filmmaking, including notions of a queer nation internal to the nation itself (see Brasell 1995). Equally important is the concomitant stress placed on the imaginative consequences of cultural diversity upon majority groups. In this context Kobena Mercer poses the question: "what is going on when whites assimilate and introject the degraded and devalued signifier of racial otherness into the cultural construction of their own identity?" (1992: 21). Julian Stringer, answering this question, argues that white appropriations of blackness and Chineseness are qualitatively different: "the racial economy in the white imagination of *True Romance* (dir. Tony Scott, writer Quentin Tarantino) is clear: you can have the Chineseness; but you can be black" (1996/7: 60). Stringer asks: "what is it that makes him [Tarantino] want to be black but not really Chinese?"

Cultural exchange mechanisms can, as these examples demonstrate, be located at macro and micro levels alike, suggesting that cultural exchange is both a constitutive component of culture itself and involves matters of cultural and economic power. As Michael Schudson observes:

271

The intertwinings of local, regional, national, and global cultures are now complex beyond reckoning. Cultures flow in, out, around, and through state borders; within states, centres radiate to peripheries but peripheries influence centres, too; in the world system the same phenomenon is repeated and culture flows in many directions. (1994: 42)

In such circumstances the critical issue is the *handling* and *standing* of such cultural exchange by agents in various cultural formations. In this both the senders and receivers, the exporters and the importers, the foreign and the host cultures are implicated. At issue is how cultural exchange mechanisms enter into and shape cultural milieux, including identities and the culture itself.

3 The Standing of Cultural Exchange

A mixed standing to cultural exchange in the film milieu and beyond is an inevitable consequence of both this sheer diversity and scope of cultural materials exchanged and the variety of levels at which such cultural exchange operates – from policy to ideas, from the circulation of people to the extension of practices, from reception contexts to industry development. Cultural exchange is part of the very furniture of the film milieu, a taken-for-granted given. And it is something very much in the foreground of consideration as some aspects of cultural exchange are made into substantive political, critical, and ethical issues by film critics, filmmakers, activists, and governments.

Our film politics, our film policy-making, our film appreciation, and our film criticism are deeply ambivalent about cultural exchange. We take it for granted, embrace it, and repel it in equal measure. We simultaneously see cultural exchange as an ordinary and integral part of the very constitution of the cinema, and as something so extraordinary as to require urgent critical and policy remedy. On the one hand we appreciate it and evolve strategies for more of it, and on the other we formulate policies designed to ensure less of it, including campaigns to diminish or enhance its standing. This ambivalence about cultural exchange is a consequence of how we encounter – remark upon or simply take for granted – the standing of cultural exchange.

Cultural exchange can have standing as simply an unexceptionable process in the film milieu, as when Kristin Thompson writes of how national cinemas are, as a matter of course, shaped by the "influences film-makers and audiences picked up from the presence of American films" (1985: ix). Describing and judging this sort of cultural exchange cuts across every facet of film study. The study of film auteurs needs to assess, for example, the influence of the British creative duo Michael Powell and Emeric Pressburger on the work of Martin Scorsese. Lesley Stern, for example, writes that "*Raging Bull* (Scorsese, 1980) bears an imprint, can be read in terms of *The Red Shoes* (Powell & Pressburger, 1948); it is as though *The Red Shoes* has bled subliminally into *Raging Bull*" (1995: 11). A strand of national cinema analysis embeds the national cinema in question into a larger international cinema, such that comparing one's own national cinema to others becomes a way to understand it. Darrell William Davis notes how one strand in the discussion of Japanese cinema "emphasises its similarities and differences to other works, usually from Western cinema" (1996: 19). The result aimed for is that of "an intertextual conversation of allusion and influence that conveys the dialectic of artistic process" within Japanese cinema (19). Cultural exchange functions here as a catalyst for understanding and reinvigorating local traditions.

Cultural exchange can be of such a character that it is not even noticed as a form of exchange. Geoff Lealand notes the naturalizing of the Hollywood screen presence on the cultural horizons of ordinary New Zealanders:

> The stories of Hollywood that persist have been long naturalised into New Zealand popular culture, so that *E. T.* seems no more alien to New Zealanders than to Americans. The images we [New Zealanders] have embraced, as well as having been naturalised, have also been "neutralised"; no longer perceived as threats to the cultural integrity of New Zealand. They are deemed as something else – "entertainment", "escapism", "fantasy", universal stories with universal appeal. (1988: 90)

Here cultural exchange is part of the wallpaper – a cause for neither celebration nor denigration, it is simply something we are to attend to if we want to understand the cinema before us and the everyday transnational conversations of which it seems a part. Its standing is literally that of any other naturalized part of the film milieu. Cultural exchange seems here to be part of us, who we are, what we think. We can no more disaggregate and disentangle it than catch the air.

Something of the mundane character of this cultural exchange can be seen in the gestation and critical uptake of Alex Proyas's recent feature film *Dark City* (1998). Proyas, whose previous feature was the cult classic *The Crow* (1994) featuring the late Brandon Lee, made *Dark City* in his native Australia in a studio part-owned by the Fox Corporation – a major Hollywood studio and multi-national film distributor. In keeping with the emerging logic of global film production that Toby Miller has explored (1996, 1998a, 1998b), *Dark City* is simultaneously a Hollywood film made in Australia, an Australian film (the studio in question was developed in conjunction with support from federal and state [provincial] governments), a film with an international cast and crew, and a film whose story coordinates are claimed by its director in French comics, sci-fi literature and the German Expressionist cinema of the 1920s (Barber and Sacchi 1998; Helms 1998).

For their part, film critics typically made sense of this film through an orgy of comparison. It was judged to be a commentary on *and* an extension of classic films as diverse as *Nosferatu, eine Symphonie des Grauens* (1922), *Metropolis* (1926), *La Bête humaine* (1938), *The Wizard of Oz* (1939), *Zardoz* (1973), *Phenomena* (1984), *Hellraiser* (1987), *Delicatessen* (1991), *The Hudsucker Proxy*

(1994), *The Crow* (1994), and *La Cité des enfants perdus* (1995).[1] The reviews on the Internet proliferated resemblances. Some critics declaimed its derivativeness. Paul Tatara (1998) claimed a "dead lift" from *Brazil* (1985): "Think of a loud, unimaginably confused (visually as well as narratively) *Brazil* with absolutely no sense of humor." Others found in its cinematic references a rich intertextual space. Roger Ebert (1998) noted that: "Its villains, in their homburgs and flapping overcoats, look like a nightmare inspired by the thugs in *M*, but their pale faces would look more at home in *The Cabinet of Dr. Caligari* (1919)."

The filmmakers and audiences (insofar as critics are indicative of the audience) alike saw the film adapting, appropriating, poaching, and remaking films, filmmaking styles, practices, and technologies drawn from various filmmaking traditions. Proyas's film was clearly entering into a dialogue with the cinema – past and present, the dominant international cinema, art cinema, and traditions of comics.

The film has no discernible Australian precedent, nor can any influence be claimed from previous Australian films, and yet it is likely to significantly impact on Australian production (Venkatasawmy and O'Regan 1998). It is a film with decidedly international precedents. While not an Australasian art film along the lines of Jane Campion's *The Piano* (1993), it takes up aspects of art cinema hitherto unexplored in its imagining of other possible worlds, its plays with the logic of representation, and its studio-based rather than location-based film practice.

With *Dark City* cultural exchange is fundamental to its very constitution in production, circulation, and significance. The debating point is the quality of this exchange. Few doubt whether it should exist (they might want less of it but could not imagine none of it) or if this is the right kind of cultural exchange (to do so would query a line of filmmaking that begins with Fritz Lang's *Metropolis*). The issue is rather if it is any good at what it does in its own terms and in terms of the sci-fi, expressionist, and film-noir traditions on which it draws. Is it parasitic on them? Does it adequately contribute to them? At issue is its cinema, not its cultural authenticity or the appropriateness of an Australian creating an American noir city in a Sydney backlot. This film and this filmmaker are not making a statement about Australia or his Greek-Australian identity. They are participating in the cinema, and this film is produced, circulated, and criticized in a transnational space.

Cultural exchange is often publicly embraced as a good thing in circumstances where the line between self and other – the domestic national cinema and the international cinema – is clearer. The public championing of cultural exchange is often tied up with how generations (of audiences, filmmakers, and critics) step in the face of their predecessors by actively seeking and lionizing certain kinds of cultural exchange as a matter of active policy. Such a searching out of available international models of film and living was part of a purposive rejection of a local film and socio-political situation by the emerging filmmakers of the New German Cinema from the 1960s. Anton Kaes contends that a "unifying force of New

German Cinema since the 1960s has been the 'uncompromising rejection of the [fascist] National Socialist film tradition' " (1989: 8). He cites directors such as Wim Wenders looking to American directors such as John Ford "for stylistic inspiration"; Volker Schlöndorff going to France "to learn filmmaking," and Herzog identifying himself with "the tradition of German Expressionism of the 1920s."

The local situation need not be as drastic as a fascist past; typically many a national filmmaker will publicly reject his or her own domestic production traditions in favor of the seemingly more expansive, even liberating, horizons and models available in the international cinema. Devaluing the national cinema and admitting to the value of Hollywood is part of how filmmakers – like Australia's Baz Luhrmann (*Strictly Ballroom*, 1992) – declare their "newness," "relevance," and "importance" in the local milieu. Hollywood enacts what the national cinema holds out, at least potentially, as its preserve – namely a natural and direct relation with the local audience. As Kim Schroder and Michael Skovmond celebrate it, "by breaking away from traditional, class-based notions of good taste, [it] could be absorbed by the actual tastes and desires of large numbers of working-class people" (1992: 7).

Governments the world over promote the educational and cultural value of international understanding in their cultural policies. They inaugurate programs for intercultural dialogue, which include the support of film festivals and the encouragement of coproductions. Indeed one of the functions of national public broadcasters in the latter part of the twentieth century – particularly in their niche and minoritarian variants – was to provide expanded opportunities for seeing and appreciating more of the world's cinema and television programming than they would otherwise have had available to them through the commercial dynamics of free-to-air broadcasting. So it is, for example, that Australia's national public broadcaster, SBS-TV, broadcasts 50 per cent of its programming in languages other than English drawn from around the world and maintains a "world movies" pay-TV channel. In a similar fashion the UK's Channel 4 has been an important screening venue and production catalyst for feature films, documentaries, and series television exploring local and international cultural diversity and including a variety of international production partnerships.

Sometimes moments of cultural exchange become defining moments for a film community and enable cultural communities to reorient their appreciation, criticism, and sense of the purposes and possibilities of filmmaking, as happened in France in the 1950s and early 1960s. Like so many of his generation, Henri Agel encountered as a revelation the American cinema largely denied him under German occupation after World War II:

> It was in the course of these nights, glistening with all the fires of the music hall, through swarming carnivals worthy of the early Rouault, in smoke-filled halls oozing with all the effluvia of Pigalle, that for some an American enchantment was born. A magic, doubtless impure and at times closer to a junkie's high, a magic too

275

tied up with tinsel and vulgarity of the Boulevard not to be ambiguous. And even so, in the trip from the icy Palace to the last metro for Etoile, everything began to decant, to regroup along certain lines of force that in the course of those weeks etched a more precise and more dense image of Hollywood, no longer the one that our professors pronounced with their lips pursed, but a crucible perpetually on the boil in which was blended fear and laughter and eroticism and violence and tenderness. Surely we were mixing thus the best and the worst. (1963: 12–13; quoted in Routt 1992: 61)

This cinema became a vehicle for both a cinephilia – a love of and commitment to the cinema – and a highly particular French "romance Americaine." In Agel's case this desire and love for a specifically American cinema is simultaneously embedded with unambiguously French landmarks and cultural references.

Love and desire are as indiscriminate here as elsewhere. The desire may just as likely be for an art cinema, a political cinema, an experimental cinema seemingly unavailable in one's own local cinema as for a popular vernacular cinema like Hollywood. (Indeed in English-speaking countries this desire for cultural exchange is more likely to manifest itself publicly in a desire for something other than Hollywood vernacular and the Anglo-American quality film, including its Australasian and Canadian variants.)

Just as cultural exchange can be so appreciated, loved, and desired, cultural exchange can be repulsed, actively and trenchantly resisted. Indeed desire and repulsion are part of the very public provenance of cultural exchange, as we see in the Agel quote. One person's (foreign or simply Other) love object is another's hate object. Agel's love for Hollywood and the cinema is matched by his professors' disdain for American cinema and "the movies." Often desire and repulsion for the same cinematic phenomena are to be found among the same people. The *Cahiers du cinéma* film critics who espoused American cinema in the 1950s and early 1960s had adopted a far less sympathetic tone toward Hollywood by the mid-1960s as directors facing American competition.

Resisting cultural exchange has long been a very public matter and has its origins in the profoundly unequal cultural flows of the international audiovisual system mentioned above. As these unequal cultural exchanges flow from capitalist dynamics which have concentrated the "power over communications" into a handful of multi-nationals, resistance to them becomes a public matter. François Mitterrand, as French President, railed against this nexus in 1982:

The distribution of information developed and controlled by a few dominant countries could mean for others the loss of their history or even their sovereignty, thus calling into question their freedom to think and decide. (cited in Mattelart et al. 1988: 19)

Various cultural, educational and religious elites make a political issue of *too much distributed cultural exchange*. The desire for cultural exchange readily turns to repulsion when it rubs up against, and is seen to compromise through sheer scale, cultural transmission and routines of identity formation. Many a Briton, Frenchman or woman, and Australian has worried publicly about the consequences for cultural maintenance, transmission of heritage, and allegiance even to the nation and community of a youth brought up on other people's pictures, knowing more of the 4th of July and apple pie than 1066, the storming of the Bastille, or Gallipoli. These worries are often registered in a public anti-Americanism, anti-market, or anti-transnational-corporation position on the part of various elites and popular movements, given Hollywood's role as the primary international cinema and the US role as the world's leading economy.

Cultural exchange with the US is actively resisted for the threats it poses to the transmission of local cultures from generation to generation. In film criticism we speak of films and filmmaking traditions being swamped by other cultural traditions. In the case of Australian and Canadian audiences and filmmakers, they not only "feel second best...forced to second guess what their authentic indigenous culture should be" but they produce a "neo-colonial 'second cinema' that consciously and unconsciously strives to reproduce the Hollywood models of production and circulation, counterfeiting the local sense of historical reality" (Dermody and Jacka 1988: 20, 23). Hollywood's effects are experienced not only in the perverted complexion of markets and investment but in the perversion of the national subject itself – the value and identity of a nation's citizens. America's offense is psychical: they are the privileged group, globally enforcing their worldview. People the world over respond by becoming identified with this American point of view, and in the process their identity, history, and culture are devalued. Agents locate an abjection among audiences and filmmakers to explain why a positive relation between the local audience and their national cinema is so difficult to achieve. Under such conditions of distorted cultural exchange filmmaking milieux can seem to become predominantly neocolonial (Dermody and Jacka 1988: 23). Repulsion is integrally tied up with matters of national pride and sour grapes: too much cultural exchange becomes a measure of national failure for the local product not only to own its domestic market but to count internationally.

There are powerful political reactions on the part of political and cultural elites to the unequal cultural exchange implicit in the international audiovisual system. Perceiving too much of one kind of cultural exchange, such as largely one-directional cultural flows, these reactions acquire a modular form. Film critics in English-speaking countries routinely lament too much American influence on local filmmakers and call for a greater openness on their part to to other cultural influences like Asian or European cinema (see, for example, Berry 1992: 48). Film agents – from critics to lobbyists – around the world call for and attempt to implement protectionist measures, including the expulsion of "foreign bodies" to recover a being, a space before "contamination": in 1975 an Australian government report claimed its legitimate business as protecting local locations from exploitation by predatory international filmmakers (Interim Board of the Australian Film Commission 1975: 36). Mainland and Taiwanese critics routinely lambast Hong Kong cinema for being "un-minzu" – for being un-Chinese in its adoption of "Western" modes of filmic expression. Domestic film-industry spokespersons routinely regard the loss of their domestic audience to Hollywood (or another dominant international cinema) as a consequence of predatory and colonizing behaviors. Sometimes resistance to cultural exchange has been exhibited in political disturbances, including acts of arson and threats accompanying the opening of the South Korean market to Hollywood films and American distributors.

Repulsion need not be founded on the schoolmaster's elitism with its implicit assumptions of low versus high culture, elite versus popular art, Europe versus America. It may instead be founded on resolutely populist and even tribalist positions. Indigenous community leaders (see Michaels 1994: 20–46) are concerned at the cultural impact of a readily available cinema, television, and video on traditional life – rituals, mores, observances, and practices – and the respect for cultural authority. But even here indigenous people are typically not against cultural exchange per se. They are more often concerned to guard against its excesses and to attempt to turn it toward community-building and cultural enhancement. Classification and censorship regimes "protect citizens" from materials that would give cultural or religious offense.

Whether this is a genuinely felt cultural need, an informed response to objective conditions of concentration and control over transmission, or simply opportunist industry posturing to secure its own advantages, such reactions license both policy programs designed to foster a local filmmaking ecology and political rhetorics aimed at reclaiming symbolicly a tradition in danger of extinction. On grounds of the cultural threat and cultural erosion following from exchange, a panoply of measures have developed internationally to inhibit, limit, and channel it. These inhibitions include a variety of governmental instruments from public policy to film-censorship regimes, from film-importing practices to curricula adjustment.

Nations around the world and jurisdictions such as the Canadian province of Quebec "use the law as a vehicle for the protection of [their] identity" (Burnett 1996: 250). So we have had long histories of regulated box office quotas and levies on films, introduced and sustained over the 1930s stretching through to the 1980s as a means of ensuring a viable local supplement alongside a vigorous international cinema. Quebec legislators, as part of their efforts to encourage the public use of French and protect a distinctive identity, have mandated not only street signage in French but also that English-language films can only "play for between eight and twelve weeks before a French dubbed version must appear in the theatres" (Burnett 1996: 257).

Various content regimes, first in the cinema and later in television, mandate amounts of local cinema and television product or specify upper limits on foreign content. Such content regimes are designed to encourage particular kinds of cultural exchange and production sources for the people's cinema enjoyment. In 1928 the New Zealand government mandated that 20 per cent of films imported into New Zealand should be British, justifying this measure on the grounds that it would "give our people, particularly the younger ones, a clearer idea of British history, of British countries and British customs and ideals" (cited in Lealand 1988: 91). Lest the colonial dominion relation evident here be seen as something of the past, just substitute for British "European" and you have the basis for much of the same supra-nation-state discourse of the contemporary European Community. For his part, the French cultural minister of the 1980s, Jack Lang, denounced multi-national and, by implication, American dominance of the international cultural exchange system in remarks that occasioned diplomatic exchanges with the Americans (cited in Mattelart et al. 1988: 19–20). Against this cultural imperialism he was concerned to construct counter-measures in a Latin audiovisual space (see Mattelart et al. 1984: *passim*).

The reactions to too much exchange of a certain kind reach into general societal reactions to perennial issues such as screen (cinema and TV) violence and classification issues. Because these controversies were associated in Australia, from the late 1950s to the mid-1970s, with imported product, the importing of that product became a political issue, whereas in the US the issue was one of influencing Hollywood's generation of product. Controversies over the same programs and films in Australia carried an additional weight in that Australian children were not just being affected by violence, they were also being "Americanized." Social and educational elites in Australia found themselves supporting Australian production as a quality alternative. Quality film and television meant non-US television and screen drama. This is quite typical. Moral crusaders the world over transpose US concerns about the effects of movie and television violence on civic, social, and family life into similar concerns couched in terms of the circulation of specifically American cinema and programming. Sometimes these reactions can become populist movements dedicated to purging the foreign presence and identifying the movies and entertainment more generally as a primary target, as in Iran under Khomeini. The standing of cultural-exchange dynamics is obviously implicated in systems and relations of power within the cinema and society more generally. And this power is not only exercised by the stronger cultural producer against the weaker cultural receivers and producers, but also by the power of domestic elites to co-determine with international distributors the shape, form, and trajectory of the cultural exchange that does take place.

This mixed standing of cultural exchange when coupled with the diversity of materials for cultural exchange has encouraged film and cultural studies alike to seek to classify it – to distinguish types and kinds of cultural exchange, and to disclose the effects of the operation of these various types of cultural exchange on different film milieux, filmmakers, and film-reception contexts. And in classifying cultural exchange, film and cultural studies have been concerned to make judgments about it. We have been concerned with "what ought to be the case" and we have therefore expressed preferences for and aligned ourselves with some rather than other forms of cultural exchange, assiduously seeking to praise and locate the best and most appropriate. We have lauded those who resisted the power dynamics of the international cinema, articulating a "third cinema" – "a cinema of research and experimentation, equidistant from both mainstream and auteurist cinema" (Stam 1993: 242). And conversely we have been vitally concerned to search out and warn of the worst excesses of cultural exchange – circulation and imitation that is destructive, whether of indigenous traditions or simply of sensibility itself. Consequently critics, like their filmmaker and policy-maker counterparts, routinely find some kinds of cultural exchange good, and others bad. We use our identification of whether cultural exchange is good or bad to figure out the standing and therefore the value of films, filmmaking traditions, and film-production entities like particular companies and indeed whole countries. Cultural exchange is consequently alternately valued and criticized, embraced and combatted. Film studies' attempts to classify and evaluate cultural exchange are irrevocably shaped not only by the communities concerned and the standing of that exchange but by the very notions of culture, identity, and exchange deployed. It is to these notions we must now turn.

4 Cultural Exchange and Cultural Identity

Our deliberations above inevitably lead us to the conclusion that cultural-exchange processes are simultaneously a blessing and a curse; they enable cultural development and identity formation and they disable the same. They help define one's own pictures and are integral to substituting other people's pictures for one's own. Cultural exchange is double-faced. It is part and parcel of the mechanisms that establish a sense of collective identity; and, equally importantly, it is part of disestablishing the same. It is inextricably tied to our notions of cultural identity, national identity, diasporic identity – for peoples and for the cinema in, for example, a national cinema. Cultural exchange is an intrinsic part of the self-same process that makes our cultural and political identities so provisional.

Insofar as identity involves notions of cultural integrity and autonomy, ideals of cultural becoming and cultural wholeness including a sense of destiny as a people, cultural exchange mechanisms diminish these. The integrity and autonomy of a culture and an identity formed in auto-identificatory fashion (constructing an identity in relation to itself rather than in relation to another) seem compromised by processes which, by definition, must question, even corrode, the bounded, coherent, and placed character of a cultural formation (adopted from Morley and Robins 1995: 122). Such cultural-exchange processes emphasize the interrelatedness and hybridity of cultural formations producing cultural fragmentation under the impact of imports as the audience for the local cultural product is fractured and seemingly "lost" to other cultures.

Such processes are often held to contribute to a perceived failure to achieve an identity. This is the classic anxiety over the incompleteness of various national and sub-national identities. We can worry whether we are sufficiently other (or even have an identity or separate culture). We are concerned about unrealized or weak identities whose very weakness is a product of the encounter with other, hegemonic cultural traditions. A leitmotif in these discussions is the recognition that the domestic cinema, the culture, and the identity under conditions of cultural exchange are decentered, unbounded, incoherent, and placeless. So it is that Susan Dermody and Elizabeth Jacka talk of how:

> Second-world countries like Canada and Australia are riddled with post-colonial ambiguity and anxieties.... Our identity becomes both clamorous and permanently obscure.... For where do "we" end and the "other" begin? Who is the other by which we define our difference, ensuring "us"? Britain? America? How are "they" to be satisfactorily disentangled from what we have internalized and hybridized from them? (1988: 20)

Sometimes film critics see this as a self-inflicted national failure – a product of cultural and social dysfunction, immaturity, and underdevelopment of cinema and other institutions. More commonly however, this failure is located elsewhere in colonial histories and neocolonial power relations embodied in critical conceptions of cultural imperialism and varieties of oppression and incapacity. These circumstances make one susceptible to other people's pictures and projections that are not one's own, and even lead to pathological and dysfunctional identities for a culture and its cinema. In the field of cultural power, we routinely speak of overpowering and vulnerable identities as some cultural identities are more powerful than others. But this is not the whole story.

Cultural-exchange processes also pose an alternative mechanism for founding a cultural identity – one that is based on the recognition of the relational and hybrid character of identity and culture. As Edward Said maintains, a culture, a self, a national identity is always produced in relation to its "others":

> the development and maintenance of every culture requires the existence of another different and competing alter ego. The construction of identity ... whether of Orient or Occident, France or Britain ... involves establishing opposites and "others" whose actuality is always subject to the continuous interpretation and reinterpretation of their differences from "us". (1995: 332)

Cultural-exchange processes clearly contribute to identity and culture formation at fundamental and basic levels. Identity is also intrinsically relational and cultures are themselves hybrid mixes. Such processes enter into the very storytelling of the vulnerable party. Olle Sjogren observes that, as a "small country," Sweden in its films and TV programs:

> is forced to transform its culturally weak position into a comedic national virtue. Comedy becomes a funny mirror for reflecting upon one's cultural weakness. It allows one to admit that one longs for a more exciting life without threatening the

life one is leading. Through parodies one can indulge one's fascination with another, more exciting culture, while simultaneously dismissing the indulgence as a joke. (1992: 157)

Cultural-exchange processes show us how "we" are different from "them"; they let us know who we are through showing us who we are not. Such processes also illuminate and clear spaces for identities other than "ourselves." As Philip Schlesinger observes:

> How we define the other and how the other simultaneously defines us are part of the unavoidable game of identity politics. We are defined, in part at least, by being different from how they are. (1994: 27)

For Schlesinger this process of hetero-identification is part of all identity politics, whether it is staged at international, national, or sub-national level. Cultural exchanges are the ordinary stuff of cultures and identities. The Canadian and Australian condition is not then special but an ordinary condition of identity formation. The difference is more one of inflection: these cultural formations routinely problematize their identities, often as a matter of civic and ethical principle (Hutchinson 1994: 164–97).

Ron Burnett details some of the issues at stake when discussing the case of Quebeckers Celine Dion and Denys Arcand, the director of *Jesus de Montréal* (1989), both of whom have been "closely identified with the nationalist wing of Quebec culture" yet want, in the case of Dion, to be successful musically in the American market and, in the case of Arcand, to become known as "an international filmmaker":

> Celine Dion and Arcand have understood that specificity as such can best be identified from the outside and that the distinctions which we so arbitrarily use to maintain our sense of identity rarely survive without being affirmed by observers from other cultures. (1996: 260)

Cultural exchange is critical to any meaningful identity. It also carries the risk of substituting local culture with that of another. International contamination becomes a necessary risk, and identity a balancing act. It's not unusual for national cultural formations to oscillate between periods where public discourse emphasizes the line between self and other and other periods where it embraces a deliberate mixing, blurring, and preparedness to confuse itself with the world. Ross Gibson, for example, acknowledges that "the audience for Australian cinema ... is now perhaps more interested in the world rather than the boundaries that could theoretically separate the nation from the remainder of the international community" which it was so preoccupied with in the 1970s (1992: 81).

Burnett seems to be suggesting continuous processes of cultural interpenetration and exchange which precede the advent of the cinema and are subsequent to it. In this scenario attention is shifted to cultural-transfer processes and the relation between them. Its premise is that there is, in Davis's words, "an international consciousness inseminating the film industries of all countries from the moment of their inception" making the cinema "an institution that is profoundly, inescapably international" (1996: 19). In such circumstances there is no original or authentic local culture or national cinema – every national cinema is consequently "'always already' touched by other cultures" (20). National cinemas become, in Elsaesser's words, "relations": "'National cinema' makes sense only as a relation, not as an essence, being dependent on other kinds of filmmaking, to which it supplies the other side of the coin" (1994a: 25–6).

When Richard Collins notes the "productivity of US cultural influences . . . on the Nouvelle Vague, the New German Cinema, or on Italian filmmakers like Sergio Leone or . . . Gianni Amelio" (1990: 157), he is finding Hollywood positively in the constitution of the national cinema product. This not only questions the idea of contamination; it suggests an informed dialogue with Hollywood. To be sure this is an asymmetrical dialogue, but a dialogue nonetheless.

But the cinema disposing the Other to produce a sense of Self raises the question as to whether the Other is displayed for him or herself or simply as a cipher to establish ourselves. Such dynamics hardly matter if the Other is a culturally stronger First-World Other, as when people of a European descent (usually Americans and Britons) and African–Americans are depicted as villains in Hong Kong cinema (such representation was aided by Hong Kong censorship under British control, which was more concerned to police representations of the mainland for fear of giving offense to a capricious People's Republic of China than to police the representation of themselves and the West). Where those Others are weaker, racially, religiously, and ethnically different, and comparatively voiceless, film critics worry about the representation of these Others functioning as "metaphors for . . . [a] sense of collective identity" (Berry 1994: 33). Obviously and throughout history preceding and subsequent to the cinema, such forms of hetero-identification have been typically discriminatory and prejudiced. A blackness helps define a whiteness; the Africans and Asians help define the European; women help define men, and so on.

But with the contemporary critical attention currently paid to diasporas, migrants, intercultural exchange, exile, and marginal, minority communities defined either by ethnicity and race or by sexual preference (it is now common to talk of the "queer" nation [Berlant and Freeman 1992]), a literature on hetero-identification has developed which has moved from denouncing an in-principle opposition to forms of hetero-identification to distinguishing between negative and positive self/other dynamics. On the one hand there is the attention paid to colonialist representational logics (Young 1990) and accompanying notions of Eurocentrism (Shohat/Stam 1994); on the other hand this has been accompanied by a deal of attention to locating and celebrating good, productive, life-and identity-affirming practices. Here hybridity and intersubjective encounters are celebrated and endorsed. So it is that Chris Berry, in writing of Denis O'Rourke's fiction documentary *The Good Woman of Bangkok* (1992), talks of a "postcolonial encounter" at the Rose Hotel between the prostitute Aoi and the filmmaker, which has also become an "intersubjective space":

> What is enacted in the intersubjective exchanges in the Rose Hotel, on the other hand, is the encounter of two very different entities, each internally incoherent and split in its own way, each caught in larger patterns. Furthermore, these entities are caught up in the unequal relationships that the hybrid, syncretic space of their own interaction creates; in the Rose Hotel they create a space that is far from utopian but is different from what went before. And what is the nature of this particular intersubjective exchange, this particular deal in Bangkok? Symbolized in the form of her rice farm, Aoi gets to exert agency, and symbolized in the haunting form of his film O'Rourke gets to be in Asia and gets Asia in him. (1994: 55)

Exemplary filmmaker theorist figures such as Trinh T. Minh-ha (1992) exemplify what ought to be in such exchanges. Theirs is a hybridity of form and function in filmmaking and film criticism. They perform an avowedly indeterminate identity – refusing any fixed identity as American or Vietnamese, for example. They insist on process rather than outcome, a becoming rather than an arriving. They occupy a space that, in being neither one thing nor another, is a liminal "in between" space appropriate to the crossing of territorial and other borders in their work and its reception. They are seen to be both "outsider-in" and "insider-out."

Culture under a dispensation that takes both national societies as its unit and various communities within and across it is routinely and inevitably a hybrid phenomenon made of past and present cultural exchanges. It cannot be an ideal purity corrupted through inappropriate cultural exchange or an ideal purity to be achieved at some point in the future. Cultures under conditions of cultural exchange are made from nonoriginary, nonorganic characteristics. They are hybrid, they are contingent, they are in process. The faultlines within film studies are centered on how we describe this international contamination and the standpoints we take on cultural exchange, and most particularly where we draw the line as to its desirable and undesirable components.

Our very ways of discussing cultural exchange and identity here make it tempting to find two models of culture: an older organic model rooted in tradition and heritage and auto-identification, and another contemporary version for our globalizing times based on hetero-identification and hybridity. But if we go back to some of the founding analyses of culture and national cultures by Herder (1993), for instance, we find the same sense of culture being formed by interactions with others – through invasions, cultural transfers, migrations, and so on, alongside the more organic nativist constructions. The issue is not then a matter of choosing between one or the other but the relation between the two – the interpenetration of auto-identificatory processes with hetero-identificatory ones. The faultlines within film studies over cultural exchange emerge over the weighting given to each and therefore the angle of incidence taken on these processes.

Embedded in this discussion is a way of understanding the double-edged character of culture itself, cultural exchange and its relation to cultural identity. Such exchange is critical to defining and transforming the self, to defining the culture and redefining it; it is also critical to processes of cultural denaturing, of eroding the culture and the sense of self, of compromising it, of ruining it, reducing it to a form of sameness. This simultaneous character of cultural exchange – both as a means for us to determine who and what we are and a powerful corrosion of who and what we are – is fundamental to cultural exchange in the cinema and bedevils film studies and the wider film milieu.

An emerging perspective in film studies has it that we need a change from *normative* approaches to cultural exchange toward *normalizing* the cultural-transfer processes intrinsic to such cultural exchanges. Film studies, at least in part, is moving from principled objections to unequal cultural exchange to a careful attention to the variety, shape, and interrelatedness of the various cultural-exchange processes. This attention focusses on the negotiation of cultural transfers by the receiving culture.

5   Negotiation of Cultural Transfers

Regardless of these various asymmetries, the international film and television milieu is configured by flows and transfers (of concepts, genres, styles, texts, fashions, etc.) which shape filmmaking, criticism, and consumption in a variety of ways. Soviet semiotician Iouri Lotman (1990) has made cultural transfers central to his understanding of national cultural formations. Elsewhere I have applied this model to thinking about Australian national cinema and cultural-transfer/exchange processes more generally (see O'Regan 1996).

For Lotman cultural transfers play a significant role in the formation of cultures. They are central to culture and cultural development generally. A culture cannot turn itself into a sending culture without being at some point a receiving culture. He distinguishes processes of cultural transfer and provides a way of linking these as the successive stages involved in the unfolding story of any culture's development. These are: a first stage where imported texts "keep their strangeness" and are valued more than those of the home culture; a second stage where "the imported text and the home culture . . . restructure each other" (so, for example, Rolf de Heer's *Bad Boy Bubby* [1994] indigenizes the Eastern European art film in an Australian context); a third stage where "a higher content is found in the imported world-view which can be separated from the national culture of the imported texts" and attached to the local product (so local films become better films than their original Hollywood exemplars); a fourth stage where "imported texts are entirely dissolved in the receiving culture" (as with Italian neorealism or the Nouvelle Vague); and a fifth stage where "the receiving culture . . . changes into a transmitting culture directing its product to other, peripheral areas of the semiosphere" (so British films such as Mike Newell's *Four Weddings and a Funeral* [1994] and Hugh Hudson's *Chariots of Fire* [1981] circulate the length and breadth of the international system) (Lotman 1990: 146).

For Lotman, national cultures need to pass through these five stages. Cultures cannot become transmitting cultures without passing through the earlier stages. As a professional historian and semiotician of culture, it makes no sense to Lotman to oppose these stages to one another, as they are part of a general and larger process. Both the abject home culture of stage one and the confident producing culture of stage four are not only part of a continuum of cultural exchange but are organically interconnected. Such natural semiotic processes are not to be criticized as such but are rather to be identified for what they are – part of the general condition of any culture and not just antipodal ones. It is also the case that these stages are co-present at any one time.

In the first stage identified by Lotman, "[t]he texts coming in from the outside keep their 'strangeness' " such that they are "read in the foreign language (both in the sense of natural language and in the semiotic sense)." Also, "[t]hey hold a high position in the scale of values, and are considered to be true, beautiful, of divine origin" (1990: 146). If Australians routinely hold Hollywood filmmaking, British cinema and television, and the European and now Asian cinema in higher esteem than the local product, they are matched by those in France like Henri Agel or Naficy's "third world audiences" wooed to the cinema by Hollywood. Industry people – distributors, filmmakers, and exhibitors – regularly report that audiences, from their perspective, are unwarrantedly resistant to quality local product, so inured are they by the almost divinized imported product. For the cinephile, American, not one's own national cinema, is "the cinephile's heaven" (Martin 1988: 92). Theirs is a loving regard for modes of filmmaking often not their own. Filmmakers can often insist upon the cultural appropriateness in other contexts of the Hollywood imaginary, berating those who would accentuate what is different about local speech and life styles and ignoring what is imaginatively held in common. For Lotman:

> Knowledge of the foreign language is a sign of belonging to "culture," to the elite, to the best. Already existing texts in "one's own" language, and that language itself, are correspondingly valued lowly, being classed as untrue, "coarse," "uncultured." (1990: 146)

Variously, the Hollywood cinema, American independents, European and Asian art films, the avant-garde, exploitation, political, multi-cultural, or feminist cinema can show up the limits and inadequacies of the local product. The film critic calls on this international repertoire to introduce to the local cinema some film-performance style, genre, or social problematization. Audiences are often animated by similar concerns, as when John Baxter reported how viewing local films left him disturbed rather than glowing with national pride – rather like a Catholic hearing mass said for the first time in English rather than Latin. There was only one proper place for making films and that was America: I didn't care to see fantasies enacted right on my doorstep. It was a common reaction. (1986: 22)

During this stage, Lotman suggests there is a "dominant psychological impulse . . . to break with the past, to idealize the 'new,' i.e. the imported world-view, and to break with tradition, while the 'new' is experienced as something salvific" (1990: 146). Instances of this stage abound in criticism, filmmaking, and film-policy development. The need for a new start is undergirded by a recognition of the worthless character of the National Socialist tradition in Germany or the cinema of papa for the French New Wave. The devaluation of British-produced culture and elevation of Hollywood and the continental international art cinema is a natural part of the British experience of the cinema and culture more generally. Hence the common conception of British cinema as a kind of cardigan (Medhurst 1995: 16).

Sometimes this first stage is referred to retrospectively and disparagingly as the "cultural cringe," where anything imported is valued, come what may. The standpoint of later stages reconstructs this stage as a false consciousness to rail against. But Lotman's first stage is essential to the introduction of new formats, critical paradigms, and combinations of filmmaking. Without it there can be no system regeneration, no second stage of indigenizing the imported culture from which to begin. It also encourages a healthy disrespect for the local product and enables people to dream of an outside from which to reposition the local.

The second stage, where the "imported texts and the home culture restructure each other," is evident in the many film-concept remakes. It is present in criticism when critics take the different theories developed for other cultural formations and sometimes apply them with only minor changes to their own context. And it is an important component in documentary cinema traditions where the substantially local character of much documentary circulation makes the original neither as publicly available nor as valued as the local copy, thus permitting often rudimentary concept remakes.

Typically, feature-filmmakers and television-drama producers operate in the more advanced stage of a full-blown adaptation – as the Hollywood, British, and European originals already have a market presence. In this second stage, Lotman insists, "translations, imitations and adaptations multiply" and "the codes imported along with the texts become part of the metalingual structure." This second stage gives rise to a relatively strict division of labor: the local is the content, the flavor, the accent, and the social text, while the international provides the underlying form, values, narrative resolutions, etc. The products of this second stage are subject to Mattelart et al.'s criticism that in them "cultural identity [is] reduced to a national label stuck on what is essentially a transnational copy" (1988: 22).

This stage also includes "a predominant tendency to restore the links with the past, to look for roots" (Lotman 1990: 147). The new is now interpreted as "an organic continuation of the old, which is thus rehabilitated." Peter Weir's *Picnic at Hanging Rock* (1975) makes sense not just as a lush and quirky European art film or a classy horror film but in its connections with longstanding Australian storytellings, based as it is upon a screen adaptation of Joan Lindsay's novel. It was connected with nativist ideas about the threatening bush and tall stories and ghost stories about child disappearance and horror met with in the bush. Lotman notes that ideas of organic development come to the fore at this stage. Films can become part of a larger narrative of a culture undergoing development and flowering maturity.

Lotman's third stage stresses:

> a tendency . . . to find within the imported world-view a higher content which can be separated from the actual national culture of the imported texts. The idea takes hold that "over there" these ideas were realized in an "untrue," confused or distorted form and that "here," in the heart of the receiving culture they will find their true, "natural" heartland. The culture which first relayed these texts falls out of favour and the national characteristics of the texts will be stressed. (146)

The third stage crucially involves perceptions. It reevaluates the home culture's product in a situation of assumed international comparison. The establishment of a film's international credentials, like success and awards at Cannes and Berlin film festivals, establishes its domestic credentials as an exemplary local product of international standard. Lotman's third stage opens out onto the heartfelt pride many producers and filmworkers feel about the quality and innovation of their product in an international frame. It is evident in the appreciation of films such as Luc Besson's *La Femme* (1990). This film reveals the complete mastery of the thriller genre. It is appreciated for its technical virtuosity and its aggressive and exuberant vitality, and its standing is confirmed by its concept remake in Hollywood.

The fourth stage assimilates the imported matrices, making them entirely its own: "the imported texts are entirely dissolved in the receiving culture." For Lotman:

> During this stage . . . the culture itself changes to a state of activity and begins rapidly to produce new texts; these new texts are based on cultural codes which in the distant past were stimulated by invasions from outside, but which now have been wholly transformed through the many asymmetrical transformations into a new and original structural model. (1990: 146)

Whether it be the Japanese cinema of the 1950s and early 1960s, the French New Wave, Italian neorealism of the 1950s and the cinema of the 1960s, German Expressionism of the 1920s, or the New German Cinema from the 1960s, this cinema is related to but not beholden to its distant "debts." There are limits to participation at this fourth stage. For some film-producing countries it happens regularly, as with the larger countries of Europe. For the vast bulk of countries, which are small- or medium-sized in population terms or are comparatively impoverished in terms of film-production funding and circulation, we can be looking at "one-person" film industries. There is not the level of production activity to sustain it, nor is there the dominance of local "symbolic" culture at the box office and on the television schedule.

In the fifth stage:

> The receiving culture, which now becomes the general centre of the semiosphere, changes into a transmitting culture and issues forth a flood of texts directed to other, peripheral areas of the semiosphere. . . . As with any dialogue, a situation of mutual attraction must precede the actual contact. (Lotman 1990: 146)

Of course the prospect of any but the larger countries being at the center of the international audiovisual semiosphere is largely chimerical. Although individual films from countries other than the US do regularly become "dominant entertainment forces" (this is particularly so if they are produced in the English language or can be dubbed into English effectively, as with Bruce Lee's Kung Fu films of the early 1970s), these tend to be the exception, not the rule. Nonetheless there is an ambition within just about every reach of cinema and criticism not only to be particular and local but also to be universal and to speak to the world. The trajectory of many actors, cinematographers and directors to Hollywood, to Hong Kong, and to the larger film industries of Europe – France for francophone Africa, for example – makes sense in this context. The move to Hollywood completes the cycle: think of how many filmmakers continued to make "their" films in Hollywood. There is, obviously, a good case to be made that Alfred Hitchcock continued to make British films throughout his Hollywood career. For Elsaesser, Hitchcock's cinema revealed "the peculiar complexion of the British dandy" (1994b: 21), while for Ken Mogg, Hitchcock remained till the end "a British filmmaker" (1995: 21).

6   Conclusion

Lotman's schema provides support for a widely held position within film theory to put more flexible and open-ended conceptions of cultural exchange at the heart of its study. These conceptions are predicated on conceptions of culture that see it as always already hybrid – products of border-crossings and other features. Lotman would agree with Davis that "an international consciousness" inseminates "the film industries of all countries from the moment of their inception" (1996: 19). He, too, would see not only the cinema as "an institution that is profoundly, inescapably international" but that every national cinema, every national or marginal cultural community is " 'always already' touched by other cultures." And he would add that this is not new but the very historical condition of culture. Clearly the normalization, divinization, and demonization of cultural exchange noted above are themselves naturally occurring features of the cultural-exchange cycle.

By normalizing cultural transfers we can shift our attention from moments of cultural exchange to its broader dynamics. In so doing analysis moves from valorizing one type of cultural exchange over others to understanding the larger cultural-exchange processes that link these moments. Lotman's own emphasis upon the cyclical character of cultural exchange makes him sanguine about it. For this historian of culture we should not take sides too quickly or take up the teleological invitation of seeing five sequential stages in which the latter stages are superior. We can afford to give each stage its due, particularly if we want system regeneration to occur and if we want to create the conditions for the cultural exchanges we prefer to occur (Lotman shows we need those other aspects of cultural exchange we might sometimes abhor). Filmmaking methods, ideas, concepts are also transformed in the encounter with local traditions. In this way cultural exchange facilitates the adaptation and reinvigoration of tradition.

Such a position not only has practical consequences for how we might secure "cultural futures," in Michaels' happy phrase (1994: 99), but also has ethical and normative consequences for our practice as policy-makers and critics alike. Burnett warns us of the dangers inherent in our very conduct of cultural exchange:

> The necessity of the other . . . makes policy necessary for culture but only if policy itself is seen as a cultural product and thus as open to change and reevaluation as any cultural production might be. Any transformation of policy into law in this regard closes off the very channels of discourse and exchange which have made the creation of culture possible in the first place. (1996: 260)

For Burnett, as for Lotman, our policies, our plans of action, our very critical vocabulary need to remain flexible and open lest they inhibit and deny the very cultural adaptations so critical to cultural maintenance and growth. Working out the contours of this practice is a central issue facing contemporary film studies, whether it focusses on cultural exchange between or within societies.

Note

1 These titles are listed as links with other titles in the Internet Movie Database pages on the film. See *http://us.imdb.com/Title?Dark+City+(1998)*. Accessed August 11, 1998.

References

Agel, Henri. 1963. *Romance americaine*, 7th edn, art 35. Paris: Les Editions du Cerf.

Barber, Lynden, and Marco Sacchi. 1998. "Shadow Player." *The Australian Magazine Supplement, Weekend Australian* (May 16–17): 32–4.

Bataille, Gretchen, and Charles Silet, eds. 1980. *The Pretend Indians*. Ames: Iowa State University Press.

Baxter, John. 1970. *Australian Cinema*. Sydney: Pacific Books.

——. 1986. *Filmstruck: Australia at the Movies*. Sydney: Australian Broadcasting Corporation.

Bazin, André. 1967, 1971. *What Is Cinema? Vols 1 & 2*. Essays selected and trans. Hugh Gray. Berkeley: University of California Press.

Bell, Philip, and Roger Bell. 1993. *Implicated: The United States in Australia*. Melbourne: Oxford University Press.

Berlant, Lauren, and Elizabeth Freeman. 1992. "Queer Nationality." *boundary* 2, 19 (spring): 149–80.

Berry, Chris. 1992. "Heterogeneity as Identity." *Metro* 91 (spring): 48–51.

——. 1994. *A Bit on the Side: East–West Topographies of Desire*. Sydney: EM Press.

Bhabha, Homi. 1994. *The Location of Culture*. London: Routledge.

Bogle, Donald. 1973. *Toms, Coons, Mulattoes, Mammies and Bucks*. New York: Viking Press.

Brasell, R. Bruce. 1995. "Queer Nationalism and the Musical Fag Bashing of John Greyson's *The Making of 'Monstors.'*" *Wide Angle* 16, 3: 26–36.

Burnett, Ron. 1996. "The National Question in Quebec and Its Impact on Canadian Cultural Policy." In *Film Policy: International, National and Regional Perspectives*. Ed. Albert Moran. London: Routledge. 249–61.

Butler, Alison. 1992. "New Film Histories and the Politics of Location." *Screen* 33, 4 (winter): 413–26.

Caughie, John. 1990. "Playing at Being American: Games and Tactics." In *Logics of Television*. Ed. Patricia Mellencamp. Bloomington: Indiana University Press. 44–58.

Collins, Richard. 1990. *Television: Culture and Policy*. London and Cambridge: Unwin Hyman.

Davis, Darrell William. 1996. *Picturing Japaneseness*. New York: Columbia University Press.

Dermody, Susan, and Elizabeth Jacka. 1988. *The Screening of Australia Vol. 2: Anatomy of a National Cinema*. Sydney: Currency Press.

De Usabel, Gaizka S. 1982. *The High Noon of American Films in Latin America*. Ann Arbor: UMI Research Press.

Downing, John. 1996. *Internationalizing Media Theory*. London: Sage.

Ebert, Roger. 1998. "*Dark City*." *Chicago Sun Times* (March 11). <http://www.suntimes.com/ebert/ebert_reviews/1998/02/022704.html > Accessed Aug. 14, 1998.

Elsaesser, Thomas. 1989. *New German Cinema: A History*. London: BFI/Macmillan.

——. 1994a. "Putting on a Show: The European Art Movie." *Sight and Sound* 4 (April): 22–7.

——. 1994b. "The Dandy in Hitchcock." *Maguffin* 14: 15–23.

"Foreign Market." 1922. *The Moving Picture World* (Jan. 7): 30.

Gibson, Ross. 1992. *South of the West*. Bloomington and Indianapolis: Indiana University Press.

Guback, Thomas. 1969. *The International Film Industry*. Bloomington: Indiana University Press.

Helms, Michael. 1998. *"Dark City"* Interview with Andrew Mason and Alex Proyas. *Cinema Papers* 124 (May): 18–21, 45.

Herder, Johann. 1993. *Against Pure Reason: Writings on Religion, Language, and History*. Trans. and ed. Marcia Bunge. Minneapolis: Fortress Press.

Hutchinson, John. 1994. *Modern Nationalism*. London: Fontana Press.

Interim Board of the Australian Film Commission. 1975. *Report of the Interim Board of the Australian Film Commission*. Canberra (February).

Jenkins, Henry. 1992. *Textual Poachers*. London: Routledge.

Kaes, Anton. 1989. *From Hitler to Heimat: The Return of History as Film*. Cambridge: Harvard University Press.

Koval, Ramona. 1992. *One to One*. Sydney: ABC Books.

Lealand, Geoff. 1988. *A Foreign Egg in Our Nest? American Popular Culture in New Zealand*. Wellington: Victoria University Press.

Lotman, Iouri M. 1990. *The Universe of the Mind: A Semiotic Theory of Culture*. Trans. Ann Shukman. Bloomington and Indianapolis: Indiana University Press.

MacDonald, Kevin. 1994. *Emeric Pressburger: The Life and Death of a Screenwriter*. London: Faber and Faber.

McQuail, Denis. 1994. *Mass Communication Theory: An Introduction*, 3rd edn. London: Sage Publications.

Martin, Adrian. 1988. "Nurturing the Next Wave: What Is Cinema?" In *Back of Beyond: Discovering Australian Film and Television*. Ed. Peter Broderick. Sydney: Australian Film Commission. 90–101.

Mattelart, Armand, Xavier Delcourt, and Michèle Mattelart. 1984. *International Image Markets: In Search of an Alternative Perspective*. Trans. David Buxton. London: Comedia Publishing Group in association with Marion Boyars.

———. 1988. "International Image Markets." In *Global Television*. Ed. Cynthia Schneider and Brian Wallis. New York: Wedge Press. 13–34.

Medhurst, Andy. 1995. "Inside the British Wardrobe." *Sight and Sound* (March): 16–17.

Mercer, Kobena. 1992. "Skin Head Sex Thing: Racial Difference and Homoerotic Imaginary." *New Formations* 16 (spring): 1–23.

Michaels, Eric. 1990. "A Model of Teleported Texts (With Reference to Aboriginal Television)." *Continuum: The Australian Journal of Media and Culture*, 3, 2: 8–31.

———. 1994. *Bad Aboriginal Art: Tradition, Media and Technological Horizons*. Sydney: Allen and Unwin; Minneapolis: University of Minnesota Press.

Miller, Toby. 1996. "The Crime of Monsieur Lang: GATT, the Screen and the New International Division of Culture Labour." In *Film Policy*. Ed. Albert Moran. London: Routledge. 72–84.

———. 1998a. "Hollywood and the World." In *The Oxford Guide to Film Studies*. Ed. John Hill and Pamela Church Gibson. Oxford: Oxford University Press.

———. 1998b. *Technologies of Truth: Cultural Citizenship and the Popular Media*. Minneapolis: University of Minnesota Press.

Mogg, Ken. 1995. "'How about I Pump Hitler?': Hitchcock's *Foreign Correspondent* (1940) and Its Sources." *Maguffin* 16: 11–26.

292

Morley, David, and Kevin Robins. 1995. *Spaces of Identity: Global Media, Electronic Landscapes and Cultural Boundaries*. London: Routledge.

Naficy, Hamid. 1993. "Exile Discourse and Televisual Fetishization." In *Otherness and the Media: The Ethnography of the Imagined and the Imaged*. Ed. Hamid Naficy and Teshome H. Gabriel. Longhorne: Harwood Academic Publishers.

——. 1996. "Theorizing 'Third World' Film Spectatorship." *Wide Angle* 18, 4: 3–26.

Nichols, Bill. 1994. "Global Image Consumption in Late Capitalism." *East–West Film Journal* 8, 1: 68–85.

O'Regan, Tom. 1996. *Australian National Cinema*. London: Routledge.

Orr, John. 1993. *Cinema and Modernity*. Cambridge and Oxford: Polity Press.

Routt, William D. 1992. "L'Evidence." *Continuum: The Australian Journal of Media and Culture* 3, 2: 40–67.

Said, Edward. 1995. *Orientalism*. Ringwood, Melbourne: Penguin Books.

Schiller, Herbert. 1969. *Mass Communications and American Empire*. New York: Augustus M. Kelley.

Schlesinger, Philip R. 1994. "Europe's Contradictory Communicative Space." *Daedalus* 123, 2: 25–52.

Schroder, Kim Christian, and Michael Skovmond. 1992. "Introduction." *Media Cultures: Appraising Transnational Media*. Ed. K. C. Schroder and M. Skovmond (London and New York: Routledge).

Schudson, Michael. 1994. "Culture and the Integration of National Societies." In *The Sociology of Culture*. Ed. Diane Crane. Cambridge and Oxford: Blackwell.

Sepstrup, Preben. 1990. *Transnationalization of Television in Western Europe*. Academic Research Monograph 5. London: John Libbey.

Shohat, Ella/Robert Stam. 1994. *Unthinking Eurocentrism: Multiculturalism and the Media*. London and New York: Routledge.

Sinclair, John, Elizabeth Jacka, and Stuart Cunningham, eds. 1996. *New Patterns in Global Television*. Oxford and New York: Oxford University Press.

Sjogren, Olle. 1992. "The Swedish Star-Spangled Banner: An Essay on Blended Images in Film." In *Networks of Americanization*. Ed. R. Lurden and E. Asard. Abstract by Richard Holm, pp. 156–60. Uppsala and Stockholm: Almqvist and Wiksel International.

Stam, Robert. 1993. "Review Essay: Eurocentrism, Afrocentrism, Polycentrism: Theories of Third Cinema." In *Otherness and the Media: The Ethnography of the Imagined and the Imaged*. Ed. Hamid Naficy and Teshome H. Gabriel. Langhorne: Harwood Academic Publishers. 233–54.

Stern, Lesley. 1995. *The Scorsese Connection*. London and Bloomington: BFI/Indiana University Press.

Stringer, Julian. 1996/7. "Problems with the Treatment of Hong Kong Cinema as Camp." *Asian Cinema* 8, 2: 44–65.

Tatara, Paul. 1998. "Someone in *Dark City* Needs to Lighten up." *CNN Interactive* (10 March). <http://cnn.com/SHOWBIZ/9803/10/dark.city.review/ > Accessed Aug. 14, 1998.

Thompson, Kristin. 1985. *Exporting Entertainment: America in the World Film Market 1907–1934*. London: BFI.

Thomson, David. 1980. *A Biographical Dictionary of the Cinema*. London: Secker and Warburg.

Tomaselli, Keyan, and Arnold Shepperson. 1996. "Misreading Theory, Sloganising Analysis: The Development of South African Media and Film Policy." *South African Theatre Journal* 10, 2: 161–75.

Tomlinson, John. 1992. *Cultural Imperialism*. Baltimore: Johns Hopkins University Press.

Trinh T. Minh-ha. 1992. *Framer Framed*. London and New York: Routledge.

Tunstall, Jeremy. 1977. *The Media Are American: Anglo-American Media in the World*. London: Constable.

Varis, Tapio. 1988. "Trends in International Television Flow." In *Global Television*. Ed. Cynthia Schneider and Brian Wallis. New York: Wedge Press. 95–108.

Venkatasawmy, Rama, and Tom O'Regan. 1998. "Only One Day at the Beach: *Dark City* and Australian Filmmaking." *Metro* 117 (November).

Wasko, Janet. 1994. *Hollywood in the Information Age*. Cambridge: Polity Press.

Wildman, Steven, and Stephen Siwek. 1988. *International Trade in Films and Television Programs*. Cambridge: Ballinger Publishing.

Willemen, Paul. 1994. *Looks and Frictions: Essays in Cultural Studies and Film Theory*. London and Bloomington: BFI/Indiana University Press.

Williamson, J. W. 1995. *Hillbillyland: What the Movies Did to the Mountains and What the Mountains Did to the Movies*. Chapel Hill: University of North Carolina Press.

Young, Robert. 1990. *White Mythologies*. London: Routledge.

CHAPTER SIXTEEN

Shooting Back: From Ethnographic Film to Indigenous Production/ Ethnography of Media

Faye Ginsburg

We live in a world in which, increasingly, people learn of their own and other cultures and histories through a range of visual media – film, television, and video – that have emerged as powerful cultural forces in the late twentieth century. The development of low-format inexpensive video equipment, as well as cable and satellite technologies, has placed the capacities for image-making, once monopolized by media industries, in the hands of people almost everywhere on the planet. The transnational and intercultural spread of these new communication forms has stirred many twentieth-century intellectuals to consider their transformative impact on social life. Their arguments about the effects of mass media have ranged from the dystopic – suggesting the hegemonic reach of state and corporate powers into everyday lives – to the utopian – heralding the potential of new technologies to create electronic democracies and global villages. Only recently have these assumptions been measured against the lived realities of the production, circulation, and reception of visual media representations in different societies. New discussions are emerging, in and outside of academia, concerning the multiple ways that culture is encoded in film, TV, and video – whether dominant or alternative – and how these representations are interpreted as they mediate across disjunctures of time, culture, and prejudice.

This chapter is a response to the transformative impact of these developments on the field of visual anthropology, as media (including ethnographic film) are no longer simply vehicles for documentation but are now objects of social and cultural analyses. Without an expanded intellectual and empirical base, visual anthropology and the practice of ethnographic film are in danger of becoming atavistic and myopic, especially as images of other cultures are interpellated increasingly into the spectacles of cinema and the seamless flows of television. To resituate ethnographic film as part of a continuum of representational practices aligns our project with a more general revision of a number of fields – anthropology, cultural and media studies, cinema studies – that are concerned with the contested and complex nature of cultural production. This shift to expand our range, then, is one that can effectively address contemporary critiques of ethnographic film and revive its contemporary purpose.

The distinguished theorist and filmmaker David MacDougall suggests the term "intertextual cinema" (1997) to draw attention to the multiple positions of those engaged in the creation and consumption of screen representations of culture. Now anthropologists are expanding on that model in order to understand media in the context of broader social relations that are constituted and reimagined in film and video works explicitly engaged in representing culture. This in no way dismisses the value of the text itself, which often embodies in its own internal structure and meaning the forms and values of the social relations they mediate, making text and context interdependent. If we recognize the cinematic or video text as a mediating object – as we might look at a ritual or a commodity – then its formal qualities cannot be considered apart from the complex contexts of production and interpretation that shape its construction.

The expanded framework I propose might provisionally be termed the anthropology of culture and media, a denomination I see as invoking two often neglected legacies in visual anthropology. The first legacy can be traced to Jean Rouch (1975) and his ideas of shared anthropology, ethno–fiction, and *regards compares*. These were early important efforts to juxtapose cultural commentaries of Europeans and Africans, accommodating not only diverse views but also multiple formal strategies, including fictional, parodic, and avant-garde techniques. Following Rouch's legacy, it is easy to see how his early efforts connect with contemporary ones by Third-World and indigenous mediamakers, people who are particularly engaged in the repositioning of cultural authority and experience by using satire, humor, and performance to provide multi-layered commentaries on their own identities and on the dominant society.

The second legacy I want to invoke is the work of anthropologists (and others) who took media as a serious aspect of scholarly inquiry, beginning in the 1930s with Bateson and Mead's film and photography projects in Bali and New Guinea (1942). Later, during World War II, they and other American anthropologists studied Japanese and German cinema as ethnographic documents to help them understand differences in national cultures in order to assist the allies (Bateson 1943).[1] Hortense Powdermaker's 1950 ethnographic study of Hollywood was a prescient effort that left no legacy. In the 1960s, new possibilities opened up with the work of Sol Worth at the Annenberg School of Communications, University of Pennsylvania, and Jay Ruby and Richard Chalfen who established the first visual anthropology program in America at Temple University in 1974. Together, they argued that if anthropology was going to pay serious attention to filmmaking (as was occurring in the 1960s with the ethnographic film work of Tim Asch, Robert Gardner, John Marshall, and later David and Judith MacDougall), then anthropologists needed to attend to the cultural and social dynamics of the media systems they were engaging with, what Worth called the "shift from visual anthropology to the anthropology of visual communication" (1976).[2] It took nearly two decades for that transformation to take place.

1   Modes of Imagining

In 1993, in a comprehensive review essay, Debra Spitulnik invoked the insights of Stuart Hall[3] and other sociologically grounded media scholars to call for more engagement by anthropologists with "mass media as vehicles of culture, as modes of imagining and imaging communities" (1993: 295). Five years later, a fertile domain of study – the anthropology of mass media – had emerged, along with a general reconceptualization of anthropology that addresses our changing relationship with informants as our cultural worlds grow ever closer; as the social domains we need to track to understand contemporary lives increasingly are shaped by processes of late capitalism, requiring multi-sited research strategies (Marcus 1995); and as we imagine what our work can contribute to changes that affect people around the globe who are living "in the present" (Fox 1991). For many years mass media were seen as almost a taboo topic for anthropology, too redolent of Western modernity and cultural imperialism for a field identified with tradition, the non-Western, and the vitality of the local. As media are becoming more ubiquitous even in remote locales, an increasing number of anthropologists have recognized the necessity of attending not only to their presence, but also to the significance of film, television, video, and radio as part of the everyday lives of people throughout the world as well as visual culture, broadly conceived (Pinney 1998; Poole 1997; Ruby, in press). People who are studying these forms are studying media in sites as diverse as villages in upper Egypt (Abu-Lughod 1997), fan clubs in south India (Dickey 1993), and popular television talk shows in Bolivia (Himpele 1996). Indeed, there is an even broader range of work – looking at music, print cultures, photography, and cyberspace – that, regretfully, cannot be encompassed in a single chapter.

Following the lineage outlined above, a number of scholars link their work on media to visual anthropology (Ginsburg 1998; Banks and Morphy 1997; Hughes-Freeland 1997; Ruby, in press), often bringing a critical revision of that field through the lens of postcolonial scholarship, especially on ethnographic, documentary, and popular film practices, past and present (Rony 1996; Shohat/Stam 1994; Trinh 1989). Others focus on its counterpart in the production of a variety of alternative (Juhasz 1995; Downmunt 1993; Riggins 1992), diasporic (Gillespie 1995; McLagan 1996; Naficy 1993), and small media practices (Manuel 1993; Sreberny-Mohammadi and Mohammadi 1994) made by people who, until recently, were only objects and never producers in the enterprise of cross-cultural representation.

Another related school of thought that has stimulated research is closely identified with the journal *Public Culture*; it emerges from those interested in how processes of modernity, postmodernity, and globalization actually work on the ground, tracking the cultural effects of transnational flows of people, ideas, and objects – often mediated by film, video, and television – that are instrumental in creating a sense of a social world that is rapidly "respatializing" culture and power in ways that characterize fin-de-siècle cultural life. This scholarship builds, in particular, on the work of two key scholars, which addresses the mediation of the structures and processes of nationalism and consciousness: Benedict Anderson's insights into the role of print – and now other – media in the creation of the "imagined communities" of nation states (1983), and the extension of Anderson's Durkheimian frame (via Althusser, Lacan, and Jameson) to a broader notion of the social imaginary.[4] This work also owes a debt to Jürgen Habermas's articulation of the historical emergence of the public sphere, and the ensuing debates and critiques of that model articulated by Calhoun (1992), Fraser (1993), Robbins (1993), and others. More recently, the work of Arjun Appadurai (1996) has been influential in synthesizing their frameworks with anthropological concerns and methods. In his model, media are a central part of public culture, particularly important to the articulation of national and transnational with local processes. His influential essay on "global ethnoscapes" and the neologism "mediascape" points to the significance of the spread of film, television, video, and photography throughout the world and the ways in which satellite and video technologies transcend nation-state boundaries that were once sustained more easily through print and terrestrial television. He argues that the circulation of media accounts for the increasing significance of "the imagination" in the production of culture and identity in the contemporary world as:

> more persons in more parts of the world consider a wider set of "possible" lives than they ever did before. One important source of this change is the mass media, which present a rich, ever-changing store of possible lives, some of which enter the lived imaginations of ordinary people more successfully than others. Important also are contact with, news of, and rumors about others in one's social neighborhood who have become inhabitants of these faraway worlds. The importance of media is not so much as direct sources of new images and scenarios for life possibilities but as semiotic diacritics of great power, which also inflect social contact with the metropolitan world facilitated by other channels. (1991: 198)[5]

The significance of media as a hermeneutic for entering and comprehending the contemporary social world is especially clear in a number of recent ground-breaking projects that provide models for how programmatic claims about media can actually guide research. Lila Abu-Lughod's work on the production, circulation, and impact of Egyptian television melodrama serials is exemplary, tracking how these are intended to operate (if not always successfully) as social technologies through which modern citizens are produced and subjectivities are partially constituted. In one of her recent articles on the social life of these narrative forms as they move from producers to audiences, she demonstrates how, by staging interiorities through heightened emotional display, they encourage the embrace of individuality over kinship, a key transformation in the making of modern subjects (1999).

Finally, Pierre Bourdieu's framing of the field of cultural production (1986) – the system of relations (and struggles for power) among agents or institutions engaged in generating the value of works of art, while creating cultural capital for themselves – has been especially influential for those whose emphasis is on the institutional sites for the production of media work. For example, in a recent innovative ethnography, Barry Dornfeld draws on Bourdieu's model to understand the production of a public television series as a "cultural field" in which producers are also always prefiguring audiences in their work. This position, he argues, calls more generally for "rethinking and bridging the theoretical dichotomy between production and consumption, between producers' intentional meanings and audience members' interpreted meanings and between production studies and reception studies" (1998: 12–13).

One might think of these linked processes of the cultural production of media, its circulation as a social technology, and the relationship of mediated worlds to self-fabrication as existing on a continuum. On one end is the more self-conscious cultural activism, in which cultural material is used and strategically deployed as part of a broader project of political empowerment, providing a "third space" (Bhabha 1994) for indigenous and minoritized groups, as well as what some have called Third Cinema (Pines and Willemen 1989), often created in circumstances where political mobilization around issues of identity is incipient (Downmunt 1993; Juhasz 1995). In the middle range are reflexive but less strategic processes, in which the imaginative encounter with cinematic or televisual images and narratives may be expressive and/or constitutive of a variety of social worlds, such as the transnational links that video, television shows, films, and computer networks provide for diasporic communities (Gillespie 1995; McLagan 1997; Naficy 1993). On the other end of the continuum are the more classic formations of mass media, which require institutional framings and imply some dimension of social segregation between producers and audiences. Anthropological research on these mediations focusses on the complex and divergent ways in which national cinemas and television in Third-World settings operate, tracking the often unstable relation between intention and effect as these media are put to the task of constituting modern citizens through a variety of forms, notably in popular soap operas, telenovelas, melodramatic serials (Abu-Lughod 1993, 1995b; Mankekar 1993a, 1993b; Miller 1992; Rofel 1994; Salamandra 1998; Yang 1997), cultural programming (Hughes-Freeland 1997), and talk shows (Das 1995; Gordon 1998; Himpele 1996), and how these are intended and understood in relation to larger conjunctures and in a variety of settings from production to distribution to consumption.

Because anthropologists so frequently locate themselves in non-Western and remote places, our research offers not only a thick, vertically integrated, and multi-sited sense of the social life of media, but also engages with how this occurs outside the circuits of First-World settings which have provided an ethnocentric frame for much academic discussion of media until quite recently. Ironically, even those arguing about and against cultural imperialism (Schiller 1969, 1991) or researching the exporting of American culture through the circulation of popular film and television programs (Liebes and Katz 1990; Ang 1985, 1996) nonetheless presume the centrality of American media. In an effort to correct that, ethnographers and scholars in media studies are attending increasingly to the circulation of media in settings not dependent on Western hegemonic practices, such as the export of Hindi cinema (Pendakur and Subramanyam 1996).

At the same time, anthropological research on mass media reiterates the insufficiency of bounded concepts of culture as a way of understanding contemporary lives in our own or other societies. As Lila Abu-Lughod argued in considering the impact of Egyptian serials in the life of Zaynab, an older peasant-woman living in a peasant village in Upper Egypt:

> Television is an extraordinary technology for breaching boundaries and intensifying and multiplying encounters among life worlds, sensibilities, and ideas. . . . It brings into Zaynab's home, her conversations and her imagination a range of visions and experiences that originated outside her community. . . produced elsewhere and consumed in a variety of localities . . . . Even if it ultimately helps create something of a "national habitus" or hints of a transnational habitus, television is most interesting because of the way it provides material which is then inserted into, interpreted with, and mixed up with local but themselves socially differentiated knowledges, discourses and meaning systems . . . . Television, in short, renders more and more problematic a concept of cultures as localized communities of people suspended in shared webs of meaning. (1997: 122)

Scholars developing ethnographies of media usually begin with an interest in understanding questions generated by the phenomenon itself, often motivated by a desire to comprehend the popularity, power, and/or passion attached to certain kinds of media production and viewing (e.g. why is Indian cinema so popular in Nigeria?). It quickly becomes apparent in almost every case that answering these questions leads to an appreciation of the complexity of how people interact with media in a variety of social spaces and the resulting shifts in the sense of the local as its relation to broader social worlds becomes almost a routine part of everyday life. Understanding the social relations of media production, circulation, and reception in this way entails a grounded focus on the everyday practices and consciousness of social actors as producers and consumers of different forms of media. Their interests and responses shape and are shaped by a variety of possible subject positions: cultural, generational, gendered, local, national, regional, and transnational communities of identity requiring an increasingly complex and plural notion of audience. Indeed, these multiple identities may be part of a single social subject's repertoire of cultural resources, as is clear in this hypothetical example:

> An Egyptian immigrant in Britian, for example, might think of herself as a Glaswegian when she watches her local Scottish channel, a British resident when

she switches over to the BBC, an Islamic Arab expatriate in Europe when she tunes in to the satellite service from the Middle East and a world citizen when she channel surfs on CNN. (Sinclair et al. 1996: 25)

While our work is distinguished by an effort to track qualitatively and with the kind of cultural knowledge that enables what Geertz calls "thick description,"[6] the practices, consciousness, and distinctions that emerge for people out of their quotidian encounters with media are also always situated within the context of a broader social universe. To comprehend that reality, studies are increasingly multi-sited, tracking the various social players engaged when one follows the object – a television serial or film as it moves from elite directors to consumers (Dickey 1993; Mankekar 1993a), or cassette recorders (Manuel 1993) or radios (Spitulnik 1999) as they circulate through a variety of milieux. Whether in our own societies or elsewhere, ethnographers look at media as cultural artifacts enmeshed in daily lives to see how they are imperfectly articulated with (and sometimes created as a counter to) larger hegemonic processes of modernity, assimilation, nation-building, commercialization, and globalization, but in terms that draw attention to how those processes are being localized.

2   The Activist Imaginary[7]

Much of the work on mass media follows popular cinema, and television soap operas and melodramas, and interrogates how these apparently hegemonic forms have a more diverse interpretive life on the ground; another substantial body of research addresses counter-hegemonic fields of cultural production, most notably in the small but influential study of media – mostly video and low-power television – being produced by minoritized people as a culturally protective response to the introduction of dominant forms of mass media. For First-Nations people, this relatively new form of cultural production – which developed in the late 1970s in North America, the 1980s in Australia and New Zealand, and the 1990s in most of Latin America – was especially attractive to our profession because of its association with people in remote locations.[8] Such formations seemed particularly well suited for anthropological inquiry; small in scale and apparently a world apart from the mass-media industries that dominate late capitalist societies, they occupy a comfortable position of difference from dominant cultural assumptions about media aesthetics and practices, one that parallels the place indigenous people are meant to occupy in traditional anthropology. Indeed, the initial anthropological research on such work, which began in the 1960s with Sol Worth and John Adair's now classic study *Through Navajo Eyes* (1997),[9] set out precisely to explore the impact of cultural difference on the way the world is envisioned by teaching Navajo, who had never made or used motion pictures, to do so for the first time, without transmitting the conventions of Western production and editing, in order to see if their films would reflect a

301

distinctively Navajo film "grammar." Like much of (American) anthropology, the work was guided in part by the possibility that Navajo filmmaking might offer both a scientific insight into another culture's literal vision of the world and an alternative view – a kind of embedded cultural critique – of Western presumptions about the way media should look and how they might produce meaning.

From the late 1970s, indigenous people have had to deal with the threats and possibilities of mass media entering their lives, primarily through the imposition of satellites and commercial television, and have struggled to find ways to turn that circumstance to their advantage, a point that was effectively made by Eric Michaels who transported Sol Worth's ideas to the central desert of Australia where, in the 1980s, he worked with Warlpiri people to develop their own low-power television – what he called the invention of Aboriginal television (1986) – as an alternative to the onslaught of television introduced by the newly launched communications satellite. Michaels' work (1994) demonstrated how profoundly different Warlpiri video (and television) was from Western practices of mass media, from the complex ways in which production was organized along kinship lines (1984) to the centrality of sacred landscapes and slow movement that distinguished the formal aesthetics of pieces (1987a) to the ways in which Warlpiri watched (or were prohibited from watching certain images) and interpreted works (1987b). Since then, the work of Terry Turner with the Kayapo (1991, 1992) and Dominique Gallois and Vincent Carelli with the Waiapi and other Amazonian groups (1995; Aufderheide 1995) also shows how video is embraced as part of indigenous cultural projects of cultural revival, organized according to existing social hierarchies and very much engaged with aesthetic principles (such as repetition) that guide performance of ceremonies and rituals.

As anthropologists study the impact that media such as video might have on their communities, indigenous mediamakers are busy using the technologies for a variety of purposes, sometimes as legal documents in negotiations with encompassing states or to assert their presence televisually within national imaginaries. Such works present a kind of Faustian contract (Ginsburg 1991), or what Harald Prins calls "the paradox of primitivism" in which exotic imagery of indigenous people in documentaries about native rights, "while effective (perhaps even essential) as political agency, may pervert the cultural heritage that indigenous peoples are committed to preserving" (1997: 243). For their own people, these works are aimed at cultural preservation through the documenting of ceremonies and traditional activities with elders or creating works to teach young people literacy in their own languages; communicating among and between communities on issues such as how to confront loggers and gold prospectors; or long-distance communication among relatives separated by vast Arctic expanses.

Much of the writing and research on this topic has focussed on remote communities in the Amazon, the Australian outback, and Canada's Arctic, where media are produced and consumed primarily by members of the same community (although the work circulates to other native communities as well as to nonaboriginal audiences via film festivals and broadcasts). Indigenous people who live in or closer to metropoles also have been aspiring to be recognized as part of the broader world of media-imagery production and circulation, yet feel their claim to an indigenous identity within a more cosmopolitan framework is sometimes regarded as inauthentic, as if their comfort with aspects of modernity, including filmmaking, erased their legitimacy. Maori filmmakers were the first to break that barrier with films based on contemporary Maori life such as *Te Rua* (Barry Barclay, 1990) and *Once Were Warriors* (Lee Tamahori) which, in 1994, became the first indigenously made feature to become an international hit. Aboriginal Australian filmmakers Tracey Moffatt (*Bedevil*, 1996) and Rachel Perkins (*Radiance*, 1998) have both shown feature films at the Cannes Film Festival. Similarly, the success of the first Native-American-produced and -directed feature film *Smoke Signals* (Chris Eyre and Sheman Alexie, 1998) marked an extraordinary moment not only for its distinctive achievement, but as an index of the growth and significance of indigenous media. While such forms of cultural production clearly differ in scale and style from local community-based video, these mediamakers insist that there is no absolute dividing line that establishes one arena of indigenous production as somehow "more authentic" than another. From the remote experiments in low-power TV in native languages to feature films meant to appeal to native viewers as well as a diversity of audiences world-wide, these works are all part of the efforts of indigenous people living in a variety of situations to claim a space that is theirs in the world of modernity's representational practices.

This activist engagement with media, then, encompasses not only indigenous work but media being produced by a variety of other minoritized subjects who have become involved in creating their own representational framework as a counter to dominant systems, a framework that includes work being done by people with AIDS (Juhasz 1995), Palestinians in Israel's occupied territories (Kuttab 1993), or Tibetan Buddhist activists (McLagan 1996, 1997), to mention just a few examples. One might think of this creative and self-conscious process of objectification as a form of "cultural activism" (Ginsburg 1997), part of what George Marcus has recently termed "the activist imaginary," in which film and video are not only used by subaltern groups to "pursue traditional goals of broad-based social change through a politics of identity and representation," but also represent a utopian desire for "emancipatory projects . . . raising fresh issues about citizenship and the shape of public spheres within the frame and terms of traditional discourse on polity and civil society" (1996: 6). A particularly compelling instance for theorizing the intersection of media, culture, and power is Annabelle Sreberny-Mohammadi and Ali Mohammadi's analysis (1994) of the powerful role played by small media – audiocassette-tapes and leaflets – in the Iranian revolution that deposed the Shah, what some have called "the revolution of the television era." Similarly, Annette Hamilton's account of the role of media in the 1992 political crisis in Thailand as well as the "video crackdown" by the state, which, along with the import of American and Chinese video films, ironically undermined the Thai feature-film industry, demonstrates the often contradictory ways in which new highly mobile media technologies – video, mobile phones, cassette-recordings of international broadcasts smuggled in by airline personnel – are implicated in ongoing struggles between citizen and state (1993).

Some anthropologists have expressed alarm at these new practices, regarding them as destructive of cultural difference and the study of such work as "ersatz anthropology" (Faris 1992; Weiner 1997),[10] echoing debates first articulated by intellectuals of the Frankfurt School. Evidently, the question as to whether indigenous people can assimilate the technology to their own cultural and political concerns or are inevitably compromised by its presence still haunts much of the research and debate on this topic. Rather than passing judgment on the efforts of indigenous and other people to engage with new forms of expressive culture, a number of us see in the growing use of film and other mass media an increasing awareness and objectification of culture that are part of much larger processes of social transformation.

3   Objectifying Culture

More broadly, this work can be seen as part of a spectrum of practices engaged in the self-conscious mediation and mobilization of culture in the late twentieth century. As Daniel Miller argued in the introduction to *Worlds Apart*:

> These new technologies of objectification [such as film, video, and television]...create new possibilities of understanding at the same moment that they pose new threats of alienation and rupture. Yet our first concern is not to resolve these contradictions in theory but to observe how people sometimes resolve or more commonly live out these contradictions on local practice. (1995: 18)

This is not to deny that the presence of mass- and small-media[11] technologies in "cultural peripheries" is part of a global process of the penetration of media which has multiple and sometimes contradictory effects on local communities. However, the assumption that the center always dominates the so-called periphery too often has meant that "we get the history of the impact of the center on the periphery, rather than the history of the periphery itself" (Hannerz 1992: 207), a lack which has been addressed by much recent anthropological work on mass media. In the case of indigenous media, for example, one might read this not simply as an adaptation of Western visual culture, but as a new form of collective self-production that is being used by indigenous producers to mediate historical and cultural ruptures within their own societies and to assert their presence in the polities that encompass them (Ginsburg 1993, 1995).

Appadurai, addressing these kinds of processes in diasporic and migrant groups, suggests the word "culturalism" as another way to signify this kind of mobilization of identities in which mass media and the imagination play increasingly significant roles (1996). Such phenomena, Abu-Lughod points out, are produced out of unequal cultural encounters with others who may have pre-conceived notions of their interlocutors as cultural subjects (1997: 122). Object-ified and mediated, "culture" as such, especially for minoritized people, can become a source of values that "can be converted into political assets, both internally as bases of group solidarity and mobilization, and externally as claims on the support of other social groups, governments and public opinion all over the globe," as Terry Turner has shown regarding the work of Kayapo media-makers (1993: 424). Ethnographic studies of media offer an interesting and important perspective on the arguments of Anthony Giddens (and others) that one of the distinguishing characteristics of modernity is "the lifting out of social relations from local contexts of interaction and their restructuring across infinite spans of time-space" (1990: 21). Media practices are clearly central to these processes but not necessarily in the ways that we might have expected. It is this unpredictability and often vitality of responses that has generated much recent interest in how anthropology might increase our understanding of this restruc-turing process.

4   Parallel Modernities

A recent piece on the opinion page of the *New York Times* offered this tale of media, late capitalism, and the local declensions of globalization:

> John Burns, the New York Times New Delhi bureau chief, tells me a delightful story about his 70 year old Indian cook. Although John has four different satellite dishes on his roof top ("I'm practically running an uplink station" he says), he still couldn't get the World Cup matches off Indian TV. When he was complaining about this over breakfast, his cook invited John to come over to his house next door. When they entered, John found the cook's illiterate wife watching the BBC. I said, "What's she doing? She doesn't even speak English." The cook explained that a friend of his had started a "private" cable system and strung cable into his house along the local telephone poles – for $3.75 a month. "Then he hands me the television remote," says John, "and with increasing astonishment I start at Channel 1 and click all the way to Channel 27. He had television stations from China, Pakistan, Australia, Italy, France. With all my satellite dishes, I had only 14 stations." (Friedman 1998)

This anecdote depends for its effect on the assumption that both writer and reader are American and collaborate in the persistence of the smug, if occasion-ally guilt-ridden, assumptions that media technologies of modernity (cinema and television) or postmodernity (cable, satellites, VCRs, and computers) are securely in the hands of the West. What is meant to surprise in the story is the inversion of those assumptions, as an elderly Indian couple of modest means and apparently limited cultural sophistication have set up an inexpensive and effective cable system that gives them access to a globe's worth of television, while the rich American next door, armed with outsized technology, struggles to tune in to a soccer game. It is this world next door to the bureau chief, unanticipated by Western media theory, in which media circulates within and between non-Western countries, that a number of anthropologists (and others) argue has been ignored in contemporary scholarship, despite the strong programmatic interest in "transnational cultural flows."

Joining a slew of social theorists discussing the place of media in the emergence of alternative modernities all over the globe (Morley and Robins 1995; Sreberny-Mohammadi 1996; Tomlinson 1991), a number of recent projects exemplify the value of anthropological research on this topic. In his study of media in northern Nigeria, for example, Brian Larkin uses the trope of "parallel modernities" to account for those who are not mobile but who nonetheless "participate in the imagined realities of other cultures as part of their daily lives" through circuits in which Western media is only one of many choices that might "offer Hausa youth the choice between watching Hausa or Yoruba videos, Indian, Hong Kong or American films, or videos of Qur'anic *tafsir* (exegesis) by local preachers" (1997b: 409). The popularity of Indian cinema is evidenced not only by cinema attendance but also by a burgeoning local culture industry of *littatafan soyayya* (love stories), "pamphlet type books in which the imagined alternative of Indian romance is incorporated within local Hausa reality." The intense interest in the spectacle and plot of Indian films and their indigenization in these *soyayya* books as well as in locally produced videos (Larkin 1997a) offers Hausa youth a medium through which they can "consider what it means to be modern and what may be the place of Hausa society within that modernity" (1997b: 434). Similarly, in his study of youth in Kathmandu, Nepal, Mark Liechty argues that Bombay and Hollywood films, "teen" magazines, pirated cassettes, and interactive radio shows – the cultural economy of a transnational public sphere – provide the experience of modernity as a space of imagined possibilities contained within a commodified logic (1994: 194).

The concept of transnational encounters facilitated by mass media in the creation of new socio-political spaces also guides Mayfair Yang's recent work on mass media and transnational subjectivity in Shanghai, and what she calls a Chinese "traveling culture" created through interaction with Hong Kong and Taiwanese popular culture. She tracks how, over the last century, media played a part in transformations of the Chinese state in a series of "disembedding operations," first in the development of a new national community, then in the creation of a powerful state subjectivity. Most recently, she has analyzed the "reemergence of a transnational Chinese global media public and its effects on the modernist project of the nation-state" (1997: 287), constructing what Homi Bhabha (1994) has called "a third space" in which traditional lines of identity are blurred. She joins others in critiquing frameworks of cultural imperialism (Miller 1998), popular through the mid-1980s, that assume Western hegemony, thus often reproducing the Western-centric perspective they are critiquing. The

306

point, of course, is not to assume that power is lodged in the West, but to track how and why media are now so closely associated with power and its embodiment, such that states everywhere attempt to control the mediation of their own representations and that of others through regulation, censorship, and efforts to contain the means of distribution. In the case of China, it is not Western domination but regional/ethnic Chinese capitalist modes of power that are contesting the power of the Chinese state. Yang follows this process through the realignments of satellites, an analysis of programming, and the response of a workers' film criticism group in Shanghai to a popular television show entitled *A Beijing Native in New York*; through their identification with the protagonists who make the journey described in the show's title, they explored costs and benefits of mobility. As Yang points out: "While the nation and state continue to be imagined, now they must contend with the splintering of subjectivities into pluralized media audiences of gender, class, and rural-urban differences, as well as the emergence of a regional overseas" (1997: 311).

Like a number of other anthropologists engaged with mass media, Yang and Larkin are grappling with the effects of the increasing respatialization and privatization of cultural production and flows, querying when and whether the national provides an appropriate frame of analysis, and providing helpful periodizations of shifts in the mediation of state and popular interests. Without question, during the 1990s certain technological and institutional changes have had irreversible consequences. When broadcast television was tied primarily to a capital-intensive terrestrial technology, its range was more easily controlled and tied to state interests. The increase in satellites and cable, however, has opened up other kinds of spaces, increased privatization of media ownership, and created new geolinguistic markets for the reasonably well off, while video has become widely available to the middle classes and even the poor, providing an additional but less immediate means for the distribution of television products to diasporic communities as these media facilitate the expansion of imagined communities beyond national boundaries (Sinclair et al. 1996: 23–4). Indeed, research on video culture and other forms of decentralized small media suggests the emergence of a "new media era" that is more fragmented and diverse in its economic and social organization (Larkin 1997a), more characteristic of the expansion of informal markets under neoliberalism and the fluidity of late capitalism than the older forms of mass media.

In a number of cases, these new media are still tied to national structures of feeling, if not structures of state, as a number of scholars point out (Abu-Lughod 1993; Armbrust 1998; Ossman 1994). The national and the nation state, even under destabilizing political–economic conditions and massive technological change, are still central if increasingly contested constructs for understanding both the production and reception of media,[12] as a number of studies of Indonesian cinema (Heider 1991; Sen 1994) and television attest (Hughes-Freeland 1997.)

Despite the recent plethora of satellite dishes on Indian rooftops, India's national imaginary was still relevant in the early 1990s, as Purnima Mankekar argues in her book about the ways in which men and women interpret Indian state-run television (1999). In her research, she looks at the state's efforts to use that medium to create a pan-Indian culture, in which the discursive construct of "Indian womanhood" – a contested site through colonial, national, and post-colonial regimes – is central. She shows, for example, how women engaged with the popular televisual production of the *Mahabharata* to articulate critiques of gender inequalities as audiences (1993b), as well as how the producer, director, and star of a popular TV serial about a woman police officer struggled to sustain a feminist message within a popular narrative, and how these efforts were, in turn, interpreted. Working with the expanding middle class in New Delhi, she uses co-constructed life narratives (in relation to national narratives) to address how national television interpellates audiences as national and gendered subjects, and how a variety of subject positions – class, community, gender, age, and household position – mediate their interactions (1993a).

Other studies of melodramatic television serials in China (Rofel 1994), Egypt (Abu-Lughod 1993), and Syria (Salamandra 1998) offer helpful cross-national comparisons, suggesting that despite intentions to bolster national sympathies, televisual projects, even when sponsored by a tightly controlled state authority, can in fact foster debate and dissent. In Christa Salamandra's study of the reception of several different series produced by Syrian Arab Television in 1993 and 1994 for the popular Ramadan period, battles over who controls public representations of history became apparent in the diverse responses of Damascenes across the social spectrum, a reminder "not to assume that the presence of a state implies a strong sense of nationhood" (1998: 241). Similarly, Lisa Rofel's analysis of *Yearnings*, a seemingly innocuous 1991 Chinese television melodrama about two families during the Cultural Revolution, produced a national controversy in a post-Tienanmen world "in which intellectuals and the party-state are grappling with one another over the effects of the violent repression of intellectuals' overt challenge to state power," demonstrating the powerful constituencies and interests attached to different narratives of the nation (1994: 714).

By contrast, in neoliberal national settings such as Puerto Rico, where television is completely privatized, locally produced commercial programming serves equally as a vehicle of commerce and of social commentary, mirroring, in a sense, the way that advertising is part of everyday life. In her study of the reception of the popular TV show *El Kiosko Budweiser*, Arlene Davila (1999) argues that this televisual text – replete with the textures of quotidian speech, humor, and style – has, despite its blatant commercial sponsorship by an American corporation, become crucial to the visibility of local artists as well as everyday cultural practices, and as such has become a powerful signifier of Puerto Rican national identity. Her work suggests, once again, the complexity of categorizing by genre, producer, or sponsorship the effects media have on consciousness.

5   Circulating Culture

It is the increasingly evident necessity of linking media production and reception in broad and intersecting social and cultural fields – local, regional, national, transnational – that characterizes the anthropology of media since the 1990s. Despite that trend, ethnographies of media continue to be stereotyped as a narrowly empiricist version of market research (Sinclair et al. 1996) – questioning television-watchers in their living rooms about what they really think of certain programs, without placing them in wider structures or recognizing their complexity. These debates, it seems, have taken place more often among those in cultural studies or related fields who are attempting to use ethnographic methods (Bird 1992; Radway 1988) but sometimes in ways not recognizable to anthropologists, while anthropologists have been broadening their studies and carrying out the research for which others have pleaded (Ang 1996; Silverstone 1994).[13]

In most anthropological studies of media, audiences are varied and situated in a broad social field, which strategically includes both producers and audiences in the query as well as intertextual sources through which meaning is constituted. For example, in her study of Tamil popular cinema – an industry which has a remarkable influence in the creation of political celebrity – Sarah Dickey looks at the significance of film for urban poor of south India living in the small city of Madurai as a process of negotiation among viewers, filmmakers, film texts, and historical/political circumstances, and as part of a "vast system of popular literature, greeting cards and posters, clothing, fashions, gossip, legends, memories, and activities supporting the stars" (1993: 41), a world in which fan clubs, political activities, and popular opinions play a central role. Seemingly oblivious to this response, middle- and upper-class filmmakers, she argues, view themselves as imparting appropriate cultural ideals to what they regard as narrow and unsophisticated lower classes and unenlightened poor, while viewers "are active participants in the construction of an image that both represents them and allows them to escape who they are" (176).

Some scholars not only argue that producers and audiences should be encompassed in the same frame, but call for a radical rethinking of the very divide between production and reception and for more attention to the important but theoretically and empirically neglected area of distribution as a central process through which media helps constitute and reflect social difference, as power and status are signified through spatial and temporal dimensions of exhibition. Jeff Himpele, for example, locates his study of processes of distribution in the pluricultural metropolis of La Paz, Bolivia, where he analyzed the tensions between the circulation of transnational media and urban popular culture among different social classes and cultural groups. He did this by tracking the itinerary of *Bram Stoker's Dracula* (Sony/Tristar) from its debut in the spacious *CinemaMonje Campero* in the cosmopolitan Centro of the city as it moved up the canyon walls to the *cine popular* serving *cholos* (Aymara immigrants), while pirated video copies also proliferated, stratifying the sites through which Bolivians "emplot themselves in narratives about national development and modernity" (1996: 55). Additionally, Himpele attends to the crucial (but neglected) role played by film distributors themselves, whose "social imagination of the city clears the space for the traffic of cultural and financial flows across globally discontinuous spaces" but who also act as "timekeepers," staggering film debuts as a way to rank and separate social groups (53).

Himpele and others (Armbrust 1998; Hahn 1994) also point to the significance of exhibition sites – from the architecture of movie theaters as a diacritic of social class and modernity (or its lack) to the social space of cinema as an arena of social experimentation for young unmarried men in Egypt and Nigeria (Armbrust 1998; Larkin 1997b). Film festivals are also emerging as important sites for the analysis of new cultural formations (Lutkehaus 1995; Nichols 1994) or as an arena for claims to Indian modernity, as occurred in the Centenary Commemoration of Cinema in Bombay (Ganti 1998). These studies provide important insights into the relationship of media practices to public culture beyond the proverbial living room that has dominated reception studies as a site of analysis. They also offer an important counterpoint to Foucauldian and Marxist frameworks, which point to discourses of power as causative but fail to locate them concretely in the lives and motivations of social actors and the processes of everyday life.

6 Producing Culture

If mass media presented a kind of forbidden object to anthropologists in non-Western settings, the final boundary (breached only by Powdermaker's prescient study of Hollywood in the 1950s) was fieldwork in the social worlds and cultural logics of media institutions where "dominant ideologies" are produced, in our own as well as other societies, bringing new methods and insights to the territory already established by a small but significant body of work by sociologists of media (Gitlin 1983; Silverstone 1985), a tradition which Bourdieu has recently joined in his lectures and subsequent book on television (1998). Several recent ethnographies of media focus on a variety of institutional sites, including public television production in the US (Dornfeld 1998) and the use of a variety of media in public relations in the service of human rights (McLagan 1997) as well as capitalism (Davila 1999). Other projects focus on the world of cinema production, providing a rich set of comparative cases, from the production of culture in the Bombay film industry (Ganti 1998) to creation of film auteurs in Papua New Guinea (Sullivan 1993) and movie stars in Egypt (Abu-Lughod 1995a). Ethnographic approaches to these fields provide grounded analyses and critiques of how "technologies of power" are created and contested within the intimate institutional cultures, shaped by ideologies balanced between logics of national public service, audience appeal, aesthetics, and "the audit."

310

Ethnographies of cultural production open up the "massness" of media to interrogation as they track the ways in which structures shape the actions of professionals who are in the business of making representations of other cultures, and how structures of power affect image-making practices. Dornfeld's recent ethnography of a production unit at an American public television station is based on his participant observation of the production of a documentary project – a seven-hour cross-cultural series called *Childhood* which aired in the US in 1991 – from conception through production and editing to broadcasting and critical response. Given the television documentary's contingent relationship to the vagaries of "real life" and the constantly shifting status of the text at each point of its construction, he frames this genre as "mobile, argumentative and emergent." Drawing on insights from audience studies that look at reception as a productive act, Dornfeld argues for a "counter-reversal" in which we see television producers (and cultural producers more generally) as viewers, "not floating above society as so many approaches to the study of media forms seem to imply." Rather, he sees producers as particular types of agent, grounded in interpretive worlds through which they anticipate and accommodate the imagined audiences they anticipate will see the series (1998: 29), in this case an ideology of "televisual humanism," a paradoxical logic, he argues, which shifts authority to the presumed, predicted, and observed response of the "audience" (10).

A particularly interesting arena for studying these kinds of objectifying practice has been the use of public relations in spectacles organized by social movements for human and cultural rights to garner glamour and support for their causes. These intercultural negotiations with the media are often fraught with contradictions and cultural stereotypes on both sides, as McLagan elucidates in her groundbreaking study of the strategic deployment of Tibetan "culture" by Tibetan refugees and their Western supporters to mobilize political support (1997). Increasingly, these works underscore that oppositional logics are insufficient for grasping media practices; rather, our models must allow for the simultaneity of hegemonic and anti-hegemonic effects.

7   Complicities

Anthropologist and filmmaker Jeff Himpele describes how he "got framed as an attraction" for Bolivian television viewers in a rich reflexive analysis of the *Open Forum*, a network TV program (and base for a political party) in which urban Aymara testify to their problems and receive assistance in return. Initially hoping to do fieldwork there, he went with his Bolivian wife to the studio in La Paz where he met with the program coordinator Arturo who urged him to talk to the host of the show, Compadre Carlos Palenque. "Don't worry," Arturo advised. "It is the norm that observers also participate in the *Forum*." As any anthropologist would, Himpele complied. That evening, after seeing himself on television,

311

he recognized an ironic reversal that is one of the hazards of ethnographic work with media:

> Instead of the ethnographer representing culture for those back home, here was the local culture representation business fixing upon my difference in order to promote itself by announcing to people in their homes that a North American anthropologist thought it was worthy of study . . .

He goes on to describe a growing sense of terror that he had become like the show's host who exploits the difficulties of Bolivia's poor and indigenous people for his own professional gain. Himpele writes:

> My terror emerged because I recognized I was in the same moral sphere of engagement with the people I was studying. Is my ethnographic selection of social discourse from my informants any different from Palenque's selection and celebration of his visitors' cases and social identity in populist politics? What of anthropology's advocacy and concern for marginalized cultural processes, material inequalities, and social transformation? (in press)

Like Himpele, many ethnographers studying mass media often find themselves implicated in their object of study, in a relationship of complicity that places us increasingly in the same social universe as our subjects, if not in an activist relationship, then at times in an unanticipated reversal of authority over the representation of culture. Anthropologists have found themselves working as production assistants, extras in Indian films, or as momentary celebrities on popular talk shows (Gordon 1998).

Perhaps because of the intensity and self-consciousness of the concern with media's possible deleterious effects as well their utopian possibilities, most of us carrying out research on media with indigenous or other subaltern groups have an activist engagement with this work as well (Philipsen and Markussen 1995), as supporters and even catalyzers of activity, bringing cameras to communities and assisting in the logistics of projects (Asch 1991; Gallois and Carelli 1995; Michaels 1994; Prins 1997; Turner 1992) or helping to develop visibility, funding, and circulation systems for the work (Berger 1995; Ginsburg 1997). In a less direct but equally enaged concern, Abu-Lughod points out that studying popular television "is particularly useful for writing against the grain [of global inequalities] because it forces us to represent people in distant villages as part of the same cultural worlds we inhabit – worlds of mass media, consumption, and dispersed communities of the imagination" (1997: 128). Some have argued that these projects go beyond advocacy as authorial relations are reversed and "the anthropologist's voice supplements that of indigenous people" (Marcus, quoted in Palattella 1998), underscoring the ways in which we are increasingly complicit with our subjects when engaged with such material. In any case, increasingly we find ourselves jointly engaged in the project of objectifying and representing culture. This relationship grows even more complex as anthropologists (and fellow travelers) are beginning to study cyberspace (McLagan 1996), a site of sociality in which the research takes place (in part) through the medium of study itself.

One can see a trajectory in the theorizing of the relationship between culture and media over the last half century as the objectification of the category of culture becomes ever more widespread and the observer becomes increasingly implicated as a participant. In the early work on mass media, culture operated as a kind of unconscious Durkheimian indicator of the national, which was interpreted in metaphors of personality types in the work of Mead, Bateson, and others in the 1950s. When, in the 1990s, anthropologists began to turn their attention to film and television once again, they looked at media not so much as a reductive mirror but as a social force in which culture is a resource in struggles for hegemony over representation, from efforts to shore up state control over television to the development of the Third Cinema movement that was part of a global anti-colonial project. Most recently, this scholarship is helping us to rethink abstract notions such as globalization, to see how new technologies and economies of late modernity are being framed both by "the new international division of cultural labor" (Miller 1998) and practices on the ground (or rooftops as satellite dishes proliferate!), as people at every end of the social spectrum – from Rupert Murdoch's STAR TV to the videographers in Hmong communities dispersed across the globe – are engaging with mediascapes that increasingly escape the control of national political structures, rearranging the ways in which cultural formations are spatialized and imagined in the process. For many social theorists interested in media as a site for either social possibilities or cultural decay, the question is still open as to whether even alternative media practices inevitably "eat their young" because of the impossibility of escaping the discursive and institutional structures that even small media require or whether they can be summoned for more utopian projects. While the lack of resolution is undoubtedly healthy for intellectual debate, an unanticipated dimension of continued research during an era of ever-widening penetration and availability of media is the way in which we are increasingly implicated in the representational practices of those we study, a social fact that brings absolute and welcome closure to the tendency of anthropology to distance its objects of study in time and space (Fabian 1983).

Anthropologists at last are coming to terms with the inescapable presence of media as a contemporary cultural force engaged with the mediation of hegemonic forms and resistance to them; the growth and transnational circulation of public culture; the creation of national and activist social imaginaries with the development of media as new arenas for political expression and the production of identity. Such research offers a salutory effect on anthropology as well as media studies, opening up new questions regarding the production and circulation of film and electronic media throughout the world, in non-Western as well as Western societies, potentially resituating the "looking relations" (Gaines 1988) that take place between cultures and across boundaries of inequality.

313

Notes

Thanks to Toby Miller and Bob Stam for their editorial guidance, and numerous colleagues for their helpful readings of various drafts of this chapter, including Lila Abu-Lughod, Georgina Born, Brian Larkin, Meg McLagan, and Debra Spitulnik; and to Jeremy McClancy for catalyzing this piece in the first place.

1   During and after World War II, Margaret Mead and Gregory Bateson, as well as a number of other American anthropologists, were summoned by the US government to study Japanese and German cinema in order to help the allied effort. In order to carry out their assignment to report on "national character traits" and lacking the opportunity of doing foreign fieldwork during the war, these anthropologists used whatever data were available to them, in particular looking at popular cinema and political propaganda made available through the Museum of Modern Art and the Library of Congress, as well as interviews with expatriate populations who were living in the US. The most well-known results of this period were Ruth Benedict's best-selling book on Japanese culture, *The Chrysanthemum and the Sword* (1946) and Gregory Bateson's provocative psychoanalytically inclined analyses of a popular German propaganda film *Hitlerjunge Quex* (Bateson 1943). Research on the relationship between films and national culture continued after the war in Columbia University's Research in Contemporary Cultures Project initiated by Benedict and later directed by Mead. A collection of studies edited by Margaret Mead and Rhoda Metraux, aptly named *The Study of Culture at a Distance* (1953), was the main published work from this project, including analyses of Italian, French, Cantonese, and Soviet films.

2   Sol Worth's approach, developed in the 1970s, reflected the theoretical preoccupations of that time with structural semiotics and ethnoscience. Although he also developed an interest in the political economy and global reach of media, Worth's focus on the anthropology of visual communication looked primarily at how films made by any group of people could provide visual maps of world-views and cognitive categories, serving as a kind of window onto the native's point of view. Later, influenced by Worth's ideas and efforts, Jay Ruby, along with Worth's student Richard Chalfen, initiated the first Masters in Visual Anthropology in the US at Temple University, with a focus on culture and communication which included the social uses and cultural meanings of film, television, video, and photography.

3   Hall argues that as the mass media "have progressively *colonized* the cultural and ideological sphere" they increasingly provide "a basis on which groups construct an 'image' of the lives, and accomplishment meanings, practices, and values of *other* groups and classes" as well as "the images, representations and ideas around which the social totality . . . can be coherently grasped as a *whole*."

4   See a useful discussion of the concept of the imaginary in Lilley 1993.

5   In his 1996 edited volume *Connected: Engagements with Media*, George Marcus also focusses on electronic and visual media of various kinds and how they operate increasingly as "a direct and intimate complement to the self and self-capacity."

6   For an excellent discussion of how the notion of "thick description" enters into ethnographies of mass media, see Abu-Lughod 1997.

314

7   For a fuller accounting of this term, see Marcus 1996.
8   While "indigenous" can index a social formation "native" to a particular area (e.g. *I Love Lucy* is "indigenous" to America), I use it here in the strict sense of the term, as interchangeable with the neologism "First Peoples" to indicate the original inhabitants of areas later colonized by settler states (Australia, United States, New Zealand, Canada, most of Latin America). These people, an estimated 5 per cent of the world's population, are struggling to sustain their own identities and claims to culture and land, surviving as internal colonies within encompassing nation states. As Prins elaborates: "It is this condition of precarious survival that all indigenous peoples, regardless of their cultural differences, have in common. Shared dangers of physical extermination (genocide), political subordination, forced assimilation, and cultural repression (ethnocide) unite these culturally disparate groups as a global commonality known as the Fourth World" (1997: 245).
9   Visual anthropologist Richard Chalfen, who was a research assistant on the original research team in 1966, updated the book for the new 1997 edition, providing a thorough discussion of the importance of the Navajo project and a critical assessment of the reactions to it.
10 For the debates on this see the spring 1997 issue of *Current Anthropology* and the spring 1998 issue of *Lingua Franca*.
11 Sreberny-Mohammadi and Mohammadi (1994) use the term "small media" to refer to technologies such as video- and audiocassettes, photocopiers, faxes, and computers, which differ from older "big" mass media of cinema, television, and radio stations.
12 As Abu-Lughod argued in 1993 in the introduction to a special issue of *Public Culture* entitled "Screening Politics in a World of Nations": "While the movement of television programs across national boundaries should not be ignored, the nation-state remains crucial for the deployment of mass media . . . the locus of articulation of broadcasting policies and decisions and is the context in which viewers consume and interpret television programs."
13 Audience studies, launched by Janice Radway (1984) and David Morley (1980), opened an important new arena for research and understanding the complex effects of media, a trend developed in a number of key studies, ranging from the response of culturally diverse viewers for exported American television shows (Liebes and Katz 1990; Ang 1985) to the place of television in the construction of "the nation" (and other abstractions) in everyday life (Morley 1986; Silverstone 1994) to the creativity of an appropriative and irreverent female fan culture for television shows such as *Star Trek* and in the very construction of the notion of audience on the part of media industries (Ang 1996).

References

Abu-Lughod, Lila. 1993. "Finding a Place for Islam: Egyptian Television Serials and the National Interest." *Public Culture* 5, 3 (spring): 493–514.
——. 1995a. "Movie Stars and Islamic Moralism in Egypt." *Social Text* 42 (spring): 53–67.

——. 1995b. "The Objects of Soap Opera: Egyptian Television and the Cultural Politics of Modernity." In *Worlds Apart: Modernity Through the Prism of the Local*. Ed. Daniel Miller. London: Routledge. 190–210.

——. 1997. "The Interpretation of Culture(s) after Television." *Representations* 59: 109–33.

——. 1999. "Egyptian Melodrama and Postcolonial Difference." In *Questions of Modernity*. Ed. Tim Mitchell. Minneapolis: University of Minnesota Press.

Anderson, Benedict. 1983. *Imagined Communities: Reflections on the Origin and Spread of Nationalism*. London: Verso.

Ang, Ien. 1985. *Watching Dallas: Soap Opera and the Melodramatic Imagination*. London and New York: Methuen.

——. 1996. *Living Room Wars: Rethinking Media Audiences for a Postmodern World*. London: Routledge.

Appadurai, Arjun. 1991. "Global Ethnoscapes: Notes and Queries for a Transnational Anthropology." In *Recapturing Anthropology*. Ed. Richard Fox. Santa Fe: School of American Research Press. 191–210.

——. 1996. *Modernity at Large: Cultural Dimensions of Globalization*. Minneapolis: University of Minnesota Press.

Armbrust, Walter. 1998. "When the Lights Go Down in Cairo: Cinema as Secular Ritual." *Visual Anthropology* (special issue on visual culture in the Middle East, edited by Walter Armbrust) 10, 2–4: 413–41.

Asch, Timothy. 1991. "The Story We Now Want to Hear is Not Ours to Tell – Relinquishing Control Over Representation: Toward Sharing Visual Communication Skills with the Yanomamo." *Visual Anthropology Review* 7, 2: 102–6.

Aufderheide, Patricia. 1995. "The Video in the Villages Project: Videomaking with and by Brazilian Indians." *Visual Anthropology Review* 11, 2: 83–93.

Banks, Marcus, and Howard Morphy, eds. 1997. *Rethinking Visual Anthropology*. New Haven: Yale University Press.

Bateson, Gregory. 1943. "Cultural and Thematic Analysis of Fictional Films." *Transactions of the NY Academy of Sciences* (Series 2), 5: 72–8.

——, and Margaret Mead. 1942. *Balinese Character: A Photographic Analysis*. New York: Academy of Sciences Special Publications 2.

Batty, Philip. 1993. "Singing the Electric: Aboriginal Television in Australia." In *Channels of Resistance: Global Television and Local Empowerment*. Ed. Tony Downmunt. London: British Film Institute. 106–25.

Benedict, Ruth. 1946. *The Chrysanthemum and the Sword: Patterns of Japanese Culture*. New York: Houghton Mifflin.

Berger, Sally. 1995. "Move Over Nanook." In *Wide Angle* 17, 1–4: 177–92.

Bhabha, Homi. 1994. "The Commitment to Theory." In *The Location of Culture*. New York: Routledge. 19–39.

Bird, Elizabeth. 1992. "Travels in Nowhere Land: Ethnography and the 'Impossible' Audience." *Critical Studies in Mass Communication* 9: 250–60.

Bourdieu, Pierre. 1986. *The Field of Cultural Production*. New York: Columbia University Press.

——. 1998. *On Television*. London: Verso.

Browne, Donald. 1996. *Electronic Media and Indigenous People: A Voice of Our Own?* Ames: Iowa State University Press.

Calhoun, Craig, ed. 1992. *Habermas and the Public Sphere*. Cambridge: MIT Press.

Das, Veena. 1995. "On Soap Opera: What Kind of Anthropological Object Is It?" In *Worlds Apart: Modernity Through the Prism of the Local*. Ed. D. Miller. London: Routledge. 169–89.

Davila, Arlene. 1999. "*El Kiosko Budweiser.*" *American Ethnologist* 26, 1.

Dickey, Sarah. 1993. *Cinema and the Urban Poor in South India*. Cambridge: Cambridge University Press.

Dornfeld, Barry. 1998. *Producing Public Television*. Princeton: Princeton University Press.

Downmunt, Tony, ed. 1993. *Channels of Resistance: Global Television and Local Empowerment*. London: British Film Institute.

Fabian, Johannes. 1983. *Time and the Other: How Anthropology Makes Its Object*. New York: Columbia University Press.

Faris, James. 1992. "Anthropological Transparency, Film, Representation and Politics." In *Film as Ethnography*. Ed. P. Crawford and D. Turton. Manchester: Manchester University Press. 171–82.

Fox, Richard, ed. 1991. *Recapturing Anthropology: Working in the Present*. Santa Fe: School of American Research Press.

Fraser, Nancy. 1993. "Rethinking the Public Sphere: A Contribution to the Critique of Actually Existing Democracy." In *The Phantom Public Sphere*. Ed. B. Robbins. Minneapolis: University of Minnesota Press. 1–32.

Friedman, Thomas. 1998. "The Mouse that Roars: A Global Tale." *New York Times* (July 18): A11.

Gaines, Jane. 1988. "White Privilege and Looking Relations: Race and Gender in Feminist Film Theory." *Screen* 29, 4: 12–27.

Gallois, Dominique, and Vincent Carelli. 1995. "Video in the Villages: The Waiapi Experience." In *Advocacy and Indigenous Filmmaking*. Ed. Hans Henrik Philipsen and Birgitte Markussen. Hojberg, Denmark: Intervention Press.

Ganti, Teja. 1998. "Centenary Commemorations or Centenary Contestations?: Celebrating a Hundred Years of Cinema in Bombay." *Visual Anthropology* (special issue on Indian cinema) 11, 4: 399–420.

Giddens, Anthony. 1990. *The Consequences of Modernity*. Stanford: Stanford University Press.

Gillespie, Marie. 1995. *Television, Ethnicity, and Cultural Change*. London: Routledge.

Ginsburg, Faye. 1991. "Indigenous Media: Faustian Contract or Global Village?" *Cultural Anthropology* 6, 1: 92–112.

———. 1993. "Aboriginal Media and the Australian Imaginary." *Public Culture* (special issue on "Screening Politics in a World of Nations," ed. Lila Abu-Lughod) 5, 3: 557–78.

———. 1995. "Production Values: Indigenous Media and the Rhetoric of Self-Determination." In *The Rhetoric of Self-Making*. Ed. D. Battaglia. Berkeley: University of California Press.

———. 1997. " 'From Little Things, Big Things Grow': Indigenous Media and Cultural Activism." In *Between Resistance and Revolution: Cultural Politics and Social Protest*. Ed. R. Fox and O. Starn. London: Routledge. 118–44.

———. 1998. "Institutionalizing the Unruly: Charting a Future for Visual Anthropology." *Ethnos* 63, 2: 173–201.

Gitlin, Todd. 1983. *Inside Prime Time*. New York: Pantheon.

317

Gordon, Joel. 1998. "Becoming the Image: Words of Gold, Talk Television and Ramadan Nights on the Little Screen." *Visual Anthropology* (special issue on "Visual Culture in the Middle East," ed. Walter Armbrust) 10, 2–4: 247–64.

Habermas, Jürgen. 1989. *The Structural Transformation of the Public Sphere*. Trans. Thomas Burger with Frederick Lawrence. Cambridge: MIT Press.

Hahn, Elizabeth. 1994. "The Tongan Tradition of Going to the Movies." *Visual Anthropology Review* 10, 1: 103–11.

Hall, Stuart. 1992. "Cultural Studies and Its Theoretical Legacies." In *Cultural Studies*. Ed. L. Grossberg, et al. New York: Routledge. 277–94.

Hamilton, Annette. 1993. "Video Crackdown or the Sacrificial Pirate: Censorship and Cultural Consequences in Thailand." *Public Culture* 5, 3: 515–32.

Hannerz, Ulf. 1992. *Cultural Complexity: Studies in the Social Organization of Meaning*. New York: Columbia University Press.

Heider, Karl. 1991. *Indonesian Cinema: National Culture on Screen*. Honolulu: University of Hawaii Press.

Himpele, Jeff. 1996. "Film Distribution as Media: Mapping Difference in the Bolivian Cinemascape." *Visual Anthropology Review* 12, 1: 47–66.

——. In press. "My Tribal Terror of Self-Awareness: An Anthropology of Media Agency in the Bolivian Popular Classes." In *The Social Practice of Media*. Ed. Lila Abu-Lughod, Faye Ginsburg, and Brian Larkin. Princeton: Princeton University Press.

Hughes-Freeland, Felicia. 1997. "Balinese on Television: Representation and Response." In *Rethinking Visual Anthropology*. Ed. Marcus Banks and Howard Morphy. New Haven: Yale University Press.

Juhasz, Alexandra. 1995. *Aids TV: Identity, Community, and Alternative Video*. Durham, NC: Duke University Press.

Kuttab, Daoud. 1993. "Grass Roots TV Production in the Occupied Territories." In *Channels of Resistance: Global Television and Local Empowerment*. Ed. T. Downmunt. London: British Film Institute.

Langton, Marcia. 1993. *Well, I Heard it on the Radio and Saw it on the Television*. Sydney: Australian Film Commission.

Larkin, Brian. 1997a. "Hausa Dramas and the Rise of Video Culture in Nigeria." In *Nigerian Video Films*. Ed. Jonathan Haynes. Ibadan: Kraft Books.

——. 1997b. "Indian Films and Nigerian Lovers: Media and the Creation of Parallel Modernities." *Africa* 67, 3: 406–39.

Liebes, Tamar, and Elihu Katz. 1990. *The Export of Meaning: Cross-Cultural Readings of "Dallas"*. New York: Oxford University Press.

Liechty, Mark. 1994. "Media, Markets and Modernization: Youth Identities and the Experience of Modernity in Kathmandu, Nepal." In *Youth Cultures: A Cross-Cultural Perspective*. Ed. Vered Amit-Talai and Helena Wulff. London: Routledge. 166–201.

Lilley, Roseanne. 1993. "Claiming Identity: Film and Television in Hong Kong." *History and Anthropology* 6, 2–3: 261–92.

Lutkehaus, Nancy. 1995. "The Sundance Film Festival: Preliminary Notes Towards an Ethnography of a Film Festival." *Visual Anthropology Review* 12, 1: 19–29.

MacDougall, David. 1997. "The Visual in Anthropology." In *Rethinking Visual Anthropology*. Ed. Marcus Banks and Howard Morphy. New Haven: Yale University Press.

McLagan, Meg. 1996. "Computing for Tibet: Virtual Politics in the Post-Cold War Era." In *Connected: Engagements with Media*, Late Editions, 3. Ed. G. Marcus. Chicago: University of Chicago Press.

——. 1997. "Mystical Visions in Manhattan: Deploying Culture in the Year of Tibet." In *Tibetan Culture in the Diaspora*. Ed. E. Steinkellner. Vienna: Austrian Academy of Sciences Proceedings of the Seventh Seminar of the International Association for Tibetan Studies, Vol. 4.

Mankekar, Purnima. 1993a. "National Texts and Gendered Lives: An Ethnography of Television Viewers in a North Indian City." *American Ethnologist* 20, 3: 543–63.

——. 1993b. "Television Tales and a Woman's Rage: A Nationalist Recasting of Draupadi's Disrobing." *Public Culture* (special issue on "Screening Politics in a World of Nations") 5, 3: 469–92.

——. 1999. *Screening Culture, Viewing Politics: An Ethnography of Television, Womanhood, and Nation in Post-Colonial India*. Durham, NC: Duke University Press.

Manuel, Peter. 1993. *Cassette Culture: Popular Music and Technology in North India*. Chicago: University of Chicago Press.

Marcus, George. 1995. "Ethnography in/of the World System: The Emergence of Multi-Sited Ethnography." *Annual Review of Anthropology* 24: 95–117.

——. 1996. "Introduction." In *Connected: Engagements with Media*, Late Editions, 3. Ed. G. Marcus. Chicago: University of Chicago Press. 1–18.

Martin-Barbero, J. 1993. *Communication, Culture, and Hegemony: From the Media to Mediations*. London: Sage.

Martinez, Wilton. 1992. "Who Constructs Anthropological Knowledge? Toward a Theory of Ethnographic Film Spectatorship." In *Film as Ethnography*. Ed. P. Crawford and D. Turton. Manchester: Manchester University Press. 131–63.

Masayesva, Jr., Victor. 1995. "The Emerging Native American Aesthetics in Film and Video." In *Felix* 2, 1: 156–60.

Mead, Margaret. 1975. "Visual Anthropology in a Discipline of Words." In *Principles of Visual Anthropology*. Ed. Paul Hockings. Chicago: Aldine.

——, and Rhoda Metraux. 1953. *The Study of Culture at a Distance*. Chicago: University of Chicago Press.

Michaels, Eric (with Frances Jupurrurla Kelly). 1984. "The Social Organization of an Aboriginal Video Workplace." *Australian Aboriginal Studies* 1: 26–34.

Michaels, Eric. 1986. *The Aboriginal Invention of Television in Central Australia: 1982–1986*. Canberra: Australian Institute of Aboriginal Studies.

——. 1987a. *For a Cultural Future: Francis Jupurrurla Makes TV at Yuendumu*. Art and Criticism Monograph Series, vol. 3. Sydney: Artspace.

——. 1987b. "Hollywood Iconography: A Warlpiri Reading." In *Television and its Audience: International Research Perspectives*. Ed. P. Drummond and R. Patterson. London: British Film Institute. 109–24.

——. 1994. *Bad Aboriginal Art: Tradition, Media, and Technological Horizons*. Minneapolis: University of Minnesota Press.

Miller, Daniel. 1992. "The Young and the Restless in Trinidad: A Case of the Local and the Global in Mass Consumption." In *Consuming Technology*. Ed. R. Silverstone and E. Hirsch. London; Routledge.

——. 1995. "Introduction: Anthropology, Modernity, Consumption." In *Worlds Apart: Modernity through the Prism of the Local*. Ed. D. Miller. London: Routledge. 1–23.

Miller, Toby. 1998. "Hollywood and the World." In *The Oxford Guide to Film Studies*. Ed. J. Hill and P. C. Gibson. New York: Oxford University Press. 371–82.

Morley, David. 1980. *The "Nationwide" Audience: Structure and Decoding*. London: British Film Institute.

——. 1986. *Family Television: Cultural Power and Domestic Leisure*. London: Comedia.

——. 1992. *Television, Audiences, and Cultural Studies*. London: Routledge.

——, and Kevin Robins. 1995. *Spaces of Identity: Global Media, Electronic Landscapes, and Cultural Boundaries*. London: Routledge.

Naficy, Hamid. 1993. *The Making of Exile Cultures: Iranian Television in Los Angeles*. Minneapolis: University of Minnesota Press.

Nicholas, Bill. 1994. "Discovering Form, Inferring Meaning: New Cinemas and the Film Festival Circuit." *Film Quarterly* 47, 3: 16–30.

Ossman, Susan. 1994. *Picturing Casablanca: Portraits of Power in a Modern City*. Berkeley: University of California Press.

Palattella, John. 1998. "Pictures of Us." *Lingua Franca* (July/August): 50–8.

Pendakur, Manjunath, and Radha Subramanyam. 1996. "Indian Cinema beyond National Borders." In *New Patterns in Global Television: Peripheral Vision*. Ed. J. Sinclair, E. Jacka, and S. Cunningham. Oxford: Oxford University Press. 69–82.

Philipsen, Hans Henrik, and Birgitte Markussen, eds. 1995. *Advocacy and Indigenous Film-Making*. Aarhus, Denmark: Intervention Press.

Pines, Jim, and Paul Willemen, eds. 1989. *Questions of Third Cinema*. London: British Film Institute.

Pinney, Chris. 1998. *The Social Life of Photographs*. London: Blackwell.

Poole, Deborah. 1997. *Vision, Race and Modernity*. Princeton: Princeton University Press.

Powdermaker, Hortense. 1950. *Hollywood: The Dream Factory*. Boston: Houghton Mifflin.

Prins, Harald. 1997. "The Paradox of Primitivism: Native Rights and the Problem of Imagery in Cultural Survival Films." *Visual Anthropology* 9, 3–4: 243–66.

Radway, Janice. 1984. *Reading the Romance*. Chapel Hill: University of North Carolina Press.

——. 1988. "Reception Study: Ethnography and the Problems of Dispersed Audiences and Nomadic Subjects." *Cultural Studies* 2, 3: 359–76.

Riggins, Stephen Harold. 1992. *Ethnic Minority Media: An International Perspective*. London: Sage.

Robbins, Bruce, ed. 1993. *The Phantom Public Sphere*. Minneapolis: University of Minnesota Press.

Rofel, Lisa. 1994. "*Yearnings*: Televisual Love and Melodramatic Politics in Contemporary China." *American Ethnologist* 21, 4: 700–22.

Rony, Fatima. 1996. *The Third Eye: Race, Cinema, and Ethnographic Spectacle*. Durham: Duke University Press.

Rouch, Jean. 1975. "The Camera and the Man." *Principles of Visual Anthropology*. Ed. P. Hockings. Chicago: Aldine. 83–102.

Ruby, Jay. 1995. "The Moral Burden of Authorship in Ethnographic Film." *Visual Anthropology Review* 11, 2: 83–93.

——. In press. *Philosophical Toys: Explorations of Film and Anthropology*. Chicago: University of Chicago Press.

Salamandra, Christa. 1998. "Moustache Hairs Lost: Ramadan Television Serials and the Construction of Identity in Damascus, Syria." *Visual Anthropology* (special issue on "Visual Culture in the Middle East," ed. Walter Armbrust) 10, 2–4: 227–46.

Schiller, Herbert. 1969. *Mass Communications and American Empire*. New York: Augustus Kelley.

———. 1991. "Not Yet the Post-Imperialist Era." *Critical Studies in Mass Communication* 8: 13–28.

Sen, Krishna. 1994. *Indonesian Cinema: Framing the New Order*. London: Zed Books.

Shohat, Ella/Robert Stam. 1994. *Unthinking Eurocentrism: Multiculturalism and the Media*. New York: Routledge.

Silverstone, Roger. 1985. *Framing Science: The Making of a BBC Documentary*. London: British Film Institute.

———. 1994. *Television and Everyday Life*. London: Routledge.

Sinclair, John, Elizabeth Jacka, and Stuart Cunningham, eds. 1996. *New Patterns in Global Television: Peripheral Vision*. Oxford: Oxford University Press.

Spitulnik, Debra. 1993. "Anthropology and Mass Media." *Annual Review of Anthropology*, vol. 22. Palo Alto: Annual Reviews Inc.

———. 1999. *Producing National Publics: Audience Constructions and the Electronic Media in Zambia*. Durham, NC, and London: Duke University Press.

Sreberny-Mohammadi, Annabelle. 1996. "The Global in the Local in International Communications." In *Mass Media and Society*, 2nd edn. Ed. J. Curran and M. Gurevitch. London: Edward Arnold. 177–203.

———, and Ali Mohammadi. 1994. *Small Media, Big Revolution: Communication, Culture, and the Iranian Revolution*. Minneapolis: University of Minnesota Press.

Sullivan, Nancy. 1993. "Film and Television Production in Papua New Guinea: How Media Become the Message." *Public Culture* 5, 3 (spring): 533–56.

Tomlinson, John. 1991. *Cultural Imperialism: A Critical Introduction*. London: Pinter.

Trinh T. Minh-ha. 1989. "Outside In Inside Out." In *Questions of Third Cinema*. Ed. Jim Pines and Paul Willemen. London, British Film Institute. 133–49.

Turner, Terence. 1991. "The Social Dynamics of Video Media in an Indigenous Society: The Cultural Meaning and the Personal Politics of Video-Making in Kayapo Communities." *Visual Anthropology Review* 7, 2 (fall): 68–76.

———. 1992. "Defiant Images: The Kayapo Appropriation of Video." *Anthropology Today* 8, 6: 5–16.

———. 1993. "Anthropology and Multiculturalism: What is Anthropology that Multiculturalists Should Be Mindful of It?" *Cultural Anthropology* 8, 4: 411–29.

Weatherford, Elizabeth. 1983. "Native American Media Makers at Work." *The Independent* (April): 17–19.

Weiner, James. 1997. "Televisualist Anthropology: Representation, Aesthetics, Politics." *Current Anthropology* 38, 2: 197–236.

Wilk, Richard. 1994. "Colonial Time and TV Time: Television and Temporality in Belize." *Visual Anthropology Review* 10, 1: 94–102.

Willemen, Paul. 1989. "The Third Cinema Question: Notes and Reflections." In *Questions of Third Cinema*. Ed. Jim Pines and Paul Willemen. London: British Film Institute. 1–29.

Worth, Sol. 1972. "Toward an Anthropological Politics of Symbolic Forms." In *Reinventing Anthropology*. Ed. D. Hymes. New York: Vintage. 335–64.

———. 1976. "Margaret Mead and the Shift from 'Visual Anthropology' to the 'Anthropology of Visual Communication.'" *Studies in Visual Communication* 6, 1 (spring): 15–22.

———, John Adair, and Richard Chalfen. 1997. *Through Navajo Eyes.* New intro., afterword and notes by R. Chalfen. Albuquerque: University of New Mexico Press.

Yang, Mayfair Mei-hui. 1997. "Mass Media and Transnational Subjectivity in Shanghai: Notes on (Re) Cosmopolitanism in a Chinese Metropolis." In *Ungrounded Empires: The Cultural Politics of Modern Chinese Transnationalism.* Ed. Aihwa Ong and D. Nonini. New York: Routledge. 287–319.

CHAPTER SEVENTEEN

Psycho's Bad Timing: The Sensual Obsessions of Film Theory

Toby Miller

As we have seen, screen studies is a contested area, with a plurality of methods vying for authority. And it is sometimes ignorant, because when these methods are not debating each other, they rarely converse. Here, I look at ways of reading two films, *Psycho* (Alfred Hitchcock, 1960) and *Bad Timing: A Sensual Obsession* (Nicolas Roeg, 1980), to showcase different interpretative methods drawn from the humanities and social sciences and identify such potential conversations (the References section of this chapter lists some of the critical writing on these texts).

Psycho is canonical in both film theory and production, not to mention popular appreciation of Hitchcock and the horror genre. *Bad Timing* is peripheral by comparison. Nevertheless, it has inspired a wide range of interpretative proto-cols, which are "fresher" in film theory than those applied to *Psycho*; and it won the top award at the 1980 Toronto Film Festival. Whereas Hitchcock has come to be seen as the *voyeur par excellence*, whose spying gaze peeps in on people, Roeg has been described as "Hitchcock with the ice melted...an eye in overdrive" (Penman 1998: 85).

In each case, it becomes clear that a discourse about a film produced by a critic can *transform* the meaning of the object it supposedly seeks to *explicate*. One critical discourse may make the text incommensurate with that generated by another, despite the fact that they appear to commence with an identical object of inquiry. The purpose of this chapter is to encourage readers to utilize every possible method of understanding a film prior to pronouncing on it. To do less is to be satisfactorily neat, but to miss the meanings that accrue to movies as they move through time and space. After all, we are here to comprehend cinema, not just to trot out film theory as practiced within some priesthood of the elect.

1 Psycho

Prior to the release of Gus Van Sant's shot-by-shot remake of *Psycho* (1998), billboards across Los Angeles showed a hand on a shower curtain above the

323

following text: "Check in. Unpack. Relax. Take a shower." There was no need even to mention the film in order to promote it, so central is the original in popular knowledge. *Psycho* is, in this sense, very public property – not in legal–economic terms, but in intellectual ones. How has this come to pass?

David Bordwell looks at seven models for reading meanings into and out of Hitchcock's *Psycho* (1989: 224–48), in which spectators always feature centrally. For Jean Douchet (1960), the viewer of *Psycho* moves through three distinct spheres: the everyday world of office life, the problem of a mystery in need of solution, and finally a confrontation with base desires and craziness. There is also an auteur search going on here: Hitchcock is understood (thanks to his endorsement in an interview of intentionality as a hermeneutic key) to be encouraging viewers to feel terror and to believe in the occult. Robin Wood (1965) develops this auteurism. He positions the director as a great artist pointing to the human potential for degradation, specifically the Holocaust. The film encourages awareness of evil and the need to treat it. We learn this by identifying, as spectators, with Marion Crane (Janet Leigh) and with Norman Bates (Anthony Perkins) – her evident terror no more discomforting than his disguised evil, potentially secreted somewhere within everyone. Hitchcock always insisted that his wish in making the film was to produce a sense of "fun." Wood's auteurism requires him to address such a remark, so he reads it symptomatically, as indicative of Hitchcock misrecognizing his own artistry. Raymond Durgnat (1967) segments the text in three: Marion's story, her death, and the demise of the pursuing investigator. Durgnat says that the text comprises emotional fractures. It attacks the American way of life via critiques of mother-love, money-love, country-love, adultery, and marriage. Identification is conditional, because all the characters are prey to these malaises. By the late 1960s, spectators know what happens in *Psycho*. They are aware that Marion "has" to be punished for theft because of the Hays Code, and that the text's horror-genre visual cues are also cues to pleasure based on filmic memory. V. F. Perkins (1972) stresses the film's organic unity, which he illustrates via a New-Critical reading of the shower scene that focusses on symbolism: descending birds, beaks, and knives mirror the descent of Marion's life, as do windshield-wipers in the rain (an arc of meaning that is also called up in the sequence of events in the shower scene).

Raymond Bellour (1979) finds perversion in *Psycho*, using psychoanalysis and a notion of fractured classical film: the highway patrol officer's dark glasses are said to signify surveillance and fetishistic psychosis, as power is both expressed and unmasked. Barbara Klinger (1982) says the text institutionalizes women's sexuality as a problem of narrative and masculinity. It breaks formal and informal laws of monogamy, sexual ownership, and the monetary economy in ways that are exposed and then suppressed, as the narrative shifts from Marion's crime to Norman's. Leland Poague (1986) restores capitalism to the center: *Psycho* assaults the role of money in US life, as Ford motor cars destroy harmony, and Marion's NFB number plate is found to be the initials for Norman Ford Bates, which suggests a connection between the murderer and assembly-line capitalism's strangulation of individuality (Bordwell 1989: 239–42). Truly!

Writing after Bordwell's summary of these authors, Andrew Tudor sees *Psycho* as a response to and sign of the acceleration by capitalist economies out of post-war repression, toward a sex- and gratification-driven market economy. The service industries and personal identity stand at the apex of life. *Psycho* marks the violent, egregious side to this development, displacing the mad-scientist theme of 1950s proto-horror with a melodramatically inflected monster within, a perversion not of technology and science, but of the very essence of being. Tudor notes how unusual the film is for its time in the careful chronicling of violence and the sense that terror is constituted within normal life rather than imported from communism, fluoride, or outer space. This is doubly shocking in the context of a documentary-style naturalism, the city establishing shot and teletext information about time and place. This generic revolution displaces *grand guignol*, hyperbole, and invasion by the terror of the quotidian: mundane theft, driving, and psychosis. Ultimately, insanity is understood not via a coherent psychological or social explication, but as an everyday possibility. And the superimposition in the finale of mother's head on Norman counteracts the psychiatrist's "official" version of events, as if even custody and psychoanalysis cannot deal with the horror of the unconscious (Tudor 1989: 192–5).

Barbara Creed utilizes the theory of woman as both castrator and castrated to explain the film's theme of femininity as monstrous, simultaneously a threatening force of desire and a bodily testament to dismemberment. Horror concentrates on son–mother lesions and ties, generally theorized via oedipal repressed desire, fear of the castrating female parent, the abjection of emotions, and attacks *in extremis*. In *Psycho*, Norman is psychically and physically threatened by his mother. He must castrate her before she castrates him: so he kills her and then becomes her. Marion is equally important. She embodies these contradictions, and not just for Norman: consider the discussion of mothers she has with her boyfriend Sam. Marion overhears Norman's monologue that is played out as a discussion with his mother, in which he represents the voice of peace and sweet male reason and she is the mistrustful, misogynistic figure who hates women for their power over simpleton males. Mothers are associated throughout with birds of prey, as in classical mythology, when they would fly out as night vultures in search of the blood and flesh of children. In *Psycho*, the beak is a castrating device, part of woman's capacity to swallow and diminish maleness. The shower-scene murder might be understood either as an expression of the wish for mother to remove a threat to her hold on Norman's affections, or as a form of rape. Creed favors an account where mother is fearsome because she is the bathroom disciplinarian who polices washing the naked male and prohibits masturbation with the threat of punishment: symbolic castration. And Marion is sometimes thought to be engaged in self-abuse under that shower rose (Creed 1993: 139–48).

Clearly, film theory's "take" on *Psycho* uses two forms of knowledge. The first (close reading) relies on formal/stylistic cues and codes in the original text (generally as viewed on a television monitor via tape, with frequent use of the rewind function). This approach pays minimal or no attention to context: the means of production, distribution, and exhibition, the occasion of viewing, popular public response, media criticism, or cultural difference. The second form of knowledge (the human sciences), generally used in tandem with the first, draws on techniques from a variety of theoretical systems: auteurism, genre studies, Freudian, Lacanian, and Kleinian psychoanalysis, feminisms, Marxisms, and thematic criticism. As far as I know, postcolonial/multi-cultural critique has not thus far been deployed to highlight, for example, the unmarked nature of whiteness or symptomatic African-American metaphorizations in the text. Both close reading and the human sciences utilize the material sounds and images of the apparently originary film to underwrite their accounts, shoring up the theoretical apparatus (be it "understanding the text" or "exposing the suppressed 'other'") with reference to *Psycho*. Norman's psychosis becomes the critic's alibi.

2 Bad Timing

I examine film theory's account of *Bad Timing* for four reasons: first, the film disrupts the continuity system that characterizes Hollywood and most other cinemas; second, it can produce considerable displeasure in audiences because of its complex narrative and cultural politics; third, it connects psychoanalysis, detection, and confession, recurring themes in film theory and central to *Psycho*; and finally, it has been read from a variety of different positions, many of which are less central to orthodox film theory than those adumbrated above. In this sense, *Bad Timing* "performs" film theory diegetically as well as indicating how criticism creates its own object. The six discourses I enumerate with reference to the film are Foucauldian feminist theory, style and form, conversation analysis, mimetic desire, biographical criticism, and Jungian mythology. Each summary is brief and schematic, intended to encourage the reader to imagine a discussion between these discourses.

The feminist account comes from Teresa de Lauretis. It is especially significant as the film was initially picketed by feminists because of its depiction of Theresa Russell's character, Milena Vodnik/Flaherty (for example, cutting from sex to an emergency tracheotomy, or shooting from between her legs and over her thighs). The distributor, the Rank Organization, complained that the text was pornographic and removed its logo from British prints (Lanza 1989: 55), publicly deriding the film as "a sick film made by sick people for sick people" (quoted in Penman 1998: 91). For de Lauretis, though, *Bad Timing* is a much more revelatory, and hence potentially liberatory, text than such protests would suggest. She sees the cinema as a site where sex and desire are constructed through techniques of confession, concealment, and the drive for truthful knowledge about motivation, character, and occasion. *Bad Timing* problematizes the imbrication of power and sex to produce "unpleasure" by refusing the audience's "right to understand" assumed in the "classic realist text" (MacCabe 1981). This is not just a matter of visual complexity, but a demand that viewers consider their own voyeurism and will to know, just as they observe the will to know of the police, psychiatry, and military intelligence inside the film's story (Roeg referred to its capacity to expose viewers' "voyeuristic appetite for detachment" [quoted in Kennedy 1980: 25]). And the treatment of Milena is, for de Lauretis, emblematic of dominant male power structures: the law, the repressive state apparatus, medicine, and the psy-complexes. It illustrates their inner workings and mutual complicity in the regulation of women's bodies. Inspector Frederich Netusil (Harvey Keitel) and Dr. Alex Linden (Art Garfunkel), one a police officer and investigator, the other a psychoanalyst and suspect, are bonded, for example, when the film cuts between their two homes with *Fidelio* a thematic overture binding the two sites. And *our* desire to know what is going on in the text parallels Netusil's drive to hear a complete confession, itself a critical component of religion, therapy, and detection – the will to know. Some critics refer to *Bad Timing* as "the ultimate detective film" (quoted in Barber 1980: 46). The film is finally triumphant for Milena. The scar on her neck in the penultimate scene identifies her and inscribes her experience, even as she walks away from a helpless Alex stuck in a Manhattan cab. She is not *free* of the patriarchal laws and lovers that have sought to circumscribe her sexuality, but she *is* aware of them, her body a mnemonic of the damage they have wrought and the vitality of her resistance.

Where de Lauretis maintains that *Bad Timing* denies the viewer pleasure by preventing identification with its narrative or visuals, through the displacement of conventional informational flows and a chain of events and feelings, Bordwell sees this as a typical distantiating trope of art cinema, a convention of the genre well known by spectators (1985: 268). But there *is* something special in the style of *Bad Timing*: the film regularly cuts on the look, moving from an expressive, gazing face to a shot of something other than what was being looked at. This technique heaves us violently across time and space. The flashback scenes in which Alex ravishes Milena are managed via a cut on the look of Inspector Netusil, which conventionally suggests, through notions of the eyeline match or an interior monologue, that he is seeing or remembering what follows. But we know he was not present at the time. So we ask whether this is happening in Netusil's fantasy. That questioning produces an essential ambiguity, beyond the moral issues of individual characters or indeed the stance of the filmmakers toward their product. No one confesses, and we never receive an omniscient narrative perspective unclouded by this cutting on the look (King 1992: 174–5).

At the same time, the film's art direction offers some consistency, for example in the polysemous August Klimt paintings that Milena looks at in the opening sequence, repeated flashes of Egon Schiele's pictures of coupled morbidity in the background, and Milena's sense of color in clothing, which stands for the cluster of complex human forms she iterates. Similarly, the differences between Alex and Milena as personality types, and the decay she suffers, are signified by the comparative tidiness of their domestic spaces, while incessant smoking references

327

both tension and the dirt they share and spread around (Izod 1992: 109–11). Recurrent blasts of "Who Are You?" – by The Who – call up the issue of how Alex can truly know Milena (and why he wants to "know"/control her) as well as providing an aural match to sudden visual cuts. These recurring symbols build up the spectator's store of information about the characters, in sharp contrast to the film's unforgiving editing, which destroys any sense of etiology or flow.

In terms of its narrative form, *Bad Timing* fuses two stories. One lasts the five hours between when Milena swallows too many sleeping pills and Alex and Frederich debate the circumstances. The other diegesis is the five months when Alex and Milena are dating their way to obsession. The tumultuous meeting of these narratives is hinted at in advance. Milena reads *The Sheltering Sky* by Paul Bowles, a novel that details failed Moroccan romance and parallels her rejection (in Marrakech) of Alex's marriage proposal. There is a further parallel, of divided characters, torn between national, individual, and intellectual loyalties. When Alex tells Milena that "to be in between is to be no place at all," this applies as much to their geopolitical position as her marital status and his frustrated rage at her liminality (her last name refers to a Czech legend about a serpent of indeterminate power and form while *his* last name refers to the Czech national tree, a symbol of national strength and community). The visual corollary finds the camera panning between their faces in a university cloister. And the place where Milena parts from her ex-husband Stefan (Denholm Elliott) is literally liminal, the corridor owned by no one that marks the border of Vienna and Bratislava over the Danube. On this occasion, the literary mirror is a German-language edition of Harold Pinter's *No Man's Land*, symbolizing her entrapment between Eastern and Western men (Lanza 1989: 103–4, 135–6; Izod 1992: 107). For Roeg, her *liminality* drives Alex to apoplexy in just the way his *criminality* absorbs Frederich – each man pursues order and tidiness in his affairs, "pliant to their wills" (Roeg, quoted in Kennedy 1980: 25). This logocentric interdependence connects men whose subject positions seem quite distinct. Netusil complains to Linden of women that "[t]hey challenge our will to master reality." What is happening between the two men when these words are uttered?

I turn next to dialogue, exploring conversation analysis (CA). CA grew out of ethno-methodology. It has not been very influential in film studies, in keeping with the area's comparative neglect of speech in favor of narrative, music, and image and its bizarre ignorance of social theory (even while mobilizing the *nostra* of race, gender, and class). CA uses the concept of membership categorization devices (MCDs), utterances made by people to characterize their relationship with others. MCDs set up rules of exclusion, inclusion, and conduct. They function only as they are being applied and responded to, not as overarching categories, such as role theory, which stand outside their moment of utterance. David Silverman (1993) finds CA useful in understanding the interrogation by the police of Dr. Linden. Consider this extract:

Hospital Policeman: Husband?

Linden: no
Hospital Policeman: Relation?
Linden: no
Hospital Policeman: er boyfriend?
()
Hospital Policeman: look what connection do you have with her?
Linden: you could say I'm a friend

The authorities want to know about Alex's relationship to Milena. Each description they present connotes certain obligations and practices, which vary with the degree of commitment and closeness implied. The least clearly defined MCD is "boyfriend," which has no status in law or lineage. The hospital policeman pauses before naming Linden in this way, because there is a delicacy, an uncertainty, an ambiguity in that relation. Similarly, complex MCD work has to be done later when Netusil is interrogating Linden about ravishment.

Netusil: poor silly girl(.) how old is this girl?
(2.0)
Netusil: just a question
Linden: twenty-four twenty-five
Netusil: a nice age
(3.0)
Netusil: she had difficulty speaking?
(1.0)
Linden: she seemed normal (.) it sounded like a joke
Netusil: but it wasn't though
Linden: how do you know?
Netusil: if someone rings you and says they're going to kill themselves now that
     isn't normal (1.0) at least for normal people (.) would you agree?

How might we go about analyzing this as a piece of audio text? We could emphasize the pregnancy of the two-second space between Netusil's first question and his own metatextual response, which sets up an adjacency pair for Linden to complete. Or we might look at MCDs to see how the conversants establish boundaries, such as the distinction between what is funny and what is normal. Whereas Netusil offers abundant commentary, Linden restricts himself to empirical information and definitional remarks. He thereby denies any connection to Netusil or the experience that Netusil's interpretations imply, that Linden would be involved with a "silly girl" or himself be irresponsible in some way.

There are other options for analyzing this complicated male relationship. Consider the literary anthropologist René Girard's concept of mimetic desire. For Girard, desire is essentially imitative. Human subjects attract each other because of their desirability in the eyes of others. Stuart Cunningham uses Girard's work to examine the misogyny of Netusil and Linden, finding some interesting information about the controlling sub-text of such exchanges. In a scene where Netusil says women envy men's capacity to bend their wills and create culture through a transcendent self, he is both differentiating himself *from*, and connecting himself *to*, Linden's act of rape. We are presented with two monsters, doubling each other in refracted form. In this reading, *Bad Timing* becomes a series of triangular narratives between woman, boyfriend, lover, husband, detective, and psychoanalyst. Linden is engaged, enraged, and excited by Milena's relationships with her husband Stefan, her revolutionary Conrad, and her dead sibling. Netusil and Linden are rivals over the status and meaning of her body and their respective parental human sciences: criminology and psychoanalysis (Cunningham 1983: 108–10). As the investigator puts it to his logocentrically interdependent adversary, "We are not unalike." Just as Linden claims to know Milena but is forever uncertain as to her history and current activities, so Netusil wonders how good a detective he is (in a reference to Milena's husband being from Bratislava, "Netusil" translates as "he had no idea" in Czech). And there is authorial support for such a reading in the director's statement that the "Keitel and Garfunkel characters were the same man." Many of his characters masquerade as the other, like Linden quiet in mascara and Milena hysterical in quasi-drag (Roeg, quoted in Lanza 1989: 130).

What of biographical critique? This places the film inside the artistic, industrial, and psychological contexts of its key participants. Such an approach might find some continuity between Garfunkel's performance as Linden and his role in *Carnal Knowledge* (Mike Nichols, 1971) or between Keitel as Netusil and his charismatic, tortured figure from Martin Scorsese's *Mean Streets* (1973) and *Taxi Driver* (1976) (Cunningham 1983: 110). It would also note that *Bad Timing* was the third of Roeg's five pictures up to that time to feature a popular singer (Kennedy 1980: 26). In directorial terms, this analysis would locate Roeg at a turning-point in his career: after *The Man Who Fell to Earth* (1976), he was caught between the status of a cult figure and a potential Hollywood machinist. In a history of cinema, the film could be seen as his homage to and comment upon Carol Reed's *The Third Man* (1949). Each is set in Vienna, an urban atmosphere of deceit, desire, and spying. The search for Harry Lime is echoed when Alex tries to learn about Milena's past from an unidentified figure, while Netusil is very like Trevor Howard's Major Calloway from the earlier picture. It is part of Roeg's modus operandi to form composite characters that borrow from earlier actants and are hence always already intertextual (Lanza 1989: 56, 131).

Alternatively, we could look for the signified of the text in the psyches of its progenitors, notably Roeg. Joseph Lanza's method-mirroring montage biography of the director emphasizes Roeg and Russell's relationship as constitutive of the text's final meaning. The director's choice of her for the part is read against their later parenting and marriage. Russell becomes understood as a figure drawn to – and inside – Roeg's quixotic personality, her on-screen career producing bizarre portrayals of femininity across a series of features he directs. For Roeg, her youthfulness pulls at his life urges, encouraging him to look for himself in his other. As for Garfunkel, much is made of his account of the filmic process, how he felt that Roeg's careful evaluation of every gesture and the darkness of his role brought him closer to his own unconscious, and that, during the shoot, Garfunkel had an off-screen vision of his fiancée, Laurie Bird, dying. (Just before the crew returned to the US, she overdosed on pills, like Milena in the text.) But then we also have to deal with Roeg's statement about Garfunkel, who thought "he was really playing me. But I told him that he was only part of it. I challenged him to decipher when I was wearing the trousers and when I was wearing the dress" (quoted in Lanza 1989: 57–8, 148, 131). The director assesses the film as having "fucked up more people in my crew than anything else I've done. I know five people whose lives were turned over by that movie, including the cameraman, producer and executive producer. I'm kind of glad it got a limited release" (quoted in Lanza 1989: 58).

Lastly, I turn to myth criticism, derived from the legacy of Carl Jung, which adopts a semi-spiritual stance on the text. Such an approach cannot understand feminist concerns about Milena being unconscious for the duration of the plot, because it holds that scenes presented from her point of view have emerged as metaphors from her unconscious, aching to be pardoned by her husband for transgressing his will and their contract. In such an account, her strong desire for repentance animates the narrative. The scene where she rejects Alex's proposal of marriage is read as symbolizing the ties between libidinous energy and death: the characters are sitting above Marrakech's Place of the Dead, where a physical double of Alex appears among men performing dangerous rituals with snakes (Milena's danger signs, which are called up once more in the finale with Arabic music). And the interrogation scenes are driven by the Janus face of love and power, the shadows of one cast by the brightness of the other, and each perennially vulnerable to displacement. Netusil's work inclines him to exercise his will over people, but his other side finds expression in opera and family. Alex's profession is supposedly dedicated to healing but functions by exercising power over people. Locked together as they inexorably are, these characters miss the boat, the way out. Only Milena is ultimately transcendent, in ways that surprisingly connect this mythopoeic analysis to de Lauretis's account. Her trials and tribulations heroize her. She achieves an individuation only dreamed of by the men, purifying her conscious mind of father-love and overturning her need for Alex and his kind (Izod 1992: 107, 116–17, 120–2).

While some analyses of *Bad Timing* seem incommensurate – such as Milena's being unconscious either revealing the power structure of patriarchy or the mental structure of her guilt, Jungian versus mimetic desire, or role theory versus CA – others can usefully be combined to look at the operation of style, language, intersubjectivity, filmmaking agency, and the unconscious. Together, they offer rich and politically suggestive ways of knowing a complex film. The kind of conversation we have proposed in this volume can only occur if such meetings are staged as an everyday part of film theory.

Note

Thanks go to Terezka Carolina Korinek.

References

Barber, Susan. 1980. *"Bad Timing / A Sensual Obsession." Film Quarterly* 35, 1: 46–50.

Bordwell, David. 1985. *Narration in the Fiction Film.* Madison: University of Wisconsin Press.

———. 1989. *Making Meaning: Inference and Rhetoric in the Interpretation of Cinema.* Cambridge: Harvard University Press.

Creed, Barbara. 1993. *The Monstrous-Feminine: Film, Feminism, Psychoanalysis.* New York: Routledge.

Cunningham, Stuart. 1983. "Good Timing: Bad Timing." *Australian Journal of Screen Theory* 15–16: 101–12.

de Lauretis, Teresa. 1984. *Alice Doesn't: Feminism, Semiotics, Cinema.* Bloomington: Indiana University Press.

Izod, John. 1992. *The Films of Nicolas Roeg: Myth and Mind.* New York: St. Martin's Press.

Kennedy, Harlan. 1980. "The Illusions of Nicolas Roeg." *American Film* 5, 4: 22–7.

King, Noel. 1992. "Critical Occasions: *Making Meaning* and Film Criticism." *Continuum* 6, 1: 163–85.

Lanza, Joseph. 1989. *Fragile Geometry: The Films, Philosophy, and Misadventures of Nicolas Roeg.* New York: PAJ Publications.

MacCabe, Colin. 1981. "Realism and the Cinema: Notes on Some Brechtian Theses." In *Popular Television and Film.* Ed. Tony Bennett, Susan Boyd-Bowman, Colin Mercer, and Janet Woollacott. London: British Film Institute / Open University Press. 216–35.

Penman, Ian. 1998. *Vital Signs: Music, Movies and Other Manias.* London: Serpent's Tail.

Silverman, David. 1993. "Unfixing the Subject: Viewing *Bad Timing*." In *Cultural Reproduction.* Ed. Chris Jenks. London: Routledge. 163–87.

Tudor, Andrew. 1989. *Monsters and Mad Scientists: A Cultural History of the Horror Movie.* Oxford: Blackwell.

CHAPTER EIGHTEEN

Historical Allegory

Ismail Xavier

1   The New Status of Allegory

Since the early 1970s, when Walter Benjamin's ideas on modernity gained special attention in literary theory and film studies, the reevaluation of allegory – not only as a language trope but above all as a key notion in the characterization of the crisis of culture in modernity – has become a significant topic of research and cultural debate. Contemporary theory has established an essential connection between allegory and the vicissitudes of human experience in time. A sense of history as implying an uninterrupted process of production, change, and dissolution of meanings de-authorizes old conceptions of signs and discursive practices as able to produce universally valid and stable interpretations with an organic and necessary connection to the ultimate truths of life. Modern culture is haunted by the radical assumption of instability, condemned to explore the implications of the fact that the meaning of signs – especially new cultural contexts of complex combination of signs – can be forgotten, displaced, and twisted when faced with historical forces and power systems. This new awareness of instability only enhances an old perception of the problematic character of signifying processes, a perception that nowadays is taking us away from the lost paradise of transparent languages.

Allegory has come to the foreground, and one strong reason for its reawakening in modern times is the fact that it has always been the signifying process most identified with the presence of *mediation*, with the idea of a cultural artifact that requires specific frames of reference to be read, quite distant from any sense of the "natural." Moreover, allegory has acquired its preeminence in criticism because the accumulation of historical experience related to cultural shock, slavery, repression, and violence has shown its central role in the interaction of different cultural systems. The "conflict of interpretations" concerning basic values and canonic texts is a territory within which opposed traditions must confront or appease, struggle for their "purity" and domination, or converge to create a new configuration of values and lifestyle. Allegories usually rise from controversies. In ancient times, it was the debate on the legitimacy of mythic narratives in the Greek world that became a privileged occasion for the development of allegorical strategies of reading to account for a new conception of the function of myth in culture and society. And it was through a particular kind of allegorical reading of the Jewish Bible that the Fathers of the Christian Church set the ground for the new religion and built its conception of history (see Auerbach 1974; Pépin 1976). Later, in its search for universal validity and domination, Christianity submitted different kinds of symbolic system and religious artifact to allegorical readings meant to inscribe the Other within the Christian frame of reference. Similarly, in different moments of a multi-focal historical process, the dialectics of identity and alterity has provoked a variety of reading strategies by which new meanings were ascribed to old signifiers, where new cultural hegemonies were built on the ruins of defeated symbolic systems, in a process that largely obeyed, although in complex ways, the material power and the will of the winners of history.[1]

I say "complex ways" because not only particular cultural features but also overall cultural systems can outlive the material defeat of their subjects, as used to be said about Greek culture in the time of the Roman Empire, and as we are learning to say about the cultural features that came from Africa and, having outlived centuries of colonialism and slavery, have been showing all their strength in the contemporary Americas. Allegory is not a one-way process. If Christians allegorized pagan culture in order to dominate it, the "Others" could use similar strategies to give continuity to their own traditions – under disguise when the times were too hard, as occurred in Brazil when the African slaves maintained their religious traditions and rituals under the cover of Catholic saints and images (see Stam 1997).

Within this general process of change and confrontation, modern history, with all its accelerated transformations, has shown how the unifying principles that provide social cohesion of shared identity depend on cultural constructs – for example, the idea of the nation. Together with economic and institutional support, the nation is produced by narration and other forms of representation, implying a particular blending of historical ground and mythic accounts of past experiences (see Anderson 1983; Bhabha 1990). We are all familiar with the typical mobilization of allegorical narratives in which the lives of particular individuals are presented as figuring the foundational moment or the destiny of a group, or in which the recapitulation of the past is taken as a disguised discussion of present dilemmas.[2]

Novels from the nineteenth century[3] and films from our times – like Griffith's *Intolerance*, John Ford's *The Man Who Shot Liberty Valance*, Fritz Lang's *Metropolis*, Glauber Rocha's *Land in Anguish*, Fassbinder's *The Marriage of Maria Braun*, the Taviani Brothers' *Good Morning Babylon*, Manoel de Oliveira's *Non: A vã glória de mandar* – give us examples of deliberate national allegories. Dealing directly with present issues and experiences, or connecting past and present in different ways, they show the variety of allegorical strategies available to the filmmaker who wants to thematize the position of his or her country in human history. The representation of national destinies through an encoded storytelling process is a recurrent fact in film history. Both First- and Third-World films have offered us different versions of the so-called "overt allegory" – when the reference to national experience results from an intentional process of encoding. Moreover, the presence of national allegories in film history goes beyond the examples of overt and intentional encoding, as I hope the observation of films teaches us and the examples given in my text will show. Alongside intentional allegories there are also "unconscious" allegories, where the intervention of a "competent reader" is indispensable. Recognizing an allegorical dimension in a text requires the ability to perceive homologies, and national allegories require the understanding of private lives as representative of public destinies.

This issue of the reader's capacity to detect the collective and political dimensions beneath the surface of the storytelling process has been at the center of a recent polemic involving allegory in contemporary fiction. According to Fredric Jameson (1986), this kind of perception has been inhibited by the dominant logic of postmodern culture, especially when one thinks of literary production and its audience. For him, the separation of the private and the public spheres has produced, in First-World countries, a kind of literary fiction less concerned with politics, one that circulates in a cultural context where readers are not concerned with national questions. In contrast, he calls our attention to what he sees as the primacy of national allegories in Third-World literatures. Jameson's claims about national allegory rework the question of the "competent reader," stressing this intimate connection with specific reading practices and highlighting the role of diverse social structures that can encourage, or inhabit, allegorical interpretation. His controversial move was to posit a clear divide separating two dominant modes of literary production and interpretation, each closely corresponding to a certain stage of social and economic development. His provocative discussion of the connection between reading practices and society ends up, unfortunately, by presenting a schematic vision of Third-World societies and culture. The idea of national allegory as "Thirdworldish" has been shown to be a reductive image, one that provoked negative critical reactions, especially in the Third World (see Ahmad 1987).

My purpose here is not to give a full account of the debate between Jameson and his opponents; I take it only as further evidence that critics cannot discuss allegory without dealing with both the structure of texts and their reception within specific cultural and social contexts. The dynamics of expression (production) and interpretation (consumption) here become unusually complex, even in those cases in which producer and reader share the same references and are able to close the circle of encoding and decoding without much "noise" in their communication. Jameson's article brought allegory to the fore at a time when literary criticism had already familiarized us with distinctions between overt and unconscious allegory or, more generally, between the author's understanding of

335

his or her own text and that of the readers. The consideration of allegory always seems to lead us back to some of the major questions derived from the more complex nature of interpretation within the literary (and art) system implicated in a modern culture already aware of the debates about the "intentional fallacy" (W. K. Wimsatt) and the "death of the author" (Michel Foucault).

The interesting debates provoked by Jameson's polemical text form part of a more general discussion that has taken place not only in the English-speaking world but also in other contexts, usually involving the debate about the political efficiency and/or the aesthetic legitimacy of allegorical strategies when raising social questions, or involving the debate about the particular affinities between the modern ideas of nation and the allegorical mode. Here, I take Walter Benjamin's ideas and the recent debates on allegory and politics as central to my understanding of the status of allegory today, but I cannot limit myself either to Benjamin's formulations or to contemporary controversies. Although central today, Benjamin's notion is far from being the exclusive formulation of the problem, and one has to trace the history of allegory not only to provide the framework for clearer understanding of his original claims, but also for a better account of the current debates. A protean notion, allegory has been a perennial object of analysis, as Angus Fletcher pointed out (1970), one that changes definition and value according to cultural context. It is this multiplicity that I address here.

Conceptions of the allegorical process vary depending on the specific location of a text within the cultural process (one should add "but not depending exclusively on the geopolitical location of a text as Third- or First-World artwork"). The notion of allegory, in its modern form, has, on the one hand, taken part in the construction of "high" reflexive modernism in the making of complex works endowed with a sharp consciousness of language; on the other hand, allegory, in its more traditional forms, takes part in the routinized mass-media production, particularly within the tradition of popular genres – horror films, science fiction, melodrama, westerns, films noirs, musical comedies.

Keeping in mind all these instances of the practice of allegorical expression and interpretation, I will present here a brief discussion of some structural aspects of allegory as a mode of discourse, buttressed with historical information that helps us to understand its basic mechanisms and its most common motivations within the cultural process. I will deal with how allegories function and with what kind of demand most allegories try to answer. I will also address the internal logic of allegorical productions of meaning – the relationship between signifier and signified – but I will not be engaged in a technical debate on the synchretic semiotics of image-and-sound.

Analysts have already established the ways allegory can circulate through written texts, pictorial images, icons, and practically any kind of discourse, from artworks to advertising slogans and political speeches. In the twentieth century, cinema forms part of the very texture of our culture. It asserts values and produces meaning in a variety of ways, and allegory operates both in experimental non-narrative films and in more conventional film genres. When conveyed by a narrative film, allegory is not simply produced by a storytelling process involving agents and actions, but also results from visual compositions that, in many cases, establish a clear dialogue with particular iconographical traditions, ancient and modern. Depending on the particular editing strategy adopted, a filmmaker can privilege the horizontal, narratological, succession of shots to create specific space–time structures of action, or can privilege the vertical relationships created by the interaction of image and sound, or by the intertextual connections between the film's pictorial composition and cultural codes deriving from painting and photography. Therefore, reading films allegorically is always a multi-focal cultural gesture, requiring the capacity to explore what is suggested both by the horizontal succession of shots and by the vertical effects of visual compositions or cultural codes embedded on its soundtrack.

I begin with a description of different kinds of allegory, presented in connection with their historical origins and contexts. Then I refer to different examples of the allegorical process in cinema.

2 Allegorical Intention and Interpretation

The classical tradition lends us a notion of allegory – etymologically *allos* (other) + *agoreuein* (to speak in a public place) – as a kind of utterance in which someone says one thing but means another, or makes manifest one thing to allude to something else. This definition, however, is overly generic. It identifies allegory among the other figures of speech systematized by the ancient rhetoricians, yet it is nonetheless helpful in our contemporary discussion. The essential element implied by this generic notion is the idea of a gap between the spirit (meaning) and the letter (words), the sense that an utterance points to a concealed or disguised meaning beyond its apparent content. One finds here the acknowledgment of language as a nontransparent instance of meaning, a place of conventions and contextualized processes that mediate the connection between words (or images) and lived experience. Nevertheless, this short definition does not say anything about the structure of allegorical speeches, or texts, or images. We must therefore ask: what, within the text, signals those other meanings, and where can the reader find the indices of allegorical intention?

When we look for these signs or marks, we imply that we can clearly discriminate allegory from what is not allegory, and we assume that the allegorical interpretation on the reader's part corresponds to an allegorical intention at the source of the message. But this is not usually the case. The answer to my first question about the marks of allegorical discourse would be simple if one could conceive allegory as an intrinsic property of a text or image. But the nature of language is such that sometimes there is no sign of an allegorical intention that can be easily "fingered." Critical motions of polysemy and ambiguity make it clear that the chain of intention–utterance–interpretation is complex, creating effects beyond the control of the sender of the message, whatever the text's structure. Since we live within history, the conditions under which we practice reading change in space and time.

The dynamics that typify allegory undoubtedly allow for the identification of encoding processes. A poet, for example, creates allegorical effects by using certain techniques designed to be detected by a trained reader who shares his or her cultural background. But this hypothesis corresponds to very particular cases; it does not serve as a general rule of allegory in history. In the theory of allegory, these questions have been raised since the beginning, whether in classical Greece or in the Jewish tradition, and they were seen as intimately connected with the basic sources of allegorical practice. The Middle Ages established a tradition of underlining the difference between allegorical expression (the so-called "allegory of the poets") and allegorical interpretation (the so-called "allegory of the theologians"). In that period, the distinction between allegory as a writer's performance and allegory as a reader's performance was formulated to acknowledge the distinction between an utterance produced by an identifiable historical subject endowed with specific talents and methods giving concrete form to an intention, and utterances found in canonical and traditional texts, produced in the remote past, not from clearly identifiable sources, requiring specific and debatable techniques of reading.

Allegorical expression meant the particular rhetorical strategies set, among others, by Greek and Latin poets who encoded their verses through the controlled construction of disguised meanings and indirect language. Here allegory is a secular practice, one mode of poetic representation among others. Allegorical interpretation meant specific strategies of reading established around the fifth century AC by the philosophers who understood that the corpus of Greek mythology could not be accepted as literal truth or as a constellation of narratives referring to a factual past, but should be read as a body of disguised messages conveying ancient wisdom and the basic values of Greek culture. This new understanding – the separation of the spirit from the letter – was a symptom of a crisis in the cultural status of mythology. The old narratives were no longer seen as accounts of true facts or the real behavior of the gods. They were just the product of a storytelling practice whose value lay in the mythic conveying of the conceptual knowledge made tangible by the narrative. This crisis affecting the status of ancient narratives implied a dialectics of devaluation (the myths are only a fiction) and recuperation (even as fiction they carry lessons about the essential truths of the culture, contingent only on competent interpretation).

Taking visible stories and actions as figures for concepts, the philosophers inaugurated a technique of reading that saw narrative agents as personifications, as bodily equivalents for abstract thought. In this sense, the myth of Saturn eating his sons can be read as allegorizing the concept of Time. If Saturn is Time, Apollo is the Sun, Athene is the intellect, while Neptune is the deification of water, to mention some examples of what Jean Pépin calls the physical allegorism of the Stoics. But Pépin also tells us how allegory, as deployed by other philosophical schools, could have an ethical dimension, as when the myth of Tantalus was taken as an allegory of greed, Achilles as the personification of friendship, and Sysiphus as a rather peculiar personification of an always failing ambition to "stay on top" (1976: 145).

From ancient Greece on, this kind of reading has been performed in many different cultural contexts and based on many different conceptual frameworks. What is common is the idea that a story (conveyed by a speech, a written text, or a film) or an image (a pictorial composition, like Caravaggio's portrait of Fame, or the emblems of the Renaissance and Baroque cultures) embodies a concept, an idea, or a moral. Other examples of pedagogical narratives that feature personifications can be taken from the medieval tradition, like the battles of Virtue against Vice, of which *Psychomachia*, the narrative poem written by Prudentius, is a well-known example. In terms of film, D. W. Griffith's *The White Rose* (1923) reworks the principles of *Psychomachia*, this time as part of a modern story of sin and repentance. In this connection, one can also mention La Fontaine's fables, or the modern melodrama with its central conflict of Good and Evil. In modern times, the atmosphere created by the industrial revolution and accelerated technical developments in Europe engendered allegories dealing with the "dangerous powers" placed at our disposal by scientific progress, as personified, for example, by the figure of Frankenstein. Other fears triggered by the labyrinthian paranoias of urban life in the twentieth century found expression in a gallery of malevolent "geniuses" seen as the perverse embodiment of privileged intellect. Fritz Lang's Mabuse, for example, personifies the shadowy side of modern technology and urban development, thus inaugurating a series of "conspiracy" films that Hollywood cinema has been reworking throughout the century, with a gradual intensification of abstract, invisible, and relatively autonomous intelligence systems. In this connection, Fredric Jameson (1992) pointed out how the compression of space and time produced by postmodernity, together with the concentration of world power in a few "imperial" nations that can act on a global scale, gave a new impulse to what he calls "conspiratorial texts," schematic allegories in which totality features as conspiracy, involving complex networks of high-tech systems and a sinister "bureaucratic impersonality."

Apart from this less obvious allegorical turn fostered by the maze-like impression triggered by contemporary society, there are other kinds of more traditional film genre in which a character-oriented classic narrative produces a set of industrialized personifications – one might call them stereotypes. Here, simplified views of social problems, or reductive explanations of historical causality, place on certain characters' shoulders the burden of representation, of an entire class, or an ethnic group, or a nationality. The specific physical, psychological, and moral features of a single character are very often taken as belonging to a class (a worker and his or her personal qualities becoming the Worker), a gender (a particular woman becoming the Woman), or an ethnic identity (the African, the Latino, and so on). Stereotype, undoubtedly, has an allegorical dimension, since it corresponds to a form of representation through which a general idea (namely, a preconceived idea) about a social group finds its "illustration," or embodiment, in a single image or narrative specially composed to confirm that false generalization. In fact, stereotypical representations provide a good example of interpretations that result from a point of view located at a distance from the targeted subject. They symptomatically project the reader's own predicaments onto the person or group under observation (whether a class, an ethnic group, a gender, or an entire nation). Here the reader and his or her cultural bias – that is to say, the pole of interpretation – become the major instance responsible for the allegory.

Social groups can be seen as embodying moral values like Good and Evil. And certain historical scenes or faces can be seen as emblems (one could say allegories) of Reason, like those analyzed by Jean Starobinski in *The Emblems of Reason*, which focusses on the iconography of the eighteenth-century Enlightenment and the French Revolution (see Starobinski 1979). Many national allegories are based on personifications, as when a single character is taken as standing for the nation, like Maria Braun or Alexander Nevsky, or when the very idea of the nation is condensed in familial tropes, like Mother Russia or Mother India. And one can add to the allegorical realm all kinds of readings addressed to natural phenomena as expressing the action of cosmic entities understood as subjectivities, gods or goddesses. This very common, and sometimes unconscious, process of personification is very frequently identified with allegory per se (as the example of fables featuring animals suggests), but allegory, as a mode of representation, is more complex than this single mechanism, despite its position as the most popular instance of the allegorical process, often found in mass-media products.

Personification can emerge from a narrative or from a single image, and its detection in the texture of a message isn't obvious or always planned by the source of the message. Even this most canonical process of allegory involves different degrees of ambiguity involving the multiple relationship between expression and interpretation, the two poles of the allegorical experience that only present a term-to-term correspondence in restricted didactic fables based on commonly acknowledged similarities.

The most interesting instances of allegory are those in which the surface of the text either gives unsatisfactory answers to readers' interrogations or remains overly enigmatic, thus inducing a sense of recognition of the opacity of language and mandating the search for the concealed meaning. Apart from mythical narratives, we are all familiar with fragmentary utterances, apparently interrupted messages, suggestive juxtapositions of images that would seem enigmatic or "completely illogical" if our reading was restricted to what is literally there on the surface. The prestige of allegorical exegesis derives from its claims of solving a textual problem, of illuminating the crucial aspects of the text that are at the root of enigmas.

The performance of this kind of reading depends heavily on a capacity to perceive "analogies," correspondences that are not easily inserted in culturally acknowledged lines of causation, at least not in modern times. Not surprisingly, some authors see allegory as a mode of expression and interpretation more akin to a pre-modern mentality – from either the Middle Ages or the Renaissance, periods more attentive to the "linked analogies" and correspondences frequently at the core of allegory. While this suggestion of an elective affinity between the allegorical sensibility and specific historical times has its grain of truth, we should not understand the historical changes that fostered modernization as an evolution from magic to rational thought, correlated with the passage from allegory to realism. The "disenchantment of the world" – implied in the development of scientific thought and the overall process of rationalization pointed out by Max Weber – does not mean the end of allegory. Scientific theories – like psycho-analysis – create their own system of reference for the construction of allegories (and personifications) in order to solve enigmas and go beyond the surface of gestures or words, as clearly expressed in formulae like "father figure", Oedipus complex, or in the topology ego, id, and super-ego.

In cases where scientific theories provide systems of reference for allegorical interpretations of fictional texts, the acts of reading presumably do not involve any supposed allegorical intention. Such cases are normally instances of uncon-scious allegory, which cannot be seen either as an intrinsic property of the text or as the product of a writer's intention. Here the allegory results from specific reading strategies that, whatever their validity in relation to the text (or fact) under scrutiny, depend heavily upon the context of reading itself. In this sense, allegory comes to express the historicity of human experience and values, even when rooted in an impulse to achieve a timeless truth. Allegory, as a particular method of reading historical facts, or supposedly historical facts, tries to reconcile the imperative of "fixed truths" with the acknowledgment that time is an essential dimension of human experience. This method has engendered a kind of allegorical reading that has had a clear impact on human history in the last 2,000 years. I am referring to the rise and consolidation of Christianity by means of an original performance of reading addressed to the Jewish Bible in order to turn it into a set of narratives and specific imagery bearing the signs, the prophecies, of the advent of Christ as the Messiah.

Within Christian "figural realism," to borrow Eric Auerbach's phrase, two historical facts, widely separated in time, illuminate each other and show a specific connection that confirms the idea of God's design in history. The first fact "prefigures" the second, which is announced by it, fulfilling the prophecy inherent in the first. Moses' act of leading his people to salvation from slavery in Egypt prefigures the act of Christ who, through his sacrifice, saves all human-kind. This allegorical operation is also called "typology," referring to the "ver-tical relationship" established by the type and anti-type, complementary figures that occur in different moments of history but are the reiterated signs of the unfolding of a teleological process in time. What is essential in this Christian conception of allegory is its temporal dimension: we go from one historical fact to another, in contrast with the connection between a narrative and a temporal abstraction found in the Greek understanding of allegory. This allegorical read-ing opens up an entire set of relationships, beginning with the sense that the "cosmic order" endows human history with an internal logic that leads the succession of apparently disconnected events toward a specific final term – the *telos*. This conception will have many consequences in Western thought, especially in the development of a historical consciousness that opposes itself to the circular view of time in classical culture. In modern fiction, it will be present in many novels and films as a guiding principle presiding over the character's destiny, particularly in works in which Providers form part of the set of determinations shaping the unfolding of the plot, this hidden force that can save the heroes and help them punish the villains, assuring the final triumph of Justice. Canonical melodramas from the nineteenth-century popular theater and from industrial cinema, especially from the silent period, follow this guiding principle. The exaggerated appeal to coincidence in the overall design toward salvation becomes one of the typical marks of providential fictions that, even when covered by a tapestry of realistic presentation, reveal their allegorical overtone in the way they shape the characters' final destiny.

Considering the primary formulation of Christian allegory by the Fathers of the Church, we can see it as a modality of allegorical interpretation addressed to given texts produced in a remote past under unknown circumstances by unknown authors, texts that are endowed with a sacred dimension within the culture. Allegorical interpretations addressed to remote or sacred texts, whatever their content and context, respond to a demand for identity and continuity over time, revealing an impulse to "heal the gap between the present and a disappearing past which, without interpretation, would be otherwise irretrievable and foreclosed" (Fineman 1980: 49).

These examples suggest that whatever its method, the process of allegorical reading in the past involved an operation of unveiling the concealed truth, a sense that meaning had an origin in the past and the work of interpretation corresponded to a removal of the layers added by time, providing the conditions for the revelation of naked truth. In our period, different kinds of reading can be performed without the old concerns for the degree of consciousness or intention experienced by the supposed subject who is taken as the source of the message. In our cultural process readers are no longer searching for "intended" or conscious meanings, but for what the interpreter can say on the occasion of his or her encounter with the text, an encounter that cannot, however, be seen as only a dual (reader-plus-text) relationship, isolated from all kinds of contextual influences. If today the text is seen as acquiring different and sometimes unexpected meanings regardless of the intentions of the author, the dominant reading practices tend to inscribe it within a network of intertextual connections that also form part of the interpretation. The very nature of this process fosters allegorical strategies that refer the given text (or narrative) to a Master Code or Narrative taken as a key reference. In this sense, it is curious to see various scientific or para-scientific theories replace the Bible as the Great Code that readers take as the guide for interpretation. As pointed out above, different conceptual systems – psychoanalysis, linguistics, anthropology, Marxist social theory, physics, or biology –

can be the reference mobilized by the reader to interpret some passages or an entire text that can become an allegory of class struggle, or an allegory of the formation of the subject, or an allegory of language itself when allegory is set in motion by deconstructionist readings.

Given that allegory is not necessarily an intrinsic property of a text, one can ask whether it is still possible to discriminate between allegorical and nonallegorical texts. Given this question, Northrop Frye might claim that the structure of the text is "neutral" with regard to allegory. But this would be an unfortunate move. One might better acknowledge the importance of form and syntax with the condition that, instead of speaking of a text "with an allegorical structure" as opposed to texts "with no allegorical structure," one should propose the distinction between texts which, by their structure, encourage an allegorical reading and texts which, by their structure, do not encourage any special decipherment. In this sense, the more enigmatic a text, the greater its chance of provoking allegorical interpretations. Texts that give us a sense of incompleteness or fragmentation (the sense that something is lacking) are more susceptible to allegorical readings than texts that seem clear and satisfactory in a first reading. Indeed, Angus Fletcher's discussion of allegory implies exactly this line of opposition. On the one hand, he links the invitation to allegorical readings with incompleteness, opacity; on the other, he suggests that typically naturalist narratives, like those found in classical cinema, with a clear, amusing or easily read story-plot, are also entitled to allegorization. In other words, there are structures that lend themselves to a secondary reading more convincingly than others, but any text can be submitted to what Frye calls "alegorises," such as a move from narrative and images to ideas and concepts, because after all this is the canonical task of critics.

3   The Dialectics of Fragmentation and Totalization

Angus Fletcher also comments on the discontinuous nature of allegorical imagery. While discussing the "analytic frame of mind" into which allegory forces its reader, he reminds us that "any fragmentary utterance takes on the appearance of a coded message needing to be deciphered" (1970: 37). His contention implies a connection between allegory and incompleteness that goes beyond the modern configuration of the process, reminding us of the theological disputes derived from the lacunae perceived in sacred texts. The traditional conception of allegory as a text to be deciphered implied the idea of an a priori "concealed meaning," a conception that turned the production and reception of allegory into a circular movement composed of two complementary impulses, one of concealing the truth beneath the surface, the other of making the truth emerge again. It is this circular movement that Jean Pépin posits in his understanding of the dynamics of allegorical expression and interpretation. Pépin's analysis is more concerned with theology, a realm in which the "fragmentary utterance" is seen as something akin to an "intentional" disguise, necessary for the safeguarding of "truth." Sacred texts present various degrees of concealment in order not to be understood by the uninitiated, or their allegorical dimension is seen as fulfilling a pedagogical function, since the dissembling surface is understood as a stimulus to the reader, increasing the pleasure of revelation following an effort of decoding.

The encoding of messages, understood as a deliberate concealment, can present similar operational schemes, regardless of the motivation behind the allegorical strategy. Apart from theological motives, more pragmatic and less metaphysical motives often lie behind the production of disguise, as when the analyst needs to outwit censorship in a specific political conjuncture. Throughout history, the powers that be (religious or secular) have protected their interests by censoring texts and images, and allegory has been a frequent weapon against authoritarian rules.

In modern times, critics are suspicious of calculated allegories when they result in too obviously didactic fables from which the reader can easily draw a conventional moral lesson. And their objection to allegory becomes stronger when disguise and opacity are seen as merely a matter of rhetoric, without any special challenge or any difficult question at stake. Apart from those occasions where a clear political motive justifies this kind of allegory as a form of resistance to oppression, the effect of the encoded message becomes weaker, especially when the only obvious intention seems to be embellishment. Away from the immediate challenges of the political arena, the rhetoric of pedagogical allegory runs the risk of reducing art to a schematic but elegant illustration of a priori ideas, a piece which engages our senses to communicate worn-out ideas or abstract theories. Allegory as illustration becomes an exploration of terrains already well mapped, a confirmation of established meanings, which is precisely how the romantics saw the neoclassical allegory, given its subordination to conventional thought.

In defense of their own creative process, the romantics privileged the symbol, a form of expression that would offer a particular experience for which there is no theoretical system. For them the symbol epitomized an organic movement toward expression. The irreducible experience of the artwork would guarantee access to a truth which could never be grasped using other channels. In opposition to allegory, the symbol corresponded to a fresh and genuine intuition about experience. Untranslatable into concepts, the symbol had its own value and original meaning, resulting from a process that provided a direct expression of human experience in a revealing text, object, or image. According to Goethe, allegory takes us from the general concept to the particular configuration presented to the senses, while symbol takes us from the particular (sensible) to the universal idea, without the help of established conventions. This distinction can be seen as a reductive definition of allegory, conceived to fit the romantic strategy of defense against classicism; however, in its own terms it had enormous resonance in the aesthetic debate ever since its formulation in the late eighteenth century. Just to remember one example, Georg Lukács grounded his aesthetic theory in the romantic hierarchy of symbol over allegory in order to criticize the fragmentation of modern art. The incapacity for totalizing simply would be a new

344

version of the allegorical enterprise as one that appeals to transcendent principles to talk about social experience. In opposition, realism, as a form of representation, would be akin to the symbol (as conceived by the romantics) in its power to grasp the historical movement of society in its immanence, providing an organic and illuminating expression of totality. Given this formulation, it was not an accident that Lukács, in *Realism in Our Time*, written in the 1950s, engaged himself in a polemical dialogue with Benjamin's *The Origins of the Baroque Tragic Drama* (1916) (see Lukács 1964; Benjamin 1977). On the one hand, he acknowledged Benjamin's acute characterization of the baroque (and its affinities with modern art); on the other, he took the very applicability of the notion of allegory to modern texts as all the more reason to question them.

In our century, the Lukács vs. Benjamin confrontation has been one of the key chapters of the debate on modern art, and on allegory as well. And its point of departure – Benjamin's 1916 dissertation – was a seminal book for the aesthetic thought of the twentieth century. It combined, in a single movement, various critiques – of the symbol as conceived by the romantics, of the Christian teleology of history, of the secular version of the latter embodied by the bourgeois notion of progress, and of the reformist social democratic theories also based on a tele-ological view of history.

From Benjamin's reflections on baroque disenchantment and from his melancholy view of history as catastrophe, there emerges a peculiar theory of allegory, now taken as the primary expression of the temporal dimension of human experience when seen as separated from God and condemned to natural decay. Christian (and Hegelian) teleology took that temporal dimension as the gradual unfolding of a destiny of salvation in whose path every pain had a meaning; but Benjamin states that the sense of progress in history can only be experienced by those who win and dominate others, and who as a consequence can regard time as the continuous and gradual expansion of the same positive principles. In opposition to what he characterizes as the winner's view, his theory of history is grounded on the notion of disaster, time as a force of destruction and corrosion. Instead of a manifestation of embodied Spirit in its path toward self-conscious-ness and totalization, history is a realm of suffering and permanent conflict, not a purely logical chain of constructive events, but a directionless piling up of violence. There is no teleology, but only a collection of discontinuous, ephemeral configurations of culture. On the surface of our planet, time crystallizes itself in ruins that give a fragmentary and devitalized testimony of past experiences; in the realm of thought, allegories do the same, crystallizing in fragmentary utterances the action of time on culture, emphasizing what remains incomplete. Allegory does not take our own time or the future as a fulfillment; rather it reminds us of our own status in the future, we whose traces are bound to be a fragment among others within a collection of cultural fossils available for allegorical readings performed at a distance. The allegorists of the future, for their part, will perhaps have a chance to "communicate" with our own present, depending on specific analogies, like those existing between modernity and the baroque seventeenth century, both haunted by a deep sense of crisis, alienation from God or from any meaningful History. For Benjamin this is why allegory refuses to provide humanity with an aesthetic redemption of the world in perfect forms, or beautiful totalities that celebrate an illusory sense of unity and harmony. Rather allegory tends to interact with historical fractures and violence, especially when observed from the point of view of the defeated. For him, the privileging of the symbol as the beautiful form that offers an immediate intuition of Truth is a kind of mythic regression, the residue of Adam's legend in Paradise – harmony between man and his environment – or simply the optimistic rationalization of the winners.

With his notion of mythical regression applied to more conventional art forms (like those more frequent in mass media), Benjamin introduces a more politicized version of the same attack that modernist thought has launched toward the notion of symbol, now seen as a residue of the "age of innocence" in its assumption of an organic continuity, close identification of language and experience, signifier and signified. Modernity questions this transparency, underlining a kind of inevitable discontinuity between experience and its expression, between past and present, humankind and nature. An acute sense of language as bearing a degree of opacity consolidates the sense that interpretation is always a problematic task, and the modern sensibility, to avoid what it considers past illusions, has to deal with a multi-leveled gap implied in any reading process: that between what is given to the senses and its meaning, that between a past which must be read and a present which must read the past, and that between the first text and a second substitute text which renders apparently explicit the thought behind the surface. This gap corresponds, in its own way, to the theological tradition – of conceiving deity as a "hidden God" – acknowledged as the starting point of the allegorical process; but that tradition saw totalization and the access to Truth as its horizon, provided that one could perform the correct reading of signs and utter the right prophecies. Now the multi-leveled gap acquires a different sense, coming to the foreground as the beginning and end of the process. Instead of being attacked or reduced to its more pedagogical versions, allegory is revealed by Benjamin and his followers, and taken as that privileged process that brings to light the reiterated tension between the impulse to totalize and its inevitable incompleteness. The necessary connection between allegory and fragmentation is seen in a different perspective: the enigmatic surface does not derive from concealment of an existing meaning; rather it is conceived as expressing the very nature of allegory as a discourse whose texture is a privileged instance of the consciousness of language.

In this new theoretical framework, the romantic opposition symbol/allegory, which degrades allegorical expression as arbitrary, nonorganic, mechanical, is reversed. The idea of an unmediated experience of meaning embodied in the symbol is now seen as an illusory attempt to deny the mediation of language, and allegory is redeemed as the discourse that immerses itself "into the depths which separate visual being from meaning" (Benjamin 1977: 165).[4]

This modern conception of the allegorical has derived from the ongoing debate that involves different ideological positions within the realm of art criticism, since the changes in the philosophy of art in this century owe much to artistic practices. Modernist art elicited the perceptions and critical discourses adequate to its own processes and generated the categories adequate to describe it. The modern characterization of allegory as a fragmented and incomplete discourse matches the view that posits modernist art as an instance of discontinuity and opacity, incompleteness and ambiguity. The impact of French surrealism on Walter Benjamin is well known, and the effect of modern art on the development of contemporary research concerning the baroque has been acknowledged. Fletcher cites surrealism and the work of Eisenstein as vivid examples of the principle of allegorical juxtaposition, emphasizing their common anti-realist techniques of isolation (the perfect delineation of contours, the relative autonomy of each image forming part of the montage).

In terms of filmic structure, the issues of fragmentation, opacity, and discontinuity arise within the context of the critique of illusionism. The rejection of the dominant codes in classical narrative, based on spatio-temporal continuity, have been unevenly radical, bringing to film production a dialogue with modern art that had its special moments in film history. Modernism first entered the filmic sphere after World War I, when German Expressionism, the French avant-garde, and Soviet constructivism exemplified a film practice that associated the critique of illusionism with different, sometimes antithetical, allegorical strategies. In *Caligari* (Robert Wiene, 1919), new codes of mise-en-scène, scenery, and lighting, all taken from the German theater of the time, were central for the construction of that sense of estrangement derived from an allegorical space in which enigmatic characters lived their drama. Other experimental filmmakers, dialoguing with the historical avant-gardes (futurism, cubism, surrealism), created a more intimate connection between film and the modern allegorical strategies of space fragmentation, consolidating the montage principle in the new medium. In surrealist films like *Un Chien Andalou* (1928), despite all the polemical claims from Buñuel concerning the refusal of any interpretation, an enigmatic sequence of images and discontinuous action elicited all kinds of allegorical interpretations, starting with the most directly associated with its internal logic – the psychoanalytical reading that searched for figures of desire in Buñuel's imagery. In another context of the 1920s, the montage principle typical of modernist prose provided the ground for Eisenstein's intellectual cinema, which refused a more conventional political pedagogy based on classical narrative and proposed instead a rich variety of experiments in film language that triggered a level of conceptualization rejected by the Soviet bureaucracy and by film industries everywhere. Instead of a straightforward narrative, Eisenstein wanted his spectators to learn how to think dialectically based on the way he presented and commented on historical facts. The succession of images should not follow a line of action within a continuous space–time, but a line of conceptual thought concerning the facts evoked on the screen. As occurs with other allegorical texts, commentary prevails over narration, discontinuous juxtaposition of images over continuous evolution of action and drama.

Eisenstein's intellectual cinema, as a modernist text, faced a major challenge: to reconcile its ruptures – with conventional forms of perception and historical narration – with the pedagogical dimension of a cinema designed to perform immediate political tasks. On the one hand, his film affirmed the principle of fragmentation of space and time, allowing for enigmatic juxtapositions of images, typical features of modern allegory, which he incorporated in his constructivist way; on the other, the overall design of each film implied an ultimate movement toward totalization and toward a clear diagnosis of recent political conflicts, "unequivocal" imagery able to express a teleology of history constructed to legitimize the 1917 revolution. These tensions shaped the peculiar drama of his cinema and his thought, as a filmmaker who was deeply engaged in the purposefulness and the love for the concrete common to Marxism and constructivism, but here with an aesthetic sense akin to the metaphysical overtones common to the tradition of religious iconography and nineteenth-century symbolist art.

Within the context of narrative-dramatic cinema, the articulation of political concerns and the modernist enterprise found again a privileged manifestation in the 1960s, when the atmosphere created by the *politique des auteurs*, and particular readings of the phenomenology embedded in Italian neorealism, produced a new relationship between cinema and modern allegory, in the work of filmmakers like Jean-Luc Godard and Pier Paolo Pasolini. Godard, in particular, placed himself at the crossroads of the Bazinian-like phenomenological approach to images and the montage principle. He reworked the montage principle in terms of provocative *pop effects* created by the mixture of materials and styles – high and low, avant-garde and kitsch. Giving emphasis to voice over commentary, written texts on the screen, and documentary-like interviews, he created a new relationship between the verbal and the visual in cinema, whereby ironic anti-illusionist commentaries interact with continuous narration or naturalist drama. Intertexuality, a taste for quotations and for the disruptions of conventional cinematic procedures, made each of his films a critical essay on cinema, a conceptual work that embodied the views of the leftist filmmaker convinced that a socially critical cinema could only begin with an aesthetic critique of cinema itself. Through this deconstructive dimension, Godard's work produced a variety of allegories of cinema, giving more emphasis to a disjunctive "vertical montage" in which sound and image collide to produce those estrangement effects associated with Brecht. The filmmaker indeed borrowed some reflexive strategies from the German playwright, but Godard also searched for new methods of reflexivity typical of the 1960s, a period in which the atmosphere created by Pop Art and the challenges brought by the new stages of modernization engendered a peculiar taste for quotations, usually taken as a compromise between a critical and a sympathetic view toward industrialized culture and kitsch. Godard's style, with its mixture of different materials – film genres, high and low culture, narrative and conceptual discourse – displays, on another register, the same tension found in Eisenstein. His dialectics of fragmentation and totalization is again a way of dealing with a historical time. Now the sense of fragmentation comes from the

348

use of collage, the mixing of narrative genres and materials, while the sense of totalization results from the series of ironical allusions to French contradictions at the time of the consolidation of a consumer society in Europe. Those allusions give shape to a general diagnosis of his time that emerges from the collection of brief commentaries. In this sense, his cinema forms a kind of parallel discourse when examined in connection with Roland Barthes's constellation of short essays on mass-media mythology (Barthes 1957).

In the US, the emergence of an oppositional film culture that reworked the spirit of the historical avant-garde from the 1920s established, beginning in the late 1940s, a new context for allegorical works in the post-Benjaminian modern sense. An independent film production, more decisively engaged in the development of cinema as an art form, started a new dialogue with painters, sculptors, and poets, as had already occurred in the 1920s work of Germaine Dulac, Jean Epstein, Luis Buñuel, and Sergei Eisenstein. A succession of experiments – that began with Maya Deren films and developed in a variety of directions – made cinema share the vicissitudes of high modernism in its last stages of development. The American underground cinema, although multiple in style and concerns, has always involved a gesture of interrogation addressed to cinema as an institution and an art form (see James 1989).

4   National Allegory

Allegory, when viewed as an expression of a modern sensibility, moves away from its traditional image as conventional art concerned with pedagogical effects. It becomes a sign of a new consciousness of history where the appeal to analogies and to a vivid memory of the past is now taken not as the celebration of an identity connecting past and present, but as an experience able to teach us that repetition is always an illusion, and that old facts, like old signs, lose their "original" meaning when looked at from a new perspective. Seen from our present experience, allegories make evident their vocation to express the central role played by time in culture and in individual lives. For Paul de Man (1969), they form a kind of "rhetoric of temporality," when the impulse to memorize and identify with a previous moment (of history, of a personal life) ends up communicating the sense of crisis and separation from the irretrievable past.

While the modern view that associates allegory with an acute consciousness of time is significant in aesthetic theory today, there is more to say about the role played by allegory in our century. First, there is the question of spatiality. The process of economic expansion of globalized markets has been producing a compression of space and time that affects everyone, and it becomes more difficult to have a sense of one's own experience when one keeps looking at the real world on a local basis. Personal stories become deeply connected with large-scale social processes that transcend individual perception, establishing clear limits for any narrative concerned with the linear development of a life story in its continuity guaranteed by a circumscribed person-to-person interaction and a stable environment. The logic of lived experience has become more abstract, and modes of representation based on juxtapositions, discontinuities, and large-scale and invisible networks seem to be more able to grasp the logic of a personal action and its social destiny. In light of these changes, Fredric Jameson has proposed new developments within the Marxist tradition concerned with modes of representation, in order to grasp the social process in its totality at a given moment of history. For him, one needs to "historicize" the question of realism, acknowledging that the canonical forms of realism engendered in the nineteenth century could not accomplish that same illuminating function today; the social reality that they were able to account for was, in its internal logic, quite different from present society, belonging to a different stage of capitalist development. The new configuration of space and time and the more abstract nature of the social process in postmodern times reveal the realist form as unable to account for totality, creating the demand for new art forms able to offer not so much a representation in the classic sense, but rather a lucid "cognitive mapping" to help us understand society and our position within it (1991: 51–2). In his view, the challenges brought by postmodernity call for a revision of the entire question of allegory, and of its dialectics of fragmentation and (perhaps now impossible) totalization.

One of the challenges brought by the contemporary scene is its destabilization of otherwise consolidated political and aesthetic categories, like that of the nation, together with its correlates: national culture and national literature, art, or cinema. Nationalism had its most powerful moment in Europe and in the US in the first half of the twentieth century; from the post-World War II period to the early 1970s it became more directly associated with Third-World countries and their struggle for liberation (see Hobsbawm 1990). "The Nation," as a problematic, constantly reworked category, has had its vicissitudes in recent times, but national allegories continue to be present in our contemporary scene, although in new forms that express the ways that the new configurations of space, time, economic exchange, and political power have created a sense of crisis in this terrain. This is made evident in films that try to reach encompassing views of contemporary experience or of politics in certain regions through overt allegorical strategies. Here one might mention films like *Underground* (1995) by Emir Kusturika, *Ulysses' Dream* by Theo Angelopoulos, the Kieslovski trilogy that refers to the three colors of the French flag (Blue, White, Red) as related to the three emblematic values of the French Revolution (Liberty, Equality, Fraternity), *The Age of the Earth* (1980) by Glauber Rocha, and *El viaje* (1991) by Fernando Solanas. The list could also include numerous national allegories made in Hollywood, from the Oliver Stone films to *Short Cuts* (1993) by Robert Altman, *Wag the Dog*, and *Primary Colors*, films that express a tense relationship to myths that, in the past, reinforced a certain self-image of the United States. They present different points of view, more or less critical of the status quo, but all reveal how a general perception of the nation is crucial for a thematization not only of clearly political issues but also of private lifestyles.

The persistence of national allegory and its significant presence in our times suggest its force within the realm of representation even when the national question has lost its centrality. Recapitulating specific moments of film history in which nationalism had a stronger hand in the shaping of filmic texts, I would now like to explore the way in which narratives oriented by a teleological framework found in the category of the nation a privileged sphere within which they could operate effectively. A retrospective look at film production in the twentieth century reveals how more conventional modes of allegorical practice made a resurgence as the idea of nation came to replace religious doctrine in the creation of discursive frameworks and teleologies.

Specific trends of modernity since the late eighteenth century, nation and nationalism, as forces shaping representation, motivated and, at the same time, were produced by many narrations that became canonical texts within the allegorical tradition, first in the literary realm, later in film. As historians and political scientists have taught us, the nation is not a substance, nor a natural way of subsuming a conglomerate of people under the same category. It is a product of modernity, of market culture and industrialization, a social construct able to create a sense of totalization, a cohesive collective entity that refers to heterogeneous groups belonging to a complex society at a time when any single homogeneous community of experience is out of reach.

Benedict Anderson's (1983) idea of the nation as "imagined community" clarifies how the nation can be seen as a substitute for religion and other unifying principles related to the sense of a "cosmic order." But unlike the radical universality of the "eternal" order, the nation, in a more restricted historical scale, offers guiding principles that create a sense of totality able to establish a horizon to coordinate certain collective experiences in time, a horizon clearly manifested in problematic expressions like "national destiny" or "national character." As I pointed out earlier, "the nation," despite its secular roots in modern history, solicits personifications in fictional narratives, and other allegorical strategies as well, thus confirming its affinities with the sense of the sacred. Some of the debates mentioned in connection with allegory, myth, language, and religion emerge when we discuss the way in which historical or overtly fictional narratives treat the national question. This is especially relevant for film studies, due to the particular role cinema has been playing within the contemporary public sphere where the question of national identity has hardly disappeared.

Film as a popular medium emerged at a time in which nationalism was one of the forces shaping history in Europe and in the Americas, and film history in the first half of this century was intimately connected with the competition among national powers. Cinema took part in the expression of national rivalries in Europe and in the construction of American hegemony after World War I, a process that consolidated the United States' domination of Latin America and other "underdeveloped" regions of the globe. Given this historical context, film production – like the industrial fairs and the crystal palaces of the nineteenth

351

century – became one more forum for the exhibition of national values and technical achievements within the international arena. Film itself became an index of modernization and power, so that different countries saw their efforts to improve their cinema as a privileged strategy of national affirmation and, at times, as a celebration of hegemony. That strategy would find its ultimate fulfillment in cases where the subject of the film was national history itself or a disguised representation of a "national vocation" to conduct or to save humankind in a time of crisis.

The close connection between film and politics was obviously a central issue after the Bolshevik revolution and the official Soviet rhetoric affirming the centrality of the cinema. But in fact politics and strong national concerns have made their presence felt in film history since the very beginning of the century, paving the way for the strong political impact produced by a single film in a national context: *The Birth of a Nation*, Griffith's racist film released in 1915. The film provides a striking example of how film narrative and rhetoric was then deployed to develop an argument about American history, a theory of war and a theory of the natural role reserved for the different ethnic groups in American society. Griffith's allegory offers a lesson in the deployment of personification within a melodramatic and Manichean value system. His subsequent film *Intolerance* (1916), by far more complex and more interesting, again mobilized certain universal principles supposed to govern human history, building a historical teleology in which a trajectory of centuries was suggested as a succession of different "stages" that prepared for the emergence and consolidation of the United States in modern times as the privileged expression of God's plan, the nation that materializes the basic principles that will guarantee human salvation in the future. In *Intolerance*, Providence is taken as the guiding principle, as the spiritual force is made visible through different forms of typological relationships that connect different characters living in distant historical times. The Christian Passion and the paradigm of blessed motherhood as the natural vocation for all virtuous women are placed at the center of the intertwining of the four parallel narratives that unfold the Great Design of history: the Fall of Babylon in ancient times, the Passion, the Saint Bartholomew's Day Massacre in sixteenth-century France, and the vicissitudes of a young couple in the modern United States.[5]

During the course of film history other teleological designs place a nation at the center of the historical process. Eisenstein's *October* (1927), a film made to celebrate the tenth anniversary of the Bolshevik revolution, confirmed the sense of history as teleology but tried to displace its basic principle, contesting the hegemonic role played by the category of nation. Here the central category was that of the proletarian state, and class consciousness replaced national values as the unifying force of people in modernity. Instead of Providence as the covert force to guide the unfolding of the revolutionary teleology, Eisenstein proposed the idea of Reason as embodied by the revolutionary leadership, and his recapitulation of the events of 1917 gave more room for the theory of revolution than for any other aspect of the conquest of the Winter Palace.

This highly intellectualized sense of history, culture, and film language created severe political tensions between the filmmaker and a Soviet power suspicious of the film's modernist aesthetics and its understanding of political allegory. Eisenstein's film is an interesting example of the dialectics of fragmentation and totalization, continuity and discontinuity, typical of modern allegories, a feature detectable in other films, including *Intolerance*, as Miriam Hansen (1991) has demonstrated. Apart from her discussions of the role of Motherhood as a central moral force in the film, Hansen underlines the process by which Griffith's concern with emblems and iconography, expressed in his emphatic use of tableau-like compositions and extended visual commentaries throughout the film, collides with his concern with fluent and accelerated narrative, creating a dialectics of continuity and discontinuity in the texture of the film. *Intolerance*, with all its awkward passages, is a good example of this mixture of an impulse toward naturalism (and classical decoupage) and an impulse toward allegorical constructions based on the "graphic isolation" of images. Hansen's analysis suggests how the development of film narrative in its formative period involved something more than the acquisition of skills related to the construction of a naturalist space–time structure, verisimilar action, and psychology. At that time, as later in film history, narratives to be read required specific cultural codes, as well as logical expertise. Among those cultural codes, one finds "foundational narratives," like the Bible or more specific cultural artifacts that account for a national past and its values.

Sometimes a central love-story involves a couple whose struggle and final blessed union form an allegorical allusion to a national destiny as viewed from a restricted perspective, as occurs not only in Griffith films but also in many John Ford westerns. Observing a film like *The Searchers* (1956), we cannot fully grasp the meaning of particular actions performed by its central characters without referring their experience to the foundational narrative of the conquest of the US West. This particular Ford film is an allegory which emphasizes the territorial expansion of the American nation state, as represented on the screen by the gradual occupation of the diegetic space by the US Army. This is seen as an institutional force that brings the consolidation of law and regular family life after a time of instability and violence. As in other westerns, one finds here the elegiac celebration of the legendary hero – in this case, Ethan (John Wayne), a typically transitional figure for whom the pacification of the territory means his melancholic "retirement" and his sense of being out of place in that very order he has helped to enforce.

A variety of films from different countries provide interesting examples of the use of myth or traditional story lines to give shape to an experience lived in the present or even in the future. The genre of science fiction is full of allegorical references of a national kind. *Metropolis*, made by Fritz Lang in 1927, was one of the first major examples of a complex network of past references informing a fictional story that takes place in the future yet refers to the present. The story of the young son of the Master who commands the allegorical city brings with it all

353

kinds of Christian paradigms, combined with a gray view of technological society. Its environment exhibits high technology, skyscrapers, machines, robotized workers, alienated life, dehumanization – in short, a nightmarish view of industrial society. Nevertheless, as the story develops we encounter fragments of a gothic battle between Good and Evil, perverse science against pure feelings, the pure young virgin against the femme fatale, father against son. The melodramatic texture of actions and characters turns the critique of the dehumanization of society into a celebration of the role of a Messiah as the messenger of Love. Here again mythical paradigms shape both story line and iconography, suggesting the connections between *Metropolis* and specifically German forms of Christian piety which also played a role in German modern nationalism (see Greenfeld 1992: 278–309).

If formal analysis helps to characterize allegorical structures and identify their narrative or iconographical sources, one needs to go further and ask about the meaning that those narrative paradigms and traditional imagery acquire when incorporated by a film: that is to say, we have to understand the film as situated in its own time, the ways it can be taken as an allegory referring to the specific political juncture from which it arose. Here, our question converges with the kind of inquiry usually addressed to historical films which, while they represent the past, are taken as a disguised comment on the present. I refer to those narratives that can be seen as "pragmatic allegories," those in which the underlined analogies between past and present are taken as a piece of rhetoric, a form of raising a question about the present using the past, given that the episode focussed on by the film had similar issues at its center. In Jean Renoir's *La Marseillaise* (1936), the representation of specific episodes of the French Revolution was taken as a form of asserting the position of the Popular Front in 1930s France; Andrej Wajda's *Danton* (1982) takes the same historical event as a pretext to discuss Polish politics of the 1980s; and Ken Loach's *Land and Freedom* (1995) takes the Spanish Civil War of the 1930s to present an allegorical representation of the filmmaker's large-scale view of the shape of European history in the twentieth century.

Apart from these pragmatic allegories, there are cases where the analogies linking past and present are more than merely pedagogical references, and the film gets closer to a radically conscious figural realism of the Christian kind (Auerbach), reworking typological relationships as confirmations of the sacred truth embodied in historical facts that unfold the Grand Design administered by Providence. I have already mentioned Griffith's *Intolerance* as a major example of this, but *Intolerance*, *Metropolis*, and *October* are also suggestive examples of the construction of historical allegories where magnified visual spectacle serves as a kind of animated national monument or *tableau vivant*. The mobilization of material resources, technical skills, and the proverbial "cast of thousands" could be exhibited as a sign of a nation's (or of a social regime's) strength and legitimacy. They form instances of a self-conscious representation of a nation's role within the international order or, even more broadly, in universal history.

From the period of silent movies, Abel Gance's *Napoleon* (1928) in this sense forms a national allegory that celebrated on a monumental scale the glorious times of the French hegemony in Europe, praising the national spirit and its vocation to lead humanity toward a better future. Produced in France, the US, Germany, and the Soviet Union – that is to say, by the major forces of Western history at that point (with the exception of England) – these filmic monuments form a suggestive quartet related to the exacerbated nationalism of the early twentieth century. Political rivalries among the nation states (or the socialist confederation) had an impact on film history, as they would again in the 1930s, when the nationalist monument took the form of Riefenstahl's *Triumph of the Will* (1934), Eisenstein's *Alexander Nevsky* (1938), and Victor Fleming's *Gone with the Wind* (1939).

More recently in film history, Latin America, Asia, Eastern Europe, and Africa became privileged areas for the production of films concerned with the way in which social problems and power struggles can be shaped by particular national contexts. From the 1960s on, the rise of different national cinemas made Third-World film culture a new source of allegorical strategies of representation. At times, as in Sembene's case, historical films with allegorical overtones, like *Ceddo*, formed part of a discussion of national politics and culture that included reflection on the complex question of building a national cinema in adverse conditions (Rosen 1993). In Latin America, Brazilian Cinema Novo, "Third Cinema" from Argentina, and the Cuban post-revolutionary cinema from the 1960s took national destiny as a central theme. A concern with social issues such as poverty, labor exploitation, oligarchy, and foreign domination brought a new point of view on modern history, in opposition to the Eurocentric perspective usually expressed by North-American and European cinema. The decolonization in Asia and Africa, the anti-imperialist consciousness raised in Latin America, and the Cuban and Algerian revolutions all created a sense of a dynamic historical change issuing from the "peripheral" countries, all of which foregrounded the cinema as an instance of the affirmation of emerging national values, a key factor in the construction of national identity (at least before television began to play this role in the context of mass culture from the 1970s on).

The 1960s and early 1970s were a time of intense political debate, and film production became politicized as never before. The ideological atmosphere favored global critiques and a "state of the nation" discourse. The idea of revolution as national liberation fostered the creation of political films that focussed on past events to find examples of struggle and change with suggestive resonances for the present political movements. Here we find "pragmatic allegories" based on analogies aimed at raising class consciousness and a willingness to participate in the national struggle for liberation. The reflection on history is found in Manoel Octavio Gomez's *The First Charge of the Machete* (1969), a Cuban film that reenacts an episode of the struggle against the Spaniards in the nineteenth century in order to assert a post-revolutionary view of Cuban history. A film which also uses past events to comment on a current revolution (in

Argentina) is Hèctor Oliveira's *Rebellion in Patagonia* (1972), just as Miguel Littin's *The Promised Land* (1972) narrates an earlier episode of popular struggle as a way of raising some questions about popular unity, the politics of Salvador Allende's government in Chile. Inspired by Brecht, a bitter recapitulation of the past was performed in the Brazilian film, *The Conspirators* (1972), made by Joaquim Pedro de Andrade. The director questions the behavior of the intellectuals who led a famous rebellion against the Portuguese colonizers in 1789 in order to launch a delicate debate on intellectuals, armed struggle, and the guerrilla warfare that was taking place in Brazil at the time of the film.

Reworking the tradition of what Carlos Monsiváis calls "the cinema of the Mexican Revolution," Paul Leduc directed *Reed: Insurgent Mexico* (1971), introducing the documentary-like strategies of modern cinema in a film that placed the question of the Mexican national character in a new perspective (see Paranaguá 1995: 117–27). Leduc discards the kind of national allegory that, since the 1930s and 1940s, had turned the early-century revolution and values into a folk show (Carlos Monsiváis's term). Here we are far from the monumental, spectacular version of that crucial historical event in Latin America, an event that created special conditions for the affirmation of a national imagery before that kind of celebration of national-popular values could have a similar presence in other countries of Latin America. The experience of Mexican cinema with national allegory, by its force and specific role in society, has been unique in the continent, as one sees in its major emblem, the monumentally pictorial melodramas directed by Emilio Fernandez and photographed by Gabriel Figueiroa in the 1940s and 1950s.

Although outstanding female stars like Dolores Rios were the basis of their commercial success, Emilio Fernandez's films gave continuity to a reformist patriarchal view that celebrated the traditional roles played by men and women who personified the positive values of the nation. Latin-American cinema had to wait until the 1960s to promote woman to a central and transgressive role, understood as a condensed representation of national history. In different countries, historical films or quasi-documentary representations of present conjunctures adopted allegorical strategies, placing the female protagonist as a personification of the national predicaments or hopes within the historical process. The Cuban cinema developed even more intensively this kind of national allegory, as Marvin D'Lugo suggests (1993). The best synthesis of that tradition is Humberto Solas's *Lucia* (1968), made at a period of rich aesthetic debate and film production in Cuba. Solas's work presents a very original structure based on the allegorical juxtaposition of three stories made in different moments of Cuban history: the time of the struggle for political independence from Spain in the nineteenth century, the time of a frustrated attempt to radically change the country by liberating it from a right-wing dictatorship in the 1930s, and the time of ideological change and new proposals on gender relationships that opposed the macho tradition in the post-revolutionary 1960s. Adopting in each episode a filmic style adequate to the tone of the historical time and the specific conditions of female mentality in Cuba, *Lucia* gives us a lesson on how to use film style allegorically in order to make statements about the country's political history. "*Lucia* is not a film about a woman; it is a film about society. But within that society, I chose the most vulnerable character, the one who is most transparently affected at any given moment by contradictions and change" – this statement by Humberto Solas (quoted in D'Lugo 1993: 279) is very similar to Fassbinder's explanation of his strategy in *The Marriage of Maria Braun* (1979), a film where the construction of the female protagonist as the personification of German experience in the post-war period invited a sense of irony also produced by style and acting, as one also sees in *Lucia*.

Apart from Cuba, and its women characters as personifications, one can mention other examples of the treatment of female characters as national allegories in modern Latin-American cinema. Bodansky and Senna's *Iracema* (1974) focusses on the predatory dimension of the expansion of economic activities in the Brazilian Amazon, and centers its analysis in the pathetic and representative story of a young native female who is destroyed by her contact with people coming from Southern Brazil at the time of the construction of the transamazonian highway. *The Official Version* (1985), made by Carlos Puenzo in Argentina, adopts a melodramatic tone in its discussion of the kidnapping of children born inside the dictatorship's camps of torture and execution. The female protagonist condenses, in her own experience and in her "will to know" the truth, the experience of Argentinian society after the 1983 redemocratization occurred. The film places family affairs at the center of a humanist approach to the political question, and thus Puenzo inscribes his film within a long and diversified tradition of melodramas that work out social questions, taking a nuclear family as the exemplary microcosm that condenses the entire nation. This was typical in the American classical cinema, as one can see in Griffith, King Vidor, John Ford (remember *Young Mr. Lincoln* among others), Frank Capra, and Douglas Sirk, and in Italian cinema, from Visconti films, especially in cases like *Rocco and His Brothers* (1960), or the Taviani Brothers' films, such as *Good Morning Babylon* (1987). The modern Latin-American cinema also explored this kind of allegorical strategy, whether in Mexico in films like Arturo Ripstein's *The Castle of Purity* (1972), or in Brazil in films like Arnaldo Jabor's *It's All Right* (1972). The Ripstein and Jabor films form typical examples of the construction of the Family House as an allegorical space representing the nation, in narratives that take place almost entirely within four walls, creating a sense of claustrophobia that is unlike allegories' political conjuncture of the nation.

In opposition to this kind of allegory based on confinement and family dramas, a great number of national allegories in Latin America are based on picaresque peregrinations, or on the experience of exile, or on the migration caused by famines or chronic poverty. They explore the social experience of a continent whose modern history has been shaped by immigration and migration since the beginning of the European colonial enterprise. The displacement of human beings, the experience of the frontier, the building of new cities and the occupation of land has been an emblem throughout the Americas, and film production almost inevitably takes advantage of this historical background. Hollywood, for its part, produced the western, with its "Manifest Destiny" ideology. And in Latin America, a variety of social dramas featured migrating people observed as though reenacting a frustrated version of the search for the Supreme Good, or Eldorado. In opposition to the North-American popular fiction, the theme of the promised land has not been treated in euphoric and epic ways (a prerogative of the winners), either in the Amazon – see Oswaldo Caldeira's *Ajuricaba: The Rebel of the Amazon* (1977) and Gustavo Dahl's *Uira: An Indian in Search of God* (1972) – or in Mexico – see *Cabeza de vaca* (1990) by Nicolas Echevarria – or in the entire continent in a journey started in Patagonia – see Fernando Solanas's *El viaje* (1991).

Authoritarian regimes, censorship, and repression produced a specific motivation for journeys that inspired allegorical representations in which exiled people take the experience of separation from home and the new conditions of life to reflect upon their native land and on their national history and character. Solanas's *Tangos: The Exile of Gardel* (1985) is the most typical example of this kind of fiction in Latin America, and Tarkovsky's *Earth* is a well-known example in Europe.

The films testify to the significant presence of national allegory in modern and contemporary cinema. Although set in a changing world and increasingly circumscribed by a globalized market dynamics, allegories maintain their dramatic interest as operative totalities of reference for the fictional works engaged in the production of general statements about our historical moment. The presence of the category of the nation and the invitation to teleology that comes with it do not mean that all these national allegories can be inscribed in the more traditional type of figural totalization. Many of them are effectively engaged in reflecting on the crisis of the category of nation as a social and political framework, exhibiting most of the features of a modern fiction that problematizes its own status in the face of the real world, showing awareness of the limits of language and its discontinuity in relation to experience. No one definition of allegory can account for all the films under consideration, since artworks, even mass-mediated artworks, have confirmed that protean nature of allegory pointed out by Angus Fletcher.

The malleability of this mode of representation has been made more than evident throughout film history. Cinema, because it came late and could assimilate an enormous repertory of forms and themes, has been able to resume, in a few decades and at an accelerated pace, certain processes of change that, in other art forms, took centuries to develop. Even in a single decade or in a single country, one can follow the gradual change in the allegorical strategies that confirm this strong dialogue with the tradition and with the ruptures of modern times. The example of modernist Brazilian cinema illustrates this diversity, since a whole set of political and cultural motives engendered, in that specific national context, a rich collection of national allegories which set up an interesting play of intertextual relationships between 1964 and 1970. This happened partly because

358

of the leading role played by Glauber Rocha (a major allegorist), partly because of political censorship, and partly due to the filmmakers' strong inclination to forge a synthesis, to produce a condensed and totalizing view of national history. Before the coup d'état – therefore without the obstacles presented by political repression – an allegorical narrative expressed revolutionary hopes and used history to legitimize violence as a valid instrument within class struggle: Rocha's *Black God White Devil* (1963–4) placed the process of national liberation at the center of an ambiguous allegory, allowing for a condensed representation of society in a single story able to articulate issues concerning the entire nation. Here we have a canonical example of figural realism, or typological allegory, in cinema, with its teleological view of history. With this film on the changes in the political life of the country, from the early 1960s to the mid-1970s, there was a correlated process of transformation in the allegorical design of the narratives. After this first allegory of hope, the 1964 military coup d'état placed the leftist filmmakers in a difficult position, obliging them to perform historical revisions and a kind of autocritical recapitulation of the recent past which found its best translation in the baroque drama of disenchantment made by Rocha in 1967, *Land in Anguish*. The most celebrated political allegory made in Brazil, this film presented a hard critique of populist illusions and of the Christian-like teleological schemes incorporated by leftist thought in Latin America. Other developments included a satirical approach to the crisis of patriarchal values caused by accelerated modernization, such as in *Red Light Bandit* (1968) by Rogério Sganzerla, where allegory as collage emerged in Brazilian cinema, featuring the juxtaposition of fragments borrowed from other texts. *Macunaima*, made by Joaquim Pedro de Andrade in 1969, took an ironic view of the traditional question of a "national character" that had engaged Brazilians since the nineteenth century. The film connects the account of the adventures of Macunaima, the central personification in the film, with the ideological debate on the lack of political consciousness among the Brazilian people in the late 1960s. Finally, in the same year of 1969, a deconstructive turn addressed to old nationalist constructs engendered films like *Killed the Family and Went to the Movies* (1969) by Júlio Bressane and *Bang Bang* (1970) by Andrea Tonacci, examples of an antiteleology in which allegory performs a radical critique of narrative itself.

As a rule valid for different national contexts, allegorical representations in films have charged significantly in the 1980s and '90s, revealing the intimate connections between forms of representation and specific social conjunctures. Filmmakers from different continents now share a common historical ground that, in spite of all difficulties, challenges them to express encompassing views of the contemporary scene that engenders allegories. These end up revealing their contemporary appeal as the language of crisis, satisfying the demands presented by dramas that are typical in periods of transition and accelerated technical–economic changes which enforce people to revise their views of identity and shared values. Recent films made in Eastern Europe express the labyrinth of political ideologies and national identities that shape the contemporary history in areas that, being at the crossroads of collective migrations and economic stagnation, suffer from a chronic instability, as in the films of Kusturika and Angelopoulos.

From the 1980s on, the new debates related to a visible increase in the speed of exchange in the world market, the continuous displacement of people in search of jobs despite the big-power control of borders, and the compression of space–time created by high technology have engendered new challenges for narrative practices and visual representations of human experience. And there has been a symptomatic increase of migrating characters and cross-border love affairs (and friendships) on the screen. A new trend of story lines involving multi-national encounters of protagonists who belong to distant cultures but are led to an unexpected interaction, most of the time of a clearly private nature, is one of the main reasons for the impact created by contemporary international co-productions that engage different European countries and for the high market value of recent films made by Wim Wenders, who came to specialize in "planetary allegories" which run from Eastern Europe to Australia, crossing America, Japan, and Portugal. A Third-World film like the Macedonian *Before the Rain* can take some charm from its fresh landscape and scenes involving the local population, but there is also the allegorical dimension related to its sense of international connections created by the love affair between the photographer and the English woman.

5 Coda: Allegory in History

Allegories, as I suggested earlier, often emerge from controversies, conflicts of interpretation, confrontations related to struggles for hegemony in a world in which the shock of cultures and the network of material interests and symbolic systems tend to produce instability in people's lives. Although not an effective mode of representation when reduced to conventional pedagogical functions, allegory has acquired a new meaning in modernity – more related to the expression of social crisis and the transient nature of values, with special emphasis given to its connection with the sense of the fragmentation, discontinuity, and abstraction provided by compression of space and time in our contemporary technological world. So allegory is bound to reemerge today as an ingredient of the "spirit of the time," a privileged signifying practice that brings to light all the ambiguities related to national identity and interests, or related to an omnipresent mediasphere shaping our everyday life.

Here, I have emphasized the ways in which allegory, as a mode of representation (or a mode of expressing the crisis of representation), remains inscribed in the very dynamics of our time. And I would like to conclude by observing how the relevance of allegory in film studies does not come only from the actual conditions that surround film practice in recent years. Film studies – history and theory – will always have to deal with the question of figuration. In other words, how are certain conceptions of human experience in time or an encompassing view of history presented in a condensed way, sometimes requiring personifications, sometimes requiring an appeal to juxtapositions or to the montage principle left as a legacy by the historical avant-gardes?

Film criticism needs to explain the structure and identify the sources of a given allegorical design (given models, iconographies, narrative patterns), and should also be able to perform a historical analysis that would explain what the powers of those paradigms and iconographies are and what they mean within that specific context, given the social conjuncture into which the film is inserted. The clarification of the notion of allegory and the scholarly research on its history help to clarify the way in which a film can intervene in cultural and political debates. I have referred many times to the ambiguity of the idea of nation, and the new essays on the subject make clear the connection of this political category with historical narratives – and, I would add, with allegorical narratives. For anyone concerned with the dangers of globalized systems of domination that monopolize information and interpretation, or for anyone who lives under particular authoritarian regimes inspired by an exacerbated nationalism rooted in secular or religious doctrines, the clarification of the structure and sense of allegory in modern times is helpful in the struggle against various kinds of mythical reduction and false totalization, especially those leading toward fascism. The dynamics of allegory, with its typical dialectics of fragmentation and totalization, is far from a closed system; rather it is a signifying practice deeply involved in, and formally permeable to, the vicissitudes of historical change.

Notes

1 For allegorical strategies and projects of colonial and neocolonial domination, see Shohat and Stam 1994, especially the chapter "Tropes of Empire" (137–77).
2 *Danton*, made by Andrej Wajda in 1982, is a clear example of the use of the background provided by the French Revolution to discuss present-day politics in Poland and Eastern Europe. The debate on *Young Mr. Lincoln* launched by the critics of the *Cahiers du cinéma* in the 1970s involved a dispute about the film's allegorical references to the 1930s political scene in the US. For other examples, see Burgoyne 1997.
3 In the case of Latin American literature, see Sommer 1993.
4 Although apparently "deconstructive," Benjamin's formulation has a different sense more connected to his concern for theological questions.
5 For an analysis of *Intolerance*, see Hansen 1991: 127–241.

References

Ahmad, Aijaz. 1987. "Jameson's Rhetoric of Otherness and the 'National Allegory.'" *Social Text* 17 (summer): 3–25.

Anderson, Benedict. 1983. *Imagined Communities: Reflections on the Origin and Spread of Nationalism*. London: Verso.

Auerbach, Erich. 1974. *Mimesis: The Representations of Reality in Western Literature*. Princeton: Princeton University Press.

Barthes, Roland. 1957. *Mythologies*. Paris: Seuil.

Benjamin, Walter. 1977. *The Origin of the German Tragic Drama*. London: NLB.

Bhabha, Homi, ed. 1990. *Nation and Narration*. London: Routledge.

Burgoyne, Robert. 1997. *Film Nation: Hollywood Looks at US History*. Minneapolis: University of Minnesota Press.

de Man, Paul. 1969. "The Rhetoric of Temporality." In *Interpretation: Theory and Practice*. Ed. C. S. Singleton. Baltimore: Johns Hopkins University Press.

D'Lugo, Marvin. 1993. "Transparent Women: Gender and Nation in Cuban Cinema." In *Mediating Two Worlds: Cinematic Encounters in the Americas*. Ed. Ana López, John King, and Manuel Alvarado. London: BFI. 279–90.

Fineman, Joel. 1980. "The Structure of Allegorical Desire." *October* (spring).

Fletcher, Angus. 1970. *Allegory: The Theory of a Symbolic Mode*. Ithaca: Cornell University Press.

Frye, Northrop. 1957. *Anatomy of Criticism: Four Essays*. Princeton: Princeton University Press.

Greenfeld, Liah. 1992. *Nationalism: Five Roads to Modernity*. Cambridge: Harvard University Press.

Hansen, Miriam. 1991. *Babel and Babylon: Spectatorship in American Silent Film*. Cambridge: Harvard University Press.

Hobsbawm, E. J. 1990. *Nations and Nationalism since 1780: Programme, Myth, Reality*. Cambridge: Cambridge University Press.

James, David. 1989. *Allegories of Cinema: American Film in the Sixties*. Princeton: Princeton University Press.

Jameson, Fredric. 1986. "Third World Literature in the Era of Multinational Capitalism." *Social Text* 15 (fall): 65–88.

———. 1991. *Postmodernism, or The Cultural Logic of Late Capitalism*. Durham, NC: Duke University Press.

———. 1992. *The Geopolitical Aesthetic: Cinema and Space in the World System*. Bloomington: Indiana University Press.

Lukács, Georg. 1964. *Realism in Our Time*. New York: Harper.

Paranaguá, Paulo Antonio, ed. 1995. *Mexican Cinema*. London: BFI.

Pépin, Jean. 1976. *Mythe et allégorie: Les Origines grecques et les contestations judéo-chrétiennes*. Paris: Etudes Augustiniennes.

Rosen, Phil. 1993. "Making a Nation in Seubere's *Ceddo*." In *Otherness and the Media: The Ethnography of the Imagined and the Imaged*. Ed. Hamid Naficy and Teshome Gabriel. Longhorne: Harwood Academic Publishers.

Shohat, Ella/Robert Stam. 1994. *Unthinking Eurocentrism: Multiculturalism and the Media*. New York: Routledge.

Sommer, Doris. 1993. *Foundational Fictions: The National Romances of Latin America*. Berkeley: University of California Press.

Stam, Robert. 1997. *Tropical Multiculturalism: A Comparative History of Race in Brazilian Cinema and Culture*. Durham, NC: Duke University Press.

Starobinski, Jean. 1979. *Les Emblèmes de la raison*. Paris: Editions Flammarion.

362

CHAPTER NINETEEN

Every Picture Tells a Story: José Guadalupe Posada's Protocinematic Graphic Art

Charles Ramírez Berg

At its inception, cinema joined a larger, well-established representational system that included the fine arts (painting, sculpture, drawing, etching, engraving, print-making) and the popular media (photographs and illustrations in news-papers, pictorial magazines, advertisements, slideshows, dime novels, posters, handbills, and broadsides). Though there have been some studies of the recipro-cal influences of image media and the beginnings of First-World moving pic-tures,[1] no one has made more than a passing comment on these mediated cross-fertilizations in Mexico's early cinematic history.[2] To address this under-researched topic, I want to look at the illustrations of the prodigious penny press in Mexico, and particularly at the work of its greatest artist, José Guadalupe Posada (1852–1913). I am specifically looking for the pictorial and compositional techniques Posada developed that would eventually find their way into classical cinematic narrative practice in Mexico.

For those seeking to understand the transition in Mexico from static to moving-image narrative, Posada is a pivotal figure. In his own way, he was as important to the unfolding of Mexican cinema as Winsor McCay and his comics were to the early development of US film. To begin with, there is the length and breadth of his career. The prolific Posada was an illustrator for more than 40 years, from the pre-cinematic era (he began illustrating in León in the 1870s and moved to Mexico City around 1887) until well into Mexico's initial documentary film stage (roughly 1896–1916). Moreover, his etchings and engravings encom-passed an extremely broad range of subjects, from religious portraits to carefully drafted views of Mexico City to depictions of news events, satirical *calavera* (skeleton) drawings, and miracles.

Furthermore, Posada produced an imposing number of images. By the turn of the century, the penny press was the most popular image medium in the country, and Posada was its master graphic artist. In documenting Mexican life, legend, and folklore, he created thousands of images (most estimates have put the total at between 15,000 and 20,000, though the actual number will never be known[3]) in various media: woodcuts, type-metal engravings, and zinc relief etchings (Tyler

363

1979: 5–6). These were published in popular journalistic forms – broadsides and chapbooks – that "had virtually disappeared in Europe and the United States" (Elliott 1980: 11). It seems reasonable to assume that popular imagery affected the development of cinematic representation, and in its formative years Mexican cinema coexisted with a rich, evocative, and markedly distinct pool of images. Therefore a third important reason for studying Posada's work in the cinematic context is that at the turn of the century the common image-containing media available in Mexico were very different from those in the First World.

Yet another reason is the built-in kinship between journalism and early Mexican cinema. From 1896, when the Lumières' and Edison's representatives introduced moving pictures to the nation, until 1917, when Mexican filmmaking turned away from documentaries and embraced fiction films, the national cinema was predominantly documentary. The new medium was considered a branch of journalism and generally understood as a moving variant of illustrated magazines, which were gaining popularity in Mexico in the 1890s. Though at first these periodicals were exclusively foreign, Mexico's own production of such magazines began in 1895 with the publication of *El mundo ilustrado*, which combined engravings, lithographs, and photographs (de los Reyes 1987: 22). In those early decades of cinema, Posada and Mexican filmmakers saw themselves – and were seen by others – as essentially in the same business: reportage. Conceptually, then, the ties between the Mexican press and moving pictures were very close indeed. So much so that Antonio Vanegas Arroyo, the owner of the prominent penny press where Posada did most of his Mexico City work, was involved in the early history of film in Mexico (though it is not clear in exactly what capacity).[4]

The purpose of this essay is to look at the linkages between Mexico's early cinema – from the documentary films that dominated domestic screens from 1896 to 1916 to the fiction films that came of age in the short span of time between 1917 and 1919 – and the array of journalistic images available at the time. My main goal is to demonstrate that, in the midst of Posada's prodigious output, he discovered, developed, synthesized, and consolidated representational techniques we would call "cinematic," techniques that would eventually be available for incorporation into the classical Mexican cinema, which for me begins with *El automóvil gris* (*The Gray Automobile*) in 1919.

To do this I will focus on the dominant form of Mexican journalistic practice during this period: the ubiquitous penny press. From the 1890s to the rise of newspapers and other mass media in the 1920s, the penny press was the most widespread, accessible source of images for the Mexican public. In Mexico City in the 1890s, for example, at least 18 such presses were in operation, and from 1900 well into the 1910s, a period considered the heyday of the medium, there were more than 40 (Tyler 1979: 300–2 app. 2, 3). During this time, these presses mass-produced countless one-sheet broadsides and small newspapers, with press runs in the hundreds or thousands and sometimes in the millions.[5] These were sold by agents, newsboys, and hawkers for one or two centavos[6] "on street corners, in market places, at fairs, ranches and haciendas" (Gamboa 1944: 16). In addition, these editorial houses printed a number of other image-containing items such as board games, cookbooks, songbooks, storybooks, and chapbooks.

This wily, fertile turn-of-the-century medium surely influenced the evolution of image narrative in general in Mexico, affecting films just as it must have been affected by them. By producing and watching both the penny-press illustrations and film images projected on the screens of the new cinemas springing up around the country, Mexican artists and filmmakers learned to use images to relate a tale. That is to say, through this intertextual stream of protocinematic images, Mexican graphic artists and movie-makers acquired the skills of representational narration, a crucial step in the development of what became the classical Mexican film narrative. Simultaneously, audiences and readers learned to comprehend these carefully structured images as stories.

1   Film as Journalism: Mexican Cinema's Documentary Stage (1896–1917)

A key distinguishing feature of Mexican cinema is the fact that for its first 20 years, from 1896 until 1916, Mexican film production was almost exclusively a documentary practice. In contrast, both European and North-American cinemas gravitated toward narrative much earlier: US films, for example, made the transition during the 1903–7 period (Thompson 1985: 159–60; see also Bowser 1990; Musser 1990: ch. 11). And in the 1910s, while foreign films – mainly French, Italian, and North American – commanded more and more attention from filmgoers in Mexico, the onset of the Mexican Revolution (1910–20) provided an impetus for Mexican documentary production to continue, as news-reel footage brought events of the civil war to life for thousands of Mexican spectators.

But the rush to capture current events was not the only reason that Mexican cinema remained almost entirely a documentary practice, despite the unrelenting trend toward narrative films in First-World cinema. First of all, Mexican documentaries were enormously popular. Second, they provided native filmmakers with a ready-made market niche. Third, documentaries were cheap to make and economical to market – entrepreneurs like Enrique Rosas and Salvador Toscano shot, edited, promoted, and exhibited their films in their own theaters (see de los Reyes 1987: 25–7). Fourth, they fed the desire of Mexicans to see themselves on the silver screen.[7]

Fifth, from the 1870s, Mexico – through its intellectual and political leadership – was under the sway of positivism. As promoted by Gabino Barreda, who transplanted the French philosophical movement to Mexico, positivism was a means of moving Mexico from anarchy to liberty. This belief was based on two assumptions: first, that economic evolution preceded political evolution (and ultimately liberty), and second, that the proper means of achieving economic evolution was through order. Order, organization, a scientific approach to the nation's problems, and education of the masses were the cornerstones of Mexican positivism (see Romanell 1952: 29–53). "In that context," writes film historian Aurelio de los Reyes, "fiction cinema was rejected because of its potential to dupe the public: the cinema was a science and as such should show truths" (1995: 65).

Finally, a nationalistic side-effect of positivism led artists in the last decades of the nineteenth century toward a celebration of the native and away from the imitation of foreign traditions. As part of this movement, the representational arts, from paintings to illustrations to photographs, were called upon to depict Mexico, its people, and its culture (de los Reyes 1987: 35–8). To the degree that cinema in Mexico was regarded as a science as well as an art (early comparisons likened it to etchings, painting, and theater [de los Reyes 1987: 17–22]), it was clear that it should promote nationalism like the other representational arts. Mexico's 20-year documentary-film stage, therefore, was not simply a case of arrested development, but rather the result of the convergence of complex technological, political, economic, philosophical, and nationalistic factors.

The decline of the Mexican documentary came in 1915, when interest in nonfiction films waned significantly. By 1916, revolutionary documentaries – along with domestic documentaries in general – had all but disappeared from Mexican movie screens (de los Reyes 1983: 202). Shortly thereafter, in 1917, a small band of enterprising Mexican filmmakers initiated Mexico's first sustained fiction-film stage by producing story films. Only a fragmentary record of this early wave of narrative films survives, but it appears that they took two forms, one derivative and the other nationalistic.[8] Among the first were imitations of Italian melodramas, which were very popular in Mexico at the time. For example, Mexico's first narrative feature, *La luz* (*The Light*, 1917), was a faithful reconstruction of the Italian film *Il fouco* (1915), which had enjoyed enormous success in Mexico in 1916. The five films starring the Mexican stage actress Mimí Derba and produced by documentarian Enrique Rosas in 1917 were also clearly under the spell of Italian melodramas. A second kind of film produced were "truly nationalistic" stories that would exhibit the landscape, folkways, and customs of Mexico (such as the first film version of Federico Gamboa's popular 1904 Mexican novel *Santa* in 1918) (de los Reyes 1987: 68–72).

This brief experimental-fiction stage culminated in the national cinema's first legitimate narrative blockbuster, the docudrama *El automóvil gris* (produced by Enrique Rosas, directed by Rosas, Joaquín Coss, and Juan Canals de Homes). The film, originally released as a 12-part serial, now survives only in a two-hour version, having been reedited for a successful feature-length rerelease in the 1930s. Nevertheless, it is so accomplished cinematically that it can be said to mark the beginning of the classical era in Mexican cinema that stretches to 1960 (Berg forthcoming).

2   Narrational Representation in Turn-of-the-Century Mexico

As an image medium, cinema was subordinate to the penny presses upon its arrival in Mexico. And for more than two decades afterwards, cinema existed and competed within a spectrum of popular image-laden media – Mexico's representational discourse system. But I am not looking for causal links between penny-press illustrations and cinema. Given the fact that of the 24 feature fiction films made in Mexico up to 1919, only a few remain, and that only about 1,000 Posada images of the many thousands he produced have survived, such an argument would be impossible to support. Nevertheless, I am intrigued by the intertextual evolution of image narration in both print and moving pictures in Mexico from the 1890s to the release of *El automóvil gris* in 1919. I am seeking a better understanding of the dynamic, cross-pollinating influences that must have flowed among the media as filmmakers, still photographers, and graphic artists alike worked toward a coherent narrational system by which images could clearly and efficiently relate a tale. Artists like Posada learned how to utilize images narratively and helped develop a representational syntax, some of which would eventually find its way into the classic Mexican cinema. Early mediated images such as Posada's – together with moving images from Mexican documentary films and foreign fiction and nonfiction movies – provided a foundation from which Mexican filmmakers learned to transmit comprehensible, coherent narratives.

Before beginning my analysis, a word on the use of the term "narrative" when dealing with Posada. I use "narrative" in the Bordwellian sense, as "the activity of selecting, arranging, and rendering story material in order to achieve specific time-bound effects on a perceiver" (Bordwell 1985: xi). And although useful in categorizing the two general types of emerging early film, I deemphasize the nonfiction/fiction dichotomy when speaking of Posada's imagery because, by Bordwell's broad definition, all of his illustrations were narrations: that is, each drawing required him to select, arrange, and render story material – whether real or imagined – clearly, coherently, and emphatically, in order to provoke an interested response from a potential customer.

3   Posada's Cinematic Techniques

Surveying the work of Posada, one notes several cinematic techniques that would become part of what is now called "film language." By "cinematic" I mean characteristics unique to moving pictures, techniques that could not be duplicated by other media, that were not common practice in other media at the time, or that would be extremely difficult to achieve in other media. For example, when watching a play on a stage, a spectator is presented with the entire proscenium view. Cinema is able to capture that in a long shot (LS), and in

367

fact much of early cinema framed the action from such a front-row–center, proscenium vantage point. Later, however, cinema began to record closer shots via the medium shot (MS) and the close-up (CU). Providing more detailed information with these shots is something cinema can do that stage drama cannot and is one example of a cinematic feature of the medium. Others include cinema's capturing of serial motion through still photographs, the manipulation of time and space via editing, various moving camera shots (pans, tilts, and tracks), and dissolves and fades between one scene and the next.

Here, then, is a summary of Posada's cinematic pictorial techniques which would eventually be adopted into classical Mexican narrative film practice:[9]

3.1 Nearer vantage point to provide partial-figure and facial representations

In film these would be called medium shots and close-ups. They became prevalent with the advent of analytical editing, one of the hallmarks of Hollywood's and the greater Western cinema's classical style. It involves breaking down the action of a scene into separate shots: LSs to establish the setting, MSs to place the subject within the context of its immediate environment, and CUs to provide a significant detail of the subject or action. Early on in Western cinema history, films were made up almost exclusively of frontal, proscenium-like, full-figure LSs or medium long shots, and it was not until the mid-1910s that films began using a wider array of shots with any regularity. However, it appears that Posada created medium and close-up images of subjects frequently before they became standard cinematic practice.

Figure 1

Figure 1, *Gran fandango y francachela de todas las calaveras* (*Happy Dance and Wild Party of the Skeletons*, no date), gives an example of the frontal, proscenium style common to both illustrations and early cinema. The image is self-contained in that the entire scene is depicted, and the diegetic world – and the story – end at the image edge. Contrast it with figures 2 and 3, two of 13 images from the front and back pages of a two-sided broadside, *Una calavera chusca* (*A Funny Calavera*, no date), in which Posada and his *corrido* (ballad) lyricist poked fun at local market vendors. While some of the *calavera* characters are drawn in full figure, many are drawn in "medium shot." Of course portraits were a common artistic genre, and Posada produced many in his time. But these pictorial MSs are less posed, formal portraits than they are shots of active individuals caught in the middle of a working day. As such they have a documentary immediacy, and despite their being *calavera* figures, they possess recognizable human characteristics. These MSs approach the cinematic by providing closer details of the vendors, which identify them not only by the foods they sell, but also by costume and utensil (the fish, striped skirt, and apron-vest of Aurelia the fish vendor [figure 2]; the large knife of Doña Antonia the butcher [figure 3]). This sort of indication of individual traits was something that evolved in Hollywood and Western cinema throughout the 1910s and was standardized by around 1917.

One of Posada's best-known pieces is the close-up *calavera* of the fashionable lady, *La catrina* (figure 4). This, we could say, is a portrait, though not of a

Figure 2

369

Figure 3

Figure 4

particular person, but of a class of women. Posada's commentary – death over-taking wealth – is much more forceful in this near view, which allows the viewer to see how she clings to the pretensions of her upper-class standing, even beyond the grave: plumes and flowers decorate her fancy hat and ribbons adorn her bony, hairless skull.

A fascinating example of another Posada "medium shot" is a cinema-style two-shot in a skeleton composition (figure 5) included in the *corrido Aquí la calavera esta, señores, de toditos los buenos valedores* (*Here Is the Calavera, Gentle-men, of All the Good Friends*, 1910). Interestingly, these figures can be found as separate subjects in other broadsides (for example, *Calavera de cupido*, 1913). Someone – Posada, Vanegas Arroyo, or the person composing the later page – realized that the two-shot image could be manipulated into individual CUs, prefiguring cinematic shot selection (over-the-shoulder shots) and editing (cut-ting from a MS two-shot to individual CUs).[10]

Leaving the *calaveras* for the moment, another Posada MS is of the strange case of a man who was said to have a foot protruding from his side (figure 6, not dated or otherwise identified). Obviously the nearer vantage point is called for in order to provide important aspects of the freak occurrence and to satisfy viewer curiosity.

3.2   Framing to imply a world outside the composition

One additional feature of medium and close-up images is that their partial views insinuate a diegetic world beyond the "frame." Figure 7, *Alegoria de*

Figure 5

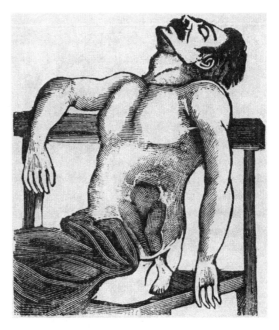

Figure 6

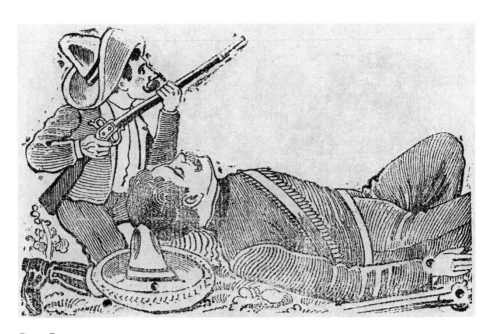

Figure 7

revolucionarios (*Allegory of the Revolutionaries*, not dated), shows the crouched, full body of one soldier, but only three-quarters of the wounded man he is protecting. The compact composition's limited information, together with the look of the soldier toward the upper right part of the composition, imply the existence of what is called in cinema "off-screen space." Another characteristic of the maturing cinematic style, the acknowledgment of and reference to off-screen space goes hand in hand with advancements in editing. Were this an image from a classical-era film, we would expect it to be part of a scene whose progression of shots would typically begin with a LS (establishing the location), then this image, then probably glance-object cutting (the next shot might well be of the person or object holding the soldier's gaze). Beyond editing, camera movement (a pan, tilt, or tracking shot) from this shot would provide important information and thus be well motivated.

3.3   Placing the viewer inside the narrative space

In Hollywood cinema, from 1909 and throughout the 1910s, cameras were positioned closer to the subject in order to feature details of a scene. The camera's entry into the space of the narrative is another clearly cinematic trait. A good example of Posada doing the same thing is figure 8, an undated, unnamed image of women who have gathered to observe Siamese twins. The viewer is placed at a very near vantage point, perhaps even closer to the twins than the women, and has clearly entered the narrative space.

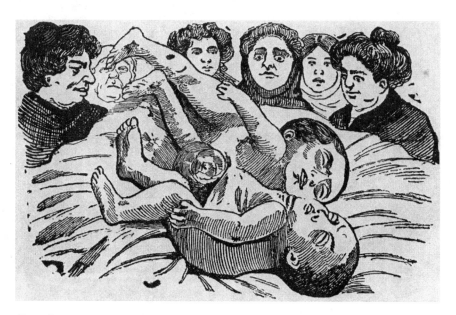

Figure 8

373

3.4 Angled compositions to accentuate depth

Two typical characteristics of early cinema compositions were their frontal, front-row-center perspective and their shallow depth, both of which drew considerably from stage conventions. By shooting actions at an angle, film-makers began emphasizing depth, something the camera could capture but which was severely limited on the stage. While Posada, in figures 1 and 17 for example, did sometimes rely on this head-on proscenium style, he often broke with it to compose the action on an angle and add depth. The broad-side image in figure 9, *Los patinadores* (*The Street Cleaners*, 1890), presents the action at an angle as films would gradually begin doing, particularly in the first decade of the new century. In those early films, a pattern of shooting seemed to be adhered to by which interior shots maintained the frontal, flattened, proscenium perspective while exteriors were angled. Interestingly, although Posada began angling on action much earlier than cinema, as with *Los patinadores*, or with figure 10, *¡Terribles y espantosísimos estragos! habidos por la suma escasez de semillas y el terrible TIFO...(Terrible and Frightful Ravages Caused by a Grain Shortage and the Terrible Typhus...*, 1893), he appears to have followed the same proscenium interior / angled exterior representational practice.

Figure 9

Figure 10

3.5   Multiple images to provide shifts in time and space

In narrativizing events, Posada sometimes found that one image was not enough to relate the tale he had to tell. This is the case with figure 11, from a broadside with the headline *Tristísimas lamentaciones de un enganchado para el Valle Nacional* (*Very Sad Lamentations of a Contracted Laborer at National Valley*, 1903). The broadside is an exposé of the oppression of humble Mexicans kidnapped or hired under false pretenses to work in the plantations of the Valle Nacional region, a common practice during the dictatorship of Porfirio Díaz. In a LS on the left, Posada illustrates a survivor relating his cautionary tale to a crowd of astonished listeners. Then, in an extreme LS enclosed in an oval bubble, he depicts the laborers working the fields. The broadside image provides views not only of two different locations, but perhaps of two different times. (Is the balloon showing what befell the worker in the past or what is still occurring as he tells his story?)

A similar example is found in figure 12, *Un sentenciado en capilla* (*A Prisoner in Solitary Confinement*, no date). Here there is more ambiguity (which the accompanying text, now unavailable, may have clarified). It is not clear in the leap in space and time from the main illustration to the bubble image whether the execution is that of the prisoner or the man's imagining of it. Similar problems in transmitting plot information existed in cinema as primitive narrational systems struggled with standardizing conventions (like thought and dream balloons) and ways to denote a character's thoughts as distinct from simultaneous or subsequent actions.

Figure 11

Figure 12

3.6 Sequential images to relate a narrative

Sometimes Posada used several illustrations to tell a complex story, the equivalent of separate film shots to capture a scene. The three images in figures 13–15, for example, all appeared on a two-sided broadside entitled *Gran Chasco que se pegó Don Chepito Mariguana: Por andar en amores con una mujer casada* (*The Great Joke Played on Don Chepito Mariguana: Because He Pursued a Married Woman*, no date). The comical *corrido*, featuring one of Posada's recurring characters, Don Chepito, tells of his ill-fated attempts to woo a married woman. Don Chepito first declares his love for her on the street (figure 13), then is accosted by the woman's husband (figure 14), and is finally taken to jail (figure 15). Of interest here is first of all Posada's rendering of sequenced events, which required him to isolate and dramatize the key incidents of the story. But beyond that is the fact that in the broadside they appeared in a different order, beginning *in medias res* on the front side with figure 14, then continuing on the back with figure 13, the start of the tale, and figure 15, the end of it. This order in effect creates a flashback from the middle of the narrative, then a flash-*forward* to its conclusion, and anticipates complex movie narratives that would be common in Mexican classical cinema.

A variation of Posada's representation of sequenced events is an illustration in which he collected four different shots in successive panels, as in a comic strip. Figure 16, *De nuestros dibujantes, momentos antes de los acontecimientos* (*From Our Artists, Moments Before the Event*, 1903), showing the attempted theft of a clock, is an illustration Posada did for a small penny periodical called *El diablito*

Figure 13

Figure 14

Figure 15

Figure 16

bromista (Bailey 1979: 116). In the first panel, a garbage collector empties a customer's household waste. In the second, he presents the bill inside to the lady of the house. When she leaves the room to get the money (panel three), he tries to steal the clock, but it chimes on the three-quarter hour and he is caught and attacked (panel four) (Tyler 1979: 230).

3.7   *Framing with partially shown figures in the foreground*

Posada's crowd scenes generally have one fascinating detail in common: they have foreground figures that are cut off by the bottom edge of the composition. For example, though one of Posada's courtroom drawings, figure 17, *Jurado* (*Trial*, no date), has the typical frontality of many of his interior drawings, it varies from the proscenium style in the way the soldiers and onlookers at the bottom of the drawing are cut off above or at the waist (even the two witnesses or defendants, seen at the center bottom, are cut off at the ankles). Another similar courtroom example is figure 18, *El jurado do los asesinos del Sr. Tomás Hernández Aguirre* (*The Trial of the Killers of Mr. Tomás Hernández Aguirre*, 1890 or 1891).

Compositions like these possess several cinematic qualities. They give viewers a privileged view they could only have if they were so close to the scene that they couldn't see the entire bodies of the nearer people: that is, it positions them

Figure 17

Figure 18

within the narrative space and gives the picture documentary immediacy. In addition, the foreground figures frame the action occurring in the middle and background, thus accentuating depth in the frame and taking viewers' eyes from

Figure 19 The trial scene from *El Automóvil Gris* (1919)

fore- to mid- to background. Despite the frontality of these drawings, they are composed in depth, a key characteristic of both Hollywood's and Mexico's classical cinema. Note that the shot from the trial of the bandits in *El automóvil gris* (figure 19) exhibits the same pictorial qualities as the Posada prints.

4 Toward a Participatory Theory of World Cinema History

An analysis of Mexico's popular image media at the turn of the century allows us to rethink some significant issues in Mexican film history. To begin with, looking at a more complete array of image media available at the time, not only cinema, suggests a different slant on Mexico's initial, documentary-intensive, cinematic experience. Maybe its 20-year love affair with the documentary film was not as developmentally stunting as it might at first appear. Perhaps Mexican cinema did not fall "behind" other national cinemas in constructing image narratives, despite its focus on nonfiction, because other segments of the country's greater representational discourse were busy developing a narrative language. From this view, Mexico's visual storytellers may have gained expertise with image narratives by creating and viewing them in various media: in domestic nonfiction films (which appear to have become more narrativized as time went on as well as longer and more complex) and in Mexico's vibrant penny press. To this, of course, must

381

be added their awareness of foreign fiction films, which dominated Mexican movie screens.

Second, the variety and compositional complexity of image narratives available in the nation's penny press may help explain one of the nagging questions of early Mexican film history. How, in the short span of time between 1916, when documentary cinema fell out of favor, to 1919 and the smashing success – and narrative sophistication – of *El automóvil gris*, did Mexican filmmakers become so quickly adept at film narrative? The easy answer, which considers the cinematic evidence exclusively, is that the film's co-director/producer/promoter Enrique Rosas (a) capitalized on his experience of two decades of documentary filmmaking and his brief foray into narrative films as director/producer of the five Mimí Derba melodramas in 1917, and (b) copied what he didn't know about narrative filmmaking from foreign models. An alternative – and more comprehensive – account would factor in advancements in narrative techniques made by all of those, like Posada, who contributed to Mexico's turn-of-the-century image discourse.

Finally, this study of Posada's graphic art and its linkages to Mexican cinema may induce us to consider the global development of narrative film conventions in a different light. One fairly standard way to think about the dominant narrative film paradigm goes like this. It was mostly (or totally) developed by Hollywood and solidified by 1917. Because of Hollywood's world-wide market dominance, other national cinemas dutifully followed suit and imitated the style which then became the standard manner in which to relate narrative in film.

This cultural imperialistic account allows for very little creative participation by filmmakers outside of North America, implying that the rest of the world's filmmakers, particularly those in the Third World, were dupes who copied the narrative conventions arrived at by pioneers in the US. Accordingly, one view of Mexican cinema is that it was in effect forced into adopting the Hollywood paradigm, having fallen so helplessly behind by concentrating on documentaries for 20 years. As Aurelio de los Reyes has put it: "While other nations developed the language of cinema and produced fiction films without neglecting newsreels, Mexico seemed permanently bound to the Lumière-style documentary tradition and to the observation of moving, proto-cinematic phenomena" (1995: 65).

Let me propose a different version of the evolution of Western movie narrative practice, in general and in Mexico. It begins with a different assumption about movie narrative that was standardized throughout the 1910s. Maybe movie narrative was not "created" by Hollywood, then imposed on and imitated by the rest of the world. Maybe, instead, it evolved out of a well-established narrative tradition in the West of representational imagery and theatrical presentation. Because of the United States' economic superiority, expanding industrial and technological base, political stability, and good fortune in not having to fight World War I on its soil, its burgeoning cinema had the best opportunity to make the most films. Therefore, US filmmaking, which migrated to Hollywood by the 1910s, was simply the first to formalize the conventions of cinematic narrative. It did so as a result of its being the leading film producer in the world, which in turn allowed it to experiment extensively in the process of making thousands of films.

From this point of view, the reason the narrative style Hollywood developed was adopted in most Western countries was that it was a fairly predictable culmination of a long history of image narratives, one that stretches from religious iconography to fine painting to magic lantern shows, comic strips, broadside illustrations, and political cartoons. To this representational lineage cinema also appropriated the parallel innovations of theatrical narration. Finally, there was the flow of films – and cinematic influences – from country to country. Indeed, due to the early cinematic cross-pollination from one country to another, Thompson and Bordwell have called the film style that emerged in the period up to World War I "international"; after that the Hollywood style was standardized and became dominant (1994: 39). What if these were not two separate styles, but rather different stages of a single evolutionary cinematic trajectory? The first, international, phase was one of synthesis – the gathering and selecting of narrational techniques from various image media. The second, "classical," stage was the consolidation and application of these techniques to the specifics of the new medium.

A couple of interesting possibilities devolve from such a hypothetical scenario. The first is that, given the right state of affairs, the classical narrative paradigm might have been developed somewhere else. The style standardized by Hollywood, and adopted by Europe and many of its colonized nations, might have been first developed in France or England or Italy had it not been for World War I. Who is to say that it might not have been developed in Mexico, but for the decade-long turmoil caused by the civil war in 1910?

This alternative hypothesis also allows us to think about national cinemas differently. Rather than seeing Hollywood's hegemonic style as superseding and effectively erasing the possibility of other national styles (e.g. the view that the Hollywood style eliminated the possibility of a "true" Mexican cinema), we might instead think of an international stylistic "template." Such a narrative style would be sophisticated and highly structured, yet flexible enough to allow for the incorporation of local representational traditions. The result would be, as with classical Mexican cinema, a narrative practice that was similar to the Hollywood paradigm but contained distinctive regional inflections. This would help explain how the classical Mexican cinema could share the same basic stylistic components as Hollywood's and at the same time remain distinctly and undeniably Mexican. Culture and ideology, within this model, exist independent of this cinematic style; rather, what is known as the classical Hollywood style has the potential to express a number of cultural traditions and/or ideological positions.

Notes

The art of José Guadalupe Posada reproduced in figures 1–18 is courtesy of the Nettie Lee Benson Latin American Collection at the University of Texas at Austin. Figure 19, the still photograph from *El automóvil gris*, is courtesy the Agrasánchez Archive of Mexican Cinema.

1 See especially Fell 1974, 1987. Charles Musser makes references to other image media throughout his excellent study, *The Emergence of Cinema* (1990). His first chapter is a very useful survey of pre-cinematic media. Similarly, Musser's *Before the Nickelodeon* (1991) makes several mentions of comic strips and newspapers in relation to early US cinema.

2 See de los Reyes 1987; Berg 1994. There is also this single tantalizing comment in one study of the work of Posada: "The relationship between popular [Mexican] graphic art... and the imaginative inventions of the earliest film-makers was strong in all countries, and there must have been cross-fertilization from the very beginning" (Berdecio and Appelbaum 1972): 152 n. 174.

3 The note to figure 234 in Tyler (1979: 297) argues that the first estimates of Posada's output numbering 20,000 prints gave Posada credit for all the images produced at the Vanegas Arroyo print shop. It is now generally agreed that other artists produced some of the prints originally attributed to Posada, not the least of whom was Posada's mentor, Manuel Manilla (who died in 1893). Another early estimation was 15,000 prints, made by Toor (in Toor et al. 1930). Most of his work has been lost, so we will never know the exact tally. Nevertheless, in more than 40 years of constant work Posada must have created several thousand prints – still a tremendous number.

4 Fernando Gamboa notes that Antonio Vanegas Arroyo, "aided by his son Blas, was one of the first to bring movies to Mexico in 1903" (1944: 17).

5 Arsacio Vanegas Arroyo, the grandson of Antonio Vanegas Arroyo, the publisher of many of Posada's etchings, claimed that some of the published ballads sold millions of copies. One children's game illustrated by Posada, "La oca" ("The Goose"), is said to have sold as many as 5,000,000 copies throughout Mexico. This astounding market saturation would make Posada without a doubt the best-known artist in Mexico at the time (Arroyo 1943).

6 Appendices 2 and 3 in Tyler (1979: 300–2) list selected penny newspapers and give their prices. Most sold for *un centavo*, though some sold for two centavos, with an occasional one selling for three or five. Some of the broadsides in the Edward Larocque Tinker collection of the Humanities Research Center at the University of Texas, Austin, had prices of five and ten centavos.

7 This was, in fact, a popular tactic of itinerant Mexican filmmakers. They would visit a town and announce that they would photograph the congregation leaving the next Sunday's mass. A crowd would gather to be captured by their camera the next Sunday, and the following Monday the same crowd would attend the screening of this local *actualitié*. See de los Reyes 1995: 64–5.

8 There had been sporadic attempts at *el filme de argumento* (narrative films) before, but never had there been a sustained effort of the kind that began in 1917.

9 In one form or another, I believe I have seen most of the approximately 1,000 Posada prints. To assemble this list of cinematic techniques, I made use of the following collections of Posada's art: several hundred images in the Edward Larocque Tinker collection of the Humanities Research Center at the University of Texas, Austin; numerous illustrations in rare books and periodicals held in the Nettie Lee Benson Latin American Collection at the University of Texas; the 272 illustrations collected in Berdecio and Appelbaum's *Posada's Popular Mexican Prints* (1972); and the several

hundred Posada images in *Posada's Mexico* (Tyler 1979), which is the catalogue of an exhibition of Posada's work held at the Library of Congress in 1980.

10 There are numerous other examples of larger etchings and engravings being cut down to smaller compositions, evidently depending on what was needed by the layout artist at the time.

References

Arroyo, Arsacio Vanegas. 1943. "José Guadalupe Posada." In *José Guadalupe Posada: 36 grabados*. Mexico City: Ediciones Arsacio Vanegas Arroyo.

Bailey, Joyce Waddell. 1979. "The Penny Press." In Tyler 1979.

Berdecio, Roberto, and Stanley Appelbaum. 1972. *Posada's Popular Mexican Prints*. New York: Dover.

Berg, Charles Ramírez. 1994. "The Cinematic Invention of Mexico: The Poetics and Politics of the Fernandez–Figueroa Style." In *The Mexican Cinema Project*. Ed. Chon Noriega and Robert Rosen. Los Angeles: UCLA Film and Television Archive. 13–24.

——. Forthcoming. "*El automóvil gris* (1919) and the Advent of Mexican Classicism." In *Visible Nations: Latin American Film and Video*. Ed. Chon Noriega. Minneapolis: University of Minnesota Press.

Bordwell, David. 1985. *Narration in the Fiction Film*. Madison: University of Wisconsin Press.

Bowser, Eileen. 1990. "The Films: Alternate Scenes." In *The Transformation of Cinema: 1907–1915*. New York: Charles Scribner's Sons.

de los Reyes, Aurelio. 1983. *Cine y sociedad en México 1896–1930: Vivar de Sueños*. Mexico City: Universidad Nacional Autónoma de México.

——. 1987. *Medio siglo de cine Mexicano (1896–1947)*. Mexico City: Editorial Trillas.

——. 1995. "The Silent Cinema." In *Mexican Cinema*. Ed. Paulo Antonio Paranaguá. London: BFI.

Elliott, David. 1980. "Orozco: A Beginning." In *¡orozco! 1883–1949*. Ed. David Elliott. Oxford: Museum of Modern Art.

Fell, John L. 1974. *Film and the Narrative Tradition*. Norman: University of Oklahoma Press.

——. 1987. "Cellulose Nitrate Roots: Popular Entertainments and the Birth of Film Narrative." In *Before Hollywood: Turn-of-the-Century American Film*. New York: Hudson Hills Press. 39–49.

Gamboa, Fernando. 1944. "José Guadalupe Posada: The Man, His Art, His Times." In *Posada, Printmaker to the Mexican People*. Chicago: The Art Institute of Chicago.

Musser, Charles. 1990. *The Emergence of Cinema: The American Screen to 1907*. New York: Charles Scribner's Sons.

——. 1991. *Before the Nickelodeon: Edwin S. Porter and the Edison Manufacturing Company*. Berkeley: University of California Press.

Romanell, Patrick. 1952. *Making of the Mexican Mind: A Study in Recent Mexican Thought*. Lincoln: University of Nebraska Press.

Thompson, Kristin. 1985. "From Primitive to Classical." In David Bordwell, Janet Staiger, and Kristin Thompson. *The Classical Hollywood Cinema: Film Style and Mode of Production to 1960*. New York: Columbia University Press.

——, and David Bordwell. 1994. *Film History: An Introduction*. New York: McGraw-Hill.

Toor, Frances, Paul O'Higgins, and Blas Vanegas Arroyo, eds. 1930. *Monografía: Las obras de José Guadalupe Posada, grabador Mexicano*. Intro. Diego Rivera. Mexico: Mexican Folkways.

Tyler, Ron, ed. 1979. *Posada's Mexico*. Washington: Library of Congress.

CHAPTER TWENTY

"Historical Poetics," Narrative, and Interpretation

Ira Bhaskar

Literature is an inseparable part of culture and it cannot be understood outside *the total context of the entire culture of a given epoch...*
Mikhail Bakhtin, "Response to a Question from the *Novy Mir* Editorial Staff" (my emphasis)

Interpretation takes as its basic subject our perceptual, cognitive and affective processes, but it does so in a roundabout way – by attributing their "output" to the text "out there." To understand a film interpretively is to subsume it to our conceptual schemes, and thus to master them more fully, if only tacitly.
David Bordwell, *Making Meaning*

I

In *Making Meaning*, David Bordwell proposes the project of "historical poetics" as an alternative to an interpretation-dominated criticism of the cinema, which, he feels, has been ill-founded precisely in that interpretive activity can be characterized by the highly suspect ascription of implicit and symptomatic meanings to a text.[1] While most scholars would not contest, but would rather welcome, Bordwell's call for a historical contextualization of the study of cinema, there would be several who would not respond as positively to his characterization of interpretive activity per se, despite the excesses of interpretation that he has outlined. Bad examples of any activity do not deny its inherent validity. However, Bordwell's objections to interpretation do not function at the level of inadequate or misplaced application of interpretive principles in current criticism. Rather it is the fundamental nature of the interpretive activity itself, which both accounts for its central place in critical practice and prevents other more worthwhile inquiries, that Bordwell finds difficult to accept or endorse. For even if the interpretive practice were revamped, it would still not "push the ascription of implicit or symptomatic meanings out of its central place in critical practice" (Bordwell 1989b: 263). The problem for Bordwell, then, seems to lie in the idea of implicit and symptomatic meanings which interpretation deals with, as opposed to referential and explicit meaning which is the domain of comprehension.

An adequate response to Bordwell's hostility to interpretive practice and the alternative of "historical poetics" that he suggests would need to confront his characterization of both interpretation and the enterprise of historical poetics, in order to examine their intrinsic worth and whether the two are in fact as inimical as Bordwell makes them out to be. This is not an unqualified view though. For despite a rhetoric of hostility to interpretation throughout *Making Meaning*, there are points at which he actually states that he would not like to repudiate interpretation altogether, but just to place it "within a broader historical inquiry" (266). In that case, "within the framework of a poetics, interpretation [would take on] its proper importance" (273). He also concedes that the work of Bazin, Burch, and some other historian–critics does indicate that the "construction of implicit and symptomatic meaning can co-exist with the study of form and style in given historical circumstances" (267). This would lead one to respond that perhaps Bordwell's problem with interpretive practice is that it does not in fact realize its potential, does not do what it is meant to do. However, that is not quite the case. For, despite his attempt to recuperate interpretation within the domain of "historical poetics" at the end of *Making Meaning*, there is throughout the book a suspicion of the enterprise per se, a suspicion that leads him to dismiss the significance of the interpretive work that he does, in fact, think has some value. There are, then, "unresolved ambiguities and tensions," not only, as Berys Gaut has pointed out, in Bordwell's neoformalist theory's key notion of construction (Gaut 1995: 9),[2] but also in his conception of the interpretive project itself.

These tensions and contradictions in Bordwell's discussion of interpretation come from a misconceived notion of the enterprise itself. Further, it is the contention of this chapter that Bordwell's misconception of interpretation comes from an inadequate understanding of narrative and its functions, effects, and significances, and an incomplete understanding of history. Bordwell sees a sharp division between comprehending the narrative of a film and interpreting its meaning, just as he sees a division between referential and explicit meanings on the one hand, and implicit and symptomatic meanings on the other. There is a similar schism in Bordwell between narrative and ideology, between form and content, and perhaps even between history and culture. At the root of these divisions lies a notion of narrative as story or "fabula" and its presentation as the plot or "syuzhet." Constructing the fabula from the syuzhet becomes the privileged activity of comprehension, so that the meanings that are relevant, according to Bordwell, are only those that have to do with the diegesis of the narrative (referential) and its explicit "moral" or "message." Any other kinds of meanings that critics see in a narrative are those that they bring to bear from semantic fields of critical institutions that lie outside the narrative.[3] Interpretation is, therefore, an activity that is suspect to Bordwell because it is always done at the expense of a consideration of the "form and style" of a film (1989b: 261), for the interpretive critic is much more involved with abstract theoretical ideas than with constructional principles and the effects of those principles.

Conceived in these terms, interpretation does seem like an extraneous activity, for all that is valuable as a response to narrative is comprehension – of its referential and explicit meanings and, beyond that, of its constructive principles and its effects. How would "historical poetics" reform the activity of interpretation? As Bordwell defines it, "historical poetics" seems much more concerned with locating the elements of style in a historical context, with studying the historical development of style and the constructive principles of films and their effects historically, than with the meanings that are central to the interpretive act. Would understanding how film style developed historically and what the effects of film have been at different points of time help us to understand the entire range of meanings that a film generates and thereby create better interpretations? The answers to problem-centered questions that neoformalist historical poetics would ask would certainly enhance our knowledge of what "constructional options" filmmakers were faced with at different "historical conjunctures" (Bordwell 1989a: 381), and what impacts those choices had on different audiences at different points in time. But in order to understand why there were certain choices before filmmakers and why there were certain effects on certain audiences, apart from the history of styles, concepts, and the determinations of the economic and technological systems of filmmaking which Bordwell emphasizes, we would also have to look at the entire field of socio-cultural life that generates what Bakhtin and Medvedev call "the ideological horizon" of an epoch (1978: 17), the determining matrix of all representational forms of the age as also of responses to those forms. Bakhtin and Medvedev's view that "the qualitative development of existence and the ideological world that is history [was] completely inaccessible to formalism" (97) can be applied in part to Bordwell's formulation of "historical poetics" as well. It is unfortunate that Bordwell did not take into account the entire Bakhtinian critique of formalism: while he does consider what Bakhtin and Medvedev would call "the unity of literature" and the "unified socio-economic laws of development," it is the missing link of "the unity of ideological and historical life" from the Bakhtinian paradigm[4] that makes Bordwell's characterization of history in his "historical poetics" inadequate. Had he acknowledged Bakhtin's formulation of "historical poetics,"[5] he might have been able to confront and enter into a dialogue/debate with the latter, which might have led to a more comprehensive notion of history that would certainly benefit the project of "historical poetics" that Bordwell proposes to revitalize the field of cinema studies.

Further, would answers to the questions regarding the constructive principles, functions, and effects of film that Bordwell's "historical poetics" proposes help us to understand the meanings of a film text – even the referential and explicit meanings that Bordwell thinks are worth pursuing? Not entirely, for the referential or diegetic implications and the explicit messages or morals of the film text form the content, which reflects, in Bakhtinian terms, "the whole of the ideological horizon" of which literature or cinema is itself a part (Bakhtin and Medvedev 1978: 17). And if content is generated by the ideological environment of an age, then implicit and symptomatic meanings would be as contained within it as referential and explicit ones. It is not just symptomatic meanings that can be traced, as Bordwell says, to "economic, political, or ideological processes" (1989b: 9; see also note 3), but all the types of meaning which are contained in both the content and the form of the work. For if we follow Bakhtin, form and structure are as ideologically shaped as themes and content.[6] Understood in this manner, interpretive activity would have to confront the meanings of a text and would therefore have to deal with the narrative at hand directly, and not in the "roundabout way" that Bordwell describes.[7]

However, this demands a view of narrative as culturally and historically rooted, as embodying within it the life-world of its times: in other words, as embodying the forms of cultural life, the life processes, the ideologies, the values, in fact the very conceptual schemes that Bordwell sees as the subject of inter-pretation. If narrative were to be understood in this way, as encoding within its fabula and syuzhet, its form and style, the vision of its world, then the inter-pretive act would not be schismatically separated from the comprehensive one, and explicit, referential meanings would carry within them the implicit, sympto-matic ones. Interpretation would not be seen as dealing with the text in a "roundabout way" by attributing our "perceptual, cognitive and affective pro-cesses" to the object "out there" (Bordwell 1989b: 257), but rather it would be possible to see interpretation as confronting the text much more directly in an empathetic, exploratory, comprehensive mode. The resultant "understanding"[8] of a narrative text would thus imply an understanding of both the cultural, historical world that has produced the narrative and the one that it represents. The reader/viewer's response to the narrative would dynamize his "perceptual, cognitive and affective processes," and the act of interpretation would then be concerned as much with understanding the text as with understanding our conceptual schemes and our temporal location in a world that may or may not be similar to the world of the text. Interpretation, then, is a dual-pronged activity – directed both outward to the text and its world and inward to ourselves and our context, in a mutually illuminating move.

What is at issue here is a conception of narrative that is implicit in Bordwell's discussion of making meaning. It can be identified with Genette's theorizing of narrative as "narrative discourse," in which his definition and distinctions of the three different meanings of the term comprise the language or means of expre-ssion, the story or content, and the act of enunciation or narration (Genette 1993: 25–6). While Genette does point out that the analysis of narrative discourse "implies a study of relationships," and that describing any one of the three aspects of narrative necessarily involves the others (27–9), he does not locate the three dimensions of narrative in culture. Without cultural and historical contextualization, the analysis of narrative discourse can become just an exposi-tion on the act of enunciation, the means of narration or expression, and when it does deal with the story or content at all, it can face the problems of unsituated auteur or thematic criticism – a fault that Bordwell has correctly related to the excesses of explicative criticism.[9]

Against Genette's theory of narrative can be juxtaposed the Bakhtinian idea of a narrative text as situated in a matrix of cultural discursivity that penetrates it and manifests itself in obvious, as well as latent, content and significance. From the Bakhtinian perspective, a narrative text cannot be understood without a decoding of the cultural meanings that are embedded, and have accrued over centuries, in the strata of popular languages, in the forms of cultural expressions, and in the "forms of thinking" that are specific to a particular culture[10] and which the text has woven together into patterns of cultural signification (Bakhtin 1986b: 5).[11] "Narrative comprehension" would therefore involve understanding how the "form" of a particular work embodies the "forms of thinking" that are specific to a particular culture. Furthermore, the Bordwellian "referential and explicit" meanings of a text are actually forms of cultural expression which carry "the implicit and symptomatic meanings" that give voice to "the powerful deep currents of culture" (3).

This is not to suggest, however, that meanings are fixed for all time and that audience experience has no role to play in making meaning, but rather that whatever orientations audiences bring to texts, they would still have to negotiate their cultural "meanings," for, as Bakhtin points out, every utterance is a historical and social act, and an "organic, historical, and actual connection is established between the meaning and act (utterance), between the act and the concrete sociohistorical situation" (Bakhtin and Medvedev 1978: 120). A historical poetics must, therefore, confront the historical context of the utterance with all the socio-cultural significances that this would imply. A Bakhtinian response would demand not only a contextual location of texts, which Bordwell does not adequately emphasize, but also the contextual location of the audience, to which he does pay attention in his proposal that since historical poetics is concerned with "effects," it will study the "practices . . . of reception" as well as those of "production" (1989b: 270). As cultural, historical situations change, there are various interpretations that become possible in contexts other than those in which the text has been produced, because of the emergence and development of newer discourses and theoretical formulations which, as Bordwell correctly points out, form the interpretations of critics. However, what Bordwell does not accept is that the institutional framework is only one of the determining elements in the process of building interpretations and would form the important other dimension of reader/spectator positioning in the active "interaction" between the text and the receiver. Bakhtin, in fact, maintains that "the work is never a ready message given once and for all," but rather it is constructed as "a kind of ideological bridge" in the interaction between the author and the reader, and that this process "causes both the thematic unity of the generating work and the form of its actual realization" (Bakhtin and Medvedev 1978: 151–2). Using the Bakhtinian perspective, then, it would be possible to avoid the kind of problem

391

that Bordwell's constructivist account is meant to overcome, that meanings of texts seem to vary historically and culturally, thereby justifying his account of meaning-making as dependent on the frameworks that spectators/readers bring to texts rather than on finding them in the text. In contrast, what the Bakhtinian perspective would suggest is that while readers/spectators bring their cultural, political awareness constituted outside the text to the literary/filmic experience, thereby inflecting it with their various "perspectival languages,"[12] they still have to negotiate the "ideological horizon" of the text, and in this interaction the "meanings" that are justifiable are those that owe some allegiance to textual features, structures, and intentions. In other words, the extrinsic theoretical frameworks that Bordwell would say critics use to interpret films would only become relevant in the text–audience interaction if there are elements in the text which respond to them: that is to say, the audience–film text interaction still functions within limits – limits imposed by textual features as much as by historical and cultural conditions and conditioning.

Read in this way, comprehending narrative would not mean just understanding how stories are constructed and the effects they have on people, though it would certainly imply that. It would also mean understanding why they have the effects they do, which would bring us face to face with the messages, both overt and covert, that narratives carry – messages that are "powerful" and evocative because they touch a deeper substratum of chords in a culture that, once touched, resonate with a multiplicity of implications that interpretation articulates. Comprehension and interpretation are thus closely imbricated, precisely because the meanings they deal with cannot be schismatically separated from each other. This imbrication of what Bordwell calls the referential, explicit and the implicit, symptomatic meanings could perhaps be better understood if one were to use the Barthesian idea of the integrated functioning of the five codes or voices which a narrative text comprises. While the hermeneutic and the proairetic codes deal with the central enigma and the actions of the narrative, the semic, the symbolic, and the cultural or the referential codes are concerned with signification and are therefore involved with the meanings that a culture articulates through its texts (Barthes 1994). The semic code articulates the emotional and cultural associations of a word/image and can thus be seen as contextualized in the referential. The symbolic is, according to Barthes, the "province of the antithesis" (17) that orchestrates the oppositions of the narrative. These oppositions are culturally determined and the play of the symbolic negotiates the antinomies through which cultural meaning is articulated. All five codes are "bound by the heavy weight of convention and tradition – centuries of what Barthes calls the 'what's already been written and done'" (Lesage 1985: 478). The Bakhtinian notion of "dialogism" as the "necessary relation of any utterance to other utterances" (cited in Stam et al. 1992: 203) that are rooted in socio-cultural life and history can thus be related to Barthes' sense that "alongside each utterance . . . offstage voices can be heard," voices that are woven together in the text and thus embody "the plurality and the circularity of the codes" (1994: 77). The Bakhtinian–Barthesian paradigm is an important counter-thrust to readings of narrative as "narrative discourse," a formulation that Bordwell implicitly identifies and sympathizes with. If the former formulation of narrative were to be used to understand the impulses of interpretive activity, the tensions and contradictions in Bordwell's response to interpretation could be easily resolved, and one would also have a historical and cultural contextualization of interpretation, without which no "historical poetics" of narrative art or cinema is either comprehensive or adequate.

II

A call to reinstate, along with Bakhtin's, the Barthesian model of narrative construction and interpretation must, however, take into account the fact that Bordwell rejects both the communication (Bakhtinian) and the signification (Saussurean) models of meaning in favor of an inferential model whereby the perceiver uses cues in the film to "execute determinable operations, of which the construction of all sorts of meanings will be a part" (1989b: 270). Bordwell does not examine or debate the values and drawbacks of the two models that he rejects, and neither does he examine the internal coherence of the inferential model that he espouses. His formulation of a neoformalist poetics, which rests on an inferential model where meanings are constructed by viewers, applying schemata to cues in the film, contradicts inherently the rational-agent explanatory scheme of filmmaking, proposed by neoformalism, which foregrounds the voluntary control over the meanings of a film that the filmmaker exerts, and which is demonstrated in the deliberate constructional choices that she or her team make during the process of filmmaking (270).

If meanings are made by filmmakers in the process of making very self-conscious choices, as the rational-agent model of filmmaking implies, then how would this position be reconciled with the inferential model, in keeping with which Bordwell asserts throughout *Making Meaning* that "meanings are not found but made" (3)? It is true that Bordwell uses the rational-agent model to explain the construction of films and the perceptual-cognitive or the inferential model to explain the "effects" of films, and he does concede that "to some extent, the filmmaker . . . can construct the film in such a way that certain cues are likely to be salient and certain inferential pathways are marked out." However, he asserts quite correctly that the filmmaker cannot control "all the semantic fields, schemata and heuristics which the perceiver may bring to bear on the film," and, therefore, audiences may "use the film for other purposes than the maker anticipated." Furthermore, he maintains that critics operating within "the institution of film criticism" are likely to "produce implicit and symptomatic meanings, regardless of the filmmaker's intent" (270). While it is true that viewers/ readers and critics often make of texts significances that may not have been intended, Bordwell does not adequately emphasize that viewers/critics do often attempt to locate their own readings in a contextual situation which not only takes the constructional choices of artists into account but also locates them in a larger context that explains why these choices were necessary.[13] The inferential model that Bordwell uses to explain reception needs both the rational–agent model and the institutional model[14] as much as it needs a larger socio-cultural contextualization if it is to adequately explain why films have the effects they do. To use different models to explain different aspects of filmmaking and reception without emphasizing the interactions between processes only foregrounds contradictory conclusions: for example, that artists voluntarily control meanings which they translate into constructional choices on the one hand, and that audiences make their own meanings which they do not find in the texts they receive on the other. These contradictions in his account of making meaning, which Bordwell neither confronts nor resolves, could be worked out if the Bakhtinian account of reception discussed above could be incorporated into Bordwell's schema. The result would be a "historical poetics" with interpretation truly absorbed within it, as Bordwell desires.

Further, Bordwell's inferential model, which grounds his theory of narrative comprehension, has been critiqued by Richard Allen, who demonstrates that since the cognitive theory of perception, upon which Bordwell's theory of narrative comprehension is based, misconceives the nature of seeing, it is not an adequate explanation for narrative comprehension (Allen 1997).[15] Berys Gaut has proved that the constructivism of Bordwell's inferential model is seriously flawed and does not explain the comprehension and interpretation of films (Gaut 1995).[16] So while Bordwell may have rejected the communication and the signification or semiotic models because they are rather simplistic and inadequate explanations of the processes of comprehension and interpretation (either of them would commit neoformalism to a detectivist view of interpretation, whereby the task of the interpreter would be either to grasp the message transmitted by a sender or to decode a previously encoded message), the inferential model to which Bordwell is committed is also contradictory and an inadequate explanation of comprehension and interpretation. Perhaps the answer lies in understanding that comprehension and interpretation do not rigidly conform to any one of these models exclusively. Rather, they use methods from all these models, and, moreover, the models are not mutually exclusive. Viewers do use schemata while comprehending and interpreting films; but they also grapple with the messages of a text, just as their response to narrative texts involves them in the activity of decoding messages that have been previously encoded. Neither the communication model nor the signification model need commit one entirely to intentionalist explanations, for by locating these models and the messages they communicate in the contexts of culture and history, we would see in the individual act of making meaning, whether in the construction of the text or in its interpretation, the life-rhythms, the values, and the belief structures of its context. By reconciling the processes of the models that Bordwell opposes, and by using the Bakhtinian and the Barthesian sense of signification, we would have a "hermeneutics" and a "poetics of interpretation"[17] that would be free from the contradictions we find in Bordwell's account.

In fact, the contradictions in Bordwell's response to interpretation persist because he insists on the division between comprehension and interpretation, with the latter seen as the ascription of implicit and symptomatic meanings to a text. There are two ruptures here that are important and that need to be addressed. The first has to do with the schism between the different kinds of meaning in a text, so that the referential and explicit meanings, which are connected with the syuzhet and the fabula of a film and are the domain of comprehension, are seen as distinct from the text's implicit and symptomatic meaning. George Wilson has demonstrated that it is impossible to see the implicit meanings of narrative film as separated from its referential ones for "the implicit meanings of a film are inextricable from the network of relationships that constitute a fabula portrayed in film" (Wilson 1997: 226). Similarly, the symptomatic meanings of a text, which Bordwell identifies with its repressed ideology, cannot be seen as a priori meanings that critics superimpose on films, for ideological questions are inherent in the constructional choices that filmmakers make – choices that relate to genre, form, style, and characterization as much as they are related to any repressed meaning that the narrative discloses, despite the director, through "its gaps and fissures."[18] Bordwell has appropriately pointed to the *Cahiers* and *Screen* critics' work for this sense of ideological determination. Thomas Schatz's work on genres also emphasizes the inextricable relationship between genres and ideologies (see Schatz 1981: esp. chs 1, 2).

As a historian of genres, forms, and styles, the neoformalist poetician begins with, Bordwell asserts, the concrete assumptions embedded in the filmmaker's craft (1989b: 269). But genres, forms, and styles involve more than the craft of the filmmaker. As Bakhtin points out, genres "accumulate forms of seeing and interpreting particular aspects of the world" (1986b: 5). Genres codify cultural responses, are semically coded, and carry within them the weight of signification from history and culture. A study of genre would have to confront the implicit and the ideological questions that genres carry within them. Thus, any attempt to understand generic, formal, and stylistic features in themselves, and purely at the level of craft, would be to divorce "form" from the particular historical and cultural "content" and context of the narrative. Even though Bordwell is ostensibly against a form–content split, by separating the referential and explicit meanings from the implicit, symptomatic ones and by privileging the study of constructional form over "thematics" he is in reality doing just that. Any "historical poetics" of genre, form, and style that does not study the implicit and symptomatic questions of a text – in other words, does not study the text holistically – would be as inadequate as a history of narrative art as it would be as an interpretation.

This brings us to the second rupture that results from Bordwell's separation of comprehension and interpretation. By seeing interpretation as the ascription of implicit and/or symptomatic meanings to a text, and with the sense that these meanings come from the schemata of critical institutions that the critic then maps almost randomly onto cues in the film, Bordwell implicitly divorces the interpretive activity, and also the text, from the world and culture of which they are a part. This is also clear from his characterization of the interpretive activity. According to Bordwell, "knowledge of the text is not the most salient effect of the interpretive enterprise," which does not aim at providing either "causal" or "functional" explanations (1989b: 257). It is not the "text" but "our perceptual, cognitive and affective processes" that are the subject of interpretation. By characterizing the activity of interpretation in these terms, Bordwell brings about a disjuncture between the text and our "perceptual, cognitive and affective processes" that are the "effects" of the text (257), thereby locking us completely outside the world of the text with no means by which to access it. The ordinary experience of comprehending and interpreting texts is otherwise. Within Bordwell's definition of interpretation, the text would function merely as a catalyst or a prompt to encourage "a disciplined speculation on the possibilities of meaning" (258). The text thus loses its specificity[19] and its value as a representation of a world, which, when we respond to it, increases our "knowledge" in the sense of "understanding"[20] understanding of a world perhaps similar to ours or perhaps even a little different, as well as of ourselves and our emotional, mental, and intellectual responses. While Bordwell is quite right in seeing that interpretation "answers to a widely felt interest in motives, intention, and ethical responsibility by showing that artworks which do not offer explicit guides for behaviour can raise significant issues of thought, feeling and action" (1989b: 258), he doesn't see that interpretation is only able to do so by explicating and interpreting the situations and the network of relationships that a text represents. If indeed interpretation "reactivates and revises our common frameworks of understanding" (257),[21] it does so only because the subject of interpretation is the text, and interpretation is about understanding the world of the text, the culture from which it is produced, and, by extension, human societies and life processes. Neither a text nor our "perceptual, cognitive, and affective processes" exist in a vacuum, and it is only when we recognize the contextual nature of life, and also speculation, that the interpretive act can be correctly valued.

It is because Bordwell values "interpretation's greatest achievement" as "its ability to encourage reflections upon our conceptual schemes"[22] that he actually undervalues the real benefits and achievements of interpretation. Having created a schism between interpretation and historical criticism, and with his heavy bias against the former, he has no option but to be either reductive or appropriative when responding to interpretations that cannot be dismissed as wayward, cavalier, or wholly "finalistic" (i.e. based upon a priori codifications of what a film must ultimately mean[23]). Speaking of the positive contribution that interpretation-dominated criticism has made to the creation of a tradition for film studies, Bordwell says:

Conceiving of the text as symptomatically revealing cultural tensions introduced a powerful frame of reference. To claim unity across an auteur's output, to posit that cinema contains three looks, and to suggest that a genre may constitute an intersection of nature and culture organized a great deal of information within a new perspective. (1989b: 256)

The benefits of interpretation as characterized by Bordwell here seem rather ineffectual, even insignificant. Do effective interpretations add only "powerful frame[s] of reference" or organize "information within a new perspective"? Does interpretation not add to our understanding of the value, the everlasting appeal and functions of narrative art in society? It is typical of Bordwell not to speak of the insights into human life, social processes, the intricate nature of human and social interaction, and the historical and cultural determination of human action that we gain from an interpretation-centered criticism. While no one would challenge Bordwell's critique of inadequate interpretations, it would be devaluing the force and function of interpretation to see its positive examples as merely "innovative frames of reference" that "have heightened our awareness of what can be noticed and appreciated in artworks" (256). To render positive interpretive activity as one that permits innovative semantic fields to pick out hitherto unperceived cues in the text impoverishes formal and stylistic, as well as thematic, analysis.

At the same time, when Bordwell does have examples of interpretive activity that also meet his demand for a "sensuous criticism" (264) and a study of formal elements, he appropriates the work as a form of "historical poetics" and states that "the construction of implicit and symptomatic meaning can co-exist with the study of form and style in given historical circumstances" (267). The writings of Bazin and Burch are examples.[24] The point is not that Bordwell is wrong in this statement, but rather whether the two activities – a sensuous criticism that recovers "art's sensuousness" (264) and the construction of implicit and symptomatic meanings, with the assumption that film's composition and effects are vehicles of the former – are mutually exclusive and contradictory. Bordwell's formulation of a difference and division between interpretation and historical criticism demands this polarity. Otherwise, a historically and culturally nuanced study of form and style that sees them as bearers of explicit, as well as implicit, symptomatic meanings can be seen as the most comprehensive form of interpretation. Just as a historical and cultural study of form and style need not be opposed to a sensuous criticism, so also an emphasis on the sensuousness of art can complement and enhance the interpretive understanding of a text and its world.

Despite his hostility and objections to interpretation, Bordwell declares at various points that to outlaw all the conventions of interpretation would be to impoverish film studies. And yet the charge remains that interpreters have scarcely paid any attention to film form and style. He seems opposed to what he calls the concentric-circle model, whereby aspects of setting or camerawork amplify or comment on characters' interaction. This would be to subordinate film style to issues considered important on other counts (260–1). While Bordwell is quite right to warn us that doctrinal readings of films can see any aspect of form and style in terms of a master narrative, and his many examples quite correctly point to the often absurd formulations that come from an approach that applies predetermined meanings to read visual images or film style (for example, to see mirrors as signifying reflexivity), it would be equally disastrous and lopsided to concentrate only on "the principles according to which films are constructed and by means of which they achieve particular effects" (1989a: 371), especially when these principles are not located in the larger socio-cultural ideological environment of the time.

The other equally important question for historical poetics is how and why these principles have arisen and changed in particular empirical circumstances. This historical study of the changing principles of film construction is commendable. However, it is important to realize that a consideration of "why" constructional principles have evolved as they have would bring us face to face with questions of economics, ideology, ethics, and the morality and values of the society in which the films are being made,[25] with questions of how and why genres uphold ideological, psychological formations and are tied into the deeper determinants of the cultural psyche – in fact, all those questions that are central to the implicit and symptomatic meanings of films, considered the domain of interpretation. And any study of constructional principles that does not confront these issues would fall short of the very yardsticks that Bordwell himself formulates for "historical poetics." In the same vein, neoformalism's identity as a historical poetics, with its emphasis "on historically changing norms, devices, systems and functions" which "requires that the analyst complement the scrutiny of single films with the study of a wide range of films" (1989a: 382), would be incomplete without a study of history, society, and culture that give form its content.[26] Form itself carries a symptomatic meaning, and therefore a hostility to the latter would mean that one does not read form at all. Bakhtin's suggestion that "scholarly poetics should be adequate to the whole generating series of literary development" (Bakhtin and Medvedev 1978: 159) would be an important corrective to Bordwell's sense of cinematic history as dealing only with filmic series in interaction with the laws of socio-economic development without any contextualizing in "other ideological series."[27]

What is at issue here is that ideological questions which Bordwell banishes to the realm of "symptomatic interpretation" are central to any understanding of form or "constructional options" open at various "historical conjunctures" (1989a: 381). Any understanding of the latter must accept a view of film history that is not a linear, teleological trajectory which moves through classical narrative cinema through Soviet montage cinema and then art cinema and so on.[28] Bordwell's understanding that Hollywood cinema, Soviet montage cinema, art cinema, and other kinds of cinema use different constructional forms (1989a: 381) must also admit that, along with historical positioning, ideological questions are important to the choices that different kinds of artist have made. So his suggestions for a "sensuous criticism" of form and style, which recovers the "palpability of the object" (Victor Shklovsky, cited in Bordwell 1989b: 264), and a historical study of particular films, with special attention to the processes that brought them into being, must accept that form can only be properly understood when all the meanings that it carries – explicit and referential, implicit and symptomatic – are allowed to body forth. Bordwell's own example of Vance Kepley's sensuous and historical reading of Dovzhenko's work demonstrates that form carries ideological and symptomatic meanings.[29] To therefore divorce the study of form from the meanings that it carries is an extremely misplaced impulse, and one that would counter the project of historical poetics. Interpretation and historical poetics may not be as inimicable as Bordwell has assumed in his account of making meaning.

Furthermore, to see meaning as related to the "effects" of a work (270) is as misplaced as divorcing meaning from form. A text's form and meaning together generate effects. In the same way it would be inadequate to deal with themes merely as "constructive principles" or "effects of constructive principles," as Bordwell proposes (1989a: 375), for themes embody the meanings of a work, meanings which structure the significance of the text's cultural context. While Bordwell sees meaning, structure, and process – the three aspects of any representational system – as central to historical poetics (376), he doesn't see the contradiction in his statement that thematics are important only if they are seen as constructional principles. Themes contain the meaning of a work, but they are structured and given form and, therefore, significance only through the constructional principles of a film. As Bakhtin would say, "there is no formless content and there is no contentless form" (Bakhtin and Medvedev 1978: 140). To deal with themes as existing outside the form and structure of a text (which Bordwell critiques) is as misplaced as what he himself suggests. For to see themes as constructive principles or their effects would be to read the meaning of a film purely in terms of "stylistic/perceptual/logical" (Carney 1989: 45) and affective principles and thus to read narrative as essentially about the means of expression and its affective implications. What is left out is the entire spectrum of situations, conflicts, and choices with their concomitant thoughts, feelings, and ideas that present the reader/viewer with hypothetical possibilities to entertain and follow, which may constitute the perennial appeal of narrative – possibilities that may not present themselves in our lives but offer explanations of our world and the human condition and equip us to deal with our own situations more appropriately.

The effects of a work are multiple and can range from pure "pleasure," which Bordwell is aware of,[30] to speculation about the potentials and possibilities open to individuals, to meditations about the human condition. Bordwell is quite right in maintaining that constructional principles and the effects they have are the results of carefully deliberated choices made by filmmakers (1989b: 268–9). However, the particular effects that a work has are not only the result of the meanings that its themes have structured, but are also deliberate ideological choices that the makers have made.[31] If poetics involves, along with a study of the construction of a text, a study of its effects, as Bordwell maintains (1989b: 270; 1989a: 383), then a study of a text's reception would involve not only an understanding of the ideology of the text, but also the assumption of its effectivity which comes from a recognition that the ideologies, the meanings, and the messages of a text will have a reception that is sympathetic. Readers/viewers do, in fact, belong to "reading communities" or "reading formations," and a text has its effects precisely because readers do interpret texts as they comprehend them, and therefore the critic does have a rhetorical warrant for his "enlightening enterprise," which Bordwell is skeptical about (1989b: 255).[32] It is ironic that in formulating a difference between the reader/viewer's activity and that of the critic, Bordwell goes against one of the fundamental assumptions of any study of the "effects" of a text: that a text can have effects only if the audience recognizes its significances. In the same way, a critic can only interpret a text if he recognizes the emotional responses and assumptions that the elements of the text are meant to evoke. And he can only do this if he participates in the ritual, in however distanced a manner. Therefore, if historical poetics is to be as much about effects as it is to be about the principles of constructive form, it must take into account all those meanings that Bordwell sees as the domain of interpretation – the highly suspect implicit and symptomatic meanings that contain symbolic and ideological implications.

III

Bordwell claims at the end of *Making Meaning* that his intention is not one of "repudiating interpretation but of situating its protocols within a broader historical inquiry" (1989b: 266). He believes that neoformalist poetics, "while concentrating on historical context, narrative form and cinematic style, does not exclude thematic interpretation. It absorbs them into a dynamic system" (1989a: 385). However, so deep is his suspicion of implicit and symptomatic meanings, and so committed is he to an exposition of form and style and their historical location without necessarily relating them to thematic significances, that his own readings of cinematic texts often end up displaying "the film as intriguing or challenging, perhaps because its operations lie beneath or beyond interpretation" (1989b: 271).[33] I will use the example of his reading of Carl Dreyer's *Ordet* to demonstrate that while Bordwell presents the film as intriguing and challenging through an analysis of its style, his reading is inadequate and impoverished because he refuses to encounter its themes or to see the embodiment of the content in the form.

Dreyer criticism is polarized between the "traditional-thematic" and the "perceptual-formalist" kinds (Carney 1989: 22). Unlike the thematic critics, David Bordwell is extremely aware of the importance of style. Holding himself at a distance from the three main kinds of critical responses before him – the religious, the humanist, and the aestheticist – Bordwell maintains that his formalist position equips him to respond adequately to the question of style, and he therefore reads Dreyer's work as essentially about "the problems of order" and "the problems of interpretation" (1981: 1–3). But, as Raymond Carney points out, Bordwell's reading reduces Dreyer's films to a "set of stylistic/perceptual/logical permutations" and completely denies the emotive and psychological dimensions of the experience. Moreover, his reading of Dreyer's style as functioning independently of the narrative is problematic, for in locating the value of his work in defamiliarizing both "ordinary perceptual reality" and the expressive forms of "other art works," Bordwell posits the only creative function of style as essentially a negative one – to deconstruct, parody, or play with forms of representation, which, as Carney points out, is "an utter trivialization of the possibilities of artistic expression" (1989: 45–8). Bordwell thus sees narrative as essentially about the means of expression and its affective implications.

The limitations of Bordwell's approach to *Ordet* become obvious in that he misses completely the contemporary significance of Dreyer's concerns because of the anachronistic form of the medieval miracle play within which Dreyer embeds his realistic narrative. So, to Bordwell, "so great was Dreyer's attachment to the ahistorical" that his films cannot be seen as "reflecting contemporary ideological positions." Even religion, which one would normally associate with ideology, Bordwell sees as taking on ideological weight only as a form of "planing the action in an asocial, atemporal frame of reference . . . validating it as representation, theorizing the film's very production of narrative" (1981: 192–3). Instead of reading the religious concerns as themes that require interpretation, Bordwell transforms them into formal elements with no thematic reverberations or significance. In doing this he misses the significance of the film and impoverishes its concerns. He sees in *Ordet* "Dreyer's typical narrative unity" which found "its most thoroughgoing justification – religion" and "Christianity becomes Dreyer's most overpowering formal device" (146–7). Bordwell's formalist reading of Christianity in *Ordet* is problematic precisely because it is a reading of the hermeneutic and proairetic codes of the narrative, without perceiving that the significance of these codes cannot be understood outside of the context of the semic, referential, and symbolic ones.[34] Christianity is not just a formal device in *Ordet*, but rather the very fabric and texture of the social and cultural life Dreyer wishes to explore, as well as what is endangered in the pervasive and destructive disbelief of the contemporary moment. In retelling an old story in a modern context, in using an older form (the miracle–mystery play) to structure the meaning of a modern experience, he not only demonstrates the generic continuity of cultural experience, but also expresses a collective wish for resurrection from the despair of doubt into which modernity has plunged Western culture. The "powerful deep currents of culture" (Bakhtin 1986b: 3) are indeed demonstrably palpable if we are sensitive enough and take the suggestions of Bakhtin and Barthes to read narrative as cultural signification.

401

Bordwell's inability to link thematic and formal issues is obvious in that he converts even thematic concerns like the examination of religion into formal devices and therefore misses the contemporary significance of Dreyer's use of forms and objects from earlier times. He sees the centrality of art objects in Dreyer's work as "symptomatic of Dreyer's tendency to impress the social into the characters' surroundings, but at one remove through decorative objects selected by the characters" (1981: 195). It is clear that Bordwell doesn't quite understand the abstraction for which the process of simplification works in Dreyer's film. The portraits of patriarchal figures on the walls of the two houses in the film subtly suggest the forces that control the forms of social interaction in this world. Interestingly, the scenes of the meeting and the discussion between Morten and Peter are composed like Rembrandt's paintings, just as earlier Inger is often shot in a Vermeer-like composition which transforms the simplicity of a routine gesture into a transcendental act. The intertextuality is not incidental, for, as Raymond Williams points out, opening a film text to a broader context traces relations between the different signifying systems of a culture (Williams 1982: 12–13; cited in Gunning 1991: 11).

It is ironic that Bordwell, who is so committed to an understanding of form and style in a historical context, misses the historical and contemporary significances of Dreyer's form. This is precisely because he does not imaginatively engage with the thematic concerns of Dreyer's work, so that his reading of form is not impregnated with the vision of the work. A brief discussion of a crucial scene in the film will make this clear. As Inger struggles with her life in labor, her daughter Maren and the supposedly mad brother-in-law Johannes briefly communicate in the parlor outside. This scene between Johannes and little Maren is in direct contrast to the one in which she comes to her grandfather with the prediction of her mother's death. While he humors her and sends her off to bed, without answering any of her questions or taking her seriously at all, Johannes and she both take each other seriously, and Maren convinces him of the power of both human love and faith, a faith that will make even the resurrection of the dead possible. Composed centrally for the first time in the film by a simultaneous arc-and-pan movement of a mobile camera, Johannes is once again semically coded as the Savior,[35] and when the movement ends with Maren and Johannes composed centrally and in the foreground, with Inger's door in the background, the vital connections between these three individuals and the forces they represent become clear. If there is a true faith, it is in this triumvirate, with the coming together of childlike faith, infinite trust in the divine, gentleness, compassion, understanding, and a vast and tender love. Despite Johannes's seeming aloofness and distractedness, he has the qualities to belong to this alternative faith and is in fact a key member, something that only Inger and Maren implicitly realize. Bordwell insightfully analyzes the technical accomplishment of this sequence. He describes the movement of the camera as it arcs and moves in one direction while it pans in the opposite one. The resultant effect is to maintain an equidistance from the figures which emerge sculpturally as the

402

space becomes dynamic (1981: 156–8). However, he fails to see the narrative significance of this movement as described above.

Any adequate analysis or description of form and style must confront its thematic and philosophical significance. The style of the film, which Dreyer believed communicated the truth of the artist's vision or personal interpretation of his reality (Dreyer 1973),[36] does not in any way work at odds with the narrative concerns of this film, for both are engaged in the task of signifying a reality and therefore a context and a culture. The universal is not a free-floating essence that needs to be either caught in the net of artistic vision or realized through a meditation on vague eternal verities. Rather, it is to be realized through the concrete specificities of a culture and a reality that is rooted in time and space. And it is such a reality that Dreyer addresses in all his films, despite the abstraction of his technique and the seeming atemporality of his subject matter. *Ordet* comes from a deep confrontation with the implications of modernity with its crisis of faith, and it is the meaning of this crisis that the film explores, providing at the same time a utopian vision of faith which, in its affirmation of Life, gifts an object lesson on the value of faith that transcends the rationalistic forces of modernity. Like other modernists, Dreyer withdraws into history to search for forms that would convey the range of meanings his themes demand. In doing that, what he actually achieves is to demonstrate the continuities of culture which persist despite the rupture of modernity. If "forms of thinking" (Bakhtin 1986b: 5) persist over time in a culture, then generic insights can be mobilized to establish a creative, meaningful relationship with tradition in the context of the divisive force of modernity, even as the past with its retrograde social structures is critiqued and the present looked to for the possibilities of an authentic form of human relatedness. In either case, it is the "map of meanings in a culture" (Hall 1972: 65; cited in Lesage 1985: 481) that narrative discourse is concerned with, so that "narrativization"[37] is merely the means by which the narrative, or the artist for that matter, signify the culture in which they are rooted. The Bakhtinian notion of a heteroglossic context[38] would be an important starting point for the examination of the Barthesian codes which form the narrative and, in the decoding of which, the reader/spectator confronts the meanings of a culture, rooted in a time and a place. Narrative discourse is thus the means of cultural signification, and it is only through the acceptance of the particular context that any universal meaning is generated.

IV

Bordwell's most serious allegations against interpretation come in his attack on SLAB theories, which, he feels, are the basis for most current interpretive practices (1989a: 385–92).[39] By setting historical poetics against SLAB theory, he critiques the latter for being doctrine centered, for not being based on systematic research, and for using concepts to construct interpretive narratives rather than explanatory propositions. Bordwell's tendency to polarize positions and impulses is problematic and ultimately unprofitable. While the excesses of SLAB-based criticism are unquestionable and need to be given up, should we throw out the baby with the bath water? SLAB theories (not the critical excesses that have followed from them) have insights into society, history, culture, and representation that would benefit any attempt at analyzing and interpreting texts. Moreover, Bordwell himself concedes that to give up the practices of interpretation would be to impoverish film studies (1989b: 258). Without interpretation, historical poetics would also be inadequate. On the other hand, with it, not only would historical poetics definitely be enriched, but also its study of form and style in historical terms can only be complete, as Bakhtin suggests, if it also addresses issues of cultural determination, ideological formation, and their various manifestations. If Bordwell were to reformulate his idea of interpretation and embed it in a Bakhtinian conception of history and a Bakhtinian–Barthesian conception of narrative, as suggested in this chapter, then the project of historical poetics, with interpretation truly absorbed within it, would definitely become the most promising and fruitful course for film studies to take.[40] This might involve a radical revisioning of its key notion of construction and meaning and its polarized opposition to interpretation. To begin with, one could start by reinstating the traditional notion of hermeneutics. Ricoeur's definition of interpretation as "deciphering the hidden meaning in the apparent meaning, in unfolding the levels of meaning implied in the literal meaning" (1980: 245; cited in Bordwell 1989b: 2) can work as a way of seeing that explicit, referential meanings contain within them implicit, symptomatic ones. And with meaning seen as embedded in history and culture, cultural representational forms would be charged with the significances that otherwise are not seen by Bordwell as relevant to historical poetics, but rather are banished to the polarized realm of interpretation. Thus, to realize the potential of his proposed revitalization of the field with historical poetics, Bordwell must confront the contradictions and tensions in his formulation and not reform interpretation with historical poetics but vitalize the latter with the values and benefits of the former.

Notes

I would like to thank Robert Stam, Richard Allen, and Malcolm Turvey for their invaluable comments on an earlier draft of this paper. The paper has benefited from their responses, and I am grateful to them for their interest.

1   In the last chapter of *Making Meaning* entitled "Why Not to Read a Film," Bordwell states that "to interpret a film is to ascribe implicit or symptomatic meanings to it" (1989b: 249). Here he brings to a culmination his critique of interpretation and examines whether it is time to bring about "the end of interpretation." He has various recommendations to rectify the excesses of interpretive criticism and feels

that the "questions of composition, function and effect that interpretive criticism sets out to answer are most directly addressed and best answered by a self-conscious historical poetics of cinema," which he defines as "the study of how, in determinate circumstances, films are put together, serve specific functions, and achieve specific effects" (266–7). He also discusses the concept in the essay "Historical Poetics of Cinema" (1989a). My discussion of Bordwell's concept of "historical poetics" is based on these two texts. However, my understanding of "historical poetics" is conditioned by Bakhtin and Medvedev's formulation of a "sociological" and "historical poetics" in their response to and critique of Russian formalism. While their "sociological poetics" shares several attitudes and features with Russian formalism, including the latter's emphasis on the problems of literary specification and the importance of understanding the "constructive functions of each of (the) elements," it critiques and is directly opposed to the loss of "full semantic meaning and ideological significance" that Russian formalism saw as necessary for the elements of the work acquiring "constructive significance." Bakhtin and Medvedev's "sociological" and "historical poetics," then, is committed to understanding the literary, artistic work in the context of the "unity of literature," which cannot be understood outside the "unity of ideological life," which in turn "cannot be studied outside the unified socioeconomic laws of development." While Bordwell's formulation of "historical poetics" takes "socioeconomic laws of [the] development" of form into consideration, it ignores the crucial, organic connection between all these dimensions. According to Bakhtin and Medvedev, the "historian must reveal the very mechanics of ideological generation," a charter that Bordwell does not think is necessary for either the historian of artistic forms or the historical critic. For Bordwell's views see *Making Meaning* (1989b). For Bakhtin and Medvedev's formulations see their *The Formal Method in Literary Scholarship* (1978: 30–1, 45, 62, 49, 27, 20).

2   Gaut's argument in this paper is that the neoformalism of Bordwell and Thompson is "seriously flawed." While Thompson and Bordwell do not confront the tensions of their theory's key notion of construction, Gaut demonstrates that viewers do not, in general, construct the meanings of films. There is a limited role for construction within a detectivist framework which is obscured by Bordwell and Thompson.

3   Bordwell believes that in the activity of comprehension, the perceiver constructs the textual world, or *referential*, diegetic meanings as also *explicit* meanings that have to do with the direct "message" of the text. The perceiver also constructs "covert, symbolic, or *implicit* meanings" that could be identified as " 'problems,' 'issues,' or 'questions.' " The spectator also constructs *repressed* or *symptomatic* meanings "that the work divulges 'involuntarily.' " *Symptomatic* meaning may either be treated as "the consequence of the artist's obsessions" or taken "as part of a social dynamic" and "traced to economic, political, or ideological processes." Implicit and symptomatic meanings are the domain of interpretation. For these definitions, see Bordwell 1989b: 8–9. For a discussion of Bordwell's notion of narrative and his constructivist model of narrative comprehension see Bordwell 1985: esp. 29–62. For a discussion of different kinds of meaning and the activity of interpretation see Bordwell 1989b: esp. 1–42, 105–45.

4   Bakhtin and Medvedev feel that "the work cannot be understood outside the unity of literature. But this whole unity...cannot be understood outside the unity of

ideological life. And this last unity ... cannot be studied outside the unified socio-economic laws of development" (1978: 27).

5   It is intriguing that Bordwell does not even refer to Bakhtin in either of the two texts in which he defines and discusses "historical poetics," especially given that one of his sharpest criticisms against the "Grand Theory" of the SLAB theorists (those who employ tenets based upon Saussurean semiotics, Lacanian psychoanalysis, Althusserian Marxism, and Barthesian textual theory, and those whose work Bordwell calls, "acronymically and a little acrimoniously, SLAB theory") is that they do no "homework in the history of [their] concepts," and that his own account of the history of criticism in *Making Meaning* is rigorously historical. See Bordwell 1989a: 385, 388, and 1989b: ch. 4, respectively. In their critique of Russian formalism, Bakhtin and Medvedev propose as a corrective a "sociological poetics" of art with "historical poetics" as a necessary corollary. According to them, the distinction between a "theoretical sociological poetics" and "historical poetics" is "more technical than methodological in nature. And theoretical poetics must be historical." That the two are closely imbricated is obvious in the development of their formulations in the entire book, while they also state clearly that "the role of historical poetics is to prepare the historical perspective for the generalizing and synthesizing definitions of sociological poetics." We can therefore assume that the social, cultural, ideological concerns of "sociological poetics" inflected with a historical perspective would be central to a "historical poetics" as conceived by Bakhtin and Medvedev. See *The Formal Method* (1978: 30–1) for the definitions. That Bakhtin was consistently interested in a "historical poetics" of literature is reflected in his other work as well. His essay "Forms of Time and of the Chronotope in the Novel" is subtitled "Notes Toward a Historical Poetics," and he attempts "a total evolution of the form being defined." See, respectively, Bakhtin 1994: 84, and Bakhtin and Medvedev 1978: 31. The Bakhtinian sense of history, then, refers not just to the resonances of the contemporary time and context, but to the entire weight of the past as it reverberates both formally and thematically in a text.

6   Bakhtin and Medvedev speak of the "deep ideological meaning to form itself" and point to plot as "the formula of ideologically refracted life" with its structure shaped by "ideological values" (1978: 49, 17).

7   "Interpretation takes as its basic subject our perceptual, cognitive, and affective processes, but it does so in a roundabout way – by attributing their 'output' to the text 'out there'" (Bordwell 1989b: 257).

8   Bordwell concedes that the aim of interpretation is not to produce "knowledge" as the natural and social sciences do, but rather to yield "understanding (verstehen)" which it may do "through a more or less disciplined speculation on the possibilities of meaning." As opposed to interpretation, the aim of historical poetics is to produce "knowledge" and therefore other "object–centered questions" about the film's "composition," and its "effects" and "functions" are important (1989b: 258, 263). Throughout Bordwell's discussion of interpretation and historical criticism there is this tension between "understanding" and "knowledge." Isn't the polarization of the two as problematic as that of interpretation and comprehension and different kinds of meanings? Bordwell's assertion that historical poetics will produce knowledge as the natural and social sciences do, and his constant emphasis on being scientific, perhaps misconceive the goals and aims of the arts. However, this question is outside the scope of this chapter.

406

9   Criticism that deals specifically with the "implicit" meanings of a text. See Bordwell 1989b: ch. 3.

10 Bakhtin states that "it is impossible to understand the concrete utterance without accustoming oneself to its values, without understanding the orientation of its evaluations in the ideological environment" (Bakhtin and Medvedev 1978: 121). Using the Bakhtinian suggestion would facilitate a confrontation of the historical and cultural resonances of a text and would prevent the kind of wild interpretations that have little to do with the text because they are much more intricately involved with working out the hypotheses of the theories or the critical institutions that have produced them, and that Bordwell rightly condemns.

11 For an understanding of Bakhtin's ideas about dialogism and the text–context relationship, I have used Bakhtin 1986b, Bakhtin and Medvedev 1978, Stam 1989, and the section on intertextuality in Stam et al. 1992: 203–6. Robert Stam's use of Bakhtin to critique Metzian cinesemiology has sharpened my own arguments against Bordwellian formalism. See Stam 1989: esp. ch. 1.

12 Robert Stam points out that the "Bakhtinian notion of heteroglossia, as the diverse perspectival languages generated by sexual, racial, economic, and generational difference, is eminently compatible with spectator-oriented approaches." While both Bakhtin and latter-day reception theorists would be in "favor of a multiplicity of spectatorial positions, sometimes coexisting within a given spectator," Stam also points out that the spectator is "historically situated . . . in both a biographical and a larger historical sense" (1989: 43).

13 This could range from the spectatorial awareness of production conditions with which they may be familiar through the circulation of journalistic discourse to the more academic kind of criticism that takes pains to research the kinds of detail that Bordwell himself suggests good criticism should do (1989b: 263).

14 Bordwell points out that neoformalism relies upon three explanatory schemes: a rational-agent model, an institutional model, and a perceptual-cognitive model. He explains the institutional model as the "social and economic system of film-making, involving tacit aesthetic assumptions, the division of labor, and technological procedures [which] forms the horizon of what is permitted or encouraged at particular moments" (1989a: 382–3).

15 Allen points out that the cognitive theory of perception misconceives the nature of seeing "since perception cannot be defined as an inferential process though some forms of looking involve making inferences e.g. a detective trying to interpret what it is that she sees . . . therefore, film cannot be conceived as something that makes explicit the inferential processes that are implicit in everyday seeing, as the theory claims." Allen also points out that narrative comprehension and narrative interpretation cannot be so sharply divided as Bordwell makes out: "By misconceiving narrative comprehension as an objective process (based on a misconceived theory of seeing), Bordwell mistakenly draws an erroneous distinction between narrative comprehension and narrative interpretation that sounds the clarion call to abandon the activity of interpretation in *Making Meaning*" (from the abstract of the unpublished paper presented at the conference). I am grateful to Richard Allen for sharing his ideas with me.

16 Gaut extracts three different notions of construction from Bordwell's arguments and examines them to see whether any of them prove that "meanings are made, not

found." The first, "conceptual construction," in which concepts are mapped onto cues using background knowledge in keeping with the constructivist theory of perception, is no ground for thinking that the objects of perception and meaning are constructs. The second, "normative construction," according to which viewers are directed to imagine what they see, also does not prove that viewers therefore determine what they ought to imagine. And finally, the strongest version of constructivism, critical school constructivism – inherent in Bordwell's claims about the nature of interpretation as an activity in which critics map semantic fields onto films using schemata, heuristics, assumptions, and hypotheses, all of which derive their validity and effectiveness from critical institutions – is a false theory of interpretation. This is so because Gaut demonstrates that the norms that should be appealed to in interpretation are not the norms of critical institutions but the norms that govern the film in its historical context. Thus, the neoformalist has failed to prove that genuine construction lies at the heart of comprehension and interpretation of films. Gaut further suggests that Bordwell and Thompson's recommendation of "historical poetics" should be freed from the burden of general constructivism, which is actually incompatible with the renewed attention to historical context that they advocate. However, as this chapter has argued, their concept of historical context needs to be widened in its scope.

17　Bordwell opposes these two and states that he offers "not a hermeneutics – a scheme for producing valid or valuable interpretation – but a poetics of interpretation" (1989b: 273). One wonders whether the distinction between the two is as obvious as it is to Bordwell. In fact, Aristotle, from whom Bordwell would definitely claim a critical descent, seems to have done both in his *Poetics*.

18　This sense of symptomatic meaning gained critical currency from Jean-Louis Comolli and Jean Narboni's editorial "Cinema/Ideology/Criticism" in *Cahiers du cinéma* in 1969. Subsequently it formed the impetus for much critical interpretation in the 1970s, especially in *Cahiers* and *Screen*. Bordwell's chapter 4 of *Making Meaning*, "Symptomatic Interpretation," is a very comprehensive and useful account of the history of critical ideas and movements in film studies and criticism. While the descriptive account is very valuable and is a wonderful example of a historical poetics of criticism, it is not very clear in the chapter what Bordwell's objections are to the forms he is describing.

19　The argument against Bordwell here is similar to the one that Malcolm Turvey makes about Murray Smith and Noël Carroll's theory of the spectator's emotional response to fiction films in Turvey 1997. Turvey argues that by identifying a mental entity – i.e. imagination or thought – as the "causal agent of the spectator's emotion during her viewing of fiction films," Smith and Carroll divorce the spectator's emotional response from "the sensuous particularit[y] of the cinematic medium," a position that is contradicted by "ordinary language descriptions of the experience of fiction films," and is one that Smith and Carroll find difficult to either prove or bypass. See pp. 432–8 for this argument.

20　See note 8.

21　Bordwell sees "interpretation's greatest achievement" as "its ability to encourage . . . reflections upon our conceptual schemes. By taming the new and sharpening the known, the interpretive institution reactivates and revises our common frameworks of understanding."

22   See note 21.

23   Bordwell borrows the term and the idea from Tzvetan Todorov, who says that "it is fore knowledge of the meaning to be discovered that guides the interpretation" (1982: 254; cited in Bordwell 1989b: 260).

24   Throughout *Making Meaning* and the "Historical Poetics of Cinema," Bordwell sees Bazin's work as an example of the highest standards of historical criticism and an exemplary model of "cinematic poetics." He concedes that Bazin also does interpretive criticism. While he says that Bazin's work, along with that of Burch and the Soviet filmmakers, does demonstrate that the "construction of implicit and symptomatic meanings can co-exist with the study of form and style in given historical circumstances," he is not willing to see that this constitutes perhaps the most comprehensive form of interpretation, as it does of historical poetics (1989b: 267).

25   In "Historical Poetics of Cinema," Bordwell says that "nothing prevents the poetician from arguing that economics, ideology, the class struggle, or inherent social or psychological dispositions operate as causes of constructional devices or effects" (374). This is very much like the formalist conception of "material" that Bakhtin criticized: "the formalists called the motivation of the device, 'material', and considered everything ideologically significant to be 'material' as well." But, as Bakhtin points out, "the reduction of the material to mere motivation condemns the device to complete emptiness," and therefore "the division of the poetic construction into device and material is clearly untenable" (Bakhtin and Medvedev 1978: 112, 116).

26   To study "a wide range of films" without studying the context of those films would be to look at cinema only in terms of the filmic series with no understanding of the relatedness of the filmic series with "other ideological series." This is also Bakhtin's criticism of the formalists who, according to him, considered "the series of literary history, the series of artistic works and their constructive elements to be completely independent of the other ideological series and of socioeconomic development" (Bakhtin and Medvedev 1978: 159). While Bordwell does consider socio-economic development, he does not consider adequately enough the importance of other ideological spheres for film history.

27   See note 26.

28   Bordwell states that there is no need "to assume any one model of causation and change" when involved in the enterprise of historical poetics. He points out that Bazin, in the "Evolution of the Language of the Cinema" (1967), gives a "teleological explanation" of the development of film form (1989a: 374). Bordwell points to other models of causation than the Bazinian, teleological one. The "intentionalistic" one "centers on more localized acts of choice and avoidance." As opposed to these, his own model is a "functionalist" one "whereby the institutional dynamics of filmmaking set up constraints and preferred options that fulfill overall systemic norms" (374). While his use of a functionalist model may be true of his discussion of Hollywood cinema in *The Classical Hollywood Cinema* (Bordwell et al. 1985), his discussion of the different kinds of cinema when he emphasizes the historicizing of the different "constructional options" available to filmmakers at "various historical conjunctures" implies a teleological model of film history (1989a: 381).

29   Bordwell understands that Vance Kepley "has shown that the films' mysterious mythographic elements had concrete extratextual references for the director's audiences, and that the films' explicit messages are the trace of various, sometimes conflicting, political purposes. Kepley can go on to describe ideological projects and propose informed symptomatic readings on the basis of the sort of specific historical evidence that Macherey and the *Cahiers* critics were never able to muster." But he sees this as an example of how, by turning "to history," we "discover that films have functioned in ways that are not already known to us," without admitting that symptomatic interpretation can actually aid the understanding of how films functioned in different historical contexts (1989b: 265–6).

30   However, Bordwell is skeptical about the the pleasure of film interpretation: "in 1975 Laura Mulvey wrote that her theory sought to take the pleasure out of film viewing. Perhaps now is the time to do something more controversial: take the pleasure out of film interpretation" (1989b: 262–3).

31   A typical genre film, for example, perpetuates certain ideologies that are not only coded with those genres but are also used very consciously by the filmmakers to do so: see Thomas Schatz's work on genres, especially in *Hollywood Genres* (1981).

32   Bordwell is critical of the tendency of critics to project their interpretive activity "back onto 'ordinary' or . . . 'naive' viewers" who belong to " 'reading communities,' or are constituted by 'reading formations' " because, "by defining whatever viewers do as interpretation, the critic secures a rhetorical warrant for his more enlightened and enlightening enterprise."

33   But, as I have argued in this paper, are these two activities – that of interpreting and that of "poetics" – inherently opposed, as Bordwell makes them out to be?

34   See discussion on pp. 392–3.

35   Throughout the film, Johannes is presented in iconic terms that are semically evocative of the Christ figure, though there is some ambivalence in the presentation as well. This is clear in the first scene, when Johannes walks out onto the moors and addresses an imaginary audience, condemning them for their lack of faith in the risen Christ. While the scene is semically evocative of Christ's Sermon on the Mount, there is also a sharp contrast between the two figures through the disjuncture produced by the difference in their respective sermons, namely that Johannes condemns the imagined congregation for their lack of faith in him as the risen Christ, while Jesus' sermon to his disciples and others contained the Beatitudes and other important fundamentals of Christian teaching (see Matthew 5–7; Luke 6: 20–49). Through the ambivalence of the first scene, Dreyer indicates Johannes's delusion but at the same time suggests the possibility of vision and the potential to be a savior through the image-seme used to present him.

36   "[T]he style . . . is the artist's way of giving expression to his perception of the material. . . . Through style, he gets others to see the material through his eyes" (Dreyer 1973: 127).

37   Tom Gunning adds this fourth category to Genette's "triad of story, discourse and the act of narrating" to account for the specifically cinematic mode of narration (1991: 17–18).

38   In a different sense from Bakhtin's "heteroglossia" of popular discourses, especially in carnival forms, would be the many voices of faith and religious belief that obviously formed the context of the everyday life of the Jutland countryside that

Dreyer and Munk (on whose play the film is based) were using to contextualize their explorations of these issues.

39 See note 5 for details.

40 Bordwell states this at the end of *Making Meaning* (273–4) and in the concluding paragraph of "Historical Poetics of Cinema" (392): "In this respect, historical poetics becomes not one method but a model of basic research into cinema."

References

Allen, Richard. 1997. "On Narrative Comprehension." Paper presented at the Annual SCS Conference, Ottawa (May).

Bakhtin, Mikhail. 1986a. "Response to a Question from the *Novy Mir* Editorial Staff." In Bakhtin 1986b.

——. 1986b. *Speech Genres and Other Late Essays*. Trans. Vern W. McGee. Austin: University of Texas Press.

——. 1994 [1981]. *The Dialogic Imagination: Four Essays*. Trans. Caryl Emerson and Michael Holquist. Austin: University of Texas Press.

——, and P. N. Medvedev. 1978. *The Formal Method in Literary Scholarship: A Critical Introduction to Sociological Poetics*. Trans. Albert J. Wehrle. Baltimore and London: Johns Hopkins University Press.

Barthes, Roland. 1994 [1974]. *S/Z*. Trans Richard Miller. New York: Hill and Wang.

Bazin, André. 1967. "Evolution of the Language of the Cinema." In *What Is Cinema?* Ed. and trans. Hugh Gray. Berkeley, Los Angeles, and London: University of California Press.

Bordwell, David. 1981. *The Films of Carl Theodor Dreyer*. Berkeley, Los Angeles, and London: University of California Press.

——. 1985. *Narration in the Fiction Film*. Madison: University of Wisconsin Press.

——. 1989a. "Historical Poetics of Cinema." In *The Cinematic Text: Methods and Approaches*. Ed. R. Barton Palmer. New York: AMS Press. 369–98.

——. 1989b. *Making Meaning: Inference and Rhetoric in the Interpretation of Cinema*. Cambridge and London: Harvard University Press.

——, Janet Staiger, and Kristin Thompson, eds. 1985. *The Classical Hollywood Cinema: Film Style and Mode of Production to 1960*. New York: Columbia University Press.

Carney, Raymond. 1989. *Speaking the Language of Desire*. Cambridge and New York: Cambridge University Press.

Dreyer, Carl. 1973 [1943]. "A Little on Film Style." In *Dreyer in Double Reflection, Trans. of Carl Th. Dreyer's Writings About the Film (Om Filmen)*. Ed., with commentary and essays, Donald Skoller. New York: Dutton.

Gaut, Berys. 1995. "Making Sense of Films: Neoformalism and Its Limits." *Forum for Modern Language Studies* 31, 1: 8–23.

Genette, Gerard. 1993 [1980]. *Narrative Discourse: An Essay in Method*. Trans. Jane E. Lewin. Ithaca: Cornell University Press.

Gunning, Tom. 1991. "Theory and History: Narrative Discourse and the Narrator System." In *D. W. Griffith and the Origin of American Narrative Film*. Urbana: University of Illinois Press.

411

Hall, Stuart. 1972. "The Determinations of Newsphotographs." *Working Papers in Cultural Studies* 3: 65.

Lesage, Julia. 1985. "*S/Z* and *The Rules of the Game*." In *Movies and Methods Vol. II.* Ed. Bill Nichols. Berkeley, Los Angeles, and London: University of California Press.

Ricoeur, Paul. 1980. "Existence and Hermeneutics." In *Contemporary Hermeneutics: Hermeneutics as Method, Philosophy, and Critique*. London: Routledge and Kegan Paul.

Schatz, Thomas. 1981. *Hollywood Genres: Formulas, Filmmaking, and the Studio System*. New York: Random House.

Stam, Robert. 1989. *Subversive Pleasures: Bakhtin, Cultural Criticism, and Film*. Baltimore and London: Johns Hopkins University Press.

——, Robert Burgoyne, and Sandy Flitterman-Lewis. 1992. *New Vocabularies in Film Semiotics*. London and New York: Routledge.

Todorov, Tzvetan. 1982. *Theories of the Symbol*. Trans. Catherine Porter. Ithaca: Cornell University Press.

Turvey, Malcolm. 1997. "Seeing Theory: On Perception and Emotional Response in Current Film Theory." In *Film Theory and Philosophy*. Ed. Richard Allen and Murray Smith. Oxford: Clarendon Press. 431–57.

Williams, Raymond. 1982. *The Sociology of Culture*. New York: Schocken Books.

Wilson, George. 1997. "On Film Narrative and Narrative Meaning." In *Film Theory and Philosophy*. Ed. Richard Allen and Murray Smith. Oxford: Clarendon Press.

Index

Aarseth, Espen J. 246, 247
Abu-Lughod, Lila 298, 300, 305, 312, 315 n12
Adair, John 301
Adorno, Theodor 125, 133, 134, 203
Adrian, Robert 242
aesthetics 67–8, 248–9
affirmative action programs 184–5
Agel, Henri 275–6, 286
Agre, Phil 240–1
Akerman, Chantal 81
Aksoy, A. 229
Aldrich, Robert 11
Alexandrov, G. V. 78–9
allegory: films 336–7, 348, 353, 361; fragmentation 343–4, 348–9; Greek mythology 338; intention 337–8; interpretation 333–4, 337–8, 342; Lukács/Benjamin 336, 344–6; mediation 333–4; as mode of discourse 336, 340–1; modernism 346–7, 360; of poets/theologians 338; science fiction 353–4; space/time 349–50; and symbol 344–5, 346
allegory types: Christian 334, 341–2; historical 354; national 334–5, 340, 349–51, 357–8; overt/unconscious 335–6, 341, 344; pragmatic 354
Allen, Richard 105, 126, 129, 226, 394, 407 n15
Allen, Woody 49

Alloway, Lawrence 26, 32
Althusser, Louis: apparatus theory 135–6; and Baudry 130; genre 37; ideology 134–5, 189–90, 194; post-structural film theory 101; subject 159–60; symptomatic criticism 135, 136; working-class readings 195–6
Altman, Rick 35, 80
The American Cinema 15–16
Americanization 277, 278–9, 300
Anderson, Benedict 298, 351
Anderson, John D. 72, 73
Ang, Ien 160, 161
animation 252, 253
Ansen, David 81
anthropology 295–6, 297, 304, 309, 311, 313
Appadurai, Arjun 298, 304–5
apparatus theory 125, 131, 132, 135–6, 139–41, 170
Arcand, Denys 282
Aristotle 25, 28, 238
Arnheim, Rudolph 66, 68, 69
Arnowitz, Stanley 238–9
articulation, double 85, 92
Astruc, Alexandre 10–11
audience 35, 315 n13; and film industry 35, 205–6; genres 34, 39–40; imaginary locations 264; meaning 112–13; media 162, 241; narrative 59, 375; national cinema 286–7; representation 4; response 115–16,

413

423